THE RAND McNALLY
ENCYCLOPEDIA OF

WORLD
WAR II

# THE RAND MCNALLY ENCYCLOPEDIA OF

# WORLD WAR II

## GENERAL EDITOR JOHN KEEGAN

**RAND MCNALLY & COMPANY**
Chicago · New York · San Francisco
A Bison Book

Published in the United States by
Rand McNally & Company, 1977
First Published in the UK by Bison Books

Copyright © 1977 by Bison Books Limited
Third impression 1981

ISBN: 528-81060-X (hardbound)
ISBN: 528-88106-X (paperback)
Library of Congress Catolog Card
No. 77-75730

Printed in Hong Kong

**Editor:** S. L. Mayer

**Executive Editor:** Catherine Bradley

**Contributors:**  J. F. N. Bradley
Bill Gunston
Ronald I. Heiferman
Ian V. Hogg
John Keegan
William Koenig
S. L. Mayer
Antony Preston
John W. R. Taylor

**Designer:**  David Eldred

**Cartographer:**  Richard Natkiel

**Technical Artist:**  Helen Downton

# THE RAND MCNALLY ENCYCLOPEDIA OF

# WORLD WAR II

## From The General Editor

Encyclopedias are concerned primarily with facts, and this *Encyclopedia of World War II* is faithful to the norm. It includes detailed descriptions of every major weapon and weapons system used by the combatants on both sides throughout the war: ships and ship classes, aircraft, tanks and armored vehicles, artillery pieces and small arms. It provides hundreds of concise biographies of the leaders and notabilities of the war, civilian and military. It recounts in outline the major campaigns and battles on every front and relates the outcome of one to another.

But it attempts more than the mere provision of fact. The biographies have been so written and the campaign and battle entries so constructed as to provide a continuous and explicative narrative of the war from its outbreak to its close, and chronological lists of events are located under the headings Western Front, Desert War, Eastern Front, Mediterranean War, and Pacific Theater. It offers a reasoned analysis of the motives and expectations which underlay the grand strategy of the combatants, and a rationale of the failure or success which their strategies brought. It is, in short, a complete, many-sided history of the war as a whole, arranged in encyclopedic form and, in that respect, an entirely original undertaking.

## A–4 Rocket

The A–4, more commonly known as the V–2, was the culmination of a series of rocket designs known as the A-Series which were developed by von Braun and Dornberger for the German Army. Development began in the early 1930s at the Artillery Proving Ground at Kummersdorf and was later transferred to the Peenemünde Research Establishment on the Baltic coast. The A–2 was the first successful liquid-fueled design, and two were fired from the island of Borkum in December 1934. It was succeeded by the A–3, which was the first rocket to use a control system to maintain its flight attitude, the system being based on a gyroscope. The design is said to have been based on the shape of the German Army's standard 7.92mm rifle bullet, because of that bullet's good ballistic shape. Although intended as the test vehicle for the A–4, the A–3 only flew once and was then abandoned, an A–5 design being developed as the test rocket. This was 16 feet long and was powered by a hydrogen-peroxide motor; numerous variant designs were produced in order to test specific features.

The A–4 was planned in 1936 as a rocket to supplant heavy artillery. The motor was a bi-fuel type using liquid oxygen and alcohol and sufficient fuel was carried to give a burning time of 70 seconds. Weighing 13.6 tons at launch, it carried a warhead of one ton of high explosive which was initiated by simple impact fuzes when the rocket struck the ground at the target. Control of flight was achieved by programmed controls which turned the rocket onto a predetermined trajectory after launch; once this was achieved the motor was shut off at a point calculated to place the rocket in a ballistic trajectory terminating at the target.

The warhead was filled with Amatol, a mixture of TNT and Ammonium Nitrate; this is a

relatively weak explosive, but attempts to fill the warhead with more powerful mixtures had failed due to the skin friction of the atmosphere which heated up the warhead to such an extent that premature detonation invariably occurred several thousand feet above the earth.

The first successful flight of the A–4 was on 3 October 1942, and after some delays production began in Peenemünde. After a severe Allied bombing attack in August 1943 production was moved to an underground factory at Nordhausen in the Harz Mountains, where production eventually reached 900 missiles a month. Operational use began on 6 September 1944 when two missiles were fired against Paris; both detonated in flight without reaching their target. Two days later the bombardment of England began. At this time there was a stockpile of 1800 operational missiles and production was expected to keep pace with expenditure. Allied air attacks on railway lines, however, meant that supply was frequently interrupted.

The principal advantage of the A–4 was that it could be fired from practically any clear space of a few square yards. It was fueled and pre-

An A-4 rocket, more usually known as V-2, is launched at Peenemünde.

pared under cover, then taken to the selected launch site on a *Meillerwagen*, a vehicle which carried and then erected the missile until it was standing on its fins on a special launching platform. This platform could be revolved to orient the gyroscope control mechanism. The Meillerwagen was then removed, electrical connections made to a firing vehicle, and the rocket launched. Once launched the platform could be removed and the firing site evacuated in a few minutes, making the detection of a launching unit almost impossible. Since the missile flew at supersonic speed it was extremely difficult to detect and by the end of the war the British Army had still not satisfactorily solved the problem of defense against it.

In all, some 10,000 rockets were produced; of these, 1359 were fired against Britain killing about 2500 and injuring about 6000 people. 1341 were also fired against Antwerp in an endeavor to disrupt Allied port operations there, 65 against Brussels, 98 against Liège, 15 against Paris, five into Luxembourg and 11 at the Remagen Bridge over the Rhine.

Although the A–4 was the only rocket of the series to see service, other designs were projected; the A–4b was a winged version, the intention being to increase the range to 280 miles by the ability to glide to the target. It was hoped that this model would supersede the A–4, but the only two ever built failed in their flight tests. Another possible replacement was the A–9, a lightweight A–4b with radio control during the glide phase and with a bi-fuel motor using 90 percent sulfuric acid and 10 percent hydrocarbons. This would have increased the range to 400 miles, but although the design had been perfected by 1943 the demands for a quick

An A-10 rocket which was planned for transatlantic attacks.

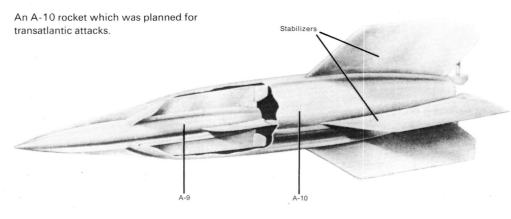

Stabilizers

A-9          A-10

and simple military solution led to the A–9 being dropped in favor of the A–4, a simpler manufacturing proposition. Finally, there was the A–10, a two-stage rocket conceived in 1940 as a trans-Atlantic bombardment missile. The A–10 was actually the first stage, a massive rocket carrying an A–4 or A–9 in its nose. After launching the A–10 would carry the A–4 into a high stratospheric trajectory and there launch it. It was hoped that a range in the region of 2800 miles would be achieved, but no constructional work was ever done on the project.

## Abbreviations

**AA**   Anti-aircraft
**AAF**   Army Air Force
**ABDA**   Australian-British-Dutch-American Command
**ACC**   Allied Control Commission
**AEAF**   Allied Expeditionary Air Force
**AEF**   Allied Expeditionary Force
**AGF**   Army Ground Force
**AIF**   Australian Imperial Force
**AKA**   Cargo ship attack
**AMGOT**   Allied Military Government
**AMMISCA**   American Military Mission in China
**ANZAC**   Australia (except for ABDA area)-New Zealand-Fijis-New Hebrides and New Caledonia Command
**AOC**   Air Officer Commanding
**ASF**   Army Service Force
**ASV**   Air-to-surface vessel radar
**AT**   Anti-tank gun
**ATC**   Air Transport Command
**ATS**   Auxiliary Territorial Service
**AVG**   American Volunteer Group (Flying Tigers)
**BCOS**   British Chief of Staff
**BEF**   British Expeditionary Force
**BEW**   Board of Economic Warfare
**CAS**   Chief of Air Staff
**CCAS**   Combined Civil Affairs Committee
**CCS**   Combined Chiefs of Staff
**CGS**   Chief of General Staff
**CIGS**   Chief of Imperial General Staff
**CINCAF**   Commander in Chief, Allied Forces
**CINCMED**   Commander in Chief, Mediterranean
**CINCPAC**   Commander in Chief, Pacific Area
**CINCSWPA**   Commander in Chief, Southwest Pacific Area
**COMINCH**   Commander in Chief, US Navy
**COMNAVEU**   Commander of US Naval Forces in Europe
**COSSAC**   Chief of Staff to Supreme Allied Commander (Designate) and invasion planning staff
**CWS**   Chemical Warfare Service
**DUKW**   Amphibious truck (duck)
**EAC**   European Advisory Commission
**Einsatzgruppe**   Operational Group of Sipo and SD for missions in occupied territory
**ETO**   European Theater of Operations
**ETOUSA**   European Theater of Operations, US Army
**FCNL**   French Committee of National Liberation
**FFI**   French Forces of the Interior
**FH**   (Allied) Forces Headquarters
**FHCIC**   (Allied) Forces Headquarters Commander in Chief
**FHCIV**   (Allied) Forces Headquarters Civil Affairs Section

**FHGCT**   (Allied) Forces Headquarters G-3
**FHINC**   (Allied) Forces Headquarters Office of Intelligence and Censorship
**FHLIA**   (Allied) Forces Headquarters Liaison Section
**FHMGS**   (Allied) Forces Headquarters Military Government Section
**FHPWO**   (Allied) Forces Headquarters Psychological Warfare Office
**FHSGS**   (Allied) Forces Headquarters Secretary of General Staff
**FHSIG**   (Allied) Forces Headquarters Signal Officer
**G-1**   Personnel Section of divisional and higher staff
**G-2**   Intelligence Section
**G-3**   Operations and Training Section
**G-4**   Logistics Section
**G-5**   Civil Affairs Section
**GESTAPO**   Geheime Staats Polizei
**GHQ**   General Headquarters
**GKO/GOKO**   State Defense Committee
**GOC**   General Officer Commanding
**HIWI**   *Hilfsfreiwillige* – Auxiliary (Russian) Volunteers
**INA**   Indian National Army
**JCS**   Joint Chiefs of Staff
**JIC**   Joint Intelligence Committee
**JPS**   Joint Planning Staff
**JSM**   Joint Staff Mission (British)
**LCA**   Landing Craft Assault
**LRPG**   Long-Range Penetration Group
**LSD**   Landing Ship Dock
**MAAF**   Mediterranean Allied Air Force
**MAC**   Mediterranean Air Command
**MT**   Motor Transport
**MTB**   Motor Torpedo Boat
**MTO**   Mediterranean Theater of Operations
**NAAF**   North Africa Air Force
**NATO**   North Africa Theater of Operations
**NCWTF**   Naval Commander Western Task Force
**NEI**   Netherlands East Indies
**Ob**   *Oberbefehlshaber* (Commander in Chief)
**OFEC**   Office of Foreign Economic Coordination
**OKH**   *Oberkommando des Heeres* (Army High Command)
**OKW**   *Oberkommando der Wehrmacht* (High Command of the Armed Forces)
**OPD**   Operations Division
**OPM**   Office of Production Management
**OSS**   Office of Strategic Services
**OWI**   Office of War Information
**PCNL**   Polish Committee of National Liberation
**PPR**   Polish Worker's Party
**PWE**   Political Warfare Executive
**RAAF**   Royal Australian Air Force
**RAF**   Royal Air Force
**RCAF**   Royal Canadian Air Force
**RCT**   Regimental Combat Team
**RFSS**   *Reichsführer SS* – Reich Leader SS
**RN**   Royal Navy
**SA**   *Sturmabteilungen* (Assault Sections)
**SACEUR**   Supreme Allied Commander in Europe
**SACMED**   Supreme Allied Commander of Mediterranean Theater
**SAS**   Special Air Service
**SCAEF**   Supreme Commander of Allied Expeditionary Force
**SD**   *Sicherheitsdienst* (Security Service)
**SEAC**   Southeast Asia Command
**SHAEF**   Supreme Headquarters of Allied Expeditionary Force
**SHCOS**   Supreme Headquarters Chief of Staff

**SHGCT**   Supreme Headquarters G-3
**SHGDS**   Supreme Headquarters G-4
**SHSAC**   Supreme Headquarters of Supreme Allied Commander
**SMC**   Staff Message Control
**SOE**   Special Operations Executive
**SOE/SO**   Special Operations Executive/Special Operations
**SOS**   Service of supply
**SS**   *Schützstaffel* (Protection Squads)
**TAF**   Tactical Air Force
**TBD**   Torpedo Boat Destroyer
**TBS**   Talk Between Ships
**TF**   Task Force
**USAAF**   US Army Air Force
**USMC**   US Marine Corps
**USN**   US Navy
**USS**   US Ship
**USSTAF**   US Strategic Air Force
**WAAC**   Women's Auxiliary Army Corps
**WAAF**   Women's Auxiliary Air Force
**WAFS**   Women's Auxiliary Ferrying Squadron
**WASP**   Women's Airforce Service Pilot
**WAVE**   Women accepted for Voluntary Emergency Service (Navy)
**WDGS**   War Department General Staff
**WPD**   War Plans Division
**WRNS**   Women's Royal Naval Service
**WSA**   War Shipping Administration
**WTF**   Western Task Force
**WVS**   Women's Voluntary Service

### *Abdiel*

This was a class of British fast minelayers which were used to run supplies through the Mediterranean to Malta in 1941–42. Being the fastest surface warships in the Royal Navy (capable of 37 knots) and also having capacious mine decks they could carry machine gun ammunition, glycol coolant and even aviation fuel for Spitfires. Their high speed which enabled them to make the trip from Gibraltar under cover of darkness combined with their capacity and good anti-aircraft armament rendered them among the most versatile small warships of World War II. Only six were built of which three were sunk, *Abdiel, Latona* and *Welshman*.

### *Achilles*
See *Ajax*

### Ack Pack
see Flamethrowers

### Adachi, Lieutenant General Hatazo, 1890–1947

Adachi was commander of the Eighteenth Army and fought a desperate battle to hold on to New Guinea. He took over command of the Japanese forces retreating on the Kokoda Trail to Buna. At the end of January 1943 Adachi had to evacuate Buna and withdraw to Sio. General MacArthur's troops forced him to evacuate Sio and then Madang. The Eighteenth Army was eventually contained at Wewak in mid-1944. He made a desperate attempt to break out in July but when he realized how futile this was, Adachi and 31,000 Japanese troops waited until the war was over. On 13 September 1945 Adachi surrendered and in 1947 he was sentenced to life imprisonment for war crimes, but killed himself.

Wreckage of the *Admiral Hipper* at Kiel Harbor.

### *Admiral Hipper*

Name-ship of the first heavy cruisers built for the new Kriegsmarine in 1935–39, the *Admiral Hipper* displaced a nominal 10,000 tons but her actual displacement was nearly 14,000 tons. Although she had an active war-career she was plagued by machinery trouble. During the Norwegian campaign she was rammed by the destroyer HMS *Glowworm*, but in 1941 she destroyed twelve merchant ships in the Atlantic. On 31 December 1942 she took part with the *Lützow* in the Battle of the Barents Sea but subsequently was sent to the Baltic for training. She was scuttled in Kiel on 3 May 1945 after suffering heavy bomb damage.

### *Admiral Scheer*

Second of the 'pocket battleships' and sister to the *Deutschland*, she served on the Non-Intervention Patrol during the Spanish Civil War in 1936–37, but in 1939–1940 she was in dock for a refit. In the autumn of 1940 she cruised the Atlantic, destroying 17 merchant ships totaling 113,223 tons and the armed merchant cruiser *Jervis Bay* on 5 November. She was later sent to Norway but finished the war on training duty in the Baltic. The *Admiral Scheer* was sunk by RAF bombers in Kiel on 9 April 1945 and the wreck was later covered with rubble when the dock was filled in.

### Admiralty

The British naval administration comprised a civilian side and a naval side; the former was headed by a political nominee, the First Lord of the Admiralty, and the latter by a naval officer, the First Sea Lord. The Board of Admiralty was composed of the following members:
First Sea Lord – Chief of the Naval Staff
Second Sea Lord – responsible for personnel, pay, recruiting and reserves etc.
Third Sea Lord – also known as the Controller – responsible for shipbuilding, research, armament etc.
Controller of Merchant Shipbuilding and Repairs – added in wartime
Fourth Sea Lord – responsible for stores and victualing
Fifth Sea Lord – responsible for naval air
Civil Lord – responsible for civilian labor in dockyards and contractors
Parliamentary Secretary – responsible for contracts and purchasing
Permanent Secretary – responsible for the Secretariat and the War Registry.
In 1939 Admiral Sir Dudley Pound took over as First Sea Lord, an office which he held until

his death in 1943. His regime was marked by excessive centralization, and his most bitterly criticized decision was the order to the PQ-17 convoy to scatter in 1942. His successor was Sir Andrew Cunningham, the former Commander in Chief of the Mediterranean Fleet.

### Afrika Korps

The Afrika Korps was a small German unit led by General (later Field Marshal) Erwin Rommel to support Italy's North African campaign. Organized in April 1941 it later expanded to the point where it dominated the Axis operations in the Desert War particularly in the Tobruk siege and the Battle of El Alamein. Its remnants capitulated to the Allies in May 1943.

German troops disembark from their Ju-52 in North Africa.

### A-Go
see Philippine Sea, Battle of the, 1944

### Aichi B7A1 Ryusei

Powered by an 1825hp Nakajima Homare radial engine, this promising naval attack aircraft became operational only after the Japanese carrier fleet no longer existed. The 100 examples flown were operated from the Japanese mainland in 1944–45, often in suicide attacks. Allied reporting name was 'Grace'.

### Aichi D3A

The Aichi D3A or 'Val' was a Japanese carrier-based dive-bomber. Aided by British and US technicians in the early 1920s, the Japanese aircraft industry quickly became competent in the manufacture of military aircraft. By the early 1930s it was being influenced more by German designs than by any others, with the important

distinction that, being an island race, the Japanese put greater emphasis on carrier-borne aircraft than did the Germans. That they had profited from their studies became clear in World War II, when the Allies were startled to encounter Japanese combat aircraft of a far higher standard than had been anticipated.

In keeping with the general change from biplane to monoplane layout in the 1930s, the Imperial Japanese Navy had issued in 1936 the 11-*shi* requirement for a new carrier-based dive-bomber. Aichi was one of three companies that tendered a design which they called the D3A. This design had benefited from studies of German Heinkel aircraft made by both the Aichi company and the Navy, and was a cantilever low-wing monoplane of all-metal construction, with a 1075hp Mitsubishi Kinsei 44 radial engine and a fixed, spatted undercarriage like that of the German Ju 87. It was not fast, but proved highly maneuverable and could defend itself with two forward-firing 7.7mm machine guns and a rear-mounted gun operated by the second crew member. More importantly, it was able to carry a 550lb bomb on a special release mechanism under the fuselage and smaller bombs under the wings. As the D3A1 Model 11 or Type 99 carrier-borne dive-bomber, it entered production in late 1937.

When, on 7 December 1941, a Japanese carrier-borne force attacked the US base at Pearl Harbor, D3A1s formed the first wave of attacking aircraft. On 4–5 April 1942 they sank the British cruisers HMS *Cornwall* and *Dorsetshire* off Ceylon, followed four days later by the

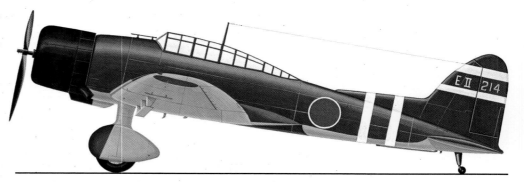

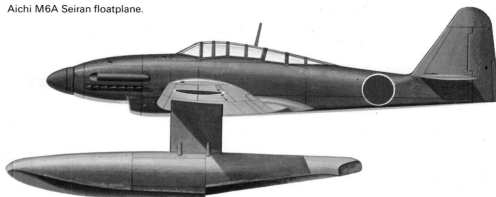
Aichi M6A Seiran floatplane.

Val dive-bomber shot down during the Pearl Harbor attack is salvaged by American crews.

aircraft carrier HMS *Hermes* and the desroyer HMS *Vampire*. The Battle of the Coral Sea, between US and Japanese carrier forces, put the carrier *Shokaku* and its D3A1s out of the subsequent Battle of Midway, and heavy losses of aircraft and experienced pilots quickly reduced the effectiveness of other D3A1 units.

D3A1 production continued until August 1942, by which time 478 had been built. Manufacture was centered consequently on the improved D3A2 Model 22, powered by a 1300hp Kinsei 54 radial engine, and about 816 of this version were delivered before production ended in early 1944. Both versions of the D3A served in most war zones where the Japanese fought, operating from both carrier and shore bases. In the final frantic effort to counter the overwhelming strength and superiority of the Americans, D3A2s were converted into single-seaters and used as suicide aircraft.

### Aichi E16A1 Zuiun

Although intended as a heavily-armed reconnaissance seaplane, the E16A1 ('Paul') was used mainly as a dive bomber with one 550lb or two132lb bombs. Production totaled 253, each with a 1300hp Mitsubishi Kinsei engine and armament of two 20mm cannon and one 12.7mm machine gun. It was deployed initially in the Philippines and later as a suicide aircraft at Okinawa.

### Aichi H9A1

Intended as a trainer for crews destined to fly the big Kawanishi H8K, this fairly large monoplane flying-boat was powered by two 710hp Nakajima Kotobuki radial engines and had a maximum speed of 202mph. Thirty-one were built in 1942–43. Some were used for anti-submarine patrols towards the end of the war, armed with two 550lb bombs or depth charges and two machine guns.

### Aichi M6A Seiran

This 292mph two-seat seaplane had folding wings and tail surfaces, so that two or three Seirans could be packed into a new class of very long-range submarines. One target for the aircraft, after leaving the submarines was to be the Panama Canal. Ten of them were en route to their initial targets, on board smaller submarines, when the end of the war led to their recall.

### Airacobra

see P-39 Airacobra, Bell

### Aircraft Carriers

Most battleships and cruisers carried floatplanes or amphibians for scouting and some navies had seaplane carriers, but the aircraft carrier was a distinct type of warship. She had a flush full-length flight-deck for launching and recovering aircraft, with elevators to move the aircraft to and from the hangars. By 1939 carriers had developed to the extent that the biggest were designated 'fleet carriers' (US designation CV), which meant that they had large aircraft capacity and sufficient speed to keep up with cruisers and battleships. In 1941 a new type appeared, the CVE or escort carrier, a merchant ship conversion which provided air cover for convoys, but these were always distinct from the fleet carriers.

The USS *Guadalcanal* (CVE-60) in 1944.

Up to 1939 carriers were limited to 23,000 tons displacement under the naval treaties, with the exception of the ex-capital ships *Lexington* and *Saratoga* (US Navy) and *Akagi* and *Kaga* (Japanese Navy). In 1937 the British introduced a new feature, an armored flight deck to allow carriers to survive prolonged bombing, and this was subsequently copied by the USN and IJN. The German Navy started work on two carriers, the *Graf Zeppelin* and *Peter Strasser*, but only the former made any progress; she was still incomplete in 1945.

The Italians belatedly tried to convert two liners, but these were also overtaken by events.

The US Navy and the Japanese Navy took carrier developments furthest; both had excellent aircraft and tactics, but under the stress of battle American carriers proved tougher. The Japanese pilot-training program could not keep up with their losses, and so the quality of their naval air force declined after 1942. By 1945 the carrier had overtaken the battleship as the most powerful unit of the fleet, and was a 'capital' ship, not only on account of its destructive power but also in size, complexity and cost.

### Ajax

Light cruiser of the *Leander* Class built 1930–35, the *Ajax* was armed with eight 6in guns and had a maximum speed of 32.5 knots. In 1939 her sisters *Leander* and *Achilles* were serving with the RN's New Zealand Division, and with *Achilles* she played a vital role in preventing the *Admiral Graf Spee* from sinking the *Exeter* in the Battle of the River Plate.

The converted aircraft carrier *Akagi*.

### Akagi

Laid down as a battlecruiser in 1920, she was converted to an aircraft carrier under the provisions of the Washington Naval Disarmament Treaty of 1922. Her sister *Amagi* was wrecked during the 1923 earthquake and had to be replaced by the battleship *Kaga*, but the two ships were converted on very similar lines, with heavy armament and large aircraft capacity. They formed the backbone of the Imperial Japanese Navy's fast carrier strike forces, and *Akagi* was the flagship of the Carrier Fleet under Admiral Nagumo. Her loss at Midway on 5 June 1942 with the other crack carriers was a blow from which the Japanese Naval Air Force never recovered.

### Akizuki

This is the class name for large Japanese destroyers, built 1940–45, which were designed to act as fleet escorts and had a heavy armament of 100mm anti-aircraft guns. As they displaced 2700 tons in light condition and had a large single funnel they were often mistaken by US observers for the light cruiser *Yubari*; US Naval Intelligence was puzzled by the apparent rapidity of her movements. Several survived the war, and two were handed over to the Soviet Union as reparations.

### Alamein (El Alamein), Battle of, 23 October–5 November 1942

This battle in the Western Desert between Montgomery's 8th (British) Army and Rommel's Italo-German army, 23 October–5 November 1942 culminated in a great British victory and Rommel's retreat into Tunisia. Montgomery arrived in North Africa on 13 August to find the 8th Army badly depressed in spirit and Rommel poised to advance on Alexandria, eighty miles from his forward positions

Australian soldiers advance at El Alamein.

near El Alamein. The Germans were, however, held in a preliminary battle, Alam Halfa, 31 August–7 September, 1942, and the British line was consolidated. Montgomery moreover had been promised reinforcements and supplies of new equipment, while Rommel was denied both by British naval activity in the Mediterranean. The British commander, who had been ordered to take the offensive by Churchill, was thus able to open the battle with a great superiority of

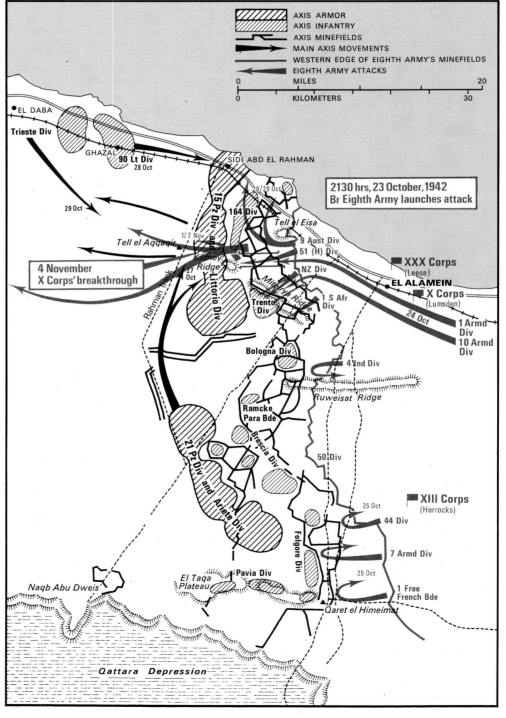

German troops of the Afrika Korps inspect British AFV (Armored Fighting Vehicle).

men and equipment: 11 divisions (two armored) against 15 (nine Italian infantry, two Italian armored, two German infantry, two German armored). The Axis divisions were all under-strength, while the British were at full complement, with a marked preponderance of tanks, about 1200 to 600; many of the German and Italian tanks were obsolescent. The British attack opened with a 1000-gun bombardment on the night of 23–24 October followed by an infantry assault on the coastal end of Rommel's line, which ran 30 miles south to the impassable Qattara Depression. German resistance held firm against it and against the subsequent armored assault. During a week of bitter fighting, losses mounted until Montgomery decided to make his major effort on 2 November at Kidney Ridge, 10 miles south of the coast where the Australians had broken in, instead of on the coastal road itself. In the ensuing tank battles, the Germans were decisively defeated and on 5 November Rommel ordered a full retreat. He was slowly followed by Montgomery who feared a trap, and made a fighting withdrawal into Tunisia, where the Anglo-American Torch landings had begun on 8 November. Alamein secured the Western Desert for the British and brought them their first clear-cut success of the war.

## Alam Halfa, Battle of, 1942

Rommel, after his success in the Gazala battle, immediately attacked the El Alamein position to which Auchinleck had withdrawn the 8th Army. A preliminary stand at Mersa Matruh was brushed aside in three days of fighting,

British 25-pounder continues its nightly barrage.

26–28 June. During July Rommel made several attacks on the Alamein position itself, 1–5 and 8–11, and was himself counterattacked successfully by Auchinleck, 14–27 July. Both sides, however, were too weak to do each other serious harm. On 13 August, despite his success in blocking Rommel's latest offensive, Auchinleck was removed by Churchill and his command transferred to Alexander and Montgomery, the latter to command 8th Army directly. Rommel, whose supply position was difficult but who received reinforcements during August, was now directed to resume the offensive, though for the first time he was reluctant to do so. He had 440 tanks, but the British 480 with more on the way. His plan was similar to that for the Gazala battle: an envelopment round the southern desert flank, followed by exploitation. Montgomery, however, had divined his intentions and fortified the Alam Halfa ridge, which ran at the rear at right angles to his main front, to contain such an envelopment if it materialized. When Rommel attacked on 31 August he at first made quick progress. But air attacks inflicted heavy losses on his tank columns and he was unable to dent the defenses of the Alam Halfa position when he reached it. Accordingly on 2 September he began to withdraw, fighting off a flank attack by the 2nd New Zealand Division. By 7 September the battle was at an end; Rommel had secured a little ground at the southern extremity of the British line but he was still 60 miles from his prize, the port of Alexandria.

## Alanbrooke, 1st Viscount
see Brooke, Field Marshal Alan

## Albacore, Fairey

Intended as a replacement for the Swordfish, the Albacore merely supplemented the older type. It was a three-seat carrier-based torpedo-bomber biplane, powered with a Bristol Taurus engine of 1065 or 1130hp. Weapon load comprised a 1605lb torpedo or 2000lb of bombs, with three machine guns for defense. About 800 Albacores were built for service with the Royal Navy. They served with distinction in the Battle of Matapan. More unusual tasks included the dropping of over 12,000 flares to illuminate German positions during the two months prior to the Battle of Alamein.

## Aleutian Islands Campaign, 1942–43

The Japanese Navy used the offensive against the Aleutians as a diversion for the Midway operation. The Aleutians were not of any strategic importance, especially since the appalling climate and barren and rocky land made an air base impossible. Two Japanese light carriers launched their aircraft to bomb the airfields at

Unalaska, but because of poor visibility they did not do much damage. On 7 June, two landing forces struck at Kiska and Attu, where they met little opposition and captured them easily. Because of the tremendous setback at Midway, Japanese propagandists built this operation up as a great success.

The Americans decided that the Aleutians would have to be recaptured before any other operation in the Central Pacific was carried out, perhaps because the islands were the only US-owned territories in North America which had fallen to the Japanese. At the beginning of August 1942 they bombarded Kiska and at the end of the month established an air base at Adak. In January 1943 they established another base at Amchitka, 90 miles east of Kiska and they decided to bypass the nearer Kiska and attack Attu first. On 11 May 1943, 7th Infantry Division invaded Attu at Holtz and Massacre Bay. The Americans numbered 11,000 but they were badly trained and badly led. Once they had been driven inland they could make little headway but managed to squeeze the Japanese garrison of 2600. On 29 May over 1000 Japanese made a desperate counterattack but were beaten back and resistance collapsed. The Japanese suffered 2350 killed and 28 captured, the US suffered 552 killed and 1140 wounded with another 500 casualties suffering because of the cold conditions.

The Americans decided to improve their chances of overrunning Kiska by a heavy bombardment of the island's defenses. On 15 August an invasion force of 29,000 Americans and 5300 Canadians landed to find that the Japanese had evacuated their garrison of 6000 in July.

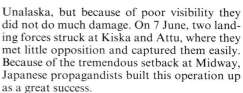

Field Marshal Alexander with King George VI.

## Alexander, Field Marshal Harold, 1891–1969

Harold Alexander was appointed to command 1st Division in the British Expeditionary Force, which he handled with great skill during the retreat to Dunkirk; he was subsequently promoted to I Corps and then to command in Burma at the beginning of the disaster there. In August 1942 Churchill sent him and Montgomery to the Western Desert to inaugurate a new regime. It was a most successful dual appointment. Alexander, Montgomery later wrote, was 'the only man under whom . . . any general . . . would gladly serve in a subordinate position' – the fruit of their relationship was born at Alamein. After the junction of the Torch and Western Desert Forces in Tunisia, he became deputy to Eisenhower and commander of the Anglo-American ground force. In that capacity he directed the invasions of Sicily and Italy and, in Eisenhower's appointment as SCAEF, succeeded him as Supreme Allied Commander in the Mediterranean. He took the German unconstitutional surrender in Italy on 29 April 1945.

## Alsace, German Offensive in, 1944

Hitler had initially thought of making his winter counteroffensive in Alsace, before his choice fell on the Ardennes, but he ranked the project as a subsidiary offensive. Codenamed *Nordwind* it began on 31 December and was a complete surprise. Of the two German corps engaged, Thirteenth SS and Nineteenth, the former was soon halted but the latter made a ten-mile advance towards Bitche and seemed to threaten Strasbourg. Eisenhower contemplated retiring to a better line in the Vosges and abandoning the city, but de Gaulle so strongly opposed the maneuver and he accordingly ordered Devers, commanding 7th Army, to hold the city at all costs. The Germans renewed the offensive with attacks on 7 and 17 January, including a surprise attack across the Rhine just north of Strasbourg, and the Americans were obliged to retire to the Moder river on 20 January, but after that the offensive lost impetus. By way of riposte, Eisenhower ordered the reduction of the Colmar pocket left over from the autumn advances and it was overrun by the French 1st and 2nd Corps, attacking concentrically, between 20 January and 9 February 1945.

## *Altmark*

The *Altmark* was a German fleet oiler and supply ship, which was secretly supplying the *Admiral Graf Spee* in the South Atlantic in 1939. In February 1940 she took on board some 300 prisoners from the *Graf Spee* and attempted to slip through the British blockade to get back to Germany. To dodge British patrols she entered Norwegian territorial waters. However the Admiralty was fully aware that she was carrying British prisoners and ordered the destroyer *Cossack* under Captain Philip Vian to free them. The *Cossack* entered Jösen Fjord and boarded the *Altmark* in classic style, but withdrew after the prisoners had been freed. The Norwegian Government protested at this highhanded action, but allowed the *Altmark* to make her way back to Germany.

## Amiot 143

The French Air Force equipped five bomber squadrons and one independent group with this twin-engined all-metal bomber, dating from the mid-thirties. They dropped leaflets and bombs on Germany in the spring of 1940. Weapon load comprised nearly 2000lb of bombs and four machine guns.

## Amphibious Tanks

Although amphibious tanks had been under development on and off since 1919, they saw very little use in the earlier part of World War II since there had been little faith in them in the interwar years. The Soviets appear to have been the most industrious researchers in this field and they introduced their T-40 in 1941. This was a light vehicle, with a two man crew and armed with machine guns. As a reconnaisance machine it was of some use, but in the early fighting against the German army it soon became evident that this and their other tanks of comparable weight and armament were useless, and it faded from view. The Germans had no proper amphibian but modified a number of their tanks to become

US amphibious DUKW crosses the Rhine.

capable of 'deep wading', using air tubes to keep the crew and engine supplied while underwater. Numbers of these tanks were used to spearhead the crossing of the River Bug during the invasion of Russia in 1941, but beyond this they saw little use.

Amphibians were developed principally by the British and US armies in order to assist seaborne landing operations, primarily on the continent of Europe. The 'DD' or 'Duplex Drive' tank, so called from its having screw propulsion as well as tracks, was developed by Nicholas Straussler, a Hungarian-born British engineer. These were standard tanks waterproofed and provided with flotation skirts which could be raised to increase bouyancy; the tank then propelled itself through the water by means of the screw system. The prime defect was that with the flotation skirt raised the tank could not use its main armament and was impotent until it reached firm ground. Valentine DD tanks were produced for training, but Sherman M4 tanks were prepared for the actual invasion, and five British, two Canadian and three US tank battalions were so equipped. Due to rough water conditions on 6 June 1944 many of the DD tanks were actually launched directly onto the beach from landing craft, but several did swim ashore. They were subsequently used in other operations involving water obstacles, notably the crossing of the Rhine and in some operations on the Scheldt, but it is doubtful if they made any decisive contribution.

## Amtracs
see Landing Vehicles, Tracked

## Anami, General Korechika, 1887–1945

As Vice Minister of War in 1940, under Konoye, and a leading member of the Army clique, Anami was involved in the power play which led to Tojo's appointment as Prime Minister.

He was later War Minister in the Suzuki Cabinet, which was maneuvering the nation towards peace. Though as convinced as most leaders of the inevitability of Japan's eventual defeat, he constantly delayed admitting this, having to save face for the army and to control his militant officers who desired a fight to the death of the whole nation. In the final days, a coup was brewing among these officers and Anami was as unable to stop them as he was unwilling to join them. However, his final refusal to join ensured that none of the highest ranking officers (except Hatanaka) joined. He committed suicide on 15 August 1945.

## Anders' Army

This was an army composed of Poles released from Russian prisons and led by Anders.

Initially, when Germany invaded Poland in September 1939, Anders and his retreating army were taken prisoner by invading Russian forces. When he, like many other Poles, refused to join the Red Army, he was imprisoned in Lubianka jail. The German invasion of Russia, June 1941, forced Stalin to come to an agreement with the Polish government in exile (London). He agreed to support a Polish army, to be organized in Russia, and appointed Anders general-in-command. Anders then attempted to trace and re-assemble all Polish POWs in Soviet labor camps, discovering in the process the enormous losses his people suffered. However, even with his army formed, the Soviets would not give him sufficient supplies nor let him fight on the Russian front, so Anders, in 1942, secured the evacuation of 159,000 Poles from Russia to Persia and Palestine. Anders estimated that over one million Poles were left in Russia. Now under the jurisdiction of the British and of the Polish Government in exile, who did not quite know what to do with him, his army received final training in Palestine until late 1943.

Anders' Army was first transferred to Quassassin, Egypt, then (January 1944) landed in Italy as part of the British 8th Army. There, they were detailed to take the heights of Monte Cassino and of Piedimonte, which barred the advance on Rome (11 May 1944) which they achieved after hand-to-hand combat and enormous casualties. In August they fought at Metauro, which drove the Germans back to the Sennio and later took Bologna.

After the German surrender, Anders' Army was a serious political embarrassment to the Allies, a wedge between Britain and the Soviets, and was therefore demobilized. Of 112,000 men, only 77 officers and 14,000 troops returned to Poland. The others were allowed to settle in Western Europe.

## Anders, General Wladyslaw, 1892–1970

Captured by the Russians after the partition of Poland in 1939, Anders was released from the Lubianka prison in 1941 to lead the Polish Prisoners of War from Russia into Persia, where the British had offered to arm and equip them to fight against the Germans in the Western Desert. This Polish II Corps became one of the most redoubtable military formations of the War. Its principal, and unforgettable, achievement was to capture Monte Cassino, 17–18 May 1944, after three attempts by other troops had failed. Anders subsequently led it in the battles up the Adriatic Coast and in the clearance of the Po Valley. Most of the II Corps chose exile at the end of the war, and Anders remained leader of their community in England until his death.

## Anson, Avro

This British reconnaissance, training, transport and rescue aircraft was in service from 1936 to 1969. The memory of 'Faithful Annie' is of utterly good-natured lumbering reliability, yet when it was new the Anson was a 'hot ship'. Except for special prototypes it was the first monoplane in the RAF, and the first aircraft with retractable landing gear, and its maximum speed of 188mph on two 350hp Armstrong Siddeley Cheetah engines, was faster than any other aircraft except single-seat interceptors. By 1939 no fewer than 760 had been delivered to 16 Bomber Command squadrons and ten of Coastal Command, most having a crew of three and carrying two machine guns, 360lb of bombs and cameras. In 1940 these highly maneuverable machines often had to fight the Luftwaffe and even shot down at least one Bf 109, but by this time the main role was that of aircrew training in Canada, where quite different versions were made in large numbers, and Rhodesia. Various engines were used, and by 1943 British production was turning to the Mk XII and later types with much larger fuselage, different structure, 425hp engines with constant-speed propellers, and hydraulic landing gear that did not have to be laboriously cranked up and down by hand. By 1952 production had reached 11,020, and they had been used for countless purposes, including search for downed aircrew, air survey, ambulance, weapon trials and finding the German radio beams that guided the Luftwaffe's attacks on Britain in 1940.

## Anti-aircraft Guns (naval)

All navies had devoted research to developing defenses against air attack during World War I, but serious progress was not made until the 1920s and 1930s. For a long time navies had pinned their faith on medium-caliber (120–152mm) guns as the main defense, but the lack of suitable fire-control made most of these weapons only partially effective. The most useful guns were light automatic close-range guns, which were most effective against dive-bombing. The British tackled the problem by designing the massive 8-barrelled pom-pom, which remained in service throughout the war. On the other hand the US Navy's 1.1in four-barrelled mounting was so unreliable that it had to be discarded in 1942. The finest AA gun was the Swedish 40mm Bofors automatic, which was used by both sides. It was built under license in Britain and the USA, and is still in service today. The lighter 20mm Oerlikon and similar guns were also widely used.

The most advanced AA fire-control system was the US Navy's Mark 37, which was used with the rugged and reliable 127mm (5in) 38 caliber dual-purpose gun on all types of warships. The standard German AA gun was the twin 10.5cm (4.1in) while the British relied on a 102mm (4in) twin. The Japanese used a 127mm medium gun and a 25mm automatic.

## Anti-tank Artillery

All the combatant nations began the war with similar anti-tank guns, all light two-wheeled models of 37-40mm caliber, firing either solid shot or piercing shell of about 2lbs weight. On average they could defeat about 50mm of homogeneous plate at 500yds range, given ideal conditions – a stationary target exactly at right-angles to the gun. The French campaign of 1940 soon showed that these guns were at the limit of their power, and new weapons were demanded. Germany developed a 5cm gun, the PAK (*Panzer Abwehr Kanone*) 38 which could defeat 78mm at 500yds with normal steel shell and 120mm with tungsten-cored shot. Britain produced the six-pounder 57mm which could beat

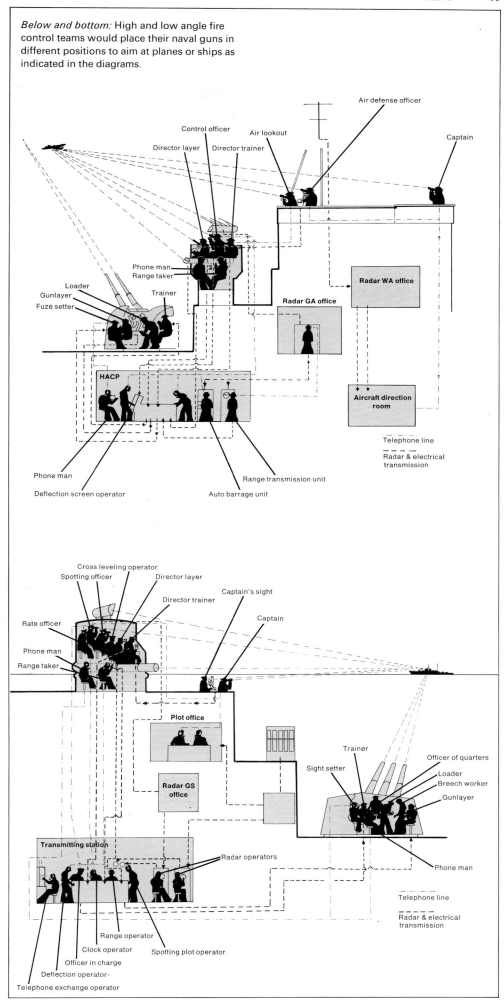

*Below and bottom:* High and low angle fire control teams would place their naval guns in different positions to aim at planes or ships as indicated in the diagrams.

US tanks advance up the Rhône Valley.

74mm at 1000yds with steel shot, 95mm with capped shot and, later, 146mm with discarding sabot shot. These guns held the ring for about a year, by which time fresh generations of tanks had appeared which demanded heavier guns to beat them. America had, by this time, adopted a 57mm which was the British gun with slight modifications, and now went to a 3in gun derived from an anti-aircraft weapon. This could defeat 105mm at 1000yds firing capped shot. Germany produced two 75mm guns, one of conventional form capable of defeating 135mm at 1000yds with tungsten shot, and one with a tapered bore which could defeat 175mm at the same range. The Germans were also, by this time, utilizing their 88mm anti-aircraft gun as an anti-tank gun and had begun to develop a 'pure' anti-tank weapon in this caliber. The Soviet Army now produced their own 57mm weapon, less powerful than either the British or US guns of this caliber, but soon followed it with a 100mm gun which could beat 185mm at 500yds.

The final generations of anti-tank guns were extremely powerful; the German 88mm PAK 43 could defeat 240mm at 1000yds; the British 17-pounder (3in), 230mm at 1000yds; and the US 90mm, 250mm at 1000yds. Even heavier guns were in the development stage; Germany produced prototypes of a 128mm gun which was capable of defeating 180mm of plate at 3000yds range, while Britain developed a 3.7in 32-pounder which probably had a similar performance – figures were never published. The penalty for this performance, however, was that the weight of the gun had reached impossible levels; the prewar guns weighed around 1000lbs and could be easily handled; the German 128mm weighed ten tons and the British 32-pounder about twelve. It was this increase in weight and decrease in agility which led to the development of recoilless guns and shoulder-fired rocket launchers and also accelerated the postwar development of anti-tank missiles. The heavy anti-tank gun, as developed during the war, has been obsolete for many years.

## Anti-tank Rifles

Anti-tank rifles were developed during the 1930s and were essentially heavy shoulder-fired rifles of conventional type firing heavy armor-piercing bullets. At the time of their introduction they were entirely capable of penetrating any service tank then known, and they were the only form of anti-tank protection available to infantry short of a towed gun. The original anti-tank rifle was, in fact, a 13mm bolt-action Mauser developed in 1918, but this did not survive the Armistice as a service weapon. The first of the new generation to enter service was the British 'Boys' rifle, named after a Captain Boys who was one of the principal designers. This rifle weighed 36lb was 63in long with a 36in barrel and fired a .55in bullet. It was a bolt action rifle; the barrel was free to recoil in its stock and the butt was heavily padded with rubber, but in spite of all this it was a difficult weapon to fire, giving a violent kick to the firer. The bullet could pierce 21mm of plate at 300 yards range.

The German Army, in the following year (1938) produced their Panzerbuchse 38. This fired a 7.92mm bullet but used a necked-down 13mm cartridge in order to generate the high velocity required for penetration. It was 51in long and it weighed 35lb and the bullet, at almost 4000ft/sec could pierce 30mm of armor at 100 yards range. The Polish Army, at this time, produced their 'WZ/35' rifle, which also used a necked-down cartridge to fire a 7.92mm bullet, but they improved performance by having a dense core of tungsten inside the bullet, an idea which was later copied by both Germany and Russia.

The Soviet Army, after some ineffectual trial models, issued their 'Degtyarev' in 1941. This fired a heavy 14.5mm bullet from a massive cartridge case; the barrel was free to recoil in its stock, an action which automatically opened the bolt after firing and ejected the spent case. The first ammunition used a steel core, but this was soon changed to a tungsten-cored bullet with which it was claimed that 25mm could be penetrated at 500 yards range. At the same time a second Soviet design, the 'Simonov' was also introduced. This was a much more complex model of self-loading rifle operated by gas piston action. It fired the same cartridge as the Degtyarev to achieve the same penetration, but in spite of its technical superiority it was a lot less robust than the Degtyarev, much heavier and much longer, and fewer were issued. Both rifles remained in service for the duration of World War II long after they had been abandoned in other armies, probably because there was no weapon in the Soviet armory capable of replacing them.

In the British and German armies though, the anti-tank rifle faded from view in about 1943 with the rise of simple shoulder-fired launchers which could fire hollow-charge projectiles. These could do far more damage to a tank, they were less difficult to fire and they were usually much easier to carry. Such devices as the PIAT, the Bazooka and the Panzerfaust pushed the anti-tank rifles aside, and there were few soldiers who wept at their passing.

## Antonescu, Marshal Ion, 1886–1946

Antonescu was dictator of Rumania during World War II. In September 1940 Antonescu was appointed Premier of Rumania and soon became dictator with the Iron Guards (a fascist organization) behind him. He immediately pledged his support to Hitler and Mussolini. He was master of his country and was allowed to repress the Iron Guards with Hitler's approval. He supported Hitler's invasion of the USSR but Rumanian divisions outside Stalingrad were blamed for the German Army's defeat. As the situation on the Eastern Front worsened, Antonescu tried unsuccessfully to pull out of his fascist alliance. In August 1944 King Michael announced a coup and Antonescu was arrested as the Red Army launched its final offensive on Rumania.

## Antonov, General Aleksei I, 1896–1962

Antonov was the Russian Chief of Staff and head of Operations from 1942–45. Son of a Tsarist artillery officer, he joined the Red Army and graduated from the Frunze Military Academy in 1921. From 1941–42 he was in action as Chief of Staff of the South and North Caucasus and then the Transcaucasus Front. General Vasilievsky chose him to be his representative in Moscow, while he was fighting on the fronts. Stalin did not like him so he was posted to the Voronezh Front, where his distinguished services led to his appointment as Deputy Chief of General Staff and Chief of Operations. His duty was to liaise with all front commanders and keep Stalin informed of the overall situation. He helped to prepare Operation Bagration (Belorussian campaign) and the Berlin Offensive. In 1944 he was the chief spokesman, putting forward Soviet military plans to the Allies at the Moscow Conference and later at Potsdam.

## Antwerp, September–November 1944

Following the Allied break-out across the Seine from Normandy in late August 1944, the German Fifteenth Army retreated at high speed across northern France into Belgium. The British 21st Army Group (Montgomery) followed, and on 3 September entered Brussels and the next day Antwerp, whose port was captured undamaged. Rather than turn his forces westward and clear the banks of the Scheldt to the North Sea 40 miles away, Montgomery persuaded Eisenhower to let him prepare an airborne advance northeastward to the Rhine (Operation Market Garden). During its execution, 17–25 September, the Fifteenth Army collected stragglers and reinforced the defenses of the Scheldt estuary, thus preventing the Allies from making use of Antwerp to resupply their armies. An acute supply shortage consequently affected their operations in the following weeks and obliged Montgomery to undertake a slow and costly clearance of the estuary (2 October–8 November), including a bloody amphibious assault on the island of Walcheren (1–8 November). The river then had to be cleared of mines, and ships did not begin to enter Antwerp until 28 November. This 85-day supply shortage was crucial in delaying the development of the Allied offensive into Germany and granted Hitler time to mount the Ardennes offensive, the main object of which was the recapture of Antwerp itself.

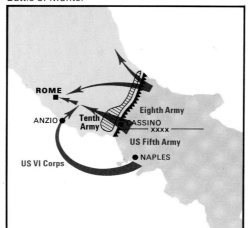

## Anzio, 21 January 1944

An Anglo-American amphibious assault, was made at Anzio south of Rome, 21 January 1944, and has since become a by-word for missed opportunity. In the winter of 1944, the Anglo-American armies in Italy, which they had invaded a year earlier, were stalemated on the Gustav Line, key point of which was Monte Cassino. Alexander and Clark, commanding the American 5th Army, planned to break the Gustav Line by two simultaneous attacks, one at Cassino itself, the other, mounted from the sea, at Anzio. It was hoped that the latter, by cutting the German Tenth Army's lines of communication, would oblige Kesselring to order the evacuation of the Gustav Line and allow the Anzio and Cassino attackers to join hands and march on Rome. The Cassino attack quickly succeeded in attracting the German reserves. But the American General Lucas, though he got

*Below:* The plan behind Anzio was to cut German communications between Rome and Cassino.
*Right:* The Germans reacted swiftly to the Allied landings.
*Bottom:* For the final breakthrough see Cassino, Battle of Monte.

his Anglo-American force easily ashore at Anzio, did not profit from the temporary weakness around his bridgehead by pressing an advance from it. When on 30 January he attempted a breakout he found the Germans organized to oppose him and was obliged thereafter to conduct a static defense. By 15 February the Germans had gathered enough strength to riposte and penetrated deeply into his positions, to be halted only by a desperate American counterattack on 19 February. The Germans then sealed in the bridgehead containing it until a general Allied offensive (11 May) permitted Truscott (who had succeeded Lucas) to break out on 23 May.

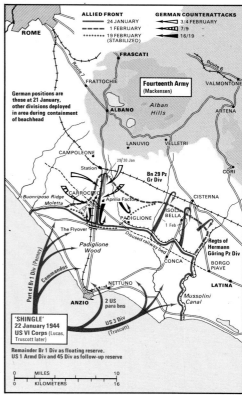

## Anvil, 15 August 1944

This was the codename for the Allied invasion of southern France, 15 August 1944. As early as August 1943 the Combined Chiefs of Staff had considered mounting an attack on southern France as a preliminary to Overlord. The British government opposed the plan, since the necessary manpower could only be found from the forces fighting in Italy, which they eventually hoped to push into Austria. Ultimately, Anvil (re-codenamed Dragoon) was adopted, but as a follow-up instead of a preliminary to the Normandy landings. Mounted by four American and three Free French divisions it began with a sea and airborne descent on the coast between Toulon and Cannes. The German Nineteenth Army (eight divisions) did not oppose it, except at Toulon and Marseilles (captured on 28 August), and the operation resolved itself into a pursuit of the retreating Germans by the Americans up the Rhône Valley. Most of the Germans escaped to fight in Alsace-Lorraine against their pursuers, the American 7th and French 1st Armies, who drove them at the end of the war into southern Germany and Austria. Its military value remains controversial.

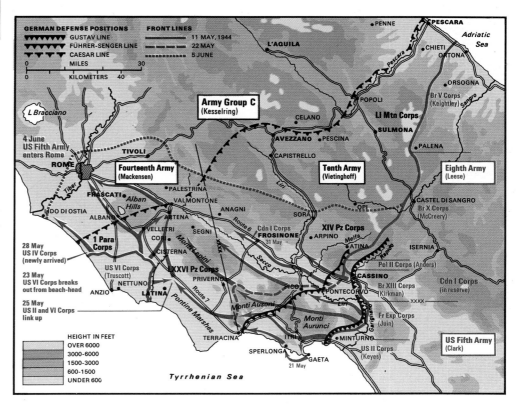

The Anzio Annie rail gun in action.

### 'Anzio Annie'

This was the nickname given to a German 28cm K5(E) railway gun which fired into the Anzio Beachhead in 1944; it was also called the 'Anzio Express'. The K5(E) was the best German railway gun of the war, and some 28 were built. It weighed 215 tons in action and was 135 feet long, including the overhang of the barrel beyond the railroad mount. The weapon was ballistically unusual in that the barrel was rifled with only 12 deep grooves and the shell was fitted with 12 curved ribs to engage with the rifling and produce the necessary spin. With the standard shell, which weighed 564lb the gun had a maximum range of 38.64 miles. A rocket-assisted shell was also produced which extended the maximum range to 53.75 miles. Towards the end of the war a 31cm smooth-bored version, firing a fin-stabilized arrow shell, reached a maximum range of 93.8 miles. The actual 'Anzio Annie' (named 'Leopold' by its German crew) is now on exhibition at the Ordnance Museum of Aberdeen Proving Ground.

---

### Aosta, Amadeo, Duke of, 1898–1942

As Governor General of Italian East Africa, and a cousin of the King of Italy, he conducted the invasion of British Somaliland in 1940 and then the defense of Abyssinia and Eritrea against the British counteroffensive in 1941. He made a last stand at Amba Alagi in May, but eventually surrendered in order to stop further useless loss of life. In testimony to his brave conduct, the British accorded him 'the Honors of War'. He died in their captivity at Nairobi.

---

### Appeasement
see Chamberlain, Prime Minister Neville

---

### Arado Ar 196

A total of 593 of these German two-seat floatplanes were built, with 960hp BMW 132K engines, maximum armament of two 20mm guns and two machine guns, and two 110lb bombs. Some flew from warships; most were used to attack submarines and small ships, and to harass Allied aircraft over the English Channel, Mediterranean and Adriatic. One forced the surrender of the submarine HMS *Seal* on 5 May 1940.

### Arado Ar 234

The Arado Ar 234 was a German jet reconnaissance-bomber, in service 1944–45. Though possibly the British turbo-jets based on Whittle's concept were more reliable, the German jet effort in World War II started much earlier and was far more diverse. In October 1940, before anyone in Britain had even thought of ordering a jet of any kind for combat duty, engineers at the Arado Flugzeugwerke had been asked to prepare studies for a jet reconnaissance aircraft. Such aircraft need the greatest possible speed and altitude, so that they can escape interception, and the Ar 234 took shape in 1941 as the first aircraft ever designed to fly faster and higher than any opponents, over enemy territory, on the power of jet engines. It was a single-seater, with the pilot in a pressurized cockpit forming the entire nose. The wing was mounted above the slim fuselage and carried the two jets in underslung nacelles. To accommodate the large amount of fuel needed, almost the whole fuselage was occupied by tankage. The main problem was that there was nowhere to put the retracted landing gear, and eventually the bold decision was taken to take off from a large trolley and land on small retractable skids under the fuselage and engines.

After extensive ground testing the first prototype flew on 15 June 1943. It was soon evident that a normal landing gear had to be provided, and the first Ar 234B, the ninth prototype, flew in March 1944 with tricycle landing gear retracting into a slightly enlarged fuselage. By September 1944 a special Sonderkommando unit had been formed to operate the Ar 234B-1 in the reconnaissance role. Powered by 1980lb-thrust Junkers Jumo 004B turbojets, this aircraft could fly at nearly 470mph at around 30,000ft and thus was immune to interception. The B-1 was used in fair numbers (about 60) over Britain and northern Italy, where no Luftwaffe aircraft had dared take photographs for months. But most of the 210 Ar 234B series that entered service were 234B-2 Blitz bombers, carrying a bomb load of up to 3086lb slung externally and also fitted with two 20mm MG 151 cannon firing directly to the rear, aimed against fighters by a pilot periscope. Many sorties were flown with 2205lb bombs against the vital Remagen bridge across the Rhine in March 1945, and at many other Allied centers. The Ar 234B was easy to fly, but it needed a long take-off run and in any case was handicapped by the Luftwaffe's desperate shortage of fuel and skilled pilots. Another Ar 234P series was under development at the end of the war.

### Arakan Offensive, Burma, December 1942–April 1943

After the British Army had retreated from Burma, they faced many problems. If they wanted to mount an offensive from Assam or Bengal, their communications and transport facilities were inadequate. They had to build airfields, roads, railways and pipelines. Britain's main effort was directed towards the Middle East and the USA was fighting in the Pacific so the India-Burma theater of war had a low priority.

General Stilwell and two Chinese 'armies' had withdrawn to India from Burma and his main objective was to reopen the Burma Road, the overland route to China. In April 1942 General Wavell planned an offensive in Northern Burma with the help of the Chinese 'armies' but when it became obvious that the lack of supplies and equipment would not allow this, Chiang Kai-shek withdrew his offer of co-operation. Wavell had to settle for a limited offensive in Arakan to recapture Akyab, for use as an air base. In December 1942 the 14th Indian Division began to advance through the swamps and jungle, but its advance was so slow that the Japanese were able to bring forward reinforcements and prepare a counteroffensive. In March 1943 the Japanese were ready to attack the 14th Division's rear at Htizwe on the Mayu River and soon they were heading for the Maungdaw-Buthidaung line.

On 14 April General Slim of 15th Indian Corps took over command and found the men were exhausted from the long march and from the lack of medicine for those men suffering from malaria. Slim decided to make a strategic withdrawal to more open territory. However his forces could not hold on to Buthidaung, which was abandoned on 6 May and shortly afterwards they left Maungdaw. The Japanese decided to halt their advance on this line. The operation was a complete fiasco for the British. Although their chances of success were poor, Wavell had insisted that the 14th continue its advance. This led the Allies completely to reorganize command in Southeast Asia. Vice-Admiral Mountbatten became Supreme Allied Commander of Southeast Asia Command (SEAC) and Wavell became Viceroy of India in June 1943.

---

### Archer

British self-propelled anti-tank gun, consisting of the 17-pounder gun mounted on a Valentine tank chassis. No turret was used, the gun being fixed so as to fire over the rear of the vehicle. In spite of this drawback it was a highly maneuverable weapon and served to good purpose in the northwest European campaign.

---

### Ardennes Offensive 1944
see Bulge, Battle of the, 1944

---

### Ardennes, Passage of, 1940

The German attack plan for the invasion of France (the Manstein Plan), placed the center of effort in the Ardennes, a region of hills and woods in south Belgium between Luxembourg and the upper Meuse. Hitler and OKH rightly presumed that the Allies would dismiss the possibility of their using it as an approach route since it appeared 'untankable'. The French compounded their error of judgment by garrisoning the Meuse sector opposite it with weak and second-rate forces, two reserve divisions of Huntziger's 2nd Army and the reserve divisions of Corap's 9th Army. The forests of the Ardennes themselves were held by the lightly-equipped Belgian *Chasseurs Ardennais*. To their south the Maginot Line offered an important obstacle, which the Germans were determined to avoid; to their north stood the Belgian Field Army and the mobile elements of the French Army and the BEF. Into the Ardennes gap between them the Germans deployed the whole of Army Group A (Rundstedt) with Fourth, Twelfth and Sixteenth Armies in First Line. The edge was supplied by the seven Panzer divisions of Hoth's, Reinhardt's and Guderian's Panzer groups. In the event, the Ardennes proved distinctly difficult for their mechanized columns to negotiate but, having crossed the Belgian and Luxembourg frontiers on 10 May their spearheads reached the Meuse between 12 and 14 May. First on the river was Rommel's Seventh Panzer Division, which arrived near Dinant at nightfall on 12 May and found a weir unguarded. Using the catwalk along its top, a patrol reached the other bank and created a bridgehead which Rommel, the following morning, was able to transform into a jumping-off place a mile deep. Next day Guderian essayed an assault crossing of the river near Sedan, in the wake of ferocious Stuka dive-bombing of the French defenders. Many were disabled or killed and others panicked and fled, so that despite stout resistance by the survivors, Guderian's assault force reached the far bank. By nightfall he had erected a pontoon bridge and begun to pass his tanks across and, shaking off a counter-attack by a cavalry division of Huntziger's Army, the next day advanced deeply into French territory. His and Rommel's break-ins signaled the beginning of the French collapse even though elsewhere on the Meuse at Monthermé and Mézières, Reinhardt's divisions were initially turned back and did not succeed in crossing in strength until 15 May.

## Arisaka Rifle

The Arisaka rifle was the basic infantry weapon of the Japanese Army from 1897 until 1945. It was developed by a commission headed by Colonel Arisaka and leaned heavily on the German Mauser for its inspiration. Introduced in 1895 as the 'Meiji 30th Year Rifle', this original Arisaka was in line with contemporary thought; a five-round magazine rifle in 6.5mm caliber, bolt action, 50in long and weighing 8.5lb. It first saw combat use in the Russo-Japanese War, after which it ran through several modifications in subsequent years.

At the outbreak of war in 1939 the standard Arisaka models in service were the 38th Year Rifle, dating from 1905 and differing from the original in various details; the 38th Year Carbine, similar to the rifle in mechanical detail but only 38in long; the 44th Year Carbine of 1911,

Soviet troops guard captured Arisaka rifles taken from the Kwantung Army in Manchuria.

essentially similar to the 38th Year Carbine but with a bayonet hinged beneath the fore-end; and the Type 97 Sniper's Rifle of 1937, which was little more than a selected 38th Year rifle with telescope sight. All these weapons were in the same 6.5mm caliber, but in the 1930s a 7.7mm cartridge had been developed for a new light machine gun and in 1939 a new rifle, the Type 99, was produced which used it also. In fact it was little more than the 38th Year re-barreled, but the opportunity was taken to produce a 'short rifle' in line with rifles of contemporary forces in other countries and also to redesign the mechanism to take advantage of manufacturing shortcuts. This rifle was later modified into the 'Parachutist's Rifle Type 99' by separating the barrel from the action by a quick-release joint, so that the weapon could be broken in two and carried in a more compact form by parachutists.

Although the quality of manufacture suffered during the war, the Arisaka was a robust enough rifle for the tasks it had to perform, and large numbers are still in use converted to sporting rifles.

## Arizona

Sister of the *Pennsylvania*, this battleship was armed with twelve 14in guns in four triple turrets, and had been launched in 1915. She was extensively modernized prewar and in 1940 had more AA guns and a radar set added. She was one of two battleships which were lost at Pearl Harbor on 7 December 1941, when her magazines detonated. Her hull lies there today, preserved as a tomb for her crew and as a war memorial.

Arisaka 38th Year carbine.

## Arkansas

Launched in 1911, the *Arkansas* was the oldest battleship serving in the US Navy in World War II. Her sister *Wyoming* had previously been disarmed to serve as a gunnery training ship, but the *Arkansas* was active through to 1945. She served in the Atlantic in 1941, bombarded the Normandy beaches and finally went to the Pacific for the assaults on Iwo Jima and Okinawa. She was sunk as an atom bomb target at Bikini on 25 July 1946.

## Ark Royal

The newest British fleet carrier in service in 1939, she soon achieved fame as the 'ship which the Germans could not sink'. This came about because a Luftwaffe pilot reported that he had 'probably' hit her with a bomb; the Propaganda Ministry broadcast repeated the erroneous claims that she had been sunk, until 'Where is the *Ark Royal?*' became a catchphrase of British counter-propaganda. Ironically, when the *Ark Royal* was sunk in 1941 the Germans proudly announced that they knew because it had been announced already by the BBC.

The '*Ark*' as she was affectionately known, had a short but successful career mainly in the Mediterranean in the convoy battles and with Force 'H'. Her torpedo-bombers scored the vital hit which slowed down the *Bismarck* in May 1941. The *Ark* was torpedoed by *U.81* thirty miles east of Gibraltar on 13 November 1941 and sank the next day. This need not have occurred; her damage had been relatively minor and the flooding had been caused by inefficient damage control. The case became a classic example of how not to cope with torpedo damage.

## Armed Merchant Cruiser

An ocean liner armed with cruiser-size guns and manned by a naval crew, the AMC, as she was known, was used particularly by the RN in both world wars to make up for the shortage of regular cruisers. They were intended mainly for blockade duties but inevitably when they came up against proper warships, the results were disastrous. Their thin plating, slow speed and vast bulk made them easy targets, but this did not stop the *Jervis Bay* and the *Rawalpindi* from fighting heroically against German capital ships.

By 1943 most of the British AMCs had been withdrawn and converted into landing ships to meet the growing demands of amphibious warfare. But the type re-emerged in a different guise; merchantmen were equipped with the latest warship-standard AA guns and fire-control to provide cover for convoys. These new conversions performed the same function as the AMC had; that is, they helped to make up for the lack of real cruisers. Similarly the Kriegsmarine used fast cargo ships converted to *Hilfskreuzer* or auxiliary cruisers as commerce-raiders. These ships carried concealed 15cm guns and in some cases torpedo-tubes, spotting aircraft and motor torpedo-boats, and they varied their appearance to confuse their victims. The most famous of these were the *Atlantis*, *Komet* and *Pinguin*. The *Kormorän* even achieved the distinction of sinking a regular cruiser, when she sank HMAS *Sydney* in November 1941.

Armor piercing projectiles.

6 pounder AP shot,
with penetrating and
ballistic caps.

German 76.2mm composite
shot, sectioned to show
tungsten core.

6 pounder APDS shot,
whole and sectioned

## Armor Piercing Ammunition

There are two basic methods of piercing armor; one uses *kinetic energy* and the other uses *chemical energy*. A kinetic energy attack involves firing a projectile which is a hard shot and is delivered at high velocity to smash a hole in the armor. With chemical energy the hole is made by application of high explosive. Kinetic attack originated with the ironclad ship in the 19th century but was brought to its highest pitch of development during World War II; chemical energy methods were developed and perfected entirely during World War II.

Kinetic methods began with a plain shot, a solid pointed projectile of hardened steel. This smashed through the plate and the inside of the ship or tank was damaged by the fragments the shot broke loose and by the shot itself ricocheting around inside. The piercing shell is similar but carries a small charge of explosive and a base fuze arranged to detonate the charge after the shell has passed through the plate, for maximum damaging effect. At velocities in the region of 2500ft/sec the shock of impact becomes so great that the projectile is likely to shatter on the outer surface of the plate without penetrating, and to conquer this the *capped shot* was developed; this has a soft steel cap protecting

2.8cm and 75mm PAK 41 armor piercing projectiles.

the point of the shot or shell, which, on striking, spreads the impact to the shoulders of the projectile without straining the point. The metal of the cap then yields and acts as a lubricant to facilitate penetration by the projectile. Since the piercing cap is blunt, it is often covered by a thin *ballistic cap* which gives better shape to the projectile and helps it to retain velocity during flight. Capped shot generally performs better against face-hardened armor, uncapped against homogeneous plate.

At striking velocities above 3000ft/sec even caps do no good and the designer must find a better material. Tungsten carbide is favored since it is extremely hard and can withstand impact at any practical velocity. Since it is about 1.4 times the density of steel it is not possible to make a full-sized shot of tungsten since it would be too heavy to develop a high velocity. Therefore a sub-caliber core of tungsten is used, and this is brought to the gun caliber by a light metal sheath. The first designs of this type were called *Composite Rigid shot* (UK) or *Hypervelocity* (USA) or *Panzergranat 40* (Germany) and have high velocity leaving the gun which soon drops due to the poor carrying ability of a light shot of full diameter. In order to achieve good carrying power it is necessary to reduce the diameter of the shot after leaving the gun, and the first solution to this was the 'Gerlich' taper bore gun in which the diameter of the shot was reduced during passage through the bore. A better solution was devised in Britain, the *Discarding Sabot* shot in which the light metal sheath is stripped away and discarded after shot ejection, leaving the heavy sub-projectile to fly to the target at high velocity.

The first chemical energy solution was the *hollow charge* or *shaped charge* in which a projectile carries a charge of high explosive with a cone-shaped recess in the nose lined with metal. When detonated at the rear of the explosive, the resulting forces cause the metal liner to flow into a fine fast-moving jet of molten metal and explosive gas traveling at about 20,000ft/sec and capable of penetrating armor. Projectiles of this type were used by most combatants during the war; originally fired from guns, it was soon discovered that the spinning of a gun projectile diffuses the penetrative jet and that fin-stabilized projectiles gave better results. Hollow charge was thus used for such items as 'Bazooka' and 'Panzerfaust' rockets, rifle grenades and similar low-velocity missiles.

The second method of chemical attack is the 'squash-head' (UK) or 'plastic' (US) shell in which a thin shell casing carries a charge of plastic high explosive and a base fuze. When

fired against armor the shell casing falls away in impact and the plastic filling is thrust onto the armor like a poultice. The base fuze detonates and a pressure wave is set up in the armor; when this wave reflects off the inner face of the plate it detaches a 'scab' of plate weighing up to 10lb. which is flung into the tank at high velocity. Note that in this form of attack the armor is not necessarily penetrated. These shells were originally called 'Wallbuster' shells as they were devised for defeating concrete when fired from Burney recoilless guns, but during the development of these shells their armor effect was discovered and followed up. No squash-head shell was ready for use in combat by 1945.

## Arnhem (Operation Market Garden), September 1944

This Anglo-American airborne operation was launched 17 September 1944 with the object of securing the crossings over the great Dutch rivers, Maas, Waal, Lower Rhine, and so opening a way for an armored advance into the north German plain before the onset of winter. Montgomery, commanding the British 21st Army Group, persuaded Eisenhower in early September that, such was the disorganization of the Germans in the west following their precipitated retreat from Normandy, he could

'bounce' their defense of the Low Countries and avoid the preparation of a long conventional offensive. This operation required the American 101st and 82nd Airborne Divisions to capture the bridges at Eindhoven and Nijmegen respectively and the British 1st Airborne Division to capture those at Arnhem. Simultaneously, with their parachute and glider landings (Operation Market), a ground advance of 64 miles by the British 30th Corps was to start from the Meuse-Escaut Canal along the same axis (Operation Garden). The American landings were a success but the British, whose drops were located deliberately far from their bridges, succeeded in capturing only the north end of one of them and were counterattacked fiercely on the first day. Bad weather and German assaults on the 30th Corps' armored column advancing on a 'single tank' front, denied them relief and their airhead was steadily reduced. On 25 September they were ordered to retire into the American area, which the 30th Corps had by then consolidated – 'a bridge too short' to bring victory. The German reaction, directed by Student and Model, was a model of flexible response, the Allied effort an awful lesson in the dangers of over-hasty strategic decisions.

*Below:* British troops fight their way back from Arnhem.
*Below left:* Parachutists descend near Arnhem.

### Arnold, General Henry H, 1886–1956

Henry Harley 'Hap' Arnold was one of the first American military aviators. He became commander of the Army Air Corps in 1938, and instituted the program of expansion which was to make it the greatest weapon of air power exercised in the war. He was also an enthusiastic champion of aid to Britain, and, on America's entry into the war, arrived in that country to organize the 8th Air Forces' strategic bombing campaign against Germany. A member of the Joint Chiefs of Staff and Combined Chiefs of Staffs Committees, he was a major Allied decision-maker and, by his relentless insistence on strategic bombing, a principal architect of Allied victory. His most cherished achievement occurred in 1947, when separate and equal status was granted to the United States Air Force; he became its first five-star General.

### Arras, Battle of, 21 May 1940

Conceived originally as an attempt to strengthen the British defense of Arras which was threatened by the extension of the German panzer corridor from the Meuse towards the sea, the Arras counterattack turned into the most fruitful British operation of the 1940 campaign. The mobile element of the force deployed under General Franklyn ('Frankforce') consisted of the 4th and 7th Royal Tank Regiments and the 8th and 6th Battalions Durham Light Infantry, divided into two columns with attached field and anti-tank artillery batteries; its tank strength was 58, and it was led by one of Britain's 'tank pioneers', G Le Q Martel. Moving east of Arras and southward with the aim of 'mopping up' Germans in the vicinity, its leading elements were surprised to find that the Germans were present in the area in great and organized strength. They, consisting principally of Rommel's Seventh Panzer Division and part of the SS *Totenkopf* Division, were most surprised to be attacked however, and reacted weakly and confusedly. Rommel only halted the tank in-

*Below:* German troops on their way to the Channel.
*Below left:* British troops advancing through Flemish Zeeland in 1944.

cursion by employing the 88mm guns of his anti-aircraft regiment – among the earliest recorded uses of those subsequently dominant weapons in the anti-tank role – and reported that he had been attacked by 'hundreds of enemy tanks'. His own situation maps are marked to show five British armored divisions. Despite Frankforce's eventual repulse, and the light losses to both sides, the attack played an important part in prompting Hitler to halt his Panzer groups outside the Dunkirk canal line and so allow the BEF's escape.

### Asdic (Sonar)

This British device, named after the 1917 Allied Submarine Detection Investigation Committee, was used to detect submerged objects. It operated on the following principle: an electric alternating current was passed through a quartz crystal causing it to vibrate and send sound-pulses through the water. These pulses bounced off solid objects and the lapsed time-interval between sending and receiving the impulses indicated distance, much like radar. Asdic was kept completely secret from 1921 until 1940 when the Germans found details of sets supplied to the French Navy.

In 1939, 200 destroyers were fitted with it, and it gave the Admiralty a feeling of overconfidence – the Admiralty's claim that it had defeated the U-Boat proved optimistic. Nevertheless, without Asdic the Battle of the Atlantic could not have been won, and under its American name, Sonar, it remains in use.

The early Asdic sets could only search in a 'lobe' extending in a narrow and shallow beam around the ship, and so when the final run-in to attack with depth-charges was carried out the surface escort lost contact. Initially the solution was to design ahead-firing weapons such as 'Hedgehog' which could operate while the U-Boat was still in contact. However, specially designed attack-Asdics were eventually developed. During the Second World War Asdic- and Sonar-fitted warships sank 246 U-Boats, and assisted in another 48 sinkings. Asdic turned out to be one of the most vital weapons in the Allied naval arsenal and was instrumental in the winning of the war against U-Boats.

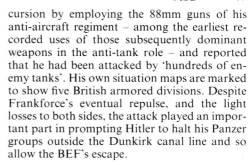

## Atlantic, Battle of, June 1940–May 1945

The biggest campaign of the entire naval war, the Battle of the Atlantic was waged between the Kriegsmarine's U-Boats, surface raiders and aircraft on the one side and the merchant shipping and navies of the Allies on the other. It is usually defined as starting with the Fall of France in June 1940, when the U-Boats were able to move along the Atlantic coast, and ending with the German surrender in May 1945. It was in addition to an Axis-Allies direct confrontation, a battle for communications and supplies between Great Britain and the North American continent. The Battle of the Atlantic also served as the link between what would otherwise have been two separate wars, the European and the Pacific. It was vital to British survival but it was also vital to American strategic aims, for had the Atlantic been dominated by U-Boats, America would have been unable to bring any pressure to bear on Hitler.

The battle divides into distinct phases:
(1) July 1940–December 1941: the USA entered World War II
(2) January 1942–March 1943: the U-Boats reached their peak in power and Allied countermeasures were only just in time to stave off defeat
(3) April-May 1943: the U-Boats suffered a severe defeat and had to be withdrawn for re-equipping
(4) June 1943–May 1945: Allied surface and air forces waged an offensive against U-Boats.

When the Battle of the Atlantic ended, 785 U-Boats had been sunk, and 11,899,732 tons (2232 ships) had been sunk in the North Atlantic alone.

---

## Atlantic Charter

The Atlantic Charter was a joint declaration of peace aims, which was signed by President Roosevelt and Prime Minister Churchill at a mid-Atlantic meeting. Although the USA was still neutral this was another step to prepare the American people for war. It contained eight principles:
(1)  no territorial aggrandizement,
(2)  no territorial changes without the consent of the people concerned,
(3)  self-government by all nations,
(4)  international economic co-operation,
(5)  improved labor standards, economic advancement, and social security for all people,
(6)  freedom from fear or want,
(7)  freedom of navigation on the high seas,
(8)  general disarmament after the war.

These eight principles were endorsed by the United Nations Declaration which was signed by 26 countries.

Churchill aboard HMS *Prince of Wales* where the Atlantic Charter was signed.

*Top:* A section of the Atlantic Wall.
*Above:* Early warning radar near Brest along the Atlantic Wall in 1942.

## Atlantic Wall

The Atlantic Wall was constructed by the Germans for the defense of Fortress Europe after their capture of France in June 1940. Although strong in places it was discovered to be dangerously weak along most of the Atlantic and Channel coasts by Rommel who reported his findings to Hitler. It was breached successfully on D-Day 6 June 1944.

---

## *Atlantis*

Known to the Admiralty as Raider 'C' and to the Germans as *Hilfskreuzer No. 2*, the *Atlantis* was one of the most successful German surface raiders. Built as the Hansa line's *Goldenfels*, she left Germany in March 1940 and cruised with remarkable success away from the busy traderoutes, pouncing on lone merchantmen by pretending to be a friendly ship. By June 1941 she had sunk 21 ships (140,900 tons) but was destined to sink only one more ship before she was caught on 22 November 1941 and sunk by the cruiser *Devonshire* in the South Atlantic.

---

## Attlee, Clement, 1883–1967

Attlee was leader of the Labor Party in the United Kingdom and Churchill's deputy throughout the war. Before the war he had op-

posed appeasement and fascism and once war broke out he devoted his energies to ensuring that the war economy was free from labor disputes. His post in the War Cabinet was Secretary of State for Dominion Affairs but his main task was to take over from Churchill when he was abroad. In July 1945 the Labor Party won the general election, Attlee became Prime Minister and attended the Potsdam and San Francisco Conferences. Although he appeared unimpressive, he had a quick mind and was a good negotiator. Called 'a sheep in sheep's clothing' by an angry Churchill, Attlee's six-year reign as Prime Minister after the war instituted the beginnings of socialism and decolonization for Britain.

---

## 'A' Type Midget Submarines

These two-man midget submarines were developed from prototypes built in 1934, and were first used at Pearl Harbor. However they proved largely unsuccessful because of their limited range; their most important success was the torpedoing of the British battleship *Ramillies* in Madagascar in 1942.

---

## Auchinleck, Field Marshal Sir Claude, 1884–1981

Auchinleck had distinguished himself as a regimental officer of the Indian Army in Mesopotamia during World War I and subsequently on the Northwest Frontier. By 1939 he was one of the most senior and distinguished officers of the Indian Army and, against established practice, was brought from it to command 4th Corps of the British Army at home. After a spell of duty in Norway in 1940, and a return to India as Commander in Chief in 1941, he was chosen by Churchill to succeed Wavell as Commander in Chief Middle East in June 1941. His task was to supervise the most difficult stage of the Desert War, when the British were at their weakest and most demoralized and Rommel at his strongest and most audacious. By July 1942 Auchinleck had sufficiently got the measure of things to inflict on Rommel his first serious defeat in the battle now generally known as First Alamein. Churchill, however, had never been able to forgive him for the fall of Tobruk, at the beginning of his period of command, and relieved him immediately after the victory. He was replaced by Alexander. 'The Auk' continued nevertheless to enjoy the respect of his soldiers both of the British Army and the Indian of which he remained Commander in Chief until after independence in 1947.

---

**Auschwitz** see Holocaust

---

## Austen Submachine Gun

As the name implies, this was the Australian version of the Sten Gun. In fact it combined the best features of the Sten with those of the German Maschinenpistole 38, the net result being a very good weapon of the type. In spite of this, the troops preferred the Owen Gun and no more than about 20,000 Austens were produced.
length 33.25in
weight 8.75lb
magazine 28 rounds
barrel 7.75in
rate of fire 500rpm

## Austria, Liberation of, 1945

On 16 March 1945 Marshal Malinovsky resumed his drive across central Europe and by 4 April was within five miles of Vienna. Vienna fell on 14 April and Malinovsky moved westwards. In late April General Patch invaded Austria from Bavaria to attack the so-called 'National Redoubt' in the Alps. His 7th Army reached the Brenner Pass but did not make contact with the US 5th Army (which was advancing from Italy) before the Germans unconditionally surrendered on 8 May.

## Avenger, Grumman TBF

This US three-seat naval torpedo-bomber was operational from 1942 to 1954. The prototype Avenger, flown on 1 August 1941, was Grumman's first torpedo-carrying aircraft and bore a strong family likeness to the company's fighters, with its 1700hp Wright R–2600 radial engine, squat fuselage and angular wings and tail. Deliveries to the US Navy began only six months later, and the TBF–1 flew into action for the first time on 4 June 1942, from a land base during the Battle of Midway. Of six aircraft dispatched, one staggered back, with its bomb doors open, one wheel dangling and a dead gunner on board. This was but one more example of a good aircraft getting off to a bad start. The Avenger proved so valuable eventually that a total of 9836 were produced by Grumman and Eastern Aircraft for the USN, Royal Navy (921) and RNZAF (63). Versions with radar, reconnaissance cameras and a searchlight appeared in 1944–45, and continued in service long after VJ-Day for anti-submarine, early warning and other specialized tasks.

*Below:* Grumman Avengers in formation.

## Axis, Berlin–Rome–Tokyo

Axis was a term coined by Mussolini to describe the common aims of his fascist regime and Hitler's Nazi Germany. These were first laid down in an agreement in October 1936 and then formalized in the Pact of Steel in May 1939. On 27 September 1940 it was made into a Tripartite pact when the Japanese joined but the USSR refused to join after some detailed negotiations. The pact spelled out the conditions under which these countries would co-operate in the event of war and were published, but it also contained a secret protocol which agreed on policy towards the USSR. Germany and Japan did not co-ordinate their war aims and although Germany promised aid to Japan, this never happened in any substantive way.

Hitler meets Mussolini prior to the signing of the Pact of Steel in 1939 which solidified the Rome–Berlin Axis.

*Below:* The Grumman TBF Avenger.

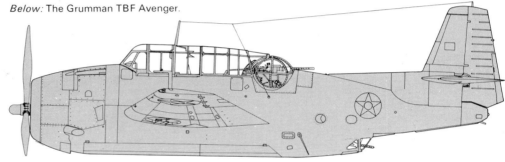

# B

## B–17 Flying Fortress, Boeing

This US heavy bomber was operational from 1937 to 1946. With smaller numbers of B–24 Liberators, Fortresses spearheaded the USAAF's daylight offensive against Europe which, with the RAF night offensive, provided round-the-clock attacks. The prototype flew on 28 July 1935, but production built up slowly as the US government was not convinced that such an aircraft was needed. The RAF bought 20 B–17C models, which it used for high-altitude raids by individual aircraft over Germany, with little success, apart from proving, in combat, that the name 'Flying Fortress' was a misnomer. RAF experience convinced the USAAF that much heavier armament was needed, particularly against attack from the rear, and that the best protection would be provided by flying large numbers of B–17s in 'box' formations, enabling them to produce heavy crossfire for mutual defense. Initial USAAF attacks on Europe, in 1942, still incurred heavy losses, but the Americans persisted with their daylight offensive, believing the greater accuracy (in a pre-radar era) to be of key importance. As de-

fensive armament built up to a staggering thirteen 0.5in guns (paired in nose, chin, dorsal, ventral and tail turrets, singly on each beam and from the radio compartment), air combat losses inflicted on the Luftwaffe began to take their toll, in parallel with a growing fuel shortage in Germany. In contrast, B–17 production grew steadily, with Boeing, Douglas and Lockheed all contributing to the final total of 12,731 of the big bombers that were built. Most numerous were the B–17Gs, with improved turbochargers on their four 1200hp Wright Cyclone engines, which enabled them to cruise at up to 35,000ft. The maximum speed of this version was 287mph. The main drawback was that the type of operations flown by the USAAF meant that the average bomb-load of a B–17 was only two tons, against a maximum of eight or nine tons that could be carried short distances. Nonetheless, so sustained was the US offensive, with so many aircraft employed, that B–17s dropped a total of 571,460 tons of bombs on European targets alone, as well as shooting down huge numbers of Luftwaffe fighters. Less well-known is that a special Luftwaffe unit, I/KG200, flew captured Fortresses in German markings to drop secret agents by parachute and keep them supplied while they performed tasks like the construction of a chain of clandestine airstrips and fuel dumps in the Western Desert. As part of the cloak and dagger act, these aircraft were known as Dornier Do 200s.

## B–18, Douglas

At the outbreak of World War II most US Army bomber squadrons flew B–18s and B–18As, which utilized the wings, tail unit and power plant of the DC–2 airliner. Many of those based in Hawaii were destroyed in the Pearl Harbor attacks; others were replaced by B–17s in 1942, after which 76 of them were fitted with nose radar and magnetic anomaly detection (MAD) gear for anti-submarine operations in the Caribbean.

*Below:* Boeing B-17G Flying Fortress.
*Bottom:* B-17 nicknamed *Yankee* refueling.

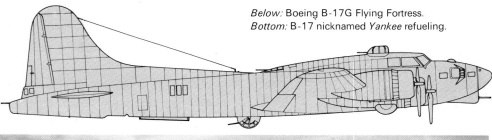

Tire and wheel maintenance on a B-24 of the 8th Air Force.

## B–24 Liberator, Consolidated

This US heavy bomber was operational from September 1941 to 1947. The B–24 was a later design than the B–17, its partner in the great US daylight bomber offensive over Europe. It dropped a smaller weight of bombs (404,025 tons) on Europe, and is reckoned to have destroyed eleven Luftwaffe aircraft per thousand sorties flown, as against 23 per thousand by B–17s. However, the total of 18,188 Liberators built for the USAAF, USN and their allies was greater than the production of any other US aircraft of World War II. The RAF acquired 1694, becoming the first air force to deploy the type operationally. Its Liberator Is helped to close the mid-Atlantic 'gap' where U-Boats had previously been beyond the reach of land-based aircraft and even the Sunderland flying-boats of Coastal Command. The effectiveness of these aircraft was enhanced by fitting them with radar and Leigh lights for illuminating submarines caught on the surface at night. In a period of six days in March 1945, aircraft from five RAF squadrons sank seven U-Boats. However, it was as a bomber that the Liberator achieved its

B-24 Liberator *Betsy* on a mission in New Guinea.

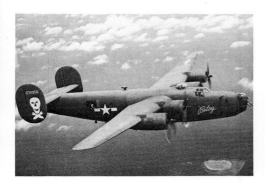

greatest fame. As well as participating in the massive 8th Air Force offensive from the UK, B–24s gave outstanding service in the Middle East. Their best-remembered raid in that theater was probably the attack on the Ploesti oilfields in Rumania on 1 August 1943, which also proved one of the most costly, with 57 of the force of 177 aircraft lost. In the Pacific B–24s almost completely replaced the shorter-range B–17s and carried the main burden of the USAAF bombing operations until the Superfortress arrived. The most-produced version was the B–24J, which carried a crew of up to ten men, an armament of ten 0.5in guns in nose, dorsal, ventral 'ball' and tail turrets and in beam positions, and a maximum bomb load of 12,800lb for short distances. Normal bomb load was about 5000lb, which could be carried on a 1700 mile round trip lasting 7.3 hours at 25,000ft. Power plant comprised four 1200hp turbocharged Pratt & Whitney R–1830 radials. Many Liberators were converted or adapted for service as C–87 transports and F–7 photographic reconnaissance aircraft.

## B–25 Mitchell, North American

This US light bomber was operational from late 1941. Like the Marauder, the Mitchell was ordered into production in August 1939, when the first flight was still a year away, on 19 August 1940. All B–25s had two 1700hp Wright R–2600 engines and a crew of up to six men; but gross weight increased progressively from the B–25A, at 27,100lb, to the B–25J, at 35,000lb, as further equipment and weapons were added. Normal bomb load of the B–25J was six 500lb or three 1000lb bombs; armament was basically seven 'point fives', with three in the nose, two in a forward upper turret and two in a tail turret. However, it was possible to fit four forward-firing guns in packages attached to the sides of the forward fuselage, and waist hatches for two more. Or the glazed nose could be replaced by

*Below:* B-25H over the Hump between India and China.
*Bottom:* B-25 Mitchell evades anti-aircraft fire in the Pacific.

a 'solid' nose housing eight 'point fives' instead of three. This raised the maximum possible number of guns to an incredible 18. Added to the eight 5in rockets which could be carried under the outer wings, it made the B–25J extremely formidable in the basic attack role. By comparison, the earlier B–25Gs and Hs, fitted with a 75mm gun and fourteen 0.5in guns, achieved little success.

Nearly 11,000 B–25s of all models were built; 9816 went to the USAAF, the rest to the USN, Royal Air Force (over 800) and other Allied air forces. The best remembered raid was that made on Tokyo in April 1942 by sixteen B–25Bs which took off at sea from the carrier *Hornet*, led by Lt Col James H Doolittle. To save weight, the dorsal turret and bombsight were removed, and two wooden poles were stuck in each rear turret to scare away would-be attackers. As a boost to US morale, at a period when the war had brought only disaster, it was a tremendous success. There was plenty of time left for Mitchells to show their genuine destructive capability in later, more orthodox operations.

## B–26 Marauder, Martin

This US light bomber was operational from 1942–48. Few aircraft have had a less promising start to their combat career than the B–26. The specification to which it was designed called for an emphasis on high speed, range and service ceiling, carrying a crew of five, four 0.3in guns and 2000lb of bombs. Nothing was said about take-off and landing performance, and the Martin proposal seemed to meet the requirement so adequately that its wing loading – the highest ever proposed for a US combat aircraft – was given scant attention. When war broke out in Europe, an order for 1100 production models was placed, under the designation B–26, long before the first aircraft flew on 25 November 1940. When delivery of operational aircraft began in the following year, the troubles started. The high wing loading, large engine nacelles, and nicely streamlined but portly fuselage gave, inevitably, such a high landing speed that accidents were frequent as pilots tried to convert from less demanding bombers. The situation was made worse when the B–26A brought provision for additional fuel in bomb-bay tanks, a 22in torpedo under the fuselage, and a switch to 0.5in guns, instead of 0.3s, in the nose and tail. Despite this, B–26As were in action as bombers over New Guinea by April 1942, and as torpedo aircraft at the Battle of Midway in June. When the B–26B entered service at a gross weight of 36,500lb, instead of the original 30,035lb, with engine output raised from 1850hp to 1920hp, something had to be done to make the take-off and landing performance less lethal. Later Bs had slotted flaps and then an increase in wing span from 65ft to 71ft. Unfortunately, weight climbed to 38,200lb at the same time, as a result of increasing the defensive armament to twelve 0.5in guns. This gave a wing loading much higher than that of the troublesome early models. Blackest day in the Marauder's history was 14 May 1943, when eleven UK-based aircraft made their first low-level attack as part of the US 8th Air Force, on Ijmuiden in Holland. None returned. High-level strategic missions were more successful, but the B–26 proved its true capability only when it was transferred to the 9th Air Force and used for tactical support. It ended the war with the lowest loss rate per thousand sorties of any US light bomber.

## B–29 Superfortress, Boeing

This US long-range bomber was operational from mid-1944 to the early fifties. The B–29 is remembered as the aircraft which brought World War II to a sudden end by dropping two atomic bombs on Japan; but such weapons did not exist when it was designed. The USAAF made known its requirement for a 'Hemisphere Defense Weapon' in February 1940, before the German blitzkrieg was launched against western Europe. The new aircraft had to be able to carry 2000lb of bombs for 5333 miles, with a speed of 400mph. It had to have heavy defensive armament and armor, self-sealing fuel tanks and a maximum bomb load of 16,000lb. The original version of the B–29, designed by Boeing, could match this specification in almost all respects except speed, which was 358mph at 25,000ft. It could carry up to 20,000lb of bombs with a crew of ten; armament comprised four remotely controlled turrets, each housing two 0.5in guns, and one 20mm or three more 0.5in guns in a tail turret. By 1941 the requirement for such an aircraft seemed so urgent that the USAAF decided production could not wait for testing of the prototype. By the time the first XB–29 flew, on 21 September 1942, orders already totalled well over 1500, each powered by four 2200hp Wright R–3350 radial engines. A year later the decision was taken to use B–29s exclusively against Japan, from bases in India and China. Tokyo came within reach of the big bombers when five bases, each able to accommodate a full 180-aircraft Wing, were opened on the Mariana Islands. High-level daylight raids began on 24 November 1944, without great success. A new and deadlier phase was initiated on 9 March 1945 when 334 B–29s made a low-level night attack on Tokyo with fire bombs. Some 80,000 Japanese died among the closely packed wooden buildings – a death toll even higher than that caused by the atomic bomb dropped on Hiroshima five months later. The intervening months brought a long succession of attacks with incendiaries on the main cities of Japan, fighter opposition being so small and ineffective that the B–29s shed all but their tail guns to save weight and so carry a heavier bomb-load. Fuel supplies for the defenses were cut further by raids on oil refineries, made more accurate by use of radar bomb-sights. The results of all attacks were recorded by camera-equipped F–13A Superfortresses. Altogether, more than 2000 Superfortresses were delivered by VJ-Day. Production ended in May 1946, with the total at 3960. Many were converted into flight refueling tankers; surviving bombers took part in the later war in Korea and 88 were lent to the RAF, as Washingtons, in 1950–58.

*Below:* B-29s hammered Japan in the last months of the war.
*Bottom:* B-29s under construction.

## Bader, Squadron Leader Sir Douglas, 1910–

One of the most well-known airmen of World War II, Bader's triumph over disablement, following the loss of both legs in a flying accident in 1931, and his subsequent acceptance back into the RAF, became as legendary as his reputation as a pilot with No 242 Squadron, RAF Fighter Command. Although greatly respected by his German adversaries, his individual approach to the problem of enemy interception (ie, the 'Big Wing' formation, during the Battle of Britain) while supported by his Group Commanding Officer, was strongly opposed by Fighter Command Headquarters. In 1941 he was captured after a mid-air collision with an enemy aircraft.

## Badoglio, Marshal Pietro, 1871–1957

Badoglio was an anti-fascist who had opposed Mussolini at first. He became Chief of Staff and successfully fought in Abyssinia and was rewarded with the title Duke of Addis Ababa. In December 1940 he resigned after Italy's failure in Greece. On 25 July 1943 he declared a coup against Mussolini and although he had kept five divisions near Rome, he could not prevent the Germans moving troops into northern Italy. He fled to Brindisi with King Victor Emmanuel and joined the Allies, who landed at the Gulf of Salerno on 8 September. Negotiations for peace with the Allies resulted in an unconditional surrender being signed on 28 September 1943, but this was too late because the Germans were now in control of most of Italy. Badoglio resigned in June 1944 and was replaced by Bonomi.

## Baetscher, Major Hans-Georg

This German bomber pilot flew 658 missions, the greatest number made in a multi-engined aircraft over enemy territory. With a career spanning the whole war, he served with the pathfinder Kampfgruppe 100, flying He 111s against Britain in 1940 and 1941, then in Russia with Kampfgeschwader 100, and finally as Commander of 111/K.G.76 which was equipped with the Arado 234 jet bomber.

## Bagramyan, Marshal Ivan K, 1897–

Bagramyan was a Front Commander in the latter half of the war who led the Russian armies into East Prussia. He graduated from the Frunze Military Academy in 1934 and his first important appointment came in 1938 when he became Operations Deputy Chief of Staff in the Kiev Military District. In 1941 he was Chief of Staff of the Southwestern Front under General Kirponos. In 1942 he became Commander of the 16th (later 11th) Guards Army and fought on the Bryansk Front, at Kursk and Kiev. On 16 November 1943 he was promoted to General and Commander of the 1st Baltic Front in place of General Yeremenko. Bagramyan was ordered to take Riga and encircled the German Army Group North in the Memel. He was held responsible for the initial failure to take Königsberg. At the end of the war he was appointed Commander of the Baltic Military District.

## Bagration
see Belorussia, Battle for, 1944

## Balaton, Battle of Lake
see Hungary, Liberation of, 1944–45

## Balck, General Hermann, 1893–

Commissioned into the Tenth (Hanoverian) *Jäger*, which Guderian had shortly before also joined, he had a distinguished career as a regimental officer in World War I. It was not until World War II, however, that his rise began, and it dated from his remarkable display of leadership in the opening stages of the Battle of France. As commander of *Schutzenregiment 1* in First Panzer Division of Guderian's Panzer Group, he established the first German bridgehead across the Meuse at Sedan. Taking advantage of a heavy air attack on the strongly defended far bank, he raced his men across in storm boats and seized sufficient ground for the divisional bridging train to set up its pontoons for the waiting tanks. For this success he was promoted to command a division in the invasion of Russia which he handled with such flair, particularly during the Russian counteroffensive of December 1941 that by the succeeding spring he had been promoted full General. In September 1944 he was given command of Army Group G in the West, in succession to Blaskowitz. His failure, against overwhelming odds, to prevent Patton's advance into Lorraine displeased Hitler however, and he finished the war commanding a mere sub-army, *Armeegruppe Balck*, opposite the Russians in Hungary. 'If Manstein was Germany's greatest strategist during World War II', wrote General Mellenthin, 'Balck has strong claims to be regarded as our finest field commander. He had a superb grasp of tactics and great qualities of leadership.'

## Balkans, Campaign in, 1941

Hitler in 1940 was anxious to extend his control over Central Europe, established by the Anschluss with Austria, the annexation of Czechoslovakia in 1938 and the occupation of western Poland in 1939, southwards into the Balkans. Italy already had a presence there, as a result of its occupation of Albania in 1939, and Mussolini had unfulfilled ambitions elsewhere in the Balkans. The dictators' first move was to impose in August 1940 a redistribution of territory on the three states most amenable to their influence, Rumania, Hungary and Bulgaria. The latter was granted a portion of Rumanian territory and Hungary was granted a major slice of Rumanian Transylvania by this so-called Vienna Award. The Rumanians, whose Bessarabian province had been compulsorily ceded to Russia in 1939, were infuriated and deposed their king, Carol II, but the regent, Michael, felt unable to outface the dictators and transferred power to a pro-Axis regime under General Antonescu. On 7 October German troops entered the country to be followed by Italians a week later. Hungary agreed to join the Axis in November and Bulgaria on 1 March 1941. On 25 March Yugoslavia's regent, Prince Paul, also agreed to sign the Tripartite Pact (Germany-Italy-Japan) but a group of patriot officers, led by Generals Simovic and Mirkovic, overthrew him two days later and organized an anti-Axis government.

This action triggered a well-prepared plan to subdue Yugoslavia by force (Operation Margarita). On 6 April 1941 two German armies, Second (Weichs) and First Panzer (Kleist) attacked in the north and south of the country, from Austria and Bulgaria respectively. They were assisted, for what it was worth, by the Third Hungarian and Second Italian Armies in the north.

The Yugoslav army, which was only partly mobilized, at once opened its own campaign against the Italians in Albania and made progress for several days. On the vital fronts, however, their resistance swiftly collapsed. On the northern frontier, the Fourth and Seventh Armies were stricken by mutinies among their Croats, the Catholic Slavs of the region whose loyalty to the artificially created and Serb-dominated kingdom had always been tepid. In the south the Panzers found the terrain a greater obstacle than the Yugoslav 5th Army. By 12 April the Germans were converging on Belgrade from three directions and the following day entered the city. An armistice was signed three days later. The Croatian area of the country became a puppet state under a pro-German (*Ustasi*) regime, the rest came under direct military administration. Almost as soon as the regular campaign had ended, however, fugitive elements of the Army, both pro-Royalists (*Četnik*) and Communist (Partisan), began guerrilla operations from the mountain regions against the German occupation forces.

## Balkans, Liberation of the, 1944–45

In August 1944 the Red Army opened up its offensive into Rumania and General Malinovsky crossed the river Pruth and captured Jassy. On 23 August King Michael of Rumania arrested Antonescu, the dictator, and dismissed the government. He announced immediate cessation of hostilities and agreed to an armistice. Many Rumanian troops changed sides and Malinovsky swept on to the Ploesti oilfields. On 31 August the Russians entered Bucharest and on the next day reached the Danube at the frontier of Bulgaria. Bulgaria proclaimed its neutrality but the Red Army marched into the country on 8 September and occupied Sofia a week later. Within two weeks the Red Army had disarmed the Germans and had gained control.

Bulgarian troops on the Eastern Front.

The Russians turned to Belgrade and Budapest, now that they had opened up a supply route up the valley of the Danube. Hitler had to order the withdrawal of his troops from Greece and Yugoslavia. Tolbukhin reached the Yugoslav border at Turnu Severin on 6 September and with Tito's partisans attacked Belgrade, which eventually fell on 20 October.

## Baltimore, Martin A–30

The rear gunner of the Maryland was separated from the other two crew members by transverse bulkheads. The Baltimore, developed from the Maryland to meet British requirements, had a deepened fuselage permitting movement between all crew positions. Performance was improved by fitting two 1660hp Wright GR–2600 engines, giving a maximum speed of 302mph, with a crew of four, 2000lb bomb load, and armament of eight or ten machine guns, which could be supplemented by four fixed rearward-firing guns. A total of 1575 were delivered to the RAF from October 1941, in five versions. They were employed on day and night bombing duties, exclusively in the Mediterranean theater until the end of the war.

## Ba Maw, Dr, 1893–

Ba Maw was a Burmese lawyer and party leader who had received his PhD from Bordeaux in 1924 and was appointed Burmese Head of State by the Japanese. Under the British, Ba Maw had been Prime Minister but had made speeches critical of Great Britain and had been imprisoned in 1940. In 1942 he was appointed national leader of Burma and opened negotiations for Burma's independence. He was often at loggerheads with the Japanese about this and was very angry when Burma was not given all of the Shan States, some going to Siam instead. In August 1943 Burma was finally made independent although the Japanese Army remained, and Ba Maw declared war on the USA and Great Britain. When the British moved back into Burma in 1944 Ba Maw went into hiding and set up the Supreme Defense Council to organize war activities against the British. Eventually captured, he was imprisoned by the Americans in Sugawo Prison in Tokyo from December 1945 to July 1946. On release he formed and led the Maha Bama (Greater Burma) Party until he was again imprisoned by the U Nu Regime from August 1947 to July 1948. Ba Maw is said to have retired from active politics in 1957 but not sufficiently to resist being imprisoned by the Ne Win regime in May 1966. His whereabouts and health at the present moment are unknown.

## Barbarossa, Operation, 1941

The preliminary planning of Barbarossa, the German invasion of the USSR, began as early as August 1940 when General Marcks presented a plan for the defeat of the USSR in nine to seventeen weeks, using 110 infantry, 24 Panzers with 12 infantry divisions. This plan involved two central Army Groups, one operating in the Ukraine and one against Moscow. After extensive war games and discussions, Barbarossa evolved as a three-pronged operation. Hitler decided that Moscow would not be his main target, as this had been Napoleon's downfall and he did not think that it was the center of power in the USSR. The southern Army Group would still aim for Kiev and the Ukraine but the two northern Groups would first aim at controlling communications to Moscow, then encircle Leningrad before knocking out Moscow. On 3 February 1941 Hitler gave his final approval to Barbarossa which now consisted of 116 infantry divisions (14 motorized), 19 Panzers and nine lines-of-communications divisions. Army Group North was commanded by Field Marshal von Leeb and consisted of the Sixteenth and Eighteenth Armies of 18 infantry divisions and the First Panzer Group under General Höpner. Army Group Center was commanded by Field Marshal von Bock and consisted of the Fourth and Ninth Armies with the Second and Third Panzer Groups under Generals Guderian and Hoth. Army Group South was commanded by General von Rundstedt and consisted of the Sixth and Seventeenth Armies, the Third and Fourth Rumanian Armies and General von Kleist's Fourth Group.

*Below:* Civilian transport helped motorized convoys advance in Operation Barbarossa in the summer offensive of 1941.

*Above:* The Wehrmacht burned its way across the Russian steppes in the summer of 1941.
*Left:* Germans advance toward Moscow in August 1941 during the Barbarossa offensive.

The Panzer Groups were used as independent groups in advance of the main army. They operated some 60 miles ahead of the infantry and encircled the Red Army units by long-range pincer movements and then wheeled inwards leaving the infantry to complete the encirclement. Guderian argued that the Panzer units should race to the Dniepr and then wheel inwards but Hitler rejected this. The date for Barbarossa had been set for April so that German armies could be transferred from Western Europe to the Eastern Front without arousing too much attention from the Russians. However Hitler then decided that his army had to intervene in Yugoslavia and this delayed the invasion until the end of June. This delay was crucial as it meant that Barbarossa was extended until December and the German army had not been prepared to fight in winter conditions. In the first week of the invasion the Luftwaffe achieved complete control of the air and destroyed 2000 Soviet planes. Although the Red Army was not prepared for the German attack, Soviet generals had been warned of the German plans and knew about the troop movements on the German border.

Army Group Center swept along Minsk-Smolensk road, Guderian's group crossed the Niemen in the north and Hoth crossed the Bug in the south. The Germans were trying to encircle the mass of the Red Army in the center, but they did not find the Red Army in 1941 as easy to defeat as the French in 1940. Brest-Litovsk was encircled on the first day but the garrison held out for a week. The Army Group Center tried to encircle pockets at Bialystok, Volkovysk and Mursk, but at least 400,000 Russians fought their way out.

Although by mid-July the Red Army had lost 164 divisions it was only when the Germans had encircled the pockets at Mogilev, Vitebsk and Smolensk that it looked as if Hitler might succeed where Napoleon had failed and conquer Russia in one campaign.

However, the German Army failed to reach Moscow and victory before the winter possibly because of Hitler's insistence on fighting another campaign in the Ukraine, depleting his resources.

## Barents Sea, Battle of

see North Cape, Battle of and *Deutschland*

## *Barham*

This British battleship of the *Queen Elizabeth* Class was built 1913–15. She was a veteran of World War I, having led the 5th Battle Squadron at Jutland, and had been partially modernized between the wars. At the outbreak of war she was part of the Home Fleet, and was torpedoed by *U.30* off the northwest coast of Scotland on 28 December 1939. When her repairs were completed three months later she was sent to reinforce the Mediterranean Fleet, and took part in several operations. She was the second ship in the battle line at the Battle of Cape Matapan on 28 March 1941.

Although the *Barham* was an old-fashioned ship which lacked the refinements of her modernized sisters *Queen Elizabeth, Valiant* and *Warspite*, she had amply proved her worth. It is all the more surprising, therefore, to find that on 15 April 1941 the Admiralty informed Admiral Cunningham that he was to sink the *Barham* in the entrance to Tripoli harbor, in an attempt to stop supplies reaching the Axis forces in North Africa. Cunningham replied tartly that if he must make a choice between sacrificing a first-class fighting unit and exposing his fleet to risks he would rather order the whole fleet to bombard Tripoli.

The argument became academic when the battle for Crete began a month later. On 27 May the *Barham* was hit by two 500lb bombs; she was not seriously damaged but needed two months' repairs at Durban. On 24 November 1941 she put to sea with the other ships of the fleet from Alexandria, and the following day she was torpedoed by *U.331* off Sollum. Three torpedoes struck her on the port side and she rolled over on her beam ends; four minutes later she blew up with the loss of 862 officers and men. The losses of the *Barham* and of the carrier *Ark Royal* and the disabling of the *Queen Elizabeth* and *Valiant* by 'human torpedoes' in Alexandria the following month marked the nadir of British fortunes in the Mediterranean. The loss of these four ships left the Royal Navy with no capital ships in the eastern Mediterranean.

## Barracuda, Fairey

Although the Barracuda was never popular, not least because of its ungainly appearance, it proved an effective combat aircraft. Its primary roles were torpedo bombing and dive bombing from carriers, and it is remembered mainly for a succession of daring attacks on the German battleship *Tirpitz* while the ship was moored in Norwegian fjords. About 2600 Barracudas were built. Typical was the Mk II, with a 1640hp Rolls-Royce Merlin engine, crew of three, armament of two machine guns in the rear cockpit, and provision for a 1620lb torpedo, 1500lb of bombs or four 450lb depth charges. Maximum speed was 228mph.

## *Bartolomeo Colleoni*

This Italian light cruiser of the 'Condottieri' or *Alberico da Barbiano* Class was built in 1928–32 and armed with eight six-inch guns. The class enjoyed a high reputation as a result of its high speed – *Alberico da Barbiano* was reputed to have made 42 knots on trials in 1930 – but the trials figures were obtained without armament, reserve fuel and feedwater on board. In service they were no faster than foreign contemporaries, as the *Bartolomeo Colleoni* found to her cost on 19 July 1940 when she ran into the Australian cruiser *Sydney* and four destroyers. Her sister *Giovanni delle Bande Nere* made her escape but the *Colleoni* was hit by a number of six-inch shells and was soon on fire. She was finally sunk by torpedoes, about six miles off Cape Spada.

## Baruch, Bernard, 1870–1965

Baruch was a US government adviser on economics. He was a successful financier who was called in by Roosevelt to help Byrnes in the Office of War Mobilization. In 1943 he produced a report outlining ways industry adjusted to wartime and he was critical of war finances. In 1946 President Truman appointed him US representative to the UN Atomic Energy Commission. He was known as 'Elder Statesman Number One' although he had never served in the Cabinet.

## Bataan, Defense of, 1942

General Homma made a bad miscalculation when he allowed General MacArthur to withdraw into the Bataan peninsula: the defense of the Philippines was extended by four months.

MacArthur had withdrawn to the Bataan peninsula with about 80,000 men and under heavy fire from the Japanese, they had taken up their defense positions on the sides of Mount Rosa. However, the Americans faced many problems; they had sufficient supplies for 100,000 men for 30 days and they had to feed 25,000 civilians; they had no mosquito nets or quinine and malaria made three-quarters of the troops unfit within a month. The Japanese also suffered from malaria and on 8 February their attacks had to be suspended as 10,000 of their troops contracted the disease. Another problem was that Homma's best division, the Forty-eighth was sent to Java in February and he had to wait for reinforcements before making the final assault.

Homma launched the offensive on 9 January with inexperienced troops, because he thought there were only 25,000 US troops in Bataan. At first the Japanese were beaten back and had heavy casualties, but by 23 January they had pushed the Americans back to their reserve positions. On 16 February MacArthur ordered an attack on the Japanese lines but by 22 February the Japanese were advancing steadily and MacArthur was persuaded to leave by his own staff. On 11 March MacArthur left by boat for Mindanao, leaving Lieutenant General Wainwright in command.

In early March the Japanese had only 3000 troops on their front lines, but reinforcements reached them at the end of the month: 22,000 fresh troops with aircraft and artillery. The Japanese attacks resumed on 3 April and the Americans were pushed back to the tip of the island. In the next week the Japanese reached Wainwright's front and caused confusion in the rear. On 8 April Wainwright withdrew to Corregidor with a small force, leaving the rest of his troops to surrender.

Six days after the surrender the Bataan Death March began. Some 70,000 Filipino and American troops were forced to march sixty miles under the tropical sun, from Mariveles in the south of Bataan to the railroad line at San Fernando. They were then packed into freight cars and taken to Camp O'Donnell. Only 54,000 survived the bestiality of the Japanese guards and the harrowing conditions.

## Battleaxe, Operation, 1941

Following Rommel's arrival on the Egyptian frontier in May 1941, Wavell decided on a counteroffensive to drive him back into Libya. The arrival of a convoy at Alexandria (a 'Tiger' convoy was the name now given to those which fought in the Mediterranean) had brought Wavell reinforcements of tanks which allowed him to rebuild his 7th Armored Divison. With this force, the Indian Division and two infantry brigades, he planned to attack the German Fifteenth Panzer Division which was supported by four Italian divisions, on the frontier and re-occupy Bardia, Sollum and Capuzzo. The offensive began on 15 June, when some ground was won. On the following day, however, progress slowed and some counterattacks were sustained. On 17 June tank losses had risen so high that the offensive was called off. About 90 of the 190 British tanks committed had been lost. It was the British Army's first encounter with the Germans' skillful use of their own armor to draw enemy tanks down onto screens of 88mm anti-tank guns. They were not to find a method of dealing with it until the following year.

Allied troops poised around Tobruk before they took the beleaguered town. Tobruk was a key point along the North African coast which both the British and German forces considered vital.

**Battlecruiser**
see Battleship

---

**Battle, Fairey**

This British three-seat light bomber was in service from 1937 to 1941. Though it marked a tremendous advance over the biplanes it replaced, the Battle proved to be a grave disappointment when it was thrust into combat over France in 1939. Powered by a 990hp Merlin, it carried only one fixed and one movable machine gun, and its speed of 240mph – once thought marvelous – was 100mph slower than the Messerschmitts. When the Blitzkrieg began on 10 May 1940, Battles were shot down in droves, and the VCs won by their heroic crews were posthumous. Of the hundreds sent to France only eight percent got back to Britain, and the Battle never again flew on operations, becoming a trainer and target tug. Total production, mostly prewar, was 2419, the last delivery being in January 1941.

---

**Battleship**

Battleships were armed with the heaviest guns available and their hulls were protected by the maximum thickness of armor consistent with reasonable size and cost, to keep out enemy shells. Although President Hoover and the British Prime Minister Ramsay Macdonald had issued a joint statement in 1930 to the effect that they confidently predicted the imminent disappearance of the battleship, the major naval powers began a new round of battleship-building in 1934.

Although the aircraft carrier was growing in importance throughout the 1920s and 1930s, in 1939 it had still not proved itself as a replacement for the battleship, for naval aircraft had neither the range nor the accuracy and heavy enough bombs to sink battleships at sea. For example, in May 1941 only battleships could finally bring the *Bismarck* to action; aircraft could hammer her but could not sink her. As long as potential enemies like Italy, Japan and Germany had battleships the British and Americans had very little choice but to follow suit.

Battleships of the Royal Navy on maneuvers in 1939.

Another factor weighing with the leading navies was the battleship 'holiday' which had been observed since 1922 – by international agreement no battleship could be laid down before 1937, apart from Italy and France, which exercised options which had been allowed for at the original Washington Conference. After fifteen years the leading navies' battleships were all growing old and despite the expenditure of vast sums on modernization they did not incorporate the latest ideas.

The Washington Treaty and later agreements limited displacement to 35,000 tons and gun-caliber to 16in, but in 1934 the Japanese gave two years' notice of their intention not to renew the agreements, and in reply the USA signified its intention of raising its limit to 45,000 tons. The British for their part said that they would be content with 40,000 tons after that date, but what either navy would have done if they had known that the Japanese were building three ships of 64,000 tons armed with nine 18in guns can only be guessed at.

Significant changes in battleship design were made. Greater speeds were achieved through machinery improvements; dual-purpose surface/anti-aircraft armament was developed; facilities for handling and maintaining reconnaissance aircraft, with built-in hangars and catapults were included, and finally, radar-assisted fire control was implemented. The enormous demands on steel and manpower and the time taken to build a battleship meant that

the only ships built during World War II were hulls which had been started in peacetime, or had at least been ordered.

The battlecruiser was a fast ship armed with the same caliber of guns as a battleship but thinner armor. If a battleship can be defined as a warship emphasizing armor, gunpower and speed in that order, the battlecruiser emphasizes the same qualities in exactly the reverse order. The increase in battleship speeds from around 23 knots to 28–30 by 1939 had rendered the battlecruiser concept obsolete, and the only examples in existence were Japanese and British ships dating from World War I and two German and two French ships built since 1934.

The 'pocket battleship' was not a battleship at all, but a phrase coined by the British press to describe Germany's *Panzerschiffe* of the *Deutschland* type built to evade the prohibitions of the Versailles Treaty. The ships could more correctly be described as heavily gunned armored cruisers, and after 1940 the Kriegsmarine re-rated them as heavy cruisers.

In 1939 battleships were still seen as having a role in fleet actions but by 1943 they were used by the Allies as escorts for carrier groups, whereas the Germans used theirs as lone commerce-raiders.

USS *North Carolina* (BB-55) off the US East Coast.

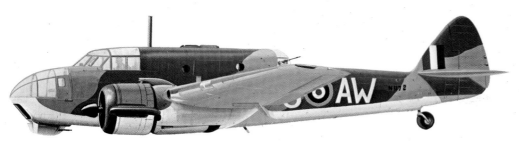

Bristol Beaufort torpedo bomber.

## Bay of Biscay

The Bay of Biscay assumed vital strategic importance after the fall of France, as it offered German U-Boats ideal bases for attacking the shipping routes converging on the Western Approaches to the British Isles, much closer than their North Sea bases. In 1943 RAF Coastal Command tried to attack U-Boats in transit from the Biscay ports to the Atlantic, and fierce air fighting resulted from German attempts to counter these patrols with their own fighters. In 1944, as D-Day approached, British warships also took a hand in the struggle to subdue the Biscay ports, and several actions were fought with destroyers.

## Bazooka
see Hollow Charge Weapons

## Beaufighter, Bristol

This British two-seat fighter and torpedo bomber/attack aircraft was in service from 1939 to 1959. The failure of the British Air Staff to order any long-range fighters, except the inadequate, converted Blenheim, upset the Bristol designers who decided to produce a fighter on their own. They used parts of the Beaufort torpedo bomber, but designed a new fuselage with the pilot in the short nose, in an excellent cockpit far better than that of the Blenheim, and an observer/navigator at the rear with a transparent cupola, and the powerful armament of four 20mm cannon under the floor firing ahead. The two engines were 1375hp Bristol Hercules sleeve-valve radials, driving large hydromatic propellers. The Air Ministry jumped at this, ordered it into production off the drawing board as the Beaufighter and two weeks later, in July 1939, watched the prototype fly. By September 1940 the first Mk I Beaufighters were in Fighter Command squadrons, and two weeks later examples arrived with AI.IV radar.

They were often thought tricky to fly, but their tremendous strength, size and power made them popular, and soon six machine guns were added in the wings to make them the most heavily armed fighters in the world. They were by far the most successful night fighter over Britain in 1940–41, and the later Mk VIF, with various radars, served the RAF and USAAF as a night fighter throughout the war. The II had Merlin engines, and the VIC was the first of a series for Coastal Command which culminated in the Mk X, with 1770hp Hercules, specially designed for attacks on shipping with a torpedo and rockets. All later aircraft were easier to fly, with a dihedral (tilted up) tailplane and large dorsal fin, and they commanded the airspace and wrought havoc over sea and land, against U-Boats and against enemies in the deserts and jungles; the Japanese called it 'Whispering death', because despite its firepower it was probably the quietest powered aircraft of the war. Total production was 5564 in UK and 364 in Australia.

## Beaufort, Bristol

This RAF reconnaissance/torpedo-bomber served as standard equipment in RAF Coastal Command from 1940 to 1943. Production totaled 1013 Beaufort Is with two 1010 or 1130hp Bristol Taurus engines, 415 Mk IIs with 1200hp Pratt & Whitney Twin Wasps, and 700 Mk VIIIs built in Australia, also with Twin Wasps. With a crew of four, the Beaufort I had a maximum speed of 265mph and carried 1500lb of bombs or a 1605lb torpedo. It gave good service over the North Sea, English Channel, Atlantic and Mediterranean, and in North Africa.

## Beaverbrook, Lord (Maxwell Aitken), 1879–1964

Beaverbrook was a Canadian-born newspaper magnate, who served in the British War Cabinet throughout the war. Before the war his motto had been 'Empire ever, Nazi-ism never', and his newspapers expounded the belief that the British Empire had no quarrel with fascism which would lead to war. Beaverbrook was an old friend of Churchill and his appointment as Minister of Aircraft Production aroused much suspicion. In fact he proved an excellent choice and worked hard to expand aircraft production from 850 aircraft to 2000, using his influence. During the war he held appointments as Minister of Supply (1942) and Lord Privy Seal (1943–45). In 1941 he went on an important mission to Moscow with Sir Stafford Cripps to negotiate Lend-Lease agreements.

## Beck, General Ludwig, 1880–1944

Beck helped to rebuild the Germany army from 1933–38. In 1938 he was appointed Chief of General Staff but he resigned a year later when it became obvious the Generals would not arrest Hitler. His opposition to Hitler was based on his belief that Germany could not sustain a war. He was a traditionalist, and became the figurehead for plots against Hitler. He was in close touch with Stauffenburg, Tresckow and Gördeler and was implicated in the July Plot of 1944. He committed suicide rather than face trial.

## Belgium, Invasion of, 1940

Hitler determined to invade Belgium though a neutral state as soon as he decided upon the principle of starting the war against France and Britain in October 1939; this Belgian operation formed part both of the *Gelb* and *Manstein* plans as well as the final OKH scheme. Originally, however, it was the main thrust which was to be delivered through north Belgium and only subsequently was that thrust transferred to the Ardennes Sector. Thus, the battle with the main body of the Belgian army in 1940, and of

the Anglo-French force which came to its support, was essentially diversionary: its object was to position the mobile element of the enemy's defense so that it might be encircled from the south and destroyed. Belgium, though suspecting that its neutrality was to be violated, scrupulously forbore from disposing its forces to meet the German attack until the threat was explicitly disclosed – even after capturing from a force-landed airplane on 7 January 1940, parts of the *Gelb* plan (which was hastily shelved by the Germans as a result of this disclosure). They also held back from full co-ordination of their plans with the Allies, who proceeded nevertheless with a scheme of their own to come to the Belgians' rescue.

The Belgian army, a conscript force, had been put on a full war footing in August 1939 and consisted of a cavalry corps (two cavalry divisions and a motorized cavalry brigade) and seven infantry corps, comprising twelve active or reserve divisions, six second rescue divisions, two divisions of *Chasseurs Ardennais* and a brigade of cyclist frontier guards. Its total strength was 650,000, which the order for general mobilization brought up to 900,000. It was, however, very weak in aircraft and anti-aircraft artillery and had no tanks and four anti-tank weapons. The Belgian war plan was to hold a 'delaying position' in central Belgium, defined by the line of the Albert Canal between Antwerp and Liège and of the Meuse between Liège and Namur. The line was defended by fortresses of which the strongest was that of Eben Emael on the Albert Canal north of Liège. The defense of the Ardennes was relegated to the lightly equipped *Chasseurs Ardennais*. The real strength of Belgium's resistance to a German invasion would be provided by the Allies, on whom the Belgians knew they could count, even though they maintained no open military relations with their high command. It was to be provided by the advance of the French 7th and 1st Armies into northern and central Belgium accompanied by the British Expeditionary Force, and of the French North Army into the Ardennes. This maneuver, Plan D, had been worked out by Gamelin and endorsed by the Allied Supreme Council in November 1939.

It played straight into Germany's hands. The

A British anti-tank position in the ruins of Louvain, 14 May 1940.

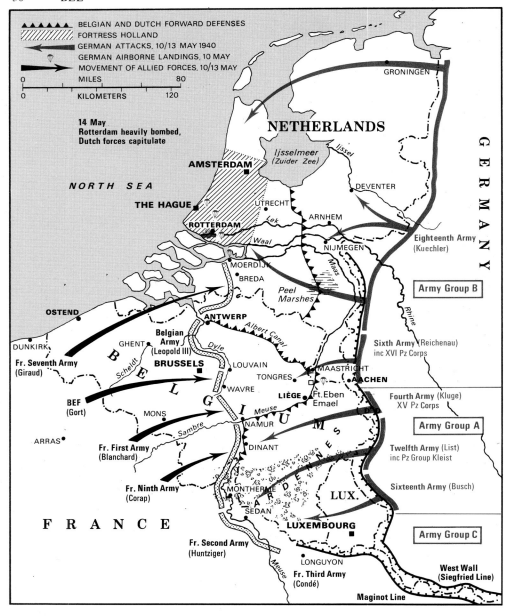

**Map legend:**
- ▲▲▲▲▲ BELGIAN AND DUTCH FORWARD DEFENSES
- ////// FORTRESS HOLLAND
- ◄━━━ GERMAN ATTACKS, 10/13 MAY 1940
- ⊕ GERMAN AIRBORNE LANDINGS, 10 MAY
- ━━► MOVEMENT OF ALLIED FORCES, 10/13 MAY

```
0          MILES          80
0        KILOMETERS       120
```

14 May
Rotterdam heavily bombed,
Dutch forces capitulate

NETHERLANDS

IJsselmeer
(Zuider Zee)

NORTH SEA

AMSTERDAM

THE HAGUE

ROTTERDAM

GRONINGEN

DEVENTER

UTRECHT

ARNHEM

NIJMEGEN

Eighteenth Army
(Kuechler)

MOERDIJK

BREDA

Peel
Marshes

Army Group B

OSTEND

ANTWERP

Albert Canal

DUNKIRK

GHENT

Belgian
Army
(Leopold III)

Fr. Seventh Army
(Giraud)

BRUSSELS

LOUVAIN

TONGRES

MAASTRICHT

AACHEN

Sixth Army (Reichenau)
inc XVI Pz Corps

WAVRE

LIÈGE

Ft. Eben
Emael

Fourth Army (Kluge)
XV Pz Corps

BEF
(Gort)

MONS

Meuse

NAMUR

Army Group A

ARRAS

Fr. First Army
(Blanchard)

Sambre

DINANT

Twelfth Army (List)
inc Pz Group Kleist

Fr. Ninth Army
(Corap)

MONTHERME

SEDAN

LUX.

Sixteenth Army (Busch)

FRANCE

LUXEMBOURG

Army Group C

Fr. Second Army
(Huntziger)

LONGUYON

Fr. Third Army
(Condé)

West Wall
(Siegfried Line)

Maginot Line

final OKH plan was for a rapid breach of the Belgian delaying position, principally at Eben Emael and a breakneck advance to catch the Anglo-French relief force in movement before it could enter the Belgians' prepared defenses. This was to be achieved by Bock's Army Group B, spearheaded by Thirty-ninth and Seven-

*Below:* German troops advance in street fighting in Flanders, 1940.

teenth Panzer Corps, which were to race across the Dutch 'Maastricht Appendix'. But the decisive stroke was to be delivered by Rundstedt's Army Group A, spearheaded by Kleist's Panzer Group (Fifteenth, Forty-first and Nineteenth Panzer Corps) which was to advance rapidly through the weakly defended Ardennes, an area discussed by the Anglo-French and Belgian high commands as 'untankable' and to crash the line of the Meuse between Givet and Sedan, to

which the Maginot Line did not quite reach. The Panzer spearheads were then to race across undefended northern France, in the rear of the Anglo-French armies, reach the Channel coast near Abbéville and then turn to encircle them. At a single blow, and in the space of ten days, most of the Allies' mobile divisions, and almost all their tanks, were to be consumed in a gigantic 'cauldron' (*Kessel*) battle.

The success of the plan exceeded expectations. The breaching of the Meuse was achieved almost without loss and they advanced across northern France at faster than anticipated speed to reach Abbéville on 20 May. Meanwhile, in Belgium, the fall of Eben Emael forced the Belgian Field Army to fall back to the line of the Dyle, on which the Allied advance guard began to join it on 12 May. The French 7th Army had meanwhile moved spearheads north of Antwerp into Holland and the 1st Army into the Gembloux gap south of Namur. Against them, however, the German Eighteenth Army (Holland) and Sixth Army (Namur Sector) developed a vigorous assault, forcing both to give ground, and with them, the BEF on the Dyle Line. The Belgian Army continued to sustain resistance between Antwerp and Brussels despite this erosion of its flanks but was forced back, with heavy losses, to the line of the Escaut on 18 May and to the Lys on 20 May. That line was breached on 24 May around Courtrai and, as the BEF withdrew towards Dunkirk, the Belgian field army found itself cast off and surrounded in Flanders. On 28 May King Leopold ordered it to surrender; the terms insisted upon by the Germans were unconditional.

## Belorussia, Battle of, Operation Bagration, June 1944

The offensive to clear Belorussia coincided with a time of great German weakness: on 20 July confusion reigned in the German High Command after Lieutenant Colonel Stauffenberg's assassination attempt.

The offensive was launched after a four-month break in activities because of the spring thaw. The Germans had a chance to regroup but received no reinforcements. Most of their air support and tanks had been sent to the West for the Ardennes Offensive. In fact on the Belorussian Front, General Busch had thinned his lines because General Model expected the Russ-

*Below:* Wehrmacht troops consult their maps during the long retreat on the Eastern Front during the 1944 campaign.

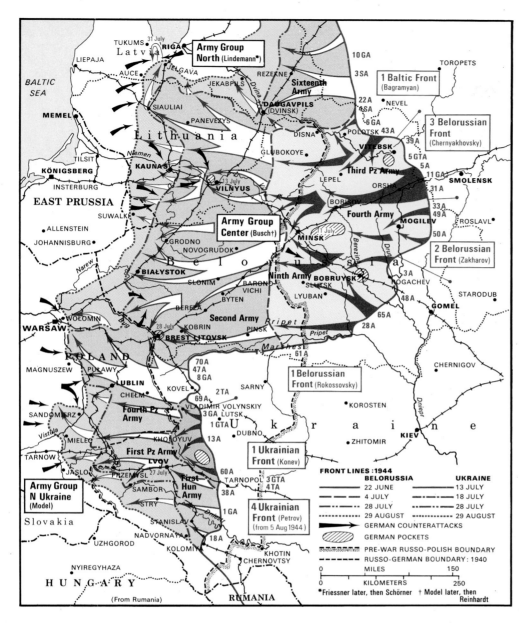

Above: The destruction of Army Group Center.
Below: Russian partisans prepare to blow up rail links as the Germans retreated.

killed 38,000 Germans. It was a resounding defeat for the Germans and Hitler dismissed Busch from the Command of Army Group Center, replacing him with Model.

## Belsen
see Holocaust

## Beneš, President Eduard, 1884–1948

Beneš was President of the Czech government-in-exile during the war. President of Czechoslovakia before the war Beneš had been forced to resign under pressure from Hitler after the Munich agreement and retired to the USA. After Nazi Germany invaded Czechoslovakia, Beneš returned to Europe and became head of the Czech National Council and tried to get Britain, France and other countries to recognize his government-in-exile and get aid for the growing resistance movement in Czechoslovakia. Beneš's government was recognized by Britain in July 1941 and Britain repudiated the Munich Agreement in August 1942. Beneš decided on a policy of co-operation with the communists and in December 1943 signed an alliance with the USSR. In Britain the Czech exiles were trained and formed units to fight Germany. Beneš gave the order to Czech underground groups to assassinate Heydrich, the Protector of Bohemia and Moravia. After the war Beneš was re-elected President of the Czech Republic.

## Bennett, Air Vice-Marshal Donald C T, 1910–

Bennett was an Australian-born RAF officer who conceived the idea of sending pathfinder aircraft ahead of a bomber force in order to pinpoint targets for attack. The Pathfinder Force which was established within Bomber Command in 1942 under Bennett's leadership, together with the Light Night Striking Force of Mosquito bombers which he also helped to found, made a vital contribution to the success of the bomber offensive against Germany between 1943 and 1944, and to the D-Day preparations.

ian offensive to be launched round Lvov. The Russians launched their attack on 22 June on four fronts with 146 infantry and 43 armored divisions. General Bagramyan's 1st Baltic and General Chernyakhovsky's 3rd Belorussian Front struck to the north and south of Vitebsk and took the city on 27 June. Chernyakhovsky's left wing then took Orsha – this meant that the Moscow-Minsk highway could now be used to threaten the German rear. To the south General Zakharov's 2nd Belorussian Front, north of the Pripet Marshes, destroyed a force of 33,000 at Bobruisk on that day. Chernyakhovsky's army now headed for Minsk: on 2 July his mobile forces reached Stolbtsy, forty miles away. Then General Rotmistrov's tanks entered Minsk on 3 July and 50,000 Germans were trapped.

The offensive pressed on to Baronovichi (8 July) and to Grodno (13 July) on the Polish border. In the south Rokossovsky cleared the Pripet Marshes taking Pinsk and Kovel on 5 July. In the north Bagramyan turned to the Baltic States and took Vilnyus in Lithuania and Daugavpils in Latvia on 13 July. This split the Army Group North in two: in East Prussia and in the Baltic States.

The Russians arrived at the Polish border within 24 days and claimed to have taken 158,000 men, 2000 tanks, 10,000 guns and 57,000 motor vehicles. They also claimed to have

## Beria, Lavrenty P, 1899–1954

Beria was the Soviet Secret Police Chief from
1938–53. On 30 July 1939 he became a member
of Stalin's State Defense Committee and kept
Stalin informed of Armed Forces' movements.
He kept dossiers on generals and threatened to
discredit some of them, for example General
Malinovsky. The NKVD, under Beria, was responsible for the deportations in Poland and the
Baltic States. From 1943–45 the NKGB carried
out deportations of Crimean Tartars and other
minority nationalities. Another of his duties was
to control Soviet partisans behind German lines
and POW camps, which were under the jurisdiction of Smersh.

## Berlin, Battle of, 1945

In April 1945 Zhukov began to prepare his
offensive against Berlin. Konev's 1st Ukrainian Front raced for the Neisse River, and
Rokossovsky's 2nd Belorussian Front headed
for the northern reaches of the Oder while
Zhukov's 1st Belorussian Front held a line
along the Oder opposite Berlin. The three Soviet
Fronts combined had 2,500,000 men, 6250
tanks, 7500 aircraft and 41,600 artillery pieces.

From 1 February to 21 April Berlin had been
bombed almost every night. On 15 April shortly
before the Russian attack, Hitler transferred
command of Berlin city defenses to Army
Group Vistula, under General Heinrici. On 16
April the 1st Belorussian Front attacked at dawn
and the 1st Ukrainian Front joined in at daylight. The 1st Belorussian Front did not make
much progress and since the 1st Ukrainian Front

had penetrated six miles on the first day Konev
was ordered to head for Berlin. On 19 April
the 1st Belorussian Front broke through and
reached the outskirts of Berlin on the next day.
Konev cut off all communication on the south
side of the city. Then the 3rd Army cut off the
Ninth Army from Berlin and one of General
Sokolovsky's tank columns joined up with
Konev's Armies west of the city on 25 April to
complete its encirclement. On the same day
Rokossovsky's 2nd Belorussian Front broke
through the Third Panzer Army's line near Stettin. Hitler did not believe he was beaten and
ordered Operational Group Steiner to attack
eastwards from Oranienburg and throw back

*Above:* Soviet tanks near the Brandenburg Gate in
Berlin.
*Below:* German officers are taken prisoner.

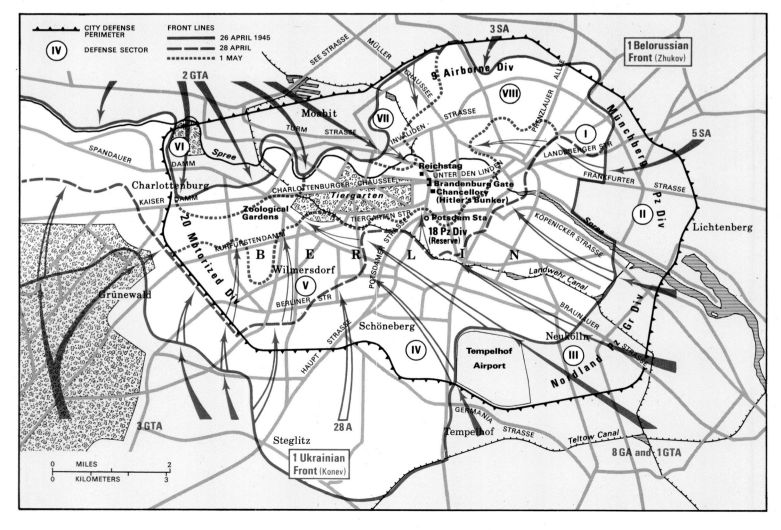

the Red Army. All German Armies were turning round to attack east so that they could surrender to the Allies.

Eight Soviet Armies destroyed Berlin's makeshift defenses and although every street was contested they made progress on 29 April. Thousands of civilians died in the intense block-by-block, house-to-house struggle, in which young boys fought alongside old men to defend the capital of the Reich. Hitler flooded the underground in a last-ditch attempt to save Berlin. In the process thousands of German civilians were drowned. On 30 April Hitler shot himself and General Krebs tried to negotiate an armistice with Chuikov. On 1 May the Reichstag surrendered after frantic resistance by SS troops and on 2 May General Weidling, Commandant of Berlin, visited Chuikov and wrote a proclamation calling on German troops to surrender. Soviet troops only joined up at Charlottenberg Chausee on 2 May and mopped up the remnants.

## Berthier Rifle

Berthier rifles were French service rifles, developed ca 1890 by a Commission headed by Andre Berthier, a French arms designer. Basically they were the Lebel M1886 action allied to a magazine derived from Mannlicher and loaded by a three-round clip. The first model to appear was the Cavalry Carbine M1890, followed by various modified designs including the basic rifles Model 1902 and Model 1907. Experience in World War I showed the futility of a three-round clip and in 1916 a modified design was produced to take a five-round clip. Finally, in 1934, the whole design was overhauled to change the caliber to 7.5mm (instead of the old 8mm Lebel cartridge) and change the magazine to a Mauser type loaded from a five-round charger. These rifles, in their various manifestations, were the principal armament of the French infantry soldier in 1939–40.

## Besa Machine Gun

This machine gun was originally designed and developed by the Czech Armaments works at Brno and marketed by them as the VZ53 (in 7.92mm caliber) and VZ60 (in 15mm caliber). Rights to both guns were bought by the British Government in 1938 and they were put into production by the BSA Company, from whence came the name Besa. Both guns were used as tank armaments, the 15mm also being used as primary armament for some armored cars.

## 'Betty'
see Mitsubishi G4M

## Beurling, Squadron Leader George F, 1922–

Beurling was a Canadian-born RAF officer, nicknamed 'Screwball' Beurling, who in the four months between July and October 1942 was awarded the DSO, DFC, DFM and Bar while stationed with 249 Squadron in Malta. A remarkable marksman, he achieved a total of 31 victories during the war.

## Biak, Battle for
see New Guinea. Biak and Wakde Islands

## Bialystok-Minsk, Battle of, June 1941

This was one of the first major disasters to befall the Red Army. General Pavlov, Commander of the Western Front, faced great difficulties because of the bad communication systems. General Guderian and General Hoth undertook a pincer movement on the Bialystok salient and managed to take Minsk at the rear of the salient on 29 June. However because of the rain and mud, the Germans did not move fast enough to trap the whole army in the pincer and about 300,000 men managed to escape. Nonetheless the Germans claimed about 290,000 Soviet prisoners, 2500 tanks and 1400 guns. As a result Pavlov was arrested and replaced by Marshal Timoshenko.

## Biddle, Francis, 1886–1968

Biddle joined President Roosevelt's Cabinet as Attorney-General in September 1941, a position he held until 1945. He had previously been Solicitor General and his main task had been to operate the Alien Registration Act of June 1940. He stood up for the rights of US citizens and tried to protect those of Italian and Japanese extraction. During his term as Attorney-General, Biddle appointed an Interdepartmental Committee on Investigations to make suggestions on procedures to ascertain loyalty. When Truman became President he asked for Biddle's resignation but then made him a member of the Military Tribunal at Nuremberg in Germany which tried Nazi leaders. He was noted for his compassion.

## Bir Hacheim
see Gazala-Bir Hacheim, Battle of, 1942

## Bishop

The Bishop was the first British self-propelled 25-pounder gun to enter service. It was built on the chassis of the Valentine tank and had limited traverse and elevation, which restricted the gun's maximum range to 6400yds. One hundred were built, commencing in October 1941, and these were used in the North African campaign in late 1942. They were replaced by the 'Sexton' and were made obsolete in October 1944.

The Bishop 25-pdr self-propelled gun.

## Bismarck

A German battleship built under the 1935 Program, she was the lead ship of a class of two, the first battleships ordered since 1918. She was not intended to form part of any battle fleet, for her role was to be that of a lone commerce-destroyer operating against British trade, and in that sense she exemplified Grand-Admiral Raeder's strategic plan to use surface warships to disrupt the convoy system.

Although nominally built to conform to the international limitation of 35,000 tons displacement, she and her sister Tirpitz had a standard displacement of 41,700 tons when completed, a discrepancy which could not be ascribed to incidental increases during building. The extra tonnage was put to good use, and the Bismarck and Tirpitz showed a marked superiority in speed to their contemporaries built under the restrictions of the Washington and London naval treaties. Yet, surprisingly, the design was by no means up-to-date. Hitler's rapid expansion of the German armed forces could not be applied to the Kriegsmarine with such rapid results, for ships take time to design and even longer to build.

The design reflects the enormous material problems facing the German Navy. Because their corps of designers had virtually ceased to exist after 1918 there was great difficulty in producing ships with the latest features in the short time allowed by Hitler. Thus the Bismarck design is little more than a faster and beamier edition of the Baden Class of 1915, with more sophisticated fire control, a heavy anti-aircraft battery and more fuel. The underwater protection against torpedoes and the armoring against shells showed little advance over ideas of 1914–1918, whereas US, British, French, Japanese and Italian designs had all made big changes to meet modern requirements. In fact the only remarkable feature of the underwater protection was the massive 118ft beam, and this had the inherent disadvantage of making the ship more liable to capsize if heavily flooded. Another old-fashioned feature was the division of the light armament into anti-surface and anti-aircraft, at a time when other battleships were provided with dual-purpose guns to save weight. The best features of the armament were the grouping of the 15in (38cm) guns into four twin mounts, and the provision of no fewer than six high-angle fire-control directors.

The career of the Bismarck was short, violent and heroic. She was completed at Hamburg at

The battleship *Bismarck* was the pride of the Kriegsmarine.

the end of 1940, but was not considered ready for battle until she had undergone a lengthy shakedown in the Baltic. It had been planned to use her in conjunction with the battlecruisers *Scharnhorst* and *Gneisenau*, which were at Brest, but by May 1941 this was no longer possible as the *Scharnhorst*'s machinery was under repair and *Gneisenau* had been hit by a torpedo. Because the *Tirpitz* was not sufficiently trained the decision was taken to send the *Bismarck* out into the Atlantic with the cruiser *Prinz Eugen*. After the raid was over the two ships would go to Brest, where they could threaten the Atlantic convoys and wait until the two battlecruisers were ready to join them for further sorties. However this was subsequently changed, and the *Bismarck* was to return to Norway or Germany, and was only to make for Brest if forced to by damage. The broad intention was that the *Bismarck* would draw off the battleships which were escorting British convoys, and so free the *Prinz Eugen* to attack shipping without risk.

After many delays the two ships sailed on 18 May, and despite precautions the British 'Ultra' cryptanalysis unit gave rapid warning of the move. They were spotted more than once and finally picked up on radar by two cruisers in the Denmark Straits between Iceland and Greenland. Their reports guided the Battle Cruiser Squadron of the Home Fleet, including the battlecruiser *Hood* and the new battleship *Prince of Wales* to an interception on the morning of 24 May. The engagement which followed was a brilliant victory for the *Bismarck* and *Prinz Eugen*, for their shells caused a magazine explosion in the *Hood*, and the British ship blew up with nearly all her crew. Fire was switched to the *Prince of Wales*, which was so new that some of her guns were not capable of firing. The British ship was roughly handled, and forced to withdraw, but not before she had scored two vital hits on the *Bismarck*. One of these ruptured fuel tanks below the waterline, making the *Bismarck* leak oil and ultimately reducing her endurance by contaminating other tanks. The aircraft carrier HMS *Victorious* launched a torpedo-bomber strike against the *Bismarck* on the night of 24 May and although a hit was obtained the 18in warhead was not big enough to cause any serious damage to a battleship's armor belt. Admiral Lütjens in the *Bismarck* decided to make for Brest as he now had insufficient fuel for an Atlantic foray, but first he decided to rid himself of the shadowing cruisers. As the *Prinz Eugen* was critically short of fuel he made a turnabout to cover her withdrawal, and in the confusion the British ships lost radar

contact. Thus from 0306 on the morning of 25 May the position of the German battleship was unknown to the Admiralty, and she was not rediscovered until she gave away her position by broadcasting a long radio message some seven hours later. Visual contact was made next day at 1030 hours by a Catalina flying boat.

To slow the *Bismarck* down the carrier *Ark Royal* launched a torpedo-strike late in the afternoon of 27 May. This was successful for a torpedo wrecked the *Bismarck*'s steering. During the night destroyers attacked with torpedoes and may have scored a further hit, but in any case the German battleship was trapped by a circle of heavy ships which were waiting to engage her at daybreak. At 0847 on 27 May the flagship of the Home Fleet, the battleship *King George V* and the *Rodney* opened fire at a range of 16,000 yards. Their heavy fire silenced the *Bismarck* within half an hour, and she was able to do no more than score a near miss against HMS *Rodney* in reply. She was a flaming shambles by 1015, but was so low in the water from flooding that the British shells were mostly passing through the unarmored parts of the superstructure without causing any further vital damage. As Admiral Tovey's force was now short of fuel he ordered the cruiser *Dorsetshire* to finish off the *Bismarck*, and at 1036 she rolled over and sank with her flag still flying.

The most important tactical error made by Admiral Lütjens was his failure to abort his mission as soon as he learned of the damage from the *Prince of Wales*' shells. By any standards this was serious battle damage, and quite sufficient to warrant a return to port, and it must be assumed that Lütjens was overconfident about his flagship's ability to withstand damage. Only later, when the British had been given time to organize powerful forces, did he accept the inevitable. Argument has raged since May 1941 about whether the *Bismarck* sank before she was scuttled, with the Germans stoutly claiming that her hull was not penetrated by British shells, and that she only sank because scuttling charges were detonated. This argument, however attractive it may be to the German Navy, has three weaknesses: (1) the testimony of the survivors *at the time* shows that the ship was a shambles below decks, and that virtually nobody from below survived, (2) the way in which the *Bismarck* sank so low in the water, indicated that serious flooding was taking place long before the sinking, and (3) tests on armor plates from her sister after 1945 showed that they had no mysterious powers of resistance to either British or American shells. From the historian's point of view the argument is irrelevant, as the *Bismarck* was on the point of sinking from one cause or another.

## Bismarck Islands
see Rabaul, 1943–44

### *Bittern*

The *Bittern* was the name-ship of a new class of British escort vessel or sloop designed to defend shipping against air attack. She was armed with the exceptionally heavy armament of three twin four-inch (102mm) AA guns, and to assist the fire control she was fitted with a new device, the Denny-Brown stabilizer, basically a pair of fins which could be actuated to reduce rolling. Small warships of the day were notorious for their poor shooting, and the stabilizer was the first major improvement in this area. Although treated with some skepticism by most naval officers, they are now an established feature of warships. The *Bittern* gunnery proved so effective during the Norwegian Campaign in April 1940 that she was singled out by the Stukas. After incessant bombing off Namsos she caught fire and sank on 30 April. She was the forerunner of the highly successful sloops which served in the Support Groups during the Battle of the Atlantic.

## Black Widow
see P-61 Black Widow, Northrop

## Blakeslee, Donald, 1915–

One of the most famous of the USAAF fighter aces, Blakeslee joined the RCAF following the outbreak of war and was posted to No 401 Ram Squadron in the UK in May 1941. He subsequently joined 133 Eagle Squadron, formed with American volunteers in 1941, and later became Commander of the USAAF 4th Fighter Group – formed by the amalgamation of 133, 71 and 121 Eagle Squadrons – which destroyed a total of 1016 enemy aircraft.

## Blamey, General Sir Thomas Albert, 1884–1951

Blamey was commander of the Australian land forces in the war. He had resigned from the army to become a policeman, but in February 1940 he was called up to take command of Australia's Infantry Force. In April 1941 he was made Lieutenant General, second in command to General Wavell. In the fall of 1941 Blamey arrived in Greece to command Anzac troops, and found himself directing some fighting but mainly preparing the evacuation. He was then posted to Alexandria and fought in Libya, but he did not like working under General Auchinleck.

After Pearl Harbor, Blamey was recalled to Australia with two divisions in March 1942, and in September was made commander of land troops in Australia. On 23 September he arrived at Port Moresby to direct operations in difficult jungle conditions. By using his Australian divisions he pushed the Japanese back along the Kokoda trail to Buna and finally took that town on 9 December.

During 1943 Blamey was not in the fore because fighting shifted northwards and MacArthur removed his American troops from under Blamey's command. He retained his position until the end of the war despite American criticism of his performance.

The Bristol Blenheim bomber.

### Blenheim, Bristol

This British three-seat light bomber and fighter was in service from 1937 to 1944. In 1935 the Bristol company delivered a civil aircraft called 'Britain First' which was the first British aircraft to introduce stressed-skin construction, flaps, retractable landing gear and variable-pitch propellers. The RAF asked if they could test it, and found its speed (307mph) to be 80mph faster than the Gauntlet fighter then just entering service. The result was obvious: a bomber version was ordered as the Blenheim, with wing raised to the mid position above a bomb bay for a 1000lb load, and with a dorsal turret with a machine gun. Another gun was fixed to fire ahead. Though rather cramped, the Blenheim reached about 270mph on its two 840hp Bristol Mercury engines, and by the outbreak of war was numerically the RAF's chief airplane with 1000 in service. From 1938 about 200 were converted into long-range fighters with four machine guns in a belly tray, and by July 1939 a few of these were becoming the first night fighters ever to go into service with radar. By this time production had switched to the Mk IV with a longer nose of curious shape giving proper accommodation for the navigator. In Canada the similar Bolingbroke was produced in various forms. Many Blenheims were exported, those in Finland going into action against the Soviet Union in 1939 on skis.

Until 1941 the Blenheim IV was the RAF's chief daylight tactical bomber, used as far afield as Germany, though losses were heavy. By this time there were two guns in the dorsal turret and two more aimed via mirrors by the nav/bomb-aimer in a turret facing aft under the nose, but during 1941 all frontline Blenheims were sent to North Africa, the Middle East and Far East, where they kept hard at work against various enemies. The Blenheim V was a much heavier tactical bomber used from 1942 in North Africa, which despite having Mercuries of 950hp had poor performance and was replaced by the Ventura or Baltimore as soon as possible. Total production of all Blenheims was 6260.

### Blitz
see Britain, Battle of, 1940

### Blitzkrieg

Blitzkrieg is the German word for 'lightning war'. This German method of warfare was based on the principle that the easiest way to defeat an enemy army was to cut it off from its supplies and communications. The Germans decided to use tanks to achieve a double envelopment of an army with air support to inspire 'fear'. This theory of war was first developed by a group of British military thinkers led by Captain Liddell Hart but the British never fully exploited the use of armor as a striking weapon.

The campaign in Poland was the first successful demonstration of this tactic and German Panzer (tank) divisions were extremely successful because the land was flat and the Polish Army equipment and tactics were not up-to-date. In 1941, in the Russian Campaign, General Guderian suggested high-speed warfare which would have sent the tanks hundreds of miles ahead operating as a completely independent unit with its own highly mobile infantry forces but the German High Command could not break away sufficiently from orthodox military tactics and did not try this in the USSR.

Sir Leslie Hore-Belisha and Captain Basil Liddell Hart, who foresaw the Blitzkrieg in the '30s.

### Bloch 151 and 152

Powered by a 920hp Gnome-Rhône 14N 35 engine, the Bloch 151 was a single-seat fighter with a maximum speed of 298mph and armament of two cannon and two machine guns or four machine guns. The 152 differed in having a 1080hp engine. A total of 593 were built for eight French Air Force groups before the June 1940 surrender.

### Blockade

The classic weapon of sea power against land power, the blockade seeks to cut off an enemy's supplies of raw materials and keep his warships confined to their harbors. It was developed and refined by the Royal Navy during the 18th century wars with France, and played a major role in the defeat of Germany in 1918. It can be said with some justification that the inhumanity of unrestricted submarine warfare against shipping was no worse than the malnutrition and deprivation suffered by the civilian populace of Germany between 1914 and 1918.

The position of the British Isles enabled the Royal Navy to dominate the exits to the Atlantic, and inevitably blockade became a fundamental part of British strategy against Germany in 1939, once again. The system was very similar, with a distant patrol line of cruisers and 'contraband control', a process of examination of neutral cargoes to ascertain whether they were genuinely destined for neutral countries or ultimately intended for Germany. Certain 'strategic commodities' such as rubber, iron ore, cotton and vegetable oil were declared contraband because they were vital to the manufacture of weapons and munitions, and ships found in the 'War Zone' with these forbidden categories of cargoes were sent to a British port for examination of manifests and documents. If a ship was judged to be carrying contraband her cargo was confiscated and sold. Whereas in World War I, ships making the captures were awarded 'prize money', a much fairer system was operated in 1939–1945 with prize money pooled in a 'Prize Fund' which was distributed after the end of the war.

When western Europe was overrun in 1940 British problems with neutral countries disappeared, as the ships of Europe's maritime nations joined the British cause. Thereafter the blockade could be made total, and some measure of its importance can be gauged by Germany's need to divert scarce shipyard resources to the construction of special blockade-running U-Boats to bring materials from Japan.

As in World War I the German reply to the British blockade was to declare a counter-blockade of the British Isles, thus conferring the right to sink all neutral shipping approaching the British Isles. The legal niceties quickly disappeared, and on 17 August 1940 Hitler declared a total blockade and gave the U-Boats orders to sink all merchant shipping on sight.

### Bloody Noose Ridge, Battle of
see Palau Islands, 1944

### Bloody Ridge, Battle of
see Guadalcanal, 1942

### *Blücher*

Sister of the *Admiral Hipper* this German heavy cruiser was part of a task force which tried to seize Oslo by surprise on 8 April 1940. With the pocket battleship *Lützow*, the light cruiser *Emden* and the gunnery training ship *Brummer* she went up Oslofjord that night. The arrival of the force had been reported to the coastal fortress of Oskarsborg on the island of Kalholmen, and although the guns were old and the gunners were elderly reservists, both were adequate to the task for which they had been designed. At

The *Blücher* on maneuvers.

0330 next morning the lookouts spotted the outline of the *Blücher* approaching in the darkness. Two 28cm (11in) shells hit her director control tower, and lighter guns demolished the bridge. Wrecked and ablaze, the *Blücher* tried to creep out of range, but as she passed the fortress two torpedoes were fired by the fixed tubes ashore. Both hit, and the *Blücher* rolled over and sank. The guns turned on the *Brummer*, and within a few minutes the whole of the force was in retreat down the fjord. The action is a classic fort–vs–ship duel, and one of the few in which coastal fortifications justified their reputation.

### Bock, Field Marshal Fedor von, 1885–1945

Scion of a traditional Prussian military family, Bock won the *Pour le Mérite* for 'reckless bravery' as a junior officer of the Fifth Foot Guards during World War I, and subsequently served as an assistant to the great Seeckt in the reconstruction of the German Army under the harsh terms of the Versailles Treaty. By 1938 he had risen to command, with Rundstedt and Leeb, one of the three 'Army Groups' into which the peacetime army was organized. At the outbreak of war he was appointed to command one of the three true Army Groups then formed, Army Group B in the campaign in the west in 1940. It overran Belgium and Holland and broke the line of the lower Seine in the Battle of France. In 1941, retitled Army Group North, it made the advance from Poland to Leningrad. Bock was relieved of command in the great purge following the Russian counteroffensive of December but was reinstated in place of Rundstedt at Army Group South in January, holding the post until July, when he was relieved and replaced by Rundstedt.

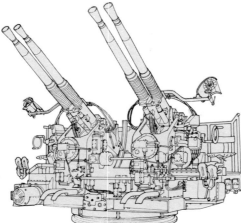

US quadruple Bofors guns for naval use.

### Bofors Gun

This is the general name for a 40mm light anti-aircraft automatic gun developed by AB Bofors of Sweden in 1929 and subsequently sold to many countries. It was adopted by the British Army in 1938 and by the US Army in 1941. The German Army also used numbers captured from France and Poland. The Bofors fired a 2lb high explosive shell at 2800ft/sec velocity and a rate of fire of 120rpm. The maximum attainable ceiling was 23,600ft, but the practical maximum was about 12,500ft. The standard mounting was a four-wheeled trailer unit, but two-wheeled units for airborne use were developed in the UK and USA, as well as self-propelled mountings for the protection of mobile columns.

### *Bolzano*

This Italian heavy cruiser was intended to be the fourth unit of the *Trento* Class but was completed to a modified design in 1933. She played an active part in the war in the Mediterranean being present at the Battle of Calabria (Italian:–Punta Stilo) on 9 July 1940 and the indecisive action off Cape Spartivento (Cape Teulada) on 26 November. On 26 August 1941 she was damaged by a torpedo from the British submarine *Triumph*, north of the Straits of Messina. She was again hit, this time by four torpedoes from HMS *Unbroken* northwest of Messina on 13 August 1942. She caught fire and was badly damaged, and had to be repaired.

She was still under repair when the Italian armistice was negotiated in September 1943, and was captured by German forces. Work proceeded slowly, and on 22 June 1944 her future was finally decided when British 'Human torpedoes' carried by an Italian motor torpedo boat penetrated the harbor and laid charges under her keel. When these detonated the *Bolzano* was a total wreck. The remains were salvaged in 1947 when the port was cleared.

### Bong, Major Richard I, 1920–1945

This American fighter pilot achieved the greatest number of victories in the USAAF. Stationed for much of the war in the Pacific theater, he flew more than 200 sorties, many of them in a P–38J Lightning named 'Marge' after his fiancée, achieving a total of 40 confirmed kills. Before his death in August 1945 while test-flying a P–80 jet, Bong had received the Congressional Medal of Honor, the DSC, two Silver Stars, seven DFCs and 15 Air Medals.

### Boomerang, Commonwealth

Designed in Australia and first flown on 29 May 1942, the Boomerang was used mainly as an interceptor, ground attack and reconnaissance fighter in support of troops in New Guinea. A total of 250 were built with a 1200hp R–1830 Twin Wasp engine; armament comprised two 20mm cannon and four 0.303in machine guns. They saw little action outside New Guinea.

### Bor-Komorowski, General Tadeusz, 1895–1966

Bor was the codename for Count Komorowski who was in command of resistance in south Poland in 1942. On 30 March 1943 Bor replaced General Rowecki as leader of the Polish Home Army and on 1 August 1944 led the Warsaw Uprising against the Germans. After fierce fighting he surrendered to the Germans on 2 October and was interned as a POW. During his imprisonment he was made Commander in Chief of Polish Forces.

### Boris III, King of Bulgaria, 1894–1943

At the outbreak of the war King Boris was anxious to keep Bulgaria out of the war. At first he resisted pressure from Germany but soon found that unless he reached an agreement with Hitler he would be deposed. In March 1941 his Prime Minister signed the Berlin-Rome-Tokyo alliance and later in that year his government declared war on the Allies. He died under mysterious circumstances after an interview with Hitler. Since none of the Secret Services claimed responsibility it is to be presumed that he died of 'natural' causes.

### Bormann, Martin, 1900–?

Bormann was Hitler's closest adviser after Hess's flight to Britain in May 1941, and alongside Himmler the second most powerful in the Reich. Bormann controlled the SA through the office of Chief of the Party Office and tried to get control of the army by attaching Nazi officials to regular units. After the battle of Kharkov Hitler turned to Bormann more and more and Bormann in turn protected him from the harsher facts of reality. Bormann continued to assure Hitler that he would win the war although the Red Army was outside Berlin. Bormann was in the Führerbunker when Hitler committed suicide and it was then that he disappeared. He may have been killed during the breakout by Hitler's staff from the Chancellery but his body was never found and rumors persist about his presence in South America. He was tried at Nuremberg in his absence and sentenced to death.

## Borneo Operations, 1945

After resistance in the Philippines had been overcome, General MacArthur decided to encourage the Australians to take Borneo. The Australian 1st Corps under Lieutenant General Morshead, undertook the biggest Australian operation of the war with the help of the US 7th Fleet. Bombardment of the coast near Tarakan began on 12 April 1945 and on 30 April the Australians took Sadau Island in the Baragan Straits so that artillery could bomb beach fortifications. This led to the landing on Tarakan on 1 May, and the town fell after four days fighting with Australian losses of 225 killed and 669 wounded compared with Japanese losses of 1540 killed. On 10 June the Australians put ashore 29,000 men in Brunei Bay, where they met little opposition and the Australians proceeded to take Balikpapan.

The main purpose of this operation was to provide the British with an advance base from which to launch an offensive against Singapore. The British wanted to use the Philippines but MacArthur would not allow this. By the time the British had prepared an air base in Borneo the Japanese had surrendered.

## Bose, Subhas Chandra, 1897–1945

Bose was an Indian revolutionary Nationalist leader who joined the Japanese. When war broke out in 1939 Bose saw it as a chance to get the British out of India. In 1940 he was imprisoned but he escaped and found his way to Berlin where he announced the setting up of an Indian National Army. In June 1943 he went to Tokyo to negotiate with the Japanese and as a result announced the setting up of a Provisional Government of Free India. Japan had 60,000 Indian POWs and Bose recruited them into his Army. He also made broadcasts to India expounding his Nationalist ideals. In 1944 Bose led his INA against the British at Kohima and Imphal but he had arguments with the Japanese commanders. He was still planning an invasion of India when he died in a plane crash in Formosa.

## Bougainville, 1943–44

After Admiral Halsey had taken New Georgia he decided to bypass Kolombangara and head for Vella Lavella and then Bougainville. On 15 August the Americans landed on Vella Lavella where they met no resistance. Almost two weeks later they landed on Arundel Island which had been reinforced by the garrison of Kolombangara, but in late September Japan's Imperial GHQ decided to abandon the Central Solomons and fall back on Bougainville, and between 28 September and 3 October, 9400 men were evacuated.

The Americans decided to bypass the Japanese troop concentrations in Bougainville and head for Empress Augusta Bay on its west coast, which had the advantages of being fairly inaccessible by land and was guarded by only 2000 Japanese. On 27 October the 3rd New Zealand Division landed on Treasury Island and took it in eleven days. To confuse the Japanese the Americans made diversionary raids on Choiseul Island and on the Shortlands Islands, then at dawn on 1 November General Vandegrift led the Marines ashore at Empress Augusta Bay to find the Japanese had fled into

the jungle. The Marines soon held enough land to build an airstrip and on 2 November bombing raids against Rabaul began, forcing Admiral Koga to withdraw his carrier aircraft. When the Japanese realized that the landing at Empress Augusta Bay was not a diversionary operation they sent a mere 475 Japanese on a raid on 7 November but they were wiped out. The Japanese Seventeenth Army did not have enough supplies or equipment to mount a full-scale operation against the Marines, and in any case committed too few troops. By the end of December, stalemate had set in and the Americans were now about 44,000 strong and had built four airfields. On 8 and 25 March the Japanese made a final attempt to dislodge the Americans. This time 15,000 Japanese marched through the jungle to join in the attack, but in very heavy fighting 5000 Japanese were killed and 263 Americans died before the Japanese were pushed back. After this most of the troops withdrew to the southern bases and the Americans left them to 'wither on the vine'.

## Bradley, General Omar, 1893–1981

An obscure divisional commander in 1941, Bradley, who had graduated with Eisenhower from West Point in 1915, was selected by him to join the American forces in Tunisia in 1942 and was soon appointed to command 2nd 2nd Corps, which he handled with great success under Patton in the final battle for Tunisia. He added further to his reputation by his handling of his forces in Sicily. Taken to Britain by Eisenhower to prepare for the D-Day landings, he was given command of the American landings and then of American 1st Army in the bridgehead battle. On the arrival of Patton to command the new 3rd Army, Bradley became his superior as commander of the US 12th Army Group, the operations of which he directed to the end of the war. They included the advance to the West Wall, the repulse of the Ardennes offensive, and the crossing of the Rhine. Unremarkable in appearance and unflamboyant in manner, Bradley was known as the 'GI's General'. It was a considerable tribute to his powers of leadership that the mercurial Patton always gracefully accepted his authority, all the more difficult to bear in that their roles had initially been reversed.

## Brand, Air Vice-Marshal Sir Quintin, 1893–1968

Brand was the South African-born Commander of No 10 Group, RAF Fighter Command, during the Battle of Britain. As a captain in the Royal Flying Corps during World War I he had served with distinction, undertaking with Murlis-Green the perilous night combat operations of 1917. He destroyed a German Gotha bomber on the night of 19–20 May 1918, in the last air raid over the UK of that war. In 1920, together with Pierre van Ryneveld, he made the first flight from London to Cape Town, via Cairo, an achievement for which both airmen received knighthoods. After holding various RAF appointments he became Director General of Civil Aviation in Egypt, retaining the post until 1936. No 10 Group Fighter Command became operational in July 1940 with the task of defending the southwest of England during the Battle of Britain. Brand retired from the RAF in 1943.

## Brauchitsch, Field Marshal Walter von, 1881–1948

On the overthrow of Fritsch, on fabricated evidence of improper conduct, in 1938, Brauchitsch was chosen by Hitler to succeed as head of OKH and Commander in Chief of the Army. Hitler would have preferred the avowed pro-Nazi Reichenau, but Rundstedt, among others, succeeded in convincing the Führer that his appointment would alienate the senior officer corps, something Hitler was not anxious to do. Rundstedt in fact hoped that Brauchitsch would preserve what was left of the Army's independence but in this he was mistaken. For all his soldierly appearance, Brauchitsch lacked the nerve to stand up to Hitler and, having lost one argument with him, never started another. Hitler made him principal scapegoat for the failure to capture Moscow in 1941, dismissed him and assumed his post himself, thus becoming the first civilian to lead the German Army. Brauchitsch was credited with saving Paris contrary to Hitler's order to demolish the city in 1944.

## Braun, Wernher von, 1912–1977

The son of a German landowner who served as minister of agriculture in Papen's government, Braun showed a schoolboy interest in rocket design and at the age of 25 was appointed technical director of the German Army's rocket research center. In 1938 he produced a rocket, the A-4, which could carry an explosive warhead eleven miles and thereby attracted the attention of Hitler who granted his institute sufficient funds to proceed with the development of the V-2. This missile, of which about 3600 were fired against Britain and the Allied bases in the Low Countries in 1944–5, had a range of up to 200 miles but carried too small a warhead to yield the strategic result Hitler anticipated. At the end of the war Braun surrendered himself, his staff, equipment and documents to the Americans and, under their aegis, went on to develop inter-continental ballistic missiles and the vehicles which carried the first men to the moon.

## Breda Machine Gun

The SA Ernesto Breda of Brescia made several machine guns for the Italian Army, starting with their *Mitriaglice Tipo* 5C in 1924. The most common of the Breda designs was the Modello 30in 6.5mm caliber. This was a blowback machine gun for infantry support; instead of a detachable magazine, the side-mounted magazine hinged forward and could be re-charged from rifle clips. Due to the blowback operation, extraction was fierce and the cartridges had to be lubricated by a built-in oil pump before being loaded into the chamber. The barrels could be changed rapidly, but there was no form of handle with which to grip the hot barrel. In spite of these defects the gun remained in Italian Army service until 1944. The standard Italian heavy machine gun was the 8mm Modello 37, a gas-operated weapon; this also required the cartridges to be lubricated, and was unusual in that feeding from a strip, the mechanism replaced the empty cases in the strip instead of ejecting them. A modified version using a top-mounted magazine was supplied for tanks and armored cars. The Modello 30 was improved in 1938 by chambering for the new 7.35mm cartridge, but relatively few of these entered service.

## Breguet 693 and 695

By the start of the German offensive in May 1940, the French Air Force had accepted 106 Breguet 693s and 33 695s, which served with five bomber groups. They were twin-engined two-seaters, with top speed of over 300mph and armed with one cannon, four machine guns and 880lb of bombs. Most memorable actions were low level attacks on German trenches in Belgium.

## Bren Gun

This was a gas-operated light machine gun used by British Commonwealth forces 1936–56. Originally designed by the Czech Armaments factory at Brno, it was manufactured at the Royal Small Arms Factory, Enfield Lock, from which names came the word 'Bren'. Magazine-fed, it was an extremely reliable weapon. The barrel could be rapidly changed to prevent over-heating, and though normally shoulder-fired from a bipod, a tripod could also be used for sustained-fire tasks. Normally in British .303in caliber, numbers were made in Canada in 7.92mm caliber for use by the Chinese Nationalist Army. Subsequent to British adoption of the 7.62mm NATO cartridge, the design of the Bren was slightly modified to suit and the gun is still in service, known now as the Machine Gun L4.

## Brereton, General Lewis, 1890–1967

Brereton was an American General who held various commands during World War II. Although a graduate of the US Naval Academy, Brereton had followed an Army career. He became an aviator in 1913, serving under Brigadier General 'Billy' Mitchell, the original although controversial US theorist of aerial warfare during World War I. In 1941, with the threat of Japanese aggression mounting, he was appointed Commander of the US Far East Air Force, under General MacArthur, with the task of preparing for the probable attack. However, with insufficient supplies, unreliable communications and untried equipment, his force suffered heavily. In 1942 he had command of the 10th Air Force in India but was subsequently transferred to the newly formed USAMEAF (US Army Middle East Air Force). He immediately initiated a series of co-ordinated attacks against enemy supply lines, and, working always in close co-operation with the RAF, had his inexperienced American pilots integrated into British squadrons to be blooded. In October 1942 he took personal command of the US Desert Air Task Force prior to the El Alamein offensive, establishing a small staff at the British Advanced HQ, both to represent US interests and to gain experience. In November 1942, the USAMEAF became the US 9th Air Force, in which role it made a vital contribution to the ending of the North African campaign and subsequently, to the occupation of Sicily and the invasion of Italy, including the notable attack on the Ploesti oil refineries on 1 August 1943.

Brereton assumed command of the newly reactivated 9th Air Force in the United Kingdom in the fall of 1943. Formed as part of the air preparations for Operation Overlord, the force which he created became one of the most formidable tactical units in the world, carrying out operations of critical importance against selected targets in northern France, in particular, the German communications system. The 9th AF's use of dive-bombing techniques against the bridges over the Rivers Seine, Oise, and Marne was especially remarkable.

Despite taking a dim view of the assignment, in August 1944 he was appointed the first Commander of the 1st Allied Airborne Army, a job which was to prove frustrating as he was unable to exploit what he considered to be the strategic potential of his force. It was his troops who fought the bitter battle at Arnhem in September 1944. Brereton was firmly convinced of the value of inter-Service, inter-Allied cooperation.

## *Bretagne*

One of three French dreadnought battleships completed in 1915–16 the *Bretagne* had been only partially modernized between 1927 and 1935 like her sister *Provence*. The *Lorraine*, on the other hand, was more comprehensively reconstructed. She blew up and capsized after several hits by British 15in shells during the action at Mers-el-Kebir on 3 July 1940.

## Bretton Woods Conference, 1–22 July 1944

The Bretton Woods conference was held to plan postwar international economic co-operation. It set up an International Monetary Fund of $8,800,000,000 to promote economic stability and encourage international trade. It also set up an International Bank for Reconstruction and Development with a capital of $10,000,000,000. It was signed by Australia, Belgium, Bolivia, Brazil, Canada, Chile, China, Columbia, Costa Rica, Cuba, Czechoslovakia, Dominican Republic, Ecuador, Egypt, El Salvador, Ethiopia, France, Greece, Guatemala, Honduras, Iceland, India, Iran, Iraq, Luxemburg, Mexico, the Netherlands, Nicaragua, Norway, Panama, Paraguay, Peru, Philippines, Poland, South Africa, the UK, the USA, Uruguay, Venezuela and Yugoslavia.

## Britain, Battle of, 1940

After the fall of France, Hitler determined to threaten Britain with invasion, since she showed no willingness to come to terms. Whether he would have actually attempted invasion is a debatable question. But as evidence of intent, he opened an air attack on Britain on 10 July with the aim of destroying the fighter defenses of the country. It was to last until the end of October. For the battle, Goering, commanding the Luftwaffe, could assemble 2800 aircraft whereas the RAF had only about 700 fighters. However the RAF had the inestimable advantage of an efficient early warning system, through the adoption of the recently discovered principle of radar. At first the Germans attacked ports and shipping in the hope of bringing the RAF into unequal battle over the Channel. When the British stopped the Channel convoys on 10 August, Goering switched to attacking the airfields along the south coast (tentative attacks on the radar towers were not pressed). On 15 August he sent 1500 airplanes, and shook the two front-

*Top:* St Paul's Cathedral in London during the Blitz.
*Right:* 'Never before in the field of human conflict have so many owed so much to so few'.

line groups of the RAF, Nos 11 and 12, badly, but also lost heavily himself. He maintained the pressure at a similar level for ten days, by which time the Luftwaffe had lost 602 aircraft to the RAF's 260. But he then switched targets again, using the pretext of a threatened attack on Berlin to open a full-scale bombing offensive against London, the 'Blitz'. The bombing began on 7 September and the attacks reached their height on 15 September – still commemorated in England as Battle of Britain Day – when 56 German planes were shot down. Having very nearly broken the RAF during August with his attacks on the airfields, Goering now had to face a severe decline of effectiveness and morale among his own units. On 17 September Hitler privately instituted an indefinite postponement of the invasion and, although daylight attacks on British cities continued to the end of the month, losses ran at such a high rate that the Luftwaffe turned at the beginning of October to night bombing which had much reduced military effectiveness. By the end of October, though the Blitz continued sporadically, the Battle of Britain was recognized to be over. Hitler's thoughts were turning eastward. During the course of the battle, the RAF had lost 790 fighters, the Luftwaffe 1389 airplanes of all types. The island base had been preserved for an eventual invasion of Hitler's own territories.

## British Army

As in 1914, the British Army which went to war in 1939 was a small, long-service force which lacked the great reserves of trained soldiers necessary to bring it up to a size equal to those of its continental allies or enemies. Its main reserve was the part-time volunteer Territorial Army, which lacked training and was underequipped. Thus it was able to send only 12 divisions to the continent in 1939 to stand beside the French. However, it had already begun to conscript young men and eventually built up fifty divisions. And it had an important source of additional strength in the forces of the empire and the dominions. The Canadian, Australian, New Zealand and South African Armies would each send several divisions into the field, while the Indian Army stood ready at the beginning of the war to deploy nearly 200,000 men.

British equipment was of mixed quality. The Army enjoyed a great advantage over its German namesake in that it was, from the start, able to provide all its divisions with sufficient motor transport to move their infantry from their own resources. British field artillery, equipped with the famous 25-pounder gun, was also good. But at the outset the medium artillery lacked proper weapons, while the anti-tank and tank units were notably deficient in modern equipment. In the I Tank (Matilda) the British began the war with a machine which the Germans could not knock out, but it was too small and undergunned to be useful as a weapon of support or exploitation. The cruiser tanks with which the British fought most of the Desert War were insufficiently protected and it was not really until they acquired the Sherman from the Americans that the Royal Armored Corps had a weapon with which it could meet the Germans on equal terms. Its better home-produced tanks of the latter stage of the war, the Churchill and Cromwell, were made in too small numbers to count seriously in the scales of battle.

The British command system, unlike the German or French, devolved considerable responsibility on to the generals in the field. Churchill, with advice from the Chief of the Imperial General Staff – for most of the war the able Alanbrooke – decided the main lines of policy, but left the theater and battlefield commanders to construct and execute their own battle plans. After American entry, British commanders came increasingly under the control of inter-Allied headquarters, of which the chiefs were usually American. The cordiality of relationships established between the headquarters of both armies was remarkable and a major contribution to the winning of the war.

## Brody-Lvov, Battle of, July 1944

The Germans expected the Russians to launch their summer offensive in 1944 around Lvov, and consequently were unprepared for the Belorussian campaign in June. On July 13 General Konev launched his offensive, which consisted of two attacks: one to cross the Bug to Lublin and join up with Rokossovsky, the other to break through the enemy's flank and take Lvov from the north. After four days Konev's left wing was heading towards Sandomierz and his tanks had trapped 40,000 men at Brody. By 21 July his troops were making no progress towards Lvov so they began the outflanking maneuver. On 27 July the Germans evacuated Lvov and on 30 July Konev crossed the Vistula to begin the sweep to the Oder.

Dancing in the street after the liberation of Lvov.

## Broke

Bearer of a name made famous in World War I, this British flotilla leader should not be confused with the flotilla leader commanded by Commander Evans during his action in the Channel in 1917. On 8 November 1942 she embarked a detachment of US Rangers whose task was to seize the port installations in Algiers harbor to prevent the French from sabotaging them. With HMS *Malcolm* she was the spearhead of the assault on Algiers which was an important part of Operation Torch, the invasion of North Africa.

The attack went wrong as the two ships failed

to find the harbor entrance and were raked by heavy gunfire. The *Malcolm* withdrew with heavy casualties but the *Broke* charged the boom four times and finally broke through to land her contingent. While withdrawing she was hit again and damaged so badly that she sank the next day.

## Brooke, Field Marshal Alan, 1883–1963

A distinguished gunner officer, Brooke succeeded Sir John Dill as British Chief of the Imperial General Staff in 1941. Thus he became Churchill's principal strategic adviser which he remained for the rest of the war. His own description of his role was that of turning Churchill's inspirations into military sense, but he also dissuaded the Prime Minister from many bad ideas, produced good ones of his own and maintained excellent relations with his American colleagues. During the Dunkirk withdrawal, he had handled 2nd Corps with great skill.

## Brooke-Popham, Air Chief Marshal Sir Robert, 1878–1953

Air Chief Marshal Brooke-Popham was Commander in Chief of all British land and air forces in Malaya, British Borneo and Hong Kong. He was told that his defense of the Far East would be based on air power, but in fact had far too few aircraft. On 1 November 1941 the British Government decided to replace Brooke-Popham by Lieutenant General Pownall but by the time war broke out the change in command had not yet taken place. Brooke-Popham knew of the Japanese landings in Siam but lost his chance to forestall them because the Cabinet would not sanction the invasion of a neutral country. His forces in the north of Malaya could do little against Japanese armor and on 27 December Brooke-Popham was relieved of his command.

## Browning Guns

John M Browning was one of America's foremost firearms designers, and the US Army relied heavily on three of his inventions during the war. These three were the Colt automatic pistol M1911A1 (qv), the Browning Automatic Rifle and the Browning Machine Gun.

Both the rifle and the machine gun were designed by Browning in 1915–16, tested in 1917 and placed in immediate production in order to arm the AEF. After the war they remained the standard automatic weapons of the US Army; improved models were developed, and in World War II they were extensively employed by the Allies.

The Browning Automatic Rifle was a gas-operated shoulder arm using a 20-round magazine. It weighed 15.5lb and had a rate of fire of about 500 rpm. Fitted with a bipod it became the 'squad automatic weapon' of the US Army, acting in the role assumed by a light machine gun in other armies, and numbers were also supplied to Britain in 1940–41 for use by the Home Guard. It was also made under license in, and adopted by the armies of, Sweden, Poland and Belgium.

Although a good design, well-suited to mass production, it was never as good a weapon as its designer hoped. It was too heavy to be a rifle,

*Top:* The Browning automatic rifle.
*Above:* The Browning machine gun.

and the vibration of the action made accurate fire from the shoulder almost impossible. On the other hand it was too light to be a good light machine gun and was unsteady on its bipod, the barrel overheated and could not be changed, and the bottom-mounted magazine was awkward to change in combat. In spite of this though, it stayed in first-line service for almost 50 years, and large numbers are still in use.

The Browning machine gun was a recoil-operated weapon feeding from a belt of cartridges. The 1917 model was, in contemporary style, water-cooled and tripod-mounted, but in the 1920s the gun was adapted to aircraft use where air-cooling was found to be sufficient. The US Cavalry then adopted the air-cooled design and found it successful in ground operations. Eventually this model was adopted throughout the US Army. The standard infantry weapon was in .30 caliber but a heavier model in .50 caliber was developed for use in tanks, aircraft, and as a heavy ground-support weapon.

This machine gun is one of the world's classic designs – robust, simple, easy to teach and maintain, utterly reliable in action; it is still the preferred machine gun for most of the countries of the free world, and will probably remain so for many years to come.

## Brummbär (Grizzly Bear)

The Brummbär was a German self-propelled gun, consisting of the standard 15cm heavy infantry gun, sIG 33, suitably modified to fit into a tank-type cradle and hemispherical mantlet and with the breech modified for electric firing, mounted into a modified Pz Kpfw IV tank chassis. The gun was frontally mounted in a raised superstructure, and there were several minor variations in the design as improvements suggested themselves. It appears to have entered service early in 1944, and some 313 units were built.

The Brummbär self-propelled gun was also known as the Sturmpanzer 43.

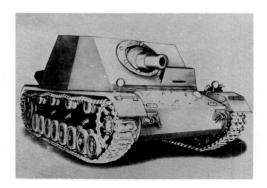

**Bryansk Pocket**

See Vyazma-Bryansk, Battle of, October 1941

## BT Series Soviet Tanks

The BT (for 'fast tank') series of vehicles were derived from the Christie M-1931 tank purchased in the USA. After examination and test, this was copied to produce the BT-1, a ten-tonner armed with two machine guns. The BT-2 followed, very similar but carrying a 37mm gun in the turret; some of these tanks were still in service in 1940. Small numbers of BT-3 and BT-4 were built during the 1930s, and then production was concentrated on the BT-5. This retained the Christie suspension but added a new engine and a larger turret carrying a 45mm gun; this tank weighed 11.5 tons, had up to 13mm of armor and could move at speeds up to 60mph. In 1938 the BT-7 appeared, another improvement on the basic design, with thicker, welded armor, a more powerful engine and better transmission – a notoriously weak point on Soviet tanks of that period. Weighing 13.8 tons and with the armor increased to 22mm, the speed dropped to 45mph, but this tank formed the bulk of the Soviet armored force when Germany invaded. It was to prove a poor opponent to the German Panzers and its armor was vulnerable to almost every German gun. It was rapidly replaced by the much superior T-34, though the BT tanks stayed in service until they were used up, several of them being captured by the Germans and used against their former owners.

*Below and bottom:* Soviet BT medium tanks.

**Buchenwald**

See Holocaust

## Buckner, Lieutenant General Simon, 1886–1945

Buckner led the US 10th Army in the last operation of the war in the Pacific. Buckner spent most of the war in Alaska commanding defense forces. He first saw action with the US 10th Army, which was used in the operation to take Okinawa. On 7 May 1945 he assumed personal control of operations and reinforced the southern front where troops were trying to destroy the defenses at Shuri. On 31 May Shuri fell and Buckner's troops now cleared the rest of the Japanese in the south. On 18 June 1945, before the Japanese had given up the fight, Buckner was killed at a forward command post, when he was hit by a piece of shrapnel in the heart.

## Budenny, Marshal Semion M, 1883–1973

Budenny and Voroshilov were the only Marshals to survive the Purges of 1938. Budenny had no great reputation as a soldier and owed his appointment as Marshal to his ability to please Stalin. He was an ex-Cavalry officer with little training in modern war tactics. On 10 July 1941 Stalin made him Commander in Chief of the Southwestern Front. Budenny's task was to co-ordinate the operations of two great armies at Uman and Kiev, a total of one and a half million soldiers. Budenny proved unequal to this task; he hesitated too long and allowed

Marshal Semion Budenny.

Rundstedt's army to cut him off from the forces at Uman, who were then captured. After this disaster, Budenny again failed to regroup his forces in a defensive formation: he planned a last-minute counterattack from Kiev which was unsuccessful and he withdrew to the Dniepr. Budenny was dismissed on 13 September and replaced by Timoshenko, but this did not prevent the other half of Budenny's army from being taken. After this debacle Budenny was never again given an active appointment.

## Buffalo, Brewster F2A

The Buffalo was the first monoplane fighter to enter service with the US Navy, in June 1939; but more than two-thirds of the total of 507 that were built, went to export customers. Only 21 were used operationally by the US, in the hands of Marine pilots at the Battle of Midway. They suffered major losses in combat with Japanese aircraft. The RAF fared no better when it bought 170 for service in the Far East and flew them against Zeros over Singapore. However, the 44 delivered to Finland served with conspicuous success for five years. The F2A–3 version flown by the US Marines had a 1200hp Wright R–1820 engine, giving a maximum speed of 321mph at 16,500ft. Armament comprised two 0.5in guns in the top cowling and two more in the wings.

## Bulganin, Political Marshal Nikolay A, 1895–1975

Bulganin was an important party official who was used to keep an eye on the activities of frontline generals. His official post was as member of the Stavka and he was sent to the Center Front in 1941 to keep an eye on Timoshenko. He was also a member of the Stavka commission to investigate the failure of Kuroshkin's Northwest Front in 1941. He then became a member of the West Front Military Council with Konev and Sokolovsky. In 1943 he was sent to the Baltic Front and was made a Colonel General in 1944. In July 1944 he was sent as a representative to the Soviet sponsored Lublin Committee of National Liberation in Poland. From 1944–46 he served as USSR Deputy People's Commissar of Defense.

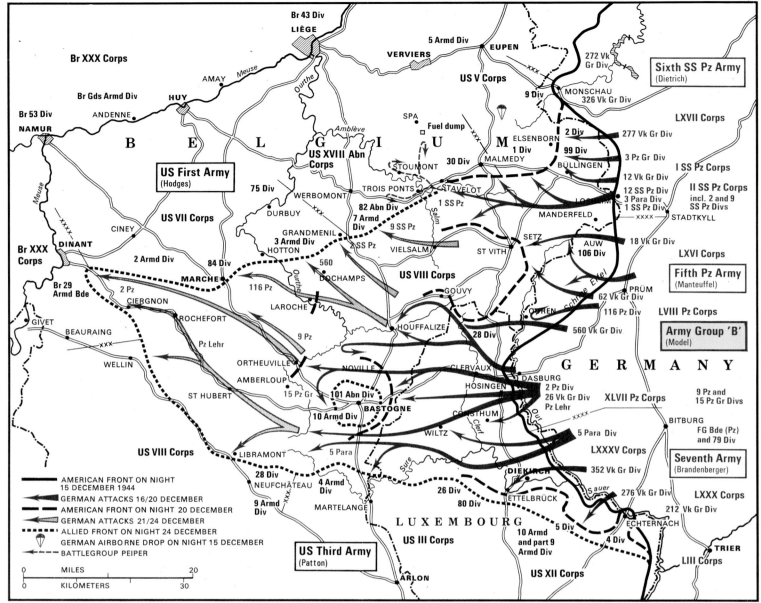

## Bulge, Battle of the, 1944

An area of wooded hills in south Belgium, through which the Germans attacked France in May 1940, and December 1944, the Ardennes offensive (Battle of the Bulge) refers generally to the latter operation. Following the German flight from France in August 1944, Montgomery's failure to capture the Rhine, crossings at Arnhem and the logistic enfeeblement of Patton's drive in Lorraine, a lull descended on the Western Front, while the Allies reconstructed and shortened their line of communications (see Antwerp). Hitler profited from it to re-equip and reinforce his garrison of the West Wall, to such effect that by December he had assembled a large enough force to undertake a counteroffensive, into the Ardennes, as weakly held in 1944 as it had been in 1940. He had conceived the germ of the plan perhaps as early as September but its exact form had been a hotly debated issue during October and November. Rundstedt (C-in-C West) and Model (Commander, Army Group B) had argued for a 'small solution' to pinch out the Aachen salient, Hitler for a 'large solution' to drive on Antwerp, thus splitting the British from the American

Generals Patton and Bradley in an anxious moment aboard a C-47 before the Bulge.

armies and capturing the Allies' main port; he insisted ultimately upon the latter. His aim was to win time in the west so as to attack later in the east, but he believed also in the possibility of forcing a separate peace on the British and Americans. On the morning of 16 December three German Armies (Fifth, Sixth, Seventh), totaling 25 divisions (11 armored) struck six unsuspecting American divisions and overran their lines. Heroic resistance by survivors, retention of two important road junctions, St Vith and Bastogne (the latter held throughout the battle) and swift reinforcement by both American and British troop units from Holland and Lorraine halted the German advance just short of the Meuse, near Dinant, on 26 December. On the same day, the Allied Air Forces, grounded by bad weather since the beginning of the battle, were able to intervene and the line was thereafter steadily pushed back and consolidated. Two associated German operations, *Bodenplatte*, the Luftwaffe's last offensive, directed against Allied airdromes on 1 January 1945, and an offensive by Army Group G in Alsace-Lorraine, 1–30 January, achieved temporary local success but were both ultimately profitless.

## Buna
see New Guinea. Port Moresby and Buna

## Burke, Captain Arleigh, 1901–

Burke was commander of Destroyer Squadron 45 which was involved in many operations off the Solomon Islands. His squadron fought in two battles off Bougainville, one at Empress Augusta Bay and another off Cape St George, where he sank three destroyers escorting transports. During these operations Burke earned the nickname '31 Knot Burke', which was a tribute to his command of destroyers. After his success in preventing the Japanese from reinforcing Bougainville, Burke was appointed Chief of Staff to Vice-Admiral Mitscher and was present at the Battles of the Philippine Sea and Leyte Gulf. In 1945 he was appointed head of the Research and Development Division of the Ordnance Bureau in Washington.

## 'Busy Lizzie'
see High Pressure Pump

## Burma, Fall of, December 1941-April 1942

The Japanese wanted to cut off the Burma Road which supplied Chiang Kai-shek's China and therefore invaded Burma. The conquest of Burma was assigned to the Japanese Fifteenth Army under General Iida. The Japanese planned to use the airfields in the extreme south of Burma to cover the main advance from Raheng along jungle track via Moulmein to Rangoon. The British only had the 1st Burma Division and the 17th Indian Brigade, which was just arriving. The 1st Burma Division was made up of three brigades which had had no collective training and which were short of artillery, engineers and transport. The forces were extremely short of aircraft: there was one squadron of 16 Buffaloes and three fighter squadrons from the American Volunteer Group, sent by Chiang Kai-shek – a total of about 30 planes. If they were needed, the British had agreed to call

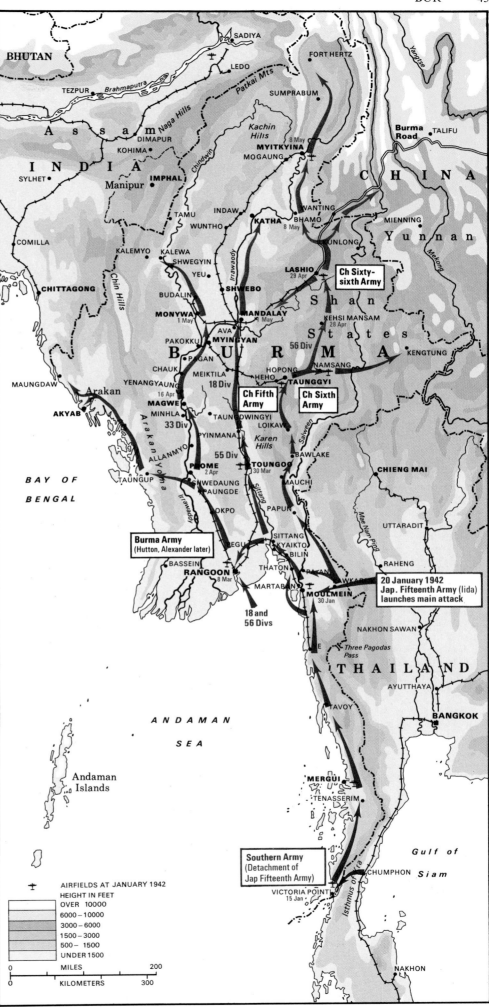

British soldier in front of the Bahe Pagoda, undamaged in the midst of fire.

in the Chinese 5th and 6th Army. Iida had only 35,000 men but he had 200 aircraft, and after the fall of Manila this figure was doubled.

The invasion began in mid-December when a detachment of the Fifteenth Army moved into Tenasserim and seized the airfield. On 15 January 1942, they took Victoria Point. The Japanese began to bomb Rangoon from these positions, but fighter planes of the AVG fought back and the bombers could only approach at night. The population of Rangoon began to flee into the jungle, causing problems for the defending army. Lieutenant General Hutton, General Wavell's Chief of Staff, suspected that the Japanese would break through from Raheng, but he wanted to protect the Shah States and deployed the 17th Indian Division and two other brigades on a front of over 400 miles from Mergui to Papun. He did, however have some of his military stocks moved from Rangoon to Meiktila, Mandalay and Myingyan in case Rangoon fell. These defensive measures were still being carried out when the Fifty-fifth Division reached Tavoy and overwhelmed the inexperienced defenders to threaten Mergui from the south.

The Japanese now controlled the three airfields in the south of Burma, so Hutton wanted to bring his forces back to a defensive position on the Sittang River. He did not want to abandon the Salween or Bilin rivers, so the experienced 2nd Burma Brigade was stationed at Moulmein on the Salween estuary. On 20 January, General Iida and his men began to advance from Raheng, carrying all their equipment with them through the jungle. Early on 30 January, the Fifty-fifth Division launched an attack on Moulmein from the south and from the east. The 2nd Burma Brigade was pushed back to the waterfront from the east, so Hutton ordered it to withdraw. Although Hutton wanted a more complete withdrawal, Wavell would not allow it, claiming it would destroy morale.

The Fifty-fifth Division was then ordered to drive the enemy from the Salween and Sittang and advance to Toungoo and destroy the Chinese troops, while the Thirty-third Division was

to take Rangoon and then progress to Mandalay and the oil-producing regions round the Irrawaddy. On 11 February the Japanese crossed the Salween at Pa-an, and although the Indian battalion resisted they were overwhelmed. On 13 February Hutton allowed a withdrawal from the Salween, but it was too late to make a stand on the Bilin River, so the troops raced back to the Sittang. The Japanese had to travel through the jungle and across fifteen miles of unpaved road, but they reached the Sittang bridge as the 48th Brigade was crossing it. The British blew up the bridge under heavy fire, leaving two-thirds of the brigade to swim across. At this point General Alexander arrived to replace Hutton on 5 March and on 19 March General Slim arrived to command the Burcorps. Alexander insisted that Rangoon be held and ordered an offensive to restore the situation, but this came to nothing. The Japanese waited until 3 March to cross the Salween in force. Alexander soon accepted that he could not hope to hold Rangoon. By 8 March the last train evacuating the population left the city, and the Japanese found Rangoon deserted. The Japanese had not approached from the north because they wanted a surprise attack, so the British narrowly avoided encirclement. The Japanese now waited for reinforcements, and early in April the Fifteenth Army moved north to Mandalay and avoided the British and Chinese lines to take the Yenangyaung oilfields on 16 April. General Stilwell devised a plan to encircle the Japanese on the Sittang but they circumvented this by outflanking the Chinese army and heading for Lashio. Alexander decided that the British should withdraw to India, where they could continue to fight the Japanese. Alexander ordered a general withdrawal across the Irrawaddy on 21 April, with Slim covering the Chinese' line of retreat.

The long retreat began on 26 April and the British had to reach India before the mid-May monsoon. The Japanese were in close pursuit. On 19 May the British rearguard reached Tamu. Two Chinese divisions also made their way cross-country to India after the Japanese cut them off by seizing Myitkyina. The British just managed to reach India before the monsoon. The whole operation in Burma had cost them 13,500 men, almost three times as many as the Japanese.

## Burma Road

The Burma Road ran from Mandalay to Lashio to Kunming in the Yunnan Province. After 1938 it was Chiang Kai-shek's only overland supply route. To please the Japanese the British closed it in July 1940. In fact they did so after consulting the Americans and shut the road during the monsoon period when it was impassable and opened it three months later. In 1942 the Japanese cut off the Burma road and Chiang Kai-shek could only receive supplies by air transport over the Hump (the Himalayas). The Americans were very insistent on opening the road up but the British were not keen because they did not have the equipment to launch an offensive to recapture Burma. In 1944 General Stilwell led the US attempt to open up the road from Ledo in Assam, India. As his Armies advanced US engineers built a road which eventually linked up with the Burma road at Lashio in February 1945. The whole road was cleared from China to Burma in June 1945 but by this time Japan was near defeat.

## Burney Gun

Burney guns were recoilless guns developed in Britain by Sir Denis Burney during the period 1941–45. The design relied on a perforated cartridge case which permitted a portion of the propellant gas to pass into an annular chamber and thence through venturi jets directed rearwards, the thrust so developed counter-balancing the recoil of the gun. Also associated with this design was a thin-walled 'Wallbuster' shell containing plastic explosive for attack of armor or concrete. Guns of 3.45in, 3.7in and 4.7in caliber were developed, and pilot quantities entered service in 1945, but too late to see combat. In addition, 95mm, 7.2in and 8in designs were also made in prototype.

## Burza

The *Burza* was a Polish destroyer built in France in 1927–30 along with her sister *Wicher* (the names meant 'Squall' and 'Hurricane' respectively). The *Wicher* was sunk during the German attack on Gdynia in September 1939 but the *Burza* escaped to England with the *Blyskawica* and *Grom*. She had a distinguished war career, and in 1951 was returned by the British Government to the Communist regime in Poland, after a wrangle over ownership.

## Bush, Vannevar, 1890–1974

Bush held the post of Director of the Office of Scientific Research and Development throughout the war. He was a distinguished scientist and engineer, President of the Carnegie Institute of Washington. He served on various committees dealing with research and in 1940 he was appointed to co-ordinate all aspects of atomic research.

## Byrnes, James, 1879–1972

Byrnes was Secretary of State in President Truman's government. Byrnes was an influential man and a clever negotiator, who helped get the Selective Service and Lend-Lease Acts through Congress. In 1942 he resigned his appointment in the Supreme Court to become director of Economic Stabilization and later of War Mobilization. He tried to stop inflation; he froze salaries and stimulated wartime production. In 1944 Byrnes was a candidate for the Vice-Presidential nomination but he withdrew in favor of Truman. Byrnes accompanied Roosevelt to Yalta, but since he had no experience in negotiating with the Russians he did not make much impact. When Roosevelt died Byrnes resigned, but Truman made him his Secretary of State. He played important roles at the Potsdam Conferences, the London Conference and the Paris Peace Conference.

Byrnes was a conservative and a hard-liner. He advocated the use of the atomic bomb against Japan. When the Japanese asked for a proviso to guarantee the Emperor's position, Byrnes sent back a reply specifying the condition that Japan would be under the rule of the Supreme Commander of US forces. He made two major contributions to peace plans. Firstly he set up the UN Atomic Energy Commission and secondly he spoke out against reparations from Germany because he wanted a free and self-sufficient Germany.

# C

## Cairo Conference, November 1943

This conference was called to formulate policy on China. Before meeting Stalin at Teheran, Roosevelt and Churchill met Chiang Kai-shek at Cairo. Roosevelt was very reassuring to Chiang and promised him full support and more operations in the Far East, such as an operation on the Andaman Islands in the Bay of Bengal. Churchill was against this and it was never carried out. Nor was he able to get agreement on British plans for operations in the eastern Mediterranean. The conference issued the Cairo declaration to boost Chinese morale which set out Allied plans for the future in the Far East. It stated that the Allies wanted Japan's unconditional surrender and that she give up her overseas empire. It also said the Manchuria, Formosa and the Pescadores Islands would be returned to China. Furthermore, the Western Powers renounced their special rights and interests in China after its reconquest.

Generalissimo Chiang Kai-shek, President Roosevelt, Prime Minister Churchill and Madame Chiang Kai-shek at the Cairo Conference, to discuss future plans for the Far East.

## Calabria, Battle of
see *Bologna* and *Eagle*

---

### *California*

This American battleship (BB–44), sistership of the *Tennessee*, was completed in 1921. She was flagship of the US Pacific Fleet from 1921 to 1941 and flagship of the Battle Force of the Battle Fleet. She was modernized in 1929–30 and was sent to Pearl Harbor in 1940. On 7 December 1941 she was at the southernmost berth in 'Battleship Row' when the Japanese struck. At 0805 a bomb exploded between decks and set off an anti-aircraft magazine and a second bomb opened up her bow plating. She slowly settled on the mud with only her superstructure above water. Her casualties totaled 98 killed and 61 wounded.

The *California* was refloated on 25 March 1942 and went into dock for repairs; she left under her own steam for Puget Sound Navy Yard just over two months later to undergo full repairs and reconstruction. When she reappeared at the end of January 1944 she was totally altered in appearance, with single streamlined stack and modern AA guns and fire-control. She took part in the bombardments of Saipan, Guam, Leyte, Iwo Jima and Okinawa, and fought in the Battle of Surigao Strait in October 1944.

---

### CAM-Ships

In mid-1941 the depredations of Focke-Wulf FW200 Condor aircraft upon British shipping on the route to Gibraltar forced the Admiralty to take special measures. Although the crisis which forced the issue occurred in June–August, when aircraft sank 94,500 tons of shipping, the Admiralty had in fact already taken steps to convert merchantmen to carry a single Hurricane fighter aircraft to be catapulted off when bombers appeared. These were known as Fighter Catapult Ships, and the first, HMS *Maplin*, *Springbank*, *Ariguani* and *Pega-*

*sus* were ready in April 1941, and they proved successful despite early and expected teething problems.

A further 50 ships were ordered to be converted to Catapult Aircraft Merchantmen of CAM-Ships, and it was under this name that they are best known. The difference between the two types was that the FCS were manned by the Royal Navy as auxiliary warships, whereas the CAM-Ships continued to serve as ordinary merchant ships, and only embarked the Hurricane aircraft and its pilot as supernumeries. The pilots of the RAF Merchantmen faced a particularly bleak prospect; once catapulted they knew there was little likelihood of landing on dry land, and would almost certainly have to parachute into the sea and hope that they would be picked up by an escort before they died of exposure. The aircraft were obsolete marks of Hurricane, but they were more than a match for the Condors in speed and armament; their loss was of less consequence than the lives of their trained pilots.

---

### Canaris, Admiral Wilhelm, 1888–1945

A World War I U-Boat commander, Canaris at the outbreak of World War II was head of the *Abwehr* (Defense), the counter-espionage agency of the German armed forces. In many ways an efficient organization, its usefulness to the German war effort was compromised by the disaffection of many of its officers, including Canaris, from the Nazi movement. Canaris himself became embroiled in the military resistance to Hitler, to which he gave important help, and after the July Plot was arrested and sent to Flossenburg concentration camp. He was executed there just before its liberation by the Allies in April 1945.

---

### *Canberra*

This Australian heavy cruiser of the British *Kent* or 'County' Class was completed in 1928 with her sister, HMAS *Australia*. She was part of an Allied force lying off Savo Island during the Guadalcanal Campaign. On the night of 9 August 1942, she and the US cruisers *Astoria*, *Quincy* and *Vincennes* were overwhelmed in a disastrous night action with Japanese surface forces. The *Canberra* was wrecked by gunfire and torpedoes, and burned fiercely until next morning. The wreck was finally sunk by the US destroyer *Ellett*.

As a compliment to their Australian allies the US Government decreed that the name *Canberra* was to be given to a new USN heavy cruiser, the only time an American warship had been named after a foreign city.

HMAS *Canberra*.

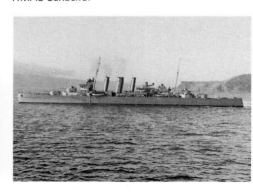

## Cant Z.506B Airone

Powered by three 750hp Alfa Romeo 126 engines, this handsome seaplane reconnaissance-bomber was used extensively for bombing or torpedo-bombing of targets in France and the Mediterranean theater, by the Italian Air Force. Priority was switched gradually to maritime reconnaissance, convoy escort and anti-submarine duties. Z.506S Airones were used for air/sea rescue by both the Italian and German air forces.

## Cant Z.1007 *bis* Alcione

Next to the S.M.79 Sparviero, the Alcione was the most important medium bomber operated by the Italian Air Force in World War II. The first prototype flew in late 1937. The main production model, the Z.1007*bis*, which was larger than the earlier Z.1007, with three 1000hp Piaggio P.XI*bis* engines and bomb load of up to 4410lb. Armament comprised two 12.7mm machine guns and two of 7.7mm. The airframe was of wood, with alternative single or twin-fin tail unit. Its durability is emphasized by the fact that units equipped with the Z.1007*bis* operated throughout the war in combat areas from North Africa to the Soviet Union. In the Mediterranean, the 172nd Strategic Reconnaissance Squadron operated in both bombing and torpedo attack roles, the latter with Alciones carrying a pair of 1000lb torpedoes.

## Cant Z.1018 Leone

Intended as an all-metal successor to the Alcione, the twin-engined Leone flew for the first time in 1940. Orders for 300 production models were placed, with alternative 1320hp Piaggio P.XII and 1350hp Alfa Romeo Tornado engines, armament of three 12.7mm and two 7.7mm machine guns, and offensive load of six 550lb bombs. Only a few became operational before the Italian surrender.

## Cape Bon, Battle of
see *Isaac Sweers*

## Cape Engaño, Battle of
see Leyte Gulf, Battle of, 1944

## Cape Esperance, Battle of, 11 October 1942

By the beginning of October 1942 the US had sufficient cruisers and destroyers to challenge the Japanese surface superiority. Under Rear Admiral Scott the US sent a Striking Force of the 8-inch cruisers *San Francisco* and *Salt Lake City*, light cruisers *Boise* and *Helena* and five destroyers. It had orders to escort a supply convoy and search and destroy enemy ships in the 'Slot', the narrow channel between the eastern and western Solomons. Before midnight 11 October 1942 Scott was steering northwest of Cape Esperance on Guadalcanal in search of Rear Admiral Goto's cruiser squadron and six destroyers. Scott formed his ships in a single line and was on a collision course with Goto's ships. At 2325 the *Helena*'s radar picked up the Japanese force 14 nautical miles away. Before Scott was informed of this he had ordered his ships to

reverse course and several destroyers were between his cruiser and the Japanese. The orders got confused and the *Duncan* attacked the Japanese alone. At 2346 the *Helena* opened fire but was told to cease because Scott was not sure where his destroyers were. The Japanese had been taken by surprise: the cruiser *Furutaka* caught fire and sank, the cruiser *Aoba* was badly damaged, the destroyer *Fubuki* also sank and Goto was mortally wounded. However the cruiser *Kinugasa* and the destroyer *Hatsuyuki* found the *Duncan* and disabled it. In the confusion the *Duncan* had been hit by US shells and the *Farenholt* had been hit by shells from the *Boise* and *Helena*. During the confusion, the *Aoba* and *Kinugasa* were able to knock out the *Boise*. The Americans believed they had sunk four cruisers and four destroyers and hailed this as a great victory. In fact the Japanese had only lost one cruiser and one destroyer. The Battle of Cape Esperance was the first time in the Pacific War that the Allies successfully attacked the Japanese despite the inconclusive results.

## Cape Matapan
see Matapan, Battle of Cape

## Cape Spartivento, Battle of
see Force H

## Capital
see Northern Burma Campaign

## Caproni Ca 309 to Ca 314

The designations Ca 309 to Ca 314 covered a series of light twin-engined aircraft that were used by the Italian and other Air Forces for duties ranging from reconnaissance and bombing to transport, training and close support. Most important version in Italian service was the Ca 313, first flown in early 1940 with 700hp Isotta-Fraschini Delta RC 35 engines, 1100lb bomb load and armament of three 12.7 and two 7.7mm machine guns. Ca 313s gave good service in Russia, and were followed by about 500 Ca 314s. These were basically similar but served with both the Italian Air Force and Navy. The Ca 314C provided close support for land forces, with two additional 12.7mm guns under its wings. The naval Ca 314RA was equipped for reconnaissance, torpedo attack, convoy escort and general support duties.

## Carlson, Brigadier Evans, 1896–1947

Carlson was the Commander of a Marine battalion which fought a guerrilla campaign in Guadalcanal and also in the Gilbert Islands. He had picked up the idea of a guerrilla unit while serving as an observer with Chiang Kai-shek's troops. He began to train a unit in early 1942 although many other officers did not approve of his methods. His most spectacular raid was a 36-day march behind Japanese lines on Guadalcanal in November 1942. He lost 17 men and pushed the Japanese further inland. After this raid his battalion was disbanded and Carlson was sent home. In November 1943 Carlson took part in the assault on Tarawa in the Gilbert Islands and advanced through the grades to become Brigadier. In 1946 Carlson retired as a result of wounds.

## Casablanca Conference, January 1943

These mainly military discussions of the Combined (US and British) Chiefs of Staff and Heads of State, showed up major differences among the Allies. The Americans wanted to wind up Mediterranean operations as soon as North Africa was cleared up and then to open a more decisive front in France. The British felt this was premature and wished to attack Sicily or Sardinia instead, to draw German troops from the Russian front and to gain control of sea lanes through the Mediterranean (convoys to India and Egypt had to go via South Africa since 1940). The British plan was accepted. The military objective was limited to Sicily, as further planning would only result in further dispute: as it was, planning for Operation Husky was very slow.

The conference made a far-reaching decision when it agreed to accept only 'unconditional surrender' from its enemies. Churchill wanted to except Italy, but Roosevelt, whose proposal it was, refused. The decision was to be a hindrance in both Italy and Japan.

A further decision taken by the US and Britain was to treat General de Gaulle and General Giraud as somewhat co-equal representatives of France (although the US favored sole trusteeship for Giraud); when they arrived at Casablanca, the two generals were induced to issue a declaration of common purpose.

## Cassino, Battle of Monte, 1944

Monte Cassino, crowned by St Benedict's monastery, overlooks the Mediterranean coastal road from Naples to Rome and is one of the strongest defensive positions in the Italian peninsula. In the winter of 1943–44 it formed the western hinge of the German Winter Line (called the Gustav Line). Following the failure of their offensive begun in December to break the Gustav Line, the Allies, now under the direction of Alexander following Eisenhower's departure in December to become Supreme Allied Commander for the invasion of France, decided on a combined land and amphibious assault. The amphibious assault, launched on 22 January, went in at Anzio south of Rome. It was intended that the troops in the beachhead there should be relieved by an offensive from the Cassino position which had been attacked by the American 2nd Corps in January, and from across the Garigliano, which was stormed by the British 10th Corps on 17 January. The 10th Corps' operation was held after it had made some ground. The 2nd Corps' attack ended in bloody failure. Cassino was to be the focus of three further battles. The next two, by the New Zealand 2nd Corps in February and by the 2nd New Zealand and 4th Indian Divisions in March also failed. So too did efforts by the French Corps to outflank it on the east, though their attack gained some mountain territory. Finally it was attacked on 11 May by the Polish 2nd Corps which, after a week of terrible fighting, finally secured the ruins of the monastery which had been devastated by aerial bombardment preceding the third battle.

*Right:* The ruins of Monte Cassino, once one of Europe's most beautiful monasteries. Permission to destroy it was granted by Pope Pius XII, after he was asked to decide by General Eisenhower. The Nazis never used the monastery as a fortress, but defended from its exterior.

## Catalina, Consolidated PBY

This US maritime reconnaissance flying-boat was operational from 1936 to the late forties. Long endurance on patrol was a supreme attributes for a reconnaissance flying-boat. None demonstrated this better than the Catalina, which often remained airborne more than 24 hours. It was a large aircraft, spanning 104ft, and carrying a crew of seven to nine men, four 1000lb bombs, two 0.3in guns in the nose turret and a tunnel in the hull, and two 0.5in beam guns. Standard power plant was two Pratt & Whitney R–1830 Twin Wasp radials of 900/1200hp. All but early PBY–1s, 2s and 3s had bulbous transparent covers over the beam gun positions. Many of the aircraft built after 1939 were amphibians, with a retractable tricycle undercarriage which greatly increased the Catalina's versatility. Altogether, 2398 PBYs were built by Consolidated. A further 892 were manufactured at the Naval Aircraft Factory in Philadelphia, 156 of them as PBN–1 Nomads, and by Canadian Vickers and Boeing in Canada. Many went to Russia, where the PBY was also produced under license as the GST. First to see action were Catalinas of RAF Coastal Command, supplied in 1941. On 26 May that year, an aircraft of 209 Squadron rediscovered the German battleship *Bismarck* after the Navy had lost contact, making its destruction possible. The 196th and last U-Boat sunk by Coastal Command was destroyed by a Catalina of 210 Squadron on the last day of the war against Germany.

## Caucasus, Battle of the, July 1942–February 1943

After the battle of Voronezh, Army Group A under Field Marshal List was ordered to capture the oilfields in the Caucasus. On 23 July the Germans took Rostov and opened the way south. The Russians were not organized for defense and the Germans captured the main pipeline in the Caucasus, thus leaving the Russians dependent on tankers in the Caspian for their oil supply. Not many Russians were captured since they were able to fall back on Stalingrad (which was being threatened by Paulus's army). As Field Marshal Kleist's First Panzer Army advanced down the Manych valley, the only setback it received was a few days halt because the valley had been flooded by the blowing up of a dam. On 9 August Kleist's right column arrived at the oil center of Maykop, some 200 miles southeast of Rostov. His center column reached Pyatigorsk, 150 miles east of Maykop and his left column was approaching Budenovsk. Despite these advances the Germans were under strain, they were running out of fuel and the railway gauges had to be changed, taking up valuable time. The country was mountainous and the Russians were beginning to put up some tough resistance.

The Caucasus Front was then divided: the first Panzer was to take Baku and the Seventeenth Army was to take the towns on the Black Sea and open the way to Batumi. In the middle of September the Seventeenth Army took Novorossiysk but it never reached Tuapse. The First Panzer was short of fuel and had no air cover. It never reached Grozny because the Russian bombers were able to pin it down. Throughout

*Right:* Russian troops pass a dead German on the Caucasus Front, January 1943.

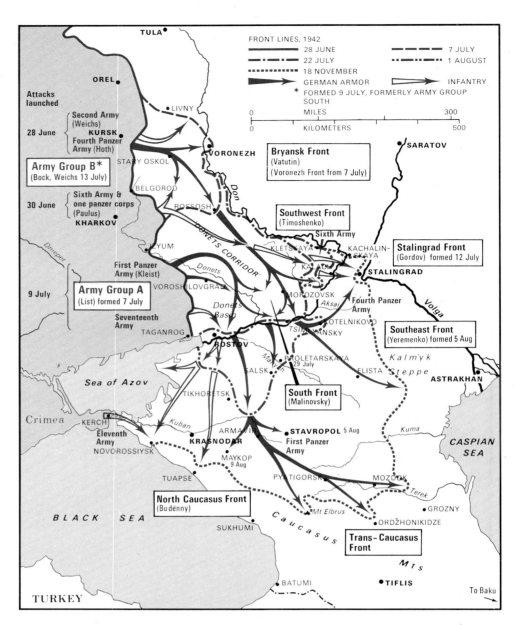

German Panzers advance in the Caucasus. This was the furthest penetration of the Soviet Union by the Wehrmacht.

September and October Kleist tried to break out of Mozdok, and in the last week of October he took Ordzhonikidze by a pincer movement. The Russians launched a counteroffensive and pushed them back. At this point the situation in Stalingrad was serious enough to prevent any action in the Caucasus.

In December General Vatutin launched an attack on the Chir and on the Donets which could have cut off the Germans in the Caucasus. Hitler vacillated but finally had to give the orders to withdraw on 1 January. Kleist was now the Commander of Army Group A and as he retreated trying to take his heavy equipment with him, communications with Rostov were threatened by a Russian advance along the Manych valley. The Seventeenth Army was told to withdraw to the Taman peninsula where it could be evacuated by sea to the Crimea. Field Marshal Manstein held the Rostov corridor long enough for the bulk of the First Panzer Army to reach Rostov by 1 February. Kleist's army had a narrow escape.

German infantry advance through the Caucasus.

**Cauldron**
see Gazala-Bir Hacheim, Battle of, 1942

## Centaur Tank

This British cruiser tank was a variant of the Cromwell, from which it differed by having a Liberty engine. Most Centaurs were later converted to Cromwells by replacing the engines with Meteor units. Original Centaurs, fitted with six-pounder guns, were used only as training tanks, but a later batch of 80 were fitted with 95mm howitzers and used by the Royal Marine Armored Support Group in the Normandy invasion. Others were converted into armored Observation Posts for artillery use and, by fitting twin 20mm Polsten cannons in the turret, as anti-aircraft tanks.

## Ceylon Raid, April 1942

After the fall of Burma, Britain was afraid that the Japanese Navy would try to establish naval bases in the Indian Ocean. General Wavell was told to hold on to Ceylon at all costs, but he had a small naval force of five battleships (four of them old) and three carriers (one old) under Admiral Somerville. The British knew that the Japanese were preparing an offensive on Ceylon, but although they (the Japanese) wanted to knock out port installations and shipping, they had no intention of actually invading Ceylon. Somerville expected the attack on 1 April 1942 and sent half his force on patrol. When the attack began these ships were 500 miles away. The Japanese force consisted of five fleet carriers and four battleships. They greatly damaged the port at Colombo and sank two cruisers, *Cornwall* and *Dorsetshire*, and an old light carrier, *Hermes*.

## Chaffee Tank

This US Light Tank M24 was named after General Adna R Chaffee, founder of the US Armored Force. The pilot model was completed in October 1943 and the first production vehicle appeared in April 1944. Orders were given for a total of 5000 to be made by Cadillac, Massey-Harris and the American Car & Foundry Co, though only the first two companies actually produced vehicles. A total of 4415 were made, at a unit cost of US $35,653. The tank saw only limited service during the war, a small number reaching Europe towards the end of 1944 and taking part in the Rhine crossing and subsequent operations.

'A prelude to a larger settlement in which all Europe may find peace', October 1938.

## Chamberlain, Prime Minister Neville, 1869–1940

Chamberlain was British Prime Minister from 1937–40 and was the principal advocate of the policy of appeasement, a policy which ceded territories to Nazi Germany in the hope that war would be avoided. It was born of a revulsion against war, but was also a policy of expediency because Chamberlain knew that Britain was not ready for war. Chamberlain negotiated the Munich Agreement in September 1938 and sincerely believed that Hitler would be satisfied with Czech Sudetenland and that peace was now secure. When Hitler invaded Czechoslovakia and contravened the agreement, Chamberlain did not respond; it was only over Hitler's invasion of Poland that he was forced to declare war on 3 September 1939. Chamberlain had given Hitler the impression that he could rely on Britain's neutrality, whatever he did. Chamberlain remained Prime Minister but was associated with defeatist policies and was replaced by Churchill. Chamberlain became seriously ill and died in November 1940.

## Channel Dash
see *Gneisenau, Prinz Eugen* and *Scharnhorst*

## Char B Tank

The Char B Tank is a member of the French heavy tank family. The Char B was the original pilot made in 1929–30 and was followed by the B1 production model in 1935. Armed with a 75mm hull gun and a 47mm turret gun, it was adequately armored but under-powered, with only 180hp to move its 30 tons. Its worst defect was that the turret held only one man, who had to command the tank, read the map, load and fire the turret gun and take tactical decisions all at once. In 1937 the B1-bis appeared, with thicker armor and a new turret, but the faults were carried over into the new design, and while the Char B was a formidable machine it fell short of its promise due to the impossible task asked of its commander.

## Chatellerault Machine Gun

Since the French Army undoubtedly had the worst light machine gun of World War I, it is not surprising that a new weapon was high on the list of postwar priorities. The Manufacture d'Armes Chatellerault developed this machine gun in the 1920s basing the design largely on that of the Browning Automatic Rifle. A new 7.5mm cartridge was developed especially for this weapon and the gun was first introduced as the Mle 1924. This turned out to be premature, and there were several unfortunate accidents during training. Further improvements were made and the cartridge redesigned, and the gun reappeared as the Mle 1924/29. This was adopted as the standard light machine gun of the French Army and remained in use until after World War II. A slightly different version, the Mle 1931, was produced for use in the Maginot Line forts and in tanks; this used a peculiar side-mounted drum magazine holding 150 rounds, instead of the more conventional top-mounted box magazine of 25 rounds found on the Mle 24/29. Both guns had a rate of fire of about 500rpm.

### Chennault, Major General Claire L, 1890–1958

Chennault was founder and organizer of the American Volunteer Group of fliers in China and with only a few planes persistently challenged Japanese superiority in the air over Burma in 1942.

Chennault had retired in 1937 to build an aviation school sponsored by Mme Chiang Kai-shek and had set up a series of air bases in China. He recruited men in the US and by November 1941 had two fully-trained squadrons and one partially-trained. These pilots fought bravely in Burma. On 24 December they intercepted Japanese bombers over Rangoon and the Japanese only sent their bombers on night flights after this. They are supposed to have destroyed almost 300 planes in the fighting over Burma, Indo-China and China.

In 1943 Chennault was made Major General and became commanding officer of 14th US (Volunteer) AAF in China. In May 1943 Chennault attended a conference in Far Eastern Strategy where he was at odds with both General Stilwell and General Wavell. Chennault was making constant demands for material support.

Chennault had cleared the air above China and tried to cut off Japanese supply lines by attacking shipping but provoked the Japanese into a counterattack: Ichi-go. Within six months Chennault's forward base at Kweilin had fallen and Chiang Kai-shek lost confidence in him.

In July 1945 Chennault resigned because he did not want his Sino-American air force disbanded.

### Chernyakhovsky, General Ivan D, 1906–1945

Chernyakhovsky was the youngest Front Commander of the Red Army and was a gifted fighter in the Belorussian campaign in 1944. At the outbreak of the war he was commander of the 3rd Tank Division and he distinguished himself in fighting around Novgorod in 1941. In February 1943 he fought in the Battle of Kursk as commander of the 60th Army. On Marshal Zhukov's suggestion he was made Commander of the 3rd Belorussian Front and was instrumental in the capture of Minsk, Vilnyus and Kaunas. He planned the tank offensive in Belorussia with Zhukov and was responsible for cutting off the German Army in East Prussia. In February 1945 at Mehlsack he was killed in close fighting.

### Cherwell, Lord, 1886–1947

Born Frederick Alexander Lindemann, of Alsatian parents but British nationality, and known in government war circles as 'The Prof', Cherwell was one of the first scientists to play an influential role in the higher direction of war. Churchill, his longtime friend, made him a member of his war cabinet and heeded his advice on a whole range of major operational questions during his war premiership. Cherwell, who had solved the problem of aircraft spin during World War I by bravely applying his own theoretical solution in solo flight, was a particular protagonist of strategic bombing, and insisted on the concentration of aerial effort upon it, even at the expense of the anti-submarine war. At the end of the war he returned to his professional chair at Oxford where he continued to enjoy as much dislike as he had generated among government scientists during his years as paymaster general.

### Cheshire, Group Captain Leonard, 1917–

This RAF officer became one of the most distinguished bomber pilots of World War II. At great personal risk, Cheshire, as leader of 617 Squadron, RAF Bomber Command, was instrumental during 1944 in perfecting the use of target indicator bombs, dropped from Mosquito bombers, to pinpoint targets for attack by the following Lancasters of his squadron. This development meant that during 1944 the RAF was able to extend its bombing capabilities to include precision as well as its more usual area attacks. He was awarded the Victoria Cross for his great skill and courage.

### Chiang Kai-shek, Generalissimo, 1887–1975

Born in Fenghwa, Chekiang, and trained as an officer in Tokyo, Chiang Kai-shek was one of the earliest disciples of Sun Yat-sen in his efforts to transform the moribund Chinese empire into a modern republican state. He became the first Commandant of the republic's Whampoa Military Academy (at which Chou En-lai served as a political commissar) and then in 1926 Commander of the Army which set out to restore to the central government the power which had been wrested from it by the local warlords and the newborn Chinese Communist Party. By diplomacy and battle he brought most of the warlords to heel within two years and achieved such

success against the Communists that they were obliged to vacate the south, where their strength lay, and make the Long March into the remote northwest. After 1931, however, his position was threatened by the Japanese, who effectively annexed Manchuria in that year, and from 1937 he found himself at open war with them. The greater military efficiency of their armies obliged him to transfer his capital from Nanking to Chungking in the interior, where, with American support, he maintained the fight both in China and Burma until the end of the war. Accepted by the world in 1945 as Asia's leading statesman, he had in fact exhausted the strength of the Nationalist Armies in the patriotic struggle and, when the Communists opened civil war against him in 1947, was unable to organize effective resistance. At the end of 1949 he and the rump of his forces were driven out of mainland China and took refuge on Formosa (Taiwan) where he continued to proclaim his status as legitimate head of state until his death.

### Chiang Kai-shek, Madame, 1898–

Mme Chiang Kai-shek was the wife of the leader of the Chinese Kuomintang. She had been educated in the West and interpreted the West for Chiang. She was also Chiang's representative in the West and in 1943 she visited Roosevelt to have talks about US aid to China. Mme Chiang Kai-shek accompanied her husband to the Cairo Conference.

### China Campaign, 1941–45

In January 1942 the Japanese attacked Burma and shortly afterwards Chiang Kai-shek's only overland supply route, the Burma Road, was cut off. The Allies now had to supply him by air, the US Air Transport Command flying supplies from India over the 500-mile Hump of the Himalayas to Kunming. Chiang was given massive aid: $500 million from the US and $50 million from Britain. He was made Supreme Commander of the Allied Forces in the China Front and had General Stilwell as his Chief of Staff. In July 1942 Lieutenant General Chennault's Flying Tigers became the US 14th Air Force, were given more planes and won local air superiority. This prompted the Japanese to launch operation Ichi-Go in 1944, with an army of almost a million Japanese troops which had been tied up in Manchuria watching the Russians from 1941 to 1944. The offensive was in two parts: first, disperse Chinese forces between the Hwang Ho and Yangtze Rivers and secure rail links from Peking to Hankow; then neutralize the 14th Air Force airfields in the Hunan and Kwangsi Provinces. On 17 April 1944 Thirty-seventh Division crossed the Hwang Ho (Yellow River), found the Chinese Armies very weak and quickly captured seven airfields in the Kiangsi and Kwangsi provinces. By June the Japanese had cleared the railway line north of the Yangtze and in the south ten Japanese divisions were heading for Hengyang in southern Hunan. On 28 June the Japanese began to assault the city but Major General Fang Hsien-chueh, Commander-in-Chief of the 10th Army, led the resistance and pushed the Japanese back with Chennault's support. Unfortunately Chiang refused to send Fang supplies, but the 10th Army fought to a man until Hengyang fell on 8 August. The 14th Air Force then attacked the Japanese and forced them to postpone their attack on Kweilin. The Japanese captured the rest of the railway line in the next four months but it was so damaged that it was of no use.

In October 1944 Stilwell was recalled at Chiang's request and General Wedemeyer took over command of US forces. He arrived to find Kweilin about to fall and Kunming, capital of Yunnan province and situated at the head of the Burma Road, about to be attacked. In fact the Japanese offensive was almost over and an offensive by Marshal Wei Li-huang from Kunming in 1944 eventually opened up the Burma Road in March 1945.

In 1945 the Chinese Armies launched an offensive to recapture the airfields and in June and July recaptured Liuchow and Kweilin. Finally on 14 August 1945 the Japanese accepted the terms of unconditional surrender and the Expeditionary Army surrendered to Chiang.

It has been estimated that the Chinese had over three million casualties during the war. Chiang's regime was more concerned though with preventing the spread of Communism than with fighting the Japanese. Millions of dollars in aid were spent on China, but the Kuomintang was corrupt and once the war with Japan was over, civil war broke out.

## China Incident, 1931–41

Japan was allowed by international agreement to maintain a force known as the Kwantung Army to guard the Southern Manchurian Railway. On 18 September 1931, an explosion on the railway led to the Kwantung's Army's occupation of Mukden. The government in Tokyo lost control of the Army which occupied Manchuria, and a puppet regime in Manchukuo (the new state) was set up in September 1932.

Manchukuo was not recognized by the League of Nations and the Japanese spent the next few years consolidating their hold and

*Above:* Japanese troop-followers in China, 1939.
*Far left:* Japanese take up a position in north China.
*Left:* Nationalist Chinese propaganda poster in Chungking.

trying to negotiate with Chiang Kai-shek's Kuomintang. On 7 July 1937 Japanese and Chinese troops clashed on the Marco Polo Bridge near Peking and war broke out because the Japanese government failed to control its Army. The main opposition to the Japanese came from Chiang Kai-shek's Kuomintang which was backed by the Western Allies but which also had a non-aggression pact with the USSR. The Communists in China also fought the Japanese but their strength was based in the countryside. Chiang's strategy was to wait for the Japanese to realize that China was too vast an area for them to control. The Japanese troops aimed to cut off the coast and communications and launched their offensive from Manchukuo. On 28 July 1937 they occupied Peking and less than a month later began the siege of Shanghai. On 5 November the Japanese threatened Shanghai from the south by invading Hangchow Bay: the Chinese began to retreat. The Japanese Armies raced each other to Nanking and Chiang gave orders to evacuate the town on 7 December, removing his Headquarters to Hankow. Nanking was defended by some 300,000 troops yet eventually fell on 12 December. However, 80,000 Japanese soldiers ran amok, systematically raped at least 20,000 women and killed 200,000 men.

By the end of 1937 the Japanese held most of Northern China, part of Inner Mongolia, and important central Chinese cities around the Yangtze River mouth. In 1938 the Japanese marched south and took Amoy on 10 May, and then invaded south China by landing at Bias Bay in October, effectively cutting off Hong Kong, a British possession, from Nationalist China. On 21 October the Japanese took Canton, after little resistance and on 25 October Hankow fell. Thus the Chinese had lost ports which handled most foreign supplies. Chiang Kai-shek was now in Chungking where he received supplies from Haiphong via Tonkin, but the Japanese thought Chiang's Armies were near collapse and did not pursue him. In November 1938 the Japanese set up a provisional government of the Chinese Republic in Peking and later a Reformed Government of the Republic of China in Nanking. The Japanese had control of major towns but they faced a hostile population; they could not control communications between their towns and were harassed by Chinese guerrilla activity. The coastal blockade successfully stopped a build-up of Chinese forces but the Japanese realized that they could not win a decisive victory.

## Chindits, 1st Operation
see Wingate, General Orde

## Chindits, 2nd Operation
see Kohima and Imphal Offensive, 1944

## Chuikov, General Vasily I, 1900–

Chuikov along with Khrushchev, Rodimtsev and Yeremenko inspired and directed the battle to hold Stalingrad. He had graduated from the Frunze Military Academy in the 1920s and had been military adviser to Chiang Kai-shek from 1926–37. In September 1942 Chuikov was made Commander of the 62nd Army isolated in Stalingrad. He used all the reserves to keep the line of defense against Paulus's Sixth Army. His tactics were to place units in isolated parts of the city and have pockets of resistance. This led the Germans to overestimate the numbers engaged

General Vasily Chuikov.

in fighting in the city. Chuikov's men lost ground but the Sixth Army's reserves of equipment, fuel and men were being exhausted in the house-to-house fighting. During Yeremenko's and Rokossovsky's offensive at Stalingrad his army stood firm. His 8th Guards Army was then sent to the Belorussian Front and it spearheaded the drive to Berlin. Chuikov had the distinction of receiving the surrender of Berlin from General Krebs. After the war he was Commander-in-Chief of Soviet Military Forces in Germany from 1949–53.

## Churchill, Prime Minister Winston Spencer, 1874–1965

After returning to the Conservative government of Neville Chamberlain to which he had been strongly opposed over its policy of appeasement of the dictators in September 1939, Churchill held the post of First Lord of the Admiralty (as he had done at the outbreak of World War I) until May 1940. Chamberlain's position had then become untenable and he yielded it gracefully to his former critic; Churchill on 11 May assumed the premiership of the coalition government and the title of Minister of Defense. Churchill's contributions to Allied victory during the next five years defy summary, but centered on four great principles: deliberate personal leadership of the British people, chiefly through the medium of broadcasting, of which he was a master; rejection of all thought of surrender, and the prosecution of offensive action against Hitler and his allies at every opportunity; unswerving friendship with the United States, even when strategic or political differences arose between the two countries; and the acceptance of alliance with any country which would join the fight against the Axis. It was fortunate that Churchill was already on friendly terms with Roosevelt before the war broke out. That friendship blossomed during the months of American neutrality and bore triumphant fruit after Pearl Harbor. Their relations were conducted on an everyday basis by letter and telephone, but their high points were the series of great international conferences (with or without Stalin) at which the strategy of the war was determined. The first wartime meeting, though it antedated America's entry, was at Argentia Bay, Newfoundland, when the Atlantic Charter

was proclaimed. The next, at Washington in December 1941, settled the 'Germany First' policy. Perhaps there were none other so important, and at those with Stalin, particularly the Teheran Conference in 1943 and the Yalta Conference of 1945, Roosevelt distanced himself from Churchill in order to win, as he thought, Stalin's confidence. Churchill's personal view, which hindsight has made appear the more realistic, was that Stalin kept his own counsel and had aims to which no right-minded westerner could acquiesce. Despite concessions granted to Russia by Roosevelt, which Churchill thought unnecessary and dangerous, the two men remained political allies and personal friends to the end. Churchill was also remarkably successful at maintaining good personal relationships with members of government and parliament. His immediate circle of advisers, though often obliged to dissuade rather than encourage, so exaggerated a form could his offensive feelings take, were devoted to him almost without exception. He also kept the loyalties of the House of Commons throughout a trying period of coalition government: the two votes of no confidence raised against his ministry were both defeated by vast majorities. The British people gave him their affection, and seemed to draw as much amusement as inspiration from his style of leadership. Their rejection of his party in the general election which followed the European victory was seen by him, therefore, and by others, as a blow of ingratitude. The truth appears to be that the electorate regarded Churchill as a war Prime Minister, whose touch in rebuilding peacetime Britain would not have been sure. In their hearts they regarded him as a hero, above tributes of gratitude, and he will undoubtedly remain the principal British hero of the twentieth century.

## Churchill Tank

Last of the British 'Infantry' tanks, this was devised in 1939 in the belief that the coming war would degenerate into a trench stalemate as had World War I. The specification therefore called for the ability to cross shell-cratered ground and trenches, surmount parapets, crush wire, and all

Winston Churchill tours the ruins of Berlin after its capitulation.

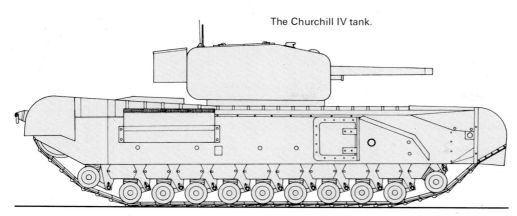
The Churchill IV tank.

the things which tanks had been expected to do in 1918. The first design was not very good, and in mid-1940 a fresh start was made by Vauxhall Motors, basing their design on a new 350hp engine they had developed. The eventual tank had a two-pounder gun in the turret and a 3in howitzer in the front plate; it weighed 39 tons in battle order and could move at 15mph in favorable conditions. The first production was done in great haste, with the threat of German invasion, and as a result the early Churchill tanks were mechanically unreliable, which contributed to their disastrous debut with the Canadians at Dieppe. They were later improved however, and given a six-pounder turret gun, the 3in howitzer being removed. As a heavy support tank they gave good service in North Africa and Italy, and they were widely used as a basis for many kinds of special-purpose tanks, flame-throwers, bridge-carriers, recovery tanks and so forth, which were extremely valuable in the Northwest European Campaign. A handful of Churchills remained in service with the Irish Army until the 1970s.

## Chu Teh, General, 1886–1977

Chu Teh was Commander-in-Chief of the Chinese Red Army from 1931 onwards. Until 1937 Chu Teh was fighting Chiang but after the Marco Polo Bridge Incident the Communist Armies were integrated into the Kuomintang and Chu Teh was given command of the predominantly Communist 8th Route Army. He scored a major success on 25 September 1937 at the Battle of Pingsinkuan when his forces ambushed the Japanese Fifth Division. Chu Teh led Communist forces in guerrilla fighting against the Japanese during the war, but he also had to fight Chiang Kai-shek's troops. When the war against Japan ended, full-scale civil war broke out.

## Ciano, Count Galeazzo, 1903–1944

Ciano was Mussolini's son-in-law and the Italian Foreign Minister from 1936–43. One of his first duties was to negotiate the Axis treaty in June 1936 which allied Italy to Nazi Germany. In 1939 he signed the Pact of Steel but soon realized that Germany meant to make war on Europe whether Italy was ready or not. Ciano advised Mussolini to avoid war but once it had broken out he commanded a bomber squadron in the Ethiopian Campaign and was involved in occasional missions until his dismissal as Foreign Minister in 1943. In July 1943 he spoke out against Mussolini during the coup against Mussolini but had to leave Rome shortly afterwards. He was tricked into giving himself up to

the Germans and was tried in Verona in January 1944. He received the death sentence, which was carried out on Mussolini's instructions. Ciano's contribution to the history of World War II also came in the form of his *Diary* in which he recorded his impressions of Mussolini and the fascist circle in Italy.

## Citadel
see Kursk, Battle of, 1943

## Clark Field
see Luzon

## Clark, Rear Admiral Joseph J, 1893–1971

Clark was commander of Task Group 58.1 one of the fast carrier groups based on the *Hornet* and *Yorktown*. At the Battle of Philippine Sea his aircraft took part in the 'Great Marianas Turkey Shoot' but Clark complained bitterly about the missed chance to destroy Vice-Admiral Ozawa's carrier force.

## Clark, General Mark Wayne, 1896–

A veteran of World War I, in which he was wounded, Clark was appointed deputy to Eisenhower in Europe in 1942 and Commander of American ground forces there. Immediately before the great Torch landings in North Africa, he was landed off Algiers by submarine and made contact with the French Commander, Admiral Darlan, with whom he concluded an armistice and recognized as Head of State. Had Darlan not soon after been assassinated by a young French royalist, this move would have greatly complicated Allied relationships with liberated France. Clark commanded the 5th Army in the invasions of Sicily and Italy, directed the unsuccessful Anzio operation, took the responsibility for the controversial decision to bomb the Monte Cassino monastery and entered Rome in triumph on 5 June 1944. He subsequently succeeded Alexander as commander in Italy and ended the war as American Commander-in-Chief in Austria. Clark is best remembered for his flair in public relations; he was also an excellent and charismatic battlefield commander.

## 'Claude'
see Mitsubishi A5M

## Coastwatchers
see New Guinea. Port Moresby and Buna

## Codenames, Allied

**Acrobat** Proposed British advance into Tripolitania, 1941

**Accolade** Proposed British attack on the Dodecanese Islands, 1944

**Anakim** First plan for the re-occupation of Burma, 1944

**Anvil** Early name for Dragoon

**Arcadia** See Conferences

**Argonaut** See Conferences

**Argument** Air attack on German aircraft industry, 20–25 February 1944

**Avalanche** Allied amphibious assault at Salerno, 9 September 1943

**Battleaxe** British offensive in Western Desert, November 1941

**Baytown** Crossing of the Straits of Messina, 3 September 1943

**Bolero** Build-up of American forces in Britain, 1942

**Brevity** British offensive in Western Desert, May 1941

**Brimstone** Projected Allied invasion of Sardinia, 1944

**Buccaneer** Projected operation against the Andaman Islands, 1944

**Bullfrog** Projected attack on Akyab, Burma, January 1945

**Buttress** Assault on the toe of Italy at Reggio, September 1943

**Capital** Re-capture of northern Burma, 1944; 'Extended Capital,' same plus capture of Meiktila.

**Catapult** British attack on French fleet in North African ports, July 1940

**Catchpole** Operations against Eniwetok and Ujelang, Marshall Islands, early 1944

**Champion** Plan for general offensive in Burma, 1943

**Clarion** Air attack on German communications, 22–23 February 1945

**Claymore** British commando raid on Lofoten Islands, March 1941

**Cobra** American break-out from Normandy bridgehead, 25 July 1944

**Compass** British counteroffensive against Italians in Egypt, December 1940

**Corkscrew** Occupation of Pantelleria, 11 June 1943

**Coronet** Planned invasion of Japan 1945

**Cromwell** Alarm signal to signify German invasion of Britain 1940

**Crossbow** Countermeasures against German V-weapon attack on Britain, 1944 (see Diver)

**Culverin** Projected operation against Western Sumatra and Malaya 1944

**Demon** British evacuation of Greece, April 1941

**Diadem** Allied operation to capture Rome, 1944

**Diver** Attacks by, and defense against, German V-1 weapons, 1944 (see Crossbow)

**Dracula** Seaborne attack on Rangoon, May 1945

**Dragoon** Allied invasion of southern France, August 1944 (see Anvil)

**Dynamo** The Dunkirk evacuation, May–June 1940

**Epsom** British offensive, west of Caen, 18 July 1944

**Eureka** See Conferences

**Exporter** British occupation of Syria, June 1941

**Firebrand** Projected invasion of Corsica, 1944

**Flintlock** Operations against Kwajalein and Majuro, Marshall Islands, early 1944

**Forager** Operation to capture Mariana Islands, early 1944

**Fortitude** Deception plan for Overlord

**Frantic** Shuttle bombing of Germany from UK, Italy and USSR

**Goodwood** British armored offensive east of Caen, July 1944

**Galvanic** Assault on Gilbert Islands, late 1943

**Grenade** American offensive in Rhineland, February 1945

**Gymnast** Early name for Torch

**Habbakuk** A projected giant floating-aïrdrome of ice

**Habforce** Expedition to Iraq, May 1941 (from Habbaniya Force)

**Harpoon** Malta convoy, June 1942

**Hercules** Plan for assault on Rhodes, early 1944

**Husky** Allied invasion of Sicily, 3 July 1943

**Imperator** Proposed large-scale raid on French Channel Coast, 1942

**Indigo** Plan for movement of US troops to Iceland, 1942

**Infatuate** British assault on Walcheren, October 1944

**Jubilee** Dieppe raid, 19 August 1942

**Jupiter** Projected invasion of northern Norway

**Lightfoot** Battle of Alamein, October 1942

**Lustre** Aid to Greece

**Magnet** Movement of US troops to Northern Ireland, early 1942

**Manhattan** Allied atomic energy program, 1942–5 (see Tube Alloys)

**Matador** Plan for British move into Kra Isthmus, 1942

**Matterhorn** Bombing of Japan from China, 1944

**Menace** Free French expedition to Dakar, September 1940

**Mincemeat** Deceptive plan for Husky

**Neptune** Internal Overlord codeword to signify cross-channel operations

**Noah's Ark** Plan for the Occupation of Greece on the German's withdrawal, 1944

**Octagon** See Conferences

**Orange** Prewar American plans for war with Japan

**Overlord** Allied invasion of Northwest Europe, 1944

**Pedestal** Malta convoy, August 1942

**Pigstick** Landing in the Mayo Peninsula

**Pilgrim** Projected capture of the Canary Islands, 1942 (and also used of operations against the Atlantic islands generally)

**Plunder** Allied crossing of the Rhine, March 1945

**Pluto** Undersea oil supply to Allied Overlord Armies, 1944 (Pipe Line Under The Ocean)

**Pointblank** The Combined Bomber Offensive against Germany

**Priceless** Allied invasion of Italy, 1943

**Puma** Projected invasion of the Canary Islands, 1942

**Quadrant** See Conferences

**Rainbow** American codename for anti-Axis operational plans, used 1939–41

**Rankin** Plan to return to continent in event of sudden German collapse

**Ratweek** Plan to attack a German withdrawal from Yugoslavia, 1944

**Ravenous** Proposed advance into upper Burma across the River Chindwin, 1944

**Roundhammer** Early name for Overlord

**Round-up** Proposed allied invasion of Northwest Europe in 1943 (see Overlord)

**Rupert** Narvik expedition, April 1940

**Saturn** Proposed introduction of an Allied force into Turkey, 1944

**Sextant** See Conferences

**Shingle** Allied landing at Anzio, January 1944

**Sickle** Movement of US Air Forces to United Kingdom, 1942

**Slapstick** British airborne landing in heel of Italy, 9 September 1943

**Sledgehammer** Proposed emergency invasion of Northwest Europe, 1942

**Springboard** Projected capture of Madeira, 1942

**Stamina** Air supply of Imphal-Kohima garrisons, 1944

**Supercharge** Follow-up to Lightfoot

**Symbol** See Conferences

**Talon** Capture of Akyab, December 1944

**Tarzan** Projected advance in Indaw/Katha area, Burma, 1944

**Terminal** See Conferences

**Thruster** Proposed expedition against the Azores, 1942

**Thursday** Second Chindit operation, Burma, 1944

**Tidal wave** Air attack on Ploesti oilfields, August 1943

**Torch** Allied invasion of French North Africa, November 1942

**Totalize** Canadian attack towards Falaise, August 1944

**Trident** See Conferences

**Tube Alloys** British atomic bomb project (see Manhattan)

**Vanguard** Plan to capture Rangoon from the sea, 1944

**Varsity** Allied airborne operation in Rhine Crossing, March 1945

**Veritable** Canadian offensive in Rhineland, February, 1945

**Vigorous** Alexandria-Malta Convoy, June 1942

**Zipper** Invasion of Malaya, 1945.

---

## Codenames, Allied Convoys (with starting dates)

**AT** USA–UK (monster liners), January 1942

**BT** Sydney–USA, January 1942

**HG** Gibraltar–UK, September 1939 (after September 1942, MK)

**HX** Halifax–UK, September 1939 (after September 1942, from New York)

**JW** Loch Ewe, Scotland–North Russia, December 1942 (see PQ)

**KM** UK–North Africa, October 1942

**ME** Malta–Alexandria, July 1940

**MG** Malta–Gibraltar, December 1940

**MK** North Africa–UK, November 1942

**MW** Alexandria–Malta, July 1940

**OB** Liverpool–North America, September 1939 (subsequently ON)

**OG** UK–Gibraltar, October, 1939 (after July 1943, sailed with KM)

**ON** Formerly OB, started July 1941

**OS** UK–West Africa, July 1941 (after April 1943 sailed with KM)

**PQ** Iceland–North Russia, September 1941 (subsequently JW)

**QP** North Russia–Iceland and UK, September 1941 (subsequently RA)

**RA** North Russia–Loch Ewe, December 1942 (see QP)

**SC** Halifax–UK, August 1940 (September 1942–March 1943, from New York)

**SL** Sierra Leone–UK, September 1939

**SW** Suez–South Africa (returning WS convoys)

**TA** Returning AT convoys

**TB** USA–Sydney, January 1942 (see BT)

**WS** UK–Middle East, via South Africa, June 1940.

---

## Codenames, Allied, Leaders

**Agent**   Prime Minister Winston Churchill

**Anfa**   the CCS, Churchill and Roosevelt at Casablanca, 1943

**Braid**   General George C Marshall

**Cargo**   President Franklin Delano Roosevelt

**Eagle**   General Mark Wayne Clark

**Eagle Tac**   General Bradley's HQ

**Kingpin**   General Henri Giraud

**Look**   General Dwight D Eisenhower

**Telegraph**   General Walter Bedell Smith

---

## Codenames, German

**Achse (Axis)** Disarmament of the Italian armed forces on the Allied invasion of Italy, 1 September 1943; also known earlier as Alarich and Konstantin (also see Schwarz)

**Aida** Advance into Egypt, 21 January 1942

**Alarich** see Achse

**Anton** Occupation of the unoccupied zone of France, 11 November 1942; also known earlier as Attila

**Barbarossa** Invasion of Russia, 22 June, 1941

**Birke (Birch Tree)** Evacuation of Finland, August 1944

**Birkhahn (Blackcock)** Evacuation of Norway, 1945

**Blau, Operation (Blue)** Offensive by northern wing of Army Group South of Voronezh, June 1942; see also Maus and Siegfried. Fall Blau (Case Blue) was also a codename for a Luftwaffe operation against England in 1938–9

**Blume (Flower)** Alert of Allied invasion of France; (i), from the Channel, (ii) on the Mediterranean Coast

**Bodenplatte (Base plate)** Luftwaffe attack against Allied airfields in the Low Countries, 1 January 1945

**Braunschweig (Brunswick)** Offensive towards Stalingrad and the Caucusus, July 1942

**Büffel-Bewegung (Buffalo Stampede)** Operation on the Russian central front 1943

**Cerberus** Breakout of *Bismarck* and *Prinz Eugen* from Brest and 'Channel Dash' to North Sea, 11–12 February 1942

**Donnerschlag (Thunderbolt)** Planned breakout of Sixth Army from Stalingrad, December 1942 (see also Wintergewitter)

**Felix** Plan to occupy Gibraltar, late 1940

**Fritz** Early codename for the Invasion of Russia (see Barbarossa)

**Gelb, Fall (Yellow, Case)** Plan for the Invasion of France, Belgium and Holland, 1939

**Gertrud** Plan to invade Turkey in the event of her alliance with the Allies

**Gisela** Plan for the occupation of Spain and Portugal, 1942

**Haifisch (Shark)** Deception plan for Barbarossa, 1941

**Herbstnebel** Evacuation of the Po plain, 1944; also an early codename for the (Autumn Mist) Ardennes Offensive (see Wacht am Rhein)

**Herkules** Operations against Malta, 1942

**Isabella** Extension of Felix

**Kamelie** Occupation of Corsica, 1942 (see Anton)

**Konstantin** See Achse

**Margarethe** Occupation of Hungary, 19 March 1944; M.II was a plan to occupy Rumania also

**Marita** Occupation of Greece, planned 1940–1; later executed also against Yugoslavia, 6 April 1941

**Maus (Mouse)** Offensive by southern wing of Army Group South into the Caucasus, July 1942 (see also Blau and Siegfried)

**Merkur (Mercury)** Airborne and sea landings on Crete, May 1941

**Mittelmeer (Mediterranean)** Air operations in that area, December 1940-January 1941

**Morgenrote (Dawn)** Counteroffensive against Anzio beachhead, January 1944

**Nord (North)** First codename for invasion of Norway (see Weserübung)

**Nordlicht (Northern Lights)** Offensive against Leningrad, Summer 1942

**Nordwind (North Wind)** Attack in north Alsace, 31 December 1944 (see Wacht am Rhein)

**Regenbogen (Rainbow)** Attack by *Lützow* and *Hipper* on Allied northern convoy, 31 December 1942

**Rheinübung (Rhine Exercise)** Atlantic raid by *Bismark* and *Prinz Eugen* 21–27 May 1941

**Rösselsprung (Knight's Move)** Attack on Allied Murmansk-Archangel Convoy, July 1942

**Rot, Operation (Red, Operation)** Second half of Battle of France, June 1940 (originally Case Red, 1935)

**Schwarz** Military take-over of Italy, 1943

**Seelöwe (Sealion)** Plan for the invasion of England, 1940

**Siegfried** Advance by center of Army Group South from Kharkov to Stalingrad, July 1942, see also Blau and Maus

**Silberfuchs (Silver Fox)** Concentration of troops in Finland for invasion of Russia, May-June 1941

**Sonnenblume (Sunflower)** Deployment of German troops to Africa, January-February 1941

**Taifun (Typhoon)** Offensive against Moscow, begun 2 October 1941

**Trojanisches Pferd (Trojan Horse)** Occupation of Budapest as part of Margarethe

**Wacht am Rhein (Guard on the Rhine)** Ardennes offensive, December 1944

**Weiss, Fall (White, Case)** Invasion of Poland, 1939

**Weserübung (Weser Exercise)** Invasion of Denmark and Norway, 9 April 1940; W. Nord = Norway (see also Nord), W. Sud = Denmark

**Wintergewitter (Winter Storm)** Attack to relieve Stalingrad, December 1942 (see Donnerschlag)

**Zitadelle (Citadel)** Attack on the Kursk salient, July 1943

There were also a large number of codenames given to operations against the Yugoslav partisans (Kügelblitz, Maibaum, Maigewitter, Napfkuchen, Rösselsprung (2), Rübezahl, Schwarz (2), Treibjagd, Waldrausch, Waldteufel, Weiss I–III and Werwolf), as well as to minor operations, strategic contingencies and fortified positions.

## Codenames, Japanese

**A-Go** Plan to bring the American fleet to battle east of the Philippines, June 1944 (Battle of the Philippine Sea)

**Ha-Go** Diversionary offensive in Arakan as preliminary to U-Go

**I** Air offensive from Rabaul against American fleet in Papua and the Solomons, April 1943

**Ichi-Go** Offensive in China, April 1944

**Ketsu-Go** Plan for defense of Japan against invasion, 1945

**Kon** Japanese reinforcement of Biak, New Guinea, May-June 1944

**Mo** Port Moresby and Coral Sea Offensive, May 1942

**Ro** Defense of Rabaul, November 1943

**Sho-Go** Battle of Leyte Gulf, October 1944

**Ta** Offensive at Bougainville, November, 1943

**Ten-Go** Naval offensive off Okinawa and Iwo Jima, April-July 1945

**U-Go** The Imphal offensive, March-July 1944

---

## Collins, Lieutenant General Joseph Lawton, 1882–1963

Collins was commander of the US 7th Corps which fought in Guadalcanal and northwestern Europe. In January 1941 Collins was Chief of Staff of the 7th Corps and he helped reorganize the Hawaiian defenses. At Guadalcanal he took over from General Vandegrift and there earned the nickname 'Lightning Joe' for his aggressive pursuit of the enemy. In December 1943 Collins was sent to England to prepare for Overlord and in February 1944 he took command of the 7th Corps. The Corps landed at Utah beach and in a 20-day campaign took Cherbourg. On 25 July 1944 he became the hero of St. Lô when his Corps broke through the German lines to the east and blocked the German counterattacks. His troops then swept through northern France and took Namur, Liège and eventually Aachen. He took part in the envelopment of the Ruhr and met Soviet forces on the Elbe, at Dessau.

---

## Colt Automatic Pistol M1911A1

This, the finest and most reliable combat pistol ever made according to many experts, originated from a design of John Browning's in 1900. With some modification, it was entered for the US Army competitive trials in 1907 and emerged a clear winner. Adopted in 1911, it was given further slight modifications in the light of

World War I experience and in June 1926 was standardized as the M1911A1. Since then it has seen no further change – it needs none. Firing a .45, 230 grain bullet at 860ft/sec to deliver 380ft-pounds of energy at the muzzle, the Colt automatic is a locked-breech pistol in which the breech is held firmly closed until the bullet has left the barrel by ribs on top of the barrel engaging in slots in the slide. As the pistol recoils, so the barrel is allowed to swing downward and to the rear by Browning's patent 'link' system, thus unlocking the breech and permitting the slide to move back so as to eject the spent case and then reload. A magazine of seven rounds is carried in the grip, and safety is assured by a manual catch, an external hammer, and a grip safety which prevents the pistol being fired unless properly held. In addition to US service use in .45 caliber, the Colt has also been made in .455 for the British Royal Navy and Royal Air Force and has been made under license in Norway and Argentina.

---

## Comet Tank

Comet was the last 'cruiser' tank to be developed in Britain, and was basically the 'Cromwell' with improved armor, electric turret drive, and a new 77mm gun. First issues were made in September 1944 and it was to remain in service until 1959. It has been said by many experts that Comet was the best and certainly the most reliable British tank to see service during the war.

---

## Commandos
see Laycock, Major General Robert

---

## Coned Bore Gun

This is an artillery piece in which the barrel caliber is sharply reduced at some point, in contrast to a 'Taper Bore' gun in which the caliber reduces gradually from breech to muzzle. The coned bore achieves the same end, of reducing the diameter of the projectile so as to enhance its armor penetrating ability, but is an easier manufacturing proposition since the cone section can be made as a separate unit and either fitted on to the muzzle (as in the British two-pounder 'Littlejohn') or built into an otherwise conventional barrel (as in the German 75mm PAK 41 gun). The Germans also experimented with coned attachments for heavy guns in order to develop extreme ranges, but none were used.

*Above:* Colt US automatic .45 pistols: M1911 (*far right*) & M1911 A1s.

**Conferences, Major Allied**

| Date | Codename | Place | Purpose |
|------|----------|-------|---------|
| 14 August 1941 | — | Argentia Bay | Churchill and Roosevelt issue Atlantic Charter and agree on 'Germany First' |
| 22 December 1941 | Arcadia | Washington | Churchill and Roosevelt re-affirm 'Germany First' and issue United Nations Declaration (First Washington Conference) |
| 25-27 June 1942 | — | Washington | Churchill and Roosevelt attempt to reach agreement on European strategy for 1942-3. (Second Washington Conference) |
| 14-23 January, 1942 | Symbol | Casablanca | Churchill and Roosevelt agree on invasion of Sicily and on invasion of France in 1944. Roosevelt issues 'Unconditional Surrender' Declaration. |
| 11-17 May, 1943 | Trident | Washington | Churchill and Roosevelt agree to prosecute war more vigorously on all fronts. (Third Washington Conference) |
| 17-24 August, 1943 | Quadrant | Quebec | Churchill and Roosevelt re-affirm decision to invade France. (First Quebec Conference) |
| 22-26 November, 1943 | Sextant | Cairo | Churchill, Roosevelt and Chiang Kai-shek agree on future of China. |
| 28 November – 1 December, 1943 | Eureka | Teheran | Churchill, Roosevelt and Stalin agree on final date for invasion of Europe. |
| 10 September, 1944 | Octagon | Quebec | Churchill and Roosevelt agree on plans for end of European war and future Pacific strategy. (Second Quebec Conference) |
| 4-12 February, 1945 | Argonaut | Yalta | Churchill, Roosevelt and Stalin agree on future governments for defeated Germany, liberated Poland and Yugoslavia, formation of United Nations and transfer of Kurile Islands to Russia. |
| 17 July – 2 August, 1945 | Terminal | Potsdam | Churchill, Attlee, Truman and Stalin agree on the redrawing of Germany's eastern boundaries, reparations and future relations with German Satellite states. |

*Below:* The Big Three meet at the Teheran Conference.

## Coningham, Air Marshal Sir Arthur, 1895–1948

Originally a soldier, he served with New Zealand troops during World War I. Coningham became an expert on long-distance flying between the wars when it was a fad, but at the outbreak was appointed to command No 4 Group of RAF Bomber Command. In 1941 he was sent to the Western Desert to take over the Desert Air Force and there pioneered the practice of close co-operation between ground and air forces. His location of his headquarters cheek by jowl with 8th Army's was revolutionary and did much to enhance the efficiency of joint air-ground operations against Rommel. He later commanded the Allied 1st Tactical Air Force in the North African and Italian campaigns and the famous 2nd Tactical Air Force in the invasion of Northwest Europe.

---

### *Conte di Cavour*
see *Giulio Cesare*

---

## Convoys

The history of convoys dates back into the mists of antiquity, but organized convoys were certainly recorded for the wine-trade between England and France in the 14th century. Through the centuries it has evolved as the basic shipping defense against commerce-raiding ships, and most of the classic sea battles of the 18th century arose through attempts to attack convoys. Briefly, the convoy is a group of merchant ships sailing together under the protection of warships.

During the long gap between the Napoleonic Wars and World War I, no attempt to wage war against merchant ships was made in any of the small wars in between (apart from a highly skilled campaign by the Confederacy during the

*Right:* Dawn breaks over an Atlantic convoy in February 1944.
*Below:* Joint UK and US convoy unloads in N Africa.

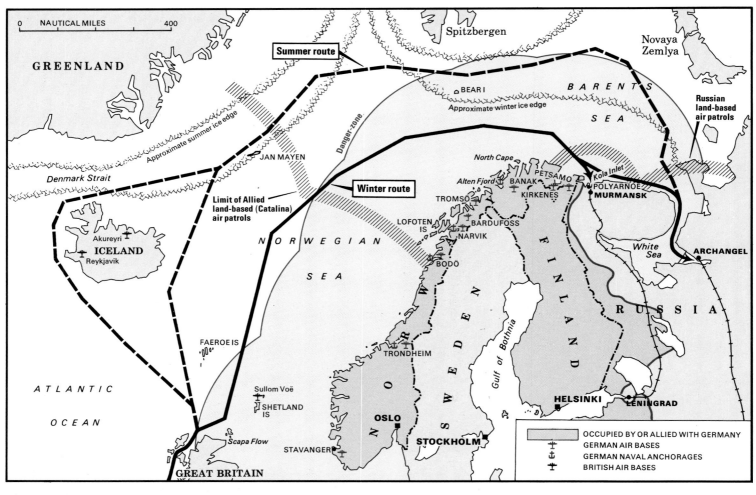

Scale: 0 to 400 NAUTICAL MILES

GREENLAND

Spitzbergen

Novaya Zemlya

Summer route

BARENTS SEA

BEAR I

Approximate winter ice edge

Russian land-based air patrols

Approximate summer ice edge

JAN MAYEN

Danger-zone

Denmark Strait

North Cape

Winter route

Alten Fjord · BANAK · PETSAMO · Kola Inlet

Limit of Allied land-based (Catalina) air patrols

TROMSO · KIRKENES · POLYARNOE · MURMANSK

ICELAND
Akureyri
Reykjavik

NORWEGIAN SEA

LOFOTEN IS · BARDUFOSS

NARVIK

BODÖ

White Sea

ARCHANGEL

FINLAND

RUSSIA

FAEROE IS

N O R W A Y

S W E D E N

Gulf of Bothnia

ATLANTIC OCEAN

TRONDHEIM

Sullom Voë

SHETLAND IS

OSLO

STOCKHOLM

HELSINKI · LENINGRAD

Scapa Flow

STAVANGER

GREAT BRITAIN

| | OCCUPIED BY OR ALLIED WITH GERMANY |
| --- | --- |
| | GERMAN AIR BASES |
| | GERMAN NAVAL ANCHORAGES |
| | BRITISH AIR BASES |

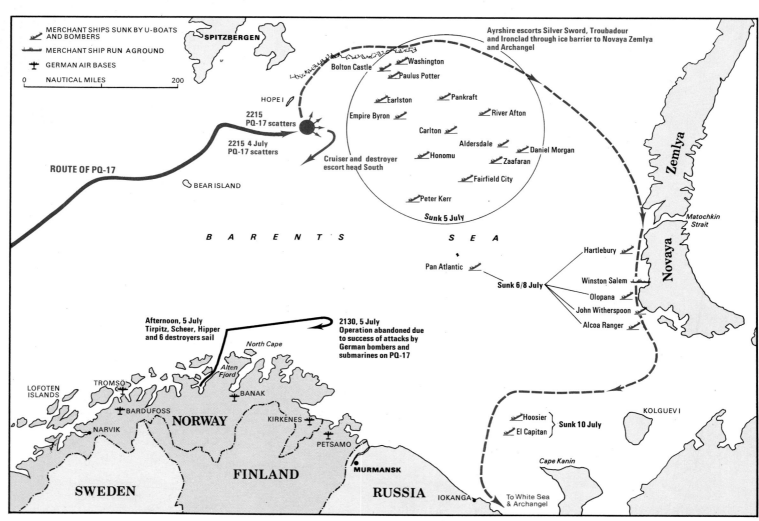

MERCHANT SHIPS SUNK BY U-BOATS AND BOMBERS

MERCHANT SHIP RUN AGROUND

GERMAN AIR BASES

0 NAUTICAL MILES 200

SPITZBERGEN

Ayrshire escorts Silver Sword, Troubadour and Ironclad through ice barrier to Novaya Zemlya and Archangel

Bolton Castle · Washington

Paulus Potter

HOPE I

Earlston · Pankraft

2215 PQ-17 scatters

Empire Byron · River Afton

2215 4 July PQ-17 scatters

Carlton

ROUTE OF PQ-17

Aldersdale · Daniel Morgan

Honomu · Zaafaran

Cruiser and destroyer escort head South

Fairfield City

BEAR ISLAND

Peter Kerr

Sunk 5 July

B A R E N T S   S E A

Zemlya

Matochkin Strait

Pan Atlantic

Hartlebury

Sunk 6/8 July

Winston Salem

Novaya Zemlya

Olopana

John Witherspoon

Alcoa Ranger

Afternoon, 5 July Tirpitz, Scheer, Hipper and 6 destroyers sail

2130, 5 July Operation abandoned due to success of attacks by German bombers and submarines on PQ-17

North Cape

Alten Fjord

LOFOTEN ISLANDS

TROMSO

BARDUFOSS · BANAK

NARVIK · NORWAY · KIRKENES

KOLGUEVI

PETSAMO

Hoosier · Sunk 10 July

El Capitan

SWEDEN

FINLAND

RUSSIA

MURMANSK

Cape Kanin

IOKANGA

To White Sea & Archangel

Civil War which almost destroyed the American mercantile marine) and the doctrine of the convoy lapsed. By 1914 it was regarded as an historical oddity, and nearly all naval thinkers seem to have ignored the possibility of any large-scale attack on shipping, or at least a 'sink on sight' policy. The staggering losses of 1916–17 were met at first by futile attempts to increase the number of warship patrols and decoy-vessels or 'Q-Ships' loitering in the shipping lanes.

Convoy was finally adopted as a measure of desperation, mainly at the behest of the far-sighted Cabinet Secretary, Maurice Hankey, although the Prime Minister Lloyd George later generously awarded himself most of the credit. The effect was immediate, and losses to U-Boat attack fell away as if by a miracle. Whereas previously it had not been possible to provide warships at every point where a submarine *might* appear, now the submarines had to try to attack targets which were heavily defended by warships. Convoy proved that it could not only protect merchant ships but also sink submarines.

At the outbreak of World War II there was no doubt in the Admiralty's mind about convoy, and elaborate plans had been drawn up prewar. Tactics and weapons changed as the war progressed, and new formations were tried, but the fundamentals remained the same. The most interesting discovery was made by Operational Research, that the larger the convoy the safer it was, for the ratio of number of merchant ships to the number of escorts needed increased. Only once, during the black days of March 1943, when merchant shipping losses rose almost to disaster level, did the Admiralty doubt that the convoy system was still valid. Fortunately the balance tilted dramatically against the U-Boats, for a decision to abandon convoying at that juncture would have lost the war for the Allies.

The US Navy despite its involvement in the convoy campaign of 1917–18 had never been indoctrinated to think of the protection of merchant shipping as its overriding task, and when the United States entered the war in December

Swordfish patrols the skies over a convoy in the Mediterranean.

Japanese carrier *Shoho* is torpedoed by US Navy planes at Coral Sea.

1941 the clock was put back to 1917. Merchant ships sailed on the east coast singly, broadcasting their positions and offering themselves as easy pickings to the U-Boats. The warships expended their fuel in 'offensive patrolling' and for the first six months of 1942 it looked as if the USA might be prevented from deploying its full strength by the sheer scale of shipping losses. Only when convoy was put into force did the losses come under control once more.

The organization of convoys demanded detailed planning and on both sides of the Atlantic administrative machinery was set up to regulate schedules and provide gun-crews.

## Coral Sea, Battle of, May 1942

In April-May 1942 the Japanese Imperial GHQ decided to try to capture Midway (in order to threaten Hawaii) and to extend their hold on the Solomon Islands (by capturing Port Moresby and isolating Australia from the USA).

The Japanese prepared the second part of the plan in April. The naval forces were commanded by Vice-Admiral Inouye at Rabaul and involved different forces meeting at Coral Sea to catch the US fleet by surprise. The Carrier Striking Force under Vice-Admiral Takagi, based on the carriers *Zuikaku* and *Shokaku* with 125 naval aircraft, was to cover the whole operation.

Admiral Nimitz knew of these plans and sent as many forces there as possible. Task Force 17, including the carrier *Yorktown* under Admiral Fletcher, was to be joined to Task Force 11, including the carrier *Lexington* under Rear Admiral Fitch. A mixed group of Australian and US cruisers under Rear Admiral Crace was to join them.

On 2 May the Japanese landed at Tulagi and took the island unopposed. At 1900 on the next day Fletcher received news of the landing, headed north, and his aircraft damaged one destroyer, three minesweepers and five seaplanes. Fletcher's pilots exaggerated the extent of the damage and he went south to meet the other two Task Forces and refuel from the tanker *Neosho*. On 6 May the Allied and Japanese carrier groups in the Coral Sea sent reconnaissance planes to look for the enemy, and although they were within 70 miles of each other there were no sightings. On 7 May Fletcher sent Crace's cruiser squadron to attack the Port Moresby Invasion Group.

Fletcher had launched his aircraft but they could not attack the Port Moresby invasion Group because of bad weather. A scout had reported sighting two carriers 225 miles away but these turned out to be cruisers. On the morning of 7 May Takagi's planes spotted a carrier and cruiser: in fact they were the tanker *Neosho* and an escorting destroyer. They were

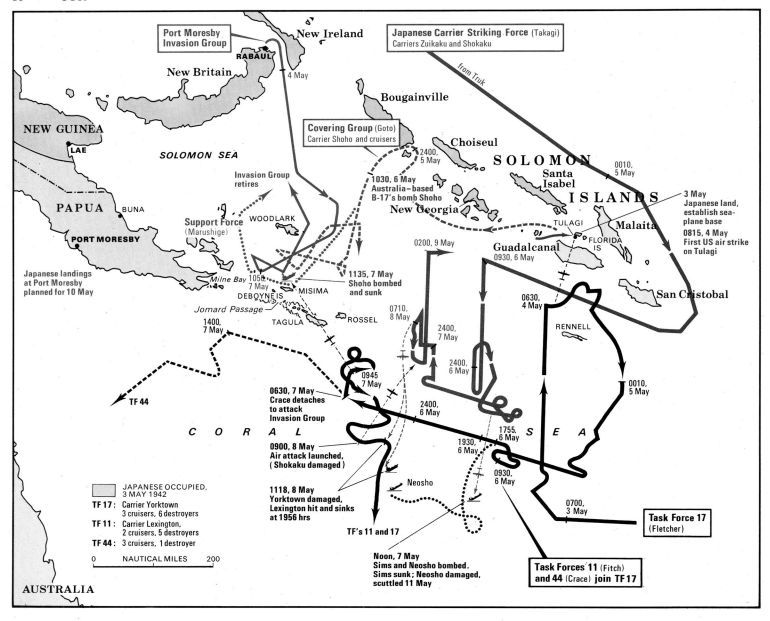

Port Moresby Invasion Group

**New Ireland**

RABAUL

4 May

**Japanese Carrier Striking Force (Takagi)**
Carriers Zuikaku and Shokaku

from Truk

**New Britain**

**Bougainville**

**NEW GUINEA**

LAE

SOLOMON SEA

Covering Group (Goto)
Carrier Shoho and cruisers

2400, 5 May

**Choiseul**

**SOLOMON**

0010, 5 May

Santa Isabel

1030, 6 May Australia–based B-17's bomb Shoho

**ISLANDS**

3 May Japanese land, establish sea-plane base

**PAPUA** BUNA

Invasion Group retires

WOODLARK

**New Georgia**

TULAGI

**Malaita**

0815, 4 May First US air strike on Tulagi

**PORT MORESBY**

Support Force (Marushige)

0200, 9 May

**Guadalcanal** 0930, 6 May

FLORIDA IS

Japanese landings at Port Moresby planned for 10 May

Milne Bay 1050, 7 May

DEBOYNE IS

MISIMA

1135, 7 May Shoho bombed and sunk

0630, 4 May

**San Cristobal**

Jomard Passage

TAGULA

ROSSEL

0710, 8 May

2400, 7 May

RENNELL

1400, 7 May

2400, 6 May

0010, 5 May

0945 7 May

0630, 7 May Crace detaches to attack Invasion Group

2400, 6 May

1755, 6 May

0350, 4 May

**TF 44**

1930, 6 May

0010, 5 May

**C O R A L**

0900, 8 May Air attack launched, (Shokaku damaged)

**S E A**

0930, 6 May

0700, 3 May

1118, 8 May Yorktown damaged, Lexington hit and sinks at 1956 hrs

Neosho

JAPANESE OCCUPIED, 3 MAY 1942

**TF 17:** Carrier Yorktown 3 cruisers, 6 destroyers

**TF 11:** Carrier Lexington, 2 cruisers, 5 destroyers

**TF 44:** 3 cruisers, 1 destroyer

0        NAUTICAL MILES        200

**AUSTRALIA**

TF's 11 and 17

Noon, 7 May Sims and Neosho bombed. Sims sunk; Neosho damaged, scuttled 11 May

**Task Force 17** (Fletcher)

**Task Forces 11 (Fitch) and 44 (Crace) join TF 17**

attacked, the destroyer sank and the *Neosho* was damaged (scuttled on 11 May). US reconnaissance planes spotted the *Shoho* and *Lexington* aircraft sank her at the cost of three planes. Admiral Inouye then decided that the Port Moresby Invasion Group should return to Rabaul. Japanese land-based aircraft attacked Crace's squadron but didn't inflict damage.

The carrier groups had still not made contact and Fletcher decided to wait until the morning. Takagi launched 27 planes at dusk but only seven of these returned. In the morning US planes attacked the Japanese carriers first and scored two hits on the *Shokaku* which was put out of action. Japanese dive bombers hit the *Lexington* which was eventually scuttled but the *Yorktown* avoided damage and Nimitz ordered withdrawal.

The Battle of Coral Sea was a strategic victory for the Allies because the Port Moresby Invasion fleet withdrew. The Americans lost a full fleet carrier but the Japanese lost a light carrier and many more aircraft. The US also were at an advantage because both the *Shokaku* and *Zuikaku* could not be used in the Battle of Midway, whereas the *Yorktown* was operational shortly afterwards.

*Left:* USS *Lexington* blows up as sailors leap for their lives.

### Cornwall

This British heavy cruiser of the *Kent* or 'County' Class was sunk by Japanese carrier dive-bombers off Ceylon on 5 April 1942 with HMS *Dorsetshire*.

### Coronado, Consolidated PB2Y

A total of 217 of these big four-engined flying-boats were built as maritime patrol bombers for the US Navy. They saw little operational service, but many were converted into transports and air ambulances for 25 stretchers, including ten PB2Y–3Bs supplied to the UK.

### Corregidor, Defense of, 1942

After the fall of Bataan on 8 April 1942, the US troops withdrew to Corregidor Island, which controlled Manila Bay. The Japanese decided to maintain heavy bombardments over the straits and continuous air attacks. Wainwright had 15,000 men for the defense, but the continuous pounding weakened morale and diminished supplies. On 4 May, 16,000 shells hit the island and on the night of 5 May, 2000 Japanese crossed the straits and landed on Cavalry Point, unable to reach their target destination of the Malinta Tunnel area because of strong currens. They met fierce resistance but the use of three tanks was enough to install a beachhead. By 1030 on 6 May the Japanese had broken through the defenses in the Malinta tunnel area and Wainwright ordered surrender. General Homma insisted that Wainwright declare a general surrender for the Philippines, but this did not prevent guerrilla activity which continued throughout the war.

### Corsair, Vought F4U

This US single-seat carrier-based fighter was operational from 1943. Arguably the best US fighter of World War II, the Corsair has many claims to fame. Only five months after its first flight, which had taken place on 29 May 1940, the XF4U–1 prototype became the first US aircraft to exceed 400mph in level flight. A production order was placed on 30 June 1941, after which the Corsair remained in production for eleven years – longer than any other US piston-engined fighter, and long enough to make it the last aircraft of that category, well into the jet age. Its combat record is equally impressive, as Corsairs achieved an 11:1 ratio of 'kills' to losses in combat with Japanese aircraft. Strange to relate, the US Navy was reluctant for a very long time to use its F4Us from carriers. After the prototype had flown, reports from Europe suggested that the design was already outdated in certain important respects. To remedy the deficiencies, Vought removed the two 0.3in and 0.5in guns from the front fuselage, and increased the wing 'point fives' from two to six. To make room for them, fuel tanks had to be relocated in the fuselage, which could be done only by moving back the cockpit three feet. The fuel tanks were made self-sealing, and armorplate was added. Unfortunately, carrier trials on the USS *Saratoga* then showed that positioning of the cockpit further rearward had seriously restricted the pilot's forward view for take-off. Landing speed was also considered too high for safe carrier operation so the Corsairs

Vought Corsairs prepare to take off from the deck of a US carrier in the Pacific.

were allocated initially to the Marines, for operation from land. After a time, the Brewster and Goodyear companies began fitting raised cockpit canopies to the Corsairs they were producing, as F3A–1s and FG–1s respectively, to supplement Vought manufacture. Vought adopted the canopy, which offered the pilot a better field of view, and the Royal Navy had no hesitation in flying the Corsairs they received under lend-lease from HMS *Victorious*. First combat sorties were flown on 3 April 1944 during attacks on the *Tirpitz*, and at last the US Navy acknowledged that F4Us were safe for shipboard use. Among the aircraft soon embarked were F4U–2 night fighters, with a radar pod on the starboard wingtip and an autopilot, and camera-carrying F4U–1Ps. Manufacture of later versions such as the F4U–4 with a 2100hp R–2800–18W engine instead of the former 2000hp R–2800–8, raising maximum speed to 446mph, continued until 1952, by which time Corsairs had played their part in another war, in Korea. Of the final total of 12,571 built, 2012 were supplied to the Royal Navy.

### Corvette

In 1938 the British Admiralty investigated ways of meeting the desperate shortage of convoy escorts and decided to adapt a whalecatcher design. Orders were placed for 56 in September 1939 and the first came into service in April 1940. As the new ships were different in many ways from previous escorts the designation 'corvette' which had not been used for 60 years was revived. To commemorate a similar expedient in World War I they were given names of flowers, with the result that reports of convoy actions were interspersed with names such as *Hollyhock* and *Petunia*.

The 'Flower' Class was put into quantity production as the standard escort, 22 being ordered for the French and a further 56 by the Canadian Navy. Eventually a total of 300 were built, and they bore the brunt of the Battle of the Atlantic. They were lively craft but very seaworthy; their

main drawback was their lack of speed. By 1941, as U-Boats realized that the Asdic set could not detect a surfaced U-Boat, they took to operating on the surface at night, and this gave them a margin of two-three knots over the 16-knot corvettes. Another advantage of speed in an escort was in rounding up stragglers and catching up with the convoy after hunting a contact, and so in 1942 a new type of escort was introduced, the 'River' Class frigate. The 'Rivers' were at first known as 'blown up corvettes' or twin-screw corvettes, but the name 'frigate' was used by the Canadians to distinguish them from the smaller corvettes.

### Cossack
see *Altmark*

### Courageous

This British aircraft carrier had been built in 1915–17 as a battlecruiser, and had taken part with her sister *Glorious* in a skirmish with German light forces off Heligoland in 1917. With high speed, virtually no armor and only four 15in guns, these two ships had no justifiable role and so they were laid up shortly after the Armistice. After the Washington Conference they were selected for conversion to aircraft carriers, to make use of the RN's allocation of tonnage in that category.

The conversion followed the general lines of that given to HMS *Furious*, but as work did not start on *Courageous* until 1924 many improvements were suggested by experience with the *Eagle* and the *Furious*. The most obvious difference was the provision of an 'island' superstructure enclosing the stack on the starboard side of the flight deck, and the first fully anti-aircraft armament given, 16 4.7in (120mm) guns. The ship was completed in 1928 and remained in frontline service until 1939. She was the first major loss suffered by the RN in World War II, being hit by three torpedoes from *U.29* on 17 September 1939. She had been used as the main unit of a 'U-Boat Hunting Group' in the Western Approaches, and the loss of such a unit showed the fallacy of this doctrine.

### Crace, Rear Admiral Sir John G, 1887–1968

Crace was the British commander of Task Force 44 in the Battle of Coral Sea. Crace had been sent to Australia to command a squadron of cruisers. During the Battle of Coral Sea, Grace patrolled the southeastern tip of New Guinea and narrowly escaped being sunk by Japanese aircraft. He retired after this and became superintendent of HM Dockyard at Chatham.

### Crerar, General Henry, 1888–1965

Crerar was a Canadian general who led the 1st Canadian Army in Northwestern Europe. Crerar first went over to Britain in November 1940 to organize the training of some 100,000 Canadians in Britain. In 1943 Crerar resigned to take up a command and saw action in Sicily and Italy. He then returned to Britain to form the 1st Canadian Army – which in fact had British, Polish, Belgian, Dutch, US and Czech divisions as well as Canadians. In June 1944 the 1st Canadian Army landed at Bernières-sur-Mer and held their ground until they pushed through to encircle the German Seventh Army at Falaise. Once the Canadians had reduced this pocket the 1st Army went on to clear the Pas de Calais, the Scheldt and the Netherlands.

### Crete, Battle of, 1941

Following their expulsion from Greece in April 1941 by the Germans, the British transferred many of the survivors to Crete, which they had occupied in October of the previous year. Its possession was of great value, since it controlled the sea routes of the eastern Mediterranean and provided a forward air base close to Germany's new Balkan flank. Moreover it looked secure, since British naval superiority in local waters made a seaborne operation too risky for the Germans to attempt. Hitler, however, was determined not to give the British the advantage of possessing the island and readily agreed to a plan proposed by General Student, Commander of the German Airborne Forces, that it should be assaulted by his parachute and glider troops. They would seize bridgeheads into which convoys could be run under cover of

*Below:* German parachutists descend over Crete in General Kurt Student's most successful operation. The Germans managed to expel the British.

darkness. For this operation the Germans could assemble 500 transport aircraft and 72 gliders, supported by 500 bombers and fighters, which were to airdrop the Seventh Parachute Division and the First Parachute Assault Regiment and to glider-land the Fifth Mountain Division. The British, who were aware of the danger of an airborne assault, could oppose this force with 42,500 troops of their own, including two brigades of New Zealanders, a brigade of Australians and a British brigade, with a few guns and 24 tanks. They were short of transport, however, and the island itself lacked roads, so that, when dispersed to cover the most likely sea and air landing places on the north coast, the units could not easily come to each other's support. This weakness was to be the undoing of the Commanding General Freyberg's scheme of defense. The German parachutists began landing on the morning of 20 May at Maleme and Canea in the west of the island and Retimo and Heraklion in the center. All the parachute units suffered very heavy losses, both during the descent and on the ground, where they were heavily and instantly attacked by the defenders. The crucial struggle developed in the west, where the Germans had to seize the airfield at Maleme if they were to bring sufficient reinforcements to rescue their parachutists before they were overwhelmed. Student sent in his last parachute reserve on 21 May. It was however a bad decision on the part of the local British commander which tipped the balance. He decided to withdraw from the airfield in order to counterattack the nearby Germans in strength. The counterattack failed and the Germans began to land planes on the runway even though it was swept by British fire. They also began to land the gliders bringing the Fifth Mountain Division on the beach west of Maleme. They soon built up a preponderance in the area and began to drive the British into the mountains. Meanwhile an intense air-sea struggle had begun on the maritime approaches to the island and, though the Royal Navy dispersed a German troop convoy with heavy loss of life on the night of 21–22 May, its losses in ships to air attack forced it to withdraw from the sea area north of the island. By 28 May Freyberg had decided that the defense of the island was impossible and ordered a retreat, already largely in progress, to Sfakia on the south coast. Nearly half the British force, however, failed to make its escape. On the other hand, the losses of elite parachutists so appalled Hitler that he forbade any future large-scale parachute operation.

### Crimea, Battle of the, 1941–1944

In October 1941 the Eleventh Army under Field Marshal Manstein had attacked the Crimea and by November it was overrun except for Sevastopol and the Kerch peninsula. In July 1942 Sevastopol surrendered (see Battle of Sevastopol) and the Germans were now masters of the peninsula. In November 1943 General Tolbukhin's drive along the northern shores of the Sea of Azov and the Black Sea cut off the German and Rumanian troops in the Crimea. The number of troops was being reduced by evacuation but the Russians were having no success in breaking through as there were only two narrow approaches. On 8 April 1944 General Tolbukhin launched a major attack consisting of a frontal assault on the defenses of the Perekop isthmus and an attack on the flank from the Sivash Lagoon. After three days of fighting Tolbukhin broke through and the German Seventeenth Army had to fall back to Sevastopol. General Yeremenko's troops attacked from the eastern part of Kerch and by the 17 April both army groups had reached Sevastopol and 37,000 German prisoners were taken because they had not retreated fast enough. The Russians then brought the heavy artillery up and Hitler finally gave the order to withdraw; however, the German garrison at Sevastopol surrendered on 9 May and some 30,000 Germans were taken prisoner in the devastated peninsula.

### Cripps, Sir Stafford, 1889–1952

Cripps was a socialist barrister who served as Britain's Ambassador to the USSR during the war. He had resigned from the Labor Party because he disagreed with the Labor Party's attitude to Chamberlain's policy of rearmament. When Churchill became Prime Minister he was sent on a mission to Moscow in May 1940. Cripps had long been pressing for an alliance with the USSR against Hitler. He became Ambassador to Moscow and worked hard to improve relations. He warned Stalin about Hitler's plan to invade the USSR, but Stalin thought this was a plant. He returned to Britain in 1942 to serve in the War Cabinet as Leader of the House of Commons but at the end of the year took the job of Minister of Aircraft Production, a non-Cabinet post. In July 1945 he was made Chancellor of the Exchequer in Attlee's Cabinet.

### Crocodile
see Flamethrowers

### Cromwell Tank

This British cruiser tank was developed in 1941 using the Rolls-Royce Meteor engine, a detuned version of the Merlin aircraft engine. Production began in January 1943, using a six-pounder gun; this was soon changed to a 75mm gun to allow ammunition interchangeability with US Army sources. The Cromwell used the Christie type of suspension and could move at 40mph, making it one of the fastest and most maneuverable tanks on the battlefield, a factor which did much to compensate for its relatively poor armament vis-à-vis its German opponents, such as the Tigers and the Panthers. The Cromwell tank made its first appearance after D-Day.

## Cruiser

The cruiser is best defined as the largest warship-type ship which could be built in numbers. Its functions were many; it was in some ways a general-purpose warship designed to escort and assist battleships, protect merchant shipping and support destroyers, as well as bearing a part of the normal naval burdens of shore bombardment, patroling and scouting. The term originated in the 18th century, when a 'cruiser' was any warship on detached duty, and by 1939 international treaties had defined two separate types; the 10,000-ton (maximum) 'heavy' cruiser armed with eight-inch guns, and the 'light' cruiser which could equal the heavy cruiser in tonnage but had guns not larger than six inches.

There was an important exception to this simple definition, the 'pocket battleship', such as the *Deutschland* which was built by Germany to express unwillingness to comply with the conditions of the Versailles Treaty. In 1940 the three *panzerschiffe* were re-classified as heavy cruisers, a term more appropriate to their function.

An important variant of the light cruiser developed in the 1930s as a direct result of the threat from air attack. This was the anti-aircraft cruiser, at first a British adaptation of obsolescent World War I cruisers of the 'C' Class, but followed by custom-built ships of the *Dido* Class armed with a new 5.25in dual-purpose gun. They inspired the US Navy to build the *Atlanta* Class, armed with eight twin five-inch mountings.

Although cruisers were not intended to engage capital ships they had a good record when they did so. Apart from the Battle of the River Plate, in which the superiority of the *Graf Spee* over her opponents was more apparent than real, the cruiser *Prinz Eugen* scored the first hits on HMS *Hood* in May 1941, and started the fire which may have caused her to blow up. Three days later it was an eight-inch shell from HMS *Dorsetshire* which knocked out the *Bismarck*'s fire control just as the *Norfolk* did to the *Scharnhorst* in December 1943. Similarly US heavy cruisers did well against the *Kirishima* at Guadalcanal.

*Top right:* USS *Chester* (CA-27) in May 1945.
*Right:* USS *Boston* (CA-69) in 1944.
*Below:* USS *Baltimore* (CA-68) in 1944.

German shell misses British artillerymen in the Western Desert.

### Crusader, Operation, 1941

Despite the failure of Operation Battleaxe, the situation in the Western Desert moved in favor of the British during the second half of 1941. They continued to receive reinforcements – released by the victory in East Africa and the disengagement from Greece – and new equipment, particularly tanks. The Germans on the other hand were starved of supplies which were now going to the Russian Front. This boded well for the success of the counteroffensive which Auchinleck, who succeeded Wavell in July, began to plan as soon as he reached Egypt. His eventual scheme was to pass his 30th Corps south of the German line on the desert flank, meanwhile ordering the Australian garrison of the besieged port of Tobruk to break through the Italian lines surrounding them and join hands with the attackers. The plan achieved surprise when launched on 18 November, but Rommel reacted strongly and held 30th Corps' armor in a fortnight-long battle in the desert. Meanwhile the Australians broke out of Tobruk, forcing Rommel to abandon an armored raid he had organized as a diversion across the Egyptian frontier. His return upset the New Zealand Division's efforts to bring permanent relief to Tobruk, which they reached on 27 November. This success was quickly offset by 30th Corps' rough handling of the Italians whom Rommel's withdrawal to Tobruk had left at its mercy, and he therefore decided to retire altogether to the west of Tobruk on 4 December. Pursued by 30th Corps' tanks, he was obliged to disengage once more and reached Gazala on 7 December. When British tanks reappeared on his desert flank, he abandoned his hopes of remaining in Cyrenaica and withdrew to El Agheila, his starting point of eight months

before. Despite their initial superiority in tanks, about 700 to 400, the British could justifiably regard Crusader as a genuine victory. General Ritchie, who with Auchinleck had relieved Cunningham at the height of the battle on 26 November, could take a personal pride in the achievement.

### Crusader Tank

In 1936 a British mission visited the Soviet Army maneuvers where it was extremely impressed by the performance of the BT tanks which had been adapted from a design by the US inventor Walter Christie. Upon returning to Britain and making its report, a Christie tank was purchased by the Nuffield Organization and work began on development of a fast cruiser tank using the Christie suspension system. Extensive re-design was needed, since Christie's tanks were merely demonstration vehicles and never carried heavy armor or armament, but by December 1938 the first production models of the A13 Covenanter tank were leaving the factory. It weighed about 14 tons and was armored

with 14mm of plate, and it was felt that a somewhat heavier design would be a good thing. The Nuffield company set to work to produce a slightly larger version, powered by one of their own engines, and this, the A15 Crusader tank appeared late in 1940. The chassis had been lengthened and additional wheels fitted, the armament was a 2-pounder gun, the armor was 30mm thick and the tank weighed about 18 tons. A later model was produced with 51mm armor and a 6-pounder gun. Crusader became the standard British tank until replaced by the US Grant and Sherman designs.

Although dogged with mechanical unreliability, a legacy of its rapid development, the Crusader performed well. It first saw action in June 1941 in Operation Battleaxe, the abortive attempt to relieve Tobruk and it was extensively employed throughout the remainder of the North African campaign. Although it ceased to be a battle tank after that, numbers were rebuilt to become specialist vehicles; mine-clearing, artillery observers, anti-aircraft tanks (fitted with 40mm Bofors guns); armored recovery tanks; anti-tank gun tractors; and armored bulldozers. In these roles the Crusader continued to play a useful role until the end of the war.

### Cunningham, Admiral Andrew Browne, 1883–1963

An outstanding sea captain in World War I, in which he won the Distinguished Service Order and two bars, he was, in 1939, acting as naval Commander in Chief in the Mediterranean, the most important of Britain's overseas naval commands, comprising her largest fleet outside home waters and three major naval bases of

Crusader Type I tank.

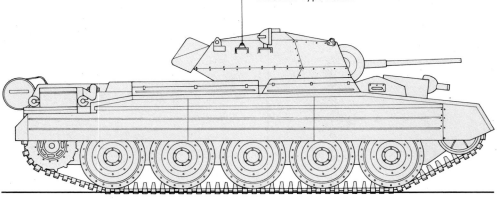

great strategic and historical importance, Gibraltar, Malta and Alexandria. Mussolini whose modern fleet formed the strongest element of Italy's armed forces, had declared his intention to turn the Mediterranean ('*Mare Nostrum*' – 'Our Sea') into an 'Italian lake' but Cunningham, by bold offensive action, quickly established British naval supremacy over it. His first victory was that of Taranto, when his Fleet Air Arm sank several major Italian ships at their moorings in November 1940; his second was the night action of Cape Matapan in March 1941. His fleet's action to deter the German seaborne invasion of Crete in the following May was less successful for, though it dispersed the German convoy with heavy losses, it itself suffered heavy damage from air attack and, following the loss of the island to parachute assault, was forced to withdraw from the area. During 1943, however, when serving as Eisenhower's naval deputy, he re-established Allied naval supremacy in the Mediterranean and then in October was transferred to London to replace Pound as First Sea Lord. In that post he acted as Churchill's principal naval adviser and strategist for the remainder of the war. Captain Roskill has said in the words of Conrad 'He stands unique amongst the leaders of fleets and sailors'.

## Cunningham, General Sir Alan, 1887–

The younger brother of Admiral Cunningham, he also was to make his name in the Mediterranean and Middle East. It was his forces which overthrew the Italians in Ethiopia and Eritrea in January–May 1941, and restored Haile Selassie to his throne. Transferred to the desert to replace the captured O'Connor in August 1941, he did not, however, match up to Rommel and was removed.

## Cunningham, Group Captain John, 1915–

A pilot of immense skill, 'Cat's Eyes' Cunningham, together with his A1 operator, Sergeant C F Rawnsley, formed the RAF's most successful night fighter crew. Flying Beaufighter aircraft with 604 Squadron, he shot down 15 aircraft in ten months from November 1940.

Generals Robertson and Gorbachov review Soviet troops in Pilsen in May 1945.

## Curtin, John, 1885–1945

Curtin was the Australian Prime Minister from 1941–45. In December 1941 Curtin declared war on Japan and looked to the USA for help. He welcomed General MacArthur from the Philippines and recalled two Australian Divisions from the Middle East to fight the Japanese. He took a keen interest in defense policy and in 1942 he became Minister of Defense. In 1943 he held a general election and was re-elected with a clear majority. In 1944 he visited Great Britain, the USA and Canada. In November 1944 he fell ill and died in July of the following year. He was a much-loved and respected war leader.

*Below:* Australians fire a 25-pounder during the Desert War. The Australians made a vital contribution to the Middle East theater.

## Czechoslovakia, Liberation of, 1944–45

In October 1944 General Petrov's 4th Ukrainian Front had begun the liberation of Czechoslovakia by invading eastern Slovakia. Marshal Malinovsky's 2nd Ukrainian Front had overrun Hungary and now joined in the reconquest of Czechoslovakia. The Germans did not put up much resistance and by May 1945 the Red Army had overrun most of Moravia. On 6 May Czech partisans staged an uprising in Prague and disrupted German communications. The only German Army left in Europe was Field Marshal Schörner's Army Group Center but its position was hopeless. On 8 May the Russian offensive began with General Konev's 1st Ukrainian Front attacking from Saxony and the 2nd, 3rd and 4th Ukrainian Fronts attacking from the south and east. The US 3rd Army, under General Patton, also advanced into Czechoslovakia and on 11 May Schörner surrendered. This was the last military offensive in the war in Europe.

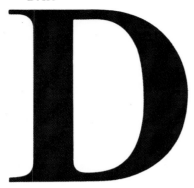

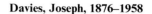

Douglas SBD-5 Dauntless.

## Dar–10F

This two-seat bomber was the only combat air-craft of Bulgarian design ever to enter squadron service. Powered by a 960hp Fiat engine, it carried 1100lb of bombs at 227mph.

## Darlan, Admiral Jean François, 1881–1942

Darlan was Commander-in-Chief of the French Navy at the outbreak of war and, after his country's defeat in the battle of France, had the difficult task of deciding how to dispose of his battle fleet, the second strongest in European waters. He assured Churchill that he would not allow it to fall into German hands and seemed at one moment willing to sail it to British ports. But, after accepting office as Minister of Marine Affairs, in Pétain's government, he sent it to North Africa, where Churchill ordered its destruction by bombardment by the British Mediterranean fleet in July 1940. In February 1941 he became deputy to Pétain in the Vichy government but, after the reconciliation of Laval with the old Marshal, was appointed Head of the French Armed Forces and High Commissioner in French North Africa. There, on the eve of the Torch landings, Mark Clark made contact with him, arranged an armistice and recognized his claims to be regarded as head of the French government. Fortunately for the future of inter-Allied relations, this extremely controversial figure was assassinated by a young French monarchist on Christmas Eve, 1942.

## Dauntless/A–24, Douglas SBD

This US carrier-based scout/dive-bomber was operational from late in 1940 to 1950. By inflicting crippling damage on the Japanese fleet in actions such as the Battle of the Coral Sea, Midway and the Solomons Campaign, the Dauntless was instrumental in turning the tide of war in the Pacific. It had its origin in the BT–1, produced for the US Navy by the prewar Northrop Corporation. When Northrop became the El Segundo Division of Douglas, engine, airframe and designation all changed. The 57 SBD–1s went to Marine Corps units; 87 SBD–2s, with extra fuel and armament increased from three to four 0.3in guns, equipped Navy squadrons on the carriers *Enterprise* and *Lexington*. By the time of the Pearl Harbor attack, they had been followed by the SBD–3, still with a 1000hp Wright R–1820 engine but with self-sealing tanks, armor, and two 0.5in forward-firing guns in place of the former 0.3in machine guns. Production was increased in 1942, and some aircraft of each version were fitted with cameras for reconnaissance and damage assessment. Soon SBD–4s, with changed electrics, and SBD–5s, with 1200hp engines, were streaming into service from El Segundo and a new factory at Tulsa respectively. Tulsa followed with the final SBD–6, with a 1350hp R–1820–66. Simultaneously with the Navy production, the USAAF acquired 953 SBD–3s, 4s and 5s as A–24s, which proved too slow, vulnerable and short of fuel when matched with Japanese shore-based aircraft in the East Indies and Australia. Production totaled 5321 of all versions.

US Navy Douglas Dauntless takes off for a bombing mission against Wake Island.

## Davies, Joseph, 1876–1958

Davies was the US ambassador to the USSR from 1937–38 and he was Cordell Hull's special assistant during the war. During Davies' stay in Moscow he attended many of the treason trials and wrote his observations in *Mission to Moscow*. This book helped the Soviet cause in the USA. During the war Davies advised President Roosevelt.

## D–Day Landings, 1944

Detailed planning for the invasion of Europe, the decision which had been finally settled at the Trident and Quadrant Conferences, was galvanized by the arrival from the Mediterranean of Generals Eisenhower and Montgomery, to be Supreme and Ground Commanders respectively, in December 1943. Montgomery in particular insisted on increasing the number of assaulting divisions from three to five and of airlanding divisions from one to three. Eisenhower was of one mind with him and secured the postponement of the landing from May to June 1944 accordingly. Its location was not in question: fighter range limited the planners to a choice between the Pas de Calais and Normandy. Normandy was preferred because of its weaker defenses. A preliminary aerial attack on the bridges and railways of northern France isolated the battlefield from the rest of the country in the Spring of 1944. Meanwhile the invasion fleet, the Tactical Air Force of 6000 airplanes and the 45 divisions which were to fight the Battle of Europe assembled in the United Kingdom. To oppose them, Rundstedt, German commander in the west, had an outnumbered air force and a non-existent navy, but over fifty divisions, including ten armored, of which 40 formed Army Group B, under Rommel, on the Channel coast.

*Above:* US troops move inland after the Utah and Omaha beaches have been secured.
*Left:* Eisenhower (center) and Montgomery (right) discuss D-Day landing plans with their staffs.
*Below:* US Forces land at Normandy in one of the first waves of the D-Day assault.
*Bottom left:* Burning landing craft tries to make it to shore during the landings on Omaha Beach.
*Bottom right:* Coast Guard-manned LC T-85 sinking off Omaha Beach.

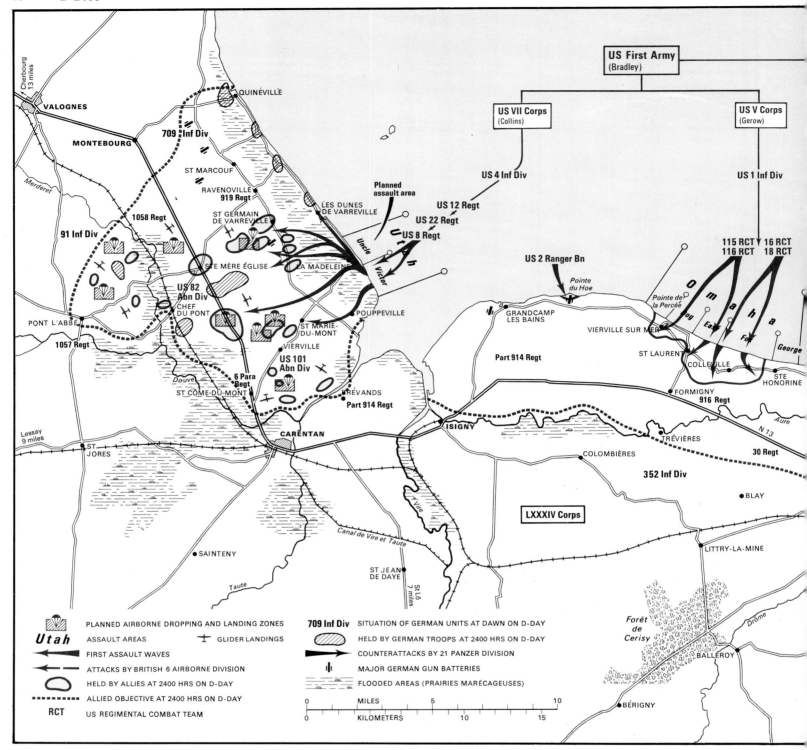

**US First Army**
(Bradley)

**US VII Corps**
(Collins)

**US V Corps**
(Gerow)

US 4 Inf Div

US 1 Inf Div

US 12 Regt

US 22 Regt

US 8 Regt

115 RCT  16 RCT
116 RCT  18 RCT

US 2 Ranger Bn

Planned
assault area

709 Inf Div

91 Inf Div

82 Abn Div

101 Abn Div

352 Inf Div

LXXXIV Corps

**Legend:**

| | PLANNED AIRBORNE DROPPING AND LANDING ZONES | **709 Inf Div** | SITUATION OF GERMAN UNITS AT DAWN ON D-DAY |
|---|---|---|---|
| **Utah** | ASSAULT AREAS | | HELD BY GERMAN TROOPS AT 2400 HRS ON D-DAY |
| | FIRST ASSAULT WAVES  GLIDER LANDINGS | | COUNTERATTACKS BY 21 PANZER DIVISION |
| | ATTACKS BY BRITISH 6 AIRBORNE DIVISION | | MAJOR GERMAN GUN BATTERIES |
| | HELD BY ALLIES AT 2400 HRS ON D-DAY | | FLOODED AREAS (PRAIRIES MARÉCAGEUSES) |
| | ALLIED OBJECTIVE AT 2400 HRS ON D-DAY | | |
| **RCT** | US REGIMENTAL COMBAT TEAM | | |

MILES    5    10
KILOMETERS    10    15

*Left:* LSTs put troops ashore on Omaha Beach
after the landings of 6 June 1944, protected by a
large flotilla and barrage balloons which were
intended to ward off aerial attack.

Rommel had greatly strengthened the fixed defenses of the shore and laid millions of mines but
he was away from the scene at the moment of
the landing on 6 June having been lulled into a
false sense of security by the extremely effective
Allied deception plan. This plan had also de-
ceived the Germans as to the direction of the
crossings and persuaded them that a fictitious
army group, as strong again as that actually
invading, was waiting in Kent to make a second
invasion across the Channel narrows. Slow reaction allowed the Allies to land on four of the
five beaches with light losses. At the fifth,
Omaha, the accompanying amphibious tanks

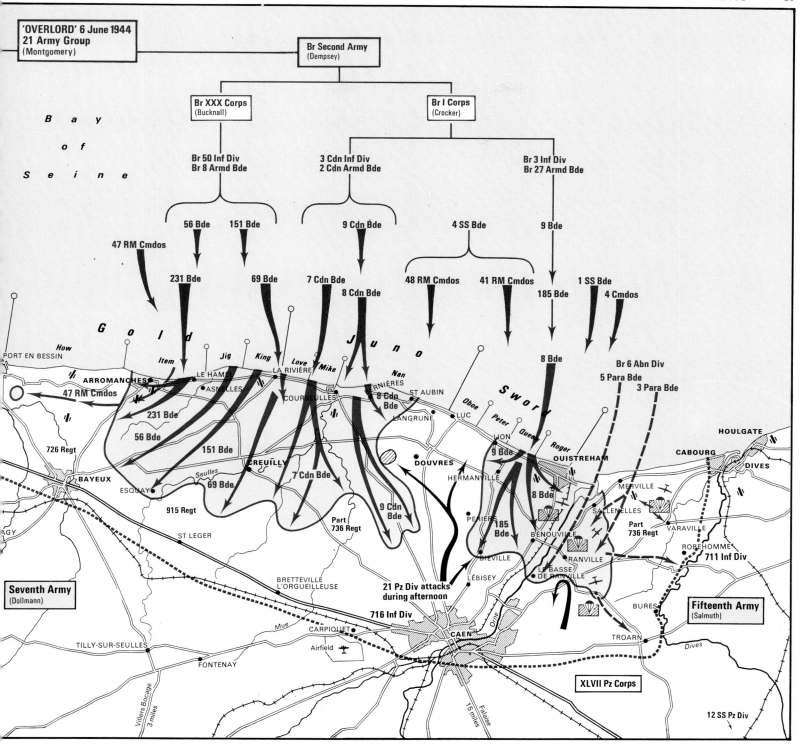

**'OVERLORD' 6 June 1944**
**21 Army Group**
(Montgomery)

Br Second Army
(Dempsey)

Br XXX Corps
(Bucknall)

Br I Corps
(Crocker)

Br 50 Inf Div
Br 8 Armd Bde

3 Cdn Inf Div
2 Cdn Armd Bde

Br 3 Inf Div
Br 27 Armd Bde

56 Bde    151 Bde

9 Cdn Bde

4 SS Bde    9 Bde

47 RM Cmdos

231 Bde    69 Bde

7 Cdn Bde
8 Cdn Bde

48 RM Cmdos    41 RM Cmdos

1 SS Bde
4 Cmdos

185 Bde

*Bay*

*of*

*Seine*

How
PORT EN BESSIN

Item    Jig    King    Love    Mike

*G o l d*

*J u n o*

Nan
ERNIERES
ST AUBIN

8 Bde

Oboe    Peter    Queen    Roger

*S w o r d*

Br 6 Abn Div
5 Para Bde    3 Para Bde

ARROMANCHES
47 RM Cmdos

LE HAMEL
ASNELLES

LA RIVIÈRE

COURSEULLES

8 Cdn Bde

LANGRUNE    LUC    LION

9 Bde

OUISTREHAM

HOULGATE

CABOURG

DIVES

726 Regt

BAYEUX

231 Bde
56 Bde
151 Bde

CREUILLY

Seulles

69 Bde

7 Cdn Bde

DOUVRES

HERMANVILLE

8 Bde

MERVILLE

SALLENELLES

ESQUAY

915 Regt

ST LEGER

9 Cdn Bde

PÉRIERS

185 Bde

BÉNOUVILLE

BIÉVILLE

RANVILLE

Part
736 Regt

VARAVILLE

ROBEHOMME
711 Inf Div

Part
736 Regt

**Seventh Army**
(Dollmann)

BRETTEVILLE
L'ORGUEILLEUSE

LÉBISEY

LE BASSE
DE RANVILLE

BURES

**Fifteenth Army**
(Salmuth)

21 Pz Div attacks
during afternoon

716 Inf Div

Mue

CARPIQUET

CAEN

Orne

TROARN

Dives

TILLY-SUR-SEULLES

Airfield

Falaise

**XLVII Pz Corps**

FONTENAY

Villers Bocage
3 miles

15 miles

**12 SS Pz Div**

were swamped and the US 1st Division suffered heavily. All five divisions, however, had secured footholds by evening, and at the flanks had made contact with the airborne divisions (US 82nd and 101st and British 6th) which had dropped in the early morning. The Germans attacked east of Caen on the evening of 6 June but were repulsed. It was the only organized counterattack of the day. During the next five days fighting intensified both at Caen in the British sector, and Carentan in the American but by 12 June the Allies had succeeded in uniting their bridgeheads and were holding a continuous front 60 miles long, and, at its maximum, 15 deep.

**Death March**
see Bataan, Defense of, 1942

**Decoy Ships**

The spectacular exploits of 'Q-Ships' in World War I, although they had not accounted for many U-Boats sunk, led the Admiralty to reintroduce them in World War II. Between October 1939 and March 1940 eight were commissioned, disguised as innocent-looking freighters with concealed guns, torpedoes and depth-charges. In fact their code-designation was 'Freighters'.

The concept was a total failure, and no U-Boats were even sighted. However, the need for total security meant that the senior officers in charge of anti-submarine warfare were not allowed to discuss them in reports, and so their failure was not acted upon until December 1940, when the idea was abandoned. One ship, the *Fidelity* was retained for undercover work in

the Mediterranean. She was eventually torpedoed off the Azores in 1942.

**Deere, Flight Lieutenant Alan**

Deere was a New Zealand-born Spitfire pilot serving with No 54 Squadron, RAF Fighter Command during the Battle of Britain. Operating with great success, he was fortunate to survive a head-on collision with a Bf 109 on 9 July 1940.

**Defiant, Boulton Paul**

This British two-seat fighter was in service from 1940 to 1941. Designed to a 1935 specification for a fighter with four machine guns in a power-operated turret, the Defiant proved to be a complete mistake. Powered by a Merlin of 1030 (Mk I) or 1260hp (Mks II and III), it was naturally heavier than a Hurricane, and so slower at about 300mph; and as the wing was smaller its maneuverability was poor. When first used against the Luftwaffe in the hectic three weeks from mid-May 1940 it shot down 65 aircraft, 38 in one day, but then the Luftwaffe learned to watch out for the turret and attack from below. By August 1940 it was clear the Defiant could not survive in daylight, and it was thereafter used only at night, later being fitted with radar. From 1942 they were almost all relegated to target towing and air/sea rescue.

**De Gaulle, General Charles André Joseph Marie, 1890–1970**

De Gaulle, who had served as a subaltern in Pétain's 33rd Regiment at the outbreak of World War I and subsequently been captured at Verdun, made a considerable reputation between the wars as a military writer and theorist, particularly by his advocacy of a professional army and of the need for mechanization. In 1940 he was appointed to command the half-formed 4th Armored Divison and with it delivered one of the few counterattacks attempted by the French against the German 'Panzer Corridor', near Laon on 19 May. A few days later he was promoted *Général de Brigade*, the highest rank he was to hold, and brought into the government as Under-Secretary for War. He was, however, not willing to acquiesce in the opening of negotiations with Hitler for an armistice and fled to England, where in June he declared the existence of 'Free France' and called on his fellow-countrymen to join him in carrying on the fight. Few at first did so, regarding him as the rebel Vichy accused him of being, and his first effort to annex French territory to Free France, the Dakar expedition of October 1940, ended in fiasco. His relations with the British and later the American governments were also less than smooth, for he insisted on regarding himself as head of the legitimate French government, even though they did not do so until after the invasion of Northwest Europe. His ecstatic welcome by the people first of Bayeux, then of Paris confirmed by popular acclamation the legitimacy of his leadership. In the aftermath of Liberation he founded a new Republic, the Fourth, and led its government until 1946 when

his impatience with the persistence of Third Republican attitudes among his political allies led him into political exile. He was to remain there until 1958, when he emerged to found yet another regime, the Fifth Republic, of which he became President and chief executive, thus finally combining in his person both the trappings and substance of power he had craved all his life. Overriding everything in his character, however, was his desire to serve France, which he achieved more generously and effectively than any man since the great Bourbon kings.

---

**Degaussing**

By the outbreak of war in 1939 three navies were experimenting with magnetic exploders for torpedoes and mines, the USN, RN and the Kriegsmarine. As so often happens, the research into magnetic fields necessary to produce such devices led to the discovery of the antidote, degaussing, which was to use an electric current to neutralize a ship's magnetism. This was very simply done at first by running a cable around the outside of the hull and running a low voltage current through it. Later the cabling was built into the ship, with control equipment to cope with changes of frequency in enemy mines and torpedoes, but this refinement only extended to warships. Small ships could be 'wiped' or 'depermed' to reduce their permanent magnetism but large ships needed to have degaussing gear on board permanently. The name 'degaussing' was taken from the unit of magnetism, the gauss.

---

**Degtyarev Machine Guns**

Vassily Degtyarev (1890–1959) left school at the age of eleven and became an outstanding weapons' designer. His principal designs were the DP (Degtyarev Pekhotnii) and DT (Degtyarev Tankovii) light machine guns and the PPD submachine gun, though he also worked in the heavy machine gun and anti-tank rifle fields. He eventually became a Major General of Engineers, Director of Technical Sciences and a Deputy of the Supreme Soviet.

The DP machine gun, in 7.62mm caliber, was

introduced in 1928 and became the standard light machine gun of the Soviet army. It was simple, robust and reliable, and was produced in astronomical numbers, many of which survive today. The gun was gas-operated and the bolt was locked by hinged flaps driven out by the forward movement of the firing pin, a simple and ingenious system. Its defects were minor; the flat pan magazine was prone to distortion if dropped, and the recoil spring beneath the barrel tended to soften from heat after prolonged firing. Degtyarev cured this by mounting the spring behind the bolt in the DPM model introduced during the war. The DT machine gun was a variant of the DP intended for hull mounting in tanks; it differed little mechanically but had a telescopic butt and a narrower and deeper magazine, both desirable features in the restricted space inside a tank.

The PPD submachine gun was first produced in 1934 in small numbers and appears to have been based largely on the German Bergmann of World War I, with some modifications taken from the Finnish Suomi design. It was a simple blowback gun with wooden stock and used a drum magazine holding 71 rounds of 7.62mm pistol ammunition. This original version is known as the Model 34/38 and it was later replaced by the Model 1940 which improved the magazine and its method of attachment. Both models of the PPD were used in the war against Finland and continued in use throughout the rest of the war years, but their design was such that they required considerable machinery to make them, and they were replaced in production by the simpler designs of Shpagin and Sudarev.

---

**De Lattre de Tassigny, General Jean Joseph Marie Gabriel, 1889–1952**

A cavalry officer, he had been severely wounded by a sword thrust in a mounted duel with German uhlans in 1914. After the fall of France he remained in the Armistice Army which the Germans allowed the Vichy Regime to have but was imprisoned for protesting at the occupation of the *'zone libre'* in 1942. He escaped and made his way to England, where he was reconciled with de Gaulle and appointed to command what

*Below:* The DPM light machine gun.
*Bottom:* The DP 1MG on its sledge.

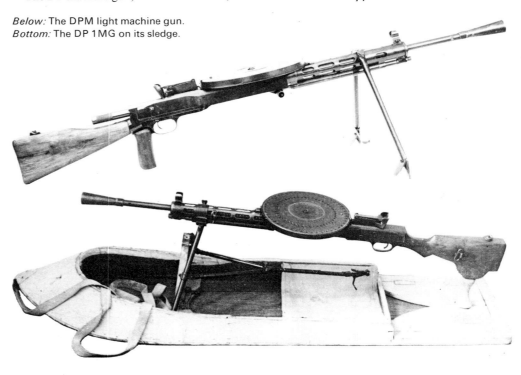

became the 1st French Army in the invasion of Italy and later of southern France. During the winter of 1944–5 he directed its operations in Alsace and eventually led it into southern Germany and Austria. After the war he achieved a remarkable victory over the Vietminh in Indo-China. He was posthumously created Marshal of France.

### Dempsey, Lieutenant General Miles, 1896–1969

Dempsey commanded the 2nd Army which overran Northern France in 1944. Dempsey had first distinguished himself during the Dunkirk evacuation, when his 13th Inf Bde fought a rear-guard action. In December 1942 Dempsey was made acting Lieutenant General of the 13th Corps and sent with the 8th Army to Libya. He took part in the early campaign in Italy and became an expert on combined operations and Montgomery chose him to command the 2nd Army in the D-Day landings. His Army fought in the toughest battles in Normandy and then drove through to Belgium and fought at the Arnhem bridgehead. He was a quiet and unassuming figure who managed to control his corps commanders and still stay in the background.

### DEMS

DEMS was the acronym for Defensively Equipped Merchant Ships, a British organization set up to provide not only guns but gun-crews for merchant ships. The program was so effective in 1939 that the threat to merchant ships of surface attack by U-Boats with gunfire which had caused so many losses in 1916–17 virtually disappeared in the Atlantic. By March 1941 a total of 4431 British and Allied merchant ships had been armed with anti-submarine or anti-aircraft guns. In addition guns and crews were provided temporarily for 'shuttle' service on certain convoy routes such as those in coastal waters. A similar organization was set up in the US to arm merchant ships in December 1941.

### Denmark, Occupation of, April 1940

Hitler had determined to occupy Denmark, despite its neutral status, at the same time as Norway, giving the operation the codename, *Weserübung (Sud)*. The Danish Army, reduced over many years of budget pruning by a pacifist government to minuscule proportions, was unfit for operations and the government, in any case, was given no warning. Three small German transports, covered by aircraft, carried a landing force into Copenhagen harbor at 0500 on 9 April, 1940, and at once seized the city center. At the same time a ground force crossed the Jutland frontier, defense of which was abandoned after a brief exchange of fire. Capitulation ensued, but the Germans left the Danish government in office until 1943, when a military administration was imposed.

### Depth-charges

As in World War I the depth-charge (also known as the depth-bomb) was the standard weapon for attacking submerged submarines. It was nothing more than a heavy (200–300lb)

The PC-551 drops a depth charge off her stern.

charge of high-explosive actuated by a hydrostatic device to explode at a pre-selected depth. The first improvement was to redesign the depth-charge to allow it to be dropped from an aircraft, as the prewar anti-submarine bomb proved totally ineffective. New explosives increased the destructive power and redesign of the shape made it sink faster. The British produced a special one ton depth-charge capable of sinking rapidly to depths of 900ft or more, as a counter to deep-diving U-Boats, and the final refinement was to design charges for firing from the 'Squid' triple mortar.

### Desert War, Chronological List of Events

Egypt, Italian Invasion of and British
    Counteroffensive, 1940
East Africa, British and Italian Campaign in,
    1940–41
Western Desert, Rommel's First Offensive,
    1941
Battleaxe, Operation, 1941
Crusader, Operation, 1941
Gazala-Bir Hacheim, Battle of, 1942
Alam Halfa, Battle of, 1942
Alamein (El Alamein), Battle of, 23 October–5
    November 1942
Torch, Operation, Allied landings in North
    Africa, 1942
Tunisia, Campaign in, 1942–43

### Destroyer

Originally a 'torpedo boat destroyer', the type evolved before World War I into a versatile fleet escort, armed primarily with torpedoes to attack the enemy battle fleet and with guns to defend its own battle fleet against enemy destroyers. Speed was the destroyer's most important asset, both to keep out of trouble and to enable her to catch her quarry. The design was highly specialized, with constant improvements in boilers, machinery and armament to increase effectiveness.

Between the two world wars the 'super-destroyer' appeared, first in Italy and then in Japan. These were extra-large destroyers with heavier armament, the idea being to increase their offensive power by curing the inherent problem of seakeeping. Small, slim craft-like destroyers were unable to maintain top speed in rough weather, and it was quite normal for a 36-knot destroyer to be capable of no more than 30 at sea. The Japanese started a series of very powerful destroyers, the *Fubuki* type, as part of a general policy of seeking maximum offensive power in each category, but too much was attempted on a limited displacement, and modifications had to be made to the vessels to improve stability. However, the 24in 'Long Lance' oxygen-driven torpedo developed for these ships gave them a big margin of superiority in surface action.

USS *Tabberer* (DE-418) comes alongside a carrier.

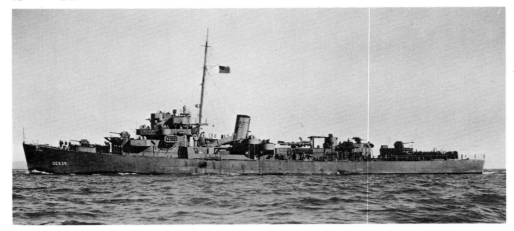

*Above:* USS *England* (DE-635) off Mare Island.
*Right:* USS *Martin Ray* (DE-338) in the Atlantic.
*Below:* Ex-US destroyer HMS *Normandy* with other British destroyers astern in the Atlantic.

The most spectacular of the super-destroyers were the French *contre-torpilleurs*, of which the finest examples were the *Fantasque* class. These destroyers were nearer to light cruisers in size, and were capable of 37 knots (on trials they reached 42–45 knots), making them the fastest warships afloat. Their range was far less than most destroyers, and their main purpose was to counter the very fast Italian cruisers. A German bid to bridge the gap by building destroyers with 5.9in (15cm) guns proved over-ambitious, and the ships were badly overloaded. Probably the best-all-round destroyer design of World War II was the US Navy's *Fletcher* Class, which remained the standard type until near the end of the war.

Destroyers played a vital role in World War II, and on many occasions were instrumental in warding off powerful surface attacks and slowing down enemy capital ships. Japanese destroyers proved tough opponents in the night-fighting around Guadalcanal in 1942, and US destroyers fought an heroic action against Japanese battleships and cruisers at Cape Engano in 1944. Similarly British destroyers added to an already full list of battle honors with such feats as the sinking of the *Scharnhorst* and the Second Battle of Sirte.

As the war progressed the destroyer's role changed, and surface torpedo-attack gave way to fleet defense as the main function. By 1945 destroyers' armament emphasized air-defense and anti-submarine warfare to a much greater

extent. In 1938 the British started building a new category, the fast escort or escort destroyer, known as the 'Hunt' Class, they were reduced versions of the standard or 'fleet' destroyer, with less speed and torpedo-armament but better anti-aircraft and anti-submarine weaponry. They were followed by the US Navy's destroyer escort or DE designs of 1941–42 which bore a similar relationship to contemporary fleet destroyers of the *Fletcher* Class.

---

### Deutschland

The prototype of the *panzerschiff* or 'pocket battleship', was ordered under the 1929 Program for the *Reichsmarine* of the Weimar Republic. Germany was limited by the Treaty of Versailles only to building replacements for her six pre-

dreadnought coast defense battleships, and they were to displace only 10,000 tons and have guns no larger than 11in (28cm) caliber.

Although this particular part of the Versailles Treaty's restrictions was no more onerous than others, the German Navy was determined to use all its technical resources to show that it could build ships to operate on the oceans. While this was not forbidden, the framers of the Washington Treaty had labored hard to ensure that no warship-type in between the 35,000-ton battleship and the 10,000-ton heavy cruiser with eight-inch guns could be built. But this was exactly what the German Navy did, without violating the conditions of either Treaty. The new ship had a nominal displacement of only 10,000 tons, had the 11in guns appropriate to a coast-defense ship, and her diesels gave her massive endurance and a good turn of speed, sufficient to make her a potent commerce-raider. She was faster than contemporary battleships but carried guns which could drive off any cruiser afloat – in short she could outfight any opponent fast enough to catch her, apart from eight British and Japanese battlecruisers built during World War I.

There was an immediate uproar when the new ship appeared. The world press immediately dubbed her a 'pocket battleship' although the German term for her was merely 'armored ship'. Examination of the design stopped there, but there was much more to the *Deutschland* than met the eye. For a start, her real standard displacement was 11,700 tons – a margin which allowed her designers some latitude. On the other hand, it did not permit more than a modest scale of armor protection, a 3·25in belt and a 3·75in deck, which was no better than the best heavy cruisers in other navies. Her speed was only 26 knots, enough to outrun contemporary battleships but nowhere near enough to outrun cruisers. Finally, her armament of two triple 11in turrets, although impressive, was ludicrously heavy for a mere commerce-raider, and not capable of rapid fire against a fast-moving target.

Although the Reichsmarine claimed the right to build five more *panzerschiffe*, only two more, the *Admiral Graf Spee* and *Admiral Scheer* were built. The diesels proved disappointing in service, and as battleship speeds soon rose to 28–30 knots the rationale of the design disappeared. As the Battle of the River Plate showed, the *panzershiff* was no match for well-handled cruisers, being too slow and having no means of coping with more than one opponent.

In February 1940 Adolf Hitler decided that the loss of a ship called after Germany could be a bad omen, and so she took the name of *Lützow*. She had been at sea with the *Admiral Graf Spee* before the outbreak of war and sank two ships. Her machinery was giving trouble and so

The pocket battleship *Deutschland (Lützow)*.

she returned to Germany for repairs in November 1939. She took part in the Norwegian campaign in 1940, and was later stationed in Northern Norway to threaten Allied convoys to Russia. On 31 December 1942 she and the *Admiral Hipper* fought an abortive action against a convoy defended by eight destroyers – the feeble performance of the *Lützow* and *Hipper* in the Battle of the Barents Sea drove Hitler to threaten to disband the Navy. This led to the resignation of Grand-Admiral Raeder and his replacement by Admiral Dönitz, but the heavy ships were later reprieved. The *Lützow* was sent to the Baltic for training duty but later supported the Army against the Russians in the Eastern Baltic. On 16 April 1945 she was badly damaged by bombs at Swinemünde and on 4 May she was blown up and scuttled. The hulk was salvaged in 1947 by the Russians and towed to Kaliningrad (Königsberg). She was beyond repair and was scrapped at Leningrad.

### Devastator, Douglas TBD

This US carrier-based torpedo-bomber was operational from 1937 to 1942. Like the British Fairey Battle, the Devastator was a good mid-thirties aircraft which remained operational too long. Powered by an 850hp Pratt & Whitney R–1830 engine, it carried a crew of three, a 1000lb bomb or torpedo under its fuselage, and two 0.3in guns, and was the US Navy's first carrier-based monoplane. Of the 129 TBD–1s built, about 100 were still available for action from February 1942. Over the Marshall and Gilbert Islands, against little opposition, they were able to make effective attacks on Japanese targets and even sank an enemy cruiser. The end came at the Battle of Midway, when Devastators became trapped between anti-aircraft fire from the ships and waiting Zeros. One complete squadron was wiped out, another so severely mauled that the TBD was relegated to training duties.

### Dewoitine D.520

This French single-seat fighter was in service from 1940 to 1945. Designed at the SNCA du Midi, one of the newly nationalized groups into which the French industry was divided just before World War II, the D.520 is generally reckoned the best fighter the Armée de l'Air possessed in 1940. Like most of the French program for combat aircraft it was late in development. Though the first prototype flew on 2 October 1938, not one D.520 got into service until 1940, though by this time SNCA du Midi's factory at Toulouse was building three a day, and before France collapsed on 25 June 1940 the output had been pushed up to ten a day.

A trim and quite small fighter, the D.520 was powered by a 910hp Hispano-Suiza 12Y–45 liquid-cooled engine, driving a Ratier electrically controlled propeller. Every production D.520 had an armament of one 20mm Hispano 404 cannon firing through the propeller hub, with a drum of 60 rounds, and four 7.5mm MAC 1934 machine guns in the wings just outboard of the landing gear. With a speed of 329mph and good maneuverability the D.520 was the only French fighter that could take on the Bf 109E on equal terms – though it was still slightly slower, and lacked the German's direct-injection engine, which allowed the Messerschmitt to do negative-g maneuvers, such as

Dewoitine French fighter.

sudden dives, without the engine cutting. From January to May 1940 only one unit, Groupe de Chasse I/3, had the new fighter, but by 25 June it had been supplied to GC II/3, III/3, III/6 and II/7. Though the pilots were not used to the Dewoitine, they scored a confirmed 114 kills and 39 'probables'.

Just before France surrendered all five D.520 units flew their surviving aircraft south across France to North Africa. The Vichy French used the D.520 as their standard fighter, operating them against the RAF over Gibraltar and in the Middle East. When Germany occupied all of France in November 1942 these formidable fighters were taken over and supplied to the Luftwaffe, Regia Aeronautica and the air forces of Bulgaria and Rumania, which used them on the Eastern Front. Altogether 610 were built.

### *Dido*

The *Dido* was the first of a class of British anti-aircraft cruisers ordered in 1937 to defend the fleet against air attack. To achieve this a new type of 5.25in dual-purpose surface/anti-aircraft twin gun-mounting was designed, disposed in an unusual way, with three superimposed positions forward and two aft. Although the gun-mounting proved something of a disappointment, as it fired a shell too large for rapid loading but not heavy enough for surface action, the class rendered good service, particularly in the Mediterranean. The *Dido* and the *Phoebe* entered service in September 1940 but wartime steel shortages meant that the last of the 16 ships built were not completed until January 1944. The *Naiad, Bonaventure* and *Hermione* were torpedoed by submarines in the Mediterranean, while the *Charybdis* was sunk in an action with German torpedo boats in the Channel in October 1943.

### 'Dinah'
see Mitsubishi Ki-46

### Dieppe Raid, 1942

Reasoned British opposition to American hopes of opening a Second Front on the continent of Europe in 1942 called into question their actual willingness to make the attempt. As a token of good faith, and also as an experiment in landing technique, Churchill decided to risk a major raid on the French coast with the aim of seizing and briefly holding a sizeable port. That chosen was Dieppe, on which a force of 5000 Canadians, 1000 British and 50 American Rangers descended on 19 August 1942. German air and sea attacks on the convoy and rapid reaction

ashore to the landing made it a disaster. Of the 5000 troops who got ashore, half were killed or captured. The conclusion which the general staffs drew from the episode was that they could not hope to capture port facilities in the opening stages of a continental invasion and would have to develop other means of supplying themselves over open beaches.

### Dietrich, SS Colonel General Josep, 1892–1976

Sepp Dietrich had been Hitler's SS bodyguard in 1928 and was close to Hitler throughout the war. He helped build up the Waffen SS and was eventually given command of an Army Group in Hungary in December 1944. He surrendered to the US at the end of the war but he was handed over to the Russians.

Sepp Dietrich (right) enjoys morning coffee on the terrace.

### Dill, Field Marshal Sir John Greer, 1881–1944

One of the intellectual leading lights of the British Army before the war when he served as both Director of Military Operations and Commandant of the Staff College, he was not made, as expected, Chief of the Imperial General Staff at the outbreak of war but appointed to command 1st Corps in France. After the retreat he did succeed Ironside as CIGS but the powers of rationality which had impressed the prewar army struck Churchill as evidence of over-caution. In December 1941 therefore he was replaced by Alan Brooke and sent as head of the military mission to Washington, where he had an immense diplomatic and personal success. In testimony of their affection for him, the Americans arranged for him to be buried, after his lamented death in harness, in Arlington National Cemetery.

### Dniepr, Battle of the, August–December 1943

After the battle of Kursk, General Vatutin, on the Voronezh Front attacked the junction between the Fourth Panzer Army and Army Detachment under Kempf which was west of Belgorod. Russian armor fanned out and on 8 August there was a thirty mile gap between the two commands. In the next week Russian pressure on Kharkov intensified. Field Marshal

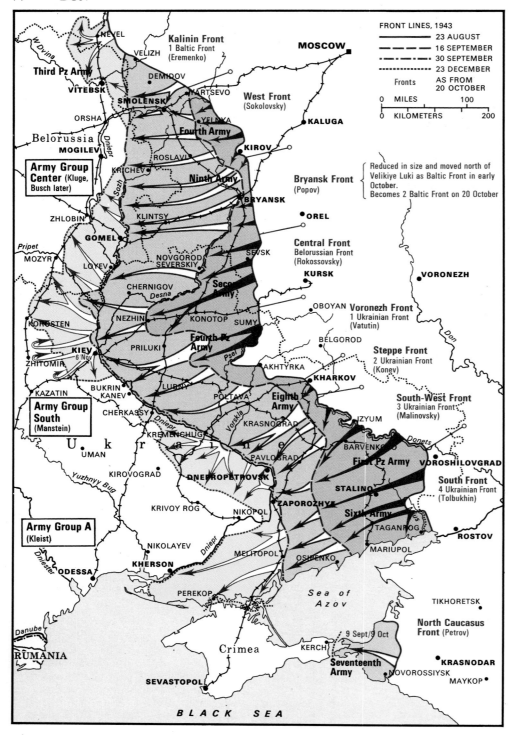

FRONT LINES, 1943
23 AUGUST
16 SEPTEMBER
30 SEPTEMBER
23 DECEMBER
Fronts AS FROM
20 OCTOBER

0    MILES    100
0    KILOMETERS    200

Reduced in size and moved north of Velikiye Luki as Baltic Front in early October.
Becomes 2 Baltic Front on 20 October

been able to make such a spectacular sweep because they were receiving US equipment. Their supply situation was still precarious since they relied on taking the food and fuel the retreating Germans left behind.

## Donets, Battle of the, February 1943

In February 1943 the Russian armies were menacing Field Marshal Manstein's left wing in Kharkov. The Russians had control over a 50 mile stretch of the Donets and had penetrated as far as Krasnoarmeiskoye and Debaltsevo. On 15 February the SS Panzer Division withdrew in a panic from Kharkov, against orders. Hitler visited the front and demanded that Kharkov be recaptured. On 21 February General Hoth attacked north of Kharkov. He faced General Popov and was greatly helped by the Tiger tanks which had 88mm guns, the only effective artillery against the T-34s. Within a week a German pincer had surrounded the Russian troops, but the Germans did not have the infantry support needed to contain the Russians and many escaped. The Germans claimed to have taken 9000 men, 615 tanks and 354 guns. By the first week of March the Germans reached the Donets but they could advance no further as the spring thaw rendered the ground impassable.

**Dönitz, Grand Admiral, Karl, 1891–1980**

An officer of the Imperial Navy, into which he had been commissioned in 1910, Dönitz was appointed head of the U-Boat service by Hitler in 1939, which he directed until January 1943. These were the 'good years' for the U-Boat crews, before the British and Americans had closed the 'air gap' in the central Atlantic and begun to win the battle of the convoys. It was fortunate, therefore, that he was promoted, on the removal of Raeder, to command the German Navy at that particular moment. Despite the decline in German naval fortunes over which he had to preside, he did not lose Hitler's confidence, perhaps because the Navy avoided both the treachery displayed by some of the leaders of the Army and the naked incompetence of the Reich Marshal of the Luftwaffe. As a result he was named in Hitler's political testament his successor as head of state, a post he assumed on 30 April 1945. He negotiated the surrender of the German Forces in the west with the Western Allies and was made prisoner at Flensburg, last seat of government of the Third Reich in May. Arraigned as a war criminal at Nuremberg, he was sentenced to ten years imprisonment for war crimes.

Manstein ordered Kempf to evacuate Kharkov on 22 August, despite Hitler's express orders to stand fast. Hitler reacted to this setback by dismissing Kempf for disobeying orders. In the second half of August the Russian offensive was extended: General Popov (Bryansk Front) had orders to advance from Orel to Bryansk, General Yeremenko (Kalinin Front) had orders to push for Smolensk, and Generals Rokossovsky (Central Front) and Vatutin (Voronezh Front) were heading for the Dniepr. Under this pressure, Hitler finally allowed Manstein to withdraw to the Dniepr after being asked seven times to give permission. This meant that Manstein now had a Front of 450 miles covered by 37 infantry and 17 Panzer divisions, and all his units were under strength. In the far south General Tolbukhin crossed the Mius and took Taganrog in early September. General Malinovsky (Southwest Front) struck south across

the Donets to Stalino and the Germans made a hasty retreat. On 25 September the Germans abandoned Smolensk to avoid encirclement. By the end of September the Russians had reached the banks of the Dniepr from Smolensk to Zaporozhye. In November the Germans faced a double threat: one to Kiev and another an eruption on the lower Dniepr below Kremenchug. General Konev broke out of this bridgehead and drove southwards but German reserves stopped him at Krivoi Rog. In the first week of November Vatutin launched a flanking offensive against Kiev and took the city (6 November) but the German divisions escaped. Hitler now dismissed General Hoth. Vatutin advanced west of Kiev but a German counteroffensive recaptured Zhitomir. Vatutin received reinforcements and stopped the German advance. The Russians then prepared the offensive on the Ukraine. The Russians had

## Donovan, General William, 1883–1959

Donovan was a US lawyer and Director of the OSS for most of the war. In 1940 Roosevelt sent him on a special mission to Europe during which he visited many of the uncommitted countries and tried to persuade them not to join Germany. He came back to the USA and talked of the necessity of helping Great Britain fight Germany. In July 1941 Donovan was made Co-ordinator of Information and one of his tasks was to observe resistance movements. In June 1942 President Roosevelt created the OSS by executive order and Donovan was made Director. The Office of Strategic Services was a military agency responsible to the Joint Chiefs of Staff and had units throughout the world. Donovan sent secret agents to help resistance movements everywhere but especially in France, Italy and Burma.

---

## Doolittle, Commander James Harold, 1896–

Doolittle left the Air Corps of the US Army in 1930, but on his return in 1940 was promoted to Major and worked at converting the motor car industry to aircraft production. In 1942 he was chosen to lead the spectacular raid on Tokyo. The mission was near suicidal, for it required the launching of B-25 land bombers from aircraft carriers and their landing, if at all possible, on airfields in China. The direct military impact of the raid was small but the strategic consequences were far-reaching, for the Japanese Navy's sense of shame at having allowed enemy forces near enough to the homeland to launch an attack on the imperial capital, and therefore the person of the emperor, prompted it in April 1942 to seek settlement with the US Navy. In the naval actions which followed, Coral Sea and Midway, the air striking force of the Imperial Navy was so badly damaged that it never again faced the Americans on equal terms. For his part in the raid Doolittle was awarded the Medal of Honor.

Late in 1942 he took command of the US 12th Air Force which had been created for Operation Torch and in 1943, he became Commander of the Northwest African Strategic Air Force, a part of the Mediterranean Air Command.

In 1944 Doolittle was promoted to Lieutenant General and created an Honorary KCB by King George VI. He commanded the US 8th Air Force, a strategic force whose operations included the bombing of the flying-bomb bases prior to D-Day. During the closing months of the war he transferred to the Pacific theater where he directed the 8th Air Force with equal success against the Japanese.

A skillful tactician, his aggressive and expansive nature won the loyalty of his men.

General Doolittle (bowed head) prays for flyers.

Air-to-air view of Dornier bomber formation.

## Dornier Do 17

This German three/four-seat medium bomber was in service from 1937 to 1943. When it was new this popular bomber was thought so slender it was called 'The Flying Pencil', though later versions were fatter. Originally designed as a six-passenger high-speed transport, the Do 17 was turned into a bomber – the reverse of what usually happened in the 1930s, when new bombers were disguised as airliners. One example demonstrated at a great air meeting in Zurich in 1937 startled the crowds by outpacing the best fighters, but in fact the production Do 17E, with a 1100lb bomb load, and the Do 17F, carrying only cameras, were much slower, with maximum speed around 220mph on two 750hp BMW VI engines. The last of the slender models were the Do 17M and N, both with 1000hp radial engines, and the similar Do 17P for reconnaissance and Do 17Kb exported to Yugoslavia. After Germany invaded the latter country two of the fine Dorniers flew to join the RAF in Egypt, bringing with them cargoes of gold bullion.

By 1940 the main Luftwaffe type was the Do 17Z, with 1000hp Bramo (BMW) Fafnir radial engines and a new front fuselage accommodating a crew of four with much more room and better defensive armament: six 7.92mm MG 15 machine guns, one fixed firing ahead, one aimed from the front (bomb-aimer's) windows, one aimed on each side, and one aimed above and below at the rear. By this time the bomb load had risen to 2205lb, and the speed was about 255mph at full throttle – accompanied by ample black smoke. Though rather smaller and lighter than the other Luftwaffe bombers the Do 17Z was liked by its crews, because it was extremely maneuverable, had no flight limitations (it could dive at full throttle) and had a reputation for getting home after being damaged in action. The Dorniers still took a mauling in the Battle of Britain and were withdrawn to the Russian front in the spring of 1941. By 1942 they were being withdrawn from bombing missions and used as glider tugs and for battlefield supply-dropping.

The Do 215 was a model with DB 601A

liquid-cooled engines built for export in small numbers but taken over by the Luftwaffe. About 100 were delivered as reconnaissance bombers, but by 1942 most of the 75 survivors had been rebuilt as some of the first German night fighters. They carried a 20mm MG FF cannon and four MG 17 machine guns in a 'solid' nose, and a few were fitted with infra-red or radar to help find enemy aircraft at night.

---

## Dornier Do 18

This German twin-engined flying-boat was used for coastal reconnaissance and later, in unarmed form, for air-sea rescue.

---

## Dornier Do 24

This three-engined flying-boat was used by the Luftwaffe almost entirely for air-sea rescue duties.

---

## Dornier Do 217

This German four-seat bomber and missile carrier and two/three-seat night fighter was in service from 1941 to 1945. First flown in August 1938, the Do 217 was an enlarged and more powerful Do 215 or Do 17Z, able to carry a very much greater bomb load. No less than 5550lb could be carried inside the fuselage and wing bomb cells of the first operational version, the Do 217E-1 of 1941, plus two 551lb bombs slung under the outer wings. Despite this great load the maximum speed was over 270mph on two 1580hp BMW 801A two-row radial engines, and when the bombs had been dropped the speed could reach 326mph. There were many E versions, some of the earliest having an unusual petal-type airbrake that folded out of the tail of the fuselage for steep dive bombing. Typical defensive armament comprised a 15mm MG 151/15 cannon and an MG 15 machine gun in the nose, two MG 15s in the side windows and two 13mm MG 131 heavy machine guns in the dorsal turret and rear ventral position. The elec-

The Dornier 217-E.

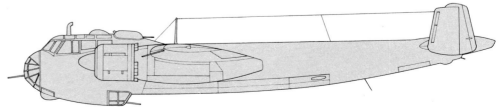

trically aimed dorsal turret was one of the first to go into service on a German aircraft. Another 'first' of the Do 217E–5 in late 1942 was that it was the first aircraft to launch guided missiles in action, carrying two Hs 293 radio-controlled glider bombs which sometimes scored devastating hits on Allied ships.

Most of the early E-series were rebuilt as Do 217J night fighters with radar and heavy forward-firing armament; many of these were passed to the Regia Aeronautica (Italian Air Force). The Do 217K had a bulbous all-glazed nose, and the K–2 had extended wings with span increased from 62 to over 81ft. Carrying FX radio-controlled bombs a small formation of K–2 bombers sank the Italian battleship *Roma* as it sailed to join the Allies and crippled other large Italian warships, in September 1943. The last model used in large numbers was the M, like a K but with 1750hp DB 603 liquid-cooled engines. A few N night fighters followed, and many Ms were also turned into Ns to help stem the tide of Allied bombers that were wrecking Germany. Only 1730 of these very capable aircraft were built, but nearly all of them saw a great deal of frontline action.

**Dornier Do 335 Pfeil**

This was one of the fastest piston-engined fighters ever built. Two 2100hp Daimler-Benz engines were installed uniquely, in nose and rear fuselage, driving conventional tractor and tail pusher propellers. Maximum speed was 474mph. The war ended before Do 335 could become operational.

___

### *Dorsetshire*

The *Dorsetshire* was a British heavy cruiser of the *Norfolk* or third 'County' Group. She fired two torpedoes into the starboard side of the battleship *Bismarck* during the final phase of the battle, and then fired a third into the port side. With the cruiser *Cornwall* she was sunk by Japanese carrier planes off the west coast of Ceylon on 5 April 1942.

___

### Douglas A–20/P–70 and F–3 Havoc and Boston

This US light bomber/night fighter and reconnaissance aircraft was operational between 1941–45. In 1936, Douglas' chief engineer Ed Heinemann believed that the USAAF would soon need a high-performance attack bomber. First to show interest were the French, who ordered an initial batch of 105 of a redesigned version of the original Heinemann prototype, as DB–7s. French contracts were taken over by the RAF after the defeat of France, and the RAF

A squadron of Douglas A-20s in formation over Tunisia during the final stages of the Desert War.

eventually received more than 1400 aircraft of the DB–7 series. First to become operational were 40 aircraft fitted with additional armor plating, airborne interception radar and an eight-gun nose, and named Havoc Is by the RAF. Havoc IIs had a 12-gun nose. Other variants were a three-seat intruder fighter which ventured out over France in 1941 in search of Luftwaffe aircraft; the LAM ('Pandora') which dropped small aerial mines in the path of enemy bombers, with no apparent success; and the Turbinlite, with radar to locate hostile night bombers and a searchlight in its nose to illuminate them for the benefit of accompanying fighters. From October 1941, the RAF began using DB–7s also for their intended role as light day bombers, with ships and targets close to the continental coastline as the main victims. These bombers, named Boston, provided close support for Allied armies in North Africa, Italy and France to the last day of the war against Hitler. Typical was the four-seat Boston III, with two 1600hp Wright Cyclone radial engines, speed of 304mph, bomb load of 2000lb and armament of four 0.303in guns, and two each in dorsal and ventral positions. Meanwhile the USAAF had been operating the DB–7 series as standard three-seat attack aircraft, designated A–20 and retaining the British name Havoc. Like the RAF aircraft, the USAAF versions operated with both glazed and 'solid' noses, the latter usually with six 0.5in nose guns, a twin-gun dorsal turret and underwing racks which doubled the bomb load to 4000lb. The USAAF aircraft flew in the Pacific, as well as in Europe and North Africa, specializing in low-altitude delivery of parachute-borne fragmentation bombs over Japanese positions in the Pacific islands. Also used by the USAAF were camera-carrying F–3s and P–70 night fighters with British radar. About 3125 Havocs of all types were sent to Russia. Production of all models totaled 7385.

___

### Douglas A–26

The XA–26 prototype of this three-seat light attack bomber flew on 10 July 1942. The first version ordered into production for the USAAF was the A–26B, with two 2000hp Pratt & Whitney R–2800 engines, armament of six

'point fives' in the nose and four more in the remotely controlled dorsal and ventral turrets. Up to 4000lb of bombs could be carried internally, with provision for carrying half this load, eight 5in rockets and two fuel tanks, or 16 rockets, under the wings. Altogether 1355 A–26Bs were built, their maximum speed of 355mph making them among the fastest bombers used by the USAAF in World War II. They flew their first operations with the 9th Air Force in Europe on 19 November 1944. Other A–26Bs, together with A–26Cs, operated in the Pacific. The 'C' had a transparent 'bombardier' nose and only two forward guns instead of six; 1091 were built. Both versions remained in service long after VJ-Day.

___

### Douglas, Air Marshal Sir W Sholto, 1893–

Douglas was a British Air Marshal who at the beginning of the war was Assistant Chief of the Air Staff, becoming Deputy Chief in 1940. In November 1940, with the Battle of Britain past its climax, he succeeded Dowding as head of RAF Fighter Command and immediately changed the emphasis of the Command's operations from defense to attack. He carried the daylight fighter battle over the Channel to France, with the major aim of forcing Germany to maintain strong defenses in the west, thereby diverting its strength from other theaters.

In January 1943 Sholto Douglas became Commander of the RAF Middle East Command and, a year later, Commander of RAF Coastal Command. With D-Day preparations gaining momentum, he described the role of his Command as putting the cork in the bottle ie, ensuring that the Channel was kept free of enemy interference particularly from German U-Boats. With the ending of the war he took command of the British Air Forces of Occupation in Germany.

___

### Dowding, Air Marshal Hugh Caswell Tremenheere, 1882–1970

An artillery officer by training, Dowding transferred to the Royal Flying Corps during World War I. Between 1930 and 1936 he was a research and development member of the Air Council, the governing body of the Royal Air Force. Here, he oversaw the development of the Spitfire and Hurricane interceptors and the

Hugh 'Stuffy' Dowding.

early experimentation with radar. He was appointed head of Fighter Command in 1936 and as such directed the Spitfire and Hurricane squadrons in the Battle of Britain, July-October 1940. His careful husbandry of his aircraft and perfect understanding of the air defense system, which he had largely created, rightly made him the 'victor' of the battle. But he was a lonely and uncharismatic figure (nicknamed 'Stuffy') and was not promoted after 1940. He retired in 1942.

## Dracula
see Rangoon, Capture of

## Dresden, Bombing of
see Strategic Bombing Offensive in Germany

## *Duke of York*

The third unit of the British *King George V* Class battleships, she joined the Home Fleet in November 1941. In December 1941 she carried the British Prime Minister, Winston Churchill, to Annapolis for a conference with President Franklin D Roosevelt. After a short spell as flagship of the Home Fleet in 1942 she was sent to the Mediterranean to join Force H as flagship for the Torch landings, but in May 1943 she was once again flagship of the Home Fleet.

On 26 December 1943 she engaged the German battlecruiser *Scharnhorst* during the Battle of North Cape, and hit her several times, causing serious damage. She herself was hit twice but the shells passed through the legs of her tripod masts. This was the first battle fought entirely by radar plotting and also the last capital ship action fought in European waters. She was on her way out to join the British Pacific Fleet, but was at Manus Island when the Japanese surrendered on 15 August; she was present, however, as the British flagship in Tokyo Bay for the formal signing of the surrender on 2 September 1945.

## Dulles, Allen, 1893–1969

Dulles was an American lawyer and head of the OSS in Switzerland. He was the President's special representative engaged in secret discussions with envoys from Himmler and Schellenberg about possible peace terms. He was also involved in Operation Sunrise which led to the surrender of German troops in northern Italy.

Dulles held negotiations with Karl Wolff, Head of the SS in Italy, who was in charge of the area behind the front and signed an agreement to surrender at the end of April 1945.

## Dumbarton Oaks Conference, 22 August – 28 September 1944

This conference was called to implement the Teheran Declaration's call for a world security organization. The only two issues not settled prior to the conference were Russia's demands for (1) separate representations for each of its sixteen Soviet Republics; and (2) the right of veto for the Great Powers, even in disputes to which they are a party (decided at Yalta Conference on right of veto except when an interested party). Nor were they settled at this conference. The Allies issued a declaration that their failure to reach agreement did not affect their solidarity regarding war with Germany.

## *Dunkerque*

The first of a class of two battlecruisers ordered by the French Navy as a reply to the German *Deutschland* Class *panzerschiffe*, the *Dunkerque* was built under the 1931 Program. Although too lightly armored to be regarded as a worthy opponent for a modern battleship, she was more than a match for the *Deutschland*, even if an expensive solution to the problem.

With her sister *Strasbourg* she was lying at Mers-el-Kebir in North Africa on 3 July 1940, when the British squadron under Admiral Somerville arrived to demand the immediate disarmament of the French ships. When negotiations broke down the British opened fire, and the *Dunkerque* was hit by four 15in shells while still trying to let go her mooring lines. She was quickly immobilized, although she managed to fire several salvos at HMS *Hood*. Then the patrol boat *Terre Neuve* blew up alongside on 6 July and caused severe damage to her hull; these two engagements cost 150 dead and 1147 wounded.

The *Dunkerque* was refloated and sailed back to Toulon in February 1942. On 27 November 1942 she was scuttled when German troops tried to seize the French Fleet. The hull was later scrapped.

## Dunkirk, Retreat to and Evacuation from, 1940

The strategy of the Allied Supreme Council placed the British Expeditionary Force in cen-

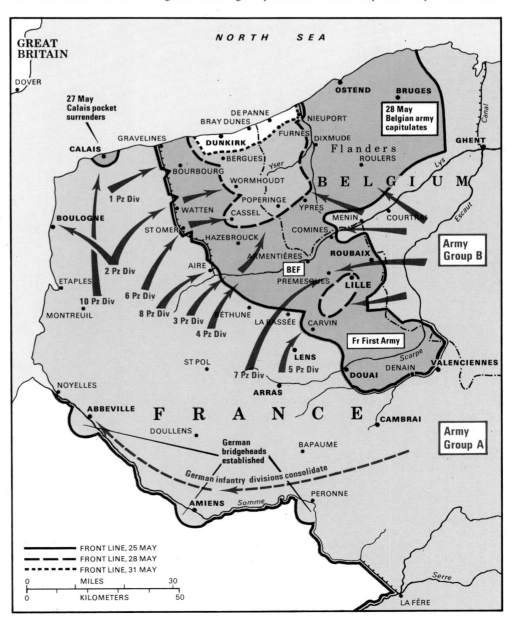

General Wavell, Supreme Commander of ABDA, with Brooke-Popham in Singapore, 1941.

tral Belgium in response to the German invasion of that country. The rapid German advance from 10–16 May obliged Gort, the British commander, to retreat from the line of the Dyle to that of the Scheldt, but before he had taken up his new position, Guderian's crossings of the Meuse had cut his line of communications with his base at Cherbourg. On 19 May the Cabinet heard that he was contemplating a withdrawal towards Dunkirk and ordered him to force his way through the German 'Panzer Corridor' to regain the French Armies south of it. He attempted such a breakthrough at Arras on 21 May but failed. His supplies and munitions had begun to dwindle and pressure on his front and flanks to increase, while the Belgians were evidently on the point of collapse. On 25 May, therefore, he boldly decided to fall back on Dunkirk and call for evacuation, organizing meanwhile the 'canal line' along the Aa, the Scarpe, and the Yser as a final position. Admiral Ramsay commanding at Dover, had been ordered by Churchill on 20 May to collect small craft 'in readiness to proceed to ports and inlets on the French coast' and on 26 May Operation Dynamo, as the Dunkirk evacuation was to be known, began. In the following eight days, 848 British, Dutch, Belgian and French ships of all sizes from destroyers to private motor cruisers carried 338,226 men, two-thirds British, from the Dunkirk port and its adjoining beaches to English shores. The achievement, remarkable in result and heroic in execution, was nevertheless

very much Hitler's doing. By ordering a final push by Hoth's and Kleist's Panzer Groups, he most certainly could have broken the canal line and captured much of the BEF intact. On 24 May however, he visited Rundstedt at the headquarters of Army Group A to ask if he (Rundstedt) did not think it wiser to preserve the Panzer Groups for the coming battle on the 'Weygand Line.' Rundstedt agreed and Hitler therefore took up Goering's offer to 'finish' the Dunkirk bridgehead by air attack. Despite the heavy losses inflicted on British units and ships by the Luftwaffe, it failed to make good its Commander's offer, and probably could not have done so even had the evacuation been protracted for another week. This reprieve of the BEF was the first of Hitler's 'fatal decisions', much though it fed French and Belgian suspicions of British perfidy.

---

### Duster

This was the nickname for the US Army Gun Motor Carriage M19, mounting twin 40mm anti-aircraft guns. It was standardized in June 1944 and consisted of two 40mm Bofors guns in a special open-topped turret on a chassis derived from the Light Tank M24. With a six-man crew and 336 rounds of ammunition it weighed 38,500lbs, and could travel at 35mph. It was extremely useful for the protection of mobile columns, and was also found to be a valuable assault gun, moving into the attack while simultaneously firing its guns at a total rate of 240 rounds a minute.

### Dutch East Indies, Fall of the, 1942

The Dutch East Indies was Japan's main objective since it could provide all the oil needed by Japan to continue fighting the war. The Japanese had conceived a three-pronged invasion. In the south the Japanese would invade Southern Sumatra, Western Java and North Borneo; the center prong would attack East Borneo and then Java; in the east the Japanese would attack the Celebes and then Eastern Java.

By the end of 1941 the Japanese had captured Davao in Mindanao, which was to be the springboard for the attacks on the Celebes and Borneo. They also held Jolo, between Mindanao and North Borneo, and Kuching in Sarawak. The Japanese transports landed off Tarakan on 11 January and although they lost two minesweepers, they overcame the garrison. In the Celebes the Japanese landed at Manado and Kema and by 12 January had captured the northern part of the island.

General Wavell, Supreme Commander of ABDA, realized that the Dutch East Indies could only be defended by naval and air power. All his ships had to be used to protect convoys and this left only three cruisers, twelve destroyers and submarines to be used against Japanese convoys. Wavell had considerable numbers under his command, some 98,000 troops in the Dutch East Indies, but without air cover he felt it was better to concentrate on defending the line of bases from Singapore to Darwin. On 23 January the Japanese landed at Balikpapan and demanded that the oil installations be handed over intact. They took the town but two US cruisers and four destroyers arrived and managed to sink three transports. In West Borneo the Japanese landed at Pemangkat on 27 January and joined up with troops from Kuching and began to overrun the western part of Borneo. In the Celebes the Japanese seized the Kendari airfield, which meant they could now strike at Java with their bombers.

Their next target was the island of Amboina, which was garrisoned by 2600 troops. On 30 January a Japanese infantry regiment and naval landing party arrived off the island. The Dutch troops surrendered 24 hours after the Japanese disembarked. On 4 February the Japanese had overcome Australian resistance and had control of the island and airfield, which meant that they had two air bases for an attack on Timor, which would breach Wavell's line of bases. On 3 and 5 February, the Japanese made air strikes against Java from Kendari. In South Borneo Japanese troops captured Bandjermasin, and took Makassar in South Celebes on 9 February. Rear Admiral Doorman had had orders to intercept these convoys but arrived too late to prevent the landings.

At this point the Western Force under Admiral Ozawa with six cruisers, one light aircraft carrier and three destroyers was heading for Sumatra. Allied bombers attacked this force but only hit one ship. Japanese transports carried paratroops to Palembang on 14 and 16 February. On 15 and 16 February the British and Dutch withdrew from Palembang to Java: within a few days the Sumatran bases had fallen. On 19 and 20 February the Japanese landed at Bali and Timor, so the British reinforcements being shipped there were sent back to Darwin. Doorman again failed to stop the invasion force in the battle of Lombok Strait. Wavell's command was dissolved, at his request since Borneo had fallen, and Lieutenant General ter Poorten became commander of all land forces in the

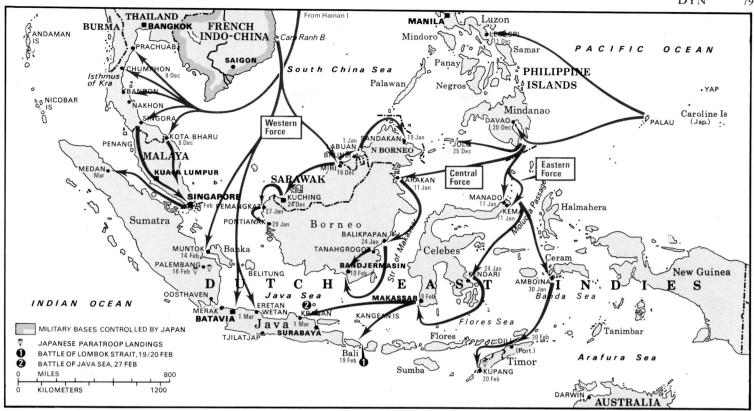

Japanese soldiers sing a hymn to the sea in celebration of their triumph in the Dutch East Indies.

Dutch East Indies and Vice-Admiral Helfrich became commander of all naval forces. On 24 February a large fleet of Japanese transports was seen south of the Makassar straits. The next day Japanese destroyers set down a landing party on Bawean Island near Surabaya and all Allied shipping was sent to Java. The Combined Striking Force was destroyed in the Battle of Java Sea. On 1 March the convoy which Door-man had failed to find, cast anchor on the north coast of Java at Kragan. The Dutch did not offer much resistance and late on 7 March the Forty-eighth Division was outside Surabaya. In western Java the Japanese force landed at Fret-anwetan and Merak on 1 March. Again the Dutch did not resist, but Hurricane fighters dam-aged at least six landing craft. The Japanese split into two columns. The first headed for Batavia, but was held up. The second was heading for Bandung, but the Dutch resisted with the aid of an Australian unit known as Blackforce (com-manded by Brigadier Blackburn). On 4 March ter Poorten decided to withdraw to Bandung, using Blackforce to cover the retreat. Black-force delayed the Japanese second column for four days suffering 150 casualties. On 5 March ter Poorten informed Major General Sitwell, the British Commanding Officer, that the Dutch could not hold Bandung but would continue to fight a guerrilla campaign. On 8 March ter Poorten issued a proclamation that organ-ized resistance in the Dutch East Indies was at an end and Sitwell decided to order the British, Australian and American units to cease fire.

**Dynamo**
see Dunkirk, Retreat to and Evacuation from

## Eagle

This British aircraft carrier was laid down in 1913 as the Chilean battleship *Almirante Cochrane* and taken over while still on the building slip in February 1918. She was renamed HMS *Eagle* when launched on 8 June 1918, and she was converted to the Royal Navy's first fleet carrier, capable of operating with the cruisers of the Grand Fleet.

Although numerous delays and the unexpected collapse of Germany prevented the *Eagle* from being tested in war service the delay in completion allowed a number of improvements to be incorporated into her design. When she finally entered full operational service in 1923 she was the first British carrier with an 'island' superstructure and had many other new features. When war broke out in 1939 she was too slow for frontline operations, and she had been sent to the China Station. In September 1939 she was refitted at Singapore and covered troop convoys from Australia to North Africa, but joined the Mediterranean Fleet in May 1940 to counter Italian intentions.

Despite her age the *Eagle* played an active part in the war in the Mediterranean, being present at the Battle of Calabria in July 1940. Although damage to her avgas system prevented her from joining in the torpedo-attack on the Italian Fleet at Taranto in November 1940, five Swordfish torpedo-bombers and eight crews were transferred to the *Illustrious* to strengthen the attack.

After a spell in the south Atlantic hunting for raiders the *Eagle* joined Force H in January 1942. She ferried Spitfires to Malta nine times between March and July 1942, and a total of 183 fighter-planes reached the beleaguered island safely. In one of these operations she was joined by the USS *Wasp*, which had been specially lent to the RN by the USN. In June the *Eagle* escorted a convoy to Malta safely, but on 11 August her luck ran out during the massive convoy battle known as Operation Pedestal. The carrier was hit by four torpedoes fired by *U.73*, and quickly took a list to port. Four minutes later she rolled over and sank, taking 160 officers and men out of a total of 953 on board.

## Eaker, Lieutenant General Ira C, 1898–

US Commander of Strategic Air Forces in Europe and an outstanding pilot, Eaker was a firm advocate of strategic bombing as a war-winning stratagem. On 17 August 1942 he led the first US bombing raid in western Europe against marshaling yards outside Rouen, with a force of 12 B–17 Flying Fortresses. As Commander of the US 8th Air Force he strove to prove the ability of heavily armed Fortresses to penetrate Germany in daylight, and without fighter escort, to precision-bomb targets. The Casablanca Conference of January 1943 was to sanction this form of strategic offensive together with the night-time area attacks of RAF Bomber Command, the two constituting the Combined Bomber Offensive. Eaker was promoted Lieutenant General in June 1943. In 1944 he succeeded Tedder as Commander in Chief of Mediterranean Air Command; based in Italy, he continued the strategic air offensive against Germany and the Balkans. In August 1944 he took command of the Allied air forces for the invasion of southern France and, despite unfavorable weather, led his units in an assault on German communications and supplies which was to contribute greatly to the success of the Allied ground operations.

## East Africa, British and Italian Campaign in, 1940–41

The Italians who had colonized Eritrea at the end of the nineteenth century and annexed the Empire of Ethiopia in 1935–36, embarked on the invasion of neighboring British Somaliland on 4 August 1940, two months after they had entered the war. The Duke of Aosta, a member of the Italian royal family, had 200,000 troops in Ethiopia and dispatched three armies into Somaliland. The British, who had only 1500 troops on the spot, took up positions at Tug Argan on the Hargeisa-Berbera road, but were outflanked and after a five-day battle, 11–16 August, withdrew, made their escape and embarked from Berbera on the night of 19 August. Mussolini hailed the occupation of British (and the undefended French) Somaliland as a great victory, and it did indeed impede the sea supply of the Middle East via the Red Sea.

The British, however, retained their base in the Sudan on Ethiopia's eastern border, and proceeded to reinforce their army there. In January 1940, under the command of General Alan Cunningham, it advanced in three columns, one into Eritrea and two towards Addis Ababa, the capital of Ethiopia. They were assisted by a fourth, from Kenya, which entered Italian Somaliland, and a seaborne force from Aden which landed at Berbera, British Somaliland, on 16 March. The Italian garrison in Eritrea was quickly driven back to the mountain stronghold of Keren which, after a siege of several weeks, surrendered on 27 March. In Ethiopia the garrison was also driven back into the mountains and the Duke of Aosta surrendered to the British on 16 May at Amba Alagi. Isolated detachments continued to hold out, the last surrendering at Gondar on 27 November. During the course of the campaign the Italian army lost about 290,000 soldiers, including those locally enlisted, almost all of whom became prisoners. The British forces, of which the majority were white South Africans (27,000) and black East Africans (33,000), lost only 1154 battle casualties on a strength of 77,000. The result of the campaign was a crushing humiliation for Mussolini, as well as a heavy diminution of his military strength. The fall of East Africa to the British secured the southern flank of Egypt. Had the Allies ignored this danger, Egypt would have been caught between the Italians and the Afrika Korps.

## Eastern Front, Chronological List of Events

Russo-Finnish War, 1939
Polish Campaign, 1939
Barbarossa, Operation, 1941
Ukraine, Battle of the, July–August 1941
Bialystok-Minsk, Battle of, June 1941
Smolensk, Battle of, July 1941
Roslavl, Battle of, August 1941
Vyazma-Bryansk, Battle of, October 1941
Rostov, Battle of, November 1941
Crimea, Battle of, October 1941 – May 1944
Leningrad, Battle and Siege of, September 1941 – January 1944
Kharkov, Battle of, 1942
Sevastopol, Battle of, May–June 1942
Voronezh, Battle of, June 1942
Caucasus, Battle of the, July 1942–February 1943
Stalingrad, Battle of, 1942–43
Kursk, Battle of, July 1943
Mius, Battle of the, 1943
Donets, Battle of the, February 1943
Dniepr, Battle of the, August–December 1943
Ukraine, Battle of the, December 1943–May 1944
Belorussia, Battle of, Operation Bagration, June 1944
Brody–Lvov, Battle of, July 1944
Poland, Liberation of, 1944–45
Warsaw Uprising, 1944
Jassy-Kishinev, Battle of, August 1944
Balkans, Liberation of the, 1944–45
Finland, Peace with, September 1944
East Prussia, Fall of, 1945
Königsberg, April 1945
Hungary, Liberation of, 1944–45
Czechoslovakia, Liberation of, 1944–45
Austria, Liberation of, 1945
East Germany, Liberation of, 1945
Berlin, Battle of, 1945

## Eastern Mediterranean War, Chronological List of Events

Greece, Italian Invasion of, 1940
Balkans, Campaign in the, 1941
Greece, Invasion of, 1941
Crete, Battle of, 1941
Iraq, Occupation of, 1941
Persia, Occupation of, 1941
Syria, British Occupation of, 1941
Greece, British Occupation of, 1944
Balkans, Liberation of the, 1944

## Eastern Solomons, Battle of, 1942

After the Battle of Savo Island, the Japanese decided to reinforce their men on Guadalcanal covered by the Combined Fleet South. The 1500 men were transported in old destroyers and escorted by Rear Admiral Tanaka's flagship *Jintsu*, supported by Vice-Admiral Mikawa's four cruisers. A Striking Force under Rear Admiral Abe was based on two carriers, *Zuikaku* and *Shokaku*. The tactical commander Vice-Admiral Kondo was in the Advance Force of six cruisers. The Japanese again used a sacrificial decoy, a small carrier *Ryujo* under Rear Admiral Hara. The Americans' air reconnaissance spotted the *Ryujo* and Admiral Fletcher's Task Force 61, the *Saratoga*, *Enterprise* and *Wasp* with the battleship *North Carolina*, nine cruisers and 17 destroyers moved to the approaches of Coral Sea. By 21 August the Americans were in position but they had lost sight of the Japanese. On 23 August planes reported Tanaka's troop convoy and Fletcher launched a strike which did not find the Japanese ships. Fletcher sent the *Wasp* to refuel, and on 24 August at 1000 the *Ryujo* was sighted 300 miles north. Fletcher launched his strike and sank the *Ryujo*. Meanwhile planes from *Shokaku* and *Zuikaku* attacked the US carriers, but fighter planes beat them off. The *Enterprise* was hit but the damage was controlled. Admiral Nagumo withdrew his carrier force and again the Japanese lost planes which could only be replaced with difficulty.

Tanaka's transports steamed on but on 25 August Marine dive bombers attacked his force and hit *Jintsu* and *Kinryu Maru* and after a further attack the Japanese ships withdrew. After this the Japanese only tried to reinforce Guadalcanal by night, using the convoys known as the 'Tokyo Express'.

---

### East Germany, Liberation of, 1945

The overwhelming offensive of January 1945 left the Red Army at the end of January on the Oder River at Küstrin less than 30 miles from Berlin. Hitler took the opportunity to launch a small counterattack on 14 February by the

Seventh SS Panzer Army. They advanced only three miles from the Oder along the Stargrad Railway and then had to retreat, but this led the Soviet High Command to overreact. The Russians now appeared to lose interest in taking Hitler's capital and paused to extend their flanks and clear up Pomerania and Silesia.

Marshal Rokossovsky's 2nd Belorussian Front aimed for the Baltic Coast east of Küstrin and split the Third Panzer Army and the Second Army. Neither Army had enough fuel, artillery or ammunition to stop him and on 1 March,

Russian artillery opens up on German positions in Silesia as the ring around Berlin tightened.

the 3rd Guard Tank Corps reached the Baltic Coast thus isolating Danzig and Gdynia (both supply depots). Zhukov's 1st Belorussian Front also reached the coast and besieged Kolberg which eventually fell on 18 March after all 80,000 inhabitants had been evacuated. On 22 March the 1st Belorussian Front, now under General Sokolovsky, erupted from a bridgehead flanking Küstrin. Two Panzer division

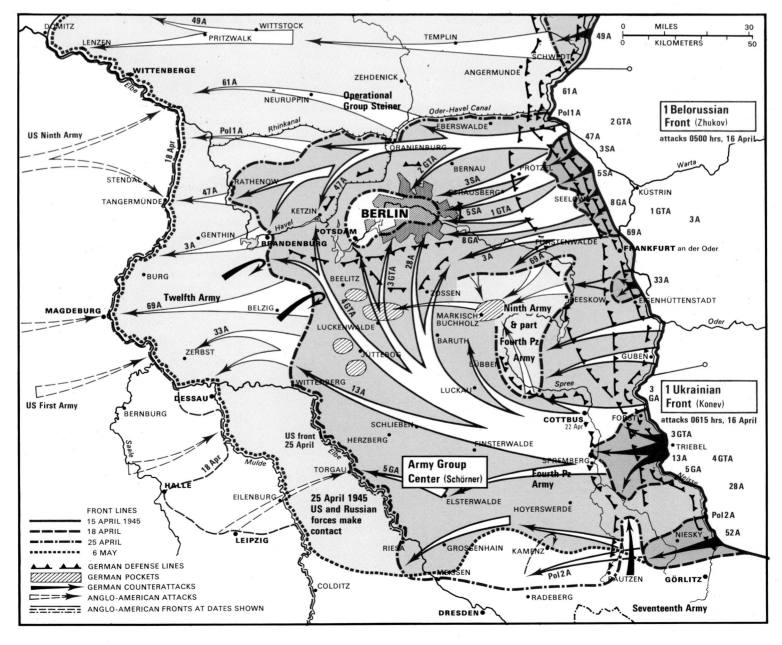

counterattacks failed and on 30 March Küstrin fell. Hitler put his Chief of Staff General Guderian on sick-leave. In the south General Konev's 1st Ukrainian Front attacked south of Grottkau and the 4th Ukrainian Front attacked Moravska Ostrava. Konev then cleared Silesia except for Breslau which fell on 7 May. In the first two weeks of April, Zhukov began to draw his forces back for an attack on Berlin.

On 16 April Zhukov's 1st Belorussian Front broke out of the Küstrin bridgehead and made for Berlin while Konev's Ukrainian Front crossed the Neisse. A few days later Rokossovsky crossed the Oder and took Stettin and then crossed northern Germany to meet Field Marshal Montgomery's 21st Army Group. In the south, Konev's troops pushed on to the Elbe River and met General Bradley's 12th Army Group at Torgau on 25 April. Soviet and Allied troops had divided Nazi Germany but it was not until 2 May that all fighting in Berlin stopped.

## East Prussia, Fall of, 1945

In summer 1944 General Chernyakhovsky pressed the Germans on the frontiers of their own land in East Prussia. His 3rd Belorussian Front drove across the Niemen and in three thrusts took Kaunas on 1 August and pressed the eastern border of East Prussia. The center thrust took Suwalki on 26 July and General Bagramyan occupied the Tukums junction on the Gulf of Riga. In September after peace with Finland, Generals Govorov and Maslenikov could advance against Schörner and within a week the Germans had fallen back on Riga. The German Army Group North was cut off in the Baltic States and further offensives in October were aimed at confining the Germans into an even smaller space. On 11 October Bagramyan's reinforced troops reached the Baltic coast to the north and south of Memel and two days later Schörner fell back on Courland. This left the Red Army free to attack East Prussia and it duly launched an offensive in mid-October. This culminated in a tank battle at Gumbinnen which was inconclusive and the offensive petered out.

After a lull, during which the Russians built up their supplies, the final offensive against Poland began on 12 January. Since a frontal attack against thick lines of defense was unlikely to succeed, General Rokossovsky's 1st Belorussian Front was ordered to cut off East Prussia by an outflanking maneuver. Rokossovsky had some 450 T-34s and a numerical superiority of three to one and so advanced rapidly through Poland. On 22 January 1945 Rokossovsky's force made contact with Marshal Zhukov's forces at Grudziadz and they wheeled north towards Danzig to cut off East Prussia. More than 500,000 Germans were caught in a pocket, but many were evacuated. On 10 February Rokossovsky reached the coast near Elbing and East Prussia was under siege from the south and east by the 3rd Belorussian Front. On 1 February Chernyakhovsky split the pocket by attacking between Elbing and Königsberg, Chernyakhovsky was killed in action and General Vasilievsky took over; he crushed a bridgehead at Braunsberg on 20 March and on 9 April Königsberg was stormed and surrendered. The German Navy succeeded in evacuating about one and a half million refugees, using every sort of ship. On 20 March Rokossovsky took Danzig and resistance in East Prussia died down.

## Eben Emael, Capture of Fort, 1940

Eben Emael was the most modern fortress in Belgium, constructed between 1931–35 and sited to guard the junction of the Albert Canal with the Meuse. These two waterlines offered the most important obstacle to an invasion of central Belgium from Germany and was the main feature of the 'delaying position' behind which the Belgian Army planned to organize its resistance. The capture of Eban Emael was therefore essential to the Germans if they were rapidly to overwhelm Belgian – and Allied – defense of the Flanders route into northern France. It could not be taken quickly by conventional assault and Hitler therefore decided, apparently on his own inspiration, to capture it by glider descent. A specially trained Storm Group of 78 engineers of Seventh Airborne Division, carried in ten gliders, was to crash-land around the fort and on its roof, blow holes through the steel and concrete with 'shaped' charges, and force the garrison, 1200 strong, to surrender. The operation went almost exactly as planned. Lieutenant Witzig kept the garrison entombed and helpless for 24 hours, 10–11 May, until the arrival of a ground spearhead of Fourth Panzer Division put the fort firmly in German hands. The attack was certainly the single most brilliant and fruitful airborne operation of the war.

## E-Boat
see Motor Torpedo Boat

## ECM Electronic Countermeasures
see Radar

### Eden, Anthony, 1897–1977

Eden was Foreign Minister in the British War Cabinet during the war. He had been Chamberlain's Foreign Minister from 1935–38 but had resigned over the Munich Agreement. He also disagreed with Britain's acceptance of Italian Intervention in Abyssinia and Spain. He returned to the government in 1939 and became Secretary of State for War and then Foreign Minister. He was extremely hard-working and enjoyed Churchill's full confidence. He attended all the major conferences during the war and backed up Churchill's policy towards Stalin.

## Egypt, Italian Invasion of and British Counteroffensive, 1940

The Italian Army in Libya under Marshal Graziani numbered about 250,000 and under the prompting of Mussolini, who wished to tie down the British before he attacked Greece from Albania, invaded Egypt on 13 September. The British, whose total strength in the Middle East was only 100,000 and who had only two divisions in the Western Desert, retreated before them and the Italians established five fortified camps between Sofafi and the sea, about sixty miles inside Egypt. After a pause of several months, while plans were laid and reinforcements gathered, Wavell ordered the Western Desert Force under O'Connor, to attack. It did so, with 30,000 men (7th Armored and 4th Indian Divisions) on 9 December. The plan was to encircle the line of forts from the desert side which, by 11 December, O'Connor had accomplished. The plan required that the operation should then halt but, so successfully was it proceeding, that Wavell took the decision to continue the advance. The Italians were falling back in confusion. The two fortified ports of Bardia and Tobruk inside Libya, fell easily to the British and O'Connor next sent some of his armor on an unexplored route across the desert to block the continuing retreat of the Italians at Beda Fomm. The British column cut the route just ahead of the Italians who, after failing to break through on the only coast road, surrendered on 7 February. The British captured 130,000 soldiers, 845 guns and 380 tanks. Their own losses were under 2000. Wavell wished to proceed to Tripoli but Churchill's orders to dispatch troops to Greece prevented him from so doing. Shortly afterwards the appearance of the German Afrika Korps in the Western Desert turned the balance against the British for nearly two years.

### Eichelberger, General Robert, 1886–1961

Eichelberger led many successful operations in the war in the Pacific. At the time of Pearl Harbor, Eichelberger was superintendent of West Point Military Academy. He was given command of the US 1st Corps and his orders were to turn back the Japanese offensive. In early 1943 General MacArthur sent Eichelberger to Papua to speed up the offensive and this led to the capture of Buna. This was a minor victory but it was one of the first repulses of the Japanese on land by the Allies.

Eichelberger then led the US 1st Corps in fighting in New Guinea on the Huon Peninsula and took part in the amphibious landings at Hollandia (April 1944). When General Krueger's 6th Army left to mount an operation on Leyte in the Philippines, Eichelberger was left in command of all US forces in Dutch New Guinea. On 1 July 1945 Eichelberger's 8th Army arrived at Luzon to finish clearing up the Japanese troops on the island. He also mounted amphibious operations to clear the islands in the South Philippines.

### Eichmann, Adolf, 1906–1962

Eichmann was a German SS officer and head of the Gestapo's department of Jewish affairs. As an expert on Jewish affairs, he put his knowledge to use in rounding up the Jews, sending them to concentration camps and destroying them. After the Wannsee Conference (January 1942) he was in charge of effecting the 'final solution', and he introduced gas chambers to replace the mass shooting. Although he was a member of the SS, he was known to have Jewish relatives and have had a Jewish mistress in Vienna. He disappeared in 1945 and escaped to South America where Israeli intelligence discovered him and kidnapped him. He was put on trial in Israel and claimed that he did not hate or kill Jews and that he had merely been doing his duty in putting the 'final solution' so ruthlessly into effect. He was found guilty and executed in 1962.

**Eisenhower, General Dwight D, 1890–1969**

A poor boy but a hard-working one with deeply religious and ambitious parents, Eisenhower secured a nomination to West Point in 1910. He was an outstandingly successful sportsman at the Academy and immensely popular, displaying to all the brilliant charm which was to make him supreme among service diplomats of World War II. Although he saw no action during World War I he enjoyed a successful interwar career largely through attracting the patronage first of MacArthur and then of Marshall, both of whom recognized his remarkable talents as a staff officer. The latter appointed him to the war division in Washington on the outbreak of war and then to head US forces in the European Theater of Operations from London in June 1942.

In November 1942 he commanded the Torch landings at Casablanca, Oran and Algiers and the eventual movement of troops into Tunisia. By February 1943 as Supreme Allied Commander in North Africa he directed the invasions of Sicily (July) and Italy (September). Because of his success in inter-Allied relations during this period he was appointed Supreme Commander of the Allied Expeditionary Force in Western Europe in December of that same year. In overseeing and directing the D-Day Landings in June 1944 (Operation Overlord) his tact and diplomacy were constantly tested as he had to weld together cosmopolitan troops, commanders and politicians – and he did so with great success. He left direct command of the

General Eisenhower (left and above) celebrates the victory over the Axis with his British and Russian colleagues.

ground forces to Montgomery until September 1944 but then assumed it himself and was at once plunged into the settlement of a major dispute between Montgomery and Patton over the strategy of the advance into Germany: each wanted the lion's share of the available supplies to make his individual 'narrow front' advance into Germany. In the interests of inter-Allied harmony, Eisenhower settled for a 'broad front' advance which satisfied neither general and perhaps delayed the conclusion of the campaign but was undoubtedly the better coalition strategy.

Eisenhower's gifts were for inspiration and conciliation and it was these which made him one of the most popular of America's postwar presidents (1953–1961).

## Electric Gun

The prospect of launching a projectile by magnetic force has attracted inventors ever since the solenoid was invented, but it has rarely been attended with success. During World War II there were two projects put forward in Germany to use electric propulsion. The first was by an engineer named Muck, consultant to the Siemens company, who proposed a solenoid-type gun to be mounted in a hillside near the Lille coalfields in France; this location was necessary since the gun would require 50,000 tons of anthracite a month to generate the necessary electric power. This weapon would then be used to bombard London from a range of 155 miles with 450lb shells. In 1943 this idea was put forward to Reichsminister Speer, but after examination by a number of technical experts it was turned down as being impractical. In 1944 another idea was put forward by Engineer Hansler of the Gesellschaft für Geratbau for a 4cm gun based on the linear motor principle. This promised a rate of fire of 6000 rounds a minute from a multiple-barreled installation, a velocity of over 6000ft/sec and a shell containing 500g of explosive. The Luftwaffe accepted the idea for use as an anti-aircraft gun and preliminary calculations indicated that the

power required, 3900 kilowatts per gun, would be easily achieved by conventional generators. Work began on a prototype gun in February 1945 but the work was not completed before the war ended. The project was closely examined by the Allies in postwar years, but it was eventually ascertained that each gun would have required the services of a power station sufficient to supply a major city. The idea has never been revived.

## Elkton Plan
see MacArthur, General Douglas

## Embry, Air Vice-Marshal Sir Basil, 1902–

This British Air Force officer led three spectacular and exacting bombing raids on Gestapo headquarters at Aarhus, Copenhagen and Odense. He had already received awards for gallantry as a bomber pilot during the Norwegian and the Low Countries and French campaigns, and had, although captured, escaped to serve in RAF Fighter Command during the Battle of Britain. In 1943 he became an Air Vice-Marshal, taking command of No 2 Bomber Group in the build-up to D-Day.

## *Emile Bertin*

This French light cruiser was designed as a minelayer but spent her life as a leader for the *contre-torpilleurs* of the *Fantasque* and *Maille Breze* Classes. In response to the threat from the Italians her design emphasized speed, and on trials she averaged 36.73 knots for eight hours, and even touched an incredible 39.66 knots for an hour. However, she had a theoretical maximum endurance of only 3600 miles at economical speed, and was not capable of such impressive speeds at full load. She took part in the Norwegian campaign in April 1940, and carried French troops to Namsos. She went to Martinique with the carrier *Béarn* in June 1940, and lay disarmed until 1943, when she went to the USA for refitting. She took part in the invasion of Southern France and was subsequently sent out to Indo-China when French colonial rule was re-established.

**'Emily'**

see Kawanishi H8K

## Enfield

This was the generic name for weapons developed at the Royal Small Arms Factory, Enfield Lock, England, notably the Lee-Enfield rifles and Enfield revolvers. The name is also used to identify the US Rifle M1917 which was derived from a design which originated in Enfield.

Shortly before World War I, on the urgings of competitive target shooters, Enfield began developing a modified Mauser system rifle, using a bolt with forward locking lugs and an integral magazine, in .276 caliber. The weapon had several defects, attributable to the powerful cartridge, and with the coming of war in 1914 the design was shelved. Later in the war, when vast numbers of rifles were needed, the design was brought out, re-worked to take the standard .303 cartridge, and contracts were placed for its manufacture in the USA. This entered service in 1916 as the 'Rifle .303 Pattern 1914 Mark 1', and numbers of them survived to be used as training and Home Guard rifles during World War II. When the USA entered the war in 1917, also in need of rifles, the Pattern 1914 design was again re-worked, this time to accept the standard US .300 cartridge, and went into production for the US Army as the M1917 rifle. Again, large numbers of these rifles survived in store and were re-issued in World War II, some for use by US forces, many being sent to Britain for Home Guard and service use.

*Above:* The Enfield .38 No 2 Mk 1 at Arnhem.
*Below:* Close-up of the above pistol.

The only Enfield revolver used during World War II was a .38 model which had been developed from an original design by Webley in the 1920s. It was a top-break six-shot model with double or single action; a variant was produced for use by Tank Corps troops in which the hammer spur was removed and the revolver could only be fired at double action.

## English Channel

For the British and the Germans this was possibly the most bitterly contested stretch of water in the whole European naval war. From the earliest hours the Dover Straits were blocked by deep defensive minefields to bar them to U-Boats, but they were never blocked to surface traffic as both the French and British needed to be free to move coastal convoys through.

The relative tranquility was shattered in May 1940 when the German Army launched its attack through the Low Countries. The evacuation of Dunkirk was achieved from Dover and the other small harbors nearby, and then followed the air battle between the RAF and the Luftwaffe. Had the invasion of the British Isles, Operation Sealion, been launched, the Channel would have seen the bloodiest fighting of all, for the British had 80 destroyers, as well as many more patrol craft in the Channel area; furthermore the Home Fleet had orders to enter the Channel if an invasion force was sighted.

The end of the Battle of Britain did not result in any respite for both sides built up their light forces, *Schnellboote* on the German side and motor torpedo boats (MTBs) and motor gun boats (MGBs) to harass the vital coastal shipping. Throughout 1941, 1942 and 1943 fierce battles were fought, mostly at night and often at point-blank range, as the Allied light forces fought hard to establish supremacy. In 1944 the build-up before the Invasion of Normandy made the English Channel even more important, and soon the ports on the Channel coast were packed with landing craft and transports.

World War II exploded one influential myth about the English Channel. During World War I it had been repeatedly stated by such leading military figures as Admiral Jellicoe that if the French Channel Ports were to fall into enemy hands, the Royal Navy could not hold the Channel and the War would be lost. From 1940 to 1944 the entire coast of Belgium (including Antwerp, Napoleon's 'pistol pointed at the heart of England', an earlier strategic shibboleth) and France down to the Bay of Biscay was in German hands, and it was even possible to shell Dover from Cap Gris Nez not more than ten miles away.

**Eniwetok**

see Marshall Islands, 1944

## Ente

The Ente was a German amphibious demolition vehicle which resembled a small tank. Full-tracked, and with a screw and rudders, it could be controlled by a driver during an approach march. On arrival at the scene of action he dismounted and the vehicle was thereafter radio-controlled. It could then be driven and swum to an obstacle where a large charge (about 1000lbs) of explosive could be dropped, with a delay-action fuze, and the vehicle brought back. In practise the delay usually failed and the vehicle was blown up with the charge. It is believed that only a small number of Ente were produced.

## *Enterprise*

This fleet carrier was the most famous US warship of World War II, and certainly saw more fighting than any other carrier in any navy, participating in nearly every major action in the Pacific. She was the second ship of the *Yorktown* Class (CVs. 5–6 and 8) and was launched on 3 October 1936 at Newport News, Va.

The *Enterprise* (CV.6) was one of the carriers which fortuitously escaped destruction at Pearl Harbor, but her planes took part in the defense of the base. Fifteen SBD Dauntless dive-bombers of Scouting Squadron (VS) 6 arrived at Ford Island airfield in between the first and second Japanese strikes. With the *Lexington* she launched strikes against the Marshall Islands early in 1942, and against Rabaul, Wake and Marcus, expensive pin-pricks but invaluable training for the future.

In mid-April 1942 she screened her sister *Hornet* when the latter launched the Doolittle Raid on Tokyo, and her aircraft sank a number of Japanese vessels serving as pickets. Both carriers returned too late for the Battle of the Coral Sea but they played a vital role at Midway a month later. Her first strike against the Japanese carriers was heavily punished, but finally she and the *Yorktown* managed to cripple the Japanese carrier flagship *Akagi* and then sank the *Kaga* and *Soryu*. The *Enterprise* and *Hornet* clinched the battle by scoring hits on the fourth carrier, *Hiryu*.

The *Enterprise* flew the flag of Rear Admiral Thomas C Kinkaid at the invasion of Guadalcanal in August 1942 when her air group was responsible for defending the invasion area on 7–8 August 1942. In the Battle of the Eastern Solomons on 24 August she was badly damaged by bombs from Japanese aircraft, which set her on fire. Fortunately the US Navy had designed its ships well, and early next morning the fires were extinguished, but the ship needed two months of repairs. She returned in time for the Battle of Santa Cruz on 26 October when she wore the flag of Rear Admiral Kinkaid, now in overall command of Task Forces 16 and 17, known collectively as TF 61. Once again she was hit by bombs; and only extraordinary ship-handling saved her from being torpedoed by Japanese carrier planes. She effected urgent repairs at Noumea, but could not be made fully battleworthy without going to a dockyard.

Before the *Enterprise* could leave the area she was recalled hastily to help repel a Japanese attack on Guadalcanal on the night of 11 November. Although her forward elevator was still out of action and the whole forepart of the ship was damaged by blast and fire, she was the only US carrier left. Despite her injuries she continued to fly off searches as she hurried north through the Coral Sea, and although her aircraft could do nothing to help the surface forces engaged in the Battle of Guadalcanal on the night of 12–13 November, they sank the damaged battleship *Hiei* the next day.

The strikes against the Japanese bombardment group played a vital part in fending off the Japanese attempt to relieve the defenders of Guadalcanal, but the aircraft of the *Enterprise* were yet to play a part in finishing the battle. Apart from 18 fighters left on board for self-defense, the entire air group was left ashore to operate from Henderson Field, and on 14 November they inflicted severe damage on the invasion convoy, which had got within 100 miles of its destination.

The *Enterprise* and her aircraft took part in the island-hopping campaign, and they were involved in the operations against the Gilbert Islands, Kwajalein, Truk, Hollandia, Palau, Iwo Jima and Saipan. In June 1944 they fought in the Battle of the Philippine Sea, and in October they fought in the Battle of Leyte Gulf. During the assault on Okinawa in April 1945 she was hit twice by kamikazes and badly damaged. She returned to the United States for repairs and saw no further service.

## Enzian

The Enzian was a German guided missile developed by Messerschmitt AG in 1943–44. It was first designed as a ground-to-air missile, but later proposals envisaged using it as a ground-to-ground or even anti-tank weapon. Of exceptional power, it carried 1000lbs of high explosive and a proximity fuze. It was powered by four solid-fuel boost rockets for take-off and a liquid-fuel sustainer motor for flight. Guidance was by radio link, an operator relying on optical or radar tracking to get the missile into the target area, after which an infra-red homing head or radar homing head would take over and

The Enzian missile on its launching pad.

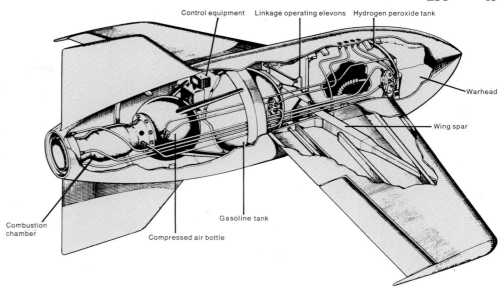

Diagram of the Enzian missile.

guide the missile to its target. About 60 rockets, of various degrees of development, were built and 38 were flown, 16 with radio guidance, but the project never reached the production or service stage.

## Epsom

see Normandy, Breakout from, 1944

## Erma

This was an acronym derived from 'Erfurter Maschinenfabrik B. Giepel GmbH, Erfurt' and known as 'Erma-Werke'. This company began manufacturing submachine guns in the late 1920s, to designs by Heinrich Vollmer and Berthold Giepel. The principal feature was the telescoping shroud over the main operating spring behind the bolt and the making of the receiver from seamless steel tubing. The design was sound and the weapons well-finished, and numbers were sold in France, Mexico and various South American countries, as well as turning up in some numbers in the Spanish Civil

War. In about 1932 the Model EMP was produced, recognizable by its perforated barrel jacket and fixed fore-grip, and numbers of these were bought by the German Army.

In 1938 the German Army, having watched events in Spain, decided to adopt a submachine gun in large numbers, and approached Erma-Werke for a new design. Giepel produced a model in which no wood was used, which had a folding steel stock, and which was to become virtually the German Army's trademark in the years ahead – the Maschinen Pistole 38. This weapon has frequently but erroneously been called the 'Schmeisser', but Schmeisser had nothing to do with the design, though it is understood that he was the manager of a sub-contracting factory for some time.

The MP38 was an outstandingly good submachine gun; in 9mm caliber, it used a 32-round box magazine and could fire at a rate of 500rpm. It weighed 10.5lbs with a full magazine and was only 24in long with the stock folded. Production continued until 1940, by which time experience had shown that some changes were needed. The principal complaint was that there was no safety device to lock the bolt in its forward position; in consequence, if the magazine was in place and the butt of the gun grounded sharply, the bolt could be jerked back sufficiently far to chamber and fire a round. The other complaint was that manufacture was too slow and difficult, since much expensive machining was required. To cure these points, the MP40 was designed; this placed a simple safety lock on the bolt handle and altered the basic design so as to use more stamped and pressed metal components. Welding and brazing was extensively used for assembly, and the cheapest grades of steel were used which would provide the necessary strength. Over one million MP40 were produced during the war at a unit price of some 60 Reichmarks each – about US $22.

## Escort

The term 'escort' could be applied to any ship allocated to screening duties, and it was even used at times to refer to capital ships, carriers and cruisers. However, technically, it is a type of warship designed specifically for protecting other ships, usually against submarine attack but also against air attack.

The British placed more emphasis on convoy escorts, primarily because they had the world's largest merchant fleet and they alone had given serious thought before World War II to the design of suitable escorts. The US Navy had hoped to rely on large numbers of over-age destroyers, but in 1942 the soaring U-Boat successes forced the introduction of the Destroyer Escort or DE. The British relied initially on prewar sloops and the small corvettes put into production in 1939, but in 1942 they produced the first frigate, a long-range escort designed specifically for working with North Atlantic convoys.

The prime armament of the escort was Asdic or Sonar in conjunction with depth-charges or the later, improved weapons such as Hedgehog. Such was the intensity of the Battle of the Atlantic that escorts often received the latest radar and communications aids before fleet destroyers. When air attack was a serious threat escorts were given heavy AA armament, and in specific cases they were given special gear, eg some of the Lend-Lease DEs serving with the RN were used as control ships against *Schnellboote* in the English Channel. As the war progressed older destroyers were often reclassified as escorts, with guns and torpedoes replaced by anti-submarine gear.

## Essex

The *Essex* Class fleet aircraft carriers were developed from the highly successful *Yorktown* Class, but without the restrictions imposed by disarmament treaties. The result was not only the most numerous class of carriers ever built but possibly the most successful in history.

The first ten (CV.9–18) were ordered in 1940 but a slightly improved class was ordered starting the week after Pearl Harbor. The two groups were divided into 'short-hull' and 'long-hull' types but there was little to choose externally between them. In all, 24 *Essex* Class carriers were completed for the US Navy, but only four of the second group were ready before the surrender of Japan.

The outstanding features of the *Essex* design were their high speed (33 knots, maximum) and high capacity (80 planes). As with the *Yorktown* Class they proved capable of absorbing terrible punishment, the *Bunker Hill* and the *Franklin* were outstanding in this respect but many of the others were badly hit. Many names of older ships were repeated in the class: *Yorktown, Hornet, Lexington* and *Wasp,* while the *Shangri-La* was specially named to commemorate the Doolittle Raid of 1942.

## Exeter

This British heavy cruiser was a 'one-off' experimental design, built with a half-sister, HMS *York* in 1927–31. They marked an effort by the British to break away from the expensive 10,000-ton eight-inch gunned cruisers built under the Washington Treaty, which were too big to be built in numbers, even if numbers had not been limited by the Treaty, and too vulnerable. The British Director of Naval Construction maintained that a class of ship with eight or nine eight-inch guns could not be adequately armored on 10,000 tons, a claim which was found to be justified when true figures of other navies' cruisers were revealed after 1945. Furthermore, British Governments of the day were anxious to see armaments scaled down, and were prepared to reduce cruiser displacement to 8000 tons.

To accommodate adequate armor, the DNC, Sir William Berry, sacrificed one twin eight-inch gun mounting, but even so it was not possible to get the *Exeter*'s tonnage below 8400, and it was decided for the future that 'small' heavy cruisers were not worth building. Nonetheless, war experience showed that the smaller type was a better-balanced design, and that large numbers of big guns would require bigger hulls; the only other way to improve protection was to reduce gun-caliber.

HMS *Exeter* was launched at Devonport Dockyard on 18 July 1929 and commissioned in July 1931. From 1932 to 1933 she served with the 2nd Cruiser Squadron, but later in 1933 she was recommissioned for service in the South American Division of the North America and West Indies Station, where she was to remain (except for a brief interval in 1936 during the Abyssinian Crisis) until August 1939. It should be noted that a standard exercise for British cruisers on foreign stations was to practise the tactics laid down by the Admiralty for dealing with a German 'pocket battleship', and in 1938 the *Exeter* played the part of the 'enemy', a curious portent for the future.

After a brief spell in the South Atlantic, the *Exeter* was transferred back to the South American Division, and Captain Henry Harwood was appointed Commodore of the division. On the morning of 13 December 1939, Harwood's division, consisting of the *Exeter* and two smaller six-inch gunned cruisers, the RN-manned *Ajax* and a New Zealand-manned sister *Achilles,* caught the German *panzerschiff Admiral Graf Spee,* about to attack shipping off the River Plate. The German ship recognized the *Exeter*'s distinctive silhouette but first mistook the two single-stack cruisers for destroyers. But in any case the *Exeter* was the most dangerous opponent so she inevitably drew the German fire.

The standard tactics laid down for such an action were simple; the force was split into two divisions to divide the German fire and to use their margin of five knots' speed to best advantage. The *Ajax* (now the flagship) and *Achilles* formed the 1st Division, while the *Exeter* operated independently, but each division carried out 'flank marking' for the other by marking the fall of shot.

The *Graf Spee* opened fire at 0418 and the *Exeter* replied two minutes later. An 11in shell passed through the ship without exploding, but

HMS *Exeter* after the sinking of the *Admiral Graf Spee,* February 1940.

a minute later 'B' turret was hit and splinters caused casualties on the bridge. More shells wrecked 'A' turret and started fires amidships, and the captain was forced to fight the ship from the emergency control position aft, by a chain of verbal messengers. By 0730 the British cruiser was listing 10° to starboard and down by the bows, and all three eight-inch turrets were silent. But she was not sunk, as the *Ajax* and *Achilles* repeatedly closed the range like picadors drawing off the bull from a wounded matador, and each time the *Graf Spee* was forced to shift target, something that her cumbersome 11in mountings were ill-suited to do. Another reason for her failure to finish off the *Exeter* was discovered later; the German 11in shells were faulty, and many either failed to burst or only partially detonated. In contrast one of *Exeter*'s shells penetrated the German ship's 102mm belt and the 38mm longitudinal bulkhead before exploding amidships. The Germans were uncomfortably surprised to see how much damage was done, and as Cdr Rasenack, one of the *Graf Spee*'s gunnery officers commented, it clearly contradicted the view that she could only be fought by a capital ship.

The *Exeter* was patched up at the Falkland Islands and limped home to a hero's welcome, for the Battle of the River Plate was the first naval action of the war and a considerable tonic to Allied morale. She was refitted at Devonport in 1940–41 and sailed for the Far East in mid-1941. When Singapore fell on 15 February 1942 she was based at Tandjong Priok in the Dutch East Indies, forming part of the ABDA (American-British-Dutch-Australian) force under the Dutch Admiral Doorman. On 25 February she sailed from Surabaya and next day fought in the hopeless Battle of the Java Sea against a superior force of Japanese cruisers and destroyers. A shell in her boiler-room reduced her speed to 11 knots, and although she later reached 15 knots she was forced to return to harbor for temporary repairs. At dusk on 28 February she sailed with the destroyers USS *Pope* and HMS *Encounter* in a desperate attempt to escape to Colombo through the Sunda Strait, but she was trapped by the Japanese cruisers next morning. Finally at 1135 she sank with colors flying, followed shortly afterwards by the two destroyers.

## Falaise Pocket

see Normandy

## 'Fat Man'

see Hiroshima and Nagasaki

## Ferdinand

This German tank destroyer was named after Dr Ferdinand Porsche, its designer. The design originated when Porsche was called upon to produce a prototype medium tank in competition with Henschel; the Henschel design was chosen for production and became the Tiger tank. The Porsche design, using gasoline-electric drive and several other mechanical novelties, was at first authorized to go into production in parallel with the Henschel design, but this was later changed and the chassis were converted into fixed-gun tank destroyers mounting an 88mm gun. Only 90 units were made, and they were later renamed 'Elefant'; some authorities say this was official, others aver that it was a name bestowed by the troops after seeing the weapons in action in the Russian mud. The Ferdinand was used to equip Panzer Abteilung 654 and first saw action in Operation Citadel, at Kursk in 1943. Due to their bulk and the fact that the guns had but 14° of traverse each side, these vehicles were extremely vulnerable to flank attack. Given a fair shot they could demolish any tank they met, but Russian infantry were able to creep up on their blind quarters and immobilize them. Numbers were lost at Kursk; more were lost in subsequent actions. The survivors were withdrawn and sent to Italy, but the conditions there were even worse for such a heavy vehicle and they were all eventually lost.

## FG-42 Paratroop Rifle

The Fallschirm Gewehr 42 was a remarkably well-designed automatic rifle developed for the German airborne forces, and one of the best firearm designs of World War II. During 1940–41 the German Army were developing their assault rifle, the MP–43, which fired a short cartridge; when this was offered to the Paratroop force they refused it, demanding a weapon which fired the full-sized 7.92mm Mauser cartridge. Since the Army disagreed with them, and since the Paratroops were supplied through the Luftwaffe, they went ahead with their own development, enlisting the Rheinmetall-Borsig company to do the work.

In 1942 they produced a design which was accepted for service, but since the Rheinmetall company had no production facilities, the rifles were actually produced by Krieghoff of Suhl.

The FG–42 was a gas-operated automatic rifle which used a rotating bolt and was able to fire at full automatic if required. It was one of the first weapons to be designed on the 'straight-line' principle, with the butt a prolongation of the barrel – a system which tends to reduce the tendency for the muzzle to rise when fired automatically. It was fed from a box magazine mounted on the left-hand side, and the mechanism of the trigger was so arranged that when firing single shots the bolt closed before the trigger was released, but when firing automatically the bolt remained open after each burst to allow a stream of cooling air to pass through the barrel. It was fitted with a bipod for use as a light machine gun and could also be fitted with a telescopic sight for sniping. For all this, it weighed just under ten pounds, a most remarkable achievement.

Unfortunately it was a difficult rifle to manufacture and the Wehrmacht's opposition made it difficult to get the necessary raw materials. As a result, only about 7000 rifles were made. It was used for the first time in the rescue of Mussolini, secondly at Rhodes and by the First German Airborne Corps at Cassino. But the decline in importance of the airborne troops in Germany also led to a falling-off in production and the rifles later found their way to all types of German units.

## Fiat B.R.20 Cicogna

When Italy entered the war in June 1940, its air force had 172 B.R.20s and slightly modified B.R.20Ms in operational use. Each carried a crew of five, up to 3525lb of bombs and a defensive armament of four machine guns. Two groups totaling 75 aircraft, made a number of daylight and sporadic night raids against the UK in 1940 from bases in Belgium. Most of the others operated over Malta, Yugoslavia, Greece and Libya. Those sent to Russia were badly mauled and soon recalled. The 81 survivors were being used mainly for reconnaissance at the time of the Italian surrender. Standard power plant was two 1000hp Fiat A.80 engines.

## Fiat C.R.32

About 400 of these 1933-model biplane fighters still flew with the Italian Air Force in June 1940. With a 600hp Fiat A.30 engine and, usually, two 12.7mm machine guns, it served mainly as a night fighter and close support aircraft in Greece and East Africa. Maximum speed was 233mph.

## Fiat C.R.42

This Italian single-seat fighter was in service from 1940 to 1945. From the 1920s the giant Italian Fiat company produced that country's main series of fighters. All were biplanes designed by Rosatelli, C.R. meaning *Caccia* (fighter) Rosatelli. Though quite ordinary, and armed with just the usual synchronized pair of machine guns firing past the propeller blades, they were outstandingly maneuverable, and ace Italian pilots gave breathtaking displays in them at all the big air meetings. Until 1936 all the C.R. fighters had water-cooled V engines, but in that year the C.R.41 was built with a radial engine. From it stemmed the C.R.42 of 1939, named Falco (Falcon). By this time other countries were giving up the old-fashioned biplane, but the Italian pilots preferred the C.R.42 to the new monoplanes. It was probably built in larger numbers than any other Italian warplane, though the total was only 1781, the last coming off the line in 1942.

It was exhilarating to fly, and few other aircraft could equal its maneuverability in a dogfight, but the 840hp Fiat A74 engine gave a speed of only 267mph and the armament was only two 12.7mm machine guns. Most could carry two 220lb bombs, and after the Falco had been shown to be no match for RAF fighters it was used mainly at night or in close-support attack missions.

## Fiat G.50 Freccia

Following a brief period of service at the end of the Spanish Civil War, this all-metal single-seat fighter entered series production for the Italian Air Force. More than 100 were in service when Italy entered the war, and were soon in action on interception, ground attack, convoy escort and bomber escort duties from bases in Belgium, Greece, the Balkans, Italy and North Africa. They were joined by 450 improved G.50*bis*, with a better view from the cockpit, armor and self-sealing tanks. An 840hp Fiat A.74 engine and armament of two 12.7mm machine guns were standard.

## Fiat Machine Gun

The Fiat Company, better known for their automobiles, entered the armament business during World War I with a contract to manufacture a medium machine gun which had been designed by Abel Revelli. Outwardly resembling the contemporary Vickers and Maxim guns, it worked on the delayed blowback system, the barrel and breech recoiling a short distance before the

The Fiat-Aviazione G.50 Freccia.

The 8mm Fiat (Revelli) Model 35 machine gun.

breech opened. The gun was fitted with an odd magazine system, the magazine box containing ten compartments into each of which five cartridges were dropped. As the gun fired so the first five rounds were used up, after which an arm pushed the whole unit inwards to present the next five rounds for firing. This was the Model 1914 machine gun, and in spite of its mechanical novelties it survived in service throughout World War II.

During the 1920s the company designed a number of machine guns for infantry use and for aircraft use. Their 1926 model light machine gun used the same delayed blowback system and again had a peculiar feed mechanism; the right-hand mounted magazine was fixed but capable of being hinged forward so that it could be re-loaded from a special clip. Usually half a dozen rounds fell out while the gunner was trying to close the magazine after reloading. Some 2000 of these guns were built, but it had little commercial success.

In 1928 Fiat abandoned the blowback system and developed a recoil-operated gun with positive breech locking. This was fed by a link belt and was intended as an aircraft gun. It was a much better design than its predecessors and was used in some numbers by the Italian Air Force.

In the early 1930s, however, Fiat decided they had better things to do than manufacture the small quantities of guns demanded in those days, and they sold out their armament interest to the Breda company. Their only subsequent involvement in machine guns came in 1935 when they redesigned their 1914 model; the water cooling system was removed and an air-cooled barrel substituted, the caliber was changed from the original 6.5mm to 8mm, and the chamber was fluted in order to make extraction of the fired case easier. In spite of these changes the Model 1935 was actually a worse gun than the one it replaced, since the air-cooling was insufficient and the gun had a nasty habit of going off on its own when a cartridge was inadvertently left loaded in a hot breech.

## Fiat R.S.14

A total of 150 of these handsome four/five-seat maritime reconnaissance seaplanes were built, each with two 840hp Fiat A.74 engines and a long underfuselage pannier for two 350lb depth charges or up to 880lb of bombs. Defensive armament was normally one 12.7mm machine gun in the dorsal turret and two 7.7mm guns in the sides of the fuselage. Operations were confined to the Mediterranean, on both sides after the Italian surrender. A variant was the air/sea rescue R.S.14C.

## Fiji

The *Fiji* Class was a new departure in British cruiser design. Ordered under the rearmament program these ships were the first to be built to the new 8000-ton limit agreed by the 1936 London Naval Treaty. Although 2000 tons smaller than the previous *Southampton* Class they retained the same heavy armament and nearly the same scale of armor by judicious economies in design. Despite the reduction in size they proved most successful, and the 11 ships had active careers. During the war a further seven were ordered to a nearly identical design.

The *Fiji* herself was sunk during the Battle of Crete, when caught by German Stuka dive-bombers with virtually no anti-aircraft ammunition left. The only other war loss was the *Trinidad*, which suffered the ignominy of torpedoing herself during a surface action in the Arctic. The water temperature was so low that

*Fiji* Class cruiser refueling a destroyer.

the torpedo's gyroscope froze, but as the ship was hotly engaged with German destroyers at the time it was assumed that she had been hit by one of their torpedoes. Only when repaired in a Russian port did the facts come to light. The ship was on her way home on 14 May 1942 when she was attacked by aircraft in the Barents Sea. The new patch in her side gave way, and further damage set her on fire so that she eventually had to be abandoned and torpedoed by one of her escorting destroyers.

## Finland, Peace with, September 1944

During the war Finland was an ally of Germany and took the opportunity to take back the land that she had lost during the Russo-Finnish War. In August 1941, the Finnish General Mannerheim was asked several times by the Germans to advance further and cut off Leningrad but Mannerheim refused. The Finns were forced to recede further territories to Russia which they had initially lost in 1940.

By June 1944, the Russians were sufficiently reinforced with air cover to launch an offensive against the Finns. After breaking through the Karelian Isthmus, General Govorov's forces captured Viipuri but they stopped at the 1940 border. The Finns, however, did not accept the armistice terms offered by Stalin because Ribbentrop had promised German aid. In September, when the Germans were obviously retreating, the Finns accepted the armistice terms (4 September) and when the Germans tried to land at Hogland in the Gulf of Finland they were repulsed.

## Firefly

Fireflies were British armored vehicles; the name was originally given to a light-armored four-wheeled truck carrying a six-pounder anti-tank gun in 1941, but few of these were made and the name fell into disuse. It was then revived and applied to a modification of the Sherman M4 tank in which the 75mm gun was removed and the British 17-pounder gun inserted into the modified turret. About 600 tanks were so adapted.

## Firefly, Fairey

This British two-seat carrier-based fighter and reconnaissance aircraft, was in service between 1943–62. Far better than the underpowered Fulmar which it replaced, the Firefly was powered by a 1730 or 1990hp Rolls-Royce Griffon, and thus could exceed 300mph even burdened by two seats and naval equipment. With four 20mm cannon it packed a good punch, and most carried 2000lb of bombs, eight rockets and often radar. Service began in October 1943, but the Firefly hit the headlines only with an attack on oil refineries in what was then called Sumatra. Most Fireflies were built in new post-war versions.

## Fitch, Rear Admiral Aubrey W

Fitch was commander of Task Group 11, based on the *Lexington*, which fought at the Battle of Coral Sea. Fitch had too few fighters and after the battle was over the *Lexington* blew up from the damage she had received and sank. In 1943 Fitch took over as commander of land-based aircraft in the South Pacific.

## *Fiume*

This Italian heavy cruiser was a unit of the *Zara* Class, and was sunk by gunfire in the Battle of Cape Matapan on the night of 28 March 1941. She was following the *Zara* when she was hit by the battleship *Valiant*'s first salvo of four 15in shells at a range of only 3000 yards. Within seconds she was a blazing wreck, and sank at about 2315 with the loss of 32 officers and 780 men out of a total of about 830.

## Flame Throwers

Introduced into warfare during the course of World War I the flame thrower has changed very little since then except in matters of detail and reliability. Basically it consists of a nozzle from which an inflammable liquid is discharged by gas pressure. This liquid is ignited as it emerges, so that a jet of flame, capable of being directed at a target, results. That being said, it has to be added that the whole thing is a good deal more complicated than it might appear. In the first place the choice of fuel is critical; ordinary gasoline, for example, will ignite readily enough and form a good jet, but there is little tenacity in it and the shock of arrival is often enough to extinguish the flames. Furthermore, such a thin liquid would immediately run off anything it hit. It is therefore necessary to thicken the fuel without reducing its flammability. Additives such as creosotes, oils, soaps, stearates and even more abstruse chemicals have all been tried at one time or another and every nation has its own formula which provides the optimum between a good trajectory and a tenacious burning mixture on the target. Once the fuel is selected, the next question is that of propelling it to the target; for this the usual medium is compressed gas. This needs to be inert otherwise it could form an explosive mixture with the fuel; nitrogen is usually selected for the job. The third problem is ignition of the emergent jet, and this can be done either by an electrical spark gap or by some form of flame-producing cartridge fired by a conventional firing-pin device. The former system has the advantage that repeated

German flame thrower blasts a Soviet pillbox.

ignitions can be made so that the weapon can fire a number of shots; the cartridge system may demand re-loading for each successive shot, or, if repetition is attained mechanically, requires a more complex mechanical arrangement necessary to present successive cartridges to the flame nozzle.

The maximum range of a flame thrower is allied to the method of carriage; if the weapon is to be man-carried then the fuel and pressure tanks must be small and this, in turn, restricts both the number of shots and their range. The British 'Ack Pack', for example, weighed 49lbs when filled with 4gal of fuel, could be fired no more than ten times, each a ten second shot, and had a maximum range of fifty yards. To achieve more range it was necessary to mount the flame thrower on some sort of vehicle, usually a modified tank. Here the nitrogen cylinders and fuel supply could be carried either inside the tank or in an armored trailer; the capacity and power of the installation was limited solely by the space available. The British 'Crocodile' flame-throwing tank was a modified Churchill towing a 6.5 ton armored trailer with 400gal of flame fuel and five pressure bottles of nitrogen. The flame gun had a range of 120yds and could fire 80 one-second bursts or a lesser number of longer shots. The US Army developed a flame-throwing version of the M4 'Sherman' tank which carried the flame gun in place of the hull machine gun and had the fuel and gas within the tank body for protection. In the German Army the flame-thrower was an engineer weapon; manpack throwers were used, similar in design to the British model and of similar performance, and a number of armored vehicles were converted to 'Flammpanzers', though less use was made of this device by the Germans than by the British.

## Fleet Air Arm

The British naval air arm alone of the major navies' air forces had been subjected to the ruthless doctrine of the indivisibility of air power. From modest beginnings in 1912–13 the Royal Naval Air Service had expanded enormously between 1914 and 1918, and had pioneered techniques of operating aircraft from ships. But on 1 April 1918, the RNAS and the land-based Royal Flying Corps were united to form the Royal Air Force, the world's first and only unified air force. Although naval aviation continued for awhile, within two years of the Armistice the RAF showed an alarming tendency to downgrade the importance of seaborne aviation in favor of strategic bombing. The RN was permitted to retain its carriers but all flight personnel belonged to the RAF. That the system worked at all was testimony to the goodwill shown on both sides, but the fact remains that the RN slipped steadily from first place in expertise and equipment to a poor third to the American and Japanese who kept their Naval Air Forces under naval control. Unfortunately too, the British senior naval officers had not had any firsthand flying knowledge. In the long run the RAF's control over aircraft design and procurement had even more dire results.

After years of bitter wrangling the politicians reversed their verdict in 1937, when the Fleet Air Arm was handed back to the Admiralty. But the equally vital shore-based maritime squadrons for reconnaissance and anti-submarine work were allowed to remain under RAF control. All the aircraft mechanics and support personnel were withdrawn from the RN. The new Fleet Air Arm was born with obsolescent aircraft and a desperate lack of trained personnel.

The two years' respite was put to good use, but the lack of good aircraft could not be remedied in the time, and throughout World War

II British aircraft carriers operated a mixture of good American aircraft supplied under Lend-Lease and mediocre to poor ones of British origin. The Fleet Air Arm nevertheless covered itself with glory. Its greatest moment was the disabling of the Italian battle fleet at Taranto in November 1940, but the obsolescent Swordfish biplane bomber also crippled the *Bismarck*, sank U-Boats in the Atlantic and even provided protection to shipping during the Normandy invasion in 1944. Finally the armored carriers of the British Pacific Fleet proved their worth off Okinawa, when they proved able to withstand even the dreaded kamikaze attacks.

### *Fletcher* Class
see Destroyers

### Fletcher, Vice-Admiral Frank, 1885–1973

Rear Admiral Fletcher was en route for Wake Island aboard the *Saratoga* when Pearl Harbor was attacked. He commanded Task Force 17 based on the carrier *Yorktown* and was given overall command during the Battle of Coral Sea since Vice-Admiral Halsey had not arrived. Although Fletcher lost the USS *Lexington*, he intercepted the Port Moresby invasion forces. His flagship, the carrier *Yorktown*, was badly damaged but was ready for the Battle of Midway in June 1942. During the battle the *Yorktown* and four Japanese carriers were sunk. Fletcher was made a Vice-Admiral and given command of the expeditionary force to protect the Guadalcanal operation. Fletcher was afraid of losing another carrier having already lost 21 planes in a day, so Vice-Admiral Ghormley allowed him to withdraw but this led to the Battle of Savo Island in which the invasion transports could have been destroyed.

Fletcher's last command was in the Battle of the Eastern Solomons during which the *Enterprise* was badly damaged. As a result of the battle Japanese reinforcements to Guadalcanal were stopped. Fletcher had sent the *Wasp* to be refueled before the battle and had not had superiority in the air. This left Nimitz with only one carrier off Guadalcanal, but this was enough to win one of the most hard-fought battles during the whole of the war in the Pacific.

### Fliegerfaust

This was a German close-range anti-aircraft weapon devised in 1944 and placed in limited production. It consisted of nine 20mm tubes mounted so that they could be fired from a man's shoulder by electric impulse. Each tube was loaded with a rocket made from a 20mm cannon shell fitted to a steel tube containing angled vents. On firing the angled vents caused the rocket to spin rapidly, so stabilizing its flight. The rockets were fired in two salvos, one of five shots and one of four, in quick succession, and the weapon could be rapidly reloaded by using a special loading clip which held another nine rockets. Maximum range was about 2000yds, though the most effective fighting range was about 500yds. Production was scheduled to begin in February 1945 but it is thought that very few were actually made.

### Flying Fortress
see B-17 Fortress, Boeing

### Flying Tigers
see Chennault, General Claire

### Focke-Wulf Fw 189

A total of 864 of these twin-boom three-seat reconnaissance, army co-operation and close support aircraft were built for the wartime Luftwaffe. One unit operated Fw 189s in North Africa, but most flew on the Russian Front. Armament included four machine guns and four 110lb bombs.

### Focke-Wulf Fw 190 and Ta 152

This German single-seat fighter and attack aircraft was in service between 1941 and 1945. The Fw 190 was first met in action by the Spitfires of the RAF in the spring of 1941. Though it had flown three months before World War II, it was unknown to British intelligence, and the only Luftwaffe fighters with a radial engine were thought to be a few old Curtiss Hawks captured from the French. But it was soon clear this was something else; it was in almost every way superior even to the RAF's latest Spitfire, the Mk VB. Powered by a beautifully installed BMW 801Dg two-row radial, rated at 1600 or 1700hp, it was smaller than any British fighter, yet carried heavier armament, the usual arrangement being four 20mm cannon and two machine guns. It had unsurpassed maneuverability, was well-protected, and had a wide-track landing gear unlike the Bf 109 and most other fighters of 1941.

By the end of 1942 about 2000 of these great fighters had been delivered. Most went to command the skies on the Russian front and in North Africa, or to drop bombs on hostile armies. A few stayed in France and dropped large bombs on British coastal towns, thereafter taking comfort in the fact that hardly any RAF aircraft could catch the nimble Focke-Wulf.

New versions appeared, including types with even heavier armament, as well as torpedo-bombers, dual-control trainers and night fighters. The Fw 190G had fewer guns and could carry a fantastic bomb, rocket or torpedo load up to 3970lb. It had strengthened landing gear, and like the 190F often carried rockets for use against Allied ground forces or bombers.

Fastest of all versions were the Fw 190D, or long-nosed 190 series, with a Jumo 213A liquid-cooled engine normally rated at 1776hp but capable of being boosted to 2240hp for short spurts at speeds up to 426mph. Towards the end of the war, when total Fw 190 production amounted to 20,051 aircraft, designer Kurt Tank had his own name applied to the final development, the Ta 152. This was a refined Fw 190D of even higher performance. Both had an inverted V–12 engine, the 190D's Jumo being used by some Ta 152 sub-types including the long-span 152H used for high-altitude combat, while the Ta 152C had the 2300hp DB 603L. Typical armament comprised one 30mm MK 108 or 103 (alone enough to blow the wing off any aircraft struck by its shells) and four 20mm MG 151 cannon. Tank himself was testing a Ta 152 when he was 'bounced' by some Mustangs, the fastest Allied fighters. He opened the throttle and they were unable to get near him. Fortunately for the Allies, only a handful of these formidable machines entered operational units, and then they were usually unable to fly because of a lack of fuel or lack of trained pilots.

### Focke-Wulf Fw 200 Condor

This German ocean-patrol aircraft was in service from 1940–45. Focke-Wulf built the Fw 200 Condor as a long-range civil airliner, and in 1937 it hit the headlines with nonstop flights to distant cities including New York. In early 1939 the Japanese ordered some Condor airliners, as

Focke-Wulf Fw 200 Condor.

*Below:* The Focke-Wulf Fw 190 F-8.

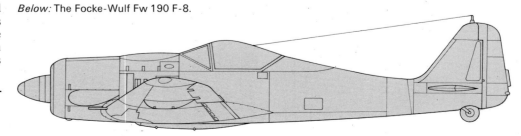

well as a single aircraft converted into a naval long-range reconnaissance bomber. These were never delivered, but at the outbreak of World War II the Luftwaffe suddenly realized that it had no long-range attack aircraft to harass Allied shipping or undertake any long-range bombing. The only answer was the Fw 200C, a specially developed Condor based on the work done for the Japanese. The Fw 200C had only modest performance, on four 1000hp Bramo (BMW) Fafnir radial engines, and was really only a lash-up built in small numbers (only 278 in all). Moreover, it kept coming apart, either the fuselage or the wing breaking either in the air or, especially, on landing. Yet it remained a thorn in the Allies' side until near the end of the war, and in 1942–43 exerted an effect on Allied Atlantic shipping which was out of all proportion to the numbers of Condors used.

Most Condors had a crew of seven or eight. Up to about 4630lb of bombs were carried in a long gondola under the fuselage and on external wing racks. Later versions had deep outboard engine nacelles to carry the Hs 293 missile. Defensive armament often comprised a 20mm cannon at the front of the gondola, a 13mm or 15mm gun in the dorsal turret, and up to five other guns aimed by hand. After the climax of the U-Boat campaign in May 1943 the big Condors found life harder, and by 1945 nearly all had been reduced to furtive missions as transports.

## Föhn

This German multiple anti-aircraft rocket launcher fired a 73mm high explosive rocket. The launcher was a simple framework of racks which held 35 rockets; it was transported on a trailer and in an emergency could be fired from it. The rocket was spin-stabilized and carried a warhead of 280g of high explosive with an impact fuze in the nose and a self-destruction device in the base which ensured that the rocket would explode in the air and not fall back to the ground unexploded. Very little information on range or effect has ever been found and it seems that relatively few were ever deployed. At the closing stage of the war it was proposed to use the Föhn rockets in the air-to-air role in the 'Natter' interceptor.

The Föhn anti-aircraft rocket was hardly ever deployed during the war.

## Fokker D.XXI

When the Germans invaded the Netherlands on 10 May 1940, the Netherlands Air Force had 29 of these single-seat fighters on its strength. Although restricted to a speed of 272mph by their 830hp Bristol Mercury engine, the D.XXIs fought well for three days, after which they were grounded for lack of ammunition. Standard armament was four 7.9mm machine guns. Other D.XXIs were used very successfully by Finland during its 'WinterWar' against Russia in 1939–40 and in later campaigns.

## Fokker G.IA

Most effective combat aircraft available to the Netherlands Air Force in May 1940, this three-seat fighter was armed with no fewer than eight 7.9mm machine guns in the nose and one more in the rear of the crew nacelle. It had a twin-boom layout, with an 830hp Bristol Mercury engine in the front of each boom. Up to 880lb of bombs could be carried for ground attack. Several of the 23 G.IAs operational on 10 May were destroyed before they could leave the ground. The others fought until all but one had been lost. They were joined by three G.IB aircraft, ordered by Spain, which Dutch workers fitted with guns stripped from other aircraft in order to offer maximum resistance to the Luftwaffe.

## Fokker T.V.

First flown on 16 October 1937, this medium bomber carried a crew of five, up to 2200lb of bombs and an armament of six or seven machine guns. Powered by two 925hp Bristol Pegasus engines, it had a maximum speed of 259mph. Only nine remained serviceable at the time of the German invasion. In a few gallant sorties they destroyed nearly 30 Luftwaffe aircraft on the airfield at Wallhaven and attacked bridges in the path of the enemy advance. All nine were destroyed, two by Dutch ground fire.

## Force H

In June 1940 the British Admiralty decided to act to fill the gap left by the loss of the French Navy and the declaration of war by Italy. A powerful striking force was to be based on Gibraltar under Vice-Admiral Sir James Somerville to cover the Western Mediterranean and the convoy routes from Gibraltar to Sierra Leone and the United Kingdom.

On 23 June the new forces arrived at Gibraltar, the carrier *Ark Royal* and the battlecruiser *Hood*, followed by the battleships *Valiant* and *Resolution* and other ships five days later. The first task was to immobilize the French Fleet at Mers-el-Kebir, an unhappy action which was achieved without loss. The most famous ships of Force H became the *Ark Royal*, the battlecruiser *Renown* and the cruiser *Sheffield*. When the *Bismarck* disappeared after sinking the *Hood* in May 1941 it was these three ships which left Gibraltar without orders, and eventually *Ark Royal*'s Swordfish torpedo-bombers scored the vital hit which slowed her down.

Force H was finally disbanded in October 1943, having covered the North African, Sicilian and Salerno landings. Apart from a brief period in April–May 1942, when its ships were

detached for the Madagascar landings, it had been the main British force in the Western Mediterranean for more than three years and the only factor preventing Axis domination of the area.

## Force Z, Sinking of, 1941

Churchill wanted Singapore to have the 'smallest number of best ships', and sent Force Z, composed of the battleship *Prince of Wales* and the battlecruiser *Repulse*, to intimidate the Japanese.

The arrival of the *Prince of Wales* in Singapore on December 2 was heralded on the BBC. Admiral Phillips had orders to impede Japanese landings and although he had no air cover he nonetheless put to sea.

Under cover of bad weather, Phillips sailed to Kota Bharu on 8 December to intercept the Japanese convoys. When the weather cleared he was spotted by three Japanese aircraft and therefore turned back to Singapore. Reports of landings at Kuantan reached him, but on arrival his destroyers found no trace of enemy activity. However, while en route their position had been spotted by Japanese submarines. The Japanese sent bombers of the Twenty-second Air Flotilla to bomb Force Z on its way back from Kuantan. On 10 December, at 1100, they started the attack. The first wave of torpedoes did little damage to the *Repulse*. However following attacks scored direct hits, and at 1233 the *Repulse* sank. Shortly after, at 1320, the *Prince of Wales* sank. The escorting destroyers rescued 2081 out of 2921 sailors, but Phillips was amongst those who were lost. The sinking of Force Z was a tremendous blow for British prestige. The action indicated the futility of sending major naval units into modern warfare without adequate air cover.

## *Formidable*

This British aircraft carrier was the second ship of the *Illustrious* Class, and was launched on 17 August 1939 by Harland & Wolff at Belfast. She joined the Home Fleet in December 1940, but after a short spell with the South Atlantic hunting raiders she went to the Mediterranean in March 1941. Her torpedo-bombers damaged the Italian battleship *Vittorio Veneto* and the heavy cruiser *Pola*, and so brought about the Battle of Cape Matapan.

After serving in the Mediterranean with conspicuous success in the Battle for Crete and the invasions of North Africa and Italy, the *Formidable* was sent to the Pacific in 1945. On 4 May 1945 off Okinawa she was hit by two kamikaze aircraft, one of which bounced off the deck and the second of which caused a bad fire but did not put her out of action. But on 18 May an accident in her hangar caused by an aircraft's guns being fired resulted in the loss of 30 aircraft and severe strain to her hull. Still she continued in action, although only able to fly off a small number of aircraft. She took part in the final onslaught on Japan, and only left Japanese waters on 11 August 1945, shortly before the surrender.

## Forrestal, James, 1892–1949

In August 1940 Forrestal was made Under-Secretary of the Navy and in May 1944 he was promoted to acting Secretary of the Navy. He advocated naval supremacy and worked hard to increase the production of ships, aircraft and guns. On two occasions he visited the South Pacific to inspect operations and at Iwo Jima he went ashore with the commanding officers. In August 1944 he visited the Mediterranean to watch the Allied landings in the south of France.

## Foss, Major J J, 1915–

Most successful pilot in the United States Marine Corps during World War II, with 26 confirmed kills.

## France, Battle of, 1940

After the overrunning of Belgium and crossing of the Meuse, the Manstein Plan required the German Army in the west to achieve three main objectives: a rapid Panzer advance to the coast beyond Abbeville on the Somme; the destruction of the mobile Franco-British Army in Flanders to the north of this 'Panzer Corridor'; and finally the overwhelming of the remains of the French army south of the 'Panzer Corridor'. The driving of the 'Panzer Corridor' to the west was the task of Army Group B, commanded by Rundstedt and comprising Fourth, Twelfth, Second, Ninth and Sixteenth Armies and three Panzer Groups, under Hoth, Reinhardt and Guderian; the latter two were overseen by Kleist. Between 14 May, when the Meuse was crossed in strength, and 16 May, the Panzer groups achieved the destruction of Corap's 9th Army and advanced into the 50-mile gap thus created as far as Rethel on the Aisne and Hirson on the Oise. Kleist hesitated there, in deference to OKH's fears of a French counter-stroke in flank (which de Gaulle's hastily formed 4th Armored Division attempted in fact to deliver at Montcornet, north of Laon, on 19 May), but Guderian argued him into permitting a 'reconnaissance in force' and resumed his headlong advance. On 18 May he took Péronne on the Somme and on 20 May reached Abbeville and the sea. Hoth's Group, spearheaded by Rommel's Seventh Panzer Division, made slightly slower progress and was effectively counterattacked by the British at Arras on 21 May. The Allied Supreme War Council now in-

*Top right:* Weary Wehrmacht troops take time out in a street in Paris.
*Right:* German soldiers fire their artillery across the Seine into the heart of Rouen during their plunge southward down the French coast.

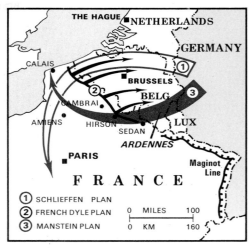

THE HAGUE ■ NETHERLANDS

GERMANY

CALAIS

BRUSSELS

② BELG ③

CAMBRAI

AMIENS

HIRSON LUX

SEDAN

ARDENNES

■ PARIS

Maginot Line

## F R A N C E

① SCHLIEFFEN PLAN
② FRENCH DYLE PLAN    0   MILES   100
③ MANSTEIN PLAN    0   KM   160

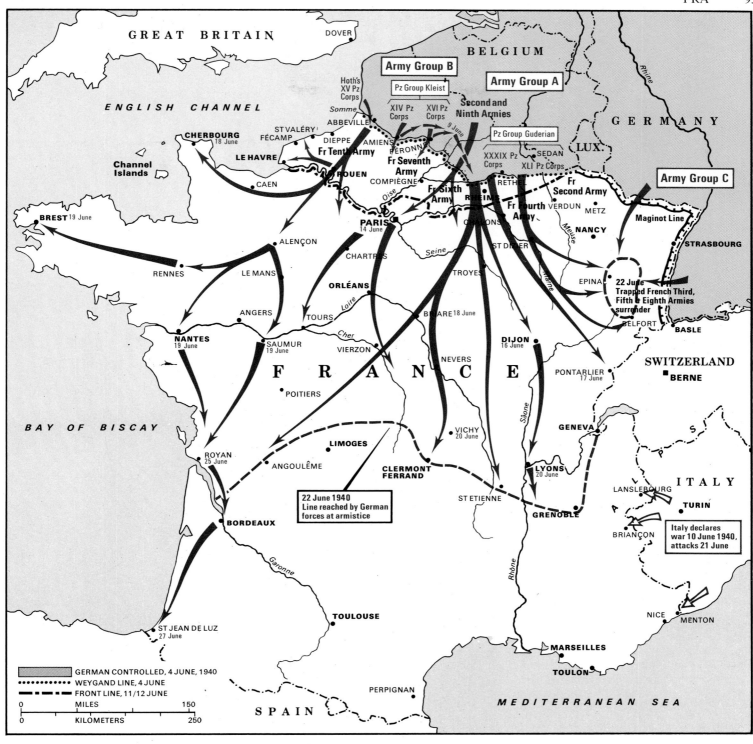

Below: The French government set up its capital at Vichy in the unoccupied zone.

stituted the so-called 'Weygand Plan' of flank attacks against the corridor but all failed, 22 May–1 June. Meanwhile the Germans were constricting the pocket around the Channel ports held by the BEF, the French 1st Army and the Belgians. The latter surrendered on 28 May, but between 24–26 May Hitler, acting on Rundstedt's advice, held the Panzer divisions back from a direct assault on the pocket. When it was resumed without tanks, the British had consolidated sufficiently to allow the orderly withdrawal of their army, and much of the French 1st, to Britain (Dunkirk). The Panzer divisions had been switched by 30 May to the Somme and Aisne fronts, on which the remnants of the French Army, still very numerous, but dispirited and short of equipment, were manning a notional 'Weygand Line' to defend the capital and interior. The balance of force was about 120 German divisions to 65,

with Kleist's Panzer groups, now under Bock's command, on the lower Somme, and Guderian, remaining with Rundstedt, on the Aisne. Their attack opened on 5 June and by 9 June Bock's Army Group B had reached the Seine below Paris. On the same day Rundstedt's Army Group A attacked, was held by local French resistance and counterattacked until 12 May when they broke through at Chalons, the attack being spearheaded by Guderian, and drove south. The French were forced into headlong retreat all along their line. Paris and much of the line of the Loire were abandoned on 13 June. The French in and behind the Maginot Line were thus isolated and by-passed. The Line itself was broken at Saarbrucken and Colmar on 14 and 15 June. On 17 June Pétain, who had become head of the French government, asked for an armistice which was granted on 22 June. But it did not take effect until Mussolini, who

Victorious German troops on a parade down the Champs Elysées after the fall of Paris.

had declared war on France on 10 June, also signed on 25 June. His efforts to win territory from the French since 20 June had been steadfastly repulsed by the numerically much inferior Army of the Alps. The terms imposed by the Germans were harsh but not extortionate. Northern France and the western and eastern frontiers, as far south as the Pyrennees and the Rivieria, came under occupation; the center, south and Mediterranean coast remained unoccupied. The French government, with its capital at Vichy, remained in existence, as did an army of about 100,000, and the fleet stayed at liberty. French overseas possessions were left under the administration of Vichy. The Germans could afford the measure of political generosity since their military success had been total. For a loss of 27,000 killed, they had destroyed the French, British, Belgian and Dutch armies; 1,900,000 Frenchmen alone had been made prisoners. Total French casualties were about 90,000 dead and 200,000 wounded; British, Belgian and Dutch casualties were 68,000, 23,000 and 10,000 respectively.

### 'Frances'
see Yokosuka P1Y1 Ginga

### Franco, General Francisco-Bahamonde, 1892–1975

Hitler courted Franco in 1940 to allow German troops freedom of movement through Spain to strike at Gibraltar and other centers of British power in the Mediterranean. Franco consistently refused, his skill in negotiation at the Hendaye meeting prompting Hitler to remark that he would rather visit the dentist to have teeth removed than do business with him again.

Hitler had in reserve a plan to invade Spain if necessary but the Caudillo managed tacitly to persuade him that in that eventuality the Spanish Army would fight. His preservation of Spanish neutrality throughout the war was a remarkable achievement, though purchased partly at the price of sending a division of volunteer anti-Bolshevists to Russia (the 'Blue Division').

### Frank, Hans, 1900–1946

Frank was the Nazi ruler of Poland from 1939–44. He was a distinguished lawyer who was Nazi minister without portfolio before the war and was then given charge of all Germany's territories in the East. He supervised the liquidation of Polish intellectuals and pursued a vigorous anti-Jewish policy. All Jewish businesses were closed down and Jews were dispatched to Auschwitz, Treblinka and other camps. He tried to resign as the Red Army approached the Polish borders on 14 occasions but it was in August 1944 that he finally resigned after announcing the collapse of the German administration. He was tried at Nuremberg and hanged on 16 October 1946.

### Frank, Karl Hermann, 1898–1946

Frank was a Sudeten German who was Secretary of State of the Protectorate of Bohemia and Moravia. Since he was Chief of Police and Senior SS Officer he was more powerful than the Protector Neurath. Frank suppressed the universities and when Heydrich became Protector he also directed the terror campaign. On Heydrich's assassination it was Frank who ordered reprisals against villages, such as Lidice. He became virtual ruler of Bohemia and Moravia until the end of the war when he tried to surrender to the Americans. He was tried by a Czech court and hanged on 22 May 1946.

### 'Frank'
see Nakajima Ki-84

### 'Frankforce'
see Arras, Battle of, 21 May 1940

### František, Sergeant Josef,

This Czech sergeant-pilot was one of the original members of No 303 (Polish) Squadron, RAF Fighter Command. Flying Hurricane aircraft, František made 17 confirmed kills, the highest individual score during the Battle of Britain. He was killed on 8 October 1940.

### Free Germany Movement
see Paulus, Field Marshal Friedrich

### French Army, (1) of 1940 and (2) Free French Army

(1) *The French Army of 1940*
This was a conscript force with a considerable proportion of regular soldiers particularly in its Colonial units. It depended upon the recall of reservists to bring its divisions up to war strength. Conscript service was for two years followed by part-time reserve service and con-

tinuing reserve obligation to the age of 42. Divisions were on several establishments: Active, consisting of regulars, conscripts and the first three-year groups of reservists; 'A' reserve divisions, consisting of the next year-groups of reservists up to the age of 32; 'B' reserve divisions, of the older reservists, with an average age of 36; Colonial divisions of white regulars, with some black or Arab regiments; and North African divisions, with some white conscripts, and a majority of Arab regulars. The cavalry, mechanized, armored, fortress and alpine divisions were a mixture of regular, active, A and B classes. These establishments provided seven Active motorized divisions, ten Active infantry, 17 'A' infantry, 19 'B' infantry (of which three were alpine), ten North African, seven Colonial, five fortress, five cavalry, three mechanized and four armored divisions; two other alpine divisions were a mixture of Active and A reservist classes. There were a number of combat units not formed into divisions, including the Foreign Legion and Polish and Czech volunteer legions.

The infantry divisions were organized into three infantry regiments of three battalions each, with two artillery regiments, given 36 field and 24 medium guns, and a reconnaissance squadron, two engineer companies and services; it had 52 light anti-tank guns (25mm). Alpine divisions were similar; fortress divisions had infantry only.

The cavalry division consisted of two horsed and one mechanized regiments and a reconnaissance group, and its artillery of 12 field and 12 medium artillery pieces and eight 47mm anti-tank guns; it had 20 light tanks and 15 armored cars. The mechanized division (*division légère mécanisée*) had two tank regiments, each of 87 light or medium tanks, a reconnaissance regiment with 40 armored cars, and three motorized infantry battalions; its artillery was 24 field and 12 medium guns and nine-47mm anti-tank guns. The armored divisions (*division cuirassée*), of which the first three were formed between January and March 1940 and the fourth (de Gaulle's) during the Battle of France itself, contained two light and two medium tank regiments, one infantry battalion in armored carriers and an artillery regiment of 24–105mm guns. Tank strength was 62 medium and 84 light tanks; anti-tank guns numbered 167. There were also about 50 independent tank battalions attached to armies.

Equipment was of mixed quality: the 75mm field and 105mm medium guns were improved World War I models; the anti-tank guns varied in caliber from the plentiful but obsolete 25mm to the excellent but scarce 47mm. Tanks were of eight types from the completely obsolete Renault F tanks of 1918 to the excellent modern Somua and B.I. models, both mounting the high-velocity 47mm gun, the latter also a 75mm low-velocity gun. Total strength was 2235.

The command system was over-complicated and slow moving. At the head stood the Supreme Commander Land Forces (Gamelin), with headquarters located at the Fort de Vincennes, near Paris; subordinate to him were the front commands, the most important of which was the Commander North East Front (Georges) at La Ferté. Georges commanded three Army Groups, 1st (Billotte), 2nd (Prételat, with 35 divisions) and 3rd (Besson, with 14 divisions). Besson's and Prételat's Groups garrisoned the Maginot Line, with the 3rd, 4th, 5th and 8th Armies. Billotte commanded the field army consisting of 1st, 2nd, 7th and 9th Armies and the British Expeditionary Force (which, however, took its orders direct from Gamelin). The French Air Force had a separate command system, and its headquarters were not co-located with the Army's.

The Germans permitted a French 'Armistice Army' of 100,000 to survive in the unoccupied zone, but it was disbanded on their occupation of the zone in 1942.

The Army of Africa remained intact, and most of it was incorporated in the Free French Army following the Torch landings in 1942.

### (2) The Free French Army

Following de Gaulle's appeal to the French people in June 1940, a few units of the Army of Africa joined his small army-in-exile to form the Free French Forces (Leclerc). After the Torch landings most units of the Army of Africa came under his control, and others were raised to supplement it during the remainder of the Mediterranean Campaign, so that by the end of 1944 he had under his command, as the reborn French Army, nearly 300,000 men, comprising the First French Army of three armored and nine infantry divisions, three Moroccan 'Tabor' groups and some independent commando units. It was almost wholly American equipped.

---

### French Navy

From being an obsolescent force in World War I, the French Navy was rebuilt for World War II, largely through the efforts of three men, the energetic Minister of Marine Georges Leygues (1927–32), and his equally energetic son-in-law Admiral François Darlan, who became Chief of the Naval Staff in 1937, and another fine Minister of Marine, François Pietri (1932–35).

There had been little attempt to match the battle fleets of the three major navies, and until 1931 the option to build replacement capital ships allowed under the Washington Treaty was not exercized. Instead money was spent on a large fleet of submarines and fast torpedo craft. Spurred on by the Italian Navy's infatuation with high-speed cruisers the French developed the super-destroyer or *contre-torpilleur*, and these ultra-fast but short-legged and fragile craft soon became their area of expertise. By comparison the cruisers built under the Washington Treaty had a poor reputation both in and out of France.

Despite widespread apathy and predominantly army influence over the allocation of defense funds, Darlan did his best to modernize the material and personnel of the *Marine*

The 7000-ton cruiser *Georges Leygues* was one of the few French ships to fall into Allied hands.

The 'flight deck' of the *Georges Leygues*, which carried only one aircraft for reconnaissance purposes.

*Nationale*, and by 1939 the following strength had been achieved:
2 old battleships
3 modernized battleships
2 battlecruisers
7 heavy cruisers
12 light cruisers
32 large destroyers or *contre-torpilleurs*
38 destroyers
77 submarines

After 1936 additional rearmament was authorized:
4 35,000-ton battleships
2 aircraft carriers
3 light cruisers
4 *contre-torpilleurs*
12 destroyers
40 submarines

None of these additional ships was ready when war broke out, partly because of poor productivity in the shipyards. The catastrophe which overwhelmed France in May–June 1940 hit the Navy very hard. Those few ships which could, escaped to England or North Africa, but were instructed to obey the provisions of the Armistice. The British Government, angered at what it regarded as a betrayal by an ally who had promised not to negotiate separately with Germany and apprehensive of Italian intentions, demanded that the fleet be removed or immobilized. For a variety of reasons no compromise could be found, with the result that on 3 July 1940 the British Fleet opened fire on the main squadrons in their base at Mers-el-Kebir, Algeria. Although not annihilated, the French Navy was to all intents out of action, and the survivors fled to Toulon, while the ships which had reached colonial ports were also content to serve under the Vichy regime. In London General de Gaulle created the 'Free French' Navy

The French battleship *Lorraine* was modernized in the prewar period, with a catapult and additional anti-aircraft guns.

under the control of the government-in-exile, and it expanded rapidly with the transfer of British equipment and ships.

The Allied invasion of North Africa was opposed by local units loyal to Vichy, and further losses were incurred, but the most serious outcome was a pre-emptive strike by the Germans against the Toulon Fleet, with the intention of seizing the ships and preventing any desertion to the Allies. Tragically most of the ships were blown up and only a handful joined the Allies, but immediately all the French warships overseas joined the Allied cause, and there were no longer two French navies. Several new ships were transferred by the US and many of the existing ones were refitted by the USA. On 13 September 1944 the cruiser *Georges Leygues* led a squadron back in triumph to Toulon.

### Freyburg, 1st Baron Bernard Cyril, 1889–1963

A hero of the Gallipoli operation of 1915 and of the fighting in France where he won the Victoria Cross, Freyburg was appointed on the outbreak of World War II Commander of the New Zealand forces, a post he held throughout. After the British evacuation of Greece in 1941 he was left with the responsibility of defending Crete against the German airborne attack which followed but, despite dogged resistance, was obliged to abandon the island. After the war he became Governor-General of New Zealand. His contemporaries regarded him as the reincarnation of one of the heroes of antiquity; to Churchill, he was the 'Salamander', a warrior refreshed by passing through the fire which had scarred his body with multiple wounds.

### Frick, Wilhelm, 1877–1946

Frick was a Nazi administrator who was Reichs-Protector of Bohemia-Moravia from 1943 until the end of the war. Until 1943 he had been Minister of the Interior but had proved an ineffectual figure who had allowed Himmler to take control of the police. As Protector of Bohemia-Moravia he was merely a figurehead; Karl Frank held effective power and Frick allowed him to pursue a policy of terror and extermination in that territory. He was tried at Nuremberg, found guilty of helping to prepare a war of aggression and of committing crimes against humanity. He was hanged.

### Friedman, Colonel William, 1891–1969

Friedman was the chief cryptanalyst of the War Department, Washington, from 1941–1947. His main contribution to World War II was that he broke the Japanese diplomatic code in the summer of 1940. The US had three tracking stations intercepting messages from Tokyo to Japanese embassies throughout the world. The operation was codenamed 'Magic' and it gave Cordell Hull, the Secretary of State, an advantage in his negotiations with the Japanese ambassador, Admiral Nomura, in 1941.

### Fritsch, General Werner Freiherr von, 1880–1939

Commander of the German Army in 1938, Fritsch was impugned on evidence fabricated by Himmler of impropriety and removed from office, together with the War Minister, General Blomberg, who had made an unwise marriage. This 'Blomberg-Fritsch crisis' provided Hitler with the opportunity he required to subordinate the high command of the Army to his personal control, exercised through a new headquarters, OKW (*Oberkommando der Wehrmacht*). Fritsch was subsequently exonerated by an officers' court of honor but not reinstated. All that Hitler offered him by way of recompense was the honorary colonelcy of Artillery Regiment 12, which he insisted on accompanying to the Polish Front in September 1939. On reconnaissance outside Warsaw he was killed.

### Fritz-X

The Fritz-X was a German air-to-ground guided glide bomb, and was also known as FX-1 400 or SD-1400. It could be controlled during its drop by an observer in the parent aircraft passing commands via a radio link. It was basically a 1400kg armor-piercing bomb to which small wings and a tail unit containing the guidance mechanism had been added. Signals received by

The Fritz-X guided bomb.

the radio receiver in the bomb caused 'spoilers' on the tail surfaces to be raised into the airstream, thus modifying the bomb's trajectory. Development began in 1939 and final trials were done in Italy in early 1942. Its most notable success was the sinking of the Italian battleship *Roma* on 9 September 1943, which was achieved by hits with three Fritz-X bombs.

### Fuchida, Commander Mitsuo,

General Commander (Air) Fuchida of the Imperial Japanese Navy 1st Carrier Division led the first attack on Pearl Harbor on 7 December 1941 flying a Nakajima B5N2 'Kate'.

### Führer's Headquarters (*Führerhauptquartier*)

Hitler directed operations from ten locations during the war:
1. His special train used during the invasions of Poland in 1939 and Yugoslavia and Greece in April 1941 was parked successively at Polzin (now Potczyn Zdroj), Gross Born, Illnau Station, Oppeln (now Opole) and, in September 1940, moved to Goddentow-Lanz, where the Sopot Casino-Hotel was used as a temporary headquarters; during April 1941 it was parked at Monichkirchen in southern Austria.

There were three specially built bunkers:
2. Felsennest (Castle on a Rock), located near Rodert, Münstereifel was occupied by Hitler from 10 May to 5 June 1940.
3. Wolfsschlucht (Wolf's Glen), located in Bruly de Pêche near Givet, Belgium, was occupied by Hitler from 6-24 June 1940.
4. Tannenberg (named after the 1914 battlefield), located on the Kniebis plateau in the Black Forest, was occupied by Hitler from 25 June to 6 July 1940.

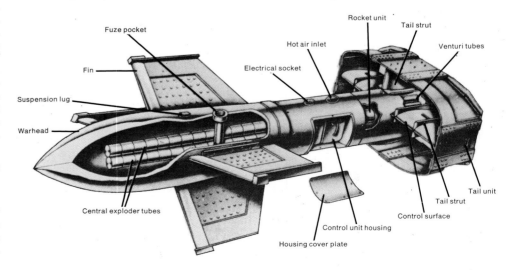

Rocket unit · Tail strut

Fuze pocket

Hot air inlet

Venturi tubes

Electrical socket

Fin

Suspension lug

Warhead

Central exploder tubes

Control unit housing

Housing cover plate

Tail unit

Tail strut

Control surface

The Japanese battleship *Fuso* displaced 34,700 tons and was armed with twelve 14-inch guns.

5. Wolfsschanze (Wolf's Lair), at Rastenburg in East Prussia was occupied with intermissions from 24 June 1941 to 20 November 1944
6. Werwolf (Wolf Man) at Vinnitsa, in the Ukraine, he occupied from 16 July to 1 November 1942 and 17 February – 13 March 1943.
7. The Berghof, his prewar holiday home at Berchtesgaden, Obersalzberg.
8. Schloss Klessheim, Salzburg, he visited to escape from the winter weather of Rastenburg.
9. Adlerhorst (Eagle's Nest) near Ziegenberg in the Taunus mountains, occupied during the Ardennes Offensive.
10. The Reich Chancellery and the Führerbunker beneath it was occupied by Hitler from 30 November 1944 until his suicide on 30 April 1945.

A Führer Headquarters (Wolfsschlucht II) was also constructed but not used at Soissons, France.

---

### Fulmar, Fairey

The first Royal Navy fighter with an eight-gun armament, the Fulmar was intended to match the firepower of the RAF's Hurricanes and Spitfires. Unfortunately, the Admiralty still insisted on carrying a crew of two, and the resulting maximum speed of only 280mph, with a Merlin engine similar to that of the RAF fighters, reduced the Fulmar's chances of success in combat. A total of 600 were built, the last 350 as Mk IIs with a 1300hp Merlin 30 engine and tropical equipment. They served fairly briefly from June 1940.

---

### *Furious*

This elderly British carrier had been laid down in 1915 as a freak 'light cruiser' or battlecruiser armed with two single 18in guns. While she was still being completed in 1917 the Admiralty decided that she would make an ideal fast aircraft carrier for working with the fleet, and so she was never completed to her original design. In June

1917 she was commissioned with a hangar and flying-off deck fitted over her forecastle in place of the forward 18in gun turret.

Between 1921 and 1925 the *Furious* was converted once again, this time to a proper fleet carrier, but with a flush deck as there was still considerable suspicion about the value of an 'island' superstructure. When she emerged she was immediately nicknamed the 'Covered Wagon', and rapidly proved her worth as the RN's first large, fast carrier. Despite her age she was refitted for frontline service between 1936 and 1939 and saw much arduous war service. She played an important part in the Norwegian campaign in April 1940, during which her aircraft flew numerous sorties in support of naval and ground forces.

She took part in the great Pedestal convoy battle in August 1942 and provided cover for the Torch landings in North Africa three months later. Her last operation was Tungsten in April 1944 when she launched Barracuda dive-bombers against the *Tirpitz*, lying in Kaafjord. In August that year, old age finally caught up with her and she was declared to be 'worn out'. She had been the platform for some of the most far-reaching experiments in naval aviation and handled a wider variety of aircraft types than any other ship afloat, from Sopwith Pups, floatplanes and balloons to Grumman Hellcat fighters.

---

### *Fuso*

This Japanese battleship was sunk by destroyer torpedoes during the prelude to the Battle of Surigao Strait on 24 October 1944. She blew up and broke in two.

---

### FZG–76

More generally known as the 'V-1' missile, this was a German mid-wing monoplane driven by a pulsating flow duct motor and carrying a 1870lb explosive warhead. Development of this device began in June 1942 at the Research Station,

Peenemünde, and the whole design was carefully thought out so as to be as simple and cheap as possible to produce. Little scarce material was used; most of the construction was from mild steel and wood; weight-saving was a minor consideration. The missile, as launched, weighed 4858lbs and had a wing-span of 17ft 6in, a length of 25ft 4.5in, and carried 150 gals of fuel. Guidance was pre-set into the missile before launch and thus the flight was secure against any form of electronic interference or jamming.

Launching took place from a fixed ramp about 50yds long, using a piston mechanism to propel the missile into the air at a speed sufficient to allow the duct motor to function and keep the missile airborne. Launch speed was about 200mph, and once the duct motor took over the speed increased to an average of 350mph. Altitude was about 3500 to 4000 feet, a zone which was particularly difficult for British AA defenses since it was too low for the heavy guns to engage effectively and too high for the light guns. Not until automatic power control was applied to the British guns was it possible to obtain worthwhile success.

The maximum range of the missile was about 130 miles, at which range some 80% of the missiles would land within an eight-mile circle of the selected target. Mass production began in March 1944 and about 35,000 were produced before the war ended. Of these, 9251 were fired against England, of which 4621 were destroyed, and 6551 against Antwerp, of which 2455 were destroyed.

The often ridiculed but feared V-1 missile.

# G

### Galissonnière, La

This class of French light cruiser was a development of the *Emile Bertin*, but much more successful. With a good balance between speed and armor they were not only the best French cruisers of their day but also among the best for their tonnage in the world. Unlike other French ships their endurance was adequate for ocean operations, and they represented a shift in emphasis from a purely Mediterranean strategy to a more flexible 'blue water' outlook.

Six were built between 1931 and 1937, and the class served in the Atlantic on convoy duty in 1939–1940. The *Georges Leygues, Gloire* and *Montcalm* left Toulon on 9 September 1940 bound for Casablanca, and eluded a British squadron. The *Gloire* was intercepted off Dakar nine days later and forced to return to Casablanca but the other two joined the Vichy forces at Dakar and helped to foil Operation Menace later that month. When Dakar joined the Allies in November 1943 all three went to the USA for refits, but the *Galissonnière, Jean de Vienne* and *Marseillaise* were all scuttled at Toulon in November 1942.

The surviving ships carried out shore bombardments at Normandy and in the South of France invasion in 1944.

---

### Galland, General Adolf, 1912–

One of the most outstanding officers of the German Luftwaffe, Galland had been a fighter pilot before the outbreak of war but had held a staff post until April 1940, when he rejoined the fighter squadrons. During the Battle of Britain he led III Gruppe of Jagdgeschwader 26, becoming one of its most successful pilots. In November 1941, he succeeded Werner Mölders, another renowned fighter ace who was killed in a flying accident, as General der Jagdflieger. A year later, at the age of 30, he was promoted to become the youngest General in the German Armed Forces. In this position, he not only inspired his squadrons with his personal prowess, being credited with 104 victories, but he also applied the knowledge he had gained in combat to improve technical and tactical aspects of the fighter arm. In recognition of his success he was awarded the coveted Knights Cross with Oak Leaves, Swords and Diamonds.

With German fortunes diminishing and the supply of urgently needed equipment running short, Galland was constantly called upon to defend the activities of his squadrons to the German High Command. Added to this,

Adolf Galland, hero of the Luftwaffe.

Goering's unwillingness to stand up to Hitler's demands that the Fighter Arm should be disbanded led ultimately to Galland's being dismissed from his post in January 1945. He returned to operational flying, commanding Jagdverband 44, equipped with the new Me 262 twin-jet fighter, until he was shot down near Munich by a P–51 Mustang on 26 April 1945.

A brilliant pilot and a farsighted Commander, Galland never fell into the trap of underestimating his enemies.

---

### Galvanic
see Gilbert Islands

---

### Gamelin, General Maurice Gustave, 1872–1958

A military technician of a 19th rather than 20th century type, Gamelin was head of the operations section at French General Headquarters throughout World War I. In the 1920s he was Chief of Staff of the Army of the Orient in Syria and then became Commander in Chief. After 1935 he held a succession of politico-military jobs – Vice-President of the War Council, Chief of the Defense Staff – and in 1939 was acting as Commander of the land forces. Unfortunately a Commander was what he was not. His instructions to his subordinates both before and during the Battle of France were abstract and philosophical rather than direct and positive. He was replaced by Weygand on 19 May 1940, too late for his sins of omission to be made good.

---

### Garand Rifle

John C Garand developed his first automatic rifle in 1920; the operation relied on the cartridge primer 'setting back' a few hundredths of an inch under the gas pressure inside the case, and this small movement was used to unlock the breech of the rifle. Once the breech was un-

locked there was still sufficient chamber pressure to drive the cartridge case backwards and thus operate the breech block. He submitted the rifle for test by the US Army, who turned it down; nevertheless, they were sufficiently impressed by Garand's ingenuity to offer him a post as a designer at Springfield Armory, and he continued to work on automatic rifle designs.

Garand now turned to the more conventional form of gas operation and after extensive trials his design was accepted by the US Army in 1932, a piece of far-sightedness which was to the Army's credit. It took some time to perfect the design, but in 1936 issues began, and the US Army was the only army to enter World War II with an automatic rifle as the standard infantryman's weapon (though at the beginning of the war there were insufficient rifles for the *entire* army). By the time production ceased in the 1950s, over five and a half million had been made plus those made under license overseas. The success of the Garand was instrumental in persuading other armies that the automatic rifle was a practical weapon.

The Garand operates in the following manner. A gas piston beneath the barrel turns and opens the rotating bolt by a cam action. Feed is from an eight round clip which is inserted into the magazine through the open action. After the last round has been fired the clip is ejected and the action remains open ready for re-loading; this is probably the only weak point of the whole design, since the magazine can only be loaded with a full clip and cannot be 'topped up' during a lull in the action. Although numerous experimental models were produced during the war for purposes of research, the only variant to reach the hands of troops was the Sniper's Rifle M1C, a standard rifle with flash suppressor, leather cheek-piece and telescopic sight.

---

### Gauss, Clarence, 1887–1960

Gauss was the US Ambassador to China from 1941 until December 1944. He was a State Department expert on Chinese affairs. Shortly after Stilwell's recall Gauss resigned.

---

### Gazala–Bir Hacheim, Battle of, 1942

Auchinleck's advance to El Agheila in pursuit of Rommel after the Crusader battle left his army as overextended as Rommel's had been on the Egyptian frontier in November. The Germans now also benefited from a sudden improvement in their supply situation, which brought Rommel the reinforcements of men and equipment he needed for a resumption of his offensive. Auchinleck's light advanced forces were driven out of their screening positions on 21 January and his forward troops from Benghazi, his advanced port, on 29 January. Auchinleck now recognized that his position was untenable and made a strategic withdrawal to a new line between Gazala and Bir Hacheim, thirty miles west of Tobruk reached on 4 February. Across that line the two desert armies faced each other for the next four months while they built up their strength. By June the British fielded about 700 tanks (of which 200 were the new American Grants, with a 75mm gun) to Rommel's 560 (of which half were Italian). Fearing that the British would continue to outstrip him in this race, Rommel decided to attack the Gazala line. He intended to outflank it round the desert strongpoint of Bir Hacheim, held by a Free French

Brigade, largely Foreign Legion in composition, and then drive to seize El Adem in the rear of the British position. He began with a frontal assault launched by the Italian infantry but supported by some German armor on 26 May. That night, however, he called the armor away and concentrated all he had in a drive at and round Bir Hacheim. His leading elements reached El Adem the following day. Ritchie, commanding the 8th Army, hastily formed an improvised line at right angles to his main front to protect 'Knightsbridge', his administrative area, and bitter tank fighting followed in the area between 30 May and 2 June. Rommel's rearward communications were also threatened, however, by the unsubdued resistance of the French at Bir Hacheim and when the Italians succeeded in breaching the British line to its north he decided therefore to withdraw immediately behind the gap they had created. While he resupplied himself the British advanced and eight days of bitter tank fighting in this 'Cauldron' ensued. On 10 June the French were finally beaten into surrender after one of the bravest defensive actions of the desert war and the British consequently were impelled to retreat from the region altogether. Despite his heavy tank losses, Rommel was able to follow them in pursuit. Tobruk, besieged on 14 June, was surrendered by its South African garrison on 21 June. Four days later Rommel bumped up against the 8th Army's new defensive position running between El Alamein on the coast and the Qattara Depression 40 miles to the south and came to a halt.

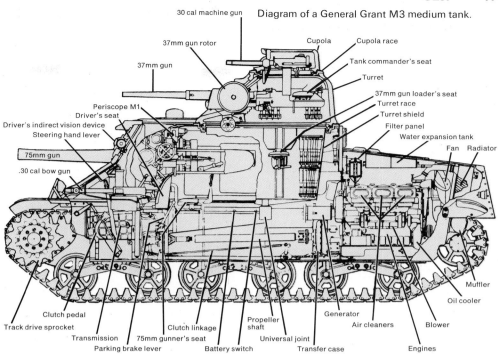

Diagram of a General Grant M3 medium tank.

**General Grant**

This was the British name given to the US M3 medium tank. This design originated in August 1940 from a demand for a medium tank with thicker armor than the service M2A1 and with a 75mm gun. Since it was recognized that a suitable turret for such a gun would take time to develop, a design was prepared in which the 75mm gun was carried in a sponson-type turret at the right side of the body. A 37mm gun was mounted in the turret. It was by no means a perfect design but it was one way of obtaining a powerful tank quickly. The pilot tank was ready in Januars 1941 and production was under-way by July. Numbers of these tanks were taken by Britain on a 'cash and carry' basis (it was be-

Grant M3 medium tank.

fore the days of Lend-Lease) and some small changes were made to suit British practice, notably the removal of the machine gun cupola on top of the turret. These tanks were delivered to North Africa in early 1942 and saw their first major action in the Battle of Gazala in May. After the passing of the Lend-Lease Act several American pattern M3s (with machine gun cupola) were sent to Britain, and these were known to the British as the 'General Lee' in order to distinguish them from the earlier 'Grant' pattern.

**'George'**
see Kawanishi NiK

**George VI, King**

George VI was King of Great Britain and the titular head of the British Commonwealth and Empire. He was a shy and modest man who came into his own during the war and found that he was able to raise British morale, even during the darkest days of the blitz. He actively encouraged the war effort by visiting troop positions overseas and traveling all over England.

He and his wife were offered the opportunity to leave for Canada but George and Elizabeth decided to stay with their people in their hour of need.

**Georges, General Joseph, 1875-1951**

In 1940 he was responsible for the conduct of operations on the Northeast Front, in direct subordination to the Commander in Chief, Gamelin, and it was his troops there which were assailed by the German invasions of Belgium, Holland and France. He had risen to eminence through his close association with a succession of French military leaders, Foch, Pétain and Maginot, whom he had served respectively as Director of Operations in 1918, Chief of Staff in the Rif war and military assistant. He had been deputy to Gamelin since 1935 but had been badly wounded in the assassination of King Alexander of Yugoslavia at Marseilles in 1934 and had not fully recovered, a condition which contributed to his faltering and slow-witted handling of the defense in May 1940.

**German Army**

Rapidly expanded by Hitler after his seizure of power in 1933 from the 100,000 men allowed Germany under the Versailles Treaty, the Army numbered at the outbreak of war some two million men, organized into 106 divisions. Another 44 divisions were raised after the Polish Campaign, so that on 10 May 1940, its full strength was three million organized into 150 divisions. Of these ten were armored (Panzer) including four recently converted from 'light' divisions; four were motorized; three were mountain; and one was cavalry. In addition, the Luftwaffe provided a parachute division and the Waffen (armed) SS, a Nazi party organization, three notional divisions. After the victories of 1940 some 45 infantry divisions were demobilized, to a greater or lesser degree, but, in preparation for the 1941 campaign in the Balkans and Russia, new divisions were raised and thereafter numbers of divisions in all categories grew until the great defeats of 1944. In all, 315

German troops moved rapidly across the Russian frontier in the summer of 1941 in the Wehrmacht's most daring and ultimately its most disastrous offensive.

infantry divisions were raised during the war, of very varied quality. Some were later reorganized either into Panzer divisions which eventually numbered 29, or motorized (Panzer Grenadier) divisions which eventually numbered 11. Besides these, the Luftwaffe organized ten infantry divisions from its surplus ground staff, as well as ten parachute divisions and one Panzer division (the famous 'Hermann Goering'), and the Waffen SS eventually fielded over 30 divisions, of which only about 12 (all Panzer or Panzer Grenadier divisions) reached full strength.

The infantry divisions, whether of good or poor quality troops, and whether fully or inadequately equipped, were all alike in their low mobility; throughout the war their artillery and transport columns were horse-drawn and the infantry were marching soldiers. Only the Panzer and motorized (Panzer Grenadier, as they were renamed in 1942) divisions possessed sufficient mechanical transport to move their soldiers independently of the railways.

One of the principal means used by the German army to expand the number of its formations during the war was to reduce establishments of existing divisions, both of men and equipment. The Panzer division of 1944, for example, was notably weaker in tanks than that of 1940, and the *Volksgrenadier* (People's Grenadier – infantry) divisions raised after the retreat from France were much smaller than those of 1939. Divisional establishments are thus difficult to summarize. In brief, infantry divisions in 1939 consisted of three infantry regiments, each of three battalions, a reconnaissance squadron, an anti-tank battalion, an engineer battalion and an artillery regiment of nine batteries of 105mm howitzers and three batteries of 150mm howitzers (48 guns in all); by 1944, infantry regiments had been reduced to two battalions and the artillery regiment to 32 guns, somewhat compensated for by the addition of better anti-tank and anti-aircraft weapons. Panzer Grenadier divisions closely resembled infantry divisions, except that each possessed a tank battalion, as well as motorized transport for the infantry and artillery, but their strength also diminished towards the end of the

war. The Panzer divisions' decline was the most marked; in 1940 it fielded 328 tanks, five motorized infantry battalions, an engineer, an anti-tank and a reconnaissance battalion and 6 artillery batteries (24–105mm howitzers); in 1944 it had only 159 tanks (if at full strength, which few were) and four motorized infantry battalions.

German equipment, however, was of consistently good quality throughout the war; the light Panzer Mark I and II tanks were quickly discarded and the Mk II and IV thereafter provided the mainstay of the armored forces until the arrival of the Mk V (Panther) in 1943. All were excellent vehicles, easily adaptable for re-engining, re-armoring and up-gunning. The long 75mm tank gun, mounted on the Panther and later models of the Mark IV was deadly. The Mark VI (Tiger) was not issued to divisions, but organized in special battalions under command of higher headquarters. Its thick armor and superb 88mm gun made it the most feared tank of World War II battlefields. German artillery was at least equal to the enemy's; German small arms, particularly the Schmeisser machine-pistol and MG42 medium machine gun, were superior weapons specially and successfully designed for rapid mass production.

The German command and staff system, derived from Prussian origins which had provided a model for the rest of Europe, retained its masterly efficiency throughout the war; German staff officers were particularly adept at improvising headquarters in moments of crisis, and routine staffwork at divisional, corps, army and army group headquarters was consistently excellent. Above that last level, control was vested either in OKH (*Oberkommando des Heeres* – Army High Command) located at Zossen near Berlin, or at OKW (*Oberkommando der Wehrmacht* – High Command of the Armed Forces) a headquarters created in 1938 by Hitler who was its head. After 1941 he so arranged things that all fronts, save the Russian, were controlled by OKW. OKH remained responsible for the Eastern Front, but its chiefs were denied a global view of the progress of the war, and thus reduced to the status of operational commanders rather than strategists. They were also, as soldiers, subordinate to Hitler after December 1941, in which month he assumed the position of Commander in Chief of the Army, the first civilian in Prussian or German history to hold that post.

## German Navy

The Kriegsmarine was the lineal descendant of the *Kaiserliche Marine*, the Imperial Navy which was disbanded under the Treaty of Versailles. During the time of the Weimar Republic the truncated Reichsmarine was only allowed to keep a token force of pre-1914 ships for coastal defense. These included six pre-dreadnought battleships, eight light cruisers and 32 destroyers and torpedo boats, of which only part could be in active commission at any time. The personnel was fixed at only 15,000 men, making it almost impossible to evade the preceding provision.

These harsh conditions acted as a stimulus and a challenge rather than a straitjacket, as most Germans regarded the Versailles Treaty as something forced on them. By 1922 the skilled design team from Krupp's Germania yard had been reformed, notably in Holland under the aegis of the *Nederlandse Scheepsbouwkantoor*. Behind this 'front', research into U-Boat design continued against the day when Germany would be allowed to build her own U-Boats once more, but the agency was also successful in obtaining genuine contracts for Finnish, Turkish and Spanish submarines, all of which served as prototypes. The story of how the clause permitting replacement of the old battleships by powerful commerce-raiding armored cruisers is described under the *Deutschland* entry. The understating of tonnage which underlay that success was also used to conceal the true size of all categories of ships built during this period so that all figures were within the figure of total tonnage allowed by the Treaty. Furthermore, it had the additional advantage of making German ships appear to be well-armed for their displacement.

The advent of Adolf Hitler was matched by a big increase in expenditure on armaments, and the newly named Kriegsmarine benefited, although the plans had been developed long before by a Staff dedicated to the ultimate regeneration of German naval power. The 1933 Program included a new capital ship, the battlecruiser *Scharnhorst*, demanded as a 'reply' to the French *Dunkerque*, which was herself a reply to the *Deutschland*. The other signatories of the Treaty chose not to make an issue of the violation, but the other vessels ordered in that year would have caused more alarm had they been published. Eight U-Boats were authorized, and the material was gathered in secret, until the moment in 1935 when Hitler chose to renounce the Versailles Treaty unilaterally. The 1934 Program included further secret orders, another battlecruiser, the *Gneisenau* and 28 U-Boats.

The formal abrogation of the Versailles Treaty in 1935 came as a great shock to the still-somnolent democracies, for a powerful German Navy seemed to have sprung out of the ground. In the absence of anything but feeble protests at the League of Nations the British decided to try to contain the German naval expansion as best they could. The Anglo-German Naval Treaty of 1935 allowed the Germans to build up to 35 percent of the Royal Navy, except in U-Boats, where the Germans stated that they did not intend to go beyond 45 percent but reserved the right to build up to 100 percent. The overall limitation was expressed in total tonnage, not number of units, and so any increase in one category would be matched by reductions in others.

In 1937 the German Navy was finally told by Hitler that war with Great Britain was no longer

Recruiting poster for the German Navy, which was far more effective beneath the seas than on them.

*Top to bottom:* The German cruisers *Leipzig, Emden* and *Nürnberg.* The *Emden* was obsolescent in World War II, but the others were more successful.

unthinkable but quite inevitable. The result was the famous 'Z' Plan, for six battleships, eight heavy cruisers, 17 light cruisers, four aircraft carriers, 223 U-Boats, all to be completed between 1943 and 1948. Just how this gigantic program was to be achieved with Germany's relatively limited naval shipbuilding capacity was never explained, nor what reaction it would provoke in other countries. Certainly the British showed themselves willing and able to lay down ships on a one-for-one ratio or even higher, and if Hitler's planned date of 1944 for the outbreak of war had been met the 'Z' Plan would have been little more than a collection of half-built ships. It could only have worked if the British had failed to order warships at all in 1937, 1938, 1939, 1940 and 1941 – hardly a proposition to be considered seriously.

The German obsession with their lack of numbers reflected itself in a desire for powerful armament in the lower categories, particularly destroyers. To make up for lack of cruisers the later destroyers were given cruiser-caliber guns, but this made them less battleworthy, and the results became painfully obvious in wartime. On the other hand, the desire to get as many submarines as possible out of the total tonnage available led the Staff to choose a U-Boat design which was ultimately too small for the Atlantic. The capital ships were competently designed but very conservative and did not compare favorably with the latest British and American designs; their chief advantage lay in the concealed margin of tonnage, which permitted more

offensive and defensive features than in ships of apparently comparable size in other navies. Thus the *Scharnhorst* was a 32,000-tonner not 26,000 tons, and the *Bismarck* a 42,000-tonner not a 35,000-tonner, which accounted for much of their apparent superiority.

The cruisers built were by and large bad bargains. The light cruisers had low endurance, a grievous shortcoming in ships required for ocean work, and the heavy cruisers were mechanically unreliable and poorly protected for their size.

A scheme to produce *spähkreuzer* or scout cruisers in place of a class of six light cruisers had to be aborted in 1941 for the simple reason that the ships would have had no heavy ships to escort.

In one area, however, the Germans produced designs of outstanding quality. In 1934 a diesel engine development contract had been given to private industry, and this produced the magnificent 20-cylinder Daimler-Benz V-form diesel. This was ideal for fast motor torpedo-boats or *schnellboote*, with high power for the weight, and virtually no fire risk from fuel. When allied with a novel hull form produced by the Lürssen boatbuilding firm, with good seakeeping qualities and a good payload of weapons, the German Navy had the world's best small strike craft, and they proved their worth in literally hundreds of actions.

Although the German scientific services were as talented and ingenious as any, the armed forces did not make the best use of their ideas. Radar was perfected, but only for gunnery purposes, and although the German Navy could boast of having fought the first radar-controlled

battle, when the *Admiral Graf Spee* fired at British cruisers at the Battle of the River Plate in December 1939, this early promise was not sustained. At the height of the Battle of the Atlantic in 1942–43, when liaison with the scientists should have been a first priority, vital information about Allied electronics was not passed on. Like the Americans, the Germans were dismayed to find that their U-Boats' torpedoes were not functioning under battle conditions, and one can only speculate about reasons for so many dismal failures in a nation so dedicated to detailed planning and staffwork, and a nation, furthermore, which had been preparing for war since 1934. Part of the problem was the current of intrigue which swirled about the Führer's 'throne' and the desire to conceal bad news lest it be construed as proof of incompetence.

Other weaknesses came to light under the stress of war. Despite clear evidence of a need to produce the new 'electro-U-Boat' as early as 1943, nothing was done to cut back production of conventional U-Boats or to stop the scientists from promoting less practical projects such as the hydrogen-peroxide Walther U-Boats, with the result that the deadly new U-Boats were not ready when they were needed.

On the tactical side the German naval staff showed that it had not exorcised the spirit of 1914–18. Commanders showed remarkably little imagination, and on many occasions superior German forces disengaged when they could have finished off their opponents. The bravery of officers and men was never in question, and the last fight of the *Bismarck* and *Scharnhorst* added lustre to the Kriegsmarine's battle honors. It has been customary to blame Hitler for all the bad decisions, but many of the timid orders were given on the spot by sea-officers who had forgotten what their ships had been built to do. However, in fairness it must be admitted that Hitler's battle orders to his admirals harped on the risks rather than the rewards, and his ignorance of sea power was a major cause of the poor performance of the surface fleet.

The last weeks of the German Navy were its most heroic, as it struggled against overwhelming air attacks to rescue thousands of troops and civilians from the east, to save them from the advancing Russians. In the east they were harried by the Russians, and in the west Allied bombers pounded the harbors and sowed the Baltic with mines. By May 1945 only two light cruisers, one heavy cruiser and a dozen destroyers were left out of the ships which had started the war.

*Strength of the German Navy in 1939*
2 old battleships
2 battlecruisers
3 armored cruisers
3 heavy cruisers
6 light cruisers
22 destroyers
20 torpedo boats/small destroyers
59 submarines

## Germany, Surrender of, 1945

While Hitler lived, surrender by any German officer, high or low, was unthinkable. His discovery on 24 April of Himmler's secret negotiations with the Allies led to the instant dismissal of that most trusted servant. Goering, assuming his own succession to power on the same day, was disinherited as quickly, and Dönitz selected in his place. But the center of government and seat of power remained in the

Russian troops lower the captured standards of Nazi Germany in Red Square in a remarkable display of the Soviet triumph in World War II.

Marshal Zhukov signs the unconditional surrender of German forces on 9 May 1945.

bunker under the Reich chancellery, isolated though it had been from the outside world since 22 April. Only when Hitler shot himself on the night of 30 April and the news reached the outside world on 1 May did the military leaders dare to begin open negotiations with the Allies. For Dönitz, pitchforked suddenly into power, surrender could not come soon enough. He nevertheless decided to delay it for as long as possible, the reason being that he had information on the boundaries chosen by the Allies to delimit their respective occupation zones in postwar Germany and, like millions of other Germans, he was frantically anxious to expedite the escape of as many civilians and soldiers as possible to the west of the future Russian boundary which ran along the Elbe. While opening negotiations with the Americans and British for a ceasefire, therefore, he also prevaricated while the troops on the Eastern Front fought a desperate rearguard action. Subsidiary surrenders were arranged which came into force in Italy on 2 May and on the British front in the north and the Franco-American front in the south on 4

May but it was not until 5 May that a delegate arrived at Eisenhower's headquarters in Rheims to arrange the surrender in the center. It was made clear to him however that Eisenhower was well aware that the Germans were now playing for time and he was obliged to ask Dönitz to agree to immediate unconditional surrender. An aghast Dönitz sent Jodl to seek better terms, but Eisenhower merely threatened him with the immediate closing of the Elbe to crossings from the east. Jodl therefore gave in and, with Dönitz's assent, signed the instrument of unconditional surrender on 7 May. It came into force the following day and, at Russian insistence, was ratified on 9 May in Berlin.

## Ghormley, Vice-Admiral Robert L, 1883–1958

After the Battle of Java Sea, Vice-Admiral Ghormley was made area commander of the South Pacific Ocean Area, a command which he held until October 1942.

In April 1942 Ghormley was sent to Auckland, New Zealand to organize US naval forces under Admiral Nimitz, who briefed him on the first sea-borne expedition to take Guadalcanal and Tulagi. Ghormley was in charge of strategy yet he made numerous mistakes: he committed all his troops from the start, inexperienced though they were in jungle fighting, and he allowed Vice-Admiral Fletcher to withdraw before all the transports were unloaded. The whole operation was rushed: Ghormley thought there were 5000 Japanese on the island (there were only 2200); his intelligence, including maps, was faulty; half the supplies were left behind so that the force could arrive on the target date. In October the first news of the operation reached the USA and by this time the Japanese had sent in reinforcements and the garrison was 20,000 strong. The Marines on the island were making no advance and could not be reinforced. Ghormley was therefore replaced by Vice-Admiral Halsey and posted back to Washington.

## Giap, General Vo Nguyen, 1910–1975

Giap was a Vietnamese leader of resistance against the Japanese. In December 1941 Giap returned from his exile in China to start an underground organization under Ho Chi Minh's leadership. Their group the Viet Minh, co-operated with the OSS and in August 1945 marched into Hanoi and proclaimed a Democratic Republic of Vietnam. Giap was named Minister of the Interior.

## Gibson, Wing Commander Guy, 1918–1944

A British RAF officer, Gibson led 617 Squadron in its spectacular and renowned attack on the Möhne and Eder dams in 1943. Awarded the Victoria Cross for his part in this operation, he was to lose his life in an air crash in the Netherlands in 1944.

## Giffard, General Sir George, 1886–1964

Giffard was a British general of the old school. In 1939 he was appointed military secretary to the Secretary of State for war and then posted to the Middle East as GOC in Palestine and Trans-Jordan under General Wavell. In June 1940 he

was sent to West Africa as Commander in Chief. Giffard's job was to train fighting formations and specialist units. This he did with great success and as the strategic importance of West Africa decreased, Wavell asked for Giffard to be sent to India as GOC for the Eastern Army. His first task was to find a way to keep his men fit in jungle conditions. He also reorganized the rear administrative services and trained men and pilots for air supply. In August 1943 SEAC was set up and Giffard was made Commander in Chief of the 11th Army. General Slim was under his command and his task was to support him. Giffard had a personality clash with General Stilwell and during the Japanese offensive against Imphal and Kohima he was dismissed by Mountbatten, Allied Supreme Commander. He remained at his post until General Leese relieved him in November 1944.

## Gilbert Islands, Battle for the, 1943

The Joint Chiefs of Staff finally decided that Admiral Nimitz should advance to Japan along the Central Pacific route in May 1943. They agreed that he should build up a fleet and begin his campaign by seizing the Gilbert Islands and then the Marshalls and Carolines.

By November 1943 a sufficient force had been massed to start the campaign. Nimitz chose Vice-Admiral Spruance to lead the naval force and Major General Holland Smith was to lead the 5th Amphibious Corps on land. The attack was divided in two: a force of 7000 was sent north to Makin and a force of 18,000 to Tarawa. On 20 November the 27th Infantry Division landed on Makin and found a weak garrison, only 800 strong. Within four days all resistance had been crushed with a loss of 65 men. The other part of Operation Galvanic, as it was known, opened on the same day with a heavy naval bombardment of Betio, the small island fortress off Tarawa. After this the 2nd Marine Division landed, but although the island's defenses looked demolished, the Marines met heavy fire and nearly one-third of them were hit as they waded ashore. Some 5000 Marines struggled ashore and managed to push the Japanese into the interior. The garrison on Tarawa was 5000 strong and they were crack units, they resisted fiercely but on the night of 22 November they made a number of suicidal counterattacks and were cut down. By the next evening the island had been secured but at a heavy price: 1009 Marines and sailors were killed and 2101 wounded. By 26 November the Gilbert Islands were in Allied hands.

## Giraud, General Henri, 1879–1949

Giraud succeeded Corap in command of 9th Army at the moment of its rout in May 1940. Taken prisoner, he escaped from Germany to Gibraltar in April 1942 and was taken by British submarine to North Africa in November. It was the Allied intention to run him as a rival to de Gaulle, whom the Americans in particular mistrusted, and on the assassination of Darlan he became High Commissioner in North Africa. De Gaulle, however, refused to work with him and such was the superior strength of the latter's personality and position that Giraud was obliged to resign as High Commissioner and Commander-in-Chief in Africa in April 1944.

## Giulio Cesare

This Italian battleship was a veteran of World War I, but had been modernized in one of the most comprehensive reconstructions of modern times. The speed was raised by 7 knots, by the expedient of removing the center triple 12in gun turret to make space for more powerful machinery. The ten 12in guns remaining were bored out to 12.6in (305mm to 320mm) and given higher elevation to increase their range. The hull was gutted and rebuilt to include a revolutionary new scheme of anti-torpedo protection design by General Umberto Pugliese. To achieve all this a virtually new ship had to be built, and the work took from 1933 to 1937. A similar job was done on the *Cesare's* sister *Conte di Cavour* and the two half-sisters *Andrea Doria* and *Duilio*.

The *Giulio Cesare* was hit by a 15in shell from the British battleship *Warspite* during the Battle of Calabria in July 1940, which caused considerable damage, but she was not put out of action. She survived the war but was handed over to Soviet Russia in 1948 and renamed *Novorossissk*. In 1956 she sank with heavy loss of life after being mined in Sevastopol harbor.

## Gladiator, Gloster

This British single-seat fighter was in service from 1937–42. Though designed to a 1930 specification, the Gladiator did not reach the RAF until it had been outclassed by the new monoplanes, but considerable numbers (backed up by carrier-based Sea Gladiators) used their maneuverability to survive and even achieve many victories. Reaching about 250mph on the 840hp Mercury engine, Gladiators had four machine guns and were used by several air forces on wheels or skis. About 767 were built, the last in April 1940. Later that year three Sea Gladiators, called *Faith, Hope* and *Charity*, defended the island of Malta against the entire Italian Air Force.

## Glorious

This British aircraft carrier had been built as a sister of the battlecruiser *Courageous* in 1915–17, and was also converted to a fleet aircraft carrier in 1924–30. The 15in guns from these two ships were used in World War II to arm a new battleship, HMS *Vanguard*.

HMS *Glorious* fought well in the Norwegian campaign in April 1940, and on 8 June evacu-

Giraud shakes the hand of a reluctant de Gaulle.

ated the last of the shore-based RAF Hurricanes and Gladiators, none of whose pilots had ever landed on a carrier before. Tragically, nearly all these pilots were lost the following afternoon when the *Glorious* ran into the German battlecruisers *Scharnhorst* and *Gneisenau* off Vestfjord. The two capital ships opened fire at 28,000 yards, a range at which the carrier's guns were useless, and despite the efforts of the two destroyers escorting her she was set on fire. Only 40 survivors were picked up. One mystery which still has not been cleared up is why the *Glorious* could not fly off a torpedo-bomber strike, which might have forced the German ships to be more wary. Possibly the confusion on the flight deck caused by the unexpected arrival of the RAF aircraft had still not been sorted out by 1600 hours.

The destroyer *Ardent* was sunk without being able to protect the carrier but the *Acasta* hit the *Scharnhorst* with a single torpedo from her final salvo, before being overwhelmed by 11in shellfire. As the British did not know about the hit they did not know that the *Scharnhorst* was damaged. The damage forced Admiral Marschall to return to Trondheim, and so his force failed to intercept an equally valuable prize, a lightly escorted convoy carrying 10,000 troops back to England.

## Glowworm

From the outbreak of World War II the British Admiralty was aware of German iron-ore ships abusing Norwegian territorial waters to carry Swedish iron ore from Narvik. The *Indreled* or Inner Leads form a 1000-mile protected channel close to the Norwegian coast, and even blockade runners from the Atlantic were able to slip in at the northern end, and evade the British contraband controls.

As early as September 1939 the First Lord of the Admiralty, Winston Churchill, was urging the War Cabinet to block the Inner Leads with a declared minefield, and thus force the illicit traffic to use the open sea – it was estimated that half of Germany's 9 million tons of Swedish iron ore could be denied to her by cutting off this route. The reported sinking of three merchant ships inside Norwegian territorial waters in January gave the War Cabinet a pretext for warning the Norwegian Government of the British intention to mine the Leads, but in the face of Norwegian and Swedish protests the matter was dropped. However, by the end of March 1940 Churchill's insistence overcame the opposition from the Foreign Office, and a minelaying operation codenamed Wilfred was planned for 5 April.

Operation Wilfred was postponed until 8 April, and three days earlier the first minelayer sailed, screened by the battlecruiser *Renown* and four destroyers, including HMS *Glowworm*. What nobody knew was that Hitler, aware of the growing British exasperation over Norway, had decided to invade Norway to forestall a possible Anglo-French invasion. Among the naval forces covering the German troopships was the heavy cruiser *Admiral Hipper*, and it was this ship that the *Glowworm* met on 8 April. The destroyer had lost a man overboard on 6 April, and had lost contact with her squadron after turning back to look for him. Although hopelessly outgunned the destroyer turned at full speed and rammed the *Hipper* abreast of 'B' turret, inflicting serious damage before being sunk.

## Gneisenau

This German battlecruiser was the sister of the *Scharnhorst*, and was completed in 1939, having been ordered secretly under the 1934 Program before Hitler abrogated the Treaty of Versailles. She had an adventurous career in company with her sister ship, culminating in the 'Channel Dash' in February 1942, but once they parted her luck seemed to run out. While lying at Kiel undergoing repairs for mine damage she was hit by an aircraft bomb on 26 July 1942; the bomb set off oil fumes in the forepart of the ship and the resulting explosion wrecked the entire forward section of the ship as far back as the gun turrets. The decision was taken to rearm her with twin 15in guns in place of the triple 11in and so she was towed to Gotenhafen (Gdynia) where she was out of reach of Allied bombers. Lack of steel and labor slowed the work down, and eventually stopped it altogether. On 28 March 1945 the giant hulk was towed out to the harbor entrance, where it was scuttled to deny Gotenhafen to the Russians.

### Goebbels, Minister Joseph, 1897–1945

One of Hitler's original and most devoted comrades who established the Nazi party in Berlin, Goebbels was also a man of some education and great ability. He became Minister of Propaganda after the 1933 seizure of power and used the machinery of the ministry to brilliant effect in rallying public morale throughout the war. At the end he insisted on remaining with Hitler in the *Führerbunker* and, after his master's suicide, had his six children poisoned and himself and his wife shot by an SS officer.

Hitler and Goebbels at a Stuttgart rally in 1933.

### Goering, Hermann, 1893–1946

An early collaborator of Hitler's, he was an unusual Nazi, being of the officer class with a distinguished record from the war, in which he had commanded the Richthofen squadron and won the reputation of an ace. On Hitler's coming to power he became head of government in Prussia, organized the Gestapo and then took charge of creating the new Air Force, the Luftwaffe, at first covertly, then, on the abrogation of the Versailles treaty in 1935, openly. Thanks to his dynamism it was, at the outbreak of the war, the most efficient instrument of air power in the world. Goering, however, lacked the concentration and consistency necessary to maintain the trend of its development and as the war progressed it declined in relation to the Allied Air Forces. He lost the Führer's favor, largely for promising results which his air force did not or could not deliver – the reduction of the Dunkirk pocket, victory in the Battle of Britain, the succoring of the Sixth Army at Stalingrad – and took refuge in fantasy, where he was always at home. At Nuremberg however, he emerged as the strongest-willed of the defendants, revelled in his status of principal captive, and cheated the hangman by committing suicide with smuggled poison on the eve of execution. His performance revealed why Hitler had created the unique rank of Reich Marshal for him.

### Goliath

Goliath was a German remote-controlled demolition device. It was a small tracked vehicle containing two converted automobile starter motors powered by batteries, one motor to each track, a simple control mechanism, and a 166lb charge of TNT. A cable was connected to the vehicle and through this the controller sent signals to vary the speed of the individual tracks and thus steer the device. Due to the heavy load on the batteries the range and cross-country capability were limited, and a later version used a Zundapp two-stroke gasoline engine. The Goliath was carried on a trailer to its place of action, then guided to an obstacle by an observer. Once arrived at the obstacle the explosive charge was fired, destroying both the obstacle and the Goliath in the process.

*Below:* The Goliath demolition robot.

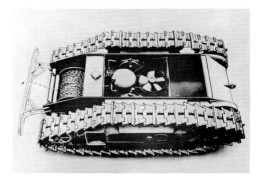

### Golikov, Colonel General Fillipp I, 1900–

Golikov was a gifted administrator who was Deputy People's Commissar of Defense from 1943–50. He was the Head of Military Intelligence and although he knew of German activities on the frontiers, advised Stalin of the unlikelihood of any German attack in 1941. From 1940–41 he was Deputy Chief of General Staff but in 1942 he was given an active command on the Voronezh Front. After Marshal Timoshenko's abortive offensive against Kharkov in May 1942 he held up Field Marshal Bock's advance with tanks at Voronezh, but when he said that he could not hold the position he was dismissed. In October he was reinstated, commanding the 10th Army in the offensive against Stalingrad. His troops crossed the Donets south of Voronezh. He ended the war as Chief of the Repatriation Mission in Moscow 1944–46.

## Golovanov, Chief Marshal of Aviation Aleksandr E, 1903–

Golovanov was the Commander of the Long Range Air Force, who became Marshal of the Air Force in 1943. In 1944 he prepared a joint artillery and air support program for the Belorussian campaign. He also planned the air offensive against Königsberg and Hungary.

## Goodwood
see Normandy, Breakout from, 1944

## Gort, Field Marshal, John, 1886–1946

Lord Gort had won the Victoria Cross as a regimental officer in World War I when he had commanded his battalion of the Grenadier Guards. In 1937 he was promoted by Hore-Belisha over hundreds of more senior officers to be Chief of the Imperial General Staff and in 1939 went to France in command of the British Expeditionary Force. His preparation for the Battle of France was unimaginative, since he allowed himself to be concerned with detail rather than principle during the phony war, but his handling of the BEF in battle was far-sighted and courageous. Despite pressure from the Cabinet to hang on, he recognized at the right moment that the battle was lost and took the decisions which allowed the Army to be evacuated from Dunkirk in the nick of time. Positive though his actions were, the essentially negative achievement of Dunkirk determined that he should move aside, and he spent the rest of the war in secondary posts, first as Governor of Malta where he sustained the siege with great resolution, and then as High Commissioner in Palestine.

## Goryunov Machine Gun

Piotr Maximovitch Goryunov (1902–1943) began his career as a locksmith, but after fighting for the Red Army in the Civil War he went to work as a gunsmith under Degtyarev. In 1940 he headed a team which developed the SG–43 machine gun for the Soviet Army which was intended as a replacement for the aging Maxim medium machine guns which had been in use since 1910. This machine gun operates by gas pressure, with the bolt locking when its rear end moves sideways into a recess in the gun body. Feed is accomplished by two arms, operated by the gas piston, which withdraw the rimmed 7.62mm cartridge from the belt and align it

with the closing bolt. The heavy air-cooled barrel can be changed quickly, and, in general, the SG–43 is a robust and simple design, considered by at least one expert to be the best air-cooled machine gun developed by any country since the Browning of 1919. The first models were mounted on wheeled or sledge mounts for infantry use, but they were later modified to become the standard tank machine guns.

## Gothic Line and Surrender in Italy, 1944–45

Having arrived on the outworks of the Gothic Line on 4 August, the Allies opened their offensive against it on 25 August. The 8th Army, secretly concentrated on the Adriatic coast, broke through quickly and captured Rimini by 21 September. In an effort to hold it, Kesselring, four of whose divisions had been withdrawn by Hitler for use elsewhere, transferred troops from the Mediterranean coast, thus offering the 5th Army the opportunity to cross the Arno and break the Gothic Line on its flank. It did so and reached to within nine miles of Bologna by 20 October. Exhaustion and mutual weakness then brought large-scale fighting to a halt for the winter, though the British mounted a minor offensive which took Ravenna in December and the Germans made a successful spoiling attack against the Americans in the Serchio valley late in the month. A stalemate ensued until March. By April the Allies had regained sufficient strength to undertake the final offensive. Attacking east of Bologna on 9 April after a massive aerial bombardment of the enemy's positions which the hopelessly outnumbered Luftwaffe was unable to prevent, the 8th Army quickly broke through. It was joined by the 5th Army in an offensive west of Bologna on 14 April. By 23 April the two had linked hands behind the city and were driving into the valley of the Po.

The Goryunov SG-43 on a Sokolov mounting.

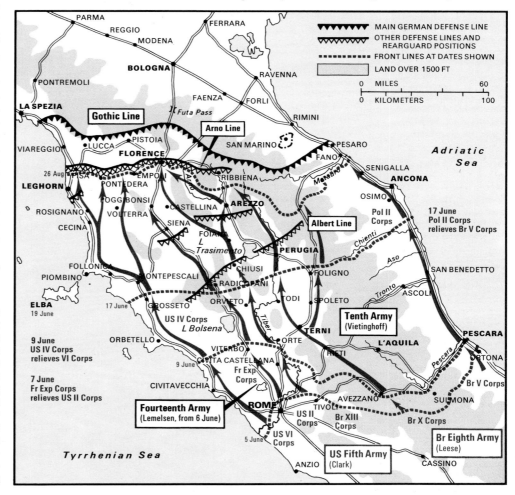
Breaking the Gothic Line and the collapse of the Italian Front, 1944–45.

Vietinghoff, who had succeeded Kesselring as Supreme Commander, managed to evacuate most of his army group across the river but its units were so scattered and his command so disorganized that he wisely decided to ask for an armistice. It was granted on 29 April and an unconditional surrender took effect on 2 May. It was the first large scale German surrender of the war, soon to be followed by those in Germany. Dulles, head of OSS in Switzerland, was the man who negotiated the surrender of the German Army in northern Italy with Wolff, the senior SS Commander. It was the only instance of a negotiated surrender in the war in Europe.

## Govorov, Marshal Leonid A, 1897–1955

Govorov was the Russian general who liberated Leningrad. In 1941 he was proscribed by the NKVD because he had fought with Admiral Kolchak, but he was spared because of Kalinin's protection. In July 1941 he was Commander of Artillery of the West Sector Reserve Front and was involved in the counteroffensive at Moscow. In December 1941 he was made commander of the Leningrad Front and carried out minor operations against Schlüsselberg which led to its liberation in 1943. In November 1943 his command was cut in two but he recovered to liberate Leningrad in January 1944. He then put Finland out of the war by storming Viborg. Afterwards he became the Stavka representative on the Baltic Front and led the assault on Lake Peipus which opened up Estonia. With General Chernyakhovsky he cut off the Germans in East Prussia and took Riga. He was made a Marshal of the Soviet Union in 1944.

---

## 'Grace'
see Aichi B7A1 Ryusei

---

## Graf Spee, Admiral

Third of the 'pocket battleships' and the best known, the *Admiral Graf Spee* was challenged off the River Plate by the British cruisers *Ajax, Achilles* and *Exeter* on 13 December 1939. Under her skilled captain Hans Langsdorff she had been cruising in the South Atlantic since the outbreak of war, and had sunk nine ships totaling 50,089 tons. The Battle of the River Plate illustrated the fundamental weakness of the *panzerschiff* concept and demolished the 'pocket battleship' myth, for the *Admiral Graf Spee* was not fast enough to dodge the three cruisers and her two triple 11in gun turrets could not cope with three fast-moving targets.

The *Graf Spee* blows up off Montevideo.

Although she crippled the *Exeter* the *Admiral Graf Spee* was damaged in the action and put into Montevideo for repairs. Skillful bluffing by the British created the impression that powerful forces were close at hand. Langsdorff was instructed by Hitler to avoid the humiliation of surrendering his ship and on 17 December the ship was scuttled in Uruguayan territorial waters.

---

## Graf Zeppelin

In 1935 Germany's first aircraft carrier was ordered, and she was launched as the *Graf Zeppelin* in December 1938. She was to provide the commerce-raiding capital ships and cruisers with air cover, and would have increased their potential for destruction considerably. A second ship, provisionally to be called *Peter Strasser* after World War I head of the naval airship squadrons, was ordered the following year, but she was canceled in 1940 to release shipyard capacity for more urgent work.

Unfortunately the Germans overreached themselves. They had no experience of all the problems which had beset the early American, British and Japanese carriers, but worst of all, the head of the Luftwaffe, Hermann Goering refused to allow his 'empire' to be encroached upon, by permitting the formation of a separate naval air force. The result was that the Navy had to try to persuade the Air Force to part with a small number of aircraft, and the wrangling went on until there was no hope of getting a carrier to sea.

Although the *Graf Zeppelin* had some advanced features she displayed her designers' lack of experience. The heavy surface armament was of little use and accounted for too much weight; the AA armament was heavy but badly sited, all on the starboard side; the radius of action was low for a fleet carrier intended to operate with the capital ships on the Atlantic shipping routes.

The *Graf Zeppelin*, Germany's first aircraft carrier.

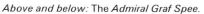
*Above and below:* The *Admiral Graf Spee*.

The wrangles over aircraft were matched by arguments over the equipment of the ship, and construction was suspended in 1940. Work started on a revised design in 1942 but was stopped in 1943, when the catapults were sent to Italy to help the Italians to complete the conversion of the *Aquila*. The hull was scuttled at Stettin on 25 April 1945 but the Russians raised it. Loaded with booty and with her hangar full of sections of U-Boats and other bulky items, she left Stettin in tow for Leningrad in August 1947; 15 miles north of Rugen on 15 August she struck a mine and sank.

### Graph

On 28 August 1941 the German submarine *U.570* imprudently surfaced beneath a Coastal Command Hudson bomber. The Hudson was soon joined by a second squadron-mate, and the two aircraft bluffed the U-Boat into surrendering, while escorts were called up from Iceland. The attempts at scuttling had been ineffectual, and the boarding parties were able to save the U-Boat, a rare prize for the RN.

*U.570* was a type VIIC, the workhorse of the U-Boat Arm, and so she was used by the British to test their own countermeasures. Renamed HMS *Graph*, she went through an exhaustive series of tests which showed principally that U-Boats had a tighter turning circle and a greater diving depth than had been thought. When the test program was finished the *Graph* was sent off on patrol off Norway, but this was a propaganda exercise and nothing more. The *Graph* was a liability, for her Germanic silhouette was likely to draw the fire of friendly ships. The story that she torpedoed another U-Boat on one of these patrols is, unfortunately, a fiction, although widely circulated by the British wartime press.

The final days of the *Graph* were spent as a target, and she was wrecked on Islay in the Hebrides on 20 March 1944.

### Graziani, Field Marshal Rudolfo, 1882–1955

Governor of Libya in 1940, Graziani responded reluctantly to Mussolini's pressure to attack the British in Egypt and in September made an advance into that country. He did not however press his attack but fortified the positions he had taken and settled down to await British reactions. Wavell and O'Connor rightly judged his desert fortress to be vulnerable to encirclement and 9 December launched a brilliantly successful counteroffensive against them. The Italians were driven back into Libya, had their lines of communication cut at Beda Fomm and lost over 100,000 prisoners. Graziani was relieved of command in February 1941 and censured by a court of enquiry. Graziani remained loyal to Mussolini however and became his Minister of Defense in the puppet Italian Social Republic erected by the Germans in north Italy after the Allied invasion in September 1943. He was captured by the Allies and sentenced by the anti-fascist government to 19 years imprisonment.

### Greater East Asia Co-Prosperity Sphere

The Greater East Asia Co-Prosperity Sphere was a concept coined by Foreign Minister Matsuoka in 1940 and used by the Japanese to give unity to their war aims. At first it was described as a defensive perimeter round Japan extending from the Aleutians in the north to Burma in the south. Another version of the Co-Prosperity Sphere included India, Australia and New Zealand and had as its ideal, Pan-Asianism or freeing the oriental countries from the colonial powers. When the Japanese had conquered Malaya, Burma, the Dutch East Indies and other territories they showed their confusion by pursuing different policies in each country. In China (Manchuria) they set up puppet governments. In Burma they declared independence and fostered anti-British feeling. In November 1943, Prime Minister Tojo held a Greater East Asia Conference attended by all the heads of state of the occupied countries, such as Ba Maw of Burma and Laurel of the Philippines.

### Great Marianas Turkey Shoot
see Philippine Sea, Battle of the, 1944

### Grechko, Marshal Andrey A, 1903–1976

Marshal Grechko is famous as Commander in Chief of the Warsaw Pact armies after the war, 1960–7. During the war he was division, corps and then army commander. In 1942 he fought in the defense of the Transcaucasus and then led one of the armies that liberated the North Caucasus and the Tamon peninsula. In 1943 he fought at Kiev and was appointed Deputy Commander of the 1st Ukrainian Front. In 1944 he fought in operations in the Carpathians and in 1945 fought at Mor Ostrava.

### Greece, British Occupation of, 1944

The Germans had maintained their hold on Greece tenaciously throughout the Mediterranean war, even mounting amphibious operations to recover the Dodecanese, which were prematurely liberated by skeleton British forces in the fall of 1943. By August 1944 it became clear however that the Germans were preparing to withdraw from Greece and the British accordingly readied themselves to move into the vacuum. Their objects were to maintain law and order, bring relief and prevent the country falling under communist domination. In September the Greek left-wing partisan movements, EAM and ELAS, met the commander of the earmarked British force, General Scobie, and Papandreou, the exiled premier, and agreed to accept the presence of British troops in Athens. The 2nd Parachute Brigade and 23rd Armored Brigade entered the country at the beginning of October and occupied Athens, on the heels of the Germans, on 13 October. The left-wing guerrillas began at once to quarrel between themselves and then with the British and by 5 December ELAS and the British were fighting for control of the capital. The arrival of the 4th Indian Division at the end of November and of the 4th British Division in mid-December swung the balance of force to the British side, while a conference chaired by Churchill on 26–27 December put forward the patriarch, Archbishop Damaskinos, as regent, with a mission of conciliation. By 5 January the British had gained complete control of Athens and the Piraeus and on 12 February EAM and ELAS agreed at Varzika to the demobilization of all revolutionary forces, release of hostages and formation of a national army. The British then occupied the whole of Greece. The underlying animosities remained, however, and were to burst forth in civil war after the world war was over.

### Greece, Invasion of, 1941

Operation Margarita, the German plan for the invasion of Yugoslavia, also included plans for the invasion of Greece, whose all too successful repulse of Mussolini's attack from Albania in November 1940 had become an embarrassment to the collective reputation of the Axis leaders. Hitler was also alarmed by the arrival of British troops in Greece, shipped from North Africa on 5 March, which threatened to establish a permanent hostile foothold on the continent. On 6 April, therefore, the German forces stationed in Bulgaria attacked Thrace and Macedonia. They consisted of 12 divisions forming the Twelfth Army under Field Marshal List. Opposite them stood the Metaxas Line defending the long Thracian frontier with Bulgaria garrisoned by three Greek divisions, and the Aliakmon Line garrisoned by three Greek divisions and the 6th Australian Divison and 1st British Armored Brigade. The Greek 1st Army, under General Papagos, was fully committed in Albania. In order to strike against the Aliakmon Line, the German Fortieth Corps had to cross southern Yugoslavia where its advance was opposed by the most fully mobilized of the Yugoslav armies, the 3rd. Nevertheless the advantage lay with the Germans since the Allied front was, in effect, divided into three segments, which were not mutuallly supporting and were separated by wide gaps. While the German Eighteenth Corps penetrated the Metaxas Line (6–9 April) and took Salonika, the Fortieth Corps making a rapid advance through southern Yugoslavia took the Aliakmon Line. It then thrust through the strategic Monastir Gap, thus forcing the British Commander, Maitland Wilson, to abandon it and retreat south of Mount Olympus. On 12 April Papagos ordered the Greek 1st Army to withdraw from Albania, but its rear was now threatened and it was forced to capitulate on 23 April. Meanwhile he also suggested to Wilson that the British troops should leave Greece if they were not also to be forced into surrender. The remainder of the campaign was fought by the British as a delaying action to cover their retreat to the ports of the Peloponnesus. Their losses during this phase were due largely to the operations of the Luftwaffe, which outnumbered the RAF by ten to one. Despite a hot pursuit, in which the remnants of the Greek army suffered severely, the British did eventually succeed in evacuating 45,000 soldiers, but they left 11,000 casualties and most of their equipment behind. Greek losses were much higher and included 270,000 men taken prisoner. German losses were a little over 5000. By comparison, however, they had lost only 500 in the invasion of Yugoslavia.

German troops move through Macedonia in their invasion of Greece to rescue an embarrassed Mussolini.

## Greece, the Italian Invasion of, 1940

Jealous of Hitler's brilliant triumphs over France and Britain and humiliated by his own army's failure to dent the French defense of their common frontier in June 1940, Mussolini decided in August to undertake his own blitzkrieg in Greece which he regarded as falling within his Mediterranean sphere of interest. He had already occupied Albania in April 1939 and from positions there launched his attack on 28 October without previously warning Hitler. His local army numbered six divisions against four Greek, and had complete air superiority. The Greeks, however, had 18 mobilizable divisions in all, were hardy and patriotic and were defending familiar home territory – the high harsh mountains of the Epirus. Despite the engagement of an eventual total of 25 divisions, the Italians were unable to make headway and in November the Greeks, under the command of Metaxas, the country's military dictator, counterattacked. The Italians were caught in snow in the mountain passes, by-passed and many forced to surrender. By the end of December the Greeks had occupied a quarter of Albania. On 9 March Mussolini personally supervised the opening of his spring counteroffensive but a week later it had to be abandoned for lack of success. It was this long drawn-out humiliation of his ally which obliged Hitler, whose anger at Mussolini's presumption in declaring war unilaterally had only slowly abated, to undertake his Balkan operation, Margarita, in the following April.

## Green Light Telegram
see Grew, Joseph

## *Greer*

The USS *Greer* (DD.145) was a unit of the *Wickes* Class of flush-decked, four-stacked destroyers turned out in large numbers in 1917–18. She was launched by the Cramp Shipbuilding Company at Philadelphia on 1 August 1918, and was one of the reserve units reactivated for patrol duties in the North Atlantic in 1940–41. On 4 September 1941 she was on passage to Iceland when a British Hudson bomber signaled to her that it was about to depth-charge a submerged U-Boat. The U-Boat, *U.652*, assumed that the depth-charges had been dropped by the *Greer*, and fired a torpedo at the destroyer.

The *Greer* counterattacked with depth-charges, and the 'Greer Incident' came to be regarded in the United States as the first major step along the road to war. However, it should be remembered that such incidents were bound to happen around Iceland, with US warships escorting supply ships and ordinary freighters. To add to the confusion the British had 50 ex-US destroyers which were very similar to the *Greer*. Hitler did his best to avoid giving the United States a reason for entering the war, but his U-Boat commanders felt exasperated at what they saw as gross provocation by the US Navy. In such circumstances the 'Greer Incident' was bound to happen.

## Grew, Joseph, 1880–1965

Grew was the American Ambassador to Japan from 1932 until the outbreak of the war. Grew was an expert on the Japanese system of government and understood the role of the Army in that system. For a long time he thought that Japan and the USA could reach a settlement but he warned Japan's ministers that they could not go too far. In September 1940 he sent a 'Green Light' telegram asking for a show of force against the Japanese and this led to the Scraps Deals Embargo (see Japanese assets). When Japan declared war on the USA, Grew was arrested but was exchanged for Japanese diplomats in the USA in the summer of 1942. He was then made adviser to the State Department on Japanese affairs.

## Grenade, Self-igniting Phosphorus No 68
see Molotov Cocktail

## Griswold, Major General Oscar W, 1886–1954

Griswold was the commander of 14th Corps and led operations in Guadalcanal, New Georgia and Luzon. After the bulk of Japanese forces had been evacuated from Guadalcanal, Griswold had to clear the last elements of resistance. In the end of 1943 Griswold took command of Occupation forces in New Georgia and cleared Munda. In January 1945 Griswold's 14th Corps and the 1st Corps drove from Lingayen Gulf down to Manila. En route Griswold had to clear resistance at Clark Field, but his forces suffered heavy casualties. To recapture Manila the 14th Corps engaged in street fighting and reduced much of the city to rubble. Griswold's task was then to fight the Shimbu group east of Manila until his force was relieved by General Hall's 11th Corps.

## Guadalcanal, 1942

After the Battle of Midway the Joint Chiefs of Staff felt ready to take the offensive against the Japanese, but the Army and Navy quarreled over who would take command. They agreed that the Solomons and New Guinea were the best bases for further advance and a three-stage program was evolved. When intelligence reports came in on 5 July describing enemy troop movements to Guadalcanal and the building of an airstrip there (Lunga Point), the Joint Chiefs changed their plan: Guadalcanal was now the primary target.

Operation Watchtower was under the overall strategic command of Vice-Admiral Ghormley with Rear Admiral Fletcher as tactical commander and Major General Vandegrift leading the landing force (19,000 Marines). It was soon nicknamed 'Operation Shoestring' because of the hastiness of preparation, the low morale of the troops and the disagreements among the commanders.

On 7 August the US carried out the first Allied landings on occupied territory of the war. The Allied bombardment of Guadalcanal began at 0900 hours: 11,000 troops were safely ashore with provisions by the evening and took the airfield the next morning. The 2200 Japanese on the island were mainly construction workers and they fled to the jungle with the first bomb. On Tulagi the story was quite different: the 6000 Marines who landed there only defeated the 1500 Japanese on the island after two days of intensive combat. All these forces under Vandegrift were left isolated and short of supplies after the Battle of Savo Island, on 8 August, when Admiral Turner's force was severely crippled by Vice-Admiral Mikawa (who, however, allowed the US transports to land). Vandegrift remained isolated until the first air squadrons arrived at Henderson Field on 20 August.

The Japanese did not make use of their advantage. Drastically underestimating the US strength, they sent a preliminary force of 915 men under Colonel Ichiki, which landed on Guadalcanal on 18 August. At the Battle of Tenaru, on 21 August, this entire force was killed at the cost of 35 US dead and 75 wounded.

After the Battle of the Eastern Solomons (23/24 August) and the build-up of US aircraft at Henderson Field, the Japanese lost daytime control of the sea. At night, however, they were able to land troops and supplies with impunity, at the same time shelling the US installations by destroyer. The Marines called this the 'Tokyo Express' and it enabled the enemy to increase their force to 6000 by early September. On 31 August Kawaguchi was landed with 3500 men. Vandegrift by now had a garrison of 19,000 troops, so that even though Henderson Field had been plowed up by naval bombardment, Kawaguchi's mission was hopeless. The battle at 'Bloody Ridge' on the night of 13/14 September was a massacre.

On 18 September Vandegrift's force was brought up to 23,000. On the same day Imperial GHQ gave top priority to the reconquest of Guadalcanal and Lieutenant General Hyakutake decided to leave Rabaul with his Seventeenth Army to direct operations on the spot.

In the meantime Vandegrift had gone over to the offensive with two forays up to the Matanikau River (27 September and 9 October). The second campaign resulted in 700 Japanese dead, which represented approximately one-third of their effective force: there were only 5000 Japanese left on Guadalcanal, less than half of whom were fit for combat. On the same evening transports and supplies began arriving from Rabaul escorted by Yamamoto and the Combined Fleet. This led to the Battle of Cape Esperance on the night of 11–12 October. This

engagement did not result in heavy losses and the troops were able to land, bringing Hyakutake's force to over 20,000 men. This was followed by the intensive bombing of Henderson Field and led to the replacement of Vice-Admiral Ghormley by Vice-Admiral Halsey.

The Japanese then began their land offensive under Maruyama. He attacked on the night of 24–25 October near the site of Bloody Ridge. He was repulsed and left 3000 Japanese dead or dying and a few hundred Marine casualties. Yamamoto received the false news that Henderson Field had fallen and sailed south, which resulted in the Battle of Santa Cruz (26 October).

On 9 November the Japanese made another attempt to reinforce Guadalcanal which resulted in the 'Naval Battle of Guadalcanal' (13 and 14–15 November). Of the 12,000 men and 10,000 tons of supplies sent from Shortland Island, only 4000 men and 5 tons of supplies arrived safely at Guadalcanal after this battle.

The Japanese were now in a hopeless situation, having lost control of sea and air and being forced to live on grass roots and water for months. After much indecision because of rivalry between Army and Navy the Japanese Imperial GHQ finally decided to evacuate Guadalcanal. The evacuation of the 13,000 Japanese (1–7 February 1943) was swift and completely bluffed the Marines, now 50,000 strong, who feared a Japanese offensive.

The Japanese lost 25,000 men during the six-month campaign, 9000 of these through starvation and disease. The Marines lost 1592 men. The greatest loss for the Japanese was 600 planes and their trained crews, who were difficult to replace. The campaign was well-covered by the American press and the boost to US morale was inestimable.

## Guadalcanal, Naval Battle of, November 1942

On 12 November 1942 Rear Admiral Callaghan received news of the approach of a Japanese group of two battleships, two cruisers and 14 destroyers. Callaghan gathered his forces: two heavy cruisers, the *San Francisco* and *Portland*, three light cruisers, the *Helena, Atlanta* and *Juneau*, and eight destroyers. Callaghan's force was inferior but he had the advantage of having radar, though he did not have it on his flagship, the *San Francisco*. Also Callaghan decided to advance in a single line because his ships had not trained together as a squadron. Even single-line formation required a greater amount of co-operation between ships than was achieved. At 0140 the *Cushing* nearly collided with two Japanese destroyers, the *Yudachi* and *Murasame*. The Americans were confused, and not until 0145 did Callaghan give the order to open fire. The Japanese shelled the *Atlanta* and killed Rear Admiral Scott and his staff. The *Cushing* was sunk by the *Hiei*, Abe's flagship, the *Laffey* was sunk and the *Sterett* disabled. The guns of the *San Francisco* and *Portland* hit the *Hiei* and damaged two destroyers, the *Akatsuki* and *Yudachi*. The *San Francisco*'s guns also crippled the *Atlanta* and at 0155 Callaghan gave the order to cease fire, thus allowing the 14-inch guns of the *Kirishima* to shell the *San Francisco*, killing Callaghan and his staff. Only one Japanese ship, the *Akatsuki*, sank, but the *Yudachi* had to be abandoned. The American cruisers *Juneau* and *Atlanta* and the destroyers *Barton, Laffey, Cushing, Monssen* and *Aaron Ward* were sunk. However, on the next day aircraft bombed and sank the *Hiei*.

The Japanese were trying to put Henderson Field out of action and land reinforcements

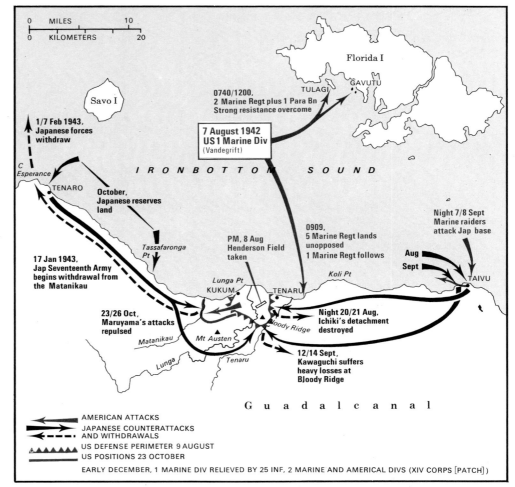

on Guadalcanal. On 13 November Admiral Mikawa's flagship *Chokai* and three heavy cruisers *Kinugasa, Suzuya* and *Maya* plus six destroyers arrived off Savo Island at midnight. Rear Admiral Kinkaid had been ordered to send in the battleships *Washington* and *South Dakota* and four destroyers, but they would not arrive before daylight. Mikawa's force bombarded Henderson Field and destroyed 18 aircraft, but next morning aircraft took off and torpedoed the *Kinugasa* and *Izuso*. Then aircraft from the *Enterprise* arrived to finish off the *Kinugasa* and also damaged the *Chokai* and *Maya*. Rear Admiral Tanaka's fleet of eleven transports sailed down the 'Slot' and was attacked by US aircraft so by nightfall there were only four transports left. On 14 November a Japanese squadron under Vice-Admiral Kondo consisting of the heavy cruisers *Atago, Takao*, and *Kirishima*, a light cruiser the *Nagara* and three destroyers, tried to bombard Henderson Field again. The US submarine *Trout* warned Rear Admiral Lee and he moved in to attack. The Japanese forces split into four groups. The cruiser *Sendai* was sent to follow the US ships. When Lee realized that the *Sendai* was tailing him, his ships opened fire, but they faced fire from the *Sendai* in the rear and the *Ayanami* and *Uranami* forward. In the gun duel, the *Walke* and *Preston* were crippled and sunk. The *South Dakota* suffered an electric failure so she could not use her guns, and the *Gwin*'s machinery was wrecked. Only one Japanese ship the *Ayanami*, was seriously damaged. Kondo and three ships then attacked the US force. Although they fired their torpedoes they all missed the *South Dakota*. The *Washington* retaliated and within a short time the *Kirishima* was crippled and sank. After this Kondo retired from battle at 0030. Tanaka ran his transports aground and landed 2000 men, 250 cases of ammunition and 1500 bags of rice. It was a feeble result.

## Guam, 1944

The invasion force heading for Guam had been turned back during the Battle of the Philippine Sea, but on 21 July it returned to land in the west of the island near Apra Harbor. The Japanese had landed in that area in 1941 when they had conquered the island, which had been a US possession. Guam was defended by 19,000 troops under General Takashina. At first they contained the advance of the Marines from the beach but on the night of 25–26 July the Japanese launched a counterattack which was beaten back. On 31 July the 3rd Marine and 77th Infantry division advanced northeastward and began to clear all opposition; by 10 August they reached the northern end of the island. This operation cost the US 1435 killed and 5646 wounded. Most of the Japanese garrison were killed or committed suicide and after 10 August 8500 died. However, some survived to fight a guerrilla campaign until the end of the war.

The Americans built up a huge base on Guam because it had runways long enough for the B-29 Superfortresses.

## Guderian, Colonel General Heinz, 1885–1953

The son of a Prussian General, Guderian was commissioned into the Tenth Hanoverian Jäger in 1908 but spent World War I as a signal and then a staff officer. After the war he specialized in military mechanical transport and helped to

Colonel General Heinz Guderian leaves a meeting, which apparently went well.

develop Germany's first tanks at a time when they were still forbidden under the Versailles Treaty. On its abrogation, he was made Commander of one of the first three Panzer divisions and in 1938 published his highly influential book on the future of armored warfare, *Achtung! Panzer!*. The book expanded his logic ideas on how German armored units should be built up. He had by then been promoted *General der Panzertruppen* and on the outbreak of war was given command of Nineteenth Corps, which he led in the Polish Campaign. For the Battle of France he was given a Panzer Group, his brilliant handling of which was a perfect demonstration of the concept of blitzkrieg – rapid armored breakthrough, supported by airpower, on a narrow front – which he had propagated in his writings. It was his tanks which were first across the Meuse, at Sedan (14 May 1940), and first to reach the Channel coast. In Russia in 1941 his Panzer group, renamed Fourth Panzer Army, led the drive on Moscow, but Hitler's midsummer decision to switch the main effort towards Kiev and Leningrad involved Guderian in an insubordinate dispute with the Führer. The rightness of his judgment did not save him and he was dismissed on 25 October 1941. Hitler, recalled him to be Inspector General of Panzer troops in February 1943 and after the 1944 Bomb Plot appointed him Chief of Staff in place of Zeitzler. Germany's military situation was hopeless and Guderian came too late. He retained the post, though constantly at odds with Hitler, until 21 March 1945, when he was finally dismissed. Guderian was a great military theorist and battlefield Commander, perhaps Germany's greatest of the war.

## Gustav

Gustav was a German 80cm (31.5in) caliber railroad gun. Design began in 1937 as a private venture by the Krupp works, the original estimate being that it would be completed by early 1940. It proved to be a more difficult task than foreseen, but the barrel was completed and proof fired towards the end of 1940, and in 1942 the entire equipment was assembled and fired at the Rugenwalde ranges. The complete weapon weighed 1328.9 tons, was 141ft long, 23ft wide and stood 38ft high. To move, it had to be dismantled by means of traveling cranes; the barrel, recoil system and top carriage were all removed and carried on railroad cars, while the lower carriage was split longitudinally as well as being dismantled downwards so as to come within the rail loading limits. Some 1400 men were required to assemble the gun, operate it, guard it and keep it in action.

After its trials it was sent to Sevastopol where it fired some forty or fifty shells in support of the siege. The shells provided were of two types, a high explosive shell weighing 4.75 tons and a concrete-piercing shell of seven tons; maximum range with these two shells was 29.2 miles and 23.6 miles respectively. One shot is recorded as having penetrated over 100 feet of earth and concrete into an underground magazine in the Soviet lines, where it detonated and destroyed the magazine.

After Sevastopol it was dismantled (a six week task) and sent to Leningrad, but before it could be placed there the Soviet Army went on the offensive and Gustav was hastily withdrawn. Its only other recorded appearance was outside Warsaw in 1944 when it was used to fire a few shells into the city during the rising. It was never seen again; parts were found in an abandoned train in Bavaria by US Army troops, but its exact fate has never been determined.

Gustav was presented to Adolf Hitler by Gustav Krupp as his contribution to the war effort, and it was named in Krupp's honor; the German gunners preferred to call it 'Dora', which accounts for the belief that there were two of these guns.

## Gustav Line
see Anzio, 21 January 1944

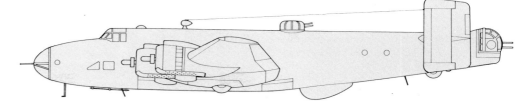

## Hacha, President Emil, 1872–1945

When Beneš resigned in October 1938, Hacha was elected his successor. Hacha became President of Czechoslovakia because he was a neutral figure, an international jurist, and would be conciliatory to Hitler. Hacha was summoned to Berlin in March 1939 and was forced to sign away Czech independence. Hitler then marched into Czechoslovakia and appointed a German administration. Hacha died in prison on 1 June 1945.

## Halder, General Franz, 1884–1971

Halder had served on the staff of the Crown Prince of Bavaria, the state from which he came, during World War I and made a reputation as an outstanding staff officer. On the resignation of Beck in 1938 he became Chief of Staff of the army – the first Bavarian and first Catholic to hold the post – and planned the invasion of Poland and later France. He was, however, an anti-Hitlerite and his planning of the Campaign in the west was marked by lack of zeal which both expressed his disapproval of the Führer's aggressive plans and undermined his standing with the head of state. He planned and directed the opening stages of the invasion of Russia but disagreed with Hitler over its conduct and was replaced by Zeitzler in September 1941. A tepid plotter against Hitler, he was arrested after the 1944 Bomb Plot and was interned at Dachau as a suspect but escaped execution.

## Halifax, Handley Page

This British heavy bomber was operational from 1941 to 1952. The Halifax was designed originally to meet the same P.13/36 requirement as the Avro Manchester. A change to four Rolls-Royce Merlin engines was made in anticipation of a shortage of Vultures, thereby avoiding the engine troubles that were to beset the Manchester in service. The first prototype flew on 25 October 1939, and the first production Halifax I on 11 October 1940. Powered by four 1280hp Merlin Xs, giving a maximum speed of 265mph, this version carried a crew of seven and up to 13,000lb of bombs. Defensive armament comprised two 0.303in machine guns in a nose turret, four in a tail turret and others in beam positions on some aircraft. The first operational sortie was made against Le Havre by six aircraft from No 35 Squadron, RAF Bomber Command, on the night of 11–12 March 1941.

*Top and above:* The Handley Page Halifax III heavy bomber.

The Halifax went on, with the Lancaster, to form a mainstay of the great RAF night offensive in Europe, dropping 227,610 tons of bombs in 75,532 sorties.

Altogether 6176 Halifaxes were built for the RAF, in many versions. Later bombers had more powerful engines, including the 1615–1800hp Bristol Hercules radial on the Mks III, VI and VII. The design was improved, with a streamlined nose instead of a turret, to improve performance and so reduce losses. Some Halifax bombers operated against the Afrika Korps, from Egypt; others flew with Special Duty Squadrons, dropping agents and arms by parachute to help the resistance movement in Europe, and as radio countermeasures aircraft with 100 Group. In other forms, Halifaxes served with distinction with Coastal Command, and as paratroop transports and glider tugs.

## Halifax, Earl of (Edward Wood), 1881–1959

The principal agent of Chamberlain's policy of appeasement, and that Prime Minister's choice as his successor in May 1940, Halifax in fact was transferred from the Foreign Secretaryship, which Churchill gave to Eden, to the Embassy in Washington. There he proved a great success, representing Britain's case with great ability and winning a wide circle of personal friends. He was one of the few 'Men of Munich' to rehabilitate themselves in mid-career, the result of evident and total integrity.

## Hall, Lieutenant General Charles P, 1886–1953

Hall was commander of the 11th Corps which liberated the Philippines. Hall became commander of the 11th Corps, part of Eichelberger's 8th Army, in 1941. He first saw action in New Guinea, where he took part in the occupation of Madang. During the invasion of Luzon, Hall landed on the beaches at San Antonio on 29 January 1945 to cut off Bataan.

When the 11th Corps joined up with the 14th Corps, Hall's men cleared the Bataan Peninsula. After the fall of Manila the 11th Corps reduced the group of Japanese who were holding the dams to the east of Manila.

## Halsey, Admiral William F, 1882–1959

Halsey became famous when he succeeded Vice-Admiral Ghormley as Commander of Naval Forces in the South Pacific Area. This put him in charge of the Solomon's campaign and he was the victor at the Naval Battle of Guadalcanal. Halsey's outbursts of temper earned him the name 'Bull'.

In April 1942 he was in command of the carrier group from which Doolittle's bomber raid on Tokyo was launched. Halsey would have been in command at Midway but he was suffering from a skin disease and was hospitalized. In October 1942 he was sent to resolve the situation at Guadalcanal. His orders were to occupy the Solomon Islands as part of the Elk-

Rear Admiral 'Bull' Halsey.

ton plan. Halsey's force was outmaneuvered at the Battle of Santa Cruz Island (October 1942) but succeeded in November 1942 in preventing Admiral Abe's bombardment force from shelling Henderson Airfield and preventing reinforcements and supplies from being landed. His forces emerged successful in the Battle of Guadalcanal, and on 26 November Halsey was made an admiral.

In March 1943 Halsey was to occupy Russell Islands west of Guadalcanal as an air and naval base and then take two islands in the Trobriand group, east of New Guinea. He was then to take Bougainville. He realized that this slow approach would encounter tougher resistance so he cut off Kolombangara, northwest of New Georgia. His next target was Bougainville and after a diversionary landing at Empress Augusta Bay he managed to establish a beachhead.

On 15 March 1943 Halsey's naval force became the 3rd Fleet and began the encirclement of Rabaul by taking Green Island. In 1944 Nimitz changed his overall strategy in the Pacific, concentrating his forces on the Central Pacific route and using Halsey's 3rd Fleet and Spruance's 5th Fleet alternatively in the advance to the Philippines and Japan. Halsey made lightning strikes on Yap, Palau Island and Mindanao durinr the summer until it was decided to head for Luzon. Halsey's task was to guard the San Bernardino Strait, but when his planes sighted Admiral Ozawa's decoy force he sailed north. He left the San Bernardino Strait unprotected and went with 64 ships to challenge a force of seventeen. The Japanese did not have sufficient strength to make the most of this brilliant maneuver.

Halsey was a brilliant exponent of naval air power and this error of judgment does not detract from his other successes.

## Hampden, Handley Page

This British four-seat bomber was in service from 1938 to 1944. Powered by two 965 or 1000hp Bristol Pegasus engines, the Hampden had an exceptional performance, carrying four times the load of the Blenheim (4000lb) twice as far, at almost as high a speed (255mph). But in the early months of the war losses in daylight were so heavy the Hampden was thereafter used almost entirely at night, the main fault being that although there were no blind spots, three machine guns were not adequate against modern fighters. Later the upper and lower rear guns were paired, and Hampdens served as minelayers and torpedo carriers around the North Sea and Baltic. Total production was 1430, 160 being built in Canada.

One of the Hampden bombers built in Canada.

## Hankow, Siege of
see China Incident, 1931–41

## *Hannover*
see *Audacity*

## *Hardy*

This destroyer was the flotilla leader for the 'H' Class, and in 1940 she was commanded by Captain Bernard Warburton-Lee, Captain (D) of the 2nd Flotilla. With the destroyers *Hotspur*, *Havock* and *Hunter* she formed part of the escort for the minelayers sent to lay minefields in the Inner Leads (see *Glowworm*) at the start of the Norwegian campaign.

The 2nd Flotilla was patrolling off Vestfjord in Northern Norway on 9 April 1940 when Captain Warburton-Lee received orders from the Commander in Chief Home Fleet to send some destroyers to the vital iron-ore port of Narvik to stop any German attempt to occupy it. Although later intelligence showed that the Germans had already arrived in strength, the 2nd Flotilla was not recalled as Warburton-Lee had no doubt about the intention behind his orders – to destroy the transports. What he did not know until later was that the six destroyers reported were in fact ten, all large powerfully armed craft which outgunned him. Fortunately another destroyer HMS *Hostile* joined his command, and he signaled at 1751 hours 'Intend attacking at dawn high water'.

At 0430 hours on 10 April the *Hardy* led the *Hunter* and *Havock* into Narvik harbor with guns blazing, and they quickly sank the German Commodore's ship, the destroyer *Wilhelm Heidkamp* and the *Anton Schmidt*, and damaged three more. The *Hotspur* and *Hostile* joined in a second attack on the transports and sank six of them. But a third attack went wrong when three German destroyers emerged from Herjangsfjord to the North. The five British destroyers withdrew, but suddenly they saw another two destroyers coming out of Ballangenfjord, cutting off their retreat. Caught between two fires, HMS *Hardy* was badly hit and Warburton-Lee was killed. The *Hunter* was sunk and the *Hotspur* badly damaged, but the German destroyers did not press their advantage, and the survivors escaped without further loss, leaving the *Hardy* to sink. To set the seal on a daring action against heavy odds, the *Havock* sank the ammunition ship *Rauenfels*, which was sighted coming up the fjord. This sealed the fate of the Germans at Narvik for she was carrying an outfit of ammunition for Commodore Bonte's flotilla; the German ships had already used a large part of their ammunition and could not fight a second action.

## Harmon, General Millard F, 1888–1945

An American General, Harmon commanded land and Air Forces in the South Pacific from mid-1942, a period which included the Solomon Island operations and, notably, the conflict at Guadalcanal. From July 1944 he commanded the USAAF for the whole of the Pacific Ocean territories and was responsible for mounting the strategic air offensive against Japan which was to give the United States absolute air supremacy.

He died in 1945 on a routine flight.

## Harriman, W Averell, 1891–

Harriman was President Roosevelt's negotiator with Stalin. In 1940 Harriman was sent to London to negotiate the Lend-Lease arrangements and then continued as Lend-Lease coordinator. In September 1941 Harriman accompanied Lord Beaverbrook to Moscow to discuss military aid to the Soviet government. In 1943 Harriman became Ambassador to Moscow and in this capacity he attended all the major Allied conferences. At Yalta he negotiated with Molotov over problems in the Far East and he warned Roosevelt about the USSR's ambitions in China. Harriman also had to deal with Stalin's demands for control of Japan's future.

## Harris, Air Chief Marshal Sir Arthur, 1892–

A South African-born Air Marshal, Harris had been a distinguished pilot during World War I and had held various posts in the 1920s and 1930s including Head of the Air Ministry Plans Branch and Air Officer Commanding RAF Palestine and Transjordan. In 1939 he commanded No 5 Bomber Group, RAF Bomber Command and in 1941, led a RAF delegation to Washington to discuss air co-operation. On his return in 1942 he became Commander in Chief, RAF Bomber Command where he was to inject new confidence and an aggressive spirit into a command that had been experiencing costly and disappointing results. Having rejected a formerly held belief in precision bombing, he immediately stepped-up the offensive, acting on a directive which instructed that operations be 'focused on the morale of the enemy civil population and in particular of the industrial workers'. This policy of area bombing because his unfaltering creed in the following months, culminating in the devastating 'Thousand Bomber' raid on Cologne on 30 May 1942. Similar raids on Essen and Bremen met with less success. The accuracy of Bomber Command's raids was improved from August 1942 by the establishment of a photo-reconnaissance force, and in September of that year, the first 8000lb blockbuster bomb was dropped on Karlsruhe.

Harris's entrenched advocacy of strategic area-bombing, as demonstrated by the massive raids on the Ruhr, on Hamburg and Berlin which caused enormous damage to these regions, was, however, opposed by his American counterparts of the US 8th Air Force who preferred attacks on specific targets which were crucial to a sector of the German industrial or economic system. These Harris dismissed as 'panacea' targets. He was, nevertheless, in full accord with Spaatz, the American strategic Commander, in totally rejecting Leigh-Mallory's transportation plan for Operation Overlord which demanded the diversion of the bombing force from its strategic offensive under the Pointblank directive to the assault on German communications and supplies in and around the invasion area prior to D-Day itself. He, furthermore, felt an intense *personal* disregard for Leigh-Mallory who, although Commander in Chief of the Allied Expeditionary Air Force, he virtually ignored. Bomber Command, nevertheless, played an invaluable part in the D-Day preparations.

The peak of Bomber Command's night offensive was achieved on 14–15 February 1945 with the devastating attack on Dresden.

A man of entrenched beliefs, Harris had an innate distrust of innovation. He feared, for example, the setting-up of the Pathfinder Force which he felt would create an elite body, detrimental to squadron morale. He maintained that by forcing the Germans to take a defensive stand, numerous Allied lives had been saved. To those he commanded, his resolution was an inspiration; his ruthlessness a total commitment to victory.

## Hart, Admiral Thomas C, 1877–1971

Admiral Hart was the overall commander of Allied naval forces in the Far East until February 1942.

At the time of Pearl Harbor, Hart's Asiatic fleet consisted of one heavy and two light cruisers, 13 destroyers, 29 submarines, six gunboats, five minesweepers and 32 flying boats. This 'fleet' could put up no resistance to the Japanese invasion force of the Philippines and in February 1942 Hart resigned his post as Commander in Chief. In January 1942 Hart had been appointed General Wavell's naval commander in charge of the fleet in the East and he directed actions in the Makassar Strait. On 11 February before the Battle of Java Sea he resigned command of the fleet and Dutch Vice-Admiral Helfrich took over. He retired from the service but was recalled in July 1942 to a seat on the naval board because of his experience. He retired again in 1945 once the war was over.

## Hartmann, Major Erich,

Germany's most successful fighter pilot of World War II, his 352 victories also constituted the highest total in the world. Hartmann was only 20 years old when he joined 9 Staffel of JG 52 operating in the Ukraine. The unit was one of the most renowned in the Luftwaffe, with several top aces in its ranks. Hartmann evidently rose to the challenge and by July 1944 he was one of only 27 men who had gained the Knights Cross with Oak Leaves, Swords and Diamonds. In October 1944 he took command of 4./JG 52 and, subsequently, of II Gruppe JG 52 in February 1945. Three months later he surrendered to the Americans.

## Heath, Lieutenant General Lewis, 1885–1954

Heath was Commander of the British 3rd Indian Corps when the Japanese invaded Malaya in December 1941. He tried to organize a stand against the Japanese in northern Malaya but after repeated failures was forced to retreat to Singapore. After the fall of Singapore Heath spent the remainder of the war as a POW.

*Right:* The He 111 bomber.

## *Hedgehog*

The inherent fault of both Asdic and Sonar in 1939 was that the narrow beam generated by the transducer could not be directed downwards. As a result the escort lost contact with its target during the last minutes of an attack – depth-charges had to be dropped by guesswork. To cure this problem the Admiralty Miscellaneous Weapons Department started work on a new weapon which could project a charge forward; in other words, one which could be aimed while the target was still held in the beam.

The project started in December 1940 and the weapon, codenamed 'Hedgehog' was ready for testing in the fall of 1941. It comprised six rows of four 'spigots' or heavy steel rods on which rested bombs with the propellant contained in a hollow tail. As the gases ignited in the tail-pipe they thrust the bomb forward off the spigot. Because the recoil was mostly absorbed in resetting the springs on the spigots, the whole weapon was light and could be mounted on a small ship's deck without much alteration. The destroyer *Westcott* took the first operational 'Hedgehog' to sea in January 1942 and appropriately it was this destroyer which claimed the first kill with it, on 2 February 1942.

The US Navy was given details immediately and produced its own version. For small escorts such as PCEs a four-bomb and eight-bomb version called 'Mousetrap' was developed. The principle was also adapted by the British as a means of clearing invasion beach obstacles, and was named 'Hedgerow'.

## Hedgehogs
see Kharkov, Battle of, 1942

## Heinkel He 59

This large twin-engined biplane was used by the Germans in seaplane form during the first half of World War II, mainly on minelaying, convoy shadowing, coastal reconnaissance and air/sea rescue duties.

## Heinkel He 111

This German four/five-seat bomber and torpedo dropper was in service from 1937–45 (Spain until 1965). Designed by the Günter brothers, who liked curving elliptical wings and tails, the He 111 made a name for itself in 1935 as a civil airliner, and later as a bomber that gained world records for high speed while carrying a heavy load. In 1938 the first mass-production versions, the four-seat He 111E and F, did very well in the Spanish civil war, dropping heavy bomb loads and proving too fast for Republican fighters to catch easily. Thus the three hand-held machine guns carried by these aircraft appeared adequate. The E, used in

large numbers by the prewar Luftwaffe, carried eight 551lb bombs, dropped tail-first from vertical cells in the beautifully streamlined fuselage to tumble end-over-end in a way that rivals said spoilt accuracy. But by the time World War II broke out the standard production model was quite different. The He 111P had broad straight-tapered wings, and an odd offset nose with no separate cockpit for the pilot. With two 1100hp DB 601A engines it was only slightly slower than the earlier models, at 247mph, but with full bomb load it was slower still. During most of the war the production version was the H-series with 1350hp Jumo 211F engines. Despite the higher power these were so burdened by bombs, missiles and extra protection that few exceeded 220mph.

It was in the Battle of Britain that the He 111 was recognized as inadequate when intercepted by modern fighters. By May 1941 the RAF's radar-equipped Beaufighters could even shoot the waddling Heinkels down at night, though in the 1940 Blitz they devastated many of Britain's cities. In Russia in 1941 they were again able to bomb effectively, but despite being laden with extra guns and armor the He 111 was never again to be a real menace. Because the Luftwaffe had no replacement, the old Heinkel, called 'The Spade' by its crews, stayed in production until the end of 1944, long after it had become obsolescent. About 7300 were built, and most of the final batches were equipped to launch the 'V-1' flying bomb against English cities after the original launch sites had been captured. There were many special versions, including torpedo carriers, magnetic-mine exploders and barrage-balloon cable-cutters, but the strangest was the He 111Z, for towing the Me 321 glider; it had two He 111s joined on a single wing, with a fifth engine in the center.

## Heinkel He 115

About 400 of these twin-engined seaplanes were produced for the Luftwaffe in 1937–44, for torpedo-bombing, minelaying and maritime reconnaissance duties. One was used also to drop agents in enemy territory, in RAF markings, after its Norwegian crew flew it to England following the occupation of their country.

The Heinkel 115 seaplane.

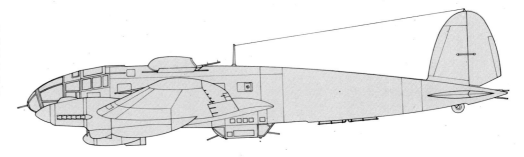

## Heinkel He 162 Salamander

This small single-seat fighter, with a 1760lb st BMW 003 turbojet pod-mounted above its fuselage, was conceived as a lightweight *Volksjäger* (People's Fighter) which could be built in huge numbers, by slave labor, from readily available materials and still have a performance better than any piston-engined type. The specification was issued on 8 September 1944. Within 15 days Heinkel completed a wooden mock-up of the He 162. On 28 September the company was awarded a large production order, and the prototype flew on 6 December – less than ten weeks from start of design. Construction was of mixed wood and metal; armament comprised two 20mm cannon. About 275 were completed before the end of the war, but few were encountered by Allied air forces. In view of the 162's instability, the end of the war may have been as fortunate for its pilots as for its enemies.

## Heinkel He 177 Greif

This German five/six-seat heavy bomber was in service from 1942 to 1945. The He 177 Greif (Griffin) was the only long-range heavy bomber built in quantity for the Luftwaffe in World War II. Fortunately for the Allies, it was one of the most troublesome and accident-prone aircraft in existence, and it was never popular with its crews or ground staff. It was designed to meet a mistaken specification of 1938 which not only demanded long range with heavy bomb load, and speed of 335mph but also stipulated the big bomber must be capable of dive-bombing. This along with many other difficulties caused great delay and added to the weight. A second big problem was that the designers wanted to use neat remotely controlled guns, and these eventually had to be discarded and ordinary turrets or hand-aimed guns used. Perhaps worst of all, to reduce drag it was decided to use four engines in two coupled pairs, so that the He 177 looked like a twin-engined aircraft. Despite great efforts by Daimler-Benz to make the 2950hp DB 610A twinned units work properly, they gave endless trouble and caught fire so often that – like an aircraft of World War I – the big Heinkel was often called 'the Flaming Coffin'. Altogether more than 1000 of many versions were built. Armed with various mixes of 20mm cannon, 13mm heavy machine guns and rifle-caliber guns, they carried up to 13,225lb of bombs or missiles, and in some versions even went into action at 'nought feet' as tank-busters carrying enormous cannon of 50 or 75mm caliber. At the end of the war new versions, the He 274 built in France and 277 built in Austria, had four separate engines; but they were too late.

## Heinkel He 219 Uhu

The *Uhu* (Owl) was the only Luftwaffe night fighter capable of stalking and fighting the RAF Mosquito on equal terms. Heinkel first offered the design in August 1940, but the German Air Ministry was not interested, believing that the war would be won before such an aircraft could be produced. Not until RAF night raids were beginning to build up in intensity, in late 1941, was it decided to go ahead with the design as a specialized night fighter. The prototype flew on 15 November 1942. The first experimental mission was flown by Major Werner Streib from Venlo, Holland on the night of 11–12 June 1943. Infiltrating a stream of RAF Lancasters bound for Berlin, he shot down five in 30 minutes. Preference continued to be given to the Ju 88G, and only 268 Uhus were completed. Basic armament was six cannon.

## Heinrici, Colonel General Gotthard

Heinrici was appointed commander of the German Fourth Army when von Kluge was made commander of Army Group Center. He gained a reputation as a defensive fighter, often holding back forces ten times the size of his own. In May 1944 he became commander of the First Panzer Army and the Hungarian First Army which he led in retreat to Silesia. In March 1945 he was given command of the defenses on the Oder and held back Marshal Zhukov for a week because he had intelligence on Soviet troop concentrations. He was the last general whom Hitler trusted and was a last-minute appointment as commander of Army Group Vistula, but even with his skills he could not hold back the Red Army. He was taken prisoner by the Russians and repatriated in October 1955.

## 'Helen'
see Nakajima Ki-49 Donryu

## Helfrich, Vice-Admiral Conrad, 1886–1962

Helfrich was a Dutch Admiral who was Commander in Chief of Dutch Navy Forces in the Far East from 1939–42. After the Japanese had launched their offensives against Malaya, the Philippines and the Dutch East Indies, Helfrich was made Commander in Chief of Allied Naval Forces in the ABDA command. He succeeded Admiral Hart and found that his ships were handicapped by their lack of sufficient air cover. His ships fought in the Battle of Java Sea but soon afterwards the ABDA command was dissolved and Helfrich was without a command because the Dutch Navy had ceased to exist. In 1945 Helfrich was the Dutch representative at the UN Conference at San Francisco and he also represented the Netherlands at the Japanese surrender in Tokyo Bay, September 1945.

## Hellcat, Grumman F6F

This was a US single-seat carrier-based fighter. To offset the unexpectedly high quality of Japanese naval aircraft, the US Navy ordered the production Hellcat with the most powerful engine available. One month after the prototype

The Grumman F6F-3 Hellcat.

Grumman Hellcats off the frozen Newfoundland coast.

XF6F–1 had flown for the first time with a 1700hp Wright R–2600 engine, on 26 June 1942, it was re-engined with a 2000hp Pratt & Whitney R–2800. With this, as the XF6F–3, it made a second 'first flight' on 30 July. Production F6F–3s flew into combat for the first time on 31 August 1943 from the carrier *Yorktown*. By the following year Hellcats were the principal USN carrier-borne fighters, and the enemy never again achieved superiority. Total number built was 12,275, with the F6F–5 of 1944 as the only other major variant. Changes were limited mainly to the engine cowling, windscreen and armament. Two of the six wing-mounted 'point five' machine guns of the F6F–3 were exchanged for 20mm cannon on most F6F–5s, which could also carry 2000lb of bombs under their center-section and six rockets under their outer wings. Night fighter versions of both the 'dash 3' and 'dash 5' had radar in a pod under their starboard wingtip. Altogether, Hellcats of the US Navy shot down 4947 enemy aircraft during operations from carriers, with another 209 victories claimed by land-based USN and Marine units. This represented almost 75 percent of all the Navy's wartime air combat 'kills'. The Royal Navy received 252 F6F–3s and 930 F6F–5s through Lend-Lease, naming them Hellcat I and II respectively.

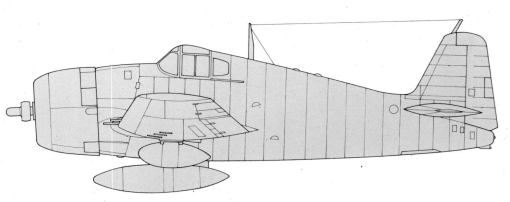

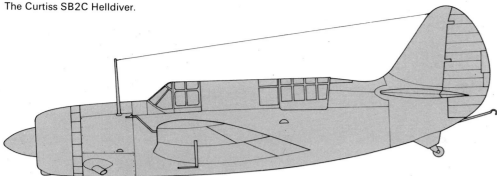

The Curtiss SB2C Helldiver.

## Helldiver, Curtiss SB2C

This US carrier-based scout-bomber was operational from November 1943 to 1949. Perpetuating the name of its biplane predecessor, the Helldiver prototype flew for the first time on 18 December 1940. The US Navy appeared undeterred when this aircraft crashed a few days later. It had already ordered the type into large-scale production and was eventually to purchase a total of 6300, in several versions, of which 1194 were built in Canadian factories. The Helldivers played such a key role in the mounting US assault on Japanese targets in the Pacific in 1944-45 that only 26 could be spared for 'export' to Britain where such a quantity was probably considered too small to put into service. The USAAF ordered 900, as A–25As, to fill an urgent need for dive-bombers; but most of these were transferred to the US Marine Corps, as SB2C–1As, although they lacked the wing folding gear and naval equipment of the carrier-based models. Most numerous of the latter were SB2C–4s, with a 1900hp Wright R–2600–20 engine which gave a top speed of 295mph and range of 1165 miles with a 1000lb bomb load: Maximum bomb load was 2000lb, and the SB2C–4 was armed with two wing-mounted 20mm cannon, plus a pair of 0.3in machine guns in the observer's cockpit. All SB2Cs were two-seaters.

The SB2C-4 Helldiver with folded wings.

## Henderson Field
see Guadalcanal, 1942

## Henschel Hs 129

A total of 841 of these tank destroyers were built for the Luftwaffe, each fitted with two 690hp Gnome-Rhône 14M radial engines found in France after the 1940 Armistice. The second Hs 129 unit lost all its aircraft in North Africa without achieving anything. In contrast, four squadrons based in the Soviet Union in July 1943 saved many German tanks from destruction during Operation Citadel, after which the Germans tried to regain their lost initiative after Stalingrad. In a continuous stream of attacks, directed at the thinly-protected flanks and rear of Soviet tanks seen to be moving towards an unsuspecting Panzer Korps, the Henschels set on fire or drove off the entire hostile force. Standard armament of the Hs 129 was one 30mm gun, two 20mm cannon and two 7.9mm machine guns. To deal with the giant Russian Josef Stalin tanks during the winter of 1944-45, some aircraft were fitted with a 75mm gun, able to fire 12 26lb shells at 1.5 second intervals. Production had ended by then, as even the Hs 129's heavily armored cockpit was failing to prevent losses of 20 percent of the pilots taking part in some missions. This plane was potentially a very effective weapon, but too few were built too late.

## Hermes

In July 1917 the Royal Navy ordered the world's first warship *designed* to operate aircraft. She was launched on 11 September 1919 as HMS *Hermes* and was completed in July 1923. Although too small (600ft long) and too slow (25 knots) to be suitable for fleet work, considerable ingenuity went into her design, especially when it is remembered that the only previous experience had been derived from a collection of makeshift conversions, and the larger *Eagle* and *Furious* had not yet entered service. Although designed to support 20 aircraft the rise in dimensions meant that she could only accommodate 12 by 1939. She served on training duties in prewar China, but in 1939 she joined the Home Fleet. She was later used for trade protection in the East Indies but joined Admiral Somerville's Eastern Fleet in 1942. She was sunk just after dawn on 9 April 1942 by D3A 'Val' dive-bombers from Admiral Nagumo's First Carrier Striking Force. The 'Vals' scored 40 hits on the small carrier in less than ten minutes.

## Hess, Deputy Rudolf, 1896–

A confidant of Hitler from 1920, Hess became his deputy in the party but failed to find an effective role in the state after the seizure of power. In May 1941 he left Germany alone in a Messerschmitt 110 and crashlanded in Scotland on a self-appointed peacemaking mission. He was disowned by Hitler and judged by the British to be insane, but was nevertheless sentenced to life imprisonment at Nuremberg after the war. He remains in captivity in Spandau prison, Berlin, the last of the unexecuted war criminals still incarcerated.

## Hetzer

The Hetzer was a German self-propelled tank destroyer which mounted the 75mm PAK 39 gun on the reworked chassis of the Czech Model 38 tank. It was developed in 1943 and remained in production until the end of the war. Although cramped inside, it was an effective machine, and almost 1600 were made. In postwar years a number were employed by the Swiss Army.

The Hetzer PzJag 38t self-propelled gun.

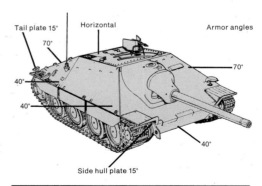

## Heydrich, Obergruppenführer Reinhard, 1904–1942

Originally a regular naval officer, Heydrich left the Kriegsmarine under a cloud. He joined the Nazi Party because it seemed most likely to offer him the rapid advancement to power and satisfaction for revenge against the German establishment that he craved, and was quickly taken into the SS and up by Himmler becoming his deputy in 1931. As head of the *Sicherheitsdienst*, the SS secret police, he quickly achieved a terrifying degree of power. His utter lack of humanity also marked him out to plan and institute the 'Final Solution of the Jewish Question', that is, the holocaust of European Jewry. In 1942 he was appointed Reichs Protector of Bohemia-Moravia (governor of occupied Czechoslovakia) and assassinated by parachuted Czech agents. The village and population of Lidice were destroyed by the Germans in retaliation.

## *Hiei*

This fast Japanese battleship had been 'demilitarized' to comply with the Washington Treaty, but in 1936 she was taken in hand for a three-year reconstruction to bring her to the same standard as her sisters of the *Kongo* Class. During the battle of Guadalcanal on the night of 12 December 1942 she was damaged by gunfire from the heavy cruisers *Portland* and *San Francisco*, and next day she was attacked by aircraft from USS *Enterprise*. The wreck was abandoned that evening.

## High and Low Pressure Gun

By 1943 the anti-tank guns in German service had reached a level of weight which made them no longer viable as an infantry-accompanying weapon capable of being pushed around the battlefield by three or four men. The only alternative seemed to be a recoilless gun firing a hollow charge shell, but these guns were inaccurate at short ranges, difficult to conceal and consumed inordinate amounts of propellant powder. But a light weapon was desperately needed and the Army asked for a lightweight gun which would use less propellant than either a recoilless gun or a rocket but which would be sufficiently accurate to hit a one meter square target at 750 meters range.

The Rheinmetall-Borsig company produced the answer utilizing a new ballistic system which they had developed and which they called the 'High and Low Pressure System'. The gun, known as the PAW (Panzer Abwehr Werfer) 600, was an 80mm smoothbore firing a fin-stabilized hollow charge bomb resembling a mortar bomb. This was attached to a conventional cartridge, but interposed between the two was a heavy steel plate with four holes and a spigot to which the bomb was attached by a shear pin. When this complete round was loaded, the bomb lay in the bore of the gun while the cartridge occupied the chamber in the usual way, but the heavy steel plate abutted a step between chamber and bore so that it could not move forward. On firing, the propellant powder exploded and generated a pressure in the chamber of about eight tons per square inch. The gas then bled through the restricting holes in the steel plate to generate a pressure of about 2.5 tons in the bore. This was sufficient to shear the pin holding the bomb and propel the bomb up the barrel and towards the target. This system meant that the barrel could be extremely light; only the chamber needed to be heavily reinforced against the pressure within, and the recoil force on the gun was relatively low. The whole gun weighed only 1323lbs while the bomb, with a muzzle velocity of 1700ft/sec

could range to 850 meters with adequate accuracy. It was capable of penetrating 5.5in of armor plate. The development of this weapon took some time, and it was not until late in 1944 that production began. About 260 guns were built before production ended in March 1945. A 105mm version was also under development but this never reached the production stage.

## High Pressure Pump

This was the cover name for a German long-range gun intended to be fired across the English Channel into the Greater London area. It was also known as 'Busy Lizzie' and 'The Millipede', both expressions arising from its configuration. It was designed as a multiple-chambered gun of 15cm caliber with a barrel 150 meters long; there was a conventional breech and a chamber at the rear end, and several auxiliary chambers arranged at 45° to the barrel at intervals of about 40 meters. The theory was that a fin-stabilized shell would be loaded into the breech, together with a propelling charge and additional propelling charges would be loaded into the side chambers. The first charge would fire and start the projectile up the bore; as it passed the first auxiliary chamber, the charge therein would be fired, producing additional gas to boost the velocity of the shell; this would be repeated as the shell passed all the chambers. With all these additional boosts, the shell would leave the muzzle at extremely high velocity – something in the order of 5000 ft/sec was forecast – and would thus be projected into the stratosphere, where the lessened air resistance would permit the projectile to reach a range of about 175 miles.

The idea was not new; it was first proposed by two Americans in the 1880s, Lyman and Haskell, and a gun built to their specification was fired. It proved unsuccessful, since the propelling gases from the first charge passed around the shell and ignited the auxiliary charges before the shell had reached them, giving an effect opposite to that desired. The idea reappeared at intervals, without having any better success, but the German proposal was put up by Engineer Conders of the Rochling Stahlwerke AG in 1941. By May 1943 he had built a 20mm prototype which appeared to work well and he had managed to get the ear of Hitler, who approved of the project and authorized Conders to proceed on his own, without the knowledge of the Army Weapons Office (who would have undoubtedly killed the idea on the spot). Full-caliber experimental guns were built and tried, all of which burst or underwent other disasters, while hundreds of workmen were set to work installing a fifty-barrel weapon in a hillside near Calais. Eventually the Weapons Office had to be called in to provide some expertise, and they managed to get the weapon working, after a fashion. However, by this time the Allied advance from Normandy had overrun the installation at Calais

High pressure pump shell.

and the project was no longer viable. Hitler had hoped to make it his 'V-3' Vengeance Weapon, but only two shortened versions of the gun were built. These were hurriedly deployed during the Ardennes battle in December 1944 and fired one or two shots without recorded result, after which they were blown up and abandoned. Fragments of the experimental gun are said to be still in existence on the Baltic coast.

Heinrich Himmler and SA Leader Ernst Röhm (right).

## Himmler, Reichsführer Heinrich, 1900–1945

An early supporter of Hitler, Himmler was made head of the *Schutzstaffel* (Protection Squad) in 1929, a small Nazi Party militia used to keep order at public meetings and provide bodyguards to the leaders. When the leaders of the SA, the mass party militia, threatened to become overmighty, Hitler used the SS to purge them (the Night of the Long Knives, 30 June 1934) and thenceforward Himmler's power rapidly increased. In 1938 he helped Hitler subordinate the Army High Command (the Blomberg-Fritsch crisis) and in 1943 became Minister of the Interior; he had been head of the police since 1936. By 1944 he therefore controlled all the organs of surveillance and repression in the Third Reich, including the Gestapo and the concentration camps. It was his *Einsatzkommando* which had carried out the mass exterminations in the east 1941–43, while he also administered a large fighting force, the Waffen SS divisions of the Field Army. In 1945 he also became a military Commander, of Army Group Vistula, but failed to show any talent for generalship. At the very end of the war he opened peace negotiations with the Allies but word reached Hitler, whom he believed incommunicado, that his most loyal servant was playing false and he was disgraced. He was subsequently captured by the British while trying to make his escape after the ceasefire and committed suicide when unmasked.

### Hirohito, Emperor, 1901–

Hirohito, the Emperor of Japan, was revered as both god and father of the Japanese people. Japanese Emperors have exercised varying amounts of direct control on political affairs and it is difficult to assess the Emperor's share in the responsibility for the war. He presided over all cabinet meetings, but according to the traditional form of government he did not utter a word at these sessions and merely gave his approval to all decisions. On one occasion he shocked his ministers by demanding an explanation of their aggressive policy in negotiating with the Americans in October 1941.

During the early successful stage in the war Hirohito was kept in the background by Prime Minister Tojo, although Japanese Admirals and Generals kept him informed and up-to-date on all important developments. Tojo submitted all new policies to the Emperor for his assent, but the defeat at Midway was kept a secret from him for a few days. After Midway Hirohito became much more involved and probed his ministers about the reversals and growing losses – he had to approve the withdrawal from Guadalcanal and Buna.

All orders were issued in Hirohito's name and it was fear for the Emperor's status after the surrender which prolonged the fighting. Many Japanese would rather fight to their death in a totally hopeless situation than allow even the possibility of a threat to the Emperor's position. The Allies declared at the Casablanca Conference that they would settle for nothing short of unconditional surrender. This was reiterated more ambiguously in the Potsdam Proclamation. In August 1945 Hirohito used his influence to help the peace movement and although the Potsdam Proclamation did not guarantee his lawful status, Hirohito said that it had to be accepted. On 15 August 1945 he announced the formal surrender to the Japanese people in a recorded message on the radio. This was the first time in history that an Emperor addressed his people directly.

Even though the Emperor told MacArthur that he was responsible for the war, MacArthur realized that he could not reconstruct Japan or maintain its political stability without the Emperor. Hirohito was not tried for war crimes, but he was required on 1 January 1946 to issue a 'non-divinity proclamation' prepared by the Allies.

### Hiroshima and Nagasaki, Atomic Attack upon, 6 and 9 August 1945

When President Truman came to power, Stimson, the Secretary of War, immediately told him about the Manhattan Project and the atomic bomb. Truman chose to regard the atom bomb as a military weapon which had to be used and ignored any moral questions raised by use of the bomb. Many influential scientists were against using the bomb, including Oppenheimer who was the Director of the Manhattan Project. However, Truman only consulted military experts in Washington. Generals Marshall and Groves advised him that Japan would not surrender and that the bomb should be used. Truman and Stimson took the final decision after the negative Japanese response to the Potsdam Declaration.

At 0245 on 6 August 1945 the B-29 superfortress 'Enola Gay', piloted by Colonel Tibbets, lifted off the special runway on Tinian. At 0815

The devastated ruins of Hiroshima after the first atomic attack, 6 August 1945.

the U-235 bomb, known as 'Little Boy', exploded 2000 feet above Hiroshima. Forty-two square miles of the city were flattened, 80,000 people were killed outright, 10,000 people went missing never to be found, 37,000 were seriously injured and many more suffered from radiation sickness. Truman declared 'This is the greatest thing in history'.

On 6 August Truman called on Japan to surrender or else face a 'rain of ruin'. While the Japanese ministers debated a response the second atom bomb fell on Nagasaki on 9 August. The bomb, known as 'Fat Man', was more powerful than the first, but because of the terrain it caused less damage. Some 35,000 were killed outright, 5000 went missing and 6000 were seriously injured. Many historians have argued that Japan would have made peace without the atom bomb. It cannot be denied that the bombing of Japan accelerated the decision to surrender.

### Hiss, Alger, 1904–

Hiss attended the Yalta Conference as one of Stettinius's chief advisers. He was accused of betraying the USA at Yalta and was tried and convicted on a perjury charge, which amounted to a charge of treason, after the war. He was generally believed to be a Communist, although he continues to deny the allegation.

### Hitler, Führer Adolf, 1889–1945

An adolescent drifter and World War I corporal, Hitler rejected his aimless Viennese past to become in Weimar Germany a demagogue of the extreme right. His party was small and he and it had many competitors, but luck, acute political talent and an instructive lesson – the failure of his *coup d'état* at Munich in November 1923 – led him out of the pack, so that by 1930 his National Socialist German Workers Party *(NSDAP)* was the second largest in the

Reichstag. The bitter effects of the world slump and the ineffectuality of a succession of center-moderate right governments in the next three years made him the majority choice of the non-Left in the January 1933 elections. In that month Hindenburg, the President, called him to the Chancellorship. He had not, however, won a majority of votes and he consolidated his power by underhand and strongarm methods. His masterstroke was to browbeat the Reichstag into voting him dictatorial powers, which he used to dissolve it, ruling thereafter by *diktat*. Between 1934 and 1939 he restored the German economy by bold deficit financing, rebuilt the armed forces after unilateral abrogation of the Versailles Treaty and established German dominance in European affairs by one dramatic and brutal *demarche* after another: in 1936 the remilitarization of the Rhineland; in 1938 the annexation of Austria and the Czech Sudetenland; in 1939 the occupation of the rump of Czechoslovakia. The logic of his foreign policy, which depended on the interminability of Anglo-French appeasement of his demands and their inability to make common cause with the Soviet Union, drove him in 1939, on the morrow of his agreement of a non-aggression pact with Russia, to declare war on Poland. But at that point France and Britain bit the bullet and made good their guarantees to the Poles. That did not save Poland but obliged Hitler after his swift defeat of that country to open war against Britain and France. The demagogue found himself obliged to become warlord, a role which he played with growing skill and confidence for the next two years; by the fall of 1941 he had subdued and occupied Holland, Belgium, Norway, Denmark, France, Yugoslavia and Greece, reduced Italy, Bulgaria, Rumania and Hungary to puppet status, isolated Great Britain and looked set to conquer Russia, as well as much of the Middle East. From December 1941 his luck changed. Russia survived his opening campaign, his ally Japan brought America into the war against the Axis and, despite a brilliant recovery on the Eastern Front in the summer of 1942, his armies began to lose battles and yield ground. Hitler's response was to isolate himself physically from the world and spiritually from

Führer and Chancellor Adolf Hitler.

reality. The last three years of his life were spent in fortified headquarters, at Berchtesgaden, in the Ukraine, but chiefly at Rastenburg in East Prussia, where he lived with his maps and saw almost no one but staff officers. There on 20 July 1944 he survived an attempt by a group of officers desperate to avoid the debacle to which his strategy was leading Germany, to kill him. Thereafter, smelling conspiracy and disloyalty on every side, he ruled and commanded even more egotistically, voicing his determination to fight 'until five past midnight' and trusting almost into his final days in the coming of some divine miracle which would reverse the odds and leave him victor. Besieged at last in the Chancellery bunker in Berlin, to which he had returned in November 1944, and faced by the inevitability of defeat, he committed suicide on 30 April 1945. A genius of evil, he made and very largely waged World War II almost single-handedly. Its history is his epitaph.

### *Hitlerjugend* and *Bund Deutscher Mädchen* (Girls' Organization within the Hitler Youth)

After Germany's invasion of Eastern Europe, Hitler decided to send German boys and girls to the occupied territories of Poland and Western Ukraine to make up the shortage of teachers. About 30,000 children were sent out after three months training and often found they were teaching racial German groups, who hardly knew any German at all.

The shortage of manpower meant that the Hitler Youth were also called on for anti-aircraft duties, to man search-light batteries and carry dispatches. After children of 12 died on anti-aircraft duties it was decided that boys under 16 should only be used to carry dispatches. Eventually the Hitler Youth organization decided to recruit boys to serve in a regiment on the frontlines. Ten thousand boys were trained in Belgium and first saw action in Normandy, in June 1944. They fought desperately and suffered tremendous losses, when they were trapped in the Falaise pocket. Eventually 600 boys managed to break out but the others were lost. The

The insignia, badges and uniforms, which were worn by the Hitler Youth.

division could never make up those lost but continued to fight in the Bastogne area and later on (1945) in Hungary.

Hitler Youth members continued to take an active part in the defense of their cities as the Allies swept over Germany. Girls manned anti-aircraft guns in Vienna and youths manned Panzerfausts on barricades. The Hitler Youth fought fanatically because they believed Goebbels's propaganda and thought the Russians and English would kill all the Germans.

### Ho Chi Minh, 1890–1969

Ho was a revolutionary Vietnamese leader who formed the Viet Minh. In 1940 Ho fled to China after an unsuccessful coup against the French and in 1941 at Changsi he founded the Viet Minh (Independence League) and sent Giap to Vietnam to find bases for their resistance movement. In 1942 the Kuomintang arrested him but he was released a year later on the insistence of OSS men, who wanted him to lead resistance against the Japanese in Vietnam. He returned to Vietnam and took command of the Viet Minh, which was supplied by the OSS. When the Japanese had been defeated his troops marched into Hanoi and he formed a coalition against the provisional government.

Ho Chi Minh.

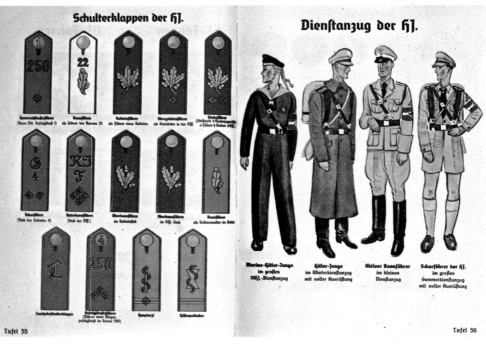

### Hodja, General Enver, 1908–

Hodja was leader of the resistance movement in Albania during the war. He also founded the Albanian communist party in 1941 and in September 1942 he was made head of the FNC (Communist National Liberation Front). He co-ordinated partisan activities and received help from Soviet, British and American officers. After the Red Army liberated Albania he became head of the Provisional Government and on 4 December 1944 announced that Albania was free of all Germans.

### Hodges, General Courtney Hicks, 1887–1966

Risen from the ranks, Hodges commanded the US 1st Army in the invasion of Europe, first under Bradley and then alone. He fought the Battle of the Reichwald, captured Aachen and in the Battle of the Bulge held the northern half of the American line. In the advance to the Rhine his troops captured the bridge at Remagen and went on to help encircle the Ruhr. After VE Day he went to the Pacific and took part in the capture of Okinawa.

### Holland, Invasion of, 1940

Holland, though neutral, was invaded by German forces on 10 May 1940, their object being both to divert Allied attention from the critical axis of attack in the Ardennes and to outflank the Belgian and Anglo-French Armies in Flanders and southern France. The Dutch Army, a conscript force, consisted of nine first-line and five second-line divisions, dependant on mobilization to make it up to full strength, and twelve air squadrons (118 planes, only 23 modern). It was particularly weak in anti-aircraft artillery. Its defense plan was based on the holding of Fortress Holland, the region north of the big rivers Maas and Waal, which was to be protected by the inundation of north-south water lines. Within it – one of the most densely populated areas in the world – an army as weak as the Dutch Army might conceivably hold out for some time. The Germans planned therefore to breach the line from the outset and

*Top:* Dutch artillerymen and their 10cm gun.
*Above:* Crippled ship of the Holland-America Line in Rotterdam harbor after the bombing of the city.
*Left:* German soldiers fire at attacking Allied aircraft on 11 May 1940. The brief Dutch defense of their country was brave but futile.

to terrorize the civil population it contained by air attack. Airborne troops were to land at bridges across the rivers at Moerdijk and Rotterdam, a bomber force was to attack Rotterdam itself if capitulation was withheld, and a Panzer division, the Ninth, was to dash across the country from the frontier to link up with the airborne landings. In the event, early landings at the Hague airfields – Valkenburg, Ockenburg and Ypenburg – were repulsed on 10 May, thus allowing the Dutch Royal Family to escape, eventually to England, but airports near Rotterdam were seized successfully as were the Moerdijk bridges. On receiving news of that setback, the French launched their 7th Army to the rescue but too late. Before it arrived, the Ninth Panzer Division had already (12 May) had a junction with the paratroops and air-landed a Jäger division outside Rotterdam.

Dutch citizens watch as the heart of Rotterdam goes up in flames.

The German Commanding General, Schmidt, had meanwhile received orders to threaten the city's destruction if its garrison did not surrender and, while terms were being negotiated on 14 May, the Second Air Fleet, from Bremen, in ignorance of an order cancelling the operation, bombed its center to destruction. About 900 Rotterdammers were killed, and General Winkelman, the Dutch Commander, ordered the Army to surrender an hour later (1700). The orders did not extend to the Dutch troops fighting alongside the French 7th Army in Zeeland who did not lay down their arms until the French themselves withdrew on 17 May. Total Dutch military casualties in the campaign were 2100 dead and 2700 wounded. The Dutch fleet and Marines continued the fight outside the homeland. Sizeable forces were left intact in the Netherlands East Indies, which would oppose the Japanese invasion in 1941–42.

## Hollow Charge Weapons

The development of hollow-charge (also called Shaped Charge) munitions was one of the foremost steps in explosive ordnance taken during World War II. It enabled the foot soldier, firing a hand-held weapon, to stop the largest tanks and provided combat engineers aith a portable method of penetrating armor or concrete fortifications. Without the hollow charge the anti-tank guided missile of today would not exist and the course of several World War II battles might have been considerably different.

The phenomenon known as 'hollow charge' was discovered in the 1880s by an American experimenter, Monroe. In the course of tests on guncotton slabs he noticed that the incised initials 'USN' on the slabs were reproduced in the surface of iron plates against which the guncotton had been detonated. Subsequent experiments led him to the discovery that if the surface of an explosive were hollowed out, when detonated in contact with a metal plate, the hollow would be reproduced in the plate, and by making the hollow deep enough it was possible to completely penetrate the plate. Beyond being an amusing laboratory demonstration there appeared to be little application of the phenomenon, which was called 'the Monroe Effect' at that time.

In the early years of the 20th century some experimenters tried to apply the idea to projectiles of war without success. After World War I a German scientist, Neumann, made further trials in which he determined that by forming the hollow in a regular shape, such as a cone, and lining it with metal, such as copper, the effect on the target plate was greater.

There the matter rested until 1938 when two Swiss announced their discovery of a 'new and powerful explosive' with special application to armor penetration. They demonstrated their explosive, requiring large license fees before parting with the secret, but to skilled ordnance engineers who saw the demonstration it was obvious that they had adapted the Neumann Effect or Hollow Charge into a workable weapon. As a result of this demonstration work began simultaneously in Britain and Germany to produce hollow charge devices.

The hollow charge, as generally perfected, consisted of a light metal casing inside which was a charge of high explosive. This charge was hollowed out in conical form at the front, and the cone was lined with a copper liner against which the explosive was in intimate contact. Initiation of the explosive had to be from the side away from the cone, so that the moving detonation wave collapsed the cone, subjecting it to intense heat and pressure and converting the liner into a fast-moving stream of finely-divided metal particles traveling along the axis of the cone towards the target. This stream, moving at some 20,000 ft/sec or more, was capable of forcing aside the metal of the target and penetrating. Provided the target was not too thick, the jet of metal burst through at high speed and temperature to damage anything behind the plate. In a tank, for example, the jet could ignite fuel or ammunition, damage armaments and engines or kill the crew.

Probably the first application of hollow charge in the war was by the German airborne troops who landed on Fort Eben Emael in 1940. These men carried hollow charge demolition devices which when placed above the armored cupolas of the fort, blasted through the armor to immobilize the guns inside, ignite ammunition and stores and injure personnel. The German

Diagram of a hollow charge shell.

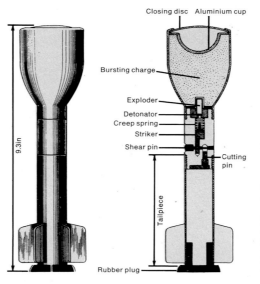

The entry hole of a 3.5in bazooka rocket in 4in thick armor.

Army then went on to develop a large range of hollow charge artillery shells which gave every gun an anti-tank capability, since the effect of a hollow charge device was independent of velocity and even a low-powered gun could inflict severe damage on a tank. Similar shells were developed in Britain and the USA.

Subsequent development, however, showed that spun projectiles were not the most effective way to employ hollow charges since centrifugal force tended to dissipate the jet and weaken its effect. Hollow charge was thus allied to fin-stabilized devices, leading to the development of such weapons as the 'Bazooka', 'PIAT', 'Panzerfaust', 'Panzerschreck' and similar shoulder-fired rocket launchers.

The hollow charge principle was also applied in other directions; naval torpedoes, aircraft rockets, booby-traps and anti-tank mines were all developed, with varying degrees of success. Indeed, one version of the ultimate weapon, the nuclear bomb, relied on a modification of the hollow charge principle to initiate the nuclear reaction.

## Holocaust

After the outbreak of World War II the Nazis began to set up concentration camps in occupied countries and to step up the campaign against the Jews. Jews were deported to ghettos and work camps where many were killed by the slave labor, starvation and sporadic mass shooting. After the Wannsee Conference (January 1942) it was decided to implement the 'Final Solution', the killing of all Jews, and special extermination camps were built at Auschwitz, Sobibor, Belsen, Chelmno, Treblinka and other places. These camps were run by the SS and had mass gassing installations and body disposal furnaces. As the Allies swept over Europe, Hitler ordered that concentration camps be evacuated and transferred into existing camps. According to the count, there were 700,000 inmates in 1945, but it is thought that 6,000,000 Jews were murdered by the Nazis.

## Home Fleet

The Home Fleet was the Royal Navy's main battle force in European waters. Originally called the Atlantic Fleet it was renamed in 1933. It comprised the main battle squadrons and the fleet carriers, and its chief responsibility was to keep the German Navy from breaking out of the North Sea. For this purpose the World War I base at Scapa Flow was reactivated as it was well-placed for interceptions of ships trying to run the blockade.

The operational areas of the Home Fleet were not circumscribed, and units were detached to other zones quite freely, but the southern parts of the North Sea and the English Channel were made separate commands for light forces, and the growing intensity of the Battle of the Atlantic led to the creation of Western Approaches Command. Only with the final disposal of the *Tirpitz* in 1944 did the Home Fleet assume a lower priority, and most of its heavy units were withdrawn to be sent to the Far East. Its Commanders in Chief during the war were Sir Charles Forbes (1939–40), Sir John Tovey (1940–42), Sir Bruce Fraser (1942–44) and Sir Henry Moore (1944–45).

## Homma, General Masaharu, 1888–1946

On 22 December 1941 Homma led the surprise attack on Luzon which led to the surrender of 65,000 Filipino and 15,000 US troops at Bataan in April 1942 (excluding the Corregidor garrison). It also led to the Bataan Death March. Homma, an intelligence and liaison officer with no previous combat experience, had 74,000 troops in Manila, many of them seasoned veterans from the rape of Nanking. He carried out his orders so strictly that he allowed Philippine guerrillas to escape to the mountains and let MacArthur get to Bataan with sufficient time to dig in. This turned what should have been an effortless rout into a major problem. When he was defeated in his initial assaults on Bataan, he was effectively relieved of command by a delegation of staff officers from Tokyo. By 3 April Homma had 50,000 of Japan's best troops, plus vast artillery and overcame US resistance.

Homma was held responsible for the Bataan Death March on which at least 10,000 died following the victory. He was arrested in September 1945, tried at Manila, and executed by firing squad in April 1946. His last combat post had been on Corregidor, April 1945.

## Hong Kong, Fall of, 1941

Hong Kong was attacked at the same time as Pearl Harbor, Malaya and the Philippines. Hong Kong was difficult to defend since the Japanese held the mainland around it and it was dependent on the mainland for its water supply. However the British could not allow its surrender. Despite the recommendation of the Armed Forces to withdraw its garrison, the

Japanese bombers over Hong Kong.

War Cabinet agreed to send two Canadian battalions as reinforcements in 1941.

On 8 December 1941 the Japanese launched their attack with nine infantry, seventeen artillery battalions and ample air cover. The British, outnumbered by two to one, had six battalions and twenty-eight guns; they drew up their forces on the Gindrinkers Line on the Kowloon Peninsula, where they hoped to make a stand. However the Japanese easily overwhelmed them and Major General Maltby ordered a speedy withdrawal to Hong Kong Island. The British managed to stop the first crossing but on the night of the 18 December, a Japanese force landed on the northeastern corner of the island. They drove through the British lines to capture the Wong Nei Chong Pass and split the defending forces in half. The garrison surrendered on the evening of Christmas Day, having held out for eighteen days. The whole garrison had numbered 12,000 men, whereas the Japanese losses were under 3000.

## *Hood*

HMS *Hood* was the world's largest warship, for she had been specially exempted from the 35,000-ton limit specified at the Washington Conference, because she had been built so recently. However, her design was already rather dated, even in 1922, and although her beautiful lines and great size earned her much attention during the peacetime years, the designers of the RN always regarded her as a liability. Her main weakness was lack of deck armor for she had been designed before the lessons of the Battle of Jutland had been learned and the post-1918 tests had been made. As one of the more modern capital ships she was low down on the priority list for modernization in the 1930s; furthermore she was used for prestige cruises, and by 1939 her machinery was in poor shape. In a prophetic note written in 1939 the Director of Naval Construction warned that the *Hood* was not fit for battle, and said that if she was not given a complete modernization there might be 'eternal cause for regret'.

The *Hood* was in action at Mers-el-Kebir on 3 July 1940, and opened fire against the French ships at 1754 hours. She was straddled twice by French shells and hit by shrapnel which caused two casualties. She fired 56 15in and 120 four-inch shells, including those fired at the shore batteries. After service with Force H she underwent a refit from January to March 1941 before joining the Home Fleet's Battlecruiser Squadron. She was the flagship of Vice-Admiral Whitworth until 8 May 1941, but he was relieved by Vice-Admiral L E C Holland.

On 24 May 1941 the *Hood* led the new

battleship *Prince of Wales* into action against the German battleship *Bismarck* and the heavy cruiser *Prinz Eugen*. On paper Holland had a superiority of firepower, 18 heavy guns against eight, but in fact the *Prince of Wales* was too new to be reliable, and he could not count on her armament remaining serviceable. But the *Hood* was equipped with radar, and as her side armor was approximately the same as the *Bismarck*'s the Admiral intended to close the range as quickly as possible with *Hood* leading. It is easy to be wise after the event, but it would hardly have been exemplary leadership to send an inexperienced ship with faulty guns first, in order to reduce the risk to the flagship.

At 0552 hours the *Hood* and *Prince of Wales* opened fire on the *Bismarck*, and the *Hood*'s Type 284 radar produced three accurate salvoes. But just as the old battlecruiser had closed the distance to the point where the trajectory of the shells would be flattening out and so make her less vulnerable, an eight-inch shell from the *Prinz Eugen* burst on the boat deck. Rocket ammunition began to blaze, and within minutes a large fire was burning. What happened thereafter will never be truly known as there is insufficient evidence, but a fifth salvo from the *Bismarck* was seen to straddle the *Hood* at a range of 16,500 yards. A pillar of flame shot up a thousand feet as a huge explosion destroyed the ship. Horrified witnesses aboard the *Prince of Wales* saw that the *Hood* had broken her back, with the bow and stern in two parts. Within a minute and a half there was nothing but a huge cloud of smoke, and the *Hood* had gone, taking with her 1416 officers and men, and leaving only three survivors.

The loss stunned the British, and Churchill recorded in his memoirs that the news ranked as a national calamity. The reasons for her loss are a matter of conjecture as two boards of enquiry failed to produce any hard evidence. The poor quality of the 15in shell which hit the *Prince of Wales* later the same day, and the fact that the *Hood* had entered her 'zone of immunity' makes the commonly held theory of a direct penetration of the main magazines unlikely. The fire on the boat deck may have had nothing whatsoever to do with the explosion, for it was nowhere near a main magazine. Other possibilities are: (1) a fire spreading to the extra anti-aircraft ammunition added in 1939–40 outside the main magazine protection, and a sympathetic detonation (2) a hit below the waterline which achieved the same effect (3) a hit in the main machinery. One thing is certain: the lack of witnesses and material evidence makes any of these theories tenable, and the design and layout of the ship makes other theories less so.

HMS *Hood*, the world's largest prewar ship.

### Hopkins, Harry, 1890–1946

Hopkins was President Roosevelt's closest and most trusted adviser. He had been Secretary of Commerce before the war, but after 1941 ill health forced him to resign so Roosevelt used him as his special envoy. Hopkins was sent to London and later Moscow to discuss the setting up of a Lend-Lease program. In October 1941 Hopkins became Chairman of the Munitions Assignment Board and later a member of the Pacific War Council and War Production Board. He attended all the major Allied conferences working closely with Roosevelt. During the London Conference in July 1942 Hopkins was involved in the arguments between General Marshall and Admiral King with Churchill about the feasibility of a landing in France. Hopkins's ill health meant he relied on drugs and he was often in pain. Nonetheless after Roosevelt's death Truman sent the weak Hopkins on his final mission to Moscow in May 1945. He discussed the problem of the Security Council of the UN with Stalin and Molotov and he broke the deadlock on the Polish question. This set the scene for the conference at Potsdam. Hopkins retired from active politics and died shortly afterwards.

### Höpner, General Erich, 1886–1944

A very successful Commander of Fourth Panzer Group in 1941, his tanks came nearest to Moscow in December. The failure of the drive to capture the city drove Hitler to dismiss many of the generals he held to blame of whom the principal one was Höpner. He was stripped of his rank. Drawn thereafter into the Stauffenberg conspiracy against the Führer, he hesitated on 20 July 1944 and was arrested on the failure of the coup that evening. He was hanged on 8 August.

### *Hornet*

The aircraft carrier *Hornet* (CV.8) was a slightly modified sister of the *Yorktown* and *Enterprise*. In her short commissioned life of 372 days' duration she earned immortal fame and made an important contribution to the US Navy's victory.

The *Hornet* was the last carrier to be commissioned before Pearl Harbor but she was still on her shakedown cruise when war broke out. But before she could be posted to the Pacific Fleet she was to perform a special mission designed to

A destroyer takes survivors off USS *Hornet*.

bolster morale and to puncture Japanese self-esteem. A squadron of B–25B Mitchell twin-engine bombers, larger aircraft than any yet flown from a carrier, were to be used to bomb Tokyo under the command of the veteran aviator Lieutenant James Doolittle.

With the *Enterprise* as escort, the *Hornet* followed the reverse course used by the Japanese carriers when they attacked Pearl Harbor. At 0558 on 18 April 1942, in a 40-knot gale all 16 bombers took off from a position about 550 miles from Japan. The raid caused little material damage but the Japanese assumption that the home islands were invincible received a rude awakening. Only one B–25 landed safely, but in neutral Russia, while the others either crash-landed or were abandoned over China. To preserve secrecy President Roosevelt described the raid as being launched from a secret base in China codenamed 'Shangri-la', the mythical land in James Hilton's *Lost Horizon*. To commemorate the exploit a new carrier was named *Shangri-la*.

The *Hornet* was not damaged in the Battle of Midway but her TBD Devastator torpedo-bombers of VT–8 were slaughtered in a hopeless, slow, low-level attack on the Japanese carriers; 15 aircraft were shot down and only one out of the 30 aircrew survived. A dive-bomber strike later missed its target completely and had to 'ditch' or land on Midway.

On 26 October 1942 while screening the invasion fleet at Guadalcanal, Task Force 16 fought the Battle of the Santa Cruz Islands. At 0910 she was attacked by about 15 dive-bombers and 12 torpedo-bombers. A bomb hit the flight deck, a bomber crashed into the stack and then two torpedoes hit on the starboard side. Within seconds another three 250kg bombs crashed into the hangar. The *Hornet* lay dead in the water, listing at 12.5° and ablaze. When it was learned that a strong Japanese task force was approaching from the north, Admiral Kinkaid ordered the *Hornet* to be scuttled. As if to endorse this decision another air attack scored a torpedo-hit. At 1800 hours the Japanese were still bombing the abandoned hulk. Unfortunately the Mark 15 torpedoes used in the destroyers proved of very little use in sinking the *Hornet*; of eight fired by the destroyer *Mustin* only three ran straight. Nine torpedo hits did not sink the carrier, a tribute to the appalling quality of the torpedoes rather than the toughness of the *Hornet*. Eventually the two destroyers, illuminated by flares dropped by Japanese floatplanes, fired 430 rounds of five-inch shells into her, leaving her to the Japanese, who finally sank her with four 'Long Lance' torpedoes. The loss of the *Hornet* put an end to the prewar carrier fleet of the United States.

### Hornisse
see Näshorn

### Horrocks, General Sir Brian, 1895–

A protégé of Montgomery who introduced him to the command of 13th Corps in the Western Desert, Horrocks commanded it with great skill in the battles of Alam Halfa and Alamein. He followed his chief to Europe for D-Day and commanded 30th Corps in the Battle of Normandy, the advance to Brussels, the Arnhem Battle and the drive into Germany.

### Horthy, Regent Miklos, 1868–1946

Admiral Horthy (the rank derived from service in the Austro-Hungarian Navy before 1918) had been Regent of his kingless country, in effect both head of state and government, since 1920. His rule was right-wing but he was not a fascist and it was through pressure that Hitler brought him to grant rights of movement to the Wehrmacht in Hungary and then the use of the Hungarian Army in the invasion of Russia. Horthy in 1944 attempted to prevent the deportation of the Hungarian Jews and to extricate his country from the war, but was obliged, as a result of Skorzeny's kidnapping of his son, to revoke his peace feelers and was deported to Berlin. He was released by the Americans in May 1945. Horthy was a Greater Hungarian nationalist – he had joined willingly in Hitler's invasion of Yugoslavia in 1941 – but he was not a Quisling.

### Horton, Admiral Sir Max, 1883–1951

A submariner of much experience, Horton in 1942 was given command of the Western Approaches, the post carrying responsibility for bringing the convoys safely from mid-Atlantic to port. It was he, therefore, who fought the Battle of the Atlantic at its most critical moment. Thanks in part to a timely closing of the 'air gap' in mid-Atlantic and to increases in the number of escorts, but also to his own shrewdness and untiring zeal, the tide of battle turned in the Allies' favor in May 1943. If any one man was victor of the Atlantic Battle, he was Horton.

### Hudson, Lockheed A–28, A–29, PBO–1

This US maritime reconnaissance, light bombing and transport aircraft was operational, 1939–45. Like the Mustang, the Hudson was designed to meet British requirements during the hasty rearmament period of the late thirties. To save time, Lockheed simply adapted their Model 14 Super Electra airliner to have more powerful (1100hp) Wright Cyclone engines, a transparent nose for a bomb-aimer, two fixed forward-firing 0.303in machine guns, an internal weapon-bay for 750lb of bombs, and provision for a twin-gun turret above the fuselage, although the turret itself was not fitted until the aircraft reached Britain. The first ones arrived in good time to begin the job of watching for German surface raiders between Scotland and Norway from the moment World War II started. As they gradually replaced Ansons in RAF Coastal Command, they logged sufficient adventures and achievements to fill a book. A Hudson

became the first RAF airplane from the UK to destroy an enemy aircraft in the war when a Dornier Do 18 flying-boat was shot down on 8 October 1939. Hudsons were the first to use radar to hunt U-Boats by night, the first to be ferried by air across the Atlantic and, on 27 August 1941, the first to force the surrender of a U-Boat to an airplane. When the crews of three 220 Squadron Hudsons spotted 40 Ju 87 dive-bombers one day, they sailed in to the attack, shot down five of the Stukas and damaged two more. In the end, the RAF took delivery of more than 2000, later aircraft having 1200hp Pratt & Whitney Twin Wasp engines and a 1000lb bomb load. They covered the Allied landings in North Africa with patrols from Gibraltar. Home-based aircraft were adapted to carry an airborne lifeboat under their fuselage, for parachuting to survivors at sea. When operational squadrons began to re-equip with new types, in 1943–44, the Hudsons were adapted for training and transport duties. When America entered the war, some aircraft were repossessed for the USAAF, the Twin Wasp versions being designated A–28, the Cyclone versions A–29. One of the latter made the first successful attack on a U-Boat by a USAAF aircraft, but was preceded by the US Navy, which had acquired 20 Cyclone-powered Hudsons as PBO–1s.

## Hull, Cordell, 1871–1955

Hull was Roosevelt's Secretary of State from 1933 to 1944. As neutrality became impossible to maintain he supported Roosevelt in drawing the USA closer to war. In 1941 his main problem was how to deal with Japan's growing dominance of the East. After Japan had seized Indo-China, Hull opened detailed negotiations with Japan on 20 November 1941. Hull had the advantage of having decoded Japanese messages from Tokyo to their embassy in Washington and adopted a hard-line policy in these negotiations. He demanded withdrawal from Indo-China and from most of China. The deadlock in the negotiations eventually led to the declaration of war on 8 December 1941.

Despite his weak health Hull played an active part in international relations during the war. He led the US delegation to the Foreign Ministers' Conference in Moscow in 1943. He played a major role at the Dumbarton Oaks Conference and laid the ground work for the San Francisco Conference. He retired in November 1944 but was a delegate at the UN Conference at San Francisco in April 1945. Roosevelt paid tribute to him by calling Hull 'the father of the United Nations'.

The *maiale* two-man human torpedo had a devastating effect on the Royal Navy in the Med.

## 'Human Torpedoes'

These first came to prominence in December 1941, when the Italian Navy knocked out the British battleships *Queen Elizabeth* and *Valiant* with two-man special assault craft. Officially named *Siluro a Lenta Corsa* (Slow-running Torpedo) or SLC but known to their crews by the more homely name *Maiale* (Pig), these were really small midget submarines driven by two operators wearing Scuba gear, sitting astride the slender body. Their purpose was to penetrate defended harbors, and the means of attack was to detach the warhead and clamp it to the keel of an enemy ship.

The British were quick to copy the SLC and called it the 'Chariot'. It was used successfully in the Mediterranean, where the water is warm, but attempts to use it in Norway proved unsuccessful. When Italy surrendered in September 1943 several Italians gallantly volunteered to attack their own ships which had fallen into German hands, and for this work one of them was decorated by the British.

## Hummel

The Hummel was a German self-propelled artillery weapon consisting of the 15cm heavy field howitzer 18 mounted on a chassis developed from components of the PzKw III and IV tanks. The hull of the vehicle was built up into a rectangular armored superstructure without roof and the gun was mounted to fire forward. It weighed 23 tons and had a crew of five.

Diagram of the Geschützwagen III/IV Hummel SdKfz 165.

## 'Hump'
see Burma Road

## Hungary, Liberation of, 1944–45

In 1944 after the liberation of Rumania, Marshal Malinovsky concentrated on two advances towards Hungary. One was direct via Cluj, but the town held out until 11 October. The indirect route via Arad led to a breakthrough on 22 September. These offensives were helped by General Petrov's 4th Ukrainian Front which broke through the Carpathian passes in the north of Hungary and on 30 October Malinovsky launched a powerful drive for Budapest. He had 64 divisions and some of his forces reached the outskirts of the capital on 4 November, but they were held up by bad weather. Marshal Tolbukhin then made a wide out-flanking maneuver from near the confluence of the Danube with the Drava on 4 December and reached Lake Balaton. The Red Army had now encircled Budapest but the city did not fall for another month. Pest, on the east bank of the Danube, fell on 18 January 1945 followed by Buda on 18 February after a bitter struggle.

The Germans held a line from the Danube to Lake Balaton to the Drava and Hitler's obsession about holding the Balaton oilfields led him to order the recapture of Budapest. The offensive opened at midnight on 5 March. After five days the Sixth Panzer Army was only advancing at the rate of five miles a day and a rapid counterattack by Tolbukhin forced the Germans to abandon the attempt. The Sixth Panzer Army escaped in time and on 20 March the Red Army reached the Bratislava Gap and the Austrian border.

## Hurley, Major General Patrick, 1883–1963

Hurley was US Ambassador to China after November 1944. He had previously served as President Hoover's Secretary of War and in January 1942 President Roosevelt gave him the job of trying to break the blockade of Bataan. This was a hopeless task and soon afterwards Hurley was made US Minister to New Zealand. Roosevelt used him as a personal envoy to the USSR, the Near East and also in China. He did some of the preliminary negotiations before the Cairo Conference. After he had become Ambassador to China Hurley opened negotiations with Mao Tse-tung and the Communists to see whether he could get more co-operation between the Kuomintang and the Communists but nothing came of this.

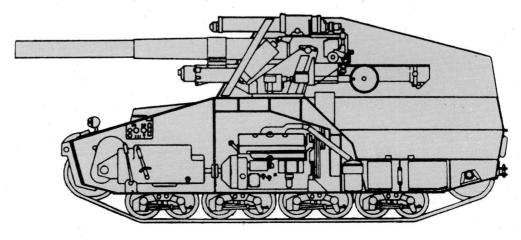

## Hurricane, Hawker

This British single-seat fighter was operational from 1937 to 1947. The prototype flew for the first time on 6 November 1935, at a period when most fighters were open-cockpit biplanes with a fixed undercarriage. In a single step it not only increased top speed by more than 35 percent, becoming the RAF's first over-300mph combat aircraft, but offered its pilots the unprecedented firepower of eight 0.303in Browning machine-guns, needing no synchronizing gear as they fired outside the propeller disc. Hurricanes first entered service in December 1937 with No 111, RAF Fighter Command. By retaining the fabric-covered metal-tube fuselage construction of his earlier biplanes, Hawker's Chief Designer, Sydney Camm, had produced an airplane easy to build, fly, service and repair. By the outbreak of war, 497 had been delivered to equip 18 squadrons. By 7 August 1940, a few days before the Battle of Britain started, the totals had grown to 2309 Hurricanes and 32 squadrons, compared with 19 squadrons of faster, but harder-to-build Spitfires. A Hurricane had been the first RAF fighter to destroy an enemy airplane in France on 30 October 1939. Squadrons had fought the Luftwaffe over Western Europe and in Norway. No. 261 had relieved the hard-pressed Gladiator biplanes in Malta, and No 274 was on its way to the Western Desert in North Africa. In the Battle of Britain they shot down more enemy aircraft than did all the other UK defenses, air and ground, combined. When German aircraft became more heavily armored, Hurricanes stepped up their firepower to 12 machine guns or four 20mm cannon. The Mk IIC, with a 1280hp Merlin XX engine instead of the earlier 1030hp Merlin II or III, added two 500lb bombs. When Rommel's tanks had to be driven back from Alamein, No. 6 Squadron used Mk IIDs, fitted with two 40mm guns, to 'open up' the enemy armor, and has worn a winged can-opener as its badge ever since. Hurricanes became the first single-seat fighters to carry ground-attack rockets, were catapulted from merchant ships and flown from carriers, as Sea Hurricanes to protect convoys at sea. They fought everywhere from Burma to Russia. Altogether, the Russians were sent 2952 of the total of 12,780 British-built and 1451 Canadian-built Hurricanes.

*Below and top:* The Hawker Hurricane I.

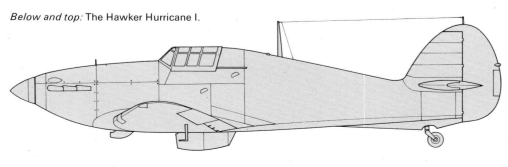

## Husky
see Sicily, Invasion of, 1943

## Husseini, Amin el (Grand Mufti of Jerusalem), 1900–

A fierce opponent of Zionist aims and the instigator of the Arab Revolt of 1936 in Palestine, the Mufti went to Iraq in October 1939 where in 1941 he was instrumental in bringing down the pro-British government of Nuri es-Said and installing Rashid Ali, a pro-German, in his place. This provoked a successful British invasion of Iraq and his own exile to Germany. He spent the rest of the war under Nazi tutelage and helped to raise for them military units of Muslims from the occupied territories. He eventually found refuge in Egypt.

## Hyakutake, Lieutenant General Harukichi

Hyakutake landed at Guadalcanal, 9 October 1942, with his fresh Seventeenth Army, to reinforce the starving and desperate Japanese forces which had been pinned down for months, and which had been defeated the night before at the Mataniko River. Additional reinforcements, artillery and ammunition were put ashore on 11 October while the US fleet was diverted by the Battle of Cape Esperance. Despite the relief given by these supplies and the destruction of Henderson Airfield by accurate and heavy Japanese aerial bombardment, Hyakutake was unable to accomplish a major offensive. Firstly, Maruyadma's force was decimated in its attempt to outflank Henderson. Secondly, Vice-Admiral Abe's transport fleet was discovered and decimated on 13 November while trying to bring more troops to Guadalcanal. (Only 4000 men arrived safely out of the 12,000 who embarked.)

By 22 November an rapidly rising average of 100 of his men starved to death every day. Malaria also took its toll. Yet, when evacuation began at the end of January, it was the front-line men who did not want to leave the island, but to die honorably in battle. Hyakutake wished to give them the chance, but finally had to acquiesce and organize the evacuation. He remained at Rabaul until the end of the war.

## Ichi-Go
see China Campaign, 1941–45

## Ickes, Harold, 1874–1952

Ickes was President Roosevelt's Secretary of the Interior. His main responsibility was the control of raw materials. He was oil and solid fuels administrator during the war and in 1943 he also took responsibility for the fisheries and coal mines. He was involved in the Washington Conferences with the British and from the start favored a hard line against Japan.

The bow wake of HMS *Illustrious*.

## *Illustrious*

In 1937 the British ordered the first of a radically new type of aircraft carrier as part of their long-deferred rearmament program. Instead of a conventional carrier in which aircraft capacity was given priority over protection, the new carriers emphasized armament and protection. This was to allow them to fight in waters where they could expect to face enemy land-based air forces, ie, Northern Europe and the Mediterranean. Given the Fleet Air Arm's lack of high-performance aircraft this philosophy made sense, but US and Japanese experience showed that an aircraft carrier should not sacrifice aircraft, as a good combat air patrol was a far better defense against any form of air attack than armor and guns. Only when the armored carriers showed their toughness by resisting kamikaze hits off Okinawa in 1945 did the US Navy begin to revise its opinions. By a strange coincidence the Japanese produced a similar design in the *Taiho*.

The 'box' hangar, with its heavy armored roof and armored sides, imposed very strict fire-precautions to reduce the risk of explosions inside the hangar. The sealed hangar was isolated from the machinery and had its own ventilation system so that gasoline vapor could not permeate the ship. It was this feature as much as the armored deck which saved the *Illustrious* and her sisters from the disastrous fires which gutted several US and Japanese carriers.

HMS *Illustrious* lived up to her name and was awarded eight battle honors. She went straight to the Mediterranean in August 1940 to reinforce the British Mediterranean Fleet. Three months later her planes had made her the scourge of the Italian Fleet, harassing shipping and protecting the Fleet against Italian attacks. She was the main unit in Operation Judgment, the air strike on the Italian Battle Fleet at its main base, Taranto. A total of 21 strike aircraft took off on the night of 11–12 November and using a total of 11 torpedoes for the loss of two aircraft, the battleship *Conte di Cavour* was sunk and the *Littorio* and *Duilio* were badly damaged.

So successful was the *Illustrious* in performing her task that the German Luftwaffe came to the aid of the Italians, by giving the crack *Fliegerkorps X* the sole task of destroying the carrier. On 10 January 1941, in an attack lasting only ten minutes a force of 50 Stuka Ju87R dive-bombers hit the carrier's deck with six 1000lb bombs, three of which set her on fire and wrecked the after-flight deck. But her system of protection saved her, for her machinery was intact and the fire did not spread. She limped into Malta's Grand Harbor with 126 dead and 91 wounded, and although the Italians and Germans continued to bomb her while she was undergoing repairs they did not cause any further serious damage. On 23 January the ship began a long trip to Norfolk Navy Yard, Virginia, where she docked on 12 May ready to begin repairs that involved the virtual rebuilding of the after-part of the ship.

The *Illustrious* was back in service in December 1941, and three months later she joined Operation Ironclad, the occupation of the French island of Madagascar to prevent it from falling into Japanese hands. With her sisters, *Formidable* and *Indomitable,* she provided air cover and tactical strikes during the landings at Diego Suarez on 5–7 May 1942. In 1943 she attended Force H covering the Salerno Invasion, and during the landings her air group flew 214 fighter-sorties in three days without a single landing-accident. In January 1944 she left for the Far East once more, and operated with the US carrier *Saratoga* in the East Indies. On 19 April the two carriers struck at the Japanese base at Sabang in Sumatra.

In June the *Illustrious* covered another raid on Sabang, this time with her sister *Victorious* and two battleships. In January 1945 two more successful strikes were made against the oil refineries at Palembang, halving the output of one and stopping the other completely.

Although having severe machinery trouble, and capable of only 24 knots the *Illustrious* joined Task Force 57, the main British Pacific Fleet force, for strikes against the Sakishima Gunto island chain in March 1945. These operations were to support the US Navy's invasion of Okinawa, 200 miles away. On 1 April the first kamikaze aircraft appeared, and one caused some damage five days later. By now the carrier was showing signs of wear-and-tear and she was sent home for full repairs.

## Ilyushin DB–3

This Soviet long-range bomber was operational from 1937. Mainstay of the Soviet long-range bomber force for a number of years, the DB–3 saw active service against both Finland and Germany during the early part of World War II. It was an all-metal monoplane, with two 960hp M–86 radial engines, which gave it a maximum speed of 253mph. It could carry up to 4850lb of bombs, some externally, a crew of three and armament of three 7.62mm machine guns, in nose and dorsal turrets and in a ventral position, firing through a trap in the floor. Despite its size and weight, it was so maneuverable that test pilot Vladimir Kokkinaki had no hesitation in looping a DB–3 during an air display at Tushino Airport, Moscow. Production totalled 1528 up to 1940, when the improved Il–4 (DB–3f) superseded the DB–3.

A German truck convoy blazes after attack from Ilyushin IL-2 Shturmoviks.

## Ilyushin Il–2

This Soviet low-level armored attack aircraft was operational from mid-1941. The original prototype of this aircraft was the two-seat TsKB–55 or BSh–2 of 1938, powered by a 1350hp AM–35 engine. The 'BSh' stood for *Bronirovanni Shturmovik* (armored ground attack), and even in wartime Britain the exploits of Russia's 'Sturmoviks' captured the popular imagination. This was fair enough. Here was an

The Il-2M3 Shturmovik.

airplane that flew through a continuous barrage of every kind of ground fire to destroy hitherto invincible German tanks with a thunder of gunfire, bombs and still-new rockets. Key to the apparent indestructibility was that the aircraft had a backbone of 7mm armor-plate, to which everything else was attached. It protected the cockpit, radiators, engine and fuel tanks, and was thickened to 12mm at the rear of the cockpit. Production aircraft, known as Il–2s were initially single-seaters, with a 1600hp AM–38 instead of the original AM–35 engine. The AM–38 produced its maximum power where it was needed, at low altitude, giving a speed of 251mph and enabling the Il–2 to carry eight 82mm RS–82 rockets or 1320lb of bombs in addition to two 23mm ShVAK cannon and two ShKAS machine guns in the wings. Tests of the TsKB–57 production prototype had still been underway at the beginning of 1941, yet a few Il–2s were able to offer opposition to the enemy attack in July-August, and 249 had been delivered by the end of the year. There were some holdups while the Soviet war industry was transferred eastward to the safety of the Urals, and for a time wood replaced metal in the outer wings and tail unit; but Stalin told the workers that Il–2s were needed by the Red Army as much as air and bread. Within twelve months the number of man-hours required to produce an Il–2 had been cut by 38 percent; the number of Il–2s in service increased 400 percent between July 1942 and July 1943. Eventual total production was 36,163, later aircraft being mostly two-seat Il–2m3s, with airframe refinements which raised top speed by 21mph, a formidable 37mm cannon in place of the ShVAK, 132mm rockets and launchers able to dispense 200 small anti-tank bombs.

## Ilyushin Il–4 (DB–3f)

This Soviet long-range bomber was operational from 1940. Except for a few Pe–8s, the DB–3 series remained the Soviet Union's only long-range bombers throughout World War II. They were also employed tactically, for a variety of tasks, including torpedo attack, photo reconnaissance, glider towing and even as transports for seven fully-equipped men. This emphasized the vital need for the Red Air Force to provide maximum support for ground forces, rather than to develop strategic bombing, but DB–3fs of a Baltic Fleet Guards torpedo bomber regiment made the first Soviet raid on Berlin as early as 8 August 1941.

Compared with the DB–3, the 3f had an entirely new front fuselage, rather like that of the German Heinkel He 111, with a universal mounting for a gun in a slim glazed nose. Performance at height was improved by fitting two 960hp M–87A engines, which developed 900hp up to 15,400ft; and the pilot was provided with 9mm back armor. Further changes came in 1942 after the aircraft industry had been moved eastwards to escape the German advance. For a period, the wing spars had to be made of wood,

The Ilyushin Il-4 (DB-3).

Sturmovik Il-2s on the assembly line. Many of these aircraft were manufactured across the Urals after 1942.

because of a shortage of light alloys. The small increase in weight was offset by introduction of new two-speed supercharged M–88B engines, giving 1100hp for take-off and 1000hp up to 20,000ft. The caliber of the gun in the dorsal turret was raised to 12.7mm. Under the revised designation system, based on the initial letters of the name of the design bureau chief, the DB–3f became the Il–4 from this time. A total of 5256 were built, production ending in 1944.

## Ilyushin Il–10

Although the Il–10 had a configuration almost identical to that of the Il–2, it was a new design embodying many improvements based on experience with the original 'shturmovik'. Power plant was a 2000hp AM–42; the gunner was better protected with armor; the size of the undercarriage fairing pods was much reduced; and a dorsal turret with a 20mm gun replaced the former machine gun. Maximum speed went up to 311mph, and the Il–10 gave excellent service with Soviet Army units advancing into Germany in the last three months of the war.

## Ilyushin, Sergey V, 1894–1977

Ilyushin was a brilliant aeronautical engineer. He designed a twin-engined bomber in 1936, the TSKB-30, which was used as a long-range bomber during the war. In 1939 he designed a dive-bomber, Il-2, which was used for ground attack. These planes enabled the USSR to control the air battles at the end of the war.

## Imphal, Battle of
see Kohima and Imphal Offensives, 1944

## Infra-red Target Detection Systems

No weapon can demonstrate its efficiency until it is presented with a target, and when combat extends into the hours of darkness, detection and acquisition of targets becomes difficult. For this reason there was much investigation of infra-red detection systems during World War II, notably by Germany. In Britain and the USA infra-red was proposed as a method of detecting enemy aircraft, but the discovery and perfection of radar soon displaced infra-red in this field. Due to the slow development of radar in Germany, infra-red had a much longer run, and several devices were placed in service.

There are two methods of using infra-red radiation, the 'active' and the 'passive'. The active method required that a source of infra-red illumination, analogous to a searchlight, be directed toward the target while detection devices searched for the reflection. The passive system relied on the natural emission of infra-red from the target, as, for example, in the form of heat from a ship's funnel, an airplane engine exhaust or a tank engine, or, at short ranges, the heat of the human body. Using suitable devices all these could be detected, usually at much greater ranges than was possible using the active system.

Examples of the active system were mainly to be found on the Allied side, with such devices as the 'Sniperscope' combined emitter-detector mounted on rifles or machine guns, and 'Tabby'

Firing a German Vampir rifle sight unit, showing the electronic pack and battery.

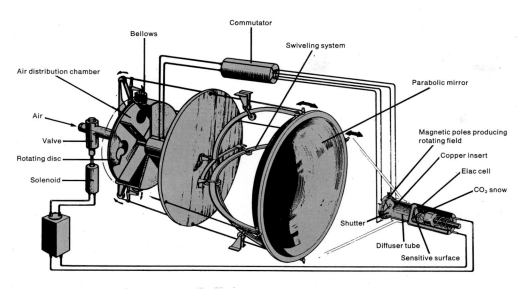

Diagram of the Madrid infra-red homing unit used with an Enzian missile.

a combined searchlight and optical viewer used as a night-driving aid. The Germans appear to have been more interested in passive systems, among which were 'Obi', a searchlight director which detected bomber exhausts and brought the normal type of searchlight to bear before exposing the light; 'Donau-60' a long-base detector used with coast artillery for detecting ship funnels; and 'Spanner', fitted to fighter aircraft to enable them to home-in on bombers at night. Night driving aids, used in conjunction with infra-red lamps alongside the road, were also in use, as was the 'Vampire' rifle sight. In spite of the many devices produced, few practical results were achieved in combat. More was achieved in the field of navigational aids.

## *Iowa*

Six *Iowa* Class battleships were ordered for the US Navy in 1939–40, but for the first time since 1921 there was no limit on size and so the displacement jumped to 45,000 tons. The principal reason for this big expansion of dimensions (and cost) was the US Navy's realization that it had no battleships fast enough to accompany the Essex Class carriers, and as armor protection was subordinated to speed they could also be described as battlecruisers. Steel shortages delayed construction and only four were completed between February 1943 and June 1944; another two were never completed.

The most famous of the class was the *Missouri* (BB. 63), the 'Mighty Mo', for the Japanese surrender was signed on her deck; the *New Jersey* also won fame as the flagship of Admiral William F Halsey Jr. These were the last battleships built for the US Navy but they did not fight in any surface action.

## Iraq, Occupation of, 1941

The kingdom of Iraq, which had been set up under British protection after World War I and was a major source of British oil supplies, was in 1941 under the pro-British government of Nuri es-Said. Anti-British feeling, fomented in part by the exiled Mufti of Jerusalem, was eagerly encouraged by the Germans, who found in Rashid Ali, an Iraqi opposition politician, a willing ally. On 3 April 1941 he organized a successful anti-British coup. It was not a situ-

ation the British could accept and, after securing the safety of the Iraq-Haifa pipeline by the dispatch of an Indian brigade to the country on 17 April, they opened hostilities against the regime's troops on 2 May. Resistance was light and on 31 May they occupied Baghdad. Rashid was removed and the regent, Emir Abdullah, and Nuri es-Said were reinstated. British troops remained in the country, however, until the end of the war. Among the remaining troops were the Iraq Levies, formed from displaced Christian Assyrian tribesmen, who had been raised to guard the great RAF airbase at Habbaniyah near Baghdad in the 1930s.

## 'Iron Annie'
see Junkers Ju 52/3m

## Ironclad
see *Illustrious*

## Ironside, Field Marshal Edmund, 1880–1959

Allegedly the model for John Buchan's fictional hero, Richard Hannay, Ironside had led an adventure story life. He had been an intelligence officer in the Boer War, Commander of the Allied Forces in North Russia, 1918–19, and spoke seven languages. At the outbreak of war Hore Belisha, who had found difficulty in working with his Chief of the Imperial General Staff, Gort, replaced him with Ironside, while Gort went to France with the Expeditionary Force, the post Ironside coveted and would perhaps have filled to greater advantage. He was relieved during the Battle of France and replaced by Dill, never having shown his best.

## 'Irving'
see Nakajima J1N1-S Gekko

## *Isaac Sweers*

When the Germans invaded the Low Countries in 1940 they found that most of the Royal Netherlands Navy ships had been sabotaged or taken to England. Four destroyers were being built at Rotterdam and Flushing, of which two had been launched. The *Isaac Sweers* was without main armament or fire control, but the bare hull was towed to England and refitted with

British guns. Her sister *Gerard Callenburgh* was scuttled on 15 May but the Germans raised her and commissioned her in 1942 as *ZH.1* (*Zerstorer Hollandse*).

The *Isaac Sweers* joined the British 19th Destroyer Flotilla in July 1941 and soon distinguished herself in the Mediterranean. After escorting convoys to Malta she and three British destroyers sank the Italian cruisers *Alberico da Barbiano* and *Alberto di Giussano*. The action, which took place at night off Cape Bon on 13 December 1941, was classic with the destroyers hiding between their victims and the shoreline. While covering Operation Torch the ship was torpedoed off Oran on the night of 13 November 1942.

## Ismay, General Sir Hastings, 1887–1965

As secretary of the Committee of Imperial Defense, a post held in World War I by the redoubtable Hankey, Ismay was the principal intermediary between Winston Churchill, in his role as Minister of Defense, and the Chiefs of Staff. His particular talent was to interpret the wishes of the former, however unrealistic, and the professional opinion of the latter, however discouraging, in the most emollient fashion possible. Both sides testified to his talent in this task and to the major contribution he made to Allied victory in so doing.

## Italian Army

The Italian Army in 1940 consisted in theory of 73 divisions, but could mobilize only 42; and it did so only by reducing the number of units within each. Some of the divisions had been active in peacetime, including a number found in Italy's African possessions and formed of local residents both settler and native, but most were reserve formations, activated by inducting reservists. In addition to the regular Army, a Fascist militia existed (*Milizia Volontaria Sicurezza Nazionale* or Blackshirts) which supplied several full divisions to the Army and a number of Legions or Cohorts (regiments or battalions) to regular formations. The bulk of the Army was infantry, but it included three armored divisions (*Ariete, Littorio, Centauro*), three *Celere* or light armored divisions, two motorized divisions (*Trento* and *Trieste*), two parachute divisions (*Nembo* and *Folgore*) and six alpine divisions. The infantry of the armored, light and motorized divisions was provided by the *Bersaglieri* (light infantry) regiments. Formations above divisions were corps and army.

A division contained two infantry regiments of three battalions each, an artillery regiment of nine batteries of four field guns each, an anti-aircraft and an anti-tank battery and an engineer company; many divisions also incorporated a Blackshirt *legion* of two battalions, reckoned to be worth a single army battalion. The armored, *Celere*, and motorized divisions consisted on paper of an armored regiment of two battalions, a *Bersaglieri* regiment of two battalions and a small self-propelled artillery regiment. The infantry divisions had little or no mechanical transport.

Italian equipment was old and poor, and in many cases lacking. Standard infantry weapons were the Mannlicher 6.5mm rifle, Hotchkiss 6.5mm light machine gun and Schwarzlose 7.92mm machine gun. Italian artillery was mostly of World War I design and the armored

Mussolini reviews his troops, who were to fight on the Eastern Front for the Axis.

vehicles were all notoriously under-armored, -powered and -gunned. The L/3, a three-ton carrier, served as the 'tank' in many armored units until well on in the war. The M/11, a true tank, had only a hull-mounted 37mm gun and the M/13, a useful vehicle with a 47mm turret gun, joined the Army only in 1941 and even then in small numbers.

Some Italian formations were excellent, particularly the alpine and Bersaglieri regiments, but the bulk of the infantry, who were badly paid, fed and cared for, had no heart for the war, which they did not see as serving the country's interests. Those sent to Russia in 1942 were quite unacclimatized. Equally, the Italian High Command (*Commando Supremo*) contained numbers of officers whose enthusiasm for Mussolini and Fascism was less than absolute. The guiding principle of the officer corps was loyalty to the Royal House of Savoy, which Mussolini had eclipsed.

## Italian Navy

More correctly known as the *Regia Navale*, the Italian Navy was large and apparently well-equipped with fast, modern ships. But behind the façade there were many shortcomings. Political interference by the Fascists in what was still predominantly a royalist navy led to friction and this was not alleviated by the attitude of some German liaison officers. Although many original designs had been produced, the builders were allowed to conduct trials with an eye to prestige abroad, and unrealistic speeds were obtained by omitting armament, for example.

The colonies in North Africa and East Africa acquired in the 1890s and in the short war with Turkey before World War I ultimately proved to be a liability. Although a large navy was built to use bases in Libya and Eritrea, the Royal Navy had Alexandria, the Suez Canal and Aden, and could easily threaten communications between the colonies and Italy. The lack of resolution in the handling of the Italian Fleet meant that the initiative quickly passed to the British, who never allowed it to slip from their grasp.

Italy's greatest naval asset was her shipbuilding industry, but German efforts to make use of it to remedy their own shortages came to nothing. Shortage of steel and labor cut the rate of building, and an acute shortage of fuel restricted the time that the Fleet could spend at sea.

Although the record of the Italian Fleet could only be described as poor, it produced one outstanding weapon, the 'human torpedo'. Known properly as the *Siluro a Lenta Corsa* or SLC (slow-running torpedo) but affectionately as the *Maiale* (pig), it was a small midget submarine 'ridden' by two operators. Its torpedo-shaped body had a detachable head, so that after it had penetrated an enemy harbor the operators could fasten the detachable warhead underneath a ship's keel. *Maiale* disabled two British battleships in Alexandria in December 1941, and after the Italian armistice in September 1943 they were used against Italian ships still in German hands.

The Italian Navy suffered two important defeats, the first at Taranto in November 1940, when British carrier planes sank a battleship and damaged two more, and the second off Cape Matapan in March 1941. The material losses were not great; the two damaged ships at Taranto were soon raised and repaired, and only three heavy cruisers were sunk at Matapan, but they sapped the confidence of the High Command. During the British evacuation of Greece and Crete in 1941 no attempt was made to attack the British Fleet, and even the success of the *maiale* against the *Queen Elizabeth* and *Valiant* was thrown away by the refusal to act offensively.

*Strength of the Italian Navy in June 1940*
6 battleships
7 heavy cruisers
14 light cruisers
1 coast defense ship
122 destroyers and torpedo boats
119 submarines

## Italy, Capitulation of, 1943

Following the Allies' invasion of Sicily on 10 July, anti-fascist feeling in Italy, which had been rising to a head, burst out in the form of a palace revolution. On 24 July a meeting of the Fascist Grand Council voted to restore the pre-Fascist system of government and return command of the armed forces to King Victor Emmanuel. On the following day, after an interview with the king, Mussolini was arrested and exiled to the island of Ponza. A new government under Marshal Badoglio was set up which at once began secret negotiations with the Allies. On 3 September an armistice was signed secretly at Syracuse and publicly announced on 8 September, the day before the landings at Salerno. It was subsequently confirmed, at Allied insistence, by an Italian acceptance of unconditional surrender on 28 September. The Germans had suspected for some time that Italy might make a separate peace and had laid plans accordingly. Reinforcements had been moved into northern Italy and on 10 September German troops seized Rome after some opposition by Italian troops, and set up a military administration in the country. Badoglio, the government and the king escaped to Allied-held territory but Mussolini, who had been moved to a mountain top hotel at Gran Sasso in the Abruzzi, was rescued by German parachutists led by Otto Skorzeny. He resurrected his regime under the title of the Italian Social Republic safe within the German-held north. The Germans recognized it but denied it effective powers. On 13 October the Badoglio government declared war on Germany, and Italian troops, henceforth known as 'co-belligerents' joined the fighting on the Allied side. A greater military threat to the Germans was presented by the partisan movements which began to organize and act behind their lines.

## Italy, Invasion of, 1943

At the Trident and Quadrant Conferences of May and August 1943, British and American differences over future strategy in the Mediterranean had finally been resolved, not altogether to the Americans' satisfaction. Marshall, American Chief of Staff, had been reluctant to commit troops any deeper into a long-drawn out Mediterranean campaign. But such was British enthusiasm for an invasion of Italy, perhaps

Victorious American troops are greeted warmly by Italian citizens as they march on Rome.

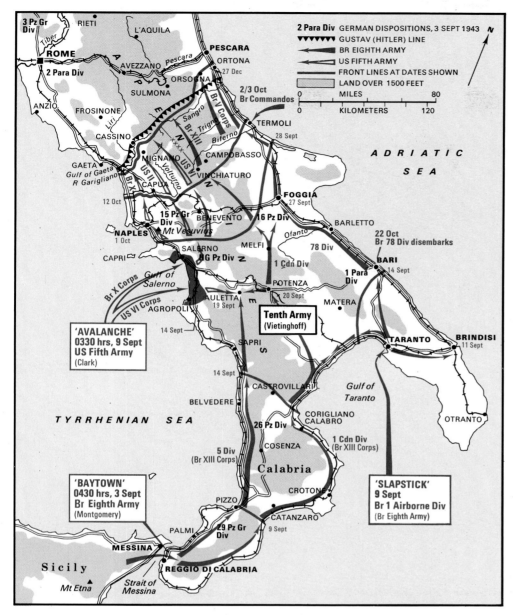

this time the largest amphibious operation of the war, seized four bridgeheads on 9 September, all but one of them in the teeth of strong opposition. That evening elements of three divisions, the British 46th and 56th and the American 36th, which had suffered heavily, were ashore, and they were joined next day by the American 45th. By 11 September, however, elements of five German Panzer divisions had arrived and between 12–14 September the bridgeheads were heavily counterattacked and some ground retaken. It seemed for a time that the safety of the whole bridgehead was threatened. It was saved chiefly by the fire support of the naval bombardment force and the Allied air forces, which broke up the final German attacks on 14 September. By then the British 7th Armored Division and other reinforcements were landing and the bridgehead was saved. The intensity of the fighting and the speed and skill of the German defensive reaction provided, however, all too accurate a foretaste of what the Italian campaign held in store.

## Italy, the Winter Line Campaign, 1943–44

Accepting their failure to repulse the Salerno landings, the Germans in Italy, directed by Kesselring, fell back slowly before the combined Anglo-American advance from the boot of Italy towards Rome. Future strategy was now determined by misunderstandings on both sides. Kesselring believed that the Allies would make use of their success to consolidate their position in the south, to build up bomber bases for the attack on Germany at the Foggia airfields and to prepare a trans-Adriatic invasion of the Balkans. He accordingly persuaded Hitler to reverse his earlier plan of holding only the north of Italy and to allow him to organize a line south of Rome. The Allies, whose intelligence had brought them word of Hitler's first plan, did not press their advance from the south with all dispatch, and therefore allowed Kesselring the time he needed for his fortification of a 'Winter Line' spanning the peninsula along the Sangro

leading to an attack into Germany through the Balkan back door, and such were the opportunities which the moment offered that the Americans had eventually agreed to landings on the Italian mainland, with the proviso that the aim must only be to tie down German troops and that American forces would be withdrawn for the coming campaign in France when needed. Planning for the invasion, begun on 27 July, committed the American 5th Army under General Mark Clark, and the British 8th under Montgomery to the enterprise. The latter was to cross the Straits of Messina and advance through Calabria to join hands with the 5th (which also included the British 10th Corps) after it had landed at Salerno. A subsidiary British landing by 1st Parachute Division in a seaborne role was to seize the Italian naval base at Taranto, thus facilitating the escape of the Italian fleet to Malta (which it in fact made good, under Luftwaffe attack which sank the flagship *Roma*). Ideally the landings would have been made further up the peninsula, with the hope of trapping German divisions in the south, but limits of fighter range from Sicilian airfields determined the points chosen.

The British landings were unopposed but their advance was hampered by German rearguards so that they did not make contact until 16 September with 5th Army. Its landings, at

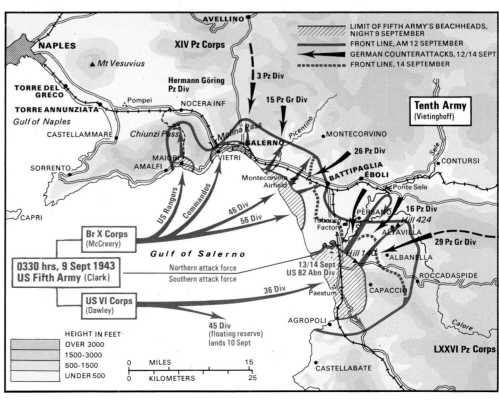

and Garigliano rivers. Defense of the line opened in October with a battle for its outworks along the Volturno river on the Mediterranean coast and for Termoli on the Adriatic. The fighting in both sectors was very bitter and when the Allies arrived on the Winter Line itself in mid-November both the British 8th Army, east of the Appennines, and the Anglo-American 5th, to the west, were tired. They nevertheless proceeded to a deliberate assault. Between 20 November and 2 December the 8th Army fought its way across the Sangro, but then got bogged down in bitter fighting, particularly for the little seaside town of Ortona. It persisted until 27 December when Montgomery, who was about to leave Italy to join the armies preparing for the invasion of France, called it off. The 5th Army, which attacked the Winter Line (known in its sector as the Gustav Line) on 1 December, made rather better progress in a longer effort. It progressively seized Mounts Camino and San Pietro, crossed the Garigliano and reached and crossed the Rapido river below Monte Cassino. There, on 15 January, 1944, its efforts petered out on the slopes of the most formidable defensive position south of Rome.

### Iwabuchi, Rear Admiral Sanji

After General Yamashita decided to abandon Manila without a fight in February 1945 and to retreat to a defensive position around Baguio, Tokyo Imperial Headquarters overrode his objections and sent in 15,000 sailors and Marines under Rear Admiral Iwabuchi. Iwabuchi contested the city street by street, demolishing it entirely with the help of the 4000 troops left by Yamashita and lost every Japanese soldier in the process.

Iwabuchi himself made a last stand at Intramuros. He showed no mercy, especially with regard to the Filipinos: the final count was 1000 US, 16,000 Japanese and 100,000 Filipino dead.

### Iwo Jima, February–May 1945

After the liberation of the Philippines, Admiral Nimitz's next step was to take Iwo Jima, Japan's so-called 'unsinkable aircraft carrier'. The island was a necessary target because it served as a radar and fighter base, and its planes in-

US Marine takes Holy Communion within 100 yards of the airstrip of Iwo Jima.

A despondent General Yoshio Tachibana signs the surrender of Iwo Jima aboard USS *Dunlap* on 3 September 1945.

tercepted the B-29s on their bombing missions over Japan. The island was heavily fortified and garrisoned by 21,000 troops under General Kuribayashi. It had the heaviest firepower and strongest defenses of all Japan's possessions in the Pacific. Iwo Jima was under constant bombardment after the fall of the Marianas, but its invasion had to be postponed when the fighting in the Philippines continued. This meant that the Japanese had a few months' grace in which to improve their formidable defenses. General Harry Schmidt's 5th Amphibious Corps was ready for the assault on 19 February and they confidently expected the island to fall in four days.

The 5th Marines landed in the south of the island but they soon became held up in the ash-like soil. Thirty thousand men landed on the first day but about 2400 of them were hit by accurate Japanese firing on the beaches. The Marines soon held a 4000 yard long beachhead, which cut off Mount Suribachi in the southwest corner of the island. The 5th Marines struck inland and took Airfield No. 1, then they

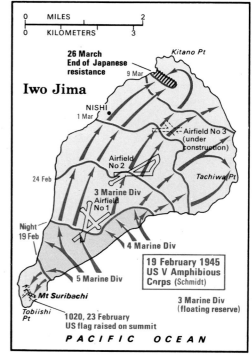

headed west to take Mount Suribachi. After the capture of the Mount on 23 February, the American flag was hoisted on its summit; this became the most famous photograph taken in World War II. The 5th Marines then turned up the west coast, while the 4th Marines fought their way up the east coast and the 3rd Marines held the center. In the northern part of the island the struggle centered on the Motoyama Plateau but on the 9th March the 3rd Marines reached the coast in the northeast and soon the Japanese were pushed back to the East Flank. By 26 March the Japanese made their last suicidal attack with 350 men and organized resistance collapsed. Fighting continued until the end of May. The action cost the Marines and Army 6812 men killed and 19,189 wounded – almost 30% of the landing force. The island did not prove to be such an asset as an airbase but it was used mainly as an emergency landing place for B-29s on missions to Japan.

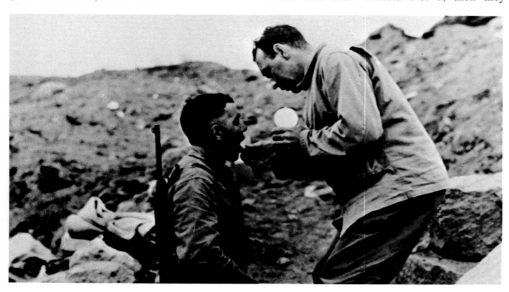

## 'Jack'

see Mitsubishi J2M Raiden

## Japanese Assets, Freezing of the, July 1941

In December 1940 the US government imposed an embargo on the sale of scrap iron and war materials to Japan. President Roosevelt and Secretary of State, Hull, were worried about Japan's increasingly war-like attitude and decided to use economic sanctions–the only measure at that time which was acceptable to the American people.

In July 1941 the Japanese invaded Indo-China in what seemed a preliminary move to threaten Southeast Asia. Roosevelt reacted firmly and froze all Japanese funds and assets in the USA. Britain and the Netherlands followed suit and this meant that Japan no longer had any currency with which to buy the oil and raw materials she needed. Japan had a strategic oil reserve of 55,000,000 barrels which would last for one and a half years of war, so unless she found an alternative source of oil she faced economic collapse. The Japanese Generals naturally considered the invasion of the Dutch East Indies which had oil fields. Thus the freezing of assets pushed Japan closer to war.

## Japanese Navy

The Imperial Japanese Navy had grown from a small force at the end of the 19th Century into the third largest fleet in the world by the end of World War I. Its brilliant victory over the Russians at Tsushima in 1905 provided confidence but also fostered dangerous delusions.

After 1920 the Japanese decided to create a navy capable of defeating the US Navy, and lavished vast sums on powerful ships. Each year startling new designs appeared, many of them bizarre. The purpose was to produce ships which were categorically superior to all possible opponents and in the 1920s and 1930s Japanese warship-designs dazzled the world. Unfortunately the Japanese designers lacked experience, and many of their innovations proved costly. Although they tried to produce a ton-for-ton superiority in speed and gunpower over US and British designs this proved impossible to achieve, and the ships exceeded their designed tonnage by a considerable margin.

The strategic problems were almost insoluble. Nearly all raw materials, notably oil, were controlled by America, Britain or Holland, and so Japan would have to expand by conquest in order to gain access to the raw materials she needed. To beat the US Navy would require a decisive margin of qualitative superiority, as numbers were limited by international treaties. To gain time to build the ships needed Japan announced her intention of opting out of the conditions established by the naval treaties, realizing that this would excite the suspicion of her potential enemies. But the Japanese, remembering the ease with which they had destroyed the Russians in 1904–5, believed that America lacked the will to fight a long war, and had sublime confidence in their own fighting ability. This was the saddest miscalculation of all, and the Japanese also misjudged the strength of their industrial base. Wartime shipbuilding output was poor and with one important exception, their ships did not enjoy the margin of superiority over their opponents that had been planned.

The greatest advantage enjoyed by the Japanese Navy was the possession of the superb 'Long Lance' torpedo, a 24in oxygen-driven weapon with high speed and very long range. In the confused night fighting around Guadalcanal in 1942 Japanese cruisers and destroyers outfought the Allies, and only radar enabled the US Navy to hold its own. As Japanese destroyers were equipped with reload torpedoes they were often able to fool opponents into thinking that they had fired all their torpedoes.

Although the Japanese had matched the US Navy's development of fast carrier strikes as the right strategic weapon for the Pacific and had provided their carriers with very good aircraft and aircrew, they were outmatched by the US Navy mostly because of the heavy losses suffered by Japanese aircrews in the Battles of the Coral Sea and Midway in 1942; the exhaustive training program produced excellent pilots but did not turn them out fast enough to replace losses. After Midway the efficiency of the Japanese carrier task forces declined steadily until by 1944 raw pilots were being thrown into battle.

Emperor Hirohito and naval officers aboard the battleship *Musashi* at Yokosuka in June 1943.

The large submarine fleet was built to co-operate with the surface fleet, to pick off enemy ships and reduce the numerical odds. In practice this tactical doctrine proved faulty, and with a few notable exceptions Japanese submarines were ineffective. They were frittered away on attacks against well-defended warship-targets, and were eventually tied down to running supplies to far-flung army garrisons. They proved vulnerable to US anti-submarine measures and losses were heavy.

The Japanese High command stressed the need to attack which led the Navy to neglect the defense of shipping. When escorts were built they came too late to stem the US submarine offensive and proved vulnerable to submarine attack. Unlike German U-Boats in the Battle of the Atlantic, US submarines were often able to sink the convoy escorts and then pick off the merchant ships at their leisure.

Two battles stand out in the destruction of Japanese seapower; Midway when the carrier strength was crippled, and Leyte when the surface fleet was destroyed in a desperate attempt to stave off defeat. Thereafter the surviving aircrews were squandered in kamikaze attacks, while the ships lay without fuel in their harbors, waiting for destruction at the hands of the US carrier air groups.

*Strength of the Imperial Japanese Navy in December 1941*

10 battleships
8 aircraft carriers
18 heavy cruisers
20 light cruisers
108 destroyers

## Japan's Decision to Surrender

As the Americans were preparing to invade Japan in 1945, the peace faction in the Japanese Cabinet, led by Prime Minister Suzuki, tried to negotiate with the USSR. Togo, the Foreign Minister, hoped to open up communications with the Russians, which would lead to finding

Lord Mountbatten (center) draws up surrender terms of Japan flanked by Slim and Wheeler (left) and Power, Park and Browning(right).

acceptable conditions to end the war. Stalin and Molotov were reluctant to negotiate as the Red Army was preparing to attack Manchuria. Various messages were sent to Moscow, including a message from the Emperor on July 13 before the Potsdam Conference. On 6 August 1945 the Atomic Bomb was dropped on Hiroshima but this did not seem to have as much effect on the Japanese Cabinet as the Russian declaration of war on 8 August. On 9 August immediately after the news of the Nagasaki bomb Japan's Supreme War Council had a prearranged meeting with the Emperor. The Cabinet was split, because if they accepted the Potsdam Declaration there was no guarantee for the Emperor's position. Eventually the Cabinet asked for the Emperor's advice on 10 August and he told them that they must accept the Allied terms. The Japanese sent a message to the Americans with a proviso concerning the Emperor's position. Stimson and Admiral Leahy were willing to accept this but Byrnes, the Secretary of State, drafted a reply which stated that the Japanese government would be subject to the Supreme Commander of the Pacific Forces. The Cabinet could not agree on this until 14 August when these terms were accepted. A couple of army officers tried to stage a *coup d'état* but they found little support. On 2 September a nine-man Japanese delegation signed the formal surrender of Japan aboard the USS *Missouri* in Tokyo Bay.

The Japanese warned the Americans that it would take them time to notify all their troops of the surrender. In Luzon, General Yamashita surrendered on 2 September.

### Jassy-Kishinev, Battle of, August 1944

At the end of the Belorussian offensive the Russians focused their strength on taking the Balkans. A new front was created: the 4th Ukrainian with General Petrov as its commander, and with Generals Malinovsky and Tolbukhin

*Right:* Soviet tanks sweep into Rumania.

was to overrun Rumania. The Germans, under General Friessner, had been able to dig themselves into fixed defensive positions on the right bank of the Dniestr from Jassy to Kishinev but they did not have sufficient numbers, and they relied on Rumanian divisions. The Russians had prepared the way in Rumania and King Michael was ready to announce a coup d'état, once the Russians launched their offensive.

On 20 August 1944 Malinovsky's troops struck south from the Jassy, down both sides of the Serth to Galatz, threatening the salient of south Bessarabia. Tolbukhin attacked, advancing directly westwards from the lower Dniestr. On 23 August, Rumanian radio announced peace with the Allies, Marshal Antonescu was arrested and the Rumanian soldiers started fighting the Germans. Within two days an army of 200,000 men had been destroyed and as a result Russian tanks reached Bucharest on 1 September. After this victory Malinovsky and Tolbukhin were made Marshals.

### Java Sea, Battle of, February 1942

Admiral Doorman had at his command a force of Allied ships known as the Combined Striking Force. This comprised two heavy and three light cruisers and nine destroyers. He had several problems facing him: his communications were weak, he had no reconnaissance planes, his

ships had never worked together and his crews were tired. They had for several months been trying to harass Japanese convoys off the coasts of Java and Sumatra.

On 27 February at 1427 hours, as the fleet was refueling, Doorman received word that an invasion force had been spotted in the Makassar Straits. This force turned out to have an escort of two heavy and two light cruisers and fourteen destroyers under Admiral Takagi. This more than matched Doorman's strength. The battle began at 1620 hours when heavy cruisers opened fire at a range of nearly sixteen miles. Doorman tried to close the range so that he could use the light cruisers' superior power. At 1630 the Allied 6-inch cruisers opened fire on the Japanese destroyers which were within range. However this enabled the rest of the Japanese destroyers, led by the light cruiser *Jintsu* to launch their torpedoes. At 1708 the *Exeter*, one of the Allied 8-inch cruisers, was hit and badly damaged. As it dropped speed, it swung out of line and the *Houston*, *Perth* and *Java* followed. Doorman ordered a counterattack and in the ensuing chaos the *Kortenaer* was sunk by a torpedo. The *Electra* was sunk by three Japanese destroyers later at 1945. He then sent the *Exeter* back to Surabaya with the *Witte de With* and turned south to regroup. He tried to shake off the Japanese but aircraft dropped flares to mark his course. He then decided to send the four US destroyers back to Surabaya to refuel as they had no torpedoes left. Then at 2125 the *Jupiter* blew up and 35 minutes later, the fleet's last remaining destroyer, the *Encounter*, was ordered to pick up the survivors of the *Kortenaer* who were spotted in the sea. At 2300 Doorman spotted the 8-inch cruisers, *Nachi* and *Haguro*, and they opened fire. They fired twelve torpedoes and sank the *Java* at 2332. *De Ruyter*, Doorman's flagship, was hit and sank with him aboard. The two surviving cruisers, *Perth* and *Houston*, retired to Western Java, where they were sunk 12 hours later.

### Jean Bart

The battleship *Jean Bart* was the second ship of the *Richelieu* Class and was launched at St Nazaire in March 1940. With only half her machinery in working order and guns in one turret, she made her escape to Casablanca on the night of 18–19 June 1940. In November 1942 she fired on US troops landing at Casa blanca but was quickly silenced by 16in shells from the US battleship *Massachusetts*. She finally returned to France for repairs at the end of 1945.

## Jeschonnek, General Hans 1899–1943

Jeschonnek was the German General who succeeded Stumpff as Chief of the Air Staff in 1939. He had had a distinguished career up until then, being an army lieutenant by the age of fifteen, serving as a fighter pilot during World War I and being directly involved with the formation of the secret air force commanding the Lehrgeschwader at Greifswald. He was, therefore, able to contribute considerable practical knowledge and an appreciation of new aircraft types to the Air Staff. A firm believer in the potential of the problematic Ju 88 high-speed bomber, he had earlier advocated the strategic bombing of London although Hitler did not permit this until September 1940. Clashes of personality were rife amongst the German Commanders, a trend aggravated by the autonomous nature of Hitler's direction. The mutual contempt felt by Jeschonnek and Milch was renowned, and as German fortunes began to wane, so Jeschonnek's position became gradually more precarious. By August 1943 Germany was obliged to concentrate on self-defense, a situation with which Jeschonnek was relatively unfamiliar. Goering became intolerable, completely bypassing his Chief of the Air Staff. The final crisis came on the night of the RAF raid on the Peenemünde rocket research station, when Jeschonnek mistakenly ordered the Berlin flak to open fire on two hundred incorrectly assembled Luftwaffe fighters. Leaving a note which stated 'It is impossible to work with Goering any longer. Long live the Führer', he shot himself.

## 'Jill'

see Nakajima B6N

## Jodl, General Alfred, 1890–1946

A Bavarian gunner officer, like Halder, Jodl was appointed in 1938 head of the operations section of OKW *(Oberkommando der Wehrmacht)*, the inter-service staff with which Hitler had replaced the old War Ministry and deposed the High Command. His role was executive rather than decision making, but he performed it brilliantly, giving concrete military form to the Führer's strategic decisions. He attended all the twice-daily situation conferences and was the principal source of technical information and advice. As a 'planner of aggressive war' he was tried and executed at Nuremberg.

## Johnson, Group Captain J E

This British RAF officer was England's leading scorer in the aerial war destroying 38 enemy aircraft. His career spanned the whole of World War II with operational experience including the Battle of Britain, the Dieppe Raid, and the D-Day build-up where he flew as a fighter-bomber pilot.

## Johnson Rifle and Machine Gun

Captain Melvin M Johnson Jr (USMCR) produced his first working semi-automatic rifle in 1936, though it was to go through several changes and modifications before it was perfected. In 1940 he submitted it as a possible service rifle for the US forces, and a bitter partisan wrangle ensued between supporters of Johnson and those in favor of the Garand. But the facts were beyond dispute. The Garand had been in production for four years; 50,000 were in service, and the 'bugs' were out of it, whereas the Johnson was a relatively unknown quantity which would take quite a while to reach the same state of perfection – and 1940 was no time for the US Army to change horses in midstream.

However, others were in more desperate straits and the Netherlands East Indies Army ordered 50,000 rifles. Manufacture began, and the US Marine Corps, unable to obtain Garand rifles as fast as it needed them, also bought several thousand. Production continued throughout the war, though the USMC gradually replaced the Johnson with the Garand as supplies became available and the Johnson was only used by OSS and similar special forces in the end. Its reliability was not as good as the Garand and it was continually being modified during production in the hope of improving matters.

The Johnson rifle was unusual in that it operated on the short recoil principle, probably the only successful military rifle ever to do so. It had several ingenious features, notably the rotary magazine which could be 'topped up' at any time, even with the bolt closed. The barrel could be removed for carrying, a feature which attracted interest from the US Airborne forces who used some of them. After the war, however, the Johnson rifle was withdrawn and has not been produced since.

Johnson also produced a machine gun which used the same operating principle as did the rifle. It was fitted with a bipod and fed from a box magazine on the left side which could be 'topped up' from the right-hand side of the gun without having to remove it. It was offered to the US Army and turned down, but the Dutch Government ordered several thousand for use in the Netherlands East Indies. Before this order was completed the Japanese overran the Indies and the balance of the production order was taken by the US Army Rangers and US Marines. Though it was an excellent design and made to a high standard, it was too delicate to stand the rough and tumble of combat and was prone to jam at inconvenient moments.

## Josef Stalin Tank

The Josef Stalin tank was derived from the earlier Klim Voroshilov design of heavy tank. The KV was fitted with an 85mm gun, and by 1943 it appeared that even heavier armament would be required. A variety of designs for a new heavy tank were put forward, but the most convenient solution was to redesign the KV body and chassis to accept a wider turret capable of taking larger guns. Due to problems in producing the guns, the first models (JS-1) in fact carried the same 85mm gun as the KV, but this was soon changed to a 100mm gun derived from a service anti-aircraft gun. Even this was not deemed sufficient and in 1944 a 122mm gun was fitted making the JS-1 the heaviest-armed tank of the time. Weighing 44 tons and with a crew of four it had a 513hp diesel engine and could travel at 20–25mph.

Late in 1944 the JS-1 was replaced by the JS-2, a redesign which produced a better hull shape, and a small reduction in weight. This became the major production model and over 2200 were built. In the early part of 1945 a further redesign was done, resulting in the JS-3 model. This was considerably different to the earlier versions which reflected combat experience. The whole tank was lowered, and the armor of hull and turret more severely sloped for maximum shot deflection. Relatively few reached the front before the end of the war and the first public knowledge of the JS-3 occurred when it appeared in the victory parade in Berlin in 1945. It was undoubtedly the most advanced and formidable tank at that time and its design had considerable influence on subsequent developments in other countries.

## Joubert de la Ferté, Air Chief Marshal Sir Philip B, 1897–1965

This British Air Marshal headed RAF Coastal Command between 1941 and 1943. At the outbreak of war he had been Air Officer Commanding in India but returned as Assistant Chief of the Air Staff to advise on air co-operation with the Navy and on radar. On his appointment to Coastal Command, a post which he had previously held between September 1936 and August 1937, he initiated a 'planned flying' scheme in an endeavor to combat the serious deficiencies which existed within the Command, including the lack of a practicable anti-submarine weapon and the limited number of available aircraft.

He was appointed Deputy Chief of Staff for Information and Civil Affairs on the staff of Lord Mountbatten in Southeast Asia in the Autumn of 1943.

## Joyce, William 'Lord Haw-Haw', 1906–1946

Ideologically one of the most interesting figures of World War II, Joyce literally made his name by his wartime pro-Nazi broadcasts to England, delivered in a curious parody of an English upper-class accent. His origins were mixed: born of an English mother and an Irish father in Brooklyn, New York, he had settled with his

The Josef Stalin II heavy tank.

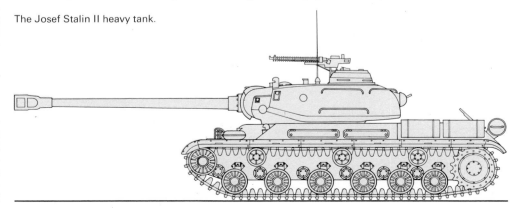

family in England in 1921 and remained there until the outbreak of the war, when he had gone to Germany. His only defense at his trial for treason at the end of the war was that he had possessed American nationality for the first nine months of the war after which he was granted German citizenship. The prosecution's case was that he held a British passport at the time of his defection, and was therefore a beneficiary of the Crown, to which he also held duties. An intellectual of the extreme right, who had broken with Mosley before the war, his treason was caused by Britain's breach with Germany.

**Judgment**
see *Illustrious*

**'Judy'**
see Yokosuka D4Y Suisei

**Juin, Marshal Alphonse Pierre, 1888–1967**

Captured commanding a division in 1940, Juin was released at the request of Pétain and made by him Commander in Chief in North Africa in succession to Weygand. After the Allied landings of November 1942, he enthusiastically attached himself to the Allies' cause and commanded the French Expeditionary Force in Italy. After the liberation of France he became Chief of Staff. A patriot and a fine fighting soldier, he was posthumously created Marshal of France by General de Gaulle, a fellow St Cyrien of the class from which Juin had first graduated.

**July Plot, 1944**

The key figures in the July Plot were Gördler, Beck, Olbricht, Tresckow, von Stauffenberg, and indirectly other noted anti-Hitlerites such as Canaris, Oster and Stülpnagel. Stauffenberg had been introduced to anti-Hitler circles in autumn 1943 and Tresckow had told him about Plan Valkyrie to take over the German government at the assassination of Hitler. Stieff had obtained bombs from England and Tresckow had already unsuccessfully tried to assassinate Hitler in March 1943, but since he had to return to active duty on the Eastern Front he handed the bombs to Stauffenberg. Stauffenberg was a Catholic Bavarian, who apparently wanted the support of Socialist circles in the plot and also wanted to negotiate with Stalin and obtain a settlement favorable to Germany. The collapse of Army Group Center at Bobruisk in June 1944 led Stauffenberg to believe that the Red Army would soon overrun Eastern Europe and so Stauffenberg decided to try to get a favorable settlement with the USSR by trying to kill Hitler, Himmler and Goering. On two occasions Stauffenberg took the bomb to the Führer's Headquarters but both times he abandoned his attempt because Goering and Himmler were absent. On 20 July 1944 he decided that he must go through with his attempt and arrived at Rastenberg with his bomb. Unfortunately the ventilation system of Hitler's bunker was not working and the conference took place in a wooden hut outside. Stauffenberg had the bomb in a briefcase which he placed under the table and then he left the room to make a telephone call. One of the staff officers kicked the briefcase over and it went off. Hitler was only wounded.

The message that Hitler was dead was sent to the *Bendlerstrasse* (the War Ministry) but Olbricht did not act immediately. He had authority over all troops stationed in the Reich and he arrested General Fromm, Commander of the Home Army and sent news of Hitler's death to General Stülpnagel, the Governor of France. Stülpnagel ordered a coup and arrested all SS and Gestapo men in Paris but he could not convince von Kluge to join the coup (Kluge knew Hitler was still alive). The news soon came through that Hitler was alive and Fromm regained his authority and arrested Olbricht and Stauffenberg and had them shot. Fromm allowed Beck to commit suicide. Kluge suspended Stülpnagel who was sent back to Berlin and after an unsuccessful suicide attempt was tried and hanged. Thousands of people implicated in the plot were arrested, tortured and killed during the following nine months. The plot increased Hitler's suspicion of the Army and reinforced Himmler's position as second-in-command by virtue of his command of the SS and thereafter of the Replacement Army.

**Jungle Carbine**
see Lee Enfield Rifle

**Junkers Ju 52/3m**

Deservedly famous as a German counterpart to the US DC–3, 'Iron Annie' was a typical Junkers design, with corrugated metal skinning and few concessions to elegance. It entered service with the newly-formed Luftwaffe as a bomber in the early thirties, and was used as such during the Spanish Civil War. Features included a belly gunner who sat in a sort of open bucket under the fuselage, aft of the fixed spatted main wheels. Most of the 4845 Ju 52/3ms built had three 575hp BMW 132A engines, which gave a cruising speed of only 124mph. They were used as troop transports during every German invasion, but Crete alone cost more than 170 of the 493 Ju 52/3ms engaged in the operation. In 17 days of April 1943, hundreds more were lost to Allied fighters as they tried to ferry supplies across the Mediterranean to Rommel's hard-pressed Afrika Korps. Yet the Ju 52s were still trying to help stave off defeat when the war ended.

The Ju 52 was first used in the Spanish Civil War.

**Junkers Ju 86**

In February 1940, Junkers flew the prototype Ju 86P, a new version of the already-retired Ju 86 bomber with a pressure cabin for a crew of two in an entirely new nose section and special 950hp Jumo 207A Diesel engines fitted with twin superchargers. A later prototype had wings of 84ft span, compared with the normal 73ft 9.75in, and could fly at heights up to 39,360ft. After proving that the 86P could operate over Britain without fear of interception at such an altitude, 40 of the former bombers were converted into Ju 86P–1 bombers and Ju 86P–2 photo reconnaissance aircraft for the Luftwaffe. For two years these aircraft dropped 2200lb bombs and took photos with impunity, over Britain, the Soviet Union and North Africa. Then, on 24 August 1942, a specially modified Spitfire climbed to 42,000ft and destroyed a Ju 86P. Soon, two others were destroyed in the same way, and the Ps were withdrawn from service in May 1943. Attempts to maintain viability by the use of more powerful engines and wings of even greater span on the Ju 86R–1 and R–2 achieved little success.

**Junkers Ju 87**

This German two-seat dive bomber and close-support aircraft was in service between 1937–45. One of the most famous warplanes of history, the Ju 87 is better known as the Stuka, a name abbreviated from the German word for a dive bomber. It was the US Navy that pioneered the technique of aiming bombs by diving steeply on the target and aiming the whole aircraft in the way a fighter pilot does to bring his guns to bear. The need for an aircraft of this type was ignored by the RAF but eagerly accepted by the reborn Luftwaffe, and the first Ju 87 flew in 1935. After much development the Ju 87A–1 was delivered in numbers from April 1937. It was an odd-looking machine, resembling a bird of prey with a W-form cranked wing, high cockpit canopy, square tail and swept-forward 'trousered' landing gears like talons. In the nose was a 610hp Jumo 210 engine, and under the belly a 551 or 1000lb bomb was carried on pivoted arms. At the bottom of the screaming dive these arms swung the bomb clear of the propeller.

Tested in the Spanish Civil War both this version and the much improved Ju 87B demon-

strated amazing pinpoint accuracy. They had airbrakes in the form of hinged plates under the wings, to keep the speed down so that the pilot would have more time to aim. The Ju 87B had spatted wheels and a 1100hp Jumo 211D engine driving a constant-speed propeller. As well as the main bomb it could carry four 110lb bombs under the wings, and it carried three machine guns, two fixed in the wings and one aimed by the man in the rear cockpit. In Poland the dreaded Stukas smashed a path for the German armies, and they repeated the technique even more forcefully in the invasion through the Low Countries into France in May 1940. By this time cardboard sirens were added to the Stukas and to their bombs to strike even greater terror into those underneath. Over Britain the almost defenseless Ju 87 was easy meat, and soon had to be withdrawn, but in Russia and over Greece and Crete it did its deadly work and caused heavy losses to ships of the Royal Navy.

By late 1944 at least 5000 Ju 87s had been built. Most were of a more powerful and more streamlined type, the 87D, with 1400hp Jumo 211J with which a bomb load of 3960lb could be carried. Some versions were equipped for night attack missions, and the 87G was a family fitted with two 37mm tank-busting cannon instead of bombs. Many were used as glider tugs and trainers, and one version was planned to operate from the carrier *Graf Zeppelin* but the ship was never commissioned.

## Junkers Ju 88

This German two/five-seat bomber, close-support aircraft, night fighter and reconnaissance aircraft was in service 1939–45. With the Mosquito the Ju 88 ranks as the most versatile combat machine of all time. It was originally designed by a small group led by two Americans who were experienced in modern all-metal 'stressed-skin' construction, and the first prototype flew in December 1936. It gained speed records, but the design had to be greatly altered before the Ju 88A–1 entered service with the Luftwaffe in late 1939. It was easily the fastest of the three chief types of German tactical bomber, having a speed close to 300mph when unloaded. The bomb load was large, 3960lb being carried in an internal bay and on four large inner-wing racks. The engines were two 1200hp Jumo 211Bs, and the crew of three or four sat close together in the efficient forward

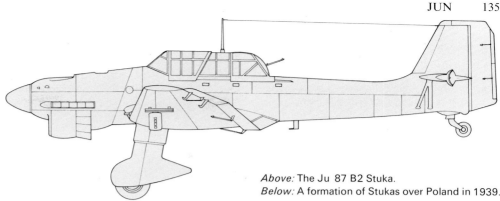

*Above:* The Ju 87 B2 Stuka.
*Below:* A formation of Stukas over Poland in 1939.

fuselage with perfect all-round view and usual armament of three hand-aimed machine guns. The 88, called 'the Three-Fingered 88' because of its long engine cowlings (which looked like radials because of the circular cooling radiators), was extremely strong and very maneuverable, but in the Battle of Britain it was shot down as easily as the other day bombers. Desperate defensive measures included four separate MG 15 machine guns all aimed by one man.

Large numbers were built of the Ju 88A–4 with longer wings to carry the heavy loads, the bomb load being increased to 5500 or 6614lb. Despite this the 88 continued to operate from rough sod airstrips, especially on the Russian front, its big mainwheels riding over the squashy surface and then turning through 90° to lie flat in the rear of the nacelles. Dive brakes under the wings were seldom used, most 88 missions being level bombing at high or very low altitudes. Versions were produced for torpedo dropping, night attack, training and various special duties, while the 88D series were tailored to long-range reconnaissance. The last of the bomber and reconnaissance versions was the slim streamlined Ju 88s, usually with 1700hp BMW 801G radials, or 1810hp 801TJ or 1750hp Jumo 213E. Altogether 10,774 of all these versions were built.

In 1938 the Ju 88B had been planned as a fighter. In July 1939 the first fighter 88 to be built, the C–0, made its maiden flight. Eventually large numbers of C-series fighters were built, with Jumo 211 or BMW 801 engines and 'solid' noses housing a battery of cannon and machine guns. In 1943–45 most production centered on the Ju 88G family, with the bigger tail of the Ju 188 to improve control at weights as high as 32,350lb (50 percent greater than the early bombers). The G was a night fighter, with 801 or 213 engines, speed up to 400mph and typical armament of two 30mm and four to six 20mm cannon all firing ahead of diagonally upwards to destroy bombers with a short burst. Many Ju 88s were turned into pilotless missiles in the Mistel composite aircraft aimed by a piloted fighter originally carried on top.

*Right:* The Ju 88 C66 on a German airstrip.
*Below:* The Ju 88 A-4.
*Bottom:* This Ju 88 was found much the worse for wear by the Allies when Brunswick was overrun.

### Junkers Ju 290

Only a small number of these very large four-engined aircraft were put into service as maritime patrol and reconnaissance bombers. Typical were eleven Ju 290A–5s, based with squadron 1/FAGr 5 at Mont de Marsan, France, and used to locate targets in the Atlantic for Focke-Wulf Fw 200 bombers and U-Boats. Each was powered by four 1700hp BMW 801D engines, carried a crew of nine and had a defensive armament of at least five 20mm guns.

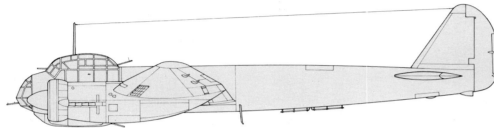

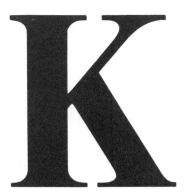

# K

## Kain, Edgar, 1918–1940

A New Zealand-born fighter pilot in the RAF, Kain was one of World War II's earliest aces. In seven months, between November 1939 and his death in June 1940 in a flying accident, he was accredited with 17 German aircraft destroyed.

## Kaltenbrunner, Ernst, 1902–1946

Head of the Austrian SS before the *Anschluss*, he was chosen in 1943 to succeed Heydrich as head of the *Sicherheitsdienst*; in 1944, following the arrest of Canaris, he also became head of the *Abwehr*. He used his immense power to buttress the Nazi system and the ascendancy of Hitler to the very end. His loyalty to the Führer was even more intense than Himmler's and his heart seems to have been even harder; 'Oppression', he once told Himmler, 'is the essence of power'. He was hanged at Nuremberg.

## Kamikaze

Kamikaze pilots were inspired by a wish to die a useful death for their country and regarded their suicide missions as part of their duty. Admiral Onishi began to train pilots in kamikaze techniques after the fall of Saipan. Recruits received intensive training for as little as a week, during which time they learnt to fly Zero fighters or Judy bombers in formation. There were two

Kamikaze pilots drink their ceremonial cup of sake prior to their fatal flights.

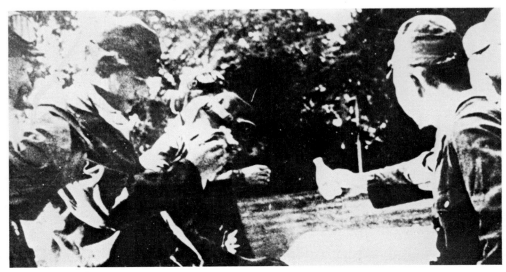

approaches for these suicide flights: a high altitude approach, which meant the plane could not dive at a very steep angle because the lack of control and speed would make it miss its target, and a low altitude approach, which made the plane vulnerable to anti-aircraft guns and fighters. The pilots of the kamikaze aircraft aimed for the central elevator on an aircraft carrier, the base of the bridge on larger ships and for any place between the bridge and the center of smaller warships and transports.

At first kamikaze planes inflicted heavy damage on the US fleets off the Philippines but the US Navy soon learned how to avoid these planes. The Japanese were short of planes and for these missions to be a success they should have sent four aircraft against one carrier, instead they sent one plane for one warship. Once the kamikaze technique stopped achieving results, it was not possible to improve their tactics because the pilots never reported back and the Japanese stubbornly continued to send out inexperienced pilots on kamikaze missions.

Kamikaze pilot receives orders for his final sortie, in 1945.

## Kanga Force
see New Guinea Huon Peninsula

## Karl

This is a class name for a group of German self-propelled howitzers, more properly known as the 'Gerat 040' series. First demanded by the German Army in 1935, the original model was a 60cm (23.6in) short-barrelled howitzer on a tracked chassis intended as a siege gun to deal with fortifications out of reach of railway artillery. The first gun was completed by Rheinmetall-Borsig in 1939 and after a series of trials two service weapons were built. Christened 'Thor' and 'Eva' these were used at the Siege of Sevastopol, at Brest-Litovsk and Leningrad, firing a 1.55 ton high explosive shell to a range of 7325yds or a 2.16 ton concrete-piercing shell to 4900yds. The German Army requested a better performance and to obtain this four 54cm (21.25in) caliber barrels were built and assembled to four more chassis. The exact number of barrels in each caliber is not known, since their external dimensions were the same and they could be, and were, interchanged between chassis. The 54cm weapon fired a 1.3 ton concrete-piercing shell to 11,485yds range. Propulsion for the chassis came from a Mercedes-Benz V-12 engine driving the tracks; for longer moves the weapons could be partially dismantled and carried on special transporters, and for very long-distance moves the complete weapon could be slung between two special railroad flatcars. It was a brilliant technical achievement; weighing 123 tons it was the heaviest self-propelled gun ever developed. But the amount of money and effort spent on them was out of all proportion to their limited tactical value.

## *Karlsruhe*

This German light cruiser was torpedoed on 10 April 1940 off Kristiansund, Norway. She was torpedoed by the British submarine *Truant* shortly after landing troops during the invasion of Norway, and had to be sunk by her escort after the crew had been rescued.

## Kasserine, Battle of
see Tunisia, Campaign in, 1942–43

## 'Kate'
see Nakajima B5N

## Kato, Lieutenant Colonel Tateo

This Japanese Commander was one of the Army Air Force's most prominent figures. In May 1942 he was shot down over Akyab in Burma while intercepting a flight of British Blenheim bombers.

## Katyn Wood Incident, Spring 1940

On 13 April 1943 Radio Berlin announced the discovery of a mass grave of 10,000 Polish officers in Katyn Forest, near Smolensk. They had been shot, methodically and expertly, by pistol in the back of the head by the NKVD in Spring 1940. The Nazis attempted to make political capital out of the atrocity, flying many

Polish POWs to the site. The Poles were shocked: they had been asking the Soviets for information concerning these men since their disappearance following the Russian invasion of Poland in 1939. The Russians denied their responsibility for the massacre on 15 April and blamed the Nazis. The Poles then appealed to the Red Cross and other agencies, which gave the Russian Government the pretext for breaking off diplomatic relations with the Polish Government in Exile (London) on 26 April 1943.

The German report was somewhat inaccurate: only 4500 officers, whom the Russians had failed to indoctrinate, were murdered.

## Katyusha
see Rockets

## Kawabe, Lieutenant General Masakuzu, 1886–

Kawabe was Chief of General Staff of the Japanese Army in China and was then appointed Commander of Japanese Forces in Burma. He planned the offensive against Kohima and Imphal at the beginning of 1944. The offensive failed because of supply problems and difficult conditions. Kawabe returned to Japan and was made Commander of the Japanese Air Force.

## Kawanishi H6K

Although of prewar design, this large four-engined flying-boat, 'Mavis' to the Allies, was used operationally until the end of 1942. It was powered by four 1000/1070hp Mitsubishi Kinsei engines, had a maximum speed of 211mph, and was defended by four 7.7mm machine guns and a cannon in the tail. Offensive weapons included two 1765lb torpedoes or bombs.

## Kawanishi H8K

'Emily' to the Allies, the H8K is generally considered to have been the best flying-boat used in World War II, in terms of both hydrodynamic design and performance. The H8K2 version, of

Kawanishi H6K5 Mavis.

which more than 100 were built, was powered by four 1850hp Mitsubishi Kasei engines, which gave it a maximum speed of 290mph. With an endurance of up to 24 hours, it ranged all over the Pacific war area, carrying two 1765lb torpedoes or eight 550lb bombs for attack, and defended by five 20mm cannon and four machine guns. The crew were well protected by heavy armor, and search radar was fitted to assist in locating the flying-boat's prey. On some missions range was extended by rendezvous with a refueling submarine. Thirty-six H8K2–Ls were built in 1943 as 64-seat troop transports, with only two guns.

## Kawanishi NiK

Japanese single-seat fighter was in service 1944–45. Unlike almost all other fighters the N1K1–J Shiden (Violet Lightning) was developed from a float-seaplane. Conversion began in November 1942 and the first prototype flew in July 1943. Powered by a 1990hp Nakajima Homare 18-cylinder radial, a very powerful but troublesome engine, the N1K1–J showed great promise with a speed of 362mph and very good maneuverability. It suffered from many drawbacks, two of which were legacies from the floatplane origin. It had a mid-wing and large propeller, needing a long landing gear which often broke, and pilot view was blocked by the wing. But general combat performance was so good that 1007 were quickly delivered, and these were given the name 'George' by the Allies (who had devised a scheme of giving names to Japanese aircraft partly because their true designations were not known and partly because the true designation were too complicated for pilots to remember in the heat of battle). George could turn inside almost all Allied fighters, and it had powerful armament, usually four 20mm cannon and two machine guns.

In April 1944 Kawanishi flew the first N1K2–J, which was completely redesigned with a low wing and fewer parts. Much easier to make, this was an excellent fighter but Allied bombing so delayed production that only just over 400 were completed.

## Kawanishi N1K1 Kyofu

First flown on 1 August 1942, the *Kyofu*, or Mighty Wind ('Rex' to the Allies) was designed to provide support for Japanese forces during their conquest of islands in the SW Pacific, independently of land bases. It was a large single-seat seaplane, powered by a Mitsubishi Kasei engine, and was encountered mainly in Borneo and as a home defense fighter. After 97 had been delivered, production was switched to the N1K1–J Shiden landplane. In retrospect, the Kyofu, which had a single main float and smaller stabilizing floats, is seen as the best seaplane fighter of its day.

## Kawasaki Ki–45

This Japanese two-seat escort and night fighter and attack aircraft was in service from 1942–45. In 1936 the Imperial Japanese Army issued a specification for a twin-engined escort fighter similar to the German Bf 110. The first Ki–45 flew in January 1939 and, after long development with engines and landing gear, it entered production in October 1941 as the Ki–45 Toryu (Dragon Slayer), officially classed as a 'heavy fighter'. Powered by two 1080hp Mitsubishi Ha–102 radial engines, it reached 336mph and carried modest armament of two 12.7mm in the nose and two light machine guns aimed from the rear cockpit. Most were later fitted with a big 37mm cannon in the nose, and one version even had a 75mm cannon for use against ships. Nearly all could also carry two 551lb bombs under the wings. Though only 1698 of all versions were built, and these were often out of action for modification, the Ki–45 was met all over the Pacific War, being named 'Nick' by the Allies. Some were used for suicide attacks, and by 1945 most surviving examples were being modified into Ki–45–Kai–C night fighters with various mixes of 12.7, 20 and 37mm cannon in the nose or firing diagonally upwards. On 7 April 1944 these night fighters claimed seven victories over B–29 Superfortresses, which usually flew so high and fast that no fighter could get within firing range.

## Kawasaki Ki–48

This Japanese four-seat light bomber was in service, 1940–45. Though 1997 were delivered, this bomber, called 'Lily' by the Allies, was not a great success. It was quite small, so that it could reach about 300mph on two 1130hp Nakajima Ha–115 radial engines, or 1000hp Ha–25 engines in early versions, but the bomb load was only 792lb and defensive armament comprised only three or four hand-aimed machine guns. First used in China in 1940, the Ki–48 proved easy meat when encountered by Allied fighters, and most served as high-level or dive bombers. The Ki–48–II had additional armor, and could carry a 1765lb bomb load, and there were many versions built in small numbers. One formation bombed Port Darwin in Australia, but 'Lily' never bothered the Allies much.

## Kawasaki Ki–61

This Japanese single-seat fighter was in service, 1942–45. In 1937 Kawasaki acquired a license from Daimler-Benz to make the DB 601 engine, as used in the Bf 109E, and by 1940 was in

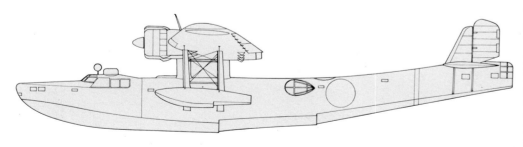

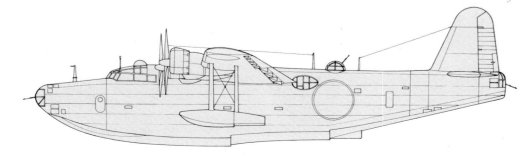

The Kawanishi H8K2 Emily flying boat.

production with a modified and lightened version called Ha–40, rated at 1175hp. This was used in the first type of Ki–61, flown in December 1941 after flight trials with the earlier Ki–60 started the previous March. Armed with two of the excellent German MG 151 cannon and two machine guns, the Ki–61 reached 348mph and from entry to service in July 1942 proved an excellent aircraft. Called 'Tony' by the Allies, the Ki–61 was constantly in action with the Imperial Japanese Army in China and throughout the other war fronts against the Allies. Total production was 2654, later versions having the unreliable 1450hp Kawasaki Ha–140 engine and modified wings with two 30mm or four Ho–5 20mm cannon. In early 1945 the shortage of Ha–140 engines led to a hasty lash-up conversion of one airframe with the 1500hp Mitsubishi Ha–112 radial. The result was an outstandingly good fighter, greatly superior to any Ki–61! As a result the liquid-cooled engine was discarded and every effort put into producing the radial-engined version, called Ki–100. In its first battle, over Okinawa, the first Ki–100 unit claimed 14 Hellcats for no loss of their own number. The Ki–100 could also intercept the B–29, but only 99 were built.

## Kawasaki Ki–100

The best fighter used by the Japanese Army during the war, the Ki–100 was developed almost by accident. Having 275 Ki–61–II Hien airframes minus engines, and unlikely to get them rapidly, Kawasaki adapted the 2.5ft-wide fuselage to take a 4ft diameter Mitsubishi Ha–112–II engine of 1500hp. To everyone's surprise, the resulting Ki–100–Ia outperformed the Ki–61 in terms of speed, climb, maneuverability and ease of servicing. Its ceiling was good enough to enable it to reach the USAAF's high-flying B–29s, and it was at least equal to any US fighters it met, with a powerful armament of two 20mm and two 12.7mm guns. Kawasaki built 99 of an improved version from scratch, the Ki–100–Ib, with improved rearward field of view, before their factory was bombed.

## Kawasaki Ki–102

The Ki–102B, known as 'Randy' to the Allies, was put into production in 1944 as an anti-shipping attack development of the Ki–45. It was formidably armed for its task, with a 57mm cannon and two 20mm cannon concentrated in the nose, and a 12.7mm machine gun at the rear of the two-seat cockpit. During a test flight, one of the pre-production Ki–102s spotted a formation of B–29s and demolished an engine of one of the bombers with a single shot from its heavy gun. Having decided already to modify six of the pre-production aircraft as high-altitude interceptors, this was encouraging for Kawasaki; but they had time to produce only 15 production Ki–102A interceptors, with turbochargers on the 1500hp Mitsubishi Ha–112 engines, before the war ended. Most of the 218 aircraft built were Ki–102Bs, which entered service at about the end of 1944. They had to operate as fighters, in an effort to stem the USAAF bomber offensive that was growing in intensity. Two were completed as night fighters, with primitive search radar – too late, as the B–29s had by that time knocked out the factories in which such aircraft might have been manufactured.

## Keitel, Field Marshal Wilhelm, 1882–1946

On his dissolution of the War Ministry in 1938, Hitler asked its disgraced chief, Blomberg, if his assistant, Keitel, would make a suitable professional head. On being told that he was 'simply the man who runs my office', Hitler said, 'That's exactly the man I want'. For the rest of the war, Keitel acted as Hitler's principal military mouthpiece. Known as *Lakaitel* to the rest of the High Command (*Lakai* meaning lackey) he never disagreed with the Führer, but did nothing else to justify his Marshal's baton. The real work of OKW was carried out by Jodl. Nevertheless they were both judged guilty of war crimes at Nuremberg and hanged.

## *Kelly*

HMS *Kelly* was the most famous British destroyer of World War II. She was commanded by Lord Louis Mountbatten from the outbreak of war and fought in several actions being badly damaged twice. After a distinguished career in the Mediterranean she was sunk by Stuka dive-bombers during the Battle of Crete on 23 May 1941.

## Kennedy, Joseph, 1888–1970

Kennedy was US Ambassador to Great Britain from 1937–41 and he was a firm believer in US isolationism. He did not understand Chamberlain's policy of appeasement and felt that Britain could not possibly fight a war against Germany. He told Roosevelt that he expected Germany to win the war. In November 1940 he resigned and returned to the USA where he became a supporter of the Lend-Lease program.

## Kenney, General George, 1889–

Kenney was the Commander in Chief of the US Far East Air Forces in the Southwest Pacific Area. He was General MacArthur's principal air officer and he streamlined the organization of his staff. He separated the USAAF and the RAAF and the American force became the 5th USAF. During the New Guinea campaign he had some 207 bombers and 127 fighters under his command. He modified his bombers so that they could be used to attack surface ships with skip bombs, equipped with 5-second delay fuses. He also developed the use of air transport in New Guinea. In the operation to capture the Philippines, Kenney had 2500 aircraft and he began to use napalm bombs in Corregidor and at Clark Field. He was a man of great drive and determination and was present at the Japanese surrender in Tokyo Bay on 2 September.

## Kesselring, Field Marshal Albrecht, 1885–1960

A Bavarian gunner officer who transferred to the expanding secret air force in 1933, Kesselring rose to command Luftwaffe units in the Polish invasion of 1939, and in the Belgium invasion of 1940, authorizing the bombardment of Warsaw, of Rotterdam and of the retreating troops during the Dunkirk evacuation. During the Battle of Britain he directed *Luftflotte II* in its intensive campaign against the air bases of southeast England, the success of which was

Kesselring and Goering in an anxious moment.

ultimately wasted when the German High Command decided to divert the major air offensive to London.

In 1941, as Commander in Chief, South, he jointly directed the North African Campaign with Rommel, leading the Axis withdrawal from Tunisia. Subsequently, as Commander in Chief in Italy, he conducted an outstanding campaign against the Allies, skillfully rebuilding his defensive line after the delayed Allied victory at Monte Cassino and hindering their advance northwards for more than a year. However, his task was fundamentally hopeless; the High Command's seeming indifference to Allied air superiority meant that Kesselring failed to receive the equipment and supplies he considered necessary to the situation he was facing.

In March 1945, with the German position on the Western Front becoming grave, Hitler ordered Kesselring to take over General von Rundstedt's command. The situation had by then, however, deteriorated too far and Kesselring was forced to surrender on 7 May. His death sentence was commuted to life imprisonment.

## Khalkin-Gol, Battle of
see Nomonhan Incident

## Kharkov, Battle of, 1942

Kharkov was an important base for the Germans. It formed part of the system of fortified points known as the 'hedgehogs'. This was a line of bastion towns: Schlüsselburg, Novgorod, Rzhev, Vyazma, Bryansk, Orel, Kharkov, and Taganrog, which served as winter bases for the Germans during the Russian counteroffensive of December 1941. The Russians were able to penetrate the territory between these bastions but were unable to take them.

After a break in hostilities because of the thaw, Marshal Timoshenko decided to launch an offensive against what he thought was the weakest link: Kharkov. He concentrated 854 tanks in the area, about two-thirds of his armored strength. The attack was launched on 12 May 1942 and the tanks were able to penetrate quite deeply behind the enemy to the rear of Kharkov. Hitler had decided to launch an attack in that area and had built up General Paulus's Sixth Army for that purpose. The Russian tanks were strung out over 70 miles and were an easy target for Kleist's Panzers. On 19 May General Kleist took the Izyum salient and cut off the Russians, who were forbidden to retreat by Stalin. The Germans claim to have taken 241,000 prisoners and about 600 tanks. This left the route down the Donets corridor to Stalingrad open for Paulus.

In February 1943 Kharkov was the focus in the Battle of the Donets.

**Kharkov, Capture of**
see Dniepr, Battle of, August-December 1943

**Khrushchev, Nikita S, 1894-1973**

During the war Khrushchev was the political commissar on the Southwest Front and took part in the defense of Stalingrad. As Marshal Budenny's political commissar he dismantled the industry in the Ukraine. He remained on the Southwest Front after Budenny's and Timoshenko's dismissal. He built up a good relationship with General Yeremenko. After 1944 he was on the 1st Ukrainian Front and undertook purges in the Ukraine.

**Kiev, Capture of**
see Dniepr, Battle of, August-December 1943

**Kiev Pocket**
see Ukraine, Battle of, July-August 1941

**Kimmel, Admiral Husband E, 1882-1968**

Admiral Kimmel was the admiral in command at the time of the Pearl Harbor attack and was removed almost immediately on 17 December 1941. Kimmel had been unexpectedly appointed Commander-in-Chief of the US Fleet on 1 February 1941. He was held responsible for the failure to protect Pearl Harbor from attack. Although Kimmel had received a war warning and had sent out his carriers on maneuvers, he expected the Japanese to attack the Philippines first. He did not liaise with General Short, the Army Commander at Pearl Harbor, and so did not have radar information. Kimmel applied for retirement and took no part in the war.

**King, Admiral Ernest, 1878-1956**

King was the most important figure behind the American Navy's success in the Pacific. After Admiral Kimmel had been dismissed, King became Commander-in-Chief of the US Fleet. In March 1942 King was made Chief of Naval Operations and had complete command of the Navy. King served on the Combined Chiefs of Staff Committee and was constantly arguing that more resources and men should be diverted to the Pacific. As Chief of Naval Operations King learned his lessons from early Japanese victories and shifted emphasis in fighting to aircraft carriers and to greater co-operation with land-based aircraft. Since he had control over landing craft he could hamper the progress of other operations. When General MacArthur demanded carrier units, landing craft and Marines, for his operation in the Solomons, King told him that the Navy would undertake the operations to take Guadalcanal.

King was a gruff man who did not hesitate to say what he felt. This involved him in many arguments with the British, especially at the Casablanca Conference in January 1943. His constant demands for more resources in the Pacific upset the British, who felt that Hitler should be defeated before Japan.

King had to deal with supply and logistics problems on a scale never experienced before. He helped devise the 'fleet train' system which allowed carriers to remain at sea for long periods of time. In December 1944 King was made

a full fleet admiral and although President Roosevelt found him a difficult man to work with, he could not deny that King was the architect of victory in the Pacific.

**Kingcobra**
see P-63 Kingcobra, Bell

*King George V*

The five ships in the *King George V* Class were the latest British battleships at the outbreak of World War II. Started in 1937, they incorporated all the lessons learned after World War I and had many novel features: the first dual-purpose high-angle/low-angle secondary armament, the first integral aircraft and catapult and the first British ships with quadruple gun-mountings.

An overriding requirement was that the first two ships should be ready by the spring of 1940, and when the politicians suggested in 1936 that it might be possible to negotiate a reduction of gun-caliber to 14in, a reluctant Admiralty was forced to accept 14in guns in place of the 16in guns allowed by the existing treaties. This was regarded at the time as a weak point of the design but subsequent events handsomely vindicated the Admiralty's decision. Delays and wartime shortages meant that *King George V* was the only one commissioned in 1940; *Prince of Wales* did not join the Fleet until May 1941, *Duke of York* at the end of that year and the *Howe* and *Anson* in 1942.

Apart from the Japanese giants the *King George V* Class had the heaviest armor of any of the battleships of the period, including the *Bismarck*. The speed, 28.5 knots, was considered adequate to meet tactical requirements, a decision reached by the US Navy independently for its own *North Carolina* and *Washington* Classes. The loss of the *Prince of Wales* to air attack led to the incorporation of many internal improvements to the survivors.

The outstanding event in the career of the *King George V* was the sinking of the *Bismarck* on 27 May 1941. As the flagship of the Home Fleet under Admiral Tovey she and the *Rodney* engaged the German battleship at first light. The Commander in Chief sent the *Rodney* in to fire at short range, while his flagship stood off to 14,000 yards to get plunging hits against the *Bismarck*'s deck armor. Finally when her repeated hits had turned the target into a blazing wreck she left the scene, for the long chase had left her short of fuel. No damage was suffered in the action.

The four ships went out to join the British Pacific Fleet in 1944-45 for the final drive against Japan, and two bombarded Miyako during the Okinawa invasion in 1945. During the final stages of the war the *King George V* shelled industrial targets near Tokyo, making her the last British battleship to fire her guns in anger.

**King, Prime Minister William Mackenzie, 1874-1950**

King was the Liberal Prime Minister of Canada throughout the war. King was elected in 1940 with a huge majority to continue his policy against participation in the war. He soon decided to win over the Canadians to war gradually and in this he was successful. By April 1942

he initiated and passed a measure to allow conscription. King liked to play the intermediary between President Roosevelt and Prime Minister Churchill and he was the host at two conferences in Quebec in August 1943 and in September 1944. Towards the end of 1944 he faced a crisis because of the rising number of Canadian casualties but he resolved this by getting his Defense Minister to resign.

**King Tiger**

This German battle tank was also known as 'Tiger B' and 'Royal Tiger' and was the last major German tank design to see service during the war. It went into production late in 1943 and first saw action on the Russian Front in May 1944. It was born of a demand from the Army Weapons Office in August 1942 for a redesigned 'Tiger' tank incorporating thicker armor, sloped plates to deflect shot, and an 88mm gun. Both Porsche and Henschel were asked to submit designs. Both their first designs were rejected; Porsche then submitted a fresh one but this was turned down because it used an electric transmission which demanded excessive amounts of copper, and Henschel's second try, known as the VK4503(H), was accepted. Delays were occasioned when the Army Weapons Office demanded some changes in design to make production easier, and the first prototype was not delivered for test until October 1943. The pilot model left the production line in December 1943, and first production models began to reach the Army late in February 1944, a commendable speed in view of the difficulties facing manufacturers in Germany by that time. Production was hoped to reach 145 tanks a month by the end of 1944, but bombing of facilities and shortages of raw materials prevented this, and the best figure ever reached was 85 tanks in August 1944. By the end of the war some 484 King Tigers had been produced.

In effect, the King Tiger was a logical improvement of the 'Tiger', incorporating various features which experience had shown were desirable; notably the front glacis plate, which was now sloped as on the 'Panther' and Soviet T-34 tanks instead of squarely vertical as on the original Tiger. The armor protection was the heaviest yet seen: the front plate was 150mm set at a 40° angle, the turret face 180mm thick, and the side and tail plates 80mm thick. Frontal attack of this tank, by any weapon available to the Allies, was out of the question. The gun was an 88mm of 71 calibers in length, firing a 23lb shell at 3280ft/sec and capable of piercing 6.25in of armor at 2000yds range, a truly formidable performance.

**Kinkaid, Vice-Admiral Thomas, 1888-1972**

Kinkaid was involved in many operations in the Pacific war and eventually rose to become commander of the 7th fleet. Kinkaid was commander of Task Force 16, built around the carriers *Enterprise* and *Hornet*, at the Battle of Santa Cruz Islands, November 1942. During this battle the *Hornet* was lost and the *Enterprise* badly damaged, but many Japanese aircraft were shot down. After the Naval Battle of Guadalcanal in November 1942, Kinkaid was made commander of Task Force 67, a cruiser squadron, and he drew up guidelines on nightfighting for his men. These cruiser squadrons helped prevent Japanese transports from reaching Guadalcanal. In May 1943 Kinkaid was commander of Northern Pacific Forces in the operation to regain the Aleutians. After this he was promoted to be commander of the 7th Fleet and was involved in operations off New Guinea. The 7th Fleet was a convoy and support fleet composed of old battleships and small escort carriers. It transported the 6th Army to Leyte in October 1944 and during the Battle of Leyte Gulf one of its Task Forces staved off an onslaught from Vice-Admiral Kurita's guns. In January 1945 the 8th Fleet transported the 6th Army to Luzon. In April 1945 Kinkaid was promoted to Admiral. Kinkaid was one of Nimitz's most highly regarded naval commanders.

### Kirishima

This fast Japanese battleship was engaged by the US battleships *South Dakota* and *Washington* on the night of 14 November 1942. She scored a hit with her 14in guns on the *South Dakota* but did not observe the approach of the *Washington*. Hit by nine 16in and 40 five-inch shells she caught fire and had to be abandoned at 0320 the next morning.

### Kirponos, Colonel General Mikhail P, 1892–1941

Kirponos was the only Russian general who managed to hold up the German advance in 1941. In 1939–40 he commanded the 70th Infantry Division on the Northwest Front against Finland and captured Viborg in a daring advance over the thin ice of the Gulf of Finland. In June 1941 he was commander of the Kiev Military District and used his tank force to hold up Generals Kleist and Reichenau at the Polish border. In early July he was forced back and he retreated to Kiev. He was encircled there and died while leading a breakout attempt.

### Kittyhawk
see P-40 Warhawk, Curtiss

### Kleist, Field Marshal Paul von, 1881–1954

Kleist had overall command of the two Panzer groups of Guderian and Hoth in the crossing of the Meuse and the Battle of France, 1940. As commander of Panzer Group I in Russia in 1941 he led the advance of Army Group South towards Kiev – the slowest of the three Panzer drives of that summer, though culminating in the largest encirclement – and in the following year was appointed to command Army Group A. Its task was to advance into the Caucasus, but it was halted as soon as the Stalingrad battle began. Kleist then became embroiled in the defensive battle in southern Russia. A steadfast rather than a brilliant field Commander, he died in Russian captivity.

### Klubov, Alexander, 1918–1944

Klubov was the fifth-ranking Soviet ace of World War II with 50 accredited victories. Klubov had the reputation of being a natural leader and a born fighter pilot, capable of maintaining a cool composure even at the height of an aerial combat.

### Kluge, Field Marshal Gunther von, 1882–1944

A senior general at the outbreak of war, Kluge commanded the Fourth Army in the Polish and Western campaigns. In 1941 he was Guderian's superior on the central front in Russia and consistently and acrimoniously disagreed with him. In the following year he was promoted to command Army Group Center, which he did with conspicuous success, particularly in the defensive battle which followed the failure of the Kursk offensive in the summer of 1943. Appointed to command in Normandy in succession to Rundstedt, he made too obvious his agreement with his predecessor's pessimistic reports. He did not agree with Hitler's orders to hold everything and attempted a counteroffensive at Avranches. He then tried to withdraw but too late – his men were trapped at Falaise. He urged Hitler to surrender and was dismissed on 17 August. Aware that Hitler suspected him of complicity in the July Plot, and even of having made contact with the Allies, he committed suicide while on the way back to Berlin. Known as *Kluger Hans* (Clever John) to his contemporaries, he was one of the most competent of German World War II generals.

### Knox, W Frank, 1874–1944

Knox was an ex-publisher of the *Chicago Daily News* and a Republican, whom Roosevelt chose to be the Secretary of the Navy. He held that appointment from July 1940 to April 1944. One of his first tasks was to investigate the failure of defenses at Pearl Harbor. Knox received all the decoded Japanese messages and he gave news of Admiral Yamamoto's flight from Rabaul to the pilots at Henderson Field.

### Koenig, General Marie Pierre Joseph François, 1898–1970

A veteran of the French colonial wars and the Norway campaign of 1940, Koenig was one of the more senior French officers to rally to de Gaulle, and was given command of a force in the Western Desert, largely composed of the Foreign Legion, which conducted a heroic defense of Bir Hacheim during the Gazala Battle of June 1941. After the invasion of Europe, he was appointed commander of the forces of the interior – the resistance – which he brought under government control. After the liberation of Paris he became military governor of the city and re-established law and order.

### Koga, Admiral Mineichi, 1885–1943

Admiral Koga replaced Admiral Yamamoto as Commander–in–Chief of the Combined Fleet after the latter's death on 20 May 1943. Unflamboyant, efficient and cool, he was nonetheless seduced by the idea of the 'Decisive Battle' with the Allied Fleet, a do or die conflict which would decide the nation's fate. He completed plans for this battle (Operation Z) on 8 March 1944 but he knew the chances of a victory were slim. On 31 March 1944 he set out to die on a plane which disappeared in a storm, without trace. His Chief of Staff, Admiral Shigeru Fukudome, also flew off with a copy of the plans for Operation Z, but he was captured by guerrillas on Cebu in the Philippines and MacArthur obtained the plans.

Japanese troops move toward Imphal in 1944.

### Kohima and Imphal Offensives, 1944

By early 1944 the British in India were ready to begin the reconquest of Burma. The British planned to reoccupy northern Burma and open up the overland route to China. There was to be a secondary attack in Arakan and a diversionary attack by the Chindits at Indaw, deep in Japanese-held territory. General Slim was in command of the 14th Army, which comprised General Christison's 15th Corps in Arakan and General Scoones's 4th Corps. General Kawabe was the overall commander of Japanese troops in Burma. He had three 'armies': Thirty-third Army under General Honda in Northern Burma, the Twenty-eighth Army under General Sakurai on the Arakan Front and the Fifteenth Army under General Mutaguchi. Mutaguchi's three divisions were to forestall the Allied offensive by capturing Imphal and Kohima.

The Japanese offensive opened up in the south. The advance in the Arakan was supposed to be a diversion for the main attack on Imphal but Mutaguchi's army had supply problems and had to wait for the arrival of the Fifteenth Division from Siam. At the beginning of 1944 Christison's 15th Corps gradually advanced south and this gave them a chance to use new jungle tactics. In early February 5000 troops of the Fifty-fifth Division passed through the front of the 7th Indian Division near the Ngakyedauk Pass at night and overran the 7th Divisions HQ. By 7 February the Japanese were advancing to Bawli Bazar. Within a few days the British had enough transport aircraft to be able to supply the 7th Division by air. By 19 February the Japanese were running short of supplies and

RAF and Australian troops take up a defensive position in the Imphal Valley in Burma in August 1944.

ammunition and on 23 February the Japanese were driven back from Ngakyedauk Pass. On 24 February Sakurai called off the offensive.

To the north the 4th Corps under Scoones had advanced from Imphal but at the end of January Scoones received news of the likelihood of a Japanese offensive in the area. Scoones began to withdraw his troops but when the Japanese advanced his three divisions were not in defensive positions. In the first week of March Mutaguchi's Thirty-third Division were to march towards Tiddim and then swing north for Imphal. In the center the Fifteenth Division was to advance westwards to take Ukhrul and then threaten the supply line to Imphal from Dimapur before heading south and attacking Imphal. Further north the Thirty-first Division was to capture the gateway of Assam and to cut off Kohima.

This was a very ambitious plan for an army with supply problems, but at some stages the offensive looked like being a success. On 7 March the Japanese began their advance to Tiddim and on 13 March Scoones told his 17th Division to withdraw but they were cut off by the Japanese on the following day. Scoones had to use his reserve to extricate the division so Slim sent the 5th Indian Division as a reserve and allocated more aircraft to supply the troops that were cut off. All three Japanese divisions continued to advance and on 19 March Ukhrul was attacked and the British realized that Kohima was being threatened as well as Imphal. On 29 March the Fifteenth Division reached the Dimapur-Kohima-Imphal road to the north of Imphal and cut off the city. There were 155,000 men in Imphal but they had five weeks' supplies and could receive supplies by air. The British had sent forward two more divisions and had four divisions on the Imphal Plain but Kohima was held by a garrison of 1500. Kawabe did not give Mutaguchi permission to take Dimapur. If Dimapur had been captured it would have given the Japanese control of communications and held up the British efforts to relieve Kohima.

The 33rd Corps under General Stopford was brought forward and on 2 April Stopford was given command of the Dimapur-Kohima area. Scoones's forces had been defending themselves in hand-to-hand fighting and now he began to regroup his men for a counterattack from the Imphal Plain. On 10 April Slim ordered a general counteroffensive and by 14 April a fresh brigade had regained control of the main road to Kohima. A week later two brigades broke through to raise the siege of Kohima and drive the Japanese back to the surrounding mountains. On the next day fighting on the Imphal Plain intensified and the Fifty-fifth Division abandoned the attempt to take Imphal and went on the defensive. Mutaguchi did not want to accept failure but his subordinates refused to obey his orders so the Japanese withdrawal was chaotic. General Sato refused to obey Mutaguchi's order to advance as late as 19 June and he fell back to the Chindwin River. On 22 June British troops finally joined up on the Kohima-Imphal road near Kang Pokpi and raised the siege of Imphal. The monsoon then broke and Mutaguchi was finally given orders to retreat on 4 July.

The Japanese had opened the offensive with 84,280 troops but only 30,775 were fit for duty at the end of July, and many of these were suffering from malnutrition. The British had casualties of less than 17,000 and they had started the campaign with a greater number of men. Mutaguchi and Kawabe came close to success but failure led to their dismissal at the end of August 1944.

## Koiso, Lieutenant General Kuniaki, 1880–1950

Koiso, a reserve general with experience in intelligence but not in combat, was appointed Prime Minister after the resignation of Tojo on 18 June 1944. He was to share power with Admiral Yonai (Navy Minister and assistant Prime Minister), who was associated with Konoye, Kido and the Emperor and therefore with the peace faction. Koiso was never more than an unstable interim leader, having the support of neither the peace faction nor of the militarists,

and therefore having no influence on the prosecution of the war nor on preparations for peace. In this position he presided over defeat after defeat. He had publicly committed his government to victory in Leyte in a radio broadcast on 8 November 1944. The December decision to abandon Leyte, followed by the defeat at Iwo Jima, brought his government near collapse. The decision to either fight to the last or to replace Koiso's government with a surrender cabinet had to be taken.

Koiso tried to hold on to power, naïvely believing that the key to a favorable peace was peace with Chiang Kai-shek. He appointed as negotiator a disreputable schemer named Miao Pin who alienated his cabinet and failed utterly.

Koiso resigned 24 March 1945 and was later tried for war crimes.

## Kolombangara, Battle of, 1943

In July 1943 the 'Tokyo Express' was still trying to reinforce Kolombangara. The force was led by Rear-Admiral Izaki though the five destroyers were led by Admiral Tanaka in his flagship *Jintsu*. Rear Admiral Ainsworth's Task Force 18 was sent to intercept it on the night of 12 July 1943. Ainsworth soon found on his radar that the Japanese were heading for Kula Gulf, but Izaki also knew the whereabouts of the US ships. Both sides maneuvered into a favorable position and opened fire at the same time. A few minutes later Ainsworth ordered his radar-controlled guns to open fire and then devastated the *Jintsu*. Only one of the Japanese torpedoes found its mark and hit the *Leander* which withdrew, escorted by two destroyers. The destroyer *Mikazuki* lost touch with the other four Japanese destroyers which continued to fire torpedoes. The US ships were confused and could not see the Japanese ships except by starshell fire. Then the *St Louis*, *Honolulu* and *Gwin* were hit by torpedo but only the *Gwin* sank. This battle showed the superb night-fighting skill of the Japanese. Nevertheless this battle did not break Japan's outer defense perimeter.

## Kon
see New Guinea. Biak and Wakde Islands

## Kondo, Vice-Admiral Nobutake, 1886–1953

In December 1941 Kondo was commander of the Japanese Southern Force which sank Force Z (the *Repulse* and *Prince of Wales*) in the battle for Singapore. Following this he commanded the Midway Occupation Force, with direct command over the Covering Force. In April 1942 Kondo, with Nagumo, made many successful raids on merchant shipping. Now fighting in the Solomon Islands, Kondo was ordered to lure the US fleet into a direct conventional naval battle. He set a trap for this purpose, which the US fleet avoided, in the Battle of the Eastern Solomons (24 August 1942). In October 1942, providing sea support for Guadalcanal, Kondo scored a victory at the Battle of Santa Cruz. In an attempt to run transports to Guadalcanal on the night of 14 November 1942, Kondo suffered a tactical defeat, but the Allies, preoccupied with this engagement, allowed the Japanese transports to be landed by Tanaka. The Allies were able to save Henderson Air Field by their defeat of Kondo.

Marshal Konev and Bokov of the Military Council study a map in 1943.

The German cruiser *Königsberg* was sunk in 1940 off Norway.

### Konev, Marshal Ivan S, 1897–1973

Konev led the armies which swept over the Ukraine, Poland, Germany and Czechoslovakia. He graduated from the Frunze Military Academy in 1926 and then had special training there. In August 1941 he served in the Smolensk sector and then from October 1941 to 1942 Konev was Commander of the Kalinin Front and he resisted the German advance on Moscow. In July 1943 he threw back the German offensive at Kursk and recaptured Orel, Belgorod and Poltava. From 1943–44 he commanded the Steppe Front which became the 2nd Ukrainian Front. He cut off ten German divisions at Korsun-Shevchenko, which the Russians regard as a very important victory, commensurate with Stalingrad. Unfortunately, although it severely weakened the Germans, they managed to break out of encirclement, with terrible losses; 20,000, not the 50,000 the Russians claim. Konev then led the 1st Ukrainian front which took Lvov. He advanced from the Vistula to the Oder with Marshal Zhukov and occupied Berlin. He reached the Elbe and made contact with the US forces at Torgau.

### Kongo

Four Japanese *Kongo* Class battlecruisers built in 1912–15 were rebuilt between 1933 and 1940 as fast battleships to act as carrier escorts. Along with her sister ships the *Hiei* and *Kirishima* she took part in the major actions off Guadalcanal. The *Kongo* survived the Battles of the Philippine Sea and Leyte Gulf until the end of 1944, when on 21 November she was torpedoed and sunk off the coast of Formosa by the US submarine *Sealion*.

### Königsberg

One of two sisters of the *Karlsruhe*, the *Königsberg* took part in the invasion of Norway in April 1940. Her presence at Bergen was noted by British reconnaissance aircraft on 10 April and word was passed to a group of 15 Skua dive-bombers left at Hatston in the Orkneys by the carrier HMS *Ark Royal*. At their maximum range the Skuas took the cruiser by surprise and sank her at her moorings with three 500lb bombs. She was the first warship to be sunk by dive-bombing.

### Königsberg, April 1945

The Russian armies, led by General Bagramyan, advanced through East Prussia in February 1945, but resistance halted them in front of Königsberg. General Vasilievsky was put in charge of operations and he decided to ignore the Germans in East Prussia and on 13 March took Heiligenbeil. In April Stalin and Novikov planned an air and artillery barrage to storm Königsberg. This was successful and the German Samland group was evacuated on 16 April and the town surrendered. This meant that all the Germans were cleared out of East Prussia.

### Kormoran

Built as the mercantile *Steiermark* in 1938, this ship was taken up by the *Kriegsmarine* in 1939 and converted to an auxiliary cruiser (*hilfskreuzer*). She was renamed *Kormoran (HS.8)*

and armed with six old 15cm guns. After a successful career in the South Atlantic and the Indian Ocean she fell in with the Australian cruiser HMAS *Sydney* on 19 November 1941. Apparently the cruiser was taken in by the disguised raider's pretense of being an innocent Dutch freighter and came too close. The concealed guns quickly inflicted serious damage and a torpedo-hit damaged the *Sydney* seriously. The cruiser replied effectively with her guns but both ships were on fire and heavily damaged. The *Sydney* drifted away and was never seen again; nothing was known about the action until months later, when a few *Kormoran* survivors were found on a South Pacific island. It was the only case of a mercantile auxiliary cruiser sinking a regular warship of any size.

### Korsun-Shevchenko(sy)
see Ukraine, Battle of the, December 1943–May 1944

### Kozhedub, Ivan, 1920–

A figure of legendary proportion in the Soviet air force, Kozhedub was the leading Russian fighter pilot with a total of 62 victories over enemy aircraft.

### Kretschmer, Commander Otto, 1912–

Regarded by both sides as the leading German submarine commander of the war, Kretschmer achieved the sinking of over 350,000 tons of Allied shipping between 1939 and 1941, largely in command of *U.99* in the Atlantic. He was forced to scuttle the boat on 27 March 1941 and taken prisoner.

The Japanese battlecruiser *Kongo*.

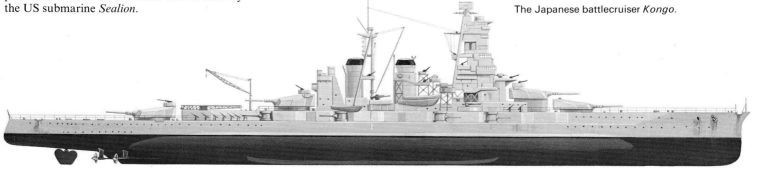

## Kromuskit

This term was used to identify recoilless guns developed in the USA during the war, and derived from the names of two scientists, Kroger and Musser, principally responsible for the design.

The first American designs of recoilless gun were no more than copies of the contemporary German 105mm LG40, and a project was originated by the Artillery Section of the Research & Development Service. But at the same time the Infantry Section of the same service began working on an idea of its own. The principal technical feature of this design was that the cartridge case was perforated with a large number of small holes, the case being lined with plastic to prevent the powder charge escaping. Moreover the shell rotating band was pre-engraved to fit the rifling of the gun without having to be forced in at high pressure, as in a conventional gun. As a result it was possible to keep the working pressure inside the gun at a low figure. When the charge was fired, gas passed through the holes in the cartridge case and were vented to the rear through a venturi nozzle, setting up a thrust which counteracted any rearward motion of the gun due to recoil. With no recoil and low pressures, it was possible to make the weapon extremely light and yet deliver a respectable performance. The first gun developed was a 57mm weighing only 35lbs, which could be fired from a man's shoulder or from a machine gun tripod. It passed trials successfully and by early in 1945 over 2000 guns had been ordered, together with supplies of high explosive, hollow-charge and white-phosphorus-filled shells. A small number of the guns reached the Pacific Theater in time to see action on Okinawa.

The 57mm was followed by a 75mm, little more than a scaled-up version of the first design. One thousand of these, with ammunition, were ordered and again only small numbers were shipped to the Pacific and to Europe in time to see action before the war ended.

## Krueger, Lieutenant General Walter, 1881–1967

As commander of the 6th Army, Krueger directed operations in the Southwest Pacific and led the reconquest of the Philippines. Krueger first saw action in New Guinea, and when MacArthur decided to separate US forces from Australian forces, Krueger's 6th Army was called the 'Alamo Force'. Krueger led the attack on New Britain, Admiralty Islands, and all operations in western New Guinea, Biak, Noemfoor and Morotai. His army was 200,000 strong when it undertook the invasions of Leyte (October 1944) and Luzon (January 1945). If the US Army had invaded Japan, Krueger would have led the operation. Krueger was a cautious commander who would halt operations if he thought his men were at risk. During the operation to capture Manila, Krueger was under pressure from General MacArthur to speed up the advance.

## Krummlauf

This German device consisted of a curved barrel attachment fitted to the MP–43 assault rifle which allowed it to shoot round corners. The device was requested in order to permit riflemen to shoot from cover without exposing them-selves and also to allow the crew of a tank to fire downwards, close to the tank side, to prevent enemy infantry coming close enough to attach explosive charges to the tank. Development was undertaken by the C G Haenel Company, and after extensive trials it was found that a simple extension would turn the bullet through 30° and deliver it accurately to the target up to a range of about 850 meters. The idea was first applied to the standard Gewehr 98 service rifle; it was then tried with the MG 34 machine gun but since the deflection altered the recoil forces the machine gun would not fire at automatic. It was finally decided to fit it to the MP–43 since this fired a shorter bullet which set up less strain when passing through the extension. In 1944 orders were given for production of 10,000 'Krummlauf' devices, though it is doubtful if anything like that number were made.

In addition to the infantry 30° model, a 90° version was made for firing from tanks. Due to the sharp bend it was impossible to hand-hold this model, and it was provided with a ball-joint which fitted into the tank armor. The design was completed in 1945, but very few were made.

## Krupp von Bohlen und Halbach, Alfried, 1907–1967

The most active member of Germany's leading industrial family in World War II, Krupp was in charge of the firm's armaments and mining branches. True to family tradition on which its fortunes had been built in the 19th century, he devoted his energy to the output of armaments for the Wehrmacht, but did not scruple about the means used to increase them. After 1942 he employed large numbers of forced laborers in his plants and mines, including 120,000 Russian Prisoners of War, often in inhumane conditions. He also built plants alongside concentration camps in order to employ their inmates. He was arrested by an American patrol in 1944, and later tried and condemned for war crimes but was eventually paroled.

## Kugelblitz

The Kugelblitz was a German anti-aircraft tank also known as 'leichte Flakpanzer IV'. It was designed to provide protection for armored columns on the move, and also to give complete protection to the crew, since earlier Flakpanzers were open-topped. The Kugelblitz used the chassis of the PzKw IV tank, with the superstructure built up to take a power-operated armored turret carrying two MK103/38–30mm cannon. It was a good design but came too late; only five were built before the war ended.

## Kula Gulf, Battle of, 1943

The Battle of Kula Gulf occurred when Japanese transports were sending reinforcements to Vila on Kolombangara and to New Georgia. The convoy included two units of three and four destroyers loaded with troops and supplies and an escort of three destroyers, *Niizuki, Suzukaze* and *Tanikaze*. The force was under the command of Rear Admiral Akiyama and he faced a Support Group commanded by Rear Admiral Ainsworth of three cruisers and four destroyers.

Akiyama arrived at Kula Gulf (on 6 July 1943), sent out the First Transport Unit to Vila at 0118 and was about to head north when the radar on the *Niizuki* picked up the American ships. The Japanese force regrouped but the US guns inflicted heavy damage on the *Niizuki*. The *Suzukaze* and *Tanikaze* launched their torpedoes and sank the cruiser *Helena*. The US guns were ready to fire but the Japanese had retreated westwards. During the night US ships sighted the Japanese destroyers, but the Japanese retreated and avoided danger.

The Americans lost one cruiser and 168 officers and men. The Japanese Admiral Akiyama was among the 300 Japanese killed, but the transports succeeded in landing their troops. This engagement was considered an American victory until after the war when it was discovered that the transports had completed their mission.

## Kuomintang

The Kuomintang was the Chinese Nationalist Party which was led by Chiang Kai-shek. Its main support came from middle classes in towns and it followed a policy of nonco-operation with the communists until 1937. After this the Kuomintang was fighting the Japanese alongside the communists but all too often its main effort was directed against Mao Tse-tung's communists. The Kuomintang received massive aid from the USA and also from the USSR. Most of these funds were misappropriated.

## Kuribayashi, General Todomichi, 1885–1945

Kuribayashi, with his One Hundred Ninth Division, conducted the suicidal defense of Iwo Jima in February–March 1945, in which 21,000 Japanese died in one month of hopeless battle. The US invaded the island on 16 and 19 February to find Kuribayashi and his forces installed in positions connected by tunnels. They suffered 26,000 Marine casualties and 900 Navy dead before the island fell.

## Kurita, Vice-Admiral Takeo

Kurita commanded the Close Support Force at Midway, but his major engagement was the Battle of Leyte Gulf in October 1944. Here he commanded the formidable First Striking Force. On his way to Leyte Gulf, he was spotted by Allied forces, attacked and forced to take evasive action. He therefore arrived at Leyte six hours late. However he still took the heavily outnumbered US transports and escorts completely by surprise. Nonetheless he was defeated in this engagement, the last in which the Japanese offered any serious challenge to the Allied navies.

## Kurochkin, Colonel General Pavel A, 1900–

Kurochkin was the Commander of the Northwest Front from 1941–44. In 1941 he fought in the defensive battles round Smolensk and was subsequently appointed Commander of the Northwest Front. He halted the German offensive at the Novgorod-Valday-Ostashkov line and in February 1942 brought off a welcome victory, when he encircled 90,000 Germans at Demyansk. In 1944 he was the Commander of the 2nd Belorussian Front but he lost Kovel and was dismissed. He then commanded the 60th Soviet Army in the Vistula-Oder operation and at Mor Ostrava.

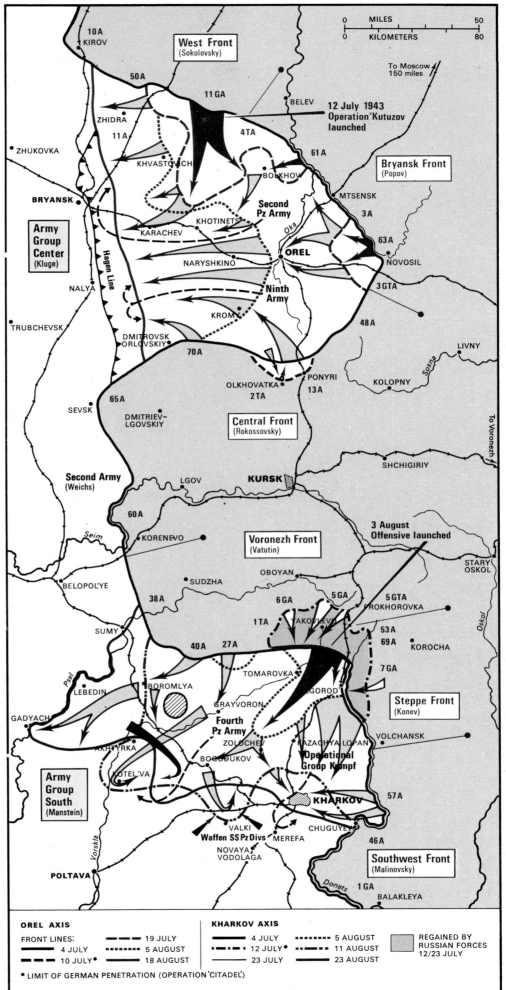

German Panzers move to the offensive in the decisive battle of Kursk.

## Kursk, Battle of, July 1943

After the fall of Stalingrad, the armies of Generals Vatutin and Golikov launched an attack to take Kharkov at the end of February 1943. Field Marshal Manstein, after a brilliant regrouping of his forces, recaptured Kharkov. Elation in the High Command led to an ambitious operation, Citadel. This was a plan to eliminate the salient round Kursk. From March to June the Germans built up their reserves and brought in more tanks. The Russians took the opportunity to build eight concentric circles of

*Below and right:* The Battle of Kursk was a double envelopment which was countered by a Soviet double envelopment.

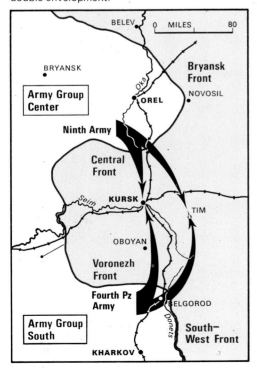

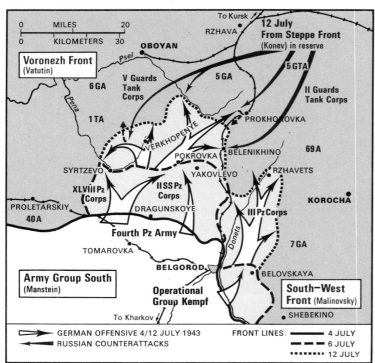

*Above:* The first Nazi attack on Kursk.
*Above right:* The Nazi attack on the Kursk southern flank taken from a reconnaissance plane.

defense and by the time the offensive was launched had a numerical superiority over the Germans in both tanks and men. The battle began on the 5 July with the Ninth Army under General Kluge attacking from the north and the Fourth Panzer Army under Manstein attacking from the south. In the north the Ninth Army penetrated a mere six miles and lost 25,000 killed, 200 tanks and 200 aircraft. In the south Manstein's army penetrated twenty-five miles, but also with great losses: 10,000 killed and 350 tanks. On 12 July the Russians launched a counteroffensive in the north against Orel and by 23 July the Germans were back where they had started. Manstein withdrew against orders to the Dniepr. This battle is known as the greatest tank battle of the war and it involved 2 million men, 6000 tanks and 4000 aircraft. It stopped the pattern of successful German offensives followed by Russian winter counteroffensives, and from that point the German armies were in retreat.

### Kuznetsov, Admiral Nikolay G, 1902–1974

Kuznetsov was the Commander-in-Chief of the Navy and was a member of the Stavka during the war. Although he did not take part in any operations he was present at all the planning meetings throughout the war. He gave Admiral Tributs, Commander of the Baltic Fleet, the order to scuttle the fleet. He participated in the Conferences at Potsdam and Yalta in 1945 and co-ordinated with the US and the British. In 1945 he took part in the defeat of the Kwantung Army but after the war he was demoted.

### Kuznetsov, General Vasiliy I, 1894–1964

Kuznetsov was one of the new generation of generals to emerge during the war, along with Konev, Govorov, Rokossovsky, Katukov and Vlasov. He fought in defense of Kiev in 1941

and has been held responsible for this disaster by the Russians but this was too easy on Marshal Budenny. He led the 1st Guards Army at Stalingrad. From 1942 to 1943 he was Deputy Commander of the Southwest Front and from 1943 to 1945 he fought in the battles of the Donbass, Eastern Pomerania and Berlin.

### KV Tanks

This Soviet heavy tank series was named for Klementi (Klim) Voroshilov, Soviet Minister of Defense at the time. The design began as a rework of an unsuccessful heavy tank, the SMK, which had been tried out during the Russo-Finnish War in 1939–40 and found to be too cumbersome. This vehicle used two turrets, demanded a seven-man crew, and placed too much strain on the commander due to his manifold tasks. The tank was therefore redesigned to

KV tanks being presented to their crews by a commune which had raised the funds.

remove one of the turrets, shorten the chassis, and incorporate many of the component parts of the T-34 which was then going into volume production. The prototypes were built sufficiently quickly to be tested in action against the Finns, and then went into volume production. The KV–1 was armed with a 76.2mm gun of 30 calibers in length, weighed 46 tons, had a crew of five men, and was propelled by a 550hp diesel engine. Frontal armor thickness was 77mm, an exceptional figure for 1940 and one which made the KV resistant to most contemporary weapons.

Later in 1940, a somewhat improved model was introduced, the KV–1A, which carried a longer (40 calibers) 76mm gun and made some small changes in the suspension. In 1941 the KV–1B was developed, having additional armor on the front and sides to give a maximum thickness of about 100mm. This model was then improved by fitting a cast turret to it instead of the earlier welded model, which afforded better protection for the occupants by virtue of its sloping surfaces.

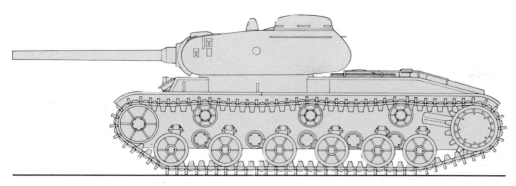

The KV-85 with a KV chassis and a T-34/85 turret.

The appearance of the KV–1 in battle gave the Germans a severe shock since it seemed to be impervious to any German tank or anti-tank gun. Indeed, the first KV to be noted by the Germans was reported as having swept through an entire Panzer regiment, with German shot bouncing off it, until it was stopped by being shot from the rear by a 150mm field gun at short range.

Nevertheless, the design was improved in 1942 by the KV–1C, with thicker armor of up to 120mm, extra side armor to give a total thickness of 130mm, and a new engine of 600hp. The tracks were made wider so as to give better performance in mud and snow.

Concurrently with the KV–1 series, a KV–2 had been produced in 1940. This was more in the nature of an assault gun than a tank, mounting a 122mm howitzer in a large, box-like turret. This was later improved by the mounting of a 152mm howitzer in the same turret. Although powerfully armed, these vehicles proved to be cumbersome in battle and not fast enough to act in the assault role, since their size and weight (53 tons) brought the speed down to only 15mph. They were withdrawn from service in 1942.

Finally, in 1943, came the KV–85; this used the same chassis as the earlier models – indeed, many were converted from early KV–1's – with the addition of a larger cast turret mounting an 85mm gun derived from a high-velocity anti-aircraft gun. Although this was a powerful and effective tank it was not produced in very great numbers, since it was treated more as an interim stage on the way to the Josef Stalin heavy tank, which was the vehicle which eventually replaced the KV in service.

## Kwajalein
see Marshall Islands, 1944

## Kwantung Army
see China Incident 1931–41

*Below:* KV tanks counterattack near Stalingrad.
*Bottom:* A Soviet KV-2 SP howitzer.

## Lacey, Sergeant J H, 1917–

Lacey was the top scoring Auxiliary pilot with the RAF during the Battle of Britain with 15 individual, plus one shared, victories.

## Lancaster, Avro

This British seven-seat heavy bomber and ocean patrol aircraft was in service from 1941 to 1954. One of the greatest bombers of all time happened as a lucky accident. When new heavy bombers were ordered in 1936, Short and Handley Page were set to building four-engined machines but Avro chose two 1760hp Rolls-Royce Vultures, in the Manchester. The Vulture proved unreliable, and in an attempt to avoid abandoning the program completely Avro fitted longer outer wings and four Merlins. The result was superb, far better than any of the rival bombers of 1941 and even a little better than the improved Halifaxes that came later. The Lancaster I carried a normal maximum bomb load of 14,000lb, and its cavernous bomb bay could take the 4000lb, 8000lb and 12,000lb 'blockbusters'. Later special Lancasters carried the Wallis 'skipping bomb' that breached the great dams, and stripped-down versions even carried the Wallis 22,000lb Earthquake bomb used at the end of the war. It was a splendid aircraft, with exceptional maneuverability, speeds up to about 280mph and ability to climb to almost 25,000ft over its heavily defended targets. It was the universal choice of the 'heavy' markers and backers-up that showed other bombers where to aim.

Nearly all the 7377 built had either the 1466hp Merlin, made by Rolls-Royce in Britain or Packard in the USA, but one batch of 300 had the 1650hp Bristol Hercules radial. The Mk II was fitted with a ventral turret, but all others had just nose, mid-upper and tail turrets, with eight machine guns (a few had a smaller number of heavy 0.5in guns), leaving the belly completely defenseless. The belly housed just the bulge for the H2S radar, which was meant to help the navigator (who in any case was guided by marker flares all along the route) but in fact served as a beacon to attract German night fighters. In the tail was a radar to warn of the approach of such aircraft, but this too was merely used by the Luftwaffe as a useful aid to interception. Losses were thus heavy, but production of Lancasters and crews more than kept pace and by 1945 this fine aircraft equipped 56 Bomber Command squadrons. They had made 156,000 sorties over Europe and dropped

The Lancaster B1 bomber.

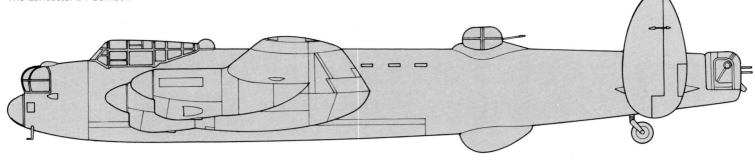

681,645 US tons of bombs. In the spring of 1945 one group of 'Lancs' was quickly equipped for FE (Far East) operations in Tiger Force, the large RAF force sent to help defeat Japan but never needed. Hundreds of others dropped food and other supplies to needy Europeans and flew prisoners of war back to Britain. Canada built 430 Lancasters, and Australia later made the Lincoln, a long-range high-altitude development.

**Lanchester Submachine Gun**

This British Navy submachine gun was named after Mr Lanchester of the Sterling Armament Company who designed it. The weapon came about by virtue of an RAF demand for weapons with which to arm airfield guards against expected German paratroop landings in 1940. Submachine gun production at that time was almost non-existent; the British Army were obtaining Thompson guns from the USA, while the Royal Navy had ordered a number of submachine guns from Smith & Wesson. In order to avoid having to work out a completely fresh design, it was suggested that the quickest way might be simply to copy an existing German pattern, the Schmeisser MP 28. In August 1940 it was decided to make 50,000 copies of this gun, production to begin late in the year since it was expected that four months would be needed to tool up and perfect the prototype. The necessary re-design to suit British machinery and manufacturing techniques was done by Lanchester, and on 8 November 1940 the first two pilots of the 'Lanchester Carbine' were tested. After some minor modifications, it was given its endurance and acceptance tests in late November,

and arrangements were made for the production to be started forthwith, output to be divided between the RAF and the Royal Navy. However, before production was very far advanced the Sten Gun was accepted for service by the Army; since this design was easier to make, the RAF also accepted it, leaving the Lanchester to be used entirely by the Royal Navy. The total number made is not known, but it was substantially less than the 50,000 originally intended.

Except for some tiny changes in dimensioning and the relocating of the selective fire lever, the Lanchester is simply a copy of the Schmeisser MP 28/11, firing the 9mm Parabellum cartridge from a 32-round magazine at about 600rpm. It remained in naval service throughout the war, a reliable and robust weapon, and was not replaced until the 1960s.

**Landing Vehicles, Tracked**

These vehicles are also known as 'Amtracs' from 'AMphibious TRACtor' and were used by US Marines for amphibious landings in the Pacific area. The LVT was developed from a design by Donald Roebling and was originally intended for rescue work in the Florida swamps. In the years 1937–39 it was evaluated by the US Marines as a possible amphibian vehicle for landing supplies and men across beaches. In early 1940 the Marines ordered their first model from Roebling, which incorporated some minor changes to make the vehicle more useful in a military role. This was delivered in October 1940 and an order was then given for 100 more, to be manufactured by the Food Machinery Corporation. This, the LVT–1, was introduced

A Lancaster takes off for another mission over Germany.

into service in July 1941, and was a 7.8 ton unarmored tracked tractor which could propel itself in the water by means of specially-shaped tracks. Capable of carrying 25 men or an equivalent load of stores, the LVT–1 was first used in action at Guadalcanal in August 1942.

The LVT–1 was followed by the LVT–2, which was simply an improved version of the original, and then the LVT–4. This moved the engine to the front to permit the fitting of a large ramp in the rear of the vehicle, allowing the occupants to dismount more easily and with less exposure to enemy fire than had the earlier method of jumping over the sides. The LVT–3, which appeared in time for the Okinawa landings, was similar to the LVT–4 but fitted with twin Cadillac engines instead of a single Continental engine.

The principal defect of the LVT was that it was not armored, and therefore after the difficult landings at Tarawa all LVTs were fitted with appliqué armor bolted on and subsequent production used lightweight armor plate for the hull. In order to endow the LVT with firepower, a fresh series of vehicles, known as the LVTA series, came into being. These were more in the nature of amphibious tanks than supply tractors, since they were covered over, armored, and fitted with guns. The LVTA–1 was the LVT–1 with the turret of the M3 light tank, complete with 37mm gun, mounted on the roof. This was soon found to be far too small to be of any value, and it was gradually replaced by the LVTA–4, an LVT–4 with the turret of the Gun Motor Carriage M8 on top, carrying a 75mm howitzer. These were used to good effect in the

*Top:* LVT(A)-4 with a 75mm howitzer.
*Above:* An LVT-4 in disembarking position.

landings on Saipan. Finally the LVTA–5 was developed, much the same as the LVTA–4 but with the howitzer given gyro stabilization and the turret fitted with power traverse; this model did not see action, coming too late in the war.

A total of 18,620 LVTs were built during the war by seven different contractors. In addition to their principal use in the Pacific, they were also used by US and British Army units in Italy (the Crossing of the Po) and Northwest Europe (the clearing of the Scheldt Estuary and the Crossing of the Rhine). But for the foresight of the US Marines in pressing for this type of vehicle in 1940, the war in the Pacific would have been a much more difficult and bloody affair.

### Langsdorff, Captain Hans, 1890–1939

The captain of the commerce raiding 'pocket battleship' *Graf Spee*, which was cornered and outmaneuvered by the British cruisers *Ajax, Exeter* and *Achilles* in the Battle of the River Plate, 13 December 1939, he was so ashamed at having to take refuge in neutral waters and forsake the fight that, after scuttling his ship, he committed suicide. A man of honor in every sense (not one British life was lost aboard any of the nine merchantmen he had sunk while cruising), he belonged to an earlier age of warfare.

He had the chance of either surrendering his ship or scuttling it. When he decided to scuttle he preferred death to the dishonour of going into captivity. He died with the Nazi flag wrapped around him.

### Latécoère 298

Eight French Navy squadrons flew these two-seat floatplanes against German troops advanced on the Somme in May 1940. An 880hp Hispano 12 Ycrs–1 engine gave a maximum speed of 180mph. The 298 was armed with three machine guns and a torpedo or two 550lb bombs.

### Laval, Pierre, 1883–1945

A successful French politician of the Third Republic, Laval decided at an early stage in the Battle of France that Germany's victory in the war was assured and that France would serve her interests best by coming to terms with Hitler. He convened the meeting of the National Assembly which on 23 June 1940 made Marshal Pétain head of government and in that government he assumed the offices of Foreign Minister and Deputy Head of State. Between December 1940 and April 1942 he was out of office, he and Pétain having fallen out, but on his return he pursued the policies with which he had begun – friendship with Germany, even at the expense of repressing dissident Frenchmen. After the invasion he was obliged to take refuge in Ger-

many accompanied by his now puppet regime; at the end of the war he was deported from Spain whither he had fled, to stand trial in France. He was condemned and executed as a traitor. Laval was vilified by the Allies, as well as the Free French and many uncommitted Frenchmen throughout the war, but he undoubtedly saw himself as a patriot, ploughing the best row he could in difficult times for his country. He was not, however, either in his appearance or methods, an attractive figure.

### Lavochkin La–5

This Soviet single-seat fighter was operational from 1942. Basically, the La–5 was a LaGG–3 with a modified front fuselage, housing a 1510hp ASh–82A radial engine in place of the former, lower-powered M–105PF in-line engine. The prototype was completed at a period when Lavochkin was so unpopular, for failing to improve the LaGG–3 as much as the authorities required, that he was thrown out of his factory, had his design team depleted, and had to keep the La–5 outdoors through lack of space in his new works. It might never have gone into production but for the personal intervention of an official test pilot who discovered the aircraft's potential, and the Lavochkin test pilot PN Nikashin who persuaded Stalin that the prototype should be given a more intensive testing. The La–5 was at once ordered in large numbers, and 1129 were completed in the last five months of 1942 – not without setbacks. The first fighters off the production line were 25–30mph slower than the prototype. Then two aircraft shed their wings in flight. Poor workmanship was behind both deficiencies. Once this had been remedied, maximum speed was established as 375mph at 21,000ft, and La–5s flew into combat at Stalingrad, armed with two 20mm guns. An improvement program during the Winter of 1942–43 produced the La–5FN, the suffix denoting installation of an ASh–82FN engine with fuel injection, rated initially at 1700hp and later at 1850hp. Weight was saved by use of metal wing spars, instead of wooden spars on later aircraft; new spats were fitted and the cowling redesigned. The result was an increase in speed to 403mph, and an improvement in handling that made the La–5FN a real 'pilot's airplane'. Among those who flew La–5s and 5FNs was Guards Colonel Ivan N Kozhedub, who ended the war as Russia's top-scoring fighter ace with 62 victories.

### Lavochkin La–7

This Soviet single-seat fighter was operational from 1944. Simultaneously produced with the late-model La–5FN with metal spars, the Lavochkin team evolved the La–7. The basic airframe, metal-spar wings and ASh–82FN engine

The Lavochkin La-7 fighter.

were unchanged, effort being devoted mainly to a general clean-up of the design. Most noticeably, the two air intakes on the cowling were combined in a single scoop under the front fuselage, giving a beautifully smooth nose and contributing to the increased maximum speed pf 423mph. Combined with an armament of three 20mm guns above the engine, the improved performance made the La–7 a match for the latest German Bf 109 G–6 and reduced-weight Fw 190 A–8 fighters, and it achieved considerable success in air combat during the last eight months of the war. The model flown by Ivan Kozhedub is preserved at the Gagarin Military Air Academy, Monino. On 15 February 1945, he made a surprise attack on an Me 262, so becoming the only Soviet pilot to engage and destroy a German jet aircraft. La–7 production totalled 5733, compared with 10,000 La–5s and 5FNs.

## Lavochkin LaGG–3

This Soviet single-seat fighter was operational from 1941. The series of wartime fighters produced by the Lavochkin design bureau seem always to be overshadowed by their Yakovlev counterparts; yet they were built in enormous numbers and had qualities that were not always obvious. For example, the LaGG–1, which flew for the first time on 30 March 1940, had a plastic-bonded wooden airframe which encountered none of the problems that affected other designs when supplies of light alloy became scarce during the war years. Inevitably, the wooden airframe proved heavier than a similar metal structure, and this was reflected in performance. The designers were conscious of this. So, they initiated a meticulous program of refinement as production got under way, to remedy the shortcomings. Weight was reduced, wing leading-edge slots were installed, and the original M–105P engine was replaced by a more powerful (1100, later 1260hp) M–105PF. The uprated fighter was given the new designation LaGG–3, and proved comparatively easy to manufacture, to the extent that 6528 were delivered in 1941–42. Equipment was sparse and unsophisticated by Western standards, as it still tends to be on many Soviet types, with a short-wave radio transceiver and lens-type reflector gunsight as the most advanced operational aids. In contrast, the fuel tanks were not only self-sealing but fireproofed by inert exhaust gases. The structure proved capable of absorbing considerable damage without failure, and armament was heavy for the time, with a 20mm cannon firing through the propeller hub, two 12.7mm guns above the engine, and underwing attachments for six 82mm rockets or 440lb of bombs. From the piloting viewpoint, acceleration and diving speed were outstanding, but maneuverability was less inspiring, with a tendency to spin out of a tight turn.

The LaGG-3 Soviet fighter.

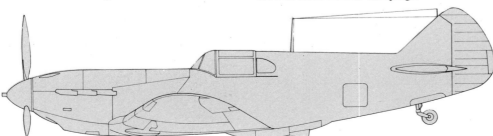

## Laycock, Major General Robert, 1907–1968

Laycock was a Commando leader and Chief of Combined Operations in the British Army during the D-Day landings. When Laycock returned from France he was told to raise and train a special unit for special operations. At the end of 1940 Laycock left Brtiain for the Middle East and raised two more units which became known as Layforce. Layforce took part on raids in Libya and Crete and had to be disbanded because of their very high casualty rate. In November 1941 Laycock led a raid on General Rommel's HQ at Sidi Raffa and although they caused much damage the raid was a failure because Rommel was away. Laycock and a sergeant were the only ones to survive the raid and spent several weeks crossing the desert to rejoin the 8th Army. After this Laycock returned to Britain to train commando units for raids on Vaagö, Dieppe, Boulogne and St Nazaire and as Chief of Combined Operations, co-ordinated operations for the D-Day landings.

## Leahy, Admiral William, 1875–1959

Leahy was President Roosevelt's personal military representative and Chief of Staff from 1942 onwards. He had been Ambassador to Vichy France until that time and once he took up his new appointment his duties were never clearly defined. He presided over JCS meetings and liaised between the Chiefs of Staff and Roosevelt. In fact he had daily conferences with Roosevelt and it was his task to present the President's views. When Roosevelt died Leahy remained to advise Truman and was involved in the long debate over whether to use the atomic bomb. Leahy came out against using it and called the bomb a 'professor's dream'.

## Leclerc, General Philippe François Marie, 1902–1947

Leclerc was the *nom de guerre* which this regular officer assumed when, in defiance of Vichy's interdict, he rallied in 1940 to de Gaulle. Sent to Africa, he first created a Free French force in Equatorial Africa and then led it northwards across the Sahara to join the British fighting in the Western Desert. He was given command of the 2nd French Armored Division for the invasion of Europe, with it fought in the Battle of Normandy and then led it into Paris on the day of liberation. Subsequently he fought in the Alsace and South German campaigns. He was killed in an air crash soon after the war. Twice a prisoner and twice an escapee in 1940, he was one of the Frenchmen of the flame-bright warrior spirit who kept alive French patriotism and self-respect during the years of occupation.

## Ledo Road
see Northern Burma Campaign

## Leeb, Field Marshal Wilhelm Ritter von, 1876–1956

By origin, like Halder, Jodl and Kesselring, a Bavarian gunner officer, Leeb had risen to the top of the prewar Army and retired after the Blomberg-Fritsch crisis of 1938. As one of its most respected minds (he had written an important theoretical study of defensive warfare) he was recalled for the Polish campaign, in which he commanded Army Group C. He commanded the same army group in the 1940 campaign, where it played the subordinate role of attacking the Maginot Line, and in Russia he commanded Army Group North, which made the advance to Leningrad. He was relieved in the great purge of generals in January 1942.

## Lee-Enfield Rifle

The standard rifle of the British Army from 1895 to 1957, the Lee-Enfield rifle took its name from James Paris Lee, Scots-born US designer who was responsible for the magazine system and parts of the bolt action mechanism, and the Royal Small Arms Factory at Enfield who developed the rifling and general design. The general design had begun with the Lee-Metford rifle, in which the rifling was suited to black powder; with the advent of smokeless powder the rifling was changed and the weapon became the Lee-Enfield.

There were no less than 27 variant models of the Lee-Enfield, but the ones most commonly used were the 'Short Magazine Lee-Enfield' and the 'Rifle Number 4'. The first was designed in 1903 and was one of the first rifles to effect a compromise in length between the 'long' infantryman's rifle of the day and the short carbine carried by cavalry and artillery. By producing an intermediate length weapon, the same rifle could be used by all troops, simplifying manufacture and supply. The SMLE had a 25.19in barrel and a ten-round magazine; it weighed 8lbs 2oz unloaded and was chambered for the standard British .303 cartridge. The most notable mechanical feature was that the bolt locked by lugs towards the rear end, turning into shoulders in the receiver; this was totally different from all other military rifles of the day which used bolt lugs at the front end which locked into recesses in the chamber. As a result the Lee-Enfield had the fastest-operating bolt action ever fitted to a service rifle, and a trained soldier could fire up to 30 aimed rounds in one minute, a performance which led the German Army, in 1914, to attribute many more machine guns to the British infantry than they in fact possessed. Its only drawback was that it was difficult to manufacture, having been designed in the days when durability was more important than mass-production. The massive demand for rifles during World War I demonstrated the dangers of such a design, and in the postwar years much work was done to simplify the design so as to suit it to mass production.

After several trial models, the Rifle Number 4 Mark 1 (the system of nomenclature had been changed in the 1920s) was introduced in February 1941. This retained the same bolt action and magazine but allied it to a more simple stock design, simpler aperture sights, and a protruding barrel on to which a spike bayonet could be fixed, replacing the sword bayonet of the earlier rifle. Although a fraction of an inch shorter than the SMLE, the No 4 was slightly heavier, weighing 9lbs 1oz. It became the stan-

An unusual version of the Enfield No 4.

dard British service rifle as the SMLE models wore out, and was used in every theater of war. It was, though, found to be somewhat heavy and cumbersome in jungle conditions, and a shortened version was produced for service in Burma. This was the 'Rifle Number 5' or 'Jungle Carbine'; the barrel was shortened by about five inches and fitted with a flash-hider; the stock was shortened, and a rubber recoil pad fitted to the butt. Although very dashing in appearance, and light and handy to carry, it was a vicious beast to fire, with excessive recoil and blast, and it was never very popular with the troops.

Although experts claimed that the Lee-Enfield could never be accurate due to the rear locking of the bolt which allowed the bolt body to compress under the firing pressure, the fact remains that as a combat rifle it was probably the best of its kind. The acceptance standard was that each rifle should put five shots into a four-inch circle at 200yds, which may not be good enough for target shooters but is amply sufficient for combat. Specially selected rifles, fitted with telescopes, were used by snipers and could make themselves felt at ranges up to 1000yds in the hands of a skilled shot. And it is noteworthy that while the standard rifle of the British Army is now an automatic, the sniping rifle is still the Lee-Enfield, albeit chambered for the 7.62mm NATO cartridge.

## Leese, General Sir Oliver, 1897–1978

A protégé of Montgomery, Leese was made (by him) commander of 30th Corps for the Battle of Alamein, and he later led it in the invasion of Sicily and Italy. He succeeded Montgomery in command of the 8th Army in Italy in January 1944. In November he handed over command to McCreery and at the end of the war became Commander of Allied land forces in Southeast Asia.

## Leigh Light

A powerful searchlight the Leigh light was used by anti-submarine aircraft in the Battle of the Atlantic. It took its name from the inventor and its purpose was to illuminate a U-Boat already detected by radar for the final run-in of the attack.

## Leigh-Mallory, Air Chief Marshal Sir Trafford L, 1892–1944

His highly successful war career began during the Battle of Britain when he had command of No 12 Group RAF Fighter Command, responsible for the defense of the Midlands region of England and of the east coast shipping routes. In advocating the use of the 'big wing' formation against the Luftwaffe as suggested by Sqn Ldr Douglas Bader, he entered into strong disagreement with Park, Commander of No 11 Group, who had the support of Dowding, Commander in Chief of Fighter Command. At the end of 1940, he was to replace Park and, under Dowding's successor, Air Chief Marshal Sir W Sholto Douglas, was to initiate offensive tactics, aimed at forcing the enemy to divert some of his defensive strength from other theaters. In August 1942, he directed the air operations for the Dieppe Raid. He also held the post of Commandant at the RAF School of Army Co-operation.

In November 1942 he became head of RAF Fighter Command, and in late 1943, was appointed Commander in Chief of the Allied Expeditionary Air Force for Operation Overlord. It was in this post that he was to encounter much criticism and opposition, in particular, from the strategic air force commanders, Spaatz and Harris. Unfortunately, his appointment directive had not given a precise definition of his powers and although his success as leader of Fighter Command was not in doubt he had no experience in heavy bomber operations. The situation was further aggravated by his personality which has been described as aggressive, bluff and dogmatic. His most valuable contribution to the success of Overlord was the Transportation Plan under which German communications, supplies, radio and radar sites in and around the invasion area were subjected to a concentrated aerial assault prior to the surface landings. Consequently, the Allies met minimum resistance in the initial phases and were able to establish a bridgehead in Normandy.

In November 1944 Leigh-Mallory was appointed Commander-in-Chief, Southeast Asia, but was killed in an air crash on his way to take up the post.

## Lemay, General Curtis, 1906–

Lemay was a pilot who became a specialist in bombing tactics over Europe and Japan. He was sent to England with US 8th AF in 1942 and began a campaign of day-time strategic bombing. His planes did not have fighter escorts so Lemay worked out that the best tactic was to have bombers flying in formation at staggered levels. He led many of these raids himself. In July 1944 he was sent to the China-Burma-India theater as Chief of 20th Bomber Command and sent B–29s from China on bombing missions over Japan. His command was then transferred to the Marianas and he decided to send bombers out on night-time low-level area bombing, which was more efficient at destroying small industrial targets. The bombing campaign continued until the end of the war when Lemay also dropped leaflets urging surrender.

Lemay was the foremost proponent of strategic bombing in World War II. He persevered in this belief throughout his conduct of both the Korean and Vietnam Wars in which he played a significant role.

## Lend-Lease Act, 1941

After the outbreak of World War II, Britain turned to the USA to buy weapons and destroyers. At the end of 1940 Britain had run out of dollars and Churchill began to press Roosevelt to give more substantial aid. Roosevelt came up with the idea of a 'destroyers for bases' deal and extended it to a Lend-Lease Act in March 1941. The Lend-Lease account allowed Britain to order war materials on credit and left the question of repayment to the President. The ownership of the supplies remained nominally with the USA. Lend-Lease arrangements were eventually extended to China and the USSR.

After the Act was passed the US helped Britain by patrolling the Atlantic and took over a base at Reykjavik, Iceland, and protected convoys from U-Boat attacks. After the USA entered World War II the Lend-Lease program covered mutual aid agreements and by the end of the war the total bill for the USA came to $4,300,000,000. In August 1945 Truman ended the Lend-Lease agreement. Britain had to borrow the $3,750,000,000 she owed from the USA.

## Leningrad, Battle and Siege of, September 1941 – January 1944

After the Fourth Panzer Army had breached the Stalin Line there was only one place where the Red Army could make a stand to halt the German advance on Leningrad. This was on the Luga River at the tip of Lake Ilmen. The Ger-

Soviet troops preparing to take action on Leningrad's perimeter.

The boats across Lake Ladoga kept a lifeline to Leningrad open during the 900-day siege.

man attack on this position was launched on 8 August 1941 and met little substantial resistance because the Russians did not have long-range artillery or tanks. However in a last-minute attempt to stop a complete collapse, and also to give the Leningrad defenders time to build trenches and a protective perimeter, the Russians counterattacked. Within two weeks they had been pushed back and the German High Command was left with the decision: whether to take the city by storm or to besiege it. They decided on the latter course, estimating that the Panzer divisions could now be used to good effect on the Central Front. This solution also bypassed the problem of what to do with the civilian population once the city had been taken. On 1 September 1941 the Germans began to bombard the city and Field Marshal von Leeb decided to disobey orders and try to take the city.

An air gunner operates a Lewis gun in 1939, when the weapons were still widely used.

He sent in General Reinhardt's Panzer Divisions on the 9 September and after initial success the Panzers could make little headway in the street fighting. A final three-sided attack on Kolpino failed and Leeb decided to withdraw the Panzers and send them south. The Germans continued to advance. They took Schlüsselburg on Lake Ladoga thus cutting off Leningrad from its major supply lines. The Finns had stopped their offensive on the 1939 Russo-Finnish borders and could not be prevailed upon to go any further.

In November 1941 the situation in Leningrad worsened as 11,000 died. During that month Tikhvin fell (9 November), the Lake Ladoga was unnavigable because of the ice and there could only be a precarious route over the ice. However the Germans had not kept a large enough force outside Leningrad and the Russians recaptured Tikhvin. The siege continued until 1944. Hitler had various plans to take the city by storm but there was no repeat of the September 1941 attempt. The most ambitious plan was conceived in the summer 1943, which was a parachute drop of two divisions onto the

city, but it was quietly discarded after the defeat at Kursk. In August 1942 the Russians tried to raise the siege by regaining the German corridor between Tosno and Lake Lagoda but although the fighting continued until September there was no breakthrough. In January 1943 the Russians launched another attempt and this time recaptured Schlüsselburg, which allowed supplies to reach Leningrad. In January 1944 a fully co-ordinated attack from all the Fronts in the north pushed the Germans back and relieved the city on 19 January 1944. The 890-day siege was over. Some 200,000 civilians had been killed by the German bombardments and at least 630,000 died of starvation.

## Leopold III, King of Belgium, 1901–

When his country was invaded by the Germans on 10 May 1940, Leopold assumed command of its armed forces, though the day to day direction of operations was executed by the General Staff. After two weeks of increasingly desperate fighting which left the Belgian Army pinned in the northeast corner of the country, Leopold made the decision to ask for an armistice which was granted on 28 May. However, there was strong opposition from the Army and the government and his action was declared illegal, though too late for it to be effectively disobeyed. Leopold further alienated his countrymen by contracting a morganatic marriage (he was a widower) during the war. At the end of the war he was in Germany where he had been taken by the Wehrmacht. After an investigation by the postwar government into his conduct during the war, a referendum was held in which the Belgian people refused to allow Leopold to return to the throne. He was not even permitted to return to Belgium until 1950.

## Lewis Gun

The Lewis Gun was a gas-operated light machine gun perfected by Colonel Isaac N Lewis, US Army, from original patents devised by Samuel N MacLean, a noted American firearms designer. Lewis demonstrated his first working guns in 1911, but for reasons never satisfactorily explained, the US Board of Ordnance turned down the design and Lewis took the gun to Belgium, where a company was formed to manufacture it. Production was subsequently taken over by the BSA company in England, and the Lewis gun became the only worthwhile light machine gun of World War I, being extensively used in both ground and aerial roles. In spite of this the US Army never adopted it, and when the US Marines, who used it, came under Army

Indian soldier operates a Lewis gun in 1939, where the weapons were still widely used.

control in France their Lewis guns were withdrawn. It has since been suggested that the root of the matter was a clash of personalities between Lewis and General Crozier, US Chief of Ordnance at the time, and given Crozier's autocratic character, this is highly likely.

Although the Lewis had been replaced in first-line service by 1939 in all the armies of the world, it nevertheless was destined to play its part in World War II. Large numbers of guns held in reserve by the British were used for training troops and also for arming trawlers and coastal vessels against air attack. In addition, 1157 Lewis guns were bought from the USA in 1940 and issued to the British Home Guard as their primary light machine gun.

## *Lexington*

The *Lexington* (CC.1) and *Saratoga* (CC.3) were laid down after World War I as two of a class of six giant, 43,500-ton battlecruisers but construction was suspended in August 1922 when agreement was reached during the Washington Conference on limiting the size of new ships. Permission was granted under the Washington Treaty to convert the two ships into aircraft carriers and the *Lexington* joined the Fleet as *CV.2* in 1937. With her sister she played a vital role in developing US naval air tactics and the techniques of fast carrier strikes. They were fast, well-armed and carried 90 aircraft, and were the most successful of all the early fleet carriers.

The *Lexington* was the flagship of Task Force 11 under Rear Admiral Fitch in the Battle of the Coral Sea and had embarked VF–2, VS–2, VB–2 and VT–2, a total of 70 aircraft. After acquitting herself well on the first day of the battle she was attacked at 1118 hours on the morning of 8 May 1942 by 69 Japanese aircraft from the *Shokaku* and *Zuikaku*. Six B5N 'Kate' torpedo-bombers attacked her, three on either bow, and two minutes later she was hit twice on the port side. D3A 'Val' dive-bombers damaged her with near-misses and scored two hits, one on the stack and one on deck.

The carrier listed seven degrees and started to burn. The aviation gasoline lines had been ruptured by the explosions, and soon the ventilation system began to distribute the explosive vapor around the ship. About an hour after the attack a large explosion took place, followed by another fire and some smaller explosions. In spite of this 39 aircraft landed and she even flew off fighters for the Combat Air Patrol. But the fires were gaining, and at 1445 hours another big explosion took place and eventually flying operations had to stop. When the fires reached the bomb-rooms and torpedo-store the ship was

The USS *Lexington* hours before she sank in the battle of the Coral Sea.

abandoned, and at 2000 hours the destroyer *Phelps* torpedoed the wreck. Casualties totaled 216 men, and 36 aircraft were lost but 2735 officers and enlisted men were picked up by the destroyers.

The name *Lexington* was given to a new carrier of the *Essex* Class (CV.16, ex-*Cabot*) and she too had an adventurous career, being torpedoed off Kwajalein in December 1943 and damaged by a kamikaze in 1944.

## Leyte, Battle for, 1944–45

The invasion of the Philippines began some two months ahead of schedule and the Joint Chiefs of Staff decided to attack Leyte first and split the Japanese defense. The largest convoy in the Pacific was sent to the Philippines and in the complex naval engagement, known as the Battle of Leyte Gulf (23–25 October) the invasion transports were nearly attacked by Admiral Kurita's Center Force. After this naval battle the Japanese Navy no longer played any part in the war since they had lost all their aircraft carriers. The only attacks the Japanese could make on naval forces came from the kamikaze pilots.

On 17 and 18 October 1944 US Rangers seized three islands at the entrance to Leyte Gulf. Admiral Kinkaid's 7th Fleet carried General Krueger's 200,000 strong 6th Army to Leyte and after a naval bombardment four infantry divisions landed on the east coast on 20 October. General Yamashita was overall com-

mander of troops in the Philippines and although he wanted to fight the US in Luzon, Imperial GHQ ordered him to fight the battle for the Philippines in Leyte. He sent in reinforcements amounting to 45,000 troops as well as supplies until early December. Four days after landing the Americans took two airfields at Dulag and Tacloban on the east coast. As they pushed further inland resistance became tougher, but by 2 November the Marines controlled the Leyte Valley from Carigara on the north coast to Abuyog on the east coast. The main problem facing the US was that the heavy rainfall turned the land into a swamp and swept away roads and airfields. By 12 November the US had captured Breakneck Ridge and took Kilay Ridge, which allowed them to approach the Japanese base at Ormoc from the north down Ormoc Valley. The Japanese landed more reinforcements at Ormoc on the west coast on 9 November, and they tried to cross the central mountains and attack the Americans' rear, but they got held up in the dense forests. General Krueger then split the Japanese defense by landing the 77th Infantry at Ipil three miles south of Ormoc. By 10 December Ormoc fell and the US controlled the entire Ormoc Valley by 22 December. Japanese resistance collapsed and the last Japanese port, Pinamopoan, fell on 25 De-

*Below:* The Allied armada at Leyte prior to the landings.
*Bottom:* A US LSM prepares for the landings on the island of Leyte after the battle of Leyte Gulf was won.

cember. Only a few hundred Japanese escaped from the island, which meant they lost six divisions, about 67,000 men. The Americans lost 3504 killed and 11,991 wounded. The whole operation took much longer than anticipated and delayed the invasion of Luzon by several months, much to MacArthur's annoyance, who wanted to liberate the Philippines quickly.

## Leyte Gulf, Battle of, 1944

The Battle of Leyte Gulf was the final battle fought by the Japanese Navy in World War II. Admiral Toyoda hoped to achieve victory in Operation Sho-Go, which turned out to be the greatest naval battle ever fought.

The Americans had the 3rd and 7th Fleet stationed off the Philippines to provide air cover for land operations on Leyte. The US Fleet was a formidable force (it had over 1000 aircraft) and Admiral Toyoda gathered all his remaining ships to face it. Two forces sailed from Japan. The first of these was Vice-Admiral Shima's Second Strike Force with two cruisers the *Nachi* and *Ashigara*, a light cruiser and four destroyers. The other was the Main Body under Vice-Admiral Ozawa, which included four carriers, the *Zuikaku, Zuiho, Chitose,* and *Chiyoda,* two battleships, three cruisers and eight destroyers. The First Striking Force sailed from Singapore under Vice-Admiral Kurita and was composed of all other heavy battleships and cruisers. Again this force was divided into two: Force A, under Kurita, was composed of five battleships, ten heavy cruisers and two light cruisers and fifteen destroyers; Force C, under Vice-Admiral Nishimura, was composed of two battleships, one cruiser and four destroyers.

The Japanese ships were ordered to arrive off Leyte in the early hours of 25 October 1944. The plan was that Kurita's Force A would head for the Mindanao Sea, the Sibuyan Sea and the San Bernardino Strait to approach Leyte from the north. Force C was to cross the Sulu Sea and approach Leyte from the south by the Surigao Strait. Ozawa's force came from Japan and since it had only 100 aircraft it was to lure Admiral Halsey's 3rd Fleet away from the San Bernardino Strait.

The Japanese plan went wrong long before any of the ships reached their destinations. Kurita's Force A was attacked by submarines, the USS *Darter* and *Dace,* and the *Atago* and *Maya* sank, whereas the *Takao* had to limp back to Singapore. On 24 October both Force A and C were sighted by reconnaissance planes of the 3rd Fleet, but before Halsey could order an air attack Admiral Fukudome's land-based bombers attacked Rear-Admiral Sherman's Task Group 38.3. The bombers were driven back, but one dive-bomber hit the *Princeton*'s avgas supply. The fire was uncontrollable and the ship sank later in the day. The *Birmingham* helped fight the fire but an explosion on the *Princeton* killed 233 of the *Birmingham*'s crew and severely wounded 400 others.

Meanwhile bombers from the *Intrepid* and *Cabot* bombed the *Musashi* and *Yamato* (the monster battleships in Kurita's force) and the *Nagato.* The planes concentrated on the *Musashi* which sank at 1935. Kurita decided that without air cover he should make for Leyte Gulf at night and withdrew. Halsey was convinced that his aircraft had beaten Kurita off and when Ozawa's force was sighted at 1540 he headed north with all the carrier groups leaving the San Bernardino Strait unprotected.

Later in the day Nishimura reached the Surigao Strait, and at 0215 on 25 October he made contact with Rear Admiral Oldendorf's force of six old battleships, four heavy and four light cruisers and a screen of destroyers. In the ensuing battle the Japanese ships were under constant fire and the *Fuso, Michishio* and *Yamagumo* sank. The *Yamashiro* was hit and the *Asagumo* withdrew. The Japanese ships were in confusion but the *Yamashiro* was able to hit the *Grant* which was towed away. Finally the *Yamashiro* was hit by two torpedoes and sank at 0419, with Nishimura aboard and then the *Mogami* retired. Shima's force approached but Shima had no news of Nishimura. When Shima saw the burning wrecks of the Japanese ships he decided to withdraw after the *Nachi,* his flagship, had collided with the *Mogami.*

Kinkaid's 7th Fleet then received the astounding news that Rear Admiral Clifton Sprague's Unit 3 of Task Group 77.4 was under fire off the coast of Samar. Kinkaid thought that Halsey had left Rear Admiral Lee's carrier group covering the San Bernardino Strait and sent urgent messages to Halsey. Sprague's destroyers fought Kurita's huge battleships. He had six escort carriers but none of his planes were equipped to fight battleships. During the two-hour battle the Japanese gained the upper hand and sank the US destroyers *Hoel, Johnston,* and *Roberts.* The *Gambier Bay,* a carrier, sank

*Below:* Japanese planes attack a US ship during the Leyte battle.
*Bottom:* The Japanese aircraft carrier *Zuiho* under attack from US aircraft off Cape Engaño.

Japanese cruiser *Kumano* is bombed by planes of Task Force 38 during the battle off Samar Strait in the Leyte Gulf action.

at 0907. The Japanese were also under heavy fire and lost the cruisers *Suzuya*, *Chokai* and *Chikuma* but as the heavy cruisers *Haguro* and *Tone* were about to finish off the battle, Kurita in his flagship *Yamato* called his ships off because he had lost touch with his force. He decided to withdraw because he thought he was fighting Halsey's carrier force and because he had no news of Nishimura.

Halsey had located Ozawa's force and sank the *Chitose*, damaged the *Zuiho*, *Zuikaku* and the light cruiser *Tama* in the first air strike. The second strike hit the *Chiyoda*, which was abandoned, and inflicted damage on the *Zuikaku* and *Zuiho* which later sank. Ozawa was left with the *Ise*, *Hyuga*, the light cruiser *Oyoda* and five destroyers. Halsey had to break off his attempt to eliminate the Japanese carriers because he was called back to the San Bernardino Strait.

In this suicidal battle the Japanese Navy was clearly defeated. Despite the fact that Kinkaid's 7th Fleet did not have adequate air cover, it defeated Japanese battleships in two engagements in the Surigao Strait and off Samar. Halsey never admitted that he had made a mistake in leaving the San Bernardino Strait unprotected, but even Admiral Nimitz joined in the criticism of Halsey's action. Most historians consider Halsey's breakaway action to have been irrelevant and even damaging to the Allied cause.

## Lidice

On 27 May 1942 two Czech volunteers trained in London, Jan Kubiš and Josef Gabčik, threw a bomb into Heydrich's car. Heydrich, the Protector of Bohemia and Moravia died a week later from his injuries. Karl Frank, his deputy, immediately threatened reprisals unless the assassins were found. Although there was very little evidence to support his assumption, Frank decided that Lidice should be punished for having harbored the assassins. On 12 June 1942 it was announced that the village of Lidice had been destroyed. Some 197 men were killed and women and children were sent to concentration camps. The village was then bulldozed and it took volunteers almost a year to raze the village completely. A few weeks later the village of Ležaky suffered the same fate. The assassins were betrayed by a fellow agent, Karel Čurda for a large sum of money. On 18 June the assassins and five other Czech resistance fighters were killed after a five hour battle in a church in Prague. Lidice became famous as an example of Nazi brutality and after the war the village was restored as a monument. One hundred and forty-three women were found and repatriated but only sixteen children were traced.

## Light Guns

The phrase 'light gun' was a German 'cover name' for their development of recoilless guns. This work began in the 1930s at the Rheinmetall-Borsig works under the direction of Dr Heinrich Klein in order to develop lightweight firepower for use by airborne troops. The guns were first used in combat during the invasion of Crete in 1941.

The German guns worked on the usual system of discharging a fast stream of gas through venturis at the rear of the breech to counter the recoil due to shot discharge. This gas stream was obtained by fitting a heavy plastic disc into the base of the cartridge case; when the charge was fired this disc held long enough to allow the shot to be started into the gun bore, after which it shattered and released the stream of gas to pass through the venturi formed in the breech block.

The first gun to be produced was the 75mm LG 1 (later re-named the LG 40 in accordance with the usual German 'year' system of nomenclature) which was designed to be readily broken into four parachute loads. It fired the standard 75mm field gun shell, weighing 12.8lbs, to a range of 6800 meters; the entire piece of equipment weighed only 320lbs in firing order. The gun was supported on a light metal tripod with small wheels, and its only tactical drawback was the need to clear an area 100 meters long immediately to the rear of the gun, because of the back blast from the venturi; this blast also made concealment of the gun very difficult.

The second standard gun was the 105mm LG 40, developed by Krupp, and more or less a scaled-up model of the smaller gun. The 75mm gun showed certain technical defects; the firing mechanism was in the center of the venturi, striking a primer in the center of the plastic cartridge base, and as a result the mechanism became severely eroded by the blast. Another problem was a severe twisting torque on the weapon due to the shell passing through the rifled barrel. These defects were cured in the 105mm model: the firing mechanism was placed on the side of the chamber, the cartridge having its primer fitted into the side. This cleared the venturi but necessitated making the cartridge case with a raised 'key' so that it could only be loaded one way, ensuring that the primer and firing mechanism mated correctly. The torque problem was cured by fitting curved vanes inside the venturi, so that the gas efflux, deflected by these vanes, set up an opposite twist to that developed by the rifling so that the two cancelled each other out.

Numerous other recoilless guns were developed once the principle was seen to be sound, but few of them reached service in great numbers. The principal drawback was that since much of the propelling charge was used up in providing the rearward blast, the recoilless gun was very demanding in propellant powder. The conventional 105mm field howitzer used a propelling charge of 3.04lbs of smokeless powder to send a 32.6lb shell to a range of 10,400 meters; the 105mm LG 40 fired the same shell but required a charge of 6.8lbs to achieve 7950 meters. Due to this demand for powder, which was becoming a critical supply problem in Germany, and since the airborne troops were no longer operating in the airborne role, the manufacture of light guns and their ammunition was brought to a stop in mid-1944 and as the existing stocks of ammunition were used up, so the guns were discarded from service.

## Lightning

see P-38 Lightning, Lockheed

## 'Lily'

see Kawasaki Ki-48

## Lioré et Olivier 451

Eight French bomber groups received 360 of these twin-engined four-seaters by June 1940, but only half of them became operational. The 451 was the only modern French medium bomber used in World War II. Two 1000hp engines gave a maximum speed of 311mph. Maximum bomb load was 3085lb.

## List, Field Marshal Wilhelm von, 1880–1971

By origin an engineer officer of the Bavarian army, List commanded the Fourteenth Army in the invasion of Poland and in 1940 the Twelfth, which spearheaded the advance into Belgium by making the crossing of the Meuse between Namur and Dinant. He was promoted to Field Marshal in the victory celebrations of 19 July 1940, and for the invasion of Greece (Operation Margarita) in the spring of 1941 was Commander in Chief of German forces. He directed Army Group A in Russia, July–October 1942, in its advance into the Caucasus.

## 'Little Boy'

see Hiroshima and Nagasaki

## *Littorio*

The *Littorio* Class battleships were the result of the abortive naval disarmament conference held in Rome in 1931 in an attempt to head off a Franco-Italian arms race.

Under the Washington Treaty both countries were entitled to build two 35,000-ton capital ships, and Italy was determined to build a reply to the French battlecruisers *Dunkerque* and *Strasbourg*.

Two ships were laid down in 1934, *Littorio* and *Vittorio Veneto*, and when France ordered the *Richelieu* and *Jean Bart*, then another pair to be named *Impero* and *Roma* were started in 1938. The *Littorio* (lictor, the bearer of the fasces in Roman times, hence the emblem of Fascism) and *Vittorio Veneto* were ready in the Spring of 1940, and joined the 1st Squadron at Taranto. They put to sea several times in response to movements of the British Mediterranean Fleet but missed the Battle of Calabria on 9 July 1940. On the night of 11 November the *Littorio* was hit by three 18in torpedoes dropped by British torpedo-bombers. She sank by the bow, but fortunately Taranto harbor is shallow, and she remained upright and could be repaired.

The *Littorio* returned to service in April 1941 and fought in the abortive Battle of Sirte the following December when she and three cruisers failed to defeat Admiral Vian's light cruisers. On 15 June 1942 she was hit by a bomb and a torpedo, and in April 1943 she was hit by a bomb while lying in harbor. On 30 July her name was changed to the non-Fascist *Italia* to celebrate the dismissal of Mussolini and two months later she was one of the group which sailed for Sardinia in a desperate attempt to avoid falling into German hands. As the squad-

Japanese troops move rapidly into Manila during their conquest of Luzon.

German Pistole '08 or Luger pistol, first used by the Germans in 1908.

ron approached Cape Corso on 9 September they were attacked by bombers armed with guided weapons. The *Roma* was hit amidships by two bombs and caught fire. Within minutes she blew up and sank, but the *Italia* was more fortunate; she was hit once and near-missed, but suffered only slight damage to her upperwork. The *Impero* was still incomplete at Trieste and fell into German hands only to be sunk later by Allied bombs.

The *Italia* was interned at Alexandria and then in the Great Bitter Lake in the Suez Canal with her sister *Vittorio Veneto*. For a while there was talk of refitting them to act as fast carrier escorts in the Pacific but they lacked the endurance; eventually they were returned to Italy.

## Litvinov, Maxim, 1876–1952

Litvinov was Commissar for Foreign Affairs until he was replaced by Molotov on 3 May 1939. He was the chief advocate of co-operation with the Western Powers against Nazi Germany, a policy which was reversed by Molotov. He was subsequently appointed Ambassador to the USA 1941–43 and was also Deputy Commissar for Foreign Affairs from 1941 to 1946. Litvinov's affable style of diplomacy made him a popular figure in Washington during the war.

## 'Lizzie'
see Lysander, Westland

## Lockwood, Rear Admiral Charles A, 1890–1967

Lockwood became Commander of US Submarines in the Pacific in 1943 and he immediately moved their refueling base from Pearl Harbor to Midway Island. This allowed the submarines greater range by saving them a journey of 2400 miles. He contributed greatly to the success of submarine operations by co-operating with Admiral Nimitz, who had begun his career as a submarine officer. In the fall of 1945 Lockwood was made naval Inspector General in recognition of his services.

## Lombok Strait, Battle of, 1942

The Combined Striking Force led by Rear Admiral Karel Doorman was given orders to intercept the Japanese convoys carrying invasion forces to Bali. The Combined Striking Force was to attack in three groups from Tjilatjap. The first group attacked at 2130 on 19 February and caught the Japanese off guard. Although they scored several hits the Japanese retaliated and sank the Dutch destroyer *Piet Hein*. The second group managed to damage one Japanse destroyer, but two Allied destroyers, the *Stewart* and the *Tromp* were hit. The third group of motor-torpedo boats could not launch their torpedoes. The attack was very disappointing and the Japanese proceeded to take Bali.

## Long-Lance Torpedoes
see Japanese Navy

## LRPG
see Wingate, Major General Orde

## Lublin Government

The Lublin committee was set up in July 1944 and combined two separate Polish communist movements: PPR (Polish Workers' Party) and UPP (Union of Polish Patriots). The USSR recognized it as the administration of liberated territories in Poland. On 31 December 1944 the Lublin committee declared itself to be the provisional government. Stalin recognized it before the Yalta Conference (February 1945) which was supposed to discuss the Polish question.

## Luger

One of the most famous and readily-recognized pistols in history, the Luger was, in fact, superseded in German Army service in 1938. In spite of that, however, it remained in use in its thousands and stayed in production until late in 1944.

The Luger pistol was developed by George Luger, who based his work on an earlier pistol designed by Hugo Borchardt. The principal

mechanical novelty of the Luger was the toggle-joint breech lock, a system of operation which demanded precise manufacture and consistent ammunition for perfect operation. Both of these were, of course, easily achieved in Germany at the turn of the century. The first formal adoption of the Luger as a military pistol was by the Swiss in 1900; it was taken by the German Navy in 1904 in 9mm caliber and by the German Army in 1908 also in 9mm caliber, becoming the 'Pistole '08' or 'P08' in Army parlance.

The P08, the most common of all the Luger designs, was 8.75in long with a 4in barrel; it weighed 1lb 15oz empty and carried an eight-shot magazine in the butt. It was first produced by Deutsche Waffen und Munitionsfabrik, but the vast demands of the Army led to other factories joining in, notably the government arsenals at Erfurt and Spandau. After World War I it was produced commercially for some years, as well as being widely supplied to other countries, until in 1930 military production began again under the auspices of the Mauser company. However, good as the Luger was, it presented many production problems and in the middle 1930s the Army settled on the Walther P-38 pistol for future service use, since it was cheaper and easier to manufacture. But production of the Luger continued, since sufficient Walther pistols could not be made for several years, and it was not until 1944 that the Mauser production line for Lugers finally closed down. Even then, there were sufficient spare parts left in stock for production to begin once more, after the war had ended, for the French Army and also to satisfy the demand for Lugers as souvenirs among the Allied troops.

As well as the standard P08, there was a long-barreled model known as the 'Artillery Model', the '1917 Model' or (correctly) as the 'Long 08 Model'. This had a 7.5in barrel and long-range sights, and was fitted with a drum magazine running into the butt which carried 32 rounds. It was originally issued to NCOs of machine gun units in World War I as a form of machine pistol, and a few of them managed to survive to see service in World War II.

## *Lutzöw*
see *Deutschland*

## Luzon, The Fall of, 1941

The Americans were not properly prepared to defend the Philippines when the Japanese struck Pearl Harbor on 8 December 1941. General MacArthur was the commanding officer of troops in the Philippines and by December he had mobilized all the Filipino reserves. He had 19,000 American and 160,000 Filipino troops and he considered that with the protection of

100 B-17s and some torpedo boats to protect his communications his defenses would be secure. On 8 December he had only 35 B-17s; half of them were stationed at Clark Field on Luzon, the other half were on Mindanao. In fact General Marshall did not think it would be possible to hold on to the Philippines, or for that matter the Dutch East Indies.

The Japanese led by General Homma decided to use a small force of two divisions, only 57,000 men, supported by two tank regiments, two infantry regiments, a battalion of medium artillery and five anti-aircraft battalions. They relied on their superiority in the air to settle the victory and had orders to complete the invasion within 50 days. On 8 December MacArthur received warning of the Pearl Harbor attack and immediately sent bombers out on patrol to avoid being caught on the ground. Fog on Formosa had held up the Japanese bombers but just after the B-17s had returned to refuel and take on their bombs, the Japanese Striking Force appeared on the horizon. Two squadrons of B-17s were caught on the ground at Clark Field and the Japanese destroyed at least 100 planes for the loss of only seven planes. The USAAF in the Philippines was reduced to seventeen heavy bombers and 40 fighters but not all were ready for action. The B-17s were not used to bomb the landing parties and were eventually withdrawn to Australia on 27 December. On 10 December the Japanese Eleventh Air Fleet returned to attack Manila and destroyed the reserve stock of torpedoes, so the US submarines were no longer of any use. MacArthur concentrated his experienced US troops around Manila, whereas the inexperienced and badly-trained Filipinos were stationed on the coast. The Japanese landings took place without any interference from MacArthur's troops. A small party landed first at Batan Island. On 10 and 12 December the second wave of landings on Luzon arrived at Vigan and Aparri in the north of the island, and at Legaspi in the southeast. MacArthur could do little to stop them, short of dispersing his troops. The main landing party disembarked in Lingayen Gulf, 120 miles north of Manila on 22 December. MacArthur decided he could not hold on to Manila, as he thought the Japanese had 100,000 men, so he declared the city open on 26 December and withdrew to the Bataan peninsula. The troops withdrawing to Bataan were harassed by the Japanese and some 13,000 Filipinos deserted.

Japanese soldiers prepare to land at Lingayen Gulf when they attacked the Philippines in December 1941.

## Luzon, The Reconquest of, 1945

As a preliminary to the invasion of Luzon, MacArthur decided to strike at the island of Mindoro, which could be used as an air base. On 15 December 1944 the Americans landed at San Jose, in the southwest of Mindoro, and met no opposition apart from kamikaze attacks. On 17 December Admiral Halsey's Task Force 38 bombarded airfields on Luzon but before they could do much damage they were hit by a typhoon and nearly 800 men were drowned.

General Yamashita had lost supplies and equipment in the battle for Leyte, so he decided to fight a defensive operation and placed his troops on three mountains. He commanded 152,000 men on the Shobu redoubt in the north. He placed 30,000 men on the Kembu redoubt in the center to protect Clark Field, and 80,000 men were on the Shimbu redoubt in the south, controlling Manila's water supply to the east. Admiral Kinkaid's 7th Fleet transported General Krueger's 6th Army to the northwest of Luzon. They landed on 9 January 1945 at Lingayen Gulf, north of the spot where the Japanese landed in 1941. By the end of the first day 68,000 men had disembarked, but there was already congestion on the beaches. At first they met little opposition, but soon the Kembu group arrived to hold up the American advance on Manila. MacArthur was impatient for success but by 29 January the 14th Corps had reached San Fernando. On 23 January Clark Field was reached, but it was only recaptured on 1 February.

On 29 January Major General Hall's 11th Corps landed at beaches at San Antonio, and by 5 February they had pushed east of Subic, joining the 14th Corps to cut off the Bataan Peninsula. On 31 January the 11th Airborne Division landed at Nasugbu Bay, 40 miles south of Manila, and the 8000 men began their march to Manila but met stiff opposition. They reached the Nichols Field on the outskirts of Manila only by 12 February.

Although Yamashita had decided not to fight for Manila and had withdrawn to the mountains, Rear-Admiral Iwabuchi, Commander of the Thirty-first Naval Base Force, had orders to defend it to the last. The 37th Infantry fought its way to the northwest edge of Manila and freed 1300 Allied POWs from the Bilibid Prison. Manila was fought for street by street and only fell on 4 March after 16,000 Japanese had died.

Before the fall of Manila, US troops had cleared the Bataan Peninsula, and on 16 February they began to clear Corregidor. Intelligence reports underestimated the numbers on

Corregidor and the operation was disastrous. Paratroops were dropped on 16 February but they missed their target and 280 men died. Amphibious landings were made on the same day and it took troops two weeks to overrun the garrison of 4000 and a further loss of 225 men killed. The other islands in Manila Bay were cleared by 16 April.

The campaign for Luzon could have ended at this point because the 172,000 Japanese troops could no longer threaten the Americans, because they were so short of supplies and equipment. However the 50,000 troops, under Lieutenant General Yokoyama, concentrated to the east of Manila posed a threat in that they controlled Manila's water supply. General Griswold attacked this Shimbu group, but he had only two divisions, and although he had superiority in the air, he found it difficult to knock out the Japanese cave defenses. In mid-March the 11th Corps was brought in which made better progress by attacking from the south, by Laguna de Bay. Further north American troops fought on until the end of May to take the Wawa and Ipo dams undamaged. This constant fighting meant the Shimbu group was no longer an effective fighting force, and it was left to guerrillas, hunger and disease to contain them.

The US 158th Regimental Combat team made an amphibious landing in the south at Legaspi on 1 April and met no opposition. It marched up the Bicol Peninsula and wiped out Japanese troops until it made contact with the 1st Cavalry Division marching from the north of the Peninsula. This meant the last group of Japanese on Luzon was the Shobu group, 110,000 strong. Baguio, Yamashita's HQ, was heavily fortified, but after continual fighting for a month and a half the town finally fell on 26 April. Most of the Japanese troops withdrew, but it still took a month for the Americans to clear the area. Fighting continued for several months until Yamashita had been driven back to Bontoc. In late June the 11th Airborne made a parachute drop at the northern end of the Cagayan Valley. Although Yamashita's troops posed no great threat they continued to tie down four US divisions. Then, on 1 July the 8th Army arrived to relieve the 6th Army which was to go on and invade Japan.

Operations in the southern and central Philippines began with a landing on Palawan on 28 February. This was followed by another 37 landings to secure the other islands. The most important landings were on the Zamboanga Peninsula, Mindanao (10 March), South Panay (18 March), Cebu (29 March), Negros (29 March) and Jolo in the Sulu Archipelago

(9 April). All these mopping up operations continued well into July and held up other operations.

Finally, on 2 September 1945, Yamashita surrendered with some 50,000 troops. The Luzon campaign had been the largest operation in the Pacific. The whole campaign to liberate the Philippines had cost the Americans about 15,000 dead and 50,000 wounded. It has been argued that the entire campaign was unnecessary in the light of the heavy casualties inflicted.

## Lysander, Westland

This British army co-operation aircraft was operational from 1938 to 1944. The first monoplane to equip RAF Army Co-operation squadrons, the 'Lizzie' was a forerunner of modern STOL (short take-off and landing) types. It was packed with clever features. For example, the inboard wing panels were inversely tapered and made progressively thinner towards the roots, to impede as little as possible the all-round view from the tandem two-seat 'glasshouse'. Automatically-opening slats and flaps gave a stalling speed of only 65mph. Each of the large spats on the main wheels housed an 0.303in machine gun, and could carry a small stub-wing fitted with racks for three light bombs. The observer in the rear seat had another gun. Four squadrons of Lysanders went to France with the Air Component in September 1939, ostensibly for reconnaissance and artillery spotting. One of them shot down the first Heinkel bomber to be destroyed over BEF territory in November. In the hectic days before the evacuation, they spent their time dropping supplies to troops defending Calais and attacking enemy positions. They performed a similar variety of tasks in the Western Desert, Greece, Palestine, India and Burma, until replaced by Tomahawks at home and Hurricanes in the Far East. They then began a new career, their slow-flying capability making them ideal for the dangerous task of transporting Allied agents into small fields in France, as well as for air/sea rescue and target towing. Altogether 1425 were built, with Bristol Mercury or Perseus engines of 870–905hp.

## M1C
see Garand Rifle

## MacArthur, General Douglas, 1880–1964

MacArthur conducted the unsuccessful defense of the Bataan Peninsula in 1942. As Allied Supreme Commander in the Southwest Pacific he directed the recapture of New Guinea, the Solomon Islands, New Britain and the Philippines and at the end of the war received the Japanese surrender, on behalf of the Allies. Before the war MacArthur had served for several years as military adviser to the Philippine government, but in July 1941 he was recalled to the active list and appointed Commanding General of US troops in the Philippines. The Philippine Army also came under his command through a previous agreement and MacArthur set about mobilizing his forces. In August he had 22,000 men under arms, but by December he had managed to raise the total to 180,000. This force, however, was not equal to the Japanese. MacArthur's artillery was obsolete; he lacked motor vehicles; the US Asiatic Fleet consisted of but a few cruisers and destroyers; they had 35

MacArthur signs the Japanese surrender aboard USS *Missouri* as Wainwright (left) looks on.

B-17s but inadequate fighter support. Nonetheless MacArthur optimistically predicted that he could hold the Philippines. Within a day of the Pearl Harbor attack MacArthur had lost half his B-17s on the ground. By 27 December MacArthur had abandoned Manila and was withdrawing to Bataan. Although his troops were short of supplies, they fought a delaying action into the spring of 1942. On 11 March MacArthur left Luzon to go to Canberra as he realized the Philippines would soon be lost. He left with the words 'I shall return'.

He flew to Melbourne to find he had only 25,000 troops under his command and 260 obsolete aircraft. From this point on, MacArthur's persistent theme was the need to defeat Japan before Germany. He was anxious to start an offensive and sent constant demands for reinforcements and supplies.

Although MacArthur was Commander of the Allied forces in the Southwest Pacific, Admiral Chester Nimitz's fleet was very much an independent force. In fact the mainspring of the Allied advance in this area was the competition between the two men as to who should reach their objective first. At the end of July 1942 Nimitz was ordered to take Santa Cruz, Tulagi and the adjacent islands and MacArthur was ordered to take the remaining ones in the Solomons and the northeast coast of New Guinea. In this campaign MacArthur developed the tactic known as 'island hopping', that is the bypassing of Japanese troop concentrations on fortified islands, to attack the weaker ones in their rear and disrupt their communications. This had the great advantage of avoiding frontal assaults and thus reducing the number of casualties.

The fight against the Japanese was tough and MacArthur overestimated their force in New Guinea. By January 1943 Buna had been encircled and had fallen and the fighting on Guadalcanal was dying down. In early 1943 MacArthur put forward the Elkton plan which proposed the seizure of airfields on the Huon peninsula, New Georgia, New Britain and Bougainville, the capture of Kavieng and the frontal assault of Rabaul. MacArthur's demands for reinforcements were rejected and it was not until October that the Solomons were secured. MacArthur compromised on the question of Rabaul and decided to take it by encirclement. By spring 1944, 100,000 Japanese soldiers were cut off at Rabaul and the Japanese Eighteenth Army was surrounded in New Guinea. In April MacArthur secured northern New Guinea by bypassing 50,000 soldiers at Wewak. In September he took Morotai and all of New Guinea was in Allied hands. On 26 July MacArthur attended a conference at Pearl Harbor where he argued against Nimitz's plan. He said that a frontal attack on Iwo Jima and Okinawa would be too costly and that the Philippines should be top priority. This question was not settled until September when the Joint Chiefs proposed that the attack on Leyte should begin on 20 December. At last MacArthur could accomplish his dream of liberating the Philippines. By the end of 1944 MacArthur had taken Leyte with the assistance of some of Nimitz's ships and on 9 January 1945 Allied troops landed at Lingayen Gulf and met little opposition. General Yamashita knew that the Japanese did not have sufficient air cover but he was determined to make a last stand in the northern Philippines. MacArthur entered Manila on 3 February. MacArthur did not think that the war would be over in that year, so he drew up plans to liberate the Dutch East Indies, even though this was not strategically necessary. He caused great offence to the British by refusing to use Mountbatten's troops. The Australians were none too happy about this and General Sir Thomas Blamey objected vociferously. MacArthur's last offensive was an amphibious attack on Balikpapan on 1 July. On 2 September MacArthur accepted Japan's formal surrender aboard Nimitz's flagship the USS *Missouri* in Tokyo Bay. After the war MacArthur became the *de facto* ruler of Japan.

MacArthur had an impressive war record: low casualties and great advances with limited resources, but historians have found that many of his claims were exaggerated. He was a superb publicist and his optimistic statements did much to lift the morale of the American people. He was isolated and aloof, not fearful of criticizing his superiors, and determined above all to maintain his view that the Pacific Theater of Operations was the most important throughout the war.

## Macchi C.200

This Italian single-seat fighter was in service in 1940–45. Though the Macchi company, led by designer Castoldi, had built speedy seaplanes to try to win the Schneider Trophy races, their first monoplane fighter was of rather poor design. Powered by a Fiat A74 radial of only 840hp (the same as was used in the Fiat C.R.42), it could only just exceed 300mph, despite the fact it was a small and light machine carrying only two 12.7mm machine guns. The prototype flew in December 1937, and proved quite maneuverable. The first production batches had enclosed cockpits and a retractable tailwheel, but the Italian pilots, like the Japanese, cared little for performance but wanted good vision and reliability, and so most C.200s had an open cockpit and fixed tailwheel. Called *Saetta* (Lightning), the C.200 was totally outclassed by all Allied fighters, even the Curtiss P–40, and though it saw more combat than any other Italian aircraft it was usually routed. One exception was the Italian Corps that went to the Russian front, where Saettas claimed 88 victories with a loss of only 15. Later batches had wings strengthened for carrying two 352lb bombs, and altogether about 1000 were built.

## Macchi C.202 and 205

This Italian single-seat fighter was in service in 1941–45. To make up for the lack of high-power Italian engines, Daimler-Benz had to supply

The Macchi C.202 Folgore.

liquid-cooled engines from Germany, and these were substituted for the small radials in most of the Italian fighters. One of the first and best conversions was the Macchi C.202 Folgore (Thunderbolt), flown in 1940 and by 1941 was being mass-produced by a team of builders. Though most of the airframe was very similar to the C.200, it had a 1200hp DB 601A engine, and as well as the two fuselage guns, added a pair of light machine guns in the wings. Speed was improved to 369mph, and altogether about 1500 were built. But though it was used on many fronts, the C.202 was still a poor fighter, being less maneuverable than the Saetta and easy meat for most Allied fighters. Most were used as fighter-bombers, or to try to intercept bombers, and though one batch had a pair of hard-hitting German MG 151 cannon slung under the wings the C.202 accomplished little.

## Macchi C.205V Veltro

As good as anything operated by the Allied air forces, the prototype of this single-seat fighter was simply a C.202 airframe fitted with a 1475hp Daimler-Benz DB 605A engine. It flew for the first time on 19 April 1942 and soon proved itself highly maneuverable, with superb handling qualities. Armament consisted of two 12.7mm machine guns and two 7.7mm guns which were soon replaced by a pair of 20mm cannon. Small bombs could also be carried. The Veltro made its first combat sortie only one month before the Italian surrender. After that a few served with the Allies; others were used by the Aviazione della RSI, which continued to fly alongside the Luftwaffe in Northern Italy and maintained production of the Veltro until 262 had been completed.

The Macchi C.205 Veltro.

## Madsen Machine Gun

This light machine gun was invented by Jens Teodor Schouboe, a Dane, and named after the then Danish Minister of War who was largely responsible for the gun's adoption. It was a remarkable weapon and one of the first light machine guns ever to be produced; it remained in military service with various nations for upwards of fifty years without major modification, yet it was never adopted officially by any major power. It did have one of the most complicated mechanisms ever seen in a machine gun.

Introduced in about 1904, the Madsen gun used recoil to operate its mechanism, and the method of breech closure was a hinged breech-block similar to that used on the Peabody or Martini rifle. Since the block moved vertically, it was necessary to provide completely separate mechanisms to extract the fired case and feed the fresh cartridge into the breech. It was contemplated for British Army use, and a few were fitted to some of the first tanks in 1916–17, but it soon acquired a bad reputation for jamming which was due entirely to the British rimmed .303 cartridge; with rimless ammunition it never gave trouble. Large numbers of Madsen guns were acquired by the German Army in 1940 when it took weapons from the Danish, Norwegian and Polish armies; many of these were modified to accept the standard German ammunition belt instead of feeding from the usual top-mounted box magazine—a modification which made the mechanism even more complicated.

## Magic
see Friedman, Colonel William

## Maginot Line

Appalled by the cost in lives of the attempts to break the German trench line in France between 1915 and 1918 and convinced of the apparent impregnability of their well-sited and constructed static defenses, the French people, government and army were at one in believing throughout the 1920s that France's eastern border must be fortified permanently against a new German invasion. Differences of opinion occurred over details and these were resolved in 1930 when the National Assembly voted overwhelmingly to provide 3000 million francs ($100 million at current exchange rates) for a scheme

Pillbox of the Maginot Line after its capture by the Germans in 1940.

proposed by the then Minister of War, André Maginot. When completed in 1935 at a cost of 7000 million francs, the program had filled the gap between Switzerland and southern Belgium with a line of interdependent 'fortified regions,' organized in three belts. On the frontier itself stood a line of pill-boxes, entanglements and anti-tank obstacles. Behind that, lay a line of larger concrete casemates and anti-tank ditches. Five miles behind that again stood the forts, three to five miles apart. It was these underground battleships with their electric railways, sun-lamp rooms and disappearing gun turrets, the largest housing 1200 men, which captured the imagination of the world press and have established the historical myth of the line as both military wonder of the world and white elephant. The facts are simple: the wall was not a white elephant since, though penetrated and encircled in 1940, not one of the line's major fortresses fell to attack; it was not a world wonder for the reason that it could be encircled. The planners, in consideration of cost and in deference to Belgian sensibilities, curtailed its construction at the tip of the Ardennes, precisely where the Germans chose to align the axis of their effort in May 1940.

**Magnetic Mine**

On 16 September 1939 the SS *City of Paris* was damaged by a mysterious explosion which did not penetrate her hull. This incident confirmed what the British Admiralty had suspected a week after the outbreak of war, that the Germans were laying a new type of influence mine, activated by the ship's own magnetism. Immediate countermeasures were put in hand (Degaussing) but what was needed was precise knowledge of the working of the German mine. This was obtained on 23 November when an air-laid mine was recovered from mudflats in the Thames Estuary off Shoeburyness.

Although the German Navy boasted of its 'secret weapon' in fact the British had laid magnetic mines of their own as far back as 1918 and had pursued the development through the interwar years. In July 1939 the first anti-magnetic sweep was tested, and production of both anti-ship and anti-submarine magnetic mines was ready to start. However, this was held up until the Germans showed their hand. When the mine-experts at HMS *Vernon* examined the Shoeburyness mine they were gratified to find that its firing mechanism was considerably cruder than their own, and easier to deactivate.

The German magnetic mine was used prematurely, as only 1500 mines had been made in September 1939. Only 470 were laid in the first three months, but even these caused considerable dislocation of coastal traffic. Magnetic mines continued to be used throughout the war, but their main disadvantage was their limited range of influence; they could only be used in relatively shallow waters.

**Magnetron**
see Radar

**Maisky, Ivan, 1884–1975**

Maisky was the Soviet Ambassador to London until his recall in 1943 when he was made Deputy Commissar for Foreign Affairs. In June 1941 he gave Stalin a warning that the Allies had information about Germany's planned invasion of Russia, but Stalin did not respond. During 1941 and 1942 Maisky pestered Churchill about the opening of a 2nd Front in Europe. Maisky negotiated with the Czech and Polish governments in exile and also met Harry Hopkins. He persuaded Hopkins to travel to Moscow and have talks with Stalin. These talks resulted in a Lend-Lease agreement between USSR and USA. After his recall, Maisky fell from prominence.

**Makin**
see Gilbert Islands

**Malan, Group Captain Adolph, 1910–1963**

A South African-born fighter pilot, Malan, with 35 victories, was the third highest-scoring RAF ace during World War II. His *Ten Rules for Air Fighting* were distributed for general instruction throughout the RAF.

**Malayan Campaign, 1941–42**

In 1941 the Japanese conquered Malaya and took Singapore, Britain's chief naval base in the Far East, in a mere 54 days.

The British had built formidable defenses at Singapore, but had not safeguarded themselves against land attacks via the Malay peninsula.

The British had 88,000 troops under General Percival in Malaya: 17,000 Malayans, 37,000 Indians, 15,000 Australians and 19,000 British. These men were poorly equipped and had been trained to fight along the roads and to avoid jungles and swamps. The British had trained for Operation Matador, which was designed to forestall land attacks by a pre-emptive invasion of Siam and the seizure of Singora. The Cabinet hesitated too long before sanctioning this plan as it did not wish to offend the USA by invading neutral Siam; thus, the Japanese had landed at Singora before the plan could be achieved.

The Japanese invasion force was surprisingly small: not more than 35,000 men, supported by 211 tanks (the British had none) and 560 aircraft (the British only had 158). The Japanese were led by Lieutenant General Yamashita and contrary to popular belief they were not jungle-trained nor did they have Malay specialists to help them negotiate the difficult terrain. They had a small budget and had to improvise (for example, many used bicycles). The Japanese's main advantage was their superiority in the air. Although the RAF had built many airfields, they had few aircraft; yet, the army had to prevent the airfields from falling into the hands of the Japanese. All too often the British fell back leaving airfields intact.

On the night of 7 December 1941 the Japanese landed a regiment of the Eighteenth Division at Kota Bharu to seize the airfields. However this was merely a diversionary attack. The British put Operation Matador into action but it was too late, and they had to fall back to a second choice position at Jitra. The Japanese landed at Singora and Patani and by 10 December the Fifth Division was on the west coast of the peninsula. On the east coast the British began to withdraw leaving the airfield at Kota Bharu intact. On 10 December the battleships *Prince of Wales* and *Repulse* were sunk off the Malay coast and the Japanese Navy had complete control of the seas.

On 11 December the British made a stand along the road at Jitra, but the Japanese tanks and artillery destroyed the line and Major General Murray-Lyon decided on a general withdrawal. Rumors of total disaster began to spread and the withdrawal was so disorganized that some brigades lost three-quarters of their men in the jungle. Lieutenant General Heath then hoped that his forces could make a stand

Japanese soldiers fight their way down a street in Kuala Lumpur.

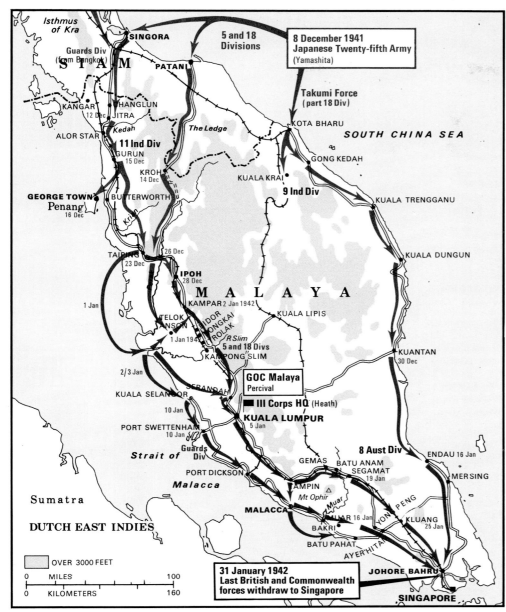

**Malinovsky, Marshal Rodion Y, 1898–1967**

Malinovsky led the Russian armies into Hungary and Czechoslovakia. At the outbreak of the war he was in Odessa and in December 1941 he was made Commander of the Southern Front. In December 1942 he defeated Manstein's attempt to free Paulus's army in Stalingrad. In 1943–44 he was Commander of the Southwest Front and then the 3rd Ukrainian Front which liberated the Donbass and Western Ukraine. In 1944 he was made Marshal. Also in that year he was Commander of the 2nd Ukrainian Front which invaded Rumania where he captured 200,000 Germans. He continued to overrun Hungary and took Budapest in February 1945. In April he overran Slovakia. In August he led the Russian armies in Manchuria.

**Malta**

Malta's situation south of Sicily made it of vital strategic importance in any naval war in the Mediterranean, particularly a war between Italy and Great Britain. It lies across the short route between Italy and North Africa, and in 1940–42 this put it astride communications with the Italian North African colonies.

Although the British Army and Air Force chiefs had declared Malta to be indefensible prewar, the RN wisely ignored their advice and insisted that it should be at least a base for light forces and submarines. The fortunes of Malta fluctuated in 1941–42, much like the fortunes of the British Army in North Africa. Strenuous efforts were made to keep the island fed, but above all aircraft were needed for defense. Aircraft carriers, including the USS *Wasp* on two occasions, ferried Spitfires and Hurricanes to within flying range of Malta, and in August 1942 a tremendous convoy battle, Operation Pedestal, was fought to save the island from surrender.

The main problem was that Malta was under continuous aerial bombardment being so close to Sicily. In 1942 the only ships which could get in and out of Malta were the very fastest, such as the minelayers *Abdiel, Manxman* and *Welshman.* Submarines were specially modified to carry supplies such as cased gasoline and machine gun ammunition, and they submerged on the harbor bottom during daylight to avoid the incessant bombing.

The relief of Malta in 1942 coincided with a

on the Perak River but his troops could not hold against the superior tanks or withstand the batteries. A strong position at Kampar was outflanked when the Japanese used small craft captured at Penang for a seaborne, outflanking maneuver. On 23 December Lieutenant General Pownall arrived in Singapore to take over from Air Chief Marshal Brooke-Popham as Commander-in-Chief of land and air forces in the Far East. He decided that the British should make a stand on the Slim River. The British used road-blocks and minefields but without anti-tank guns could not prevent the Japanese from storming through their lines.

The Japanese also used an overgrown jungle track to bypass the road and took the Slim River Bridge by surprise on 8 January 1942, cutting off the 11th Indian Division. A few days later General Wavell arrived in Singapore to take up his appointment as Supreme Commander of ABDA. Wavell decided that the policy of gradual withdrawal should be abandoned, because of the heavy losses. He decided to bring forward the Australian 8th Division, under Major General Gordon Bennett, to help the 11th Indian Division hold a line on the Muar River. Central Malaya was evacuated and the Japanese entered Kuala Lumpur on 11 January. The advance guard of the Fifth Division attacked the defense lines on 15 January. The Fourth Guards Regiment contained the Australians on the Muar,

while one of its battalions landed behind enemy lines at Batu Pahat to block their escape.

The Fifth Guards Regiment crossed the Muar using British craft and routed the remaining troops, driving them back to Bakri. Wavell then ordered Percival to fight out the battle in Johore and to prepare for withdrawal to Singapore. Percival issued the order too late to save the 45th Brigade at Batu Pahat (25 January). By 30 January British forces were in the extreme south of the Malay peninsula and all forces withdrew to Singapore, having lost much heavy equipment.

**Malenkov, Georgiy M, 1902–**

During the war Malenkov was a member of the State Defense Committee (GOKO) and responsible for technical equipment of the army and air force. He was also the political commissar on several fronts: in August 1941 he was on the Leningrad Front and then on the Moscow Front. In August 1942 he was active on the Stalingrad and Don Fronts. From 1943 to 1945 he was Chairman of the Committee for the Restoration of the Economy in the regions freed from German occupation. At the end of the war he became Deputy Chairman of the Council of Ministers and took power briefly after the death of Stalin.

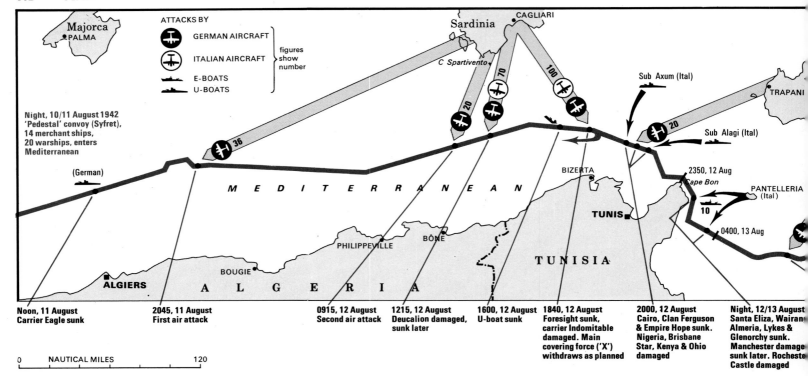

ATTACKS BY

GERMAN AIRCRAFT

ITALIAN AIRCRAFT    } figures show number

E-BOATS

U-BOATS

Night, 10/11 August 1942 'Pedestal' convoy (Syfret), 14 merchant ships, 20 warships, enters Mediterranean

**Noon, 11 August** Carrier Eagle sunk

**2045, 11 August** First air attack

**0915, 12 August** Second air attack

**1215, 12 August** Deucalion damaged, sunk later

**1600, 12 August** U-boat sunk

**1840, 12 August** Foresight sunk, carrier Indomitable damaged. Main covering force ('X') withdraws as planned

**2000, 12 August** Cairo, Clan Ferguson & Empire Hope sunk. Nigeria, Brisbane Star, Kenya & Ohio damaged

**Night, 12/13 August** Santa Eliza, Wairangi, Almeria, Lykes & Glenorchy sunk. Manchester damaged, sunk later. Rochester Castle damaged

0   NAUTICAL MILES   120

Operation Pedestal – the convoy lost nine merchantmen, one aircraft carrier, two cruisers and one destroyer.

radical improvement in the situation in North Africa after the Battle of El Alamein. As the Axis forces were squeezed between the 8th Army in the East and the US forces in Morocco, the hostile airfields were overrun. Malta became once more a forward base for powerful striking forces, and it served as an important base for the invasion of Italy in 1943. Had Malta fallen there is little doubt that the British would have lost all control of the Central Mediterranean, and this could well have led to defeat for their ground forces in Egypt and Libya, as the Germans and Italians would have been free to move reinforcements and supplies by sea.

### Manchester, Avro

This aircraft was the predecessor of the Lancaster with two 1760hp Rolls-Royce Vulture engines. About 200 were built and served with 11 squadrons of RAF Bomber Command. Unreliability of the engines led to the installation of four Merlins in the same basic design, to produce the Lancaster. Manchesters were withdrawn from service in June 1942.

### Manchuria
see China Incident, 1931–41

### Mandalay
see Meiktila and Mandalay, Battle for, 1945

### Manhattan District Project

In June 1940 President Roosevelt set up the National Defense Research Committee which had a sub-committee known as the Uranium Section to explore the possibilities of nuclear power. The original project was expanded and in September 1942 was called the Manhattan

Engineer District. Its principal laboratory was at Los Alamos where Robert Oppenheimer was in charge and it was at this laboratory that the first atomic bomb was designed and made using U235 for atomic reaction. The War Department had taken on responsibility for the project and appointed General Groves, a non-scientist, to oversee it. The whole project was extremely expensive and Congress voted it $2000 million over four years, without knowing the exact nature of the project. The atomic bomb was first tested at Alamogordo in New Mexico and on 6 August 1945 a bomb was dropped on Hiroshima in Japan.

### Mannerheim, Marshal Carl Gustav Emil Baron von, 1867–1951

An officer of the Tsar's army at the time when Finland formed part of the Russian Empire, Mannerheim returned home during the Bolshevik revolution to lead the White forces in a victorious but bloody civil war against the local Reds. Recalled in 1939 to the service of the state he had very largely founded, he conducted a brilliantly skillful resistance to the Russian invasion and helped to secure generous terms at the armistice. On Hitler's invasion of Russia in 1941, Finland resumed hostilities (the 'Continuation War') with the object of regaining the territory lost in 1940. When defeat loomed in 1944, Mannerheim, by then Head of State, again secured far better terms for an armistice from the Russians than might have been expected. A brilliant soldier and wise statesman, Mannerheim is Finland's principal national hero.

### Mannerheim Line
see Russo-Finnish War

### Mannlicher Rifles

Ferdinand Ritter von Mannlicher, is perhaps less well-known than Mauser, but as a designer of rifles and other firearms he was a good deal

more prolific. His rifles were adopted by many European nations as their standard service weapons and large numbers of them remained in first-line use until the end of World War II. His basic ideas were often taken as the starting point for variant designs, his name being added to give credit where it was due.

Mannlicher's principal rifle design was one of a straight-pull bolt action; this means that to open the bolt the handle is grasped and pulled straight to the rear without the need to lift it to rotate the bolt and unlock it. This action was achieved by placing the bolt handle not on the actual bolt but upon a sleeve surrounding the bolt; this sleeve contained helical ribs which mated into corresponding tracks cut into the bolt. Thus, pulling the bolt handle drew the sleeve back and the helical ribs forced the bolt to revolve and unlock, then to move backwards to extract the fired case. This straight-pull system was adopted by Austro-Hungary and Bulgaria in the 1880s and 1890s, and some of these weapons survived (notably with the Italian Army who had received them as reparations from Austria in 1919) until the end of World War II.

Far more practical was the Mannlicher turn-bolt system, more or less the same as any other bolt action in that it had to be turned and drawn back in two distinct moves. This was adopted by Rumania, Holland, Hungary and other countries and again many of them survived from the 1890s to take their place in the firing lines in World War II.

However the Mannlicher designs which were in major combat use during the 1939–45 period were all Mannlicher adaptations. The greatest number were the Mannlicher-Carcano rifles and carbines used by the Italian Army. These weapons were designed in 1890 under the auspices of an Italian Army Commission, and they adopted Mannlicher's clip-loaded magazine, allying it to a bolt action copied from the Belgian Army Mauser rifle with a safety mechanism invented by Salvatore Carcano, a technician at the Turin Arsenal. The rifle was in 6.5mm caliber, and used a box magazine into which six rounds were loaded in a special clip. The magazine contained a spring-loaded arm which forced the cartridges

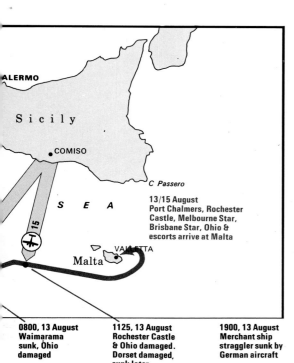

13/15 August
Port Chalmers, Rochester
Castle, Melbourne Star,
Brisbane Star, Ohio &
escorts arrive at Malta

| 0800, 13 August | 1125, 13 August | 1900, 13 August |
|---|---|---|
| Waimarama sunk, Ohio damaged | Rochester Castle & Ohio damaged. Dorset damaged, sunk later | Merchant ship straggler sunk by German aircraft |

up in the clip, and as the last cartridge was loaded into the chamber so the clip fell out of the magazine through a hole in the bottom plate. While this is an elegant engineering solution, it is slightly impractical in a combat rifle since the hole tends to scoop up dirt and mud, but in 1890 nobody thought about lying in the mud to shoot, so no objections were raised.

In addition to the rifle there were the usual carbine models produced for cavalry and specialist troops, which were no more than shortened versions of the rifle. The cavalry carbines are easily recognized because they have a folding bayonet permanently attached beneath the muzzle.

After the Ethiopian campaign in 1936 the Italian Army decided that the 6.5mm caliber was no longer sufficiently powerful, and they developed a 7.35mm cartridge. As a result a fresh design of rifle was produced, little more, in fact, than the older rifle enlarged in caliber. However the task of re-equipping the army had not begun when World War II descended upon them, and since there seemed little chance of carrying the change through the idea was dropped; most of the weapons built for 7.35mm were actually converted back again to the 6.5mm.

*Below:* 7.92mm Mannlicher rifle M1898/40.
*Bottom:* Greek 6.5mm Mannlicher rifle M1903.

The other major variant of Mannlicher's design was the Mannlicher-Schoenauer system, an alliance of the Mannlicher turnbolt with a rotary magazine developed by Otto Schoenauer, director of the Austrian Arms Factory at Steyr. This magazine was a spring-loaded spool device which could be loaded from the usual Mauser-type charger; although ingenious and compact, it shows no real advantages over the more conventional box type of magazine, though when rimmed cartridges are used it does tend to be more reliable and free of jams due to overriding rims. This rifle was offered to Austria in 1902, but they, having just completed expensive tooling-up for Mannlicher's straight-pull rifle, rejected it. It was then adopted by the Greek Army in 1903 and continued in use there until after World War II.

---

### Manstein, Field Marshal Erich von Lewinski, von, 1887–1973

Regarded by many as the greatest German field commander of the war, Manstein had been commissioned into Hindenburg's old regiment, the Third Foot Guards, and served with distinction as an infantry officer during World War I. He first attracted attention with his unorthodox proposal in 1940 to attack on a very narrow front in the Ardennes to sever the Anglo-French field army from its less mobile supports in the interior by a drive to the Channel coast. His plan was favored by Hitler, to whom Manstein had personally delivered it, and, despite the opposition of the Army High Command, to whom

Field Marshal Erich von Manstein.

Manstein was *persona non grata*, formed the basis of the 1940 strategy. Recovering from obloquy, he was appointed to command 11th Army in the capture of the Crimea in 1941 and subsequently in the advance into the Caucasus. But it was in 1943, however, that his great reputation was made. Having conceived and almost carried off the relief of Stalingrad in December 1942 (Operation Winter Storm), he achieved in February 1943 the most brilliant German counteroffensive of the Russian campaign, the recapture of Kharkov. He was then acting as Commander of Army Group Don to which he had been appointed in November 1942, and continued to direct it until March 1944, when he at last lost Hitler's favor for his ceaseless advocacy of 'fluid' tactics. That policy, to Hitler, meant surrendering ground without the guarantee that it could subsequently be recaptured. His fears might have been well-founded in the case of other commanders, but Manstein stood alone in possessing the skill to wage that dangerous form of warfare. His removal aided Russia rather than Germany.

---

### Manstein Plan, 1940

The German plan of attack in the west in 1940 is commonly known as the Manstein Plan, and though he was not the architect of its final form, his contribution to its design was so central that the appellation is just. The original plan, (*Fall Gelb* – Case Yellow) drawn up by Halder and his staff officers at Army Headquarters (OKH) in September – October 1939 and often, though misleadingly compared with the Schlieffen Plan of 1914, was designed to inflict a major defeat on the Franco-British Army in northern France and to reach the Channel coast. The main weight was to be allotted to Army Group B in the north and the axis of attack was to lie through neutral Belgium and the Dutch 'Maastricht Appendix'. It was a plan which satisfied no one, neither Hitler, who had requested OKH to prepare it, nor OKH itself; indeed that body opposed the whole project of an attack in the west which it thought militarily reckless. Least of all did it satisfy Manstein, then acting as Chief of Staff to Rundstedt's Army Group A, who believed that the operation was both more feasible than OKH thought and could be made a great deal more decisive. His 'variant' of the plan was to shift its weight from Army Group B in the north to Army Group A in the center and to direct the Axis attack through southern Belgium, with the object of separating the northern group of Franco-British Armies, attracted into Flanders by Army Group A's offensive, from the southern group. The ultimate objective again

would be the Channel coast and the piecemeal destruction of the divided enemy – 'defeat in detail'. Rundstedt communicated Manstein's plan to OKH, which, despite the accidental compromise of its *Fall Gelb*, suppressed it, partly because of Halder's dislike for its originator. It came to Hitler's ears only by chance in late November. He however had independently conceived the idea of shifting some of the weight southward, followed attentively when apprised by Manstein on 17 February of his scheme in detail, and signified his approval. On the following day Halder presented him with a scheme more drastic than that Manstein had outlined to him which gave the bulk of the armor to Rundstedt and proposed the driving of a 'Panzer Corridor' from Sedan to Abbéville on the French coast. It was this 'final OKH plan,' the product of OKH's acceptance of the superiority of Manstein's conception to their own, but refined by its own staff processes, to which the German Army attacked on 10 May.

**Mao Tse-tung, 1893–1976**

Mao Tse-tung was the Chairman of the Chinese Communist Party from 1931 until he died. In 1937 when war against the Japanese broke out in China, the Communists and the Kuomintang negotiated an alliance to fight the Japanese. This unsteady arrangement only lasted until 1940 and from then on Mao was concerned with fighting Chiang Kai-shek rather than the Japanese. He directed operations from his HQ in Yenan in the province of Shensi. In 1944 he negotiated with the US Ambassador Hurley to reach some sort of agreement with Chiang Kai-shek but it was clear that neither side was willing to compromise. When the war against Japan ended, civil war broke out.

**Maquis, the**

The Maquis was the best known resistance movement in Europe. Although it took more than a year to organize, by 1943 the Maquis had groups fighting in the Savoy, the Jura, Aveyron, Cantal and Corrèze. By 1944 the Maquis had 100,000 men working for them and had built up an intelligence network of 60 cells. They helped prepare the way for the Allied Invasion by sabotaging the French railroad system, factories and railway engines and received assistance in the form of equipment and training from the Special Operations Executive.

**Marco Polo Bridge**

see China Incident, 1931–41

**Marder**

This was the general name for a series of German self-propelled anti-tank guns. The series began in 1942 with Marder I, the 75mm PAK 40 anti-tank gun mounted in an armored barbette built on top of a captured French Lorraine armored tractor. At least 184 of these were built and used extensively in Russia. It was then followed by Marder II, a similar design using the chassis of the German PzKw II tank as a basis. The vehicle engine was moved to the rear of the chassis and the gun mounted in a fixed barbette above the driver's position. Over 1200 of these were built.

The next was Marder III, which used the ex-Czech LT38 tank as its basis. As before, the 75mm gun was mounted into a three-sided armored barbette and manned by a three-man crew. At least 418 of these were built but reports from Russia complained that the design was nose-heavy and tended to plough into snow and mud and become immobilized. As a result, the design was completely changed; the vehicle engine was moved forward to a midships position and the gun barbette was moved to the rear of the vehicle. Construction of this model began in mid-1943 and 799 were built.

Just to complicate matters there were other designs which carried the same name; a large number of Soviet 76.2mm field guns had been captured in the early days of the German invasion of Russia, so many that it was expedient for the Germans to refurbish them and re-issue them to their own troops. Numbers of these guns were fitted to the ex-Czech LT38 chassis in the cheapest and simplest way – the wheels and trail legs of the gun were removed and the remaining structure simply bolted to the top of the tank hull; an armored wall was then built around the gun. These were rushed to the Russian front in early 1942 as an interim measure until the 75mm Marders could be supplied. These vehicles were known as 'Marder II',

Marder II SdKfz 131 self-propelled 75mm on a PzKw II chassis.

though more precisely identified by adding (76mm PAK36(r)) after the name. Similarly a 76mm 'Marder III' was also produced, a similar rapid conversion based on the chassis and hull of the PzKw II tank. Few of these extempore Marder designs survived for long as they were high and presented an obvious target.

**Mareth Line**
see Tunisia, Campaign in, 1941

**Margarita**
see Balkans, Campaign in the, 1941

**Marianas**
see Saipan, Tinian, Guam and the Battle of the Philippine Sea

**Marine Corps**
See US Army

**Mariner, Martin PBM**

This US maritime patrol flying-boat was operational from 1940 to the early fifties. Of later design than the Catalina, the Mariner was judged superior in both performance and combat capability. It flew for the first time on 18 February 1939, with a 'flat' tailplane. The characteristic dihedral tail was introduced on production PBM–1s, which began to enter service in September 1940. Other changes were made on successive variants. Engine power increased from 1600hp to 2100hp with the final version, the PBM–5 changing from Wright R–2600s to Pratt & Whitney R–2800s. Sea search radar was added in a fairing above and behind the cockpit of the PBM–3Cs and 3Ds, and became standard for later versions. Postwar, 36 amphibious Mariners were produced as PBM–5As. A crew of nine was standard. Up to 2000lb of bombs or depth charges could be carried in the engine nacelles. The PBM–3S, optimized for long-range anti-submarine warfare in 1944, had 1700hp engines, and extra fuel in place of some armor-plate and the power-operated turrets.

Marlin machine gun.

## Market Garden
see Arnhem

## Marlin Machine Gun

This American aircraft machine gun was developed by the Marlin-Rockwell Company of New Haven USA in 1918 who was given a contract to produce the Colt M1895 machine gun which the company redesigned to make it more suited to aircraft use. The Colt design, known as the 'Potato-Digger' had a hinged arm which, driven by gas tapped from the barrel, swung downwards to operate the linkage to actuate the breech mechanism. This swinging arm was incompatible with aircraft installation and the Marlin engineers replaced it with the more usual sort of gas piston beneath the barrel. In this form the gun was adopted as the standard aircraft and tank machine gun for US forces in 1918, but with the end of the war production was cut back, though a total of 38,000 aircraft and 1470 tank guns were made.

In 1940–41, when Britain was desperately short of machine guns, several thousand of these were taken from store in the USA and shipped to Britain, where they were principally used for arming merchant ships against air attack and for airfield defense, in which roles they played an important, if inconspicuous, role.

## Marseille, Hauptmann Hans-Joachim, 1920–1942

This German airman was the Luftwaffe's most successful pilot against the Western Allies during World War II claiming 158 victories. Marseille served with Lehrgeschwader 2 and 4./JG 52 as an NCO/officer candidate during the final stages of the Battle of Britain and in April 1941 was posted to I Gruppe Jagdgeschwader 27 based in Libya. This was to be the scene of his greatest victories. At the time of his death in September 1942, although still only 22 years old, he had gained the Knights Cross with Oak Leaves, Swords and Diamonds, the highest award in the German system of honors.

## Marshall, General George Catlett, 1880–1959

A graduate of the private Virginia Military Institute, Marshall had fought in World War I and acted as aide to Pershing in the early years of peace. He subsequently made a reputation as one of the most thoughtful, efficient and energetic officers in the US Army and the possessor of a frightening degree of self-containment. He was appointed Chief of Staff in 1939 and held the post to the end of the war, maintaining from the first complete personal ascendancy over the officers of his own army, establishing warm working relationships with those of the Allies and winning the confidence of

all in government at Washington, from the President downward. His concrete achievements were many: he put the army on a war footing and supervised its enlargement, re-equipment and retraining; he instituted unified commands between the Allies; he restructured his own forces, dividing the army into three components, the ground forces, air forces and service forces. As the President's chief strategic adviser (he acted also as chairman of the Joint Chiefs of Staff) he was an ardent advocate not only of carrying the war into western Europe at the earliest possible moment which did not please the British, but also of the 'Germany First' priority which did. He wished, and was expected, to take up the command of the Allied Expeditionary Force for the invasion of Europe but was ultimately retained in Washington by Roosevelt who valued his services too much to lose them. After the war Marshall became Secretary of State to Truman and instituted the imaginative Marshall Plan which rebuilt the war-ruined economies of Western and part of Eastern Europe.

## Marshall Islands, 1944

The Marshall Islands consisted of hundreds of coral atolls and islets scattered over some 400,000 square miles of sea. Admiral Nimitz planned to bypass all the smaller islands and leap to the Kwajalein atoll. Vice-Admiral Spruance and Major General Holland Smith, both of whom had taken part in the costly conquest of the Gilberts, thought this was too daring.

The islands were not well defended because in September 1943 Japan's Imperial GHQ had decided that the Marshalls should be outposts on a new line of defense, stretching from the Kurile Islands through the Carolines to Timor, and therefore they could only be held for another six months. During December 1943 and January 1944 the Marshalls were subjected to bombardments by planes based in the Gilberts. The US assault troops were divided in two as in the Gilbert Campaign; one half was to attack the islets off Kwajalein, Roi and Namur, the other was to attack the island itself from the south. There were 54,000 assault troops backed up by four carrier groups, including Vice-Admiral Mitscher's fast carrier group. On 31 January the Marines took Majuro, which provided a good anchorage for US ships to bombard Kwajalein on the next day. They fired 36,000 shells and after this only 2200 combat-trained Japanese were fit to fight the Marines. The attack on Kwajalein took the Imperial GHQ completely by surprise and although the forces on the island resisted fiercely, launching counterattacks without artillery support, within a week the atoll had fallen, for the loss of 373 men.

On 17 and 18 February Spruance's 5th Fleet struck at Truk and although they did not catch Koga's heavy ships they sank two cruisers, four destroyers and over 130,000 tons of merchant shipping. This raid was countered by land-based aircraft attacks on the US Fleet, but they came to

nothing and the Japanese withdrew all their aircraft to the Bismarck Islands. On 18 February, under cover of these raids, 8000 Marines landed at Eniwetok and took the island in four days. They lost 339 men to the Japanese 2677 killed.

## *Maryland*

This battleship (BB.46) was the name-ship of a class of four authorized in 1916. They were modeled on the British *Queen Elizabeth* Class having eight 16in guns in twin turrets. Only three were completed as the fourth member, the *Washington* (BB.47), was canceled to comply with the Washington Treaty. As they were the newest ships of the battle fleet (until the completion of the *North Carolina* Class) they had not been modernized like the older ships, apart from receiving more AA guns in 1941.

The *Colorado* was being overhauled at Bremerton Navy Yard, Washington on 7 December 1941 but her sisters *Maryland* and *West Virginia* were at Pearl Harbor when the Japanese carriers struck. The *Maryland* was slightly damaged by two bomb-hits and served throughout the war with only minor alterations. Her 'cage' mainmast was cut down in 1943, and in 1945 her obsolete five-inch casemate guns were replaced by twin five-inch/38 cal. mountings. She carried out numerous bombardments, from Tarawa onwards and she took part in the Battle of Surigao Strait, the last action between battleships. She was struck twice and badly damaged by kamikazes, once at Leyte and again at Okinawa.

## Maryland, Martin 167

The Maryland light bomber and reconnaissance aircraft was another of the combat types ordered originally by France and adopted by the British services in June 1940. About 300 were acquired by the RAF, each with two 1200hp Pratt & Whitney Twin Wasp engines, bomb load of 2000lb, and armament of six machine guns. They operated mainly on reconnaissance missions from Malta and bombing sorties in North Africa. Best remembered is their photography of Taranto before and after the famous raid by FAA Swordfish on 11 November 1940.

## Maschinen Pistole

This is a German term for submachine gun. The Germans had pioneered the machine pistol with their introduction of the Schmeisser-designed Bergmann MP18 in 1918, but the terms of the Versailles Treaty denied the Army any of these weapons in postwar years. Numerous German manufacturers, however, continued to design and manufacture machine pistols for export sale and for police use. Small numbers of these weapons found their way into the German Army in the early 1930s, but it was not until the Spanish Civil War demonstrated the utility of the submachine gun in the hands of poorly-trained troops that the Germans (as well as other nations) began to take the weapon seriously. In 1937 the German Army approached the Ermawerke company, who held a number of important patents in this field and had a sizeable export business, requesting a submachine gun suitable for mass production. The resulting weapon, adopted as standard as the Maschinen Pistole 38, almost became the trade-mark of the German soldier. Known erroneously as the 'Schmeisser', it was the first submachine gun to use a folding shoulder stock, and to be almost entirely constructed of metal, abandoning the traditional wooden stock for the first time. It was an excellent weapon, but ill-suited to quantity production and it was redesigned in 1939 to utilize more steel stampings, pressed metal components and welded assemblies, and entered service in the following year as the MP40; the two are almost indistinguishable externally. Over a million and a quarter of these weapons were produced during the war.

In addition to the MP38 and MP40 there were several other designs adopted by the Germans in an effort to meet the demands of their expanding forces. The Waffen SS adopted the Bergmann MP34, a wooden stocked model resembling the original Bergmann MP18, while large numbers of the Austrian Steyr MP34(ö)s were also used, Perhaps the most remarkable German machine pistol development was that of the MP 'Potsdam' an identical copy of the British Sten gun, even down to the proof and inspector's marks, which was made by Mauserwerke in great secrecy in late 1944. These were intended for use by German guerrilla groups in Allied-occupied territory, but since these groups were never formed, the gun was never used in its intended role. It is believed that 25–30 thousand were made, but few have been preserved, probably because the imitation was so good that few people recognized them for what they were.

## Matador

see Malayan Campaign, 1941–42

## Matapan, Battle of Cape, 1941

Following the success of the air attack on Taranto, the British Mediterranean Fleet took full advantage of the Italians' weakness to reinforce their troops in Greece. The German naval liaison staff in Rome had persuaded *Supermarina* that the British had only one battleship fit to go to sea, and that the time was ripe for a sortie by the fast battleship *Vittorio Veneto*. But Admiral Cunningham had three battleships, as well as the new fleet carrier *Formidable*, and he used them in determined fashion to bring the Italians to action.

The action opened with a skirmish between the British cruisers and the Italian Fleet, some 80 miles ahead of the British main fleet. A torpedo-strike damaged the *Vittorio Veneto* at about 1500 hours in the afternoon of 28 March 1941, and although Cunningham had little hope of catching the battleship he took his heavy ships in pursuit. The news that a heavy cruiser, the *Pola*, had also been hit by a torpedo made it certain that other Italian ships would be in the vicinity, and in fact two of her sisters, the *Fiume* and *Zara* had been ordered to turn back to look after her. Confident in his ships' ability to fight a night-action, Cunningham accepted the risk of air-attack, and continued to steam westwards. At about midnight two of the cruisers were shat-

Italian guns blaze in the fateful battle of Cape Matapan which sank Mussolini's hopes for naval supremacy in the Mediterranean.

tered by 15in gunfire at a range of less than 4000 yards, while British destroyers found the damaged *Pola* and sent her to the bottom.

Matapan was not a fleet action, but coming so soon after Taranto, it showed the Italians that the British were prepared to risk anything to keep control of the Central Mediterranean. The Italian Fleet was unable to prevent the evacuation of British troops from Greece and Crete, even when the Luftwaffe inflicted heavy losses on the Royal Navy. Even when 'human torpedoes' put the battleships *Queen Elizabeth* and *Valiant* out of action in December 1941 the high command remained irresolute, and could not take advantage of the situation.

## Matilda Tank

British 'Infantry Tank Mark I' was christened 'Matilda' by General Elles, Master General of the Ordnance, because of its resemblance (due to a spindly suspension and waddling progress) to 'Matilda the Duck', a contemporary cartoon character. The design was initiated in 1934 after

Mark II tank – Matilda.

a demand by Elles for a heavily-armored tank of low speed capable of accompanying the infantry at a walking pace, virtually a reversion to World War I ideas on tanks. Since finance was short at the time, the tank was designed down to a price rather than up to a specification, and the result was an 11 tonner with a crew of two, armor 65mm thick, and armed with a single machine gun. Production began in 1936 and 139 were produced. It was soon seen that this vehicle was quite inadequate for its role, and in fact it was withdrawn from service shortly after Dunkirk, being used solely for driver training thereafter. In 1937 a new design was begun, the Matilda 2, which appeared in 1940. This bore little resemblance to Matilda 1, being based largely on an earlier experimental design, the A7. It was relatively small (only 18.5ft long) but extremely well armored – up to 78mm thickness – and weighed 26.5 tons. It carried a crew of four, was armed with the 2pr gun, and propelled by twin diesel engines to give it a speed of 15mph. A total of 2987 Matilda 2 tanks were built before production stopped in 1943.

At the time of its inception it was probably among the world's best tanks; in the hands of the 4th and 7th Royal Tank Regiments it gave the German Panzers their first setback at Arras, in 1940, and it dominated the Western Desert until the arrival of the Afrika Korps with their heavier anti-tank weapons. Only the German

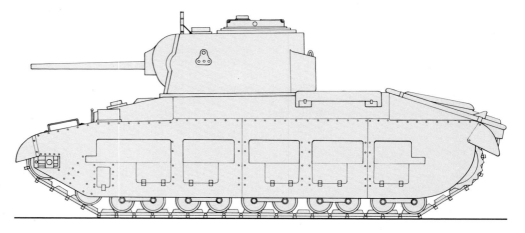

88mm gun had any chance of success against the Matilda, since its armor was far heavier than any other tank in service at that time. Unfortunately it demonstrated the basic defect in British tank design of the era; while heavily protected it was insufficiently mobile and fatally under-gunned.

## Matsuoka, Yosuke, 1880–1946

Matsuoka was the most westernized of Japanese politicians. Born to a poor samurai family, he went to Portland, Oregon in 1893 at the age of 13 with a cousin. Here he was brought up by a Methodist family, attended High School and took a degree in law from the University of Oregon in 1900, after which he returned to Japan.

A close friend of Konoye, Matsuoka divided his time between important positions in the South Manchurian Railway (including the President 1935–39) and foreign affairs. From 1932 to 1933 he headed the Japanese delegation to the League of Nations. He dramatically stormed out of the League when Japan was condemned for the invasion of Manchuria. Matsuoka was Foreign Minister from 1940 until 1941 when the entire Cabinet resigned to get rid of him (16 July). A man of many and confusing visions, he was fanatically expansionist, seeing Japan's growth (in China and the South) as a moral crusade as much as an Imperial conquest. He coined the phrase 'Greater East Asia Co-Prosperity Sphere' to describe this mission. Like Konoye he desired a totalitarian regime on the German lines and worked to ensure that Japan would get a share of the spoils when the Western democracies inevitably fell to the Axis. In pursuance of these ends, Matsuoka negotiated the Tripartite Pact with the Axis (23 September 1940) and negotiated with Molotov for Soviet neutrality (13 April 1941) in order to attack the US. After the war he was tried and executed on charges of conspiracy to rule the world.

## Mauser Arms

The Mauser company began its rise to prominence in 1871 when the German Army adopted a Mauser rifle. With this official recommendation, Mauser were soon selling rifles across the world, improvements coming rapidly with a succession of new models, culminating in the 'Gewehr 98' or Rifle of 1898 which became the German Army's standard bolt-action magazine rifle and remained so until the end of World War II. The superiority of the Mauser rifle was due to two principal features: firstly the bolt action was probably the strongest and safest such mechanism ever invented; and secondly the rifles (except in the closing months of World War II) were invariably made of the best possible materials with the best possible workmanship. Although primarily designed as a military weapon, the action was so reliable and strong that it was adopted by gunmakers throughout the world as a basis for sporting rifles, many of which were to fire cartridges far more powerful than the regulation 7.92mm × 57 German service round.

The strength of the Mauser bolt action relied upon three locking lugs, two at the front of the bolt, locking into recesses in the side of the chamber, and one at the rear, locking in front of a lug in the receiver. The price paid for this was a somewhat awkward action of the bolt since the handle extended straight out to the side and had to be lifted, rotating the bolt through 90°, before the opening stroke could begin. This was a more unwieldy action necessitating the movement of the whole of the firer's arm, than the theoretically less strong action of the Lee-Enfield rifle in which the opening of the bolt began as the rotation started, so that the firer could complete the bolt action using only his wrist. For this reason the Mauser and its derivatives could never attain the speed or rate of fire that the Lee Enfield could, an important point in combat shooting.

The original Gewehr 98 was a 'long rifle' in the current idiom, 49.4in long with a 29.15in barrel; it was to be partnered by a 'carbine' version, a short weapon with a 17in barrel for use by artillery, cavalry and other troops whose primary function in the battle was not musketry. But in 1903 the British and Americans produced their 'short rifles', weapons which were a halfway stage between the long rifle and the carbine, so that one weapon sufficed all troops. The idea was adopted in Germany and in 1908 the 'Karabiner Modell 98' was issued, 43.3in long and with a 23.6in barrel. This gradually replaced the long Gew 98 as the general service weapon of the entire German Army, though numbers of Gew 98 rifles continued to be used right through until 1945. The Kar 98 was gradually refined until it became the Kar 98k, with the same dimensions as the 1908 model, and this was the Wehrmacht's standard weapon throughout World War II. It had a five shot magazine and fired the 7.92mm bullet at 2450ft/sec.

In the pistol field, Mauser were rather less successful; a revolver developed in 1878 was not adopted by the Army, and the famous 'Mauser Military' automatic pistol, known properly as the 'C/96' and less respectfully as the 'Broomhandle Mauser' from the peculiar shape of its butt, also failed to gain official acceptance. Nevertheless it became a popular weapon, again largely due to its strength, power and reliability, and few continental army officers considered themselves properly attired for war without a Mauser pistol hanging from their belt.

The Military Model pistol is, next to the Luger, probably the most easily recognized pistol ever made, with its slender butt, box magazine in front of the trigger, long tapering barrel and prominent hammer. Until the 1970s it was the most powerful pistol ever to go into serious production, firing a 7.63mm bullet at about 1425ft/sec. It was provided with a wooden holster which could be slipped to the butt to form a shoulder-stock, turning the pistol into a short carbine; for this function the sight was grad-uated to 1000 meters, though the prospect of hitting anything at that range was slender.

Military acceptance finally came for the Mauser during World War I, when a large number were re-barreled to fire the standard 9mm service cartridge and issued to the German Army; these pistols are readily identified by having the figure '9' carved into the butt grips and stained red. After 1918 the Luger remained the standard pistol and the Mauser went out of service use, but it was to return in the 1930s in a new guise. During the late 1920s many Spanish gunmakers had prospered by producing copies of the Mauser, taking advantage of the depressed trade in Germany to undersell the original weapons, and one of the novelties produced in Spain was a Mauser copy which featured full automatic fire, turning the pistol into an inferior sort of submachine gun. In order to compete, Mauser produced a similar but better engineered weapon, calling it the 'Schnellfeuerpistole' and a number of these were adopted by the German Army as a form of lightweight submachine gun.

In the machine gun field Mauser were late starters, but they made up for this by producing two of the best machine gun designs ever seen, one of which is still in use today and which has had great influence on other designs which have appeared since. When the German Army began to re-equip in the early 1930s it was looking for a new machine gun and purchased a handful of Solothurn MG-30 guns from a Swiss company. This was quite a good weapon, with some unusual features, but it was not quite what the Army wanted and the gun was passed across to Mauser with the request that they improve it. The result, called the MG-34, bore little resemblance to the MG-30 but was a brilliant design in its own right. Recoil-operated, it had a quick-change barrel and could be fed either by a belt or by a double-drum magazine. It was laid out in the 'straight-line' configuration in which the line of the butt was a prolongation of the barrel, so that the barrel did not tend to rise in the air when the gun was fired, a feature which contributed to the gun's accuracy.

The MG-34 had one defect – it was too good. It demanded skilled and expensive machining for its manufacture and once the war was underway five factories could not keep pace with the demand. Mauser therefore looked again at the design and made some radical changes, calling in an expert on metal stamping and presswork to advise them on adapting the design to mass production. The result was the MG-42, a greatly improved gun which was easier to make, more reliable in action, and had a rate of fire of 1200

Mauser pistol Model 1932 as produced for the Chinese Nationalist Army.

rounds a minute. Such a high rate of fire soon overheated the barrel, and a quick-change mechanism was fitted which allowed the gunner to put in a new barrel in no more than five or six seconds. By the end of the war over 750,000 MG-42s had been made and it was adopted as standard in postwar years by the French Army and by many smaller nations. It was then revived by the new Bundeswehr in 1957, since, in their opinion, there was still no other comparable machine gun in the world though it is no longer made by Mauser.

In addition to these weapons, Mauser produced several models of machine gun for the Luftwaffe, small-caliber pistols for staff officers and Luftwaffe personnel, and 20mm cannon for both aircraft and anti-aircraft applications.

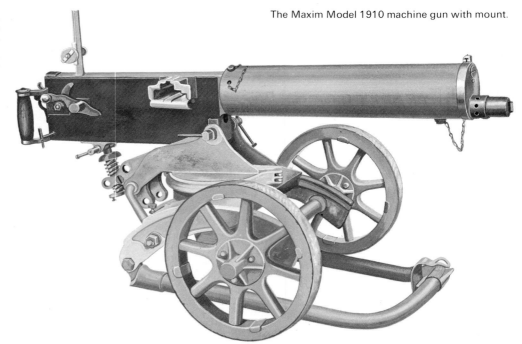

The Maxim Model 1910 machine gun with mount.

## 'Mavis'
see Kawanishi H6K

## Maxim Gun

The Maxim gun was a water-cooled, belt-fed heavy machine gun invented by Hiram Maxim in 1884. It was subsequently widely adopted, the British Army being the first to use it in service in 1888. The gun was recoil-operated, using a toggle mechanism which was extremely reliable and capable of sustained working with the heaviest cartridges. By 1939 most countries had discarded the Maxim in favor of more modern weapons, though Germany retained a number (under the terminology 'MG 08') for training purposes. The only country to use the Maxim during World War II was Russia, who had large numbers in service as their Model 1910. It was gradually superseded towards the end of the war, by the SG–43 Goryunov machine gun, but numbers of M1910 guns are still to be seen in several Asian countries and they are believed to be still held as reserve weapons in numerous Eastern Bloc countries.

The Soviet version of the Maxim differed slightly from others; the principal visual difference was the addition of a large water filler cap on the water jacket, but there were some differences in material which resulted in the Soviet gun weighing 52.5lbs, much heavier than any other Maxim. The M1910 was usually found on the 'Sokolov' mount, a peculiar tripod-cum-two wheeled cart which allowed the gun team to pull the weapon behind them and then place it in action fairly rapidly. Some were fitted with armor shields, though these (on account of their weight and limited protection) were not popular. In winter the wheels of the Sokolov mount could be replaced with sled runners.

*Above:* Red Army troops try out a Maxim gun in 1939 left over from the Tsarist Army.
*Left:* Russian Maxim Model 1910 on Sokolov mounting.

## McCain, Vice-Admiral John S, 1884–1945

McCain was one of the Task Force commanders at Leyte Gulf. He had built up his reputation as an air force commander when he had built an airstrip at Espiritu Santo in 1942. During the Guadalcanal operation McCain was the commander of all land-based aircraft in the South Pacific. Guadalcanal was out of the range of his fighters and bombers but his aircraft carried out reconnaissance missions. At Leyte Gulf McCain was Commander of Group 1 of Task

Force 38. He missed the main action because Admiral Halsey had sent him to Ulithi to refuel but his aircraft were sent in pursuit of Vice-Admiral Kurita's force. After Leyte Gulf McCain took over from Vice-Admiral Mitscher as commander of the fast carrier group 58 in Admiral Spruance's 5th Fleet. He witnessed the Japanese formal surrender on the USS *Missouri* in September 1945.

## McCreery, General Sir Richard, 1898–1967

Chief of Staff to Alexander in the Western Desert in 1942, it was McCreery who suggested to Montgomery the outline of the plan for the final stage of the Battle of Alamein. He commanded 10th Corps in the Salerno landing and succeeded Leese in command of the 8th Army in Italy in November 1944.

## Meiktila and Mandalay, Battle for Burma, 1945

In mid-October 1944 the monsoon stopped and Allied forces in Burma could resume their advance on the Central Front. General Stopford's 33rd Corps advanced down the Kabaw Valley road to take Kalemyo (14 November) and Kalewa. The 4th Corps could now advance down to the Irrawaddy at Pakokku. As the Corps advanced, British engineers built an all-weather road from Tamu to Kalewa.

General Kimura, the new Commander of Japanese forces in Burma had orders to hold the Yenangyaung oilfields and the rice-producing area in the Irrawaddy delta, so he planned to hold a line along the Irrawaddy from Lashio to Mandalay (covered by General Honda's Thirty-third Army), from Mandalay to Pakokku (covered by General Katamura's Fifteenth Army) and Yenangyaung southwards (covered by General Sakurai's Twenty-eighth Army). His troops were under strength and probably amounted to 21,000 but he hoped to have the advantage of fighting General Slim's army where its supply lines were over-extended. Slim had hoped to fight the decisive battle against the Japanese in the Yeu-Shwebo area but when he realized that they had withdrawn behind the Irrawaddy he conceived a new plan. This was for his main force to cross near Pakokku and seize Meiktila, thus strangling Japanese communications. At the same time his forces would establish bridgeheads along the Irrawaddy and give the impression that Mandalay was his main target. The operation was to be on such a wide front that the Japanese would not know where the British would strike.

Stopford's 33rd Corps reached Shwebo and after fierce fighting entered the city on 9 January 1945. On 12 January they reached Monywa. General Messervy's 4th Corps advanced due south from Kalemyo down the Myittha Valley to Gangaw and then across country to the Irrawaddy near Pakokku. On 14 February engineers began to construct a bridge in that area at Nyaungu, which was in between two Japanese commands and weakly defended. Then a striking force under General Cowan, the specially motorized 17th Division and a tank brigade, crossed the river and took Taungtha. There were severe casualties on both sides. By the end of February Cowan was ready to attack Meiktila and on 1 March he gave the order for a general attack. Although the Japanese had been taken by surprise they sent a division from Man-

British troops fighting street by street in Mandalay, 9 March 1945.

dalay and recaptured Taungtha, cutting off Cowan's force. However the British were supplied by air and kept up fierce fighting to hold their ground. By 4 March the Japanese garrison had been destroyed with a loss of 200 killed and although the Japanese counteroffensive was well under way, Cowan kept the initiative by a series of raids on Japanese positions.

In the north the 33rd Division was driving southeast to cut off the road from Maymyo to Mandalay. On 8 March they reached the northern outskirts of Mandalay and again took the Japanese by surprise. In Mandalay the Japanese HQ was situated in Fort Dufferin. This fort had such thick walls that it took several days for the British to breach the walls but by 20 March the British were able to occupy the fort, because the Japanese had withdrawn. The British force now had to clear up the Japanese counteroffensive at Meiktila so Stopford's 33rd Corps was divided in two. One force advanced via Kyaukse and Wundwin to threaten the Japanese at Meiktila and another force followed the Irrawaddy to capture the Yenangyaung oilfield. The Japanese were concentrating their attack at Nyaungu and Meiktila, but they were pushed back by the British. At Letse and Chauk a considerable Japanese attack was driven back and then Slim sent reinforcements to Cowan who was then able to launch a general offensive at Meiktila to regain control of the airfield, and finally the Japanese were pushed back.

British casualties in these battles totaled 2307 killed, 8107 wounded and almost as many sick. The Japanese lost one-third of their force and were driven back to the Shan Hills.

## Mekhlis, Political General Lev Z, 1889–1953

Mekhlis was Stalin's representative with Front Commanders and often interfered in their activities. He was sent to investigate the disaster in the Ukraine in 1941 and then he was sent to

Leningrad to speed up operations. He was sent to the Crimea where he had General Tolbukhin dismissed, but this did not prevent the fall of the Crimea (July 1942), and he was censured. He was then made a political member of Petrov's military council on the 2nd Belorussian Front, but Mekhlis had him removed, complaining about his flabbiness and illness. He was then sent to the 4th Ukrainian Front where he again succeeded in removing Petrov in April 1945.

## Meretskov, Marshal Kirill A, 1897–

Meretskov was Chief of General Staff at the outbreak of the war but was eclipsed by Zhukov during the war. During the Russo–Finnish War he commanded an army on the Vyborg flank and had conducted the breakthrough at the Mannerheim Line. From 1941 to 1945 he was the representative of GHQ on the Northwest Front. In the winter offensive of 1941 he commanded the Volkhov Front. He then served as Deputy Commander in Chief of the Western Offensive but ended the war on the Karelian Front in February 1944, where he was out of touch with Stalin and fell from favor. In August 1945 he was sent to the 1st Far Eastern Front.

## Merrill, Brigadier General Frank, 1903–1956

Merrill's Marauders were the US Special Force in North Burma in 1944. They were specially trained and used the same tactics as Wingate's Chindits.

Merrill was in Rangoon at the time of Pearl Harbor and stayed on to become General Stilwell's right hand man during the retreat from Burma. On 25 May 1942 Merrill was made Lieutenant Colonel. At this point he decided the only way to fight the Japanese was to train men in jungle fighting and use them behind Japanese lines. In February 1944 he set out with his Marauders to cut off the Japanese rear at Maingkwan. He cut off their supply line through the Hukawng Valley. His force then divided in two and headed for Shaduzup. One of his battalions was held up in fighting at Nhpum Ga.

During April, May and July, Merrill was hospitalized but his Marauders finally broke through to take Myitkyina on 4 August.

After Merrill recovered he was made Deputy US Commander in the Burma–India theater and later became Chief of Staff in the US 10th Army in the Pacific.

## Merrill's Marauders
see Northern Burma Campaign

## Mers-el-Kebir
see French Navy

## Messerschmitt Bf 109

This German single-seat fighter was in service from 1937–45 (Spain until about 1962). In 1934 Messerschmitt had never received any orders from the new Luftwaffe, but he was allowed to compete with Heinkel, Arado and Focke-Wulf in an attempt to create the chief new monoplane fighter. Nobody thought he had a chance, especially when they saw the Bf 109 prototype (designated Bf because at that time the company was called Bayerische Flugzeugwerke). It was a slim low-wing monoplane, with a very small wing fitted with slats as well as flaps, and with a rather cramped enclosed cockpit. But gradually the 109 became absolutely dominant as the leading fighter of the Luftwaffe and many other air forces. It was made in greater numbers than any other aircraft except the Russian Il–2. Exact numbers are not known but BFW and Messerschmitt AG (as the company was named in 1938) made about 12,000 and Erla of Leipzig and Wiener Neustadt Flugzeugwerke made about 13,000. Other builders in Czechoslovakia, Spain and Switzerland added about 8000, to make a grand total close to 33,000. The first flew in 1935, while the last Spanish example was completed in 1956. (By a quirk of fate, both had Rolls-Royce engines.)

The early Bf 109B and C fought well in the Spanish Civil War, but by 1939 the Luftwaffe fighter wings were equipped with the 109E, powered by the 1100hp DB 601A engine and reaching about 354mph. Most had two machine

Bf 109 flying low over the Meuse delta.

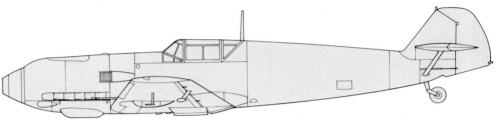

guns above the engine and two 20mm cannon in the wings. In the Battle of Britain the 109 first came up against serious opposition, and though it could dive and climb better than any RAF fighter it was fractionally slower than the Spitfire and was easily outmaneuvered by a well-flown Hurricane. The 109 was tiring to fly, and at high speed the controls were so tight that few pilots were strong enough to dogfight to the limits. Worse, the slats 'snatched' at the wings in tight turns, throwing the pilot off his aim. On the other hand the cannon were effective at ranges where the RAF's machine guns were useless. In 1941 the E (called 'Emil') was fitted to drop bombs, while the beautiful round-winged F gave the crack fighter wings higher performance that outclassed the Spitfire V. But from 1942 virtually all 109s were of the G ('Gustav') type, with big 1475hp DB 605A engines. Much

*Top:* The guns of a Bf 109 are harmonized in the North African desert.
*Above:* Messerschmitt Bf 109.

heavier, the G was armed with the world's best cannon, often carrying two 13mm and three 20mm or 30mm, as well as bombs or various rockets for bringing down Allied bombers. But it was a brute to fly, and completely outclassed by the improving Allied fighters, but it was kept in ever-increasing production because there was no better machine available. The final model was the K, which like late 109Gs had a 'Galland hood' giving a better view, a new wooden tail, and other changes. With special boost systems the engine power could be raised to 2000hp, for quick dashes at about 450mph, but by 1945 there were few experienced pilots and little fuel. In April 1945 Major Herrmann, who had masterminded use of the 109G as a free-ranging night fighter, took off with 120 young student-pilots in late-model 109s to intercept an American raid. Only 15 returned from this hazardous mission.

## Messerschmitt Bf 110

This German two/four-seat long-range escort fighter, night fighter and attack/bomber/reconnaissance aircraft was in service, 1939–45. Planned in 1934, the first Bf 110 flew in May 1936. It was intended to perform as a heavily armed escort fighter to accompany bombers deep into enemy territory, blasting a path through all opposition. When the Bf 110C joined the Luftwaffe in early 1939, special *Zerstörer* (destroyer) wings were formed, and regarded so highly that most of the best fighter pilots were posted to them. In September 1939 the ZG wings dealt easily with remnants of the Polish Air Force, which had been almost wiped out on

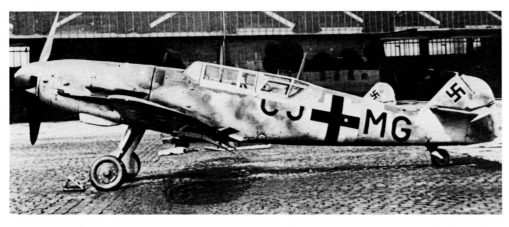

Bf 109 near its hangar in Germany.

the ground, and then proceeded to shoot down 12 out of a formation of 20 RAF Wellingtons that tried to bomb the German fleet in daylight. In April 1940 a small formation over Oslo destroyed the few Gladiators sent against them; then, as the troop transports that were to take over the airport had not appeared, they boldly landed and captured the airport by sheer bluff. But in the Battle of Britain the big fighter proved itself almost as vulnerable to Spitfires and Hurricanes as were the bombers it was supposed to protect. So the hard-pressed Bf 109s found themselves having to escort the Bf 110 escort fighters!

In 1941 virtually all the ZG wings went to North Africa, the Balkans and the Russian front, where the sky was less dangerous. The 110D had extra fuel, and the E and F, with 1300hp DB 601F engines, carried bomb loads up to 4410lb or reconnaissance cameras. Nearly all previous types had a nose armament of two 20mm cannon and four machine guns, plus a single machine gun for rear defense, but now various extra 20 or 30mm guns were added in boxes under the slim fuselage. In 1942 the old 110 was supposed to have been replaced by the Me 210, but failure of the latter led to the Bf 110G, with 1475hp DB 605B engines. Though outdated, the basic 110 was beautiful to fly, and it was better than the 109 at carrying extra burdens. The desperate need for night fighters led to a great increase in 110 production; output in 1942 was 580, but in 1943 it jumped to 1580 and in 1944 stayed at 1525. The G sometimes carried as many as four men, and nearly always three, plus extensive radar and heavy batteries of 20 or 30mm cannon firing ahead or diagonally upwards. Despite this, and large flame-dampers on the exhausts, they could exceed 300mph and were good for shooting down RAF bombers. Many even engaged US bombers by day, but when P–47 or P–51 escorts pounced, the once-proud Zerstörers had no chance.

## Messerschmitt Me 163

This German single-seat interceptor was in service from 1944 to 1945. Easily the most radical as well as the fastest aircraft of World War II, this short-range interceptor stemmed from the DFS 194 rocket test aircraft started in 1938 under the direction of Professor Alex Lippisch. In 1939 Lippisch was transferred to Messerschmitt and the project turned into a combat aircraft, finally flying on the 3750lb thrust of its Walter HWK 109–509 rocket in August 1943. A small tailless machine, the 163B Komet took off from

a trolley and landed on a sprung skid. The pilot sat in a pressurized cockpit in the nose and could fire two 30mm MK 208 cannon in the wing roots, and in many later examples also had 24 R4/M rockets which could bring down a B–17 with a single hit.

In the air the 163 was a delight, combining beautiful handling with unprecedented performance. It could climb steeply to 30,000ft in just over 2.5 minutes, and then either attack straight away or glide for quite long periods waiting for the enemy formation. It was agile and extremely difficult to hit, and most of the heavy casualties were caused by explosions on landing, when the highly reactive rocket propellants sometimes mixed together as the skid hit the ground. Later versions which did not go into service had a pressure cabin, a small auxiliary rocket for cruising, extra tankage and a bubble canopy giving all-round vision.

## Messerschmitt Me 210 and 410

This German fighter-bomber and reconnaissance aircraft was in service from 1942–45. Submitted to the German air ministry in late 1937 as a more powerful and more versatile replacement of the Bf 110, the Me 210 seemed on paper to be an extremely useful aircraft. An order for 1000 was placed before the first (with twin fins) flew on 2 September 1939, but this was a mistake. The chief test pilot said the Me 210 had 'all the least desirable attributes an aeroplane could possess'. Though it looked good and reached 385mph on two 1395hp DB 601F engines and carried 2200lb of bombs inside a bomb bay and had clever remote-controlled defensive guns at the rear, the 210 was so full of faults its production was stopped in April 1942. After complete detail redesign it emerged in 1943 as the Me 410 Hornisse (hornet), with speed around 390mph on two 1750hp DB 603A engines. The 410 served as a bomber destroyer with up to six heavy cannon, and often with a 50mm gun projecting far ahead of the nose; bomber and reconnaissance versions also saw action, but this too was most unsuccessful and production stopped in 1944.

## Messerschmitt Me 262

This German jet fighter and fighter-bomber was in service from 1944–45. Though the British Meteor beat it into service as the world's first fully operational turbojet aircraft, the Me 262 was begun far earlier in 1938, and was built during World War II in far greater numbers. The first prototype had a piston engine in the nose and tail-down landing gear, and flew in April 1941. The third prototype made the first flight on jet power only, in July 1942. Development was slow because the Nazi leaders thought they would not need such an advanced aircraft, and it was not until Hitler himself watched an Me 262 display in November 1943 that he allowed production to go ahead. Amazingly, he refused to consider it as a fighter, saying 'That is just what we need for our Blitz bomber!' Messerschmitt had to go on with the Me 262A–1a *Schwalbe* (Swallow) in secret. This was a superb machine, with excellent flying qualities and the

German Me 262 jet as seen from a US P–51 seconds before it was shot down over the Rhine.

devastating armament of four 30mm cannon. The only type officially allowed was the Me 262A–2a Sturmvogel, with pylons under the fuselage for two 1100lb bombs. Hitler's interference merely delayed the fighter by about four months. One or two were secretly used by Luftwaffe test pilots in combat missions in July 1944, but the first Development Unit did not form until September (EK 262), and the first operational fighter unit (Kommando Nowotny) formed at the end of the month. The 262 was powered by two 1980lb-thrust Jumo 004 turbojets, and could reach 540mph. Casualties were high, mainly because of engine failures and complete lack of special training. There were many versions by the end of 1944, including two-seat bombers and radar-equipped night fighters, reconnaissance versions, trainers and bomber-destroyers with R4/M rockets or the enormous 50mm MK 114 gun. More radical armament included the Jagdfaust, with twelve mortars firing heavy projectiles diagonally up at Allied bomber formations. Total production by VE-Day amounted to 1433, with hundreds more damaged in the factories by bombing, but only a few had pilots or fuel. This was lucky for the Allies because the 262 was perhaps the most formidable fighter of the war. In one month in 1945, one unit (JV 44) with an average of only six serviceable aircraft destroyed 45 of the Allies' latest warplanes. Nevertheless too few were built to have any effect.

### Messervy, Major General Frank, 1893–1974

Messervy was a British general who fought in East Africa, North Africa and Burma. In October 1940 Messervy was in command of a raiding group 'Gazelle Force', a reconnaissance unit, which operated in the East Africa campaign. During the North Africa campaign he was commander of the 4th Indian Division in the second invasion of Cyrenaica. In January 1942 he took command of the 1st Armored Division and in March of the 7th Armored Division, known as the 'Desert Rats'. His division was under heavy pressure from Rommel's troops and at one point in May 1942 he was captured but escaped after a few days. Messervy was sent to India and given command of the 7th Indian Division in 1944 and during that year his 4th Corps took part in the capture of Mandalay and Rangoon.

### Meteor, Gloster

This British single-seat jet fighter was in service from 1944 to 1961. Designed to meet a 1940 specification for a fighter using two of the Whittle-type turbojets, the first Meteor (actually the fifth prototype) flew in March 1943. Development went faster than the rival Me 262, and the Meteor F.I entered service with 616 Squadron in July 1944, soon scoring against 'V–1' flying bombs. Powered by two 1700lb-thrust Rolls-Royce Welland engines, the first Mk I Meteors could reach about 410mph. Production followed with the faster Mk III, and in 1945 a Mk IV set a speed record at 606mph, just after the war. Armament was four 20mm cannon in the sides of the fuselage. Nearly all Meteors were postwar.

### Meuse, Crossing of
see Ardennes, Passage of, 1940

## Midway, Battle of, 1942

The Battle of Coral Sea left the US with only the *Hornet* and *Enterprise* operational in the Pacific whereas the Japanese under Nagumo had four fast carriers, *Kaga*, *Akagi*, *Soryu* and *Hiryu*. Admiral Yamamoto thought there would be no carriers near Midway and devised a very complex plan. However he did not know that Admiral Nimitz knew of his plans because the Japanese Fleet's code had been broken and engineers were working hard to refit the *Yorktown*.

The Japanese fleet was divided into eight Task Forces for the Midway operation. There were two small expeditions to take two islands in the Aleutians and these were covered by a light carrier group and a group of four battleships. From the Marianas came the Midway occupation group with a close support group of cruisers and destroyers. Nagumo's First Carrier Strike Force, which had 250 planes, three battleships, two heavy cruisers and a destroyer screen, came from Japan as did the main battle fleet under Yamamoto, which included the huge 64,000 ton battleship *Yamato* with nine 18-inch guns.

The Aleutian operation was supposed to divert the Pacific Fleet to the north. This plan might have succeeded if Nimitz had not known about it. The Americans had sent two Task Forces with three carriers available and although the Japanese force was superior, the US had the advantage of surprise. On 3 June the Americans sighted Japanese transports 600 miles from Midway. Early on 4 June Nagumo launched a strike of 108 aircraft on Midway, but the pilots reported that a second strike was necessary. Thus the aircraft began to unload their

The top map traces the long route to Midway from Japan.
The bottom traces the battle itself.

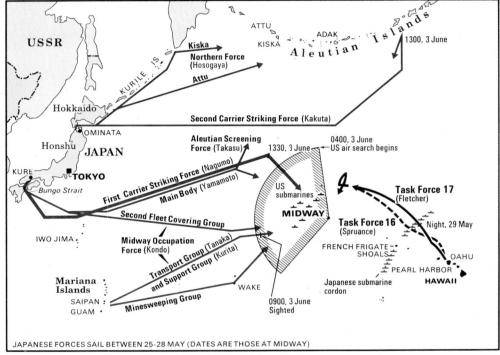

JAPANESE FORCES SAIL BETWEEN 25–28 MAY (DATES ARE THOSE AT MIDWAY)

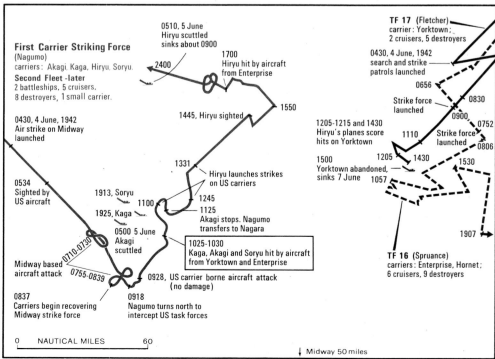

Japanese Nakajima 'Kate' passes over the USS *Yorktown* (CV-5) at Midway, dropping one of the torpedoes which sank her.

torpedoes and take on bombs. Nagumo also had to recover the aircraft from the first strike. Then at 0820 Nagumo received a report of a sighting of a carrier. Nagumo did not have any aircraft left to fight this threat and although the torpedo bombers did not inflict any damage the Dauntless dive bombers were able to hit the *Kaga*, which sank, and the *Akagi* and *Soryu*, which were abandoned. This left the *Hiryu* undamaged and it launched its aircraft which hit the *Yorktown*. Later in the day aircraft from the *Enterprise* attacked the *Hiryu*, which was scuttled on the day after. Without aircraft or carriers, Yamamoto could not challenge the US force and the Midway operation was abandoned. The Japanese had lost four fleet carriers and 250 aircraft mainly because the Japanese Task Force did not have good communications and Yamamoto had made tactical errors. Midway marked the high tide of Japanese domination of the Pacific. Japan was on the defensive for the balance of the war, although the Japanese Navy still sought a decisive battle.

## Mihajlović, General Draža, 1893–1946

Mihajlović was leader of the Serbian Četnik Resistance forces in Yugoslavia. He was a royalist army officer who was anti-communist as well as anti-fascist. After German troops invaded Yugoslavia Mihajlović went to Serbia with other soldiers and formed the Četniks. He had the support of the Royalist emigré government in Britain and he received aid from Britain and the USSR, but from the start his troops clashed with Tito's Partisans and with the understanding of the Axis forces his troops drove the Partisans out of Serbia. In January 1942 he was made War Minister in the Yugoslav government-in-exile. In 1943 the British warned him not to co-operate with the Germans in fighting the Partisans and finally in May 1944 the British decided to give Tito full support. Tito gained political control of the country and Mihajlović was eventually captured in March 1946, tried, convicted and executed by his fellow Yugoslavs.

## Mikawa, Vice-Admiral Gunichi

Recently arrived at Rabaul and in command of the Eighth Fleet when the first reports of Allied landings on Guadalcanal came in, Mikawa was one of the first to realize their import. Mikawa immediately embarked (July 1942) with a small force to slip through the Allied fleet and attack them by night. Despite being spotted three times by the Allies, Mikawa took Crutchley's Southern Force completely by surprise and went on to take Riefkohl's Northern Force equally unexpectedly. The Battle of Savo Island was a major Allied defeat: the Japanese suffered no casualties, while the Allies lost four cruisers and 1023 men.

## Mikolajczyk, Stanislaw, 1901–1967

Mikolajczyk was leader of the Polish peasant party and Premier of the Polish government-in-exile from 1943–44. In 1939 Mikolajczyk left Poland and joined the Polish National Council in Paris. In 1941 he was appointed Deputy Prime Minister to Sikorski and Minister of the Interior. His job was to co-ordinate resistance movement finances and maintain contacts with the underground in Poland. After Sikorski's death he became Premier and he had to negotiate with the Russians the question of Poland's eastern frontier. In November 1944 he resigned in protest against the Allies' lack of support for the Warsaw Uprising and over the question of the eastern frontier. He was eventually convinced to join the Lublin Committee and was the only notable Polish politician in the West to return to Poland. He was purged by the Communists.

## Mikoyan, Major General Artem I, 1905–

Mikoyan was an aircraft designer who worked with M I Gurevich. He designed a single-seat high altitude MiG-1 which was modified as MiG-3 and was widely used during the war.

## Mikoyan MiG–3

This Soviet single-seat fighter was operational from 1941. The first fighter designed by Artem Mikoyan and his colleague, mathematician Mikhail Gurevich, was the MiG–1. The prototype, known as the I–200, was built in four months and flew for the first time on 5 April 1940. The aim had been to produce the smallest aircraft that could be designed around the new 1350hp AM–35 engine. It proved to be not only an efficient high-altitude interceptor but probably the fastest production combat aircraft of its day, with a speed of 403mph at 22,000ft. Production was limited to 100 MiG–1s, as Mikoyan and Gurevich knew that their fighter would never be in the class of the contemporary LaGGs and Yaks until they improved its maneuverability and made it more pleasant to handle in a dive. The end product of their redesign was the prototype MiG–3, with increased wing dihedral; an enlarged radiator, extended forward; modified undercarriage doors; a sliding hood; and an additional fuel tank under the pilot's seat to improve the range from 445 to 775 miles. There was provision for carrying six 82mm rockets or 440lb of bombs under the wings, but, like its predecessor, the MiG–3 was best suited to high-altitude interception duties. It could match the best Luftwaffe aircraft at heights above 16,000ft until the end of 1942. Below 13,000ft it was outclassed. After 3322 had been built, production was stopped. No more AM–35 engines were to be manufactured, as the factories had to concentrate on AM–38s for Il–2s. In any case, the LaGG–3 and Yak–1 were achieving better results than the MiGs in air-to-air combat.

## Milch, Field Marshal Erhard, 1892–1972

Having commanded a fighter squadron during World War I, Milch subsequently held various appointments in industry and in commercial aviation, becoming chairman of the newly formed state airline, Lufthansa, in 1926. In this capacity he was able to exert considerable influence in the aircraft industry and also began organizing aircrew training and the development of extensive ground equipment, ostensibly for commercial purposes but, in effect, laying the foundation for the future military air arm which was to grow up in secret during the next few years.

Mikoyan MiG-3 fighter.

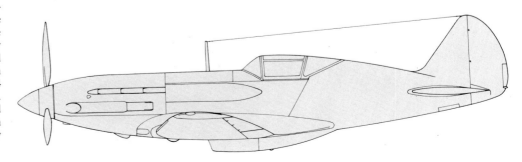

Field Marshal Erhard Milch (left) with General Christiansen.

In 1933 he became Goering's Secretary of State for Air, and as Lufthansa prospered, Milch continued to work for the clandestine military air arm. Thus, by 1935, with a body of trained air crew assured and aircraft production expanding, the Luftwaffe's existence was made known to the world.

Adopting a more cautious and realistic approach to the war situation than his heady superior officer, Milch's actions and assessments frequently were to come into question, particularly during the latter phases of the war when Germany's power was crumbling. Relations with Hitler, Goering, Speer and Jeschonnek became increasingly strained with Milch's influence gradually diminishing. By 1 August 1944 his position had deteriorated to such an extent that he was obliged to relinquish his posts as Secretary of State and Director of Armament. He was sentenced to life imprisonment at the Nuremberg Trials but was released after ten years.

## 'Millipede'
see High Pressure Pump

## Milne Bay
see New Guinea. Milne Bay, August–September 1942

## Minelaying

The first recorded use of mines occurred in the Crimean War but the Russo-Japanese War and World War I saw the first widespread use of modern mines. The success of mining in 1914–18 ensured that both sides were well-prepared for mine warfare in September 1939.

The mine proved to be an unpublicized but nonetheless deadly weapon against submarines, particularly when laid offensively *under* convoy concentration points to trap U-Boats. Aircraft proved to be far more flexible than warships as minelayers, although defensive fields were always laid by surface ships, often converted rail-ferries or large merchant ships.

Three new types of mine appeared in World War II, the magnetic, the acoustic and the pressure mine. The magnetic mine is discussed elsewhere; the acoustic mine was activated by the noise of a ship's propellers; and the pressure or 'oyster' mine was set off by the pressure of a ship passing overhead. All three were known as 'ground' mines as they had to be laid on the sea bed, and all were restricted to shallow waters. The 'oyster' mine in particular was restricted to very shallow water, and its main use was as a defense against invasion. It proved virtually unsweepable.

## Minesweeping

The traditional 'contact' or moored mine was swept in exactly the same manner as it had been 20 years before, by a warship, specially built sweeper or a converted fishing vessel, towing a submerged cutting wire. The cutter snagged the mooring rope, cut it and allowed the mine to float to the surface, where it could be sunk or exploded by small-arms fire.

'Influence' mines were swept by a strong current passed through a loop of cable (magnetic mines) or a noisemaker (acoustic mines). Many top-secret devices were tried against pressure mines, but none of them achieved any great success. The most bizarre was the 'Stirling Craft', a giant steel structure to be towed across a minefield to set up a heavy pressure wave. Its latticework iron structure was intended to allow blasts to pass through without wrecking it. Two were built and given camouflage names, HMS *Cybele* and HMS *Cyrus* but one broke adrift after D-Day and was wrecked in the Baie de la Seine.

Large numbers of minesweepers were built or taken up during the war. 'Fleet' sweepers were small warships, typical examples being the USN *Auk* Class and the British *Algerine*, but many hundreds of trawlers were requisitioned. Merchant ships were equipped with large electro-magnets in the bows to detonate magnetic mines. The German *Sperrbrecher* (barrier forcer) was a freighter with its double bottoms filled with cement, holds packed with buoyant material and electromagnet and noisemaker positioned in the forward hold. Casualties, as might be expected, were heavy on these makeshift minesweepers.

## Minsk, Battle for, 1944
see Belorussia, Battle of, 1944

*Below:* A German minesweeper in the Baltic.
*Bottom:* The British minesweeper *Clayoquot*.

*Missouri*
see *Iowa*

## Mitscher, Vice-Admiral Marc A, 1887–1947

Mitscher commanded the Fast Carrier Force in the Pacific: Task Force 58. He was the US Navy's expert in the use of naval aviation.

Mitscher commanded the task force based around the USS *Hornet* for nearly three years. In 1942 the carrier was used to launch Doolittle's bombers in the Tokyo raid and then it took part in the Battle of Midway. On 1 April 1943 Mitscher took over as Air Commander on Guadalcanal and co-ordinated the different air forces of the US Army, Navy and Marines and the New Zealand RAF. In January 1944 Mitscher was given command of the fast carrier force in Vice-Admiral Spruance's Central Pacific Force which provided an air umbrella for the troops on the Marshall Islands. As a result, on 21 March 1944, he was made Vice-Admiral. He was then sent to provide air support for the invasion of Hollandia and then sent back to the Marianas in June.

In the Battle of the Philippine Sea Mitscher played an important part by sending out his planes although they could only be recovered at night. From August to September Mitscher's planes were sent on lightning strikes on the Bonin Islands, Volcanoes, Palau and Mindanao.

When MacArthur invaded the Philippines Mitscher was engaged in raids on Formosa. During the whole of 1944 Mitscher's task force was used extensively since it had its own fleet train which meant it could remain in operation for much longer periods of time.

In February and May 1945 Mitscher's forces took part in operations at Iwo Jima and Okinawa in support of ground troops because the Japanese air force was now striking from home bases.

## Mitsubishi A5M

The A5M4 version of this open-cockpit, fixed-undercarriage fighter continued in first-line service for about six months after Pearl Harbor, over the Aleutians and other islands in the Pacific. Named 'Claude' by the Americans, this version had a 710hp Kotobuki 41 engine, armament of two 7.7mm machine guns and maximum speed of 273mph.

## Mitsubishi A6M

A Japanese carrier-based fighter, designed by a team led by Jiro Horikoshi, this neat fighter was the only design able to meet a 1937 specification of the Imperial Navy calling for a carrier-based fighter carrying two 20mm cannon and two machine guns, able to fly at 311mph and to have long range. First flown on 1 April 1939 the resulting A6M was one of the classic warplanes of history. Though it was in action over China in July 1940, flying rings round all the fighters sent against it, the detailed reports of US General Chennault were ignored in Washington. As a result it was a great shock to the Allies to discover a Japanese fighter that could out-maneuver every one of their own fighters and hit them with cannon armament. Moreover, thanks to extremely careful piloting and the use of a drop tank, the A6M had exceptional range

Mitsubishi A6M5 Zero 'Zeke' fighter, Navy type.

and could appear where no Japanese fighters had been thought possible. The A6M had gone into production in the Japanese year 5700 (our year 1940), and so one of its designations was the Type 00, or Zero-Sen. To millions the world over it became famed as the dreaded Zero, though in fact its official Allied codename was 'Zeke'.

The first major version was the A6M2, powered by a 925hp Nakajima Sakae 12 radial, which was enough for a speed of about 316mph. In 1942 the clipped-wing A6M3 appeared, with 1130hp Sakae 21; for a time this was thought to be a different aircraft, and codenamed 'Hap' and then 'Hamp', but soon was recognized as 'another Zero' and called 'Zeke 32'. The largest number of all were of the A6M5 series, with the same short-span wing with rounded tips, and with a modified engine installation with separate exhaust stacks all round. In use from the autumn of 1943, the 5a, 5b and 5c had slightly different armament, and could carry up to 700lb of bombs. During 1943 the improving Allied fighters, especially the F4U Corsair and F6F Hellcat, mastered the once-dreaded 'Zero', and many of the 10,937 built ended their lives in kamikaze suicide missions. There were various trainer and float seaplane versions.

## Mitsubishi F1M

Although developed to a 1934 specification, this two-seat reconnaissance seaplane did not enter service until 1941. It then remained in production until 1944, about 700 being built as the last frontline biplanes to serve with the Japanese Navy. The standard F1M2 ('Pete'), with an 875hp Mitsubishi Zuisei engine and armament of three 7.7mm machine guns, achieved some success as a defensive fighter during the Battle of the Solomon Islands and over Attu in the

Aleutians. Many were lost in the Coral Sea Battle, but the F1M2 continued to be met in the Philippines, New Guinea and Marshall Islands, often with two 132lb bombs under its wings.

## Mitsubishi G3M

Developed to a 1934 specification for a land-based naval attack bomber, about 275 G3M2 and G3M3 variants of this design ('Nell') still formed the basis of the Japanese Navy's long-range striking force at the time of the Pearl Habor attack. Within three days their bombs and torpedoes had sunk the British battleships *Prince of Wales* and *Repulse*. Production totaled 1103, and the G3M served throughout the war in most Pacific combat areas. The G3M3 had two 1300hp Mitsubishi Kasei engines, giving a maximum speed of 258mph.

## Mitsubishi G4M

This Japanese seven-seat bomber and torpedo carrier was in service from 1941 to 1945. In 1934 Mitsubishi flew a prototype that became the widely used G3M bomber, an outstanding aircraft with long range and excellent performance for its day. In 1937 the company was told to design an even better successor, and it could have done so more easily if the Imperial Navy had not insisted on a range of 2300 miles with full bomb load. Mitsubishi had to build the G4M extremely light to meet this long-range requirement, and the result was an aircraft which, admirable in most ways, had little armor or protection and caught fire so easily in combat it was called 'the one-shot lighter'.

Powered by two 1850hp Mitsubishi Kasei 25 radials, the G4M had quite a small wing but carried a heavy load of fuel and a crew of seven and either 2200lb of bombs or a large torpedo. Early versions had a 20mm cannon in the tail and three manually aimed machine guns, but later models had a powered dorsal turret with

Mitsubishi G4M 'Betty' bomber.

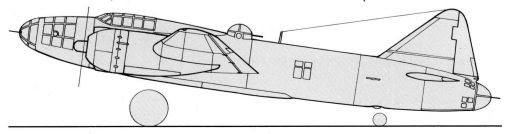

Mitsubishi G4M2 'Betty'.

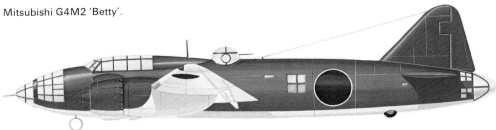

either a machine gun or a cannon. Maximum speed of all was around 270mph, though the G4M often flew with its bomb doors removed and this reduced the speed. By the time Japan entered the war in December 1941 about 200 were in service, and the Allies called the G4M 'Betty'. Eventually 2479 were delivered; late versions included the G4M2e with special mountings to carry the MXY-7 Ohka suicide missile and the G4M3 family with less fuel but much better protection. Two G4M2 bombers brought the Japanese surrender delegation to the conference table at Ie Shima at the end of the war on 19 August 1945.

## Mitsubishi J2M Raiden

It was planned that 3600 J2Ms would be built to serve as the Japanese Navy's first purpose-designed interceptors, but construction and engine problems restricted output to about 500. The most satisfactory version, of which a few were encountered by Allied bombers in 1944–45, was the J2M5, with an 1820hp Kasei engine and armament of two 20mm cannon. Maximum speed of this version of the Raiden ('Jack') was 382mph; only 35 were built.

## Mitsubishi Ki–21

Standard heavy bomber of the Japanese Army during the first two years of the Pacific War, the Ki–21 ('Sally') had two 1490hp Kinsei engines, a speed of 297mph and 2200lb bomb load in its final versions. They operated on most of the major Pacific war fronts, receiving rough handling from RAF Hurricanes in Burma. Altogether 2064 were built.

## Mitsubishi Ki–46

This Japanese two-seat reconnaissance aircraft and night fighter was in service in 1941–45. Designed solely for reconnaissance, the Ki–46 was one of the cleanest (most streamlined) aircraft of the whole war, and even with quite low-powered engines was so much faster than early Allied fighters that it was able to leave off the machine gun originally carried in the rear cockpit. The first version, flown in November 1939, reached about 336mph on two 870hp Ha–26 engines, but very soon the 1080hp Mitsubishi Ha–102 was substituted, giving a speed of about 375mph. This engine was reliable, and the whole Ki–46 always had an unsurpassed reputation for being completely free from restrictions or faults of any kind, and it was very popular. In service from the summer of 1941, it was called 'Dinah' by the Allies. It proved so successful that in 1942 it was even considered by the Germans as a possible aircraft to build in Germany for the Luftwaffe.

Most versions had the pilot and observer seated far apart in separate cockpits, without armament, but by 1943 the Ki–46–III series

appeared with more powerful 1500hp Ha–112 engines and a variety of interior arrangements. Some were IIIA reconnaissance machines with perfectly streamlined fuselage with no stepped cockpits, reaching almost 400mph and flying about 2500 miles. The III-Kai night fighter had no radar but two 20mm cannon firing ahead and a 37mm firing diagonally upwards. The IIIB was a ground attack version. Total production amounted to 1738.

## Mitsubishi Ki–51

'Sonia', as the Allies named this two-seat reconnaissance and ground attack aircraft, remained in production throughout the war. A total of 1472 were delivered with a 940hp Ha–26–II engine, armament of five machine guns, and racks for ten 44lb bombs on the attack model. They were encountered in many combat zones and were finally adapted for suicide missions in 1944–45.

## Mitsubishi Ki–67 Hiryu

The prototype of the Japanese Army's Flying Dragon heavy bomber ('Peggy') flew at the beginning of 1943, by which time its sponsors were even more aware of the need for improved maneuverability and protection for the crew and fuel tanks. Powered by two 1900hp Mitsubishi Ha–104 engines, the Hiryu carried six to eight men, 1765lb of bombs or torpedoes, and a defensive armament of one 20mm and four 12.7mm guns. It was first identified in action during the Battle of the Philippine Sea. Later, from bases on Kyushu, Ki–67s carried out frequent raids on Iwo Jima, the Marianas and Okinawa. Despite the problems under which the Japanese labored during the last year of the war, 727 Hiryus were completed.

## Mius, Battle of, 1943

On the 30 July the Third Panzer Corps attacked General Malinovsky across the Mius bridgehead. The Russians were short of tanks and within a few days the Germans had taken 1700 Russian prisoners. This was the last tactical success the Germans had in Russia but it was badly timed since it gave General Rokossovsky's troops a chance to regroup.

## Mobile Service Base or Fleet Train
see Mitscher, Vice-Admiral Marc

## Model, Field Marshal Walther, 1891–1945

Model, a rapidly promoted wartime discovery among German officers, became known as the Führer's Fireman for his success in rebuilding broken fronts. His greatest achievement was the restoration of stability in the Belo-

russian/Polish sector after the battle descriptively known as the Destruction of Army Group Center in June 1944. In August he was brought to the west to replace Kluge, whom Hitler had removed on suspicion of treason. He found the decay of the Western Front too far gone to repair, but re-established it successfully along the West Wall in September. Encircled in the Ruhr after the Allied crossing of the Rhine in April 1945, he shot himself on the grounds that 'a Field Marshal does not become a prisoner'; he had always despised Paulus for surrendering at Stalingrad.

## Mölders, Oberst Werner, 1913–1941

This German fighter pilot accredited with 115 victories, was one of the Luftwaffe's leading aces. Outstandingly proficient as a Commander during the Battle of France, the Battle of Britain – when he led JG 51 – and at the Russian Front in 1941, he was appointed Inspector of Fighter Aircraft at Luftwaffe headquarters but was killed in an air crash in November 1941.

A skillful tactician as well as a brilliant pilot, Mölders invented the 'finger four' formation which was adopted initially by the Luftwaffe, and later by the RAF. He was awarded the Knights Cross with Oak Leaves, Swords and Diamonds.

German ace Werner Mölders describing a sortie to his commandant.

## Molotov Cocktail

This general term covers any form of extemporized incendiary grenade, such as a beer-bottle filled with gasoline with a burning rag attached, to be thrown at a tank. The origin of the term is obscure; it appears to have originated during the Spanish Civil War without attracting any special name. It then re-appeared during the Russo-Finnish War, used by the Finns, and this is where the 'Molotov' name first was applied. It seems likely that it was derived from the 'Molotov Breadbasket', an aerial delivery system for incendiary bombs in which a casing was dropped and then opened during flight to release a shower of small incendiary bombs; by extension, the incendiary hand grenade attracted the same name, but it was more probably invented by a newspaper reporter than by a soldier. Molotov Cocktails achieved some measure of respectability by being developed as official grenades in several countries, notably in Britain in 1940 where they adopted the name 'Grenade, Self-Igniting Phosphorus, No. 68', a glass bottle filled with benzine, gasoline, phosphorus and latex rubber. When thrown at a tank the bottle broke and the phosphorus, ignited by contact with the air, then lit the other materials to produce a sticky burning mass which adhered to the tank and, drawn into the engine compartment, set fire to the engine and fuel supply. The American 'Frangible Hand Grenade' was a similar device, filled with Napalm or with a mixture of gasoline and alcohol.

## Molotov-Ribbentrop Pact, August 1939

Following the invasion of Czechoslovakia by the Germans, Poland appeared to be the next country threatened by Hitler's expansionist policy. Great Britain hoped that Poland could escape the same fate as Czechoslovakia and negotiated a treaty with Poland, which promised armed intervention if Poland was threatened. When Molotov replaced Litvinov, he began negotiations with Germany as well as with Great Britain. The British were suspicious of the USSR's ambitions in the Baltic and also underestimated her military potential. Molotov reached a satisfactory arrangement with Ribbentrop and on 23 August 1939 the Soviet-Nazi Pact was signed. This Pact was a non-aggression treaty for ten years. It had secret Protocols which agreed on spheres of influence in Poland, Bessarabia and the Baltic States. On 1 September the Germans invaded Poland. A further treaty on 28 September formally divided Poland between Germany and the USSR and had a special provision agreeing to the suppression of Polish agitators.

## Molotov, Vlachyslav M, 1890–

Molotov was the Soviet Commissar for Foreign Affairs from 1939 to 1952. His appointment to this post opened the way for negotiations with the Germans and led to the signing of the Nazi-Soviet Pact in August 1939. During 1940 Molotov was aware of German troop movements in Finland and Rumania and when Hitler suggested a four-power pact between Germany, the USSR, Italy and Japan, he laid the condition that German troops had to leave Finland. Hitler would not agree to this and on 18 December 1940 Hitler issued the directive for Operation Barbarossa. On 13 April 1941 Molotov concluded a non-aggression pact with Japan. On 22 June 1941 he brought news of the German invasion of Russia to Stalin.

Molotov was made a member of Stalin's State Defense Committee and his domestic duties included examining the defenses at Leningrad. During the war he was mainly kept busy by the Allied conferences. He negotiated a Mutual Assistance Pact with Great Britain through Sir Stafford Cripps, the British Ambassador in Moscow. In May 1942 he was sent to Washington to put pressure on the Allies to launch the long-talked-of Second Front and to resume the convoys to the USSR. While he was there he signed a 20-year treaty with Great Britain. In June 1943 he is supposed to have taken part in talks with Ribbentrop at Kirovograd. They talked about ending the war but discussions stopped when they could not agree on boundaries. News of this leaked out to the Allies. Despite this, Molotov continued to negotiate with Churchill over the question of convoys to Murmansk and wore down Churchill's resistance. As a result the convoys were resumed in November 1943. Molotov hosted the Foreign Ministers' Conference in Moscow that year and then went on to attend all the major conferences: Yalta, San Francisco and Potsdam.

## Montgomery, Field Marshal Bernard Law, 1887–1976

Already marked out as a strong-willed, efficient and intelligent commander and staff officer, Montgomery at the beginning of the war was commanding 3rd Divison which he took to France in 1939 and led during the 1940 campaign. He was one of the last to leave Dunkirk and was promoted to command 5th and then 12th Corps on his return. In the summer of 1942, when Churchill was searching for a new commander for the 8th Army in the Western Desert, Montgomery was chosen as the obvious successor to the Prime Minister's first choice, 'Strafer' Gott, who had been accidentally killed. His first task was to repulse Rommel's final effort to capture Alexandria in the Battle of Alam Halfa, 31 August to 7 September, and then to restore the morale and rebuild the strength of his army. He proved a master of personal publicity and managed to convince his soldiers that they were, under his leadership, to win a great victory. He was also adept at dealing with Churchill, whose urgings for premature action he gracefully deflected, while he produced a solid battle plan of his own (though owing something to the schemes of his predecessor, Auchinleck). The Battle of Alamein begun on 23 October 1942 with plentiful reinforcements and new, modern equipment did not at first break the German position as he had hoped but, after a change of front, forced Rommel into retreat and drove him towards Tunis. It was the first great British victory of the war and the last one won over the Germans single-handed. Thereafter Montgomery was to operate within the Anglo-American context, where he was not consistently successful. After the invasions of Sicily and Italy under Eisenhower's command, Montgomery joined him to act as ground commander for the invasion of Northwest Europe. His handling of the Normandy battle in the static phase was thoroughly competent but when he returned his command to Eisenhower and became a subordinate commander, his conception of strategy became over-independent. At Arnhem he attempted to gain premature entry into the Rhine plain and later, during the Battle of the Bulge, assumed temporary command of the American forces on the northern flank of the bulge with too great a display of satisfaction. None of this detracts from the fact, however, that he was a very successful practical general, a tonic to British national morale at the lowest moment of the war and a man of complete personal integrity. He was, in the postwar years, Chief of the Imperial General Staff and Deputy Supreme Allied Commander.

## Morane-Saulnier M.S.406

This French single-seat fighter was in service from 1939–1944. When the German Blitzkrieg overran France in May 1940 the M.S.406 was the only fighter available in really large numbers to try to stem the might of the Luftwaffe. Unfortunately it was only a second-rate aircraft, and though it seemed fine in 1935 when it was designed, it was outclassed in 1940. The first M.S.405 flew on 8 August 1935, and after various small improvements the production type was designated M.S.406, 1000 being ordered in March 1938. Rather knobbly and unstreamlined, the Morane had a Plymax skin of aluminium bonded to plywood over most of the wing, while the rear fuselage was covered in old-fashioned fabric. The Hispano-Suiza 12Y–31 liquid-cooled engine gave only 860hp so that the top speed only just reached 300mph. This was despite the small size and rather poor armament of one 20mm Hispano cannon firing through the propeller hub and two 7.5mm MAC 1934

Field Marshal Montgomery studies a map in France prior to Operation Market Garden, his disastrous Arnhem offensive.

machine guns in the wings just outboard of the landing gear. When the fighter was airborne a long radio mast could be pivoted down from under the cockpit, but this had to be folded back again before landing.

Despite its mediocre performance the Morane was easy to fly, maneuverable and cheap, and large numbers were bought by foreign air forces. Switzerland went into production with the D–3800 version which was the start of 20 years of Swiss fighter development, while other Moranes went to Finland and Turkey, and orders came from Poland, Lithuania and Yugoslavia. The Finnish aircraft were used against the Russians in 1939 and later flew much faster with captured Russian 1100hp engines, then being called LaGG-Moranes. But the *Armée de l'Air* had only the 'Brand X' kind of Morane, and though almost 1000 had been delivered by the end of 1939, the total actually in frontline squadrons never reached 300 because of accidents and war losses. The M.S.406 equipped 22 *Groupes de Chasse* by June 1940, with 1037 aircraft delivered, but, in the words of a French pilot, 'though nice to fly, it was too slow to catch the German bombers and too poorly armed to shoot them down; poorly armored, our own losses were high'.

## Morgenthau, Henry, 1891–1967

Morgenthau was President Roosevelt's Secretary of the Treasury. Morgenthau had to devise a way of financing the war effort. Government spending was already leading to inflation because of over-spending so Morgenthau issued Defense (later 'War') Savings Bonds. He also had to oversee the Lend-Lease arrangements and implemented the freezing of Japanese assets and economic measures against enemy-controlled companies. At the Quebec Conference in 1944 he proposed the 'Morgenthau Plan', which argued that German industry should be dismantled after the war and that the whole of Germany be converted to arable land. Roosevelt and Churchill at first endorsed this idea but when news of this plan leaked out in the press in September, Roosevelt quickly changed his mind. Morgenthau was a Jew and Goebbels used this in a successful propaganda campaign to convince the Germans that if they surrendered they would be destroyed.

## Morotai, Capture of, September 1944

The operation to take Morotai was the last preliminary before the recapture of the Philippines, and was undertaken because the Japanese had a strong base on Halmahera Island in the Moluccas. General MacArthur sent the 11th Corps to Morotai on 15 September 1944 after heavy bombardments from the 5th and 7th Fleets. The troops met little opposition and soon took the island with an American loss of 45 killed and 95 wounded and a Japanese loss of 325 killed.

## Morshead, Lieutenant General Sir Leslie, 1889–1959

Morshead was an Australian General who fought in the Middle East and in New Guinea. He commanded the Australian 9th Division which held the Germans at Tobruk in 1941 and which fought at El Alamein in October 1941,

making a decisive contribution to the victory. After this battle his division was recalled to Australia to fight the Japanese in New Guinea and was sent to make a sea-borne attack against Lae. In 1944 Morshead was made GOC of the New Guinea Force and Commander of the 2nd Australian Army. At the end of the war he directed operations in Borneo.

## Moscow, Battle of, 1941–42

After the Vyazma defeat, the Russians' situation looked hopeless. They had only 824 tanks left on their Western Front, they had no air cover and they had lost their mass armies: all that remained were a few divisions of defeated men and some improvised workers' dattalions. On 14 October General Zhukov had been given command of all the forces defending Moscow. The Germans had their Panzer divisions attacking the Russian flanks: General Hoth in the north and General Guderian in the south. Hoth then broke through at Kalinin. This meant that Moscow was now without a conventional, organized defense and on 19 October a state of siege was declared. However there were several problems facing the Germans. Whenever it rained, the roads turned into mud and they could only advance at a rate of six miles a day. At night the Russians would attack the German guards and destroy the supplies. The Germans could not advance quickly through the dense forests, north of Moscow, nor could they advance in formation. As the winter got colder much of the German equipment ceased to function: the oil in the tanks froze, the automatic firing mechanisms in the guns froze, the packing grease in the artillery froze. The men had no winter clothing, apart from overalls and they all suffered from frostbite. A first indication that the German advance was faltering badly, came to light just south of Moscow, where there were no forests and the Panzers should have made easy progress. Zhukov stationed his last independent tank force there. This was the 4th Armored Brigade, under General Katukov, which was well-trained and equipped with T-34s, the only tanks the Russians possessed whose armor could not be pierced by German artillery. At Tula, Katukov stopped the Germans' advance, so Guderian diverted his troops to Mtsensk. Road conditions were appalling and the whole group was strung out on one road, giving Katukov an easy target. On 11 October 1941 the Fourth Panzer Division was out of action.

In the north Hoth's Panzer Group continued

Russian poster calling on Soviet citizens to defend Moscow.

to advance but they were under pressure as the Russians were beginning to use their Katyusha rockets and the Red Air Force was back in action. His troops had to sleep rough as all the possible billets had been destroyed by the Russians. The other major problem was that there were only two main roads to Moscow and both were heavily congested. On 12 November Halder called a Chief of Staffs' conference at Orsha to reconsider the offensive, but it was decided to continue, especially since there were reports that the Siberian troops were being moved to the Moscow Front.

In fact Zhukov now had 1700 tanks and 1500 aircraft to defend Moscow with, but his plan was to use the Siberian troops at the last moment. He left the job of holding the Germans to the local brigades and the weather. On 15–16 November the Germans launched their final offensive, and at first they made progress because the roads were frozen and easier to move on. On 23 November Hoth entered Klin and on 28 November his Seventh Panzer Division

Soviet cavalrymen advance to defend Moscow in December 1941.

Anti-tank defenses are dug in Moscow streets. They were never required.

reached the Moscow-Volga canal some 20 miles from Moscow. In the south, however, it was obvious that Guderian would never break through: his flank was being attacked by Siberian troops and Tula was still holding out.

On 4–5 December Zhukov launched his counteroffensive, and within a couple of days the Germans were withdrawing in a panic. Generals Höpner, Kluge and Guderian were no longer in touch – their tanks were outnumbered and German casualties – up to 10,000 men suffering from frostbite – could not be replaced. Hitler appointed himself Commander in Chief. He dismissed Guderian and Höpner and the Germans were given orders to stand fast and resist the enemy. The early successes of the 1st Shock Army to the north of Moscow and of the 10th Army to the south, encouraged Stalin so much that he began to think in terms of relieving Leningrad and taking the Ukraine. Zhukov and the generals were more cautious but Stalin insisted on a further offensive which was launched on 7 January. By the end of January all the Russian reserves had been used and the front stabilized some 40 miles from Moscow.

The recovery of the Red Army was remarkable. Thanks to better planning by Zhukov and to a change in tactics – the use of smaller divisions – the Russians were able to push back the Germans. The Germans would probably not have reached Moscow in any case, since the troops were becoming more reluctant to move every time they built themselves positions. Unprepared as they were to face a Russian winter, the Germans had obviously reached their limit.

## Moscow Conference, September – December 1941

The tone of this conference was set by Russia's desperate military situation. As the Germans approached Moscow in October, Stalin called desperately to Britain and America to either open a 'second front in Europe' (Northern France) or send substantial military aid to Russia itself. Britain avoided discussing military matters at the conference as no second front was then possible and Stalin's demand for 25–30 British divisions in the Ukraine was a practical impossibility in a 'situation governed by shipping' contingencies. However, arrangements were made for a build-up of British troops in Iran and for supply convoys to Russia.

The conference ended with talks between Stalin and Anthony Eden (starting 16 December), in which Stalin demanded greater clarity in Anglo-Russian relations, with respect to war aims, strategy and postwar plans – especially the latter. He demanded a restoration of Russia to its June 1941 borders, the dismemberment of Germany and settlement of the Polish question. No decisions were made.

## Mosin-Nagant Rifle

The Mosin-Nagant was the Russian service rifle from 1891 to 1945 and is probably one of the longest-serving rifles ever made since large numbers are still in use in Vietnam and other eastern countries which purchased them cheaply after World War II. It takes its name from the combining of a bolt action designed by S I Mosin, a Russian, and a magazine designed by Emil Nagant, a Belgian. The bolt was a robust, though unnecessarily complicated design, while the magazine was unusual in that it used a control latch which secured the second and lower rounds in the magazine, relieving the top round of any pressure from beneath during the loading movement of the bolt. This was a useful feature, since the rifle was designed to use a rimmed 7.62mm cartridge, and without the control latch the cartridge rims would probably have jammed during the feed stroke. Compared with the Mauser or Mannlicher designs, the Mosin-Nagant is crude and simple, but nevertheless it is extremely strong and reliable; one can be sure that if it had not been, the Soviets would never have continued to use it.

The basic rifle was the Model 1891, 51.25in long and fitted to take a socket bayonet around the muzzle. This bayonet was so much a part of the rifle that the sights were graduated to allow for the altered point of balance when it was fitted, and, indeed, since no scabbard was issued, there was nowhere else to carry the thing. In the usual manner of the time, the long rifle

was accompanied by a shorter model, called in this case, a 'Dragoon Rifle' rather than a carbine. It was only three inches shorter because there was some doubt as to whether the smokeless powder used in the cartridge would function properly if the barrel was made any shorter. Smokeless powder was relatively new at that time, and its ballistics were not entirely understood, but experience soon showed that this fear was unjustified and in 1910 a proper carbine was introduced, with a 20in barrel and a total length of 40in.

Until 1917 these weapons were called the 'Three Line Rifles' since their caliber was three 'lines', an old Russian measurement equal to one-tenth of an inch. Similarly, their sights were graduated in 'arshins', a Russian unit of length about equal to 28 inches. Once the Soviets began to reorganize the army the rifle became known as a 7.62mm model and the sights were regraduated in meters. While many of the older weapons had the sights changed the principal change-over came in 1930 with the adoption of a new standard rifle, which was little more than the 1891 pattern shortened somewhat so that it approximated the old Dragoon Rifle. The sights were improved but there was little other change from the original design. A carbine was produced in 1938 which, in similar fashion, was simply a slight improvement on the 1910 model.

Finally, in 1944, came a fresh design of carbine which was little more than the 1938 pattern with the addition of a folding bayonet under the fore-end. Just why this weapon was developed is something of a mystery; at that time the submachine gun formed the principal armament of the Soviet Army, and a completely new automatic rifle was in the course of development. On the face of it there seems no justification for adopting such an archaic design at such a late date.

## Mosquito, De Havilland

This British two-seat fighter, bomber, reconnaissance, attack, trainer and transport aircraft was in service from 1941 to 1961. Proposed in 1938, the idea of a wooden bomber so fast it did not need heavy gun turrets struck no sparks from the Air Ministry, and it was only in December 1939 that a prototype was allowed. Then 50 were ordered, but Lord Beaverbrook, Minister of Aircraft Production, canceled them in 1940. There was a battle to keep the Mosquito alive until the first flew in November 1940. After that the sheer performance of this marvelous machine drove it ahead, and it kept demonstrating fresh capabilities. Powered by two 1230hp

*Below:* Rifle grenade launcher for the Mosin-Nagant rifle. It fixed on top of the barrel and shot a rifle grenade against enemy personnel.

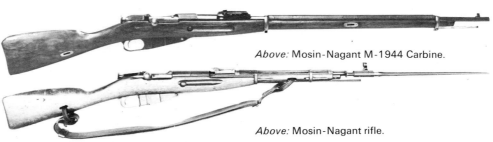

*Above:* Mosin-Nagant M-1944 Carbine.

*Above:* Mosin-Nagant rifle.

De Havilland Mosquito VI.

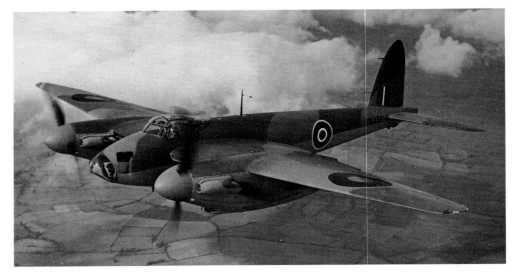

Mosquito bomber.

Rolls-Royce Merlin engines, the early reconnaissance and bomber versions delivered from November 1941 could reach 380mph and carry 2000lb of bombs over long ranges. Unexpectedly the bomb load was eventually able to be doubled, despite the addition of considerable extra fuel capacity, with speeds around 400mph with Merlins of 1630–1720hp (often made by Packard). Fighter versions appeared, with four cannon under the floor (needing a side door for the crew) and either four machine guns or radar in the nose. One model carried a six-pounder gun, while a high-altitude fighter had long pointed wings, and the most numerous of all, the Mk VI, was both a fighter and bomber.

Crews loved the 'Mozzie'. Pilot and navigator sat side-by-side and worked as a close team, flying sorties of every conceivable kind with every Allied air force in World War II, on every front. It was by far the leading Allied night fighter, scoring 600 victories over Germany alone and even catching and shooting down 600 'V–1' flying bombs. In Bomber Command it not only dropped great weights of bombs but also was the standard preliminary marking aircraft of the crack Pathfinder force, guided by 'Oboe' signals to put down bright flares of particular colors right on the center of each night's target. Altogether 7781 of these incredibly versatile aircraft were delivered in no fewer than 42 different marks; many were built in Canada and Australia. After 1945 many versions served with air forces all over the world.

### Motor Torpedo Boat

Following the success of the British Coastal Motor Boats (CMBs) and the Italian Motobarca Armata SVAN (MAS Boats) in World War I, most navies developed fast light craft armed with torpedoes. Although their supporters always claimed that 'mosquito craft'

were capable of destroying major warships with ease, war experience showed that they were best suited to attacking shipping in coastal or confined waters using 'hit and run' tactics. Destroyers were their most feared enemies, and although some isolated successes were scored against warships, set-piece attacks were easily driven off.

The Germans made the most significant progress in the 1930s with their *Schnellboote*. The development of a good hull by Lürssenwerft and a 20-cylinder V-form Daimler-Benz diesel engine proved ideal in war service. Known to the British as E-Boats they harassed coastal shipping in the English Channel and on the east coast, and fought countless battles against the Royal Navy's Coastal Forces. By 1944, however, Allied air superiority and the use of radar reduced their effectiveness considerably and losses were heavy. Many bloody fights took place against Russian light forces in the Baltic and Black Sea as well, and *Schnellboote* rank with U-Boats as the most effective units of the Kriegsmarine.

The British did little to continue their work after World War I, but in 1935 orders were placed with small boat yards specializing in fast craft. Unlike the Germans the British did not invest money in the development of fast light

MTB 238 Vosper 72.5ft.

diesel engines and so they had to rely on gasoline engines with a much higher risk of fire. The original Motor Torpedo Boat (MTB) was supplemented by the Motor Gun Boat (MGB) and by 1944 a combined MTB/MGB was in service with a good gun armament for engaging E-Boats and torpedoes for sinking shipping.

The US Navy had done even less than the Royal Navy to develop small torpedo-craft as it was felt that they had no role in the Pacific. However, British designs were procured and used as the basis for the development of the PT boats after 1941. The fighting around the Solomons was ideal for torpedo-craft and PT boats fought many confused actions with Japanese ships, including the famous ramming of PT-109 (captained by John F Kennedy) by a Japanese destroyer, but the experience was very similar to that in the European theater; the PT boats could not take on regular warships with impunity.

Two other navies had invested in torpedo boats, the Italian and the Japanese, but they achieved very little. The Italians retained the term MAS for their craft and the Japanese boats were known as *Gyoraitaei*. Like the British they developed a motor gunboat version, known as *Hayabusa-tei*.

### Mountbatten, Vice-Admiral Lord Louis, 1900–1979

Mountbatten was a distinguished Admiral, scientifically minded, who specialized in communications. He was the Supreme Allied Commander of Southeast Asia and had overall command of the operation to reconquer Burma. He was a weighty figure, a cousin of King George VI, and a suitable counterpart to the two commanders in the Pacific: General MacArthur and Admiral Nimitz.

At the outbreak of the war Mountbatten commanded the 5th Destroyer Flotilla and took part in the evacuation of Norway. In April 1941 he was sent to Malta and he saw action off Crete in May. Churchill then appointed him Adviser on Combined Operations and he undertook the preliminary planning of the invasion of Europe. In March 1942 Churchill made him a member of the Chiefs of Staff Committee. He planned the raids on St. Nazaire (March) and Dieppe (August). Mountbatten attended the Casablanca Conference in January 1943 and the Quebec Conference in July. At the latter it was decided to reorganize the command in Southeast Asia. Mountbatten was made Supreme Allied Commander of the area. His HQ was to be in Colombo and he was to be equally responsible to the British Prime Minister and the American President.

When Mountbatten arrived in Colombo he brought with him many technical advisers and set about improving communications in India and developing it as a military base for operations in Burma. He had a gift for public relations and made sure every operation was well publicized.

During heavy fighting at Kohima and Imphal, Mountbatten had to divert aircraft from China to supply his troops. Although the command had been reorganized there were still anomalies, and General Stilwell, Mountbatten's deputy, often acted completely independently. Furthermore, General Giffard, Commander of Land Forces in Burma, had his HQ in Calcutta, as did Air Chief Marshal Peirse, and they were not always in touch with Mountbatten. Another problem facing Mountbatten was that although he was expected to reconquer Burma he was not

given extra equipment. By May 1945 General Slim's 14th Army reconquered Burma by skillful use of its resources. In August 1945 the Japanese surrendered and at Singapore on 12 September Mountbatten accepted the formal surrender of about 750,000 Japanese in Southeast Asia.

---

## MP-43
see Krummlauf

---

## Mulberries

The 'Mulberries' were special artificial harbors which were used in the D-Day invasions. Churchill had urged their development from 1942 onwards, as it seemed unlikely that the Allies would capture a port installation intact. The 'Mulberries' had an outer breakwater composed of partly sunken blockships and partly concrete 'caissons', 200 feet long. They had to be towed across the Channel and were undoubtedly successful since after the first week, some 6500 vehicles and nearly 40,000 tons of stores were being landed weekly.

---

## Munich Agreement, 29 September 1938

On 29 September 1938 Chamberlain (Britain), Daladier (France), Hitler (Germany) and Mussolini (Italy) met at Munich to discuss the problem of Czech Sudetenland. Czechoslovakia possessed most of the Sudetenland which was populated by Germans and Hitler was demanding its restoration to Germany. It was decided that Czechoslovakia would give the Sudeten German border districts to Germany and also give territory to Hungary and Poland at a later date. The agreement also guaranteed the integrity of Czechoslovakia. The agreement was hailed by Chamberlain as 'peace for our time' but was violated when Hitler's army marched into Prague in March 1939.

---

## *Musashi*

The sister of the giant battleship *Yamato* was sunk by aircraft from Task Force 38 in the Sibuyan Sea on 24 October 1944. Progressive flooding from 20 torpedoes and 17 bombs got out of control and she was abandoned.

---

## Mussolini, Benito, 1883–1945

Though Mussolini, who had seized power in Italy in 1922, was an important influence upon Hitler, he himself did not make aggressive war an article of Italian Fascist policy, not, at least, within Europe; colonial conquests, however, were a different (because an easier) matter, and he conquered Abyssinia in 1935–36 and occupied the backward state of Albania in 1939. It needed Hitler's apparently effortless victories over Holland, Belgium and France to tempt him to declare war against the Allies in 1940 and even then he failed to conquer any territory in France, despite the inferiority of the French Army of the Alps to his invading force. He was scarcely more successful in Egypt later in the year when, after an unopposed invasion, his army was humiliatingly defeated by General O'Connor's Western Desert Force and driven back into Libya. The Italian Army's fortunes

Italy's Il Duce, Benito Mussolini, whose dreams of empire were all too quickly destroyed.

then became linked with those of the German Afrika Korps, which Hitler sent to its assistance. Eventually the Italian Army was captured along with the German forces in 1943. Meanwhile he had also attempted his own invasion of Greece in November 1940, which had ended in humiliating failure and obliged Hitler to come to his rescue with a full-scale Balkan invasion which delayed his invasion of Russia by a vital six weeks; Hitler did not forgive him for that, nor for his failure to warn Germany of what he had intended to do. By 1943 Italy was militarily and politically in a bad way. Her expeditionary force in Russia had suffered grievously in the Stalingrad battle, her political freedom of action had been surrendered to Germany and the Allies threatened her with invasion. In July, following the Allied invasion of Sicily, Mussolini was deposed by the Fascist Grand Council and a new government formed under Marshal Badoglio. Mussolini was confined in a hotel in the Gran Sasso in the Abruzzi mountains from which the German commando Skorzeny rescued him at Hitler's behest on 12 September. However, Mussolini never thereafter regained independent power in his country. The Germans imposed their own control over the Italian armed forces and established a military government over that portion of Italy which did not fall at once to the Allies in the invasion of September. Mussolini proclaimed his own new Italian Social Republic in the north, and punished any conspirators of July that he could find, but was allowed no jurisdiction by the German military authorities. Captured by partisans in April 1945, he was executed and the bodies of he and his mistress exposed in a Milan square. The only consolation of his declining years was that Hitler, who had abused and misused their partnership throughout the war, treated the old dictator with respect and even affection to the end.

---

## 'Mustang'
see P-51 Mustang, North American

---

## Myitkyina
see Northern Burma Campaign

---

## 'Myrt'
see Nakajima C6N Saiun

---

## Nagasaki
see Hiroshima and Nagasaki

---

## Nagumo, Vice-Admiral Chuichi, 1887–1944

Nagumo, on the flagship *Akagi*, was the commander of the Carrier Strike Force *Kido Butai* which attacked Pearl Harbor in December 1941. He and Kusaka (Chief of Staff of the First Air Fleet) cautiously decided against a third raid which, in hindsight, could have been decisive.

Nagumo commanded the same force at the Battle of Midway, June 1942, at which his flagship, the *Akagi*, sank. During this engagement, the US fleet successfully evaded the conventional naval battle which Nagumo sought: Yamamoto therefore ordered Nagumo to call off the invasion. *Kido Butai* also fought at the Battle of the Eastern Solomons and Guadalcanal; at the latter, Nagumo again lost his flagship. Nagumo also organized the defense of Saipan. In the last moments of this battle, on 6 July 1944, he committed suicide. Admiral Nagumo was one of the most formidable and courageous defenders of Japan.

---

## Nakajima B5N

This Japanese carrier-based bomber and torpedo bomber was in service from 1938–45. When it first flew in January 1937 this very ordinary-looking aircraft was actually the most advanced naval warplane in the world. Among its advanced features were all-metal stressed-skin construction, power-folding wings, retractable landing gear, flaps, integral wing tanks and a variable-pitch propeller – none of which were on the British counterpart, the Swordfish. The first B5N1 bombers went into action in 1938 in China, but the type remained apparently unknown to other countries until at Pearl Harbor on 7 December 1941 it wrought havoc among the US Pacific Fleet. Every torpedo hit on that day came from 40 of the B5N2 versions, while 103 B5N1 bombers kept up a rain of well-aimed bombs from above. Altogether at least 1200 were built, some of them by the Aichi company, and they stayed in the battlefront right to the end of the war, receiving the Allied codename 'Kate'. Their greatest feats after Pearl Harbor were the sinking of the valuable US carriers *Yorktown*, *Lexington*, *Wasp* and *Hornet*, though they stood little chance if intercepted. The B5N could reach 230mph on its 1000hp Nakajima Sakae engine, and was always popular with its crews.

The Nakajima B6N 'Jill' torpedo bomber.

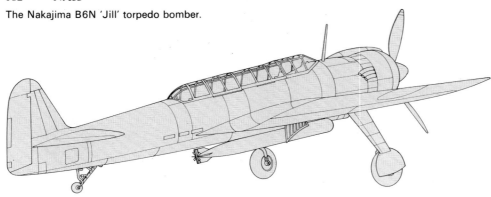

## Nakajima B6N

This Japanese three-seat carrier-based torpedo bomber was in service from 1944–45. Designed as a successor to the B5N, the B6N was just the same in layout but had a more powerful engine. When first flown in March 1942 the B6N1 had a 1870hp Nakajima Mamori 11, which gave a lot of trouble, so the B6N2 was replaced by the more reliable Mitsubishi Kasei 25 of 1850hp. With either, the B6N could reach almost 300mph once it had dropped its big 1764lb torpedo. Named Tenzan, after a heavenly mountain in China, it was a great thorn in the side of the Allies who called it 'Jill'. About 1268 were built, and though flown with great determination they suffered when the Imperial Navy's carriers were lost as well as from a shortage of skilled crews and shortage of fuel. In April–June 1945 the B6N was one of the leading types used in kamikaze suicide attacks on Allied invasion fleets. A few were equipped with some of the first flight-cleared Japanese ASV (air to surface vessel) radar, to help them find ships by night.

## Nakajima C6N Saiun

Intended as a carrier-based reconnaissance aircraft, the C6N ('Myrt') suffered from engine troubles during development; by the time it entered service, Japan no longer had much of a carrier force. Being able to out-run and out-climb most Allied fighters in 1944, the Saiun had only a 7.92mm rearward-firing gun for defense. When it was adapted into the C6N1–S night

fighter for home defense, the crew was reduced from three to two and two cannon were mounted to fire forward and upward from the rear fuselage. Others became C6N1–B model 21 torpedo-bombers. The most important successes achieved by the Saiun were to discover and reconnoiter the US task forces prior to the June 1944 assault on the Marianas and the attack on Saipan.

## Nakajima J1N1–S Gekko

Moonlight to the Japanese, 'Irving' to the Allies, the J1N1–S was evolved from the earlier J1N1–C reconnaissance aircraft. Armed with two pairs of 20mm guns, firing respectively forward-and-upward and forward-and-downward from behind the cockpit, most J1N1–S were used as night fighters. Some were fitted with early radar sets, but lacked the speed or ceiling to be effective against B–29s. A few operated in the ground attack role, with 550lb and 66lb bombs.

## Nakajima Ki–43

This Japanese single-seat fighter was in service from 1941–45. Produced in numbers second only to the Navy's 'Zero', the Ki–43 was the Imperial Army's chief fighter in World War II. Compared with the Navy fighter it was even smaller, lighter and cheaper, and though it had superb maneuverability it was so lightly armed it had difficulty in shooting down most opponents after 1941, while its light construction

*Below:* Nakajima Ki-43 Peregrine Falcon.
*Bottom:* The Nakajima C6N1 'Myrt'

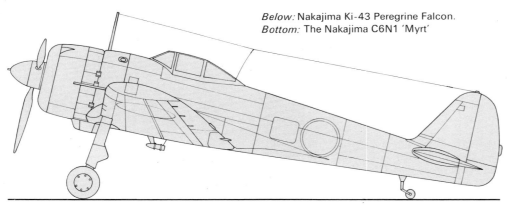

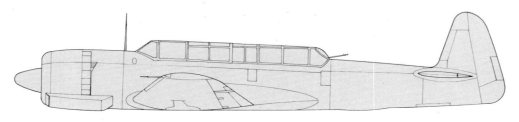

meant it often disintegrated when hit by a burst of 0.5in bullets or 20mm shells. Produced to meet a 1938 specification, the prototype flew in January 1939, and after much revision the Ki–43–I entered service in mid-1941, proudly named *Hayabusa* (Peregrine Falcon). It reached just over 300mph on the 975hp of its Nakajima Ha–25 engine, and carried two light machine guns above the forward fuselage – the same armament as fighters in 1918. By 1942 the Ki–43–II was in production, with 1105hp Sakae Ha–115 engines and the guns changed for heavier ones of 12.7mm caliber. Racks under the wings could carry two 551lb bombs. During 1942 the wing was reduced in span from near 38ft to only 35.5ft and production continued with small changes until the end of the war, two solitary prototypes in 1945 having two 20mm cannon. Altogether 5751 *Hayabusas* were delivered, and despite its obvious shortcomings it was very popular and it was the favorite mount of most of the Army's top-scoring fighter aces.

## Nakajima Ki–44 Shoki

The Shoki was conceived as a fast-climbing, heavily armed interceptor for short-range defense of the Japanese homeland. Almost all of the 1233 that were built, in several versions, were employed in this role from late 1942 to the end of the war. When Japanese Army pilots became used to handling a heavier, more bulky fighter than anything they had flown before, they achieved quite good results. In particular, pilots of the Ki–44–IIc, armed with two 40mm and two 12.7mm guns, became adept at dealing with American Liberator bombers. Allied name for the Ki–44 was 'Tojo'. Standard power plant of all late models was a 1450hp Nakajima Ha–109, giving a maximum speed of 376mph.

## Nakajima Ki–49 Donryu

Classed by the Japanese Army as a heavy bomber, the Ki–49 ('Helen') made its debut in a raid on Port Darwin, Australia, from New Guinea, on 19 February 1942. The aircraft used on that occasion were early Ki–49–Is, with 1250hp Ha–41 engines. The later Ki–49–IIs, with 1450hp engines, were more satisfactory in terms of both power and defensive armament, which was increased to one 20mm and five 12.7mm guns. It appeared everywhere from Burma and India to China, the East Indies, Formosa and the Philippines; but, after suffering particularly heavy losses in the Battle for Leyte Island, was gradually adapted for suicide missions and for coastal patrol and mine-detection duties.

## Nakajima Ki–84

This Japanese single-seat fighter was in service from 1944–45. Though it did not even fly until March 1943, and reached the Imperial Army fighter squadrons only after April 1944, the Ki–84 still made its mark in World War II, and reminded the Allies that Japanese aircraft could still give a good account of themselves in combat. Designed by a team led by T Koyama, the Ki–84 was powered by a great but troublesome engine, the 1900hp Nakajima Homare Ha–45. Poor quality control in the factories meant that landing gears often broke, brakes did not work and various systems just refused to function.

Yet the basic aircraft, named *Hayate* (Gale or Hurricane), and codenamed 'Frank' by the Allies, was so outstanding that at all times it was truly formidable. Tough, streamlined, well protected and well armed, the Ki–84 was still light enough to reach almost 400mph and to climb and maneuver better than practically all the Allied fighters. Early versions had two 20mm cannon in the wings and two 12.7mm in the fuselage, but most had four 20mm, while a few had two 20mm in the fuselage and two 30mm in the wings, packing a terrific punch. All operational versions also had two wing racks for two 551lb bombs or long-range tanks. As well as building 3513 of these excellent machines, Japanese factories also tried various experimental models with special high-altitude engines or constructed of wood or steel to save scarce aluminium.

## Nambu Pistols

These standard service pistols of the Japanese forces took their name from Colonel Kijiro Nambu, the designer. It was first demonstrated in 1909 and adopted in semi-official fashion in 1915; this was the fourth year of the Taisho era; hence the official title of the pistol as the 'Taisho 04' model. It was a locked breech automatic pistol in 8mm caliber, which was locked by a swinging wedge beneath the bolt similar to that used on the Italian Glisenti pistol. In addition to the standard model, a smaller version, chambered for a 7mm cartridge, was adopted as a staff officer's pistol.

In 1925 an improved model, known as the 'Taisho 14' was introduced, and this was the official service pistol throughout World War II. It resembles the original Nambu in external appearance and fired the same cartridge, but had some minor internal changes to facilitate mass production. A safety catch was added, replacing the grip safety device on the earlier model, and two bolt closing springs were used instead of one. After experience in Manchuria in the early 1930s a special version with a large trigger guard was produced to permit the pistol to be used with a gloved hand.

Although not a Nambu design it is useful to consider the third Japanese automatic pistol here; this was the 'Type 94', also of 8mm caliber,

The Taisho 04, the original Nambu pistol.

The Taisho 14 or improved Nambu.

introduced in about 1937. It is reputed to have been produced for commercial sale in the first instance, but almost all production was taken by the Japanese forces. It is, quite frankly, the worst automatic pistol ever adopted by a major nation. The breech-locking system relied on a vertically sliding plate holding the bolt locked, but in fact it was so badly designed that it is possible to fire the pistol without the bolt locked. Moreover the striker release mechanism is on the surface of the slide and can be pressed, releasing the striker and firing the pistol, simply by gripping the weapon firmly.

## Nanking, Rape of
see China Incident, 1931–41

## Näshorn

This German self-propelled anti-tank gun, originally known as 'Hornisse' was introduced into service in November 1942, it consisted of the 88mm anti-tank gun PAK 43 mounted into a modified PzKw IV chassis. The tank's engine was moved forward so as to leave a fighting space at the rear for the gun's crew, and the hull was built up into an armored, open-topped barbette structure with the gun pointing forward. At least 472 were built.

The Natter interceptor aircraft.

## Natter

This German piloted, rocket-propelled interceptor aircraft for the defense of vulnerable points against heavy bomber formations was basically a single-seat monoplane with a Walter rocket motor and armed with a battery of 73mm Fohn rockets in the nose or, alternatively, a battery of single-shot 30mm guns. It was to be launched vertically from a guide-rail, climbing at 425mph, with a flight duration of about four minutes, after which the pilot would glide back close to his base and parachute out, leaving the aircraft to crash-land. Work began in August 1944, and after glide tests showed the aircraft's stability to be good, a manned flight was ordered by the SS in February 1945. Against the designer's advice, this took place and the pilot was thrown out of the aircraft and killed. A total of 30 Natter aircraft were built, of which four survived to be captured by the Allies in 1945. It never achieved service status.

## 'Nell'
see Mitsubishi G3M

HMS *Nelson* fires her 16-in guns.

## *Nelson*

Under the terms of the Washington Naval Disarmament Treaty the Royal Navy was allowed to build two 35,000-ton battleships to compensate for the fact that both Japan and the USA had new ships armed with 16in guns. The British had already drawn up plans for four 48,000-ton battlecruisers, and used the information gained from this work and their tests on the surrendered German ship *Baden* to formulate their requirements; the design of the *Nelson* Class began to evolve during the Washington Conference itself.

When the two ships appeared in 1927 they did not meet with acclaim, for they presented an outlandish profile with all three triple 16in turrets forward, a massive block of superstructure and the secondary guns and a stubby stack grouped aft. Their derisive nicknames, *Nelsol* and *Rodnol*, referred to a group of oil tankers with names ending in 'ol'. However they were formidable ships incorporating massive protection and a number of ingenious ideas. They were the only battleships in the world in September 1939 designed with the full benefit of war experience, and the only modern ships available to the Royal Navy until the *King George V* Class were finished.

The *Nelson* was damaged by a magnetic mine early in the war and was torpedoed by an Italian bomber while escorting a convoy to Malta. The Italian surrender was signed on her quarterdeck, appropriately so, as her guns had played an important part in supporting the Salerno landings. After providing fire-support at Normandy she went out to the East Indies at the end of 1944 and finished the war with the Eastern Fleet.

## Nerve Gas
see Sarin, Soman and Tabun

## Nettleton, Squadron Leader John, 1917–1943

This South African-born bomber pilot in the RAF led a squadron of 12 Lancaster bombers in a raid on the submarine diesel engine works at Augsburg on 17 April 1942. A feat of immense daring with most of the mission being flown over enemy territory, only five aircraft returned. Nettleton was awarded the Victoria Cross, Britain's highest award, for his courage. He was killed in action on 12 July 1943, during a raid over Turin.

## Neurath, Konstantin von, 1873–

Neurath had held the post of Foreign Minister from 1932–38 and was appointed Reichs Protector of Bohemia-Moravia in 1939. He resigned from the Ministry, because he disapproved of Hitler's plans for aggressive war. In Czechoslovakia he administered his tasks with insufficient harshness for Hitler's taste and was forced to retire in 1941, when Heydrich replaced him. He was tried at Nuremberg and received a sentence of fifteen years, because he had intervened to mitigate the activities of the Gestapo and SD in Czechoslovakia.

## *Nevada*

The USS *Nevada* (BB.36) was built in 1912–16 as the prototype of a new type of battleship. She was the first US battleship with oil fuel and the first in the world with the revolutionary 'all-or-nothing' principle of armoring. She and her sister *Oklahoma* were completely modernized in 1927–30 with tripod masts in place of the distinctive 'cage' masts and extra AA guns.

She joined the Pacific Fleet in 1930 and was at Pearl Harbor on 7 December 1941. She alone of the eight capital ships in 'Battleship Row' was able to get up steam as she was moored by herself. She was struck by a torpedo and two or three bombs as she moved away from her berth, and then again by a bomb as she moved into the channel. To avoid the risk of blocking the entrance to Pearl Harbor she was ordered to beach herself off Hospital Point, where she lay burning for some time. Although gutted forward, with 50 killed and 109 wounded she was refloated on 12 February 1942 and was back in action three months later. However, she needed further modernization to meet wartime requirements, and she went into Norfolk Navy Yard for a refit from June 1942 to April 1944.

The *Nevada*'s first assignment was to provide fire-support for the Normandy invasion, and then she supported the invasion of Southern France. In February 1945 she arrived at Iwo Jima and spent the rest of the war on escort and bombardment duties. She received seven battle stars for her service, and in 1946 survived the second Bikini atom bomb test before being scrapped.

## New Georgia, 1943

In 1943 the American aim was to break down the barrier formed by the Bismarck Archipelago and capture the Japanese base of Rabaul. The first stage was for Admiral Halsey to occupy the Russell Islands as an air and naval base and then advance on New Georgia to take Munda airfield and then advance on Bougainville. On 21 February 1943 the first step began when the US 43rd Infantry Division landed on the Russell Islands and found that there was no Japanese garrison. Halsey's fleet continued to wear down Japanese shipping and was now in a position to stop Japanese raids down 'the Slot'. Admiral Yamamoto sent his aircraft carriers to challenge US air superiority but on a flying visit to Bougainville, on 18 April, he was shot down and this was a great blow to Japanese morale.

On 30 June 1943 the American offensive was finally launched when 43rd Infantry took Rendova Island off the coast of New Georgia. Two days later the Americans landed on New Georgia, but they made little progress in the un-

favorable conditions: wet climate, mountainous jungle and reefs on the northeast coast. The Japanese had a garrison of 10,000 which had orders to hold the island as long as possible and more supplies were sent through the 'Tokyo Express'. The Americans had planned to hop from Rendova Island to northern New Georgia and at the same time make three landings in the south at Segi Point, Wickham Anchorage and Viru Harbor. Segi Point was taken on 21 July and the Seabees soon constructed an airstrip. Wickham Anchorage was taken on 30 July and Viru Harbor the day after. This line ensured the communications for the force coming down Rendova Island. General Hyakutake thought the convoy was heading for Munda and was taken by surprise when troops landed at Zanana, east of Munda on 2 August. This boosted the morale of the troops who had been trying to take Munda for a month, and on 5 August the airfield was finally taken. The Japanese had a marked disadvantage, since their aircraft had been destroyed by American bombing raids and repeated attempts to send reinforcements were stopped by US shipping in battles in Kula Gulf and Vella Gulf.

In the next two months the rest of New Georgia was occupied. The Allies lost about 1000 killed, but many died from sickness. The Japanese lost 2500 men.

## New Guinea. Biak and Wakde Islands, 1944

After the successful operation against Hollandia, the Joint Chiefs of Staff decided that the next step would be to take Wakde Island which would be used as an air base in the capture of Biak Island.

On 17 May 1944 the US 6th Army landed a force in the Maffin Bay area and on the next day landed on Wakde Island. The Japanese garrison resisted but within two days the island was overrun. In the Maffin Bay area, fighting was heavy and it was only overcome in late June at the cost of 445 Americans killed and 1500 wounded against 4000 Japanese killed.

The conquest of Wakde was facilitated by accurate intelligence reports. However the intelligence reports on Biak Island were totally misleading. They estimated that the garrison was 4000 strong. In fact there were 11,000 Japanese on the island occupying heavily fortified positions. On 27 May the 41st Infantry landed on Biak to find that the beaches were deserted, but once they pushed inland they made little progress encountering stiff opposition from the Japanese. This was very embarrassing for General MacArthur, who had expected the island to fall in a week. Then he planned to press on to take the Philippines, using Biak as an air base.

The Japanese Imperial GHQ, and especially Admiral Toyoda, decided that the operation on Biak was the Americans' major offensive and decided to divert their reinforcements from the Marianas to Biak in Operation Kon. The US had control of the air, and the Japanese missed several opportunities to bring in the troops by being over-cautious. In the end they landed 1000 men and lost two destroyers, only to find out that the US Central Pacific Force was attacking the Marianas, where Japanese defenses were not ready.

By 20 June the US had worn down resistance on the island, although fighting continued well into August. The whole operation cost the US 474 killed and 2400 wounded, while the Japanese lost all the garrison.

## New Guinea. Hollandia and Wewak, 1943–1945

After the Allies had gained control of the Huon Peninsula, there followed another lull as General MacArthur built up his supplies. The Japanese did not have any air or naval support because their forces had been transferred to meet the threat in the Central Pacific. The Japanese now had six weak divisions in northern New Guinea to face fifteen Allied divisions.

On 2 January 1944 the US 32nd Infantry landed at Saidor, 100 miles west of the Australian divisions advancing from Finschhafen, thus cutting off 12,000 Japanese still in the Huon Peninsula. During this time the AIF 7th Division continued their advance from Dumpu via Kankiryo Saddle towards Bogadjim on the coast, west of Saidor. Finally on 24–26 April they overran Bogadjim, Madang and Alexishafen, and General Adachi's Eighteenth Army (30,000 men) retreated towards Wewak.

The Allied High Command had decided to bypass Wewak and the Hansa Bay area where there were about 30,000 Japanese troops and 20,000 civilians without supplies. On 22 April there were three amphibious landings by the US 1st Corps (led by General Eichelberger). The US 24th Infantry landed at Tanahmerah Bay while the 41st Infantry landed at Humboldt Bay, 25 miles east of Hollandia. They met little opposition and combined to take Hollandia. The third amphibious landing was at Aitape, some 125 miles further east, where a small force had to neutralize the airfield but in fact found that it had been knocked out in raids by Vice-Admiral Mitscher's Task Force 58 at the end of March.

Adachi tried to break out of this trap but by the time he had reached US lines, General Hall and the 11th Corps were ready to repulse him. Eighty-eight hundred Japanese died in the breakout attempt in July, compared with 450 US dead and 2500 wounded.

The system of bypassing major troop concentrations and leaving them to stagnate without supplies was working well, and MacArthur's next leap was to Wakde Island. The Japanese held out without any fighting until the Australian 6th Division arrived at Hollandia and decided to launch an offensive that drove through the Toricelli Mountains in terrible conditions. They took Wewak on 11 May 1945 where 442 Australians were killed and 1141 wounded and a further 16,203 had to be hospitalized. The greatly weakened Japanese lost 9000 men. Adachi and 13,500 men eventually surrendered on 13 September 1945.

## New Guinea. Huon Peninsula, 1943

After the capture of Buna, Gona and Sanananda, some 5400 Japanese managed to escape to the Lae-Salamaua-Markham Valley area which now became a major theater of war. On 30 January 1943 the Japanese cut their way through the jungle and attacked Wau, the Kanga Force base and airstrip. They were repulsed with heavy losses (1200 men) and retreated to Mubo. The Japanese received another setback when a convoy from Rabaul was destroyed in the Battle of Bismarck Sea (3 March) and 3000 troops drowned.

Stalemate set in as both sides dug in and sporadic fighting continued along a broad front from Wau to Mubo to the Francisco river. On the night of 29–30 June the Allied offensive began with an amphibious US landing of 1400

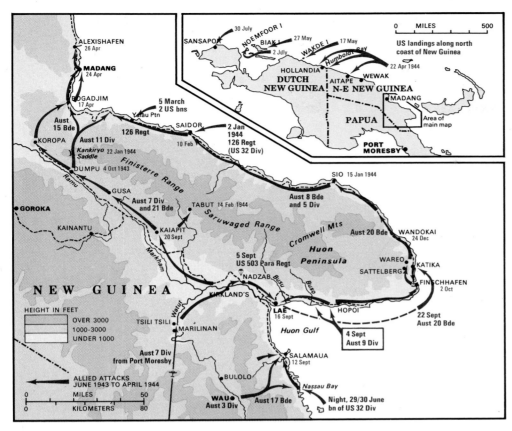

The Australians considered the protection of Port Moresby as a fight for their national security, but their small force defending New Guinea were badly trained with poor communications and very little transport. There were also 700 'Coastwatchers', who had been trained before the war to spot enemy aircraft.

The first Japanese landings in New Guinea were at Salamaua (200 miles due north of Port Moresby) on 8 March 1942. The Japanese planned to take Port Moresby and expected little opposition but their invasion force was turned back by the Battle of Coral Sea. This allowed the Australian 6th and 7th Divisions to return from Europe and by June the Allies had 104,000 AIF, 265,000 Australian militia and 38,000 US troops. They were under the overall command of General MacArthur, with General Blamey in command of land forces.

Throughout June the Allies maintained a successful guerrilla campaign against the Japanese in Markham Valley and on the Owen Stanley Range. As always this campaign of combined Coastwatchers and NGUR Kanga Force received much help from Papuan natives.

Two areas were considered crucial by both the Japanese and the Allies: Buna and Milne Bay. Buna was at the head of the Kokoda trail, a one-man wide overland track through mountains and jungle to Port Moresby. Two Australian Brigades, under Brigadier Porter, were on their way down the trail to secure Buna when 1800 Japanese landed at Sanananda (north of Buna) on the night of 21–22 July. The Australian forces made contact with the Japanese at Wairopi on 23 July, and held them for four days before falling back on Kokoda, which the Japanese took on 28 July. The Japanese then pushed forward as the Australians conducted a holding operation, often inflicting heavy casualties on the force of 13,000. The Japanese faced many problems: their troops could not cope with the climate; their supply lines were overextended; they were under continual fire from the air. On 29 August they received orders from General Hyakutake not to advance further than Ioribaiwa, some 30 miles from Port Moresby.

On 17 September the Japanese reached Ioribaiwa but eleven days later the Allies began their counteroffensive under Blamey, who was now in Port Moresby. The Australians were now experienced in jungle warfare and they met only token resistance. By the end of October they had pushed the Japanese back to Kokoda (which was reoccupied on 2 November). MacArthur was not satisfied with their speed and had Major General Allen replaced by General Vasey as commander in the field (on 27 October). The Japanese retreated throughout November and struck difficulties at Wairopi where the river bridge had been destroyed: General Horii drowned while trying to ford the Kumusi River and was succeeded by General Adachi.

The US 128th Regiment had meanwhile established air bases at Ponangi and Wanigela (east of Buna) in order to outflank Buna. The AIF were to make for Gona. The first US attacks were feeble, and provoked much criticism of the GIs fighting ability and led to the replacement of their commander, Major General Harding, by Lieutenant General Eichelberger. The Australians made two attempts on the strongly fortified Gona (on 1 and 9 December), succeeded the second time and made straight for Sanananda, the strong Japanese base. Buna was finally taken on 2 January 1943 after the veterans of Milne Bay were flown in with extra

troops at Nassau Bay, threatening Salamaua. General Adachi considered Salamaua so vital to the defense of Lae that he sent in all but 2000 of his 11,000 troops. However the AIF 17th Brigade took Mubo on 17 July. The Australians advanced behind Mubo to take Mount Tambu and the ridges surrounding Salamaua. On 11 September the Americans entered Salamaua which had been evacuated and an ambitious amphibious, airborne and overland attack on Lae had been planned. On 5 September an amphibious force landed the AIF 9th Division ten miles east of Lae and on the next day there was a parachute drop on Nadzab airfield northwest of Lae. These troops, together with the troops from Salamaua converged on Lae, which fell after heavy fighting on 16 September. This operation cost the Australians 500 killed and 1300 wounded; the US, 81 killed and 396 wounded; and the Japanese, 2722 killed among 10,300 casualties.

The Allied forces now divided: the Australian 7th Division cut straight across the Huon Peninsula down the Markham Valley towards Madang and by early October reached Dumpu some 50 miles from the town; the Americans and Australian 9th Division continued to make amphibious assaults along the coast of the Huon Peninsula. The Japanese had hoped to keep hold of Finschhafen, but on 22 September an amphibious Allied landing took Scarlet Beach and after heavy fighting on the Bumi River, advance to take Finschhafen on 2 October. The Japanese then led a counterattack on Jivevenang, half-way to Sattelberg, on 16 October. The AIF 9th Division pushed the Japanese back into mountainous country, where they had no supplies. The Australians also ran out of supplies, but they pushed on and reached Sattelberg on 25 November to find it deserted. The Japanese were now definitely in retreat. Adachi's hopes of recapturing Finschhafen and Lae had come to nothing. Amphibious landings further north would contain the Japanese.

## New Guinea. Milne Bay, August–September 1942

Milne Bay was important to both the Japanese and the Allies because it could be used for an air and sea assault on Port Moresby. The AIF 7th Brigade and US Engineers managed to occupy Milne Bay before the Japanese and built an airstrip by early August 1942.

The Japanese were trying to attack Port Moresby through the jungle on the Kokoda trail but in August they decided to attack Milne Bay as well. The Allies had some 8700 troops there under Major General Clowes and it was impossible and strategically undesirable to evacuate them. The Japanese landed at Ahioma on the night of 25–26 August and immediately Kittyhawks, Hudsons and B-17 Fortresses attacked the landing convoys destroying barges and most of the stores. The planes also strafed the enemy, a technique they continued to use with great effect during the fighting. The Japanese pushed the Australians westwards along the beach in close combat fighting by night, lying low by day. Japanese tanks were unstoppable until anti-tank guns arrived but the Japanese's ineffectual use of the bayonet and their constant frontal assaults led to heavy losses. By 31 August the Australians were on the offensive. The enemy were slowly pushed back up the beach and because the situation was critical on Guadalcanal, the Japanese could not expect reinforcements. The Japanese began evacuating on 5 September and had left by 7 September. MacArthur criticized Clowes for his 'slowness' but Milne Bay was the Allies' first land victory over the Japanese.

## New Guinea. Port Moresby and Buna, March 1942–January 1943

New Guinea marked the farthest point south reached by the Japanese in World War II, as well as the point at which they were turned back.

tanks. Together AIF and GIs captured Sana-nanda under Brigadier Porter on 22 January. By this point in the campaign the Japanese had lost 12,000 men, the Australians 5700 and the US 2800. There were three times as many casualties from disease as from the fighting.

## New Jersey

The battleship *New Jersey* (BB.62) was the second of the *Iowa* Class battleships authorized in 1940. She was launched in December 1942 and commissioned at Philadelphia on 23 May 1943. She hoisted the flag of Admiral Raymond A Spruance, Commander-in-Chief, 5th Fleet at Majuro Lagoon in February 1944 and immediately took part in a raid on Truk. Her high speed enabled her to screen the fast carriers, and in June she bombarded Saipan and Tinian in the Marianas. She covered Admiral Mitscher's carriers in the 'Marianas Turkey Shoot', and her AA fire accounted for several aircraft.

On 24 August 1944 she became the flagship of Admiral William F Halsey Jr, Commander-in-Chief 3rd Fleet, and was based at Ulithi from then until April 1945, screening the carriers as they raided far and wide across the Pacific. In January 1945 she became the flagship of Rear Admiral Badger, commanding Battleship Division 7, and took part in the invasion of Iwo Jima and Okinawa. At the end of the war she was Spruance's flagship once more, and she anchored in Tokyo Bay in September 1945.

## 'Nick'
see Kawasaki Ki-45

## Nimitz, Admiral Chester W, 1885–1966

Admiral Nimitz, Commander-in-Chief of the Pacific Fleet during the war, and had outstanding gifts as a strategist and organizer of naval combat. Unlike Admiral Yamamoto, Nimitz stayed on shore during major battles. He believed in large-scale amphibious operations.

After Pearl Harbor his main duty was to protect the Hawaiian bases and he gathered a fleet near Midway Island. In May 1942 two of his carriers were involved in the Battle of Coral Sea which paved the way for the victory at Midway. One great advantage was that the US Intelligence had cracked the Japanese Fleet's code.

Midway left Nimitz with a freer hand to direct operations. The Pacific Area had been divided into two commands: MacArthur's command was the Southwest Pacific to line 160°E longitude. Nimitz had the Central Pacific area up to that line but including Guadalcanal. This was his next target. The force sent to Guadalcanal was the first US sea-borne expedition in the war and it was beset with problems. In the many sea battles off Guadalcanal the Japanese showed their superiority in night-fighting. In October 1942 Nimitz was left with only one carrier but this crisis was overcome eventually because although the US losses in shipping matched those of the Japanese, the US fleet was able to replace ships more quickly.

In 1943 the Americans gained control of the South Solomons and Nimitz received more ships and aircraft. He came to realize that frontal assaults were not effective ways of fighting the Japanese. He favored attacking a less well-defended island to the rear of Japanese troop

Admiral Chester Nimitz at the end of 1942.

concentrations and cutting them off. He also felt that the quickest way to defeat the Japanese was to approach them via the islands in the Central Pacific; finally the Joint Chiefs of Staff agreed with this plan. In November 1943 this strategy began with the capture of Makin and Tarawa in the Gilbert Islands, and Truk and Saipan in February 1944. For these Nimitz used Admiral Halsey's 3rd Fleet and Vice-Admiral Spruance's 5th Fleet alternately. Nimitz had been a submarine specialist and his submarine arm maintained an efficient blockade of Japan by constant attack on Japanese merchant shipping.

In March 1944 Nimitz was told to speed up his advance to the Marianas and his fleet emerged victorious from the Battle of the Philippine Sea. In October the Joint Chiefs of Staff gave way to MacArthur's insistence and agreed that Nimitz's fleet should help in the conquest of Luzon and then move on to the capture of Iwo Jima and Okinawa. As part of the Luzon campaign, Vice-Admiral Kinkaid and Rear Admiral Oldendorf repulsed the Japanese fleet at the Battle of Leyte Gulf.

In February 1945 assault troops captured Iwo Jima and then in June moved on to Okinawa. Nimitz's staff were now planning operations to land on mainland Japan but the Japanese surrendered. The formal surrender of the Japanese was accepted on board Nimitz's flagship the USS *Missouri* in Tokyo Bay on 2 September 1945.

## Nomonhan Incident, 1939

In July 1938 on the Soviet-Manchurian border there was a clash between Japanese and Soviet troops at Lake Khassan. Both sides brought in tanks, artillery and air power but the Japanese were decisively beaten. In May 1939 another border dispute erupted and the Red Army poured in massive reinforcements. In August the Japanese were overwhelmingly defeated at the Battle of Khalkin-Gol and suffered 50,000 casualties. These defeats made the Japanese reluctant to take action against the Soviets.

## Nomura, Admiral Kichisaburo, 1877–

A retired admiral, respected and good natured, Nomura was appointed ambassador to Washington to spin out negotiations with Cordell Hull while Japan prepared for war with Amer-

ica. He knew almost nothing about Japan's immediate military plans even as he submitted the Japanese Declaration of War to Hull, 80 minutes after Pearl Harbor took place, on 7 December, 1941.

## Nordwind
see Alsace, German Offensive in, 1944

## Normandy, the Breakout from, 1944

Montgomery, as land commander, had a clear-cut plan for the conduct of the battle inside the bridgehead won in the week after D-Day. It was to draw the Germans onto his left around Caen in the British sector and wear down their armor, while the Americans on the right captured Cherbourg and opened it to shipping and built up their armored strength for a breakout into open country. The capture of Britanny would follow, then an advance to the Seine and, in time, to the Rhine. The timetable expected the Rhine to be reached in 11 months from D-Day. It began as planned. The base of the Cotentin peninsula was cut on 17 June and Cherbourg invested on 20 June. It fell a week later. Meanwhile the British in Operation Epsom, an infantry offensive just to the west of Caen, had advanced to the Odon river. On 8 July they seized the western half of Caen after a massive aerial bombardment had devastated the city and on 18–19 July, in the great armored offensive of Operation Goodwood, they outflanked the city from the east, though at a very high cost in tanks. The day before the battle, Rommel, the executive field commander, was shot in his staff car by an RAF fighter and very seriously wounded. The Germans had by now suffered grievous losses of humbler but irreplaceable soldiers and precious equipment. They had been forced to use their Panzer divisions piecemeal in the defense, being unable to move divisions over the broken railways from the south of France and being afraid to release divisions from the Pas de Calais in case a second invasion was launched. On 25 July they suffered the *coup de grâce*. The Americans, who had been waging a war of the hedgerows with their infantry since 3 July, had also assembled a massive force of armor under General Patton (although he did not actually arrive in France until 31 July). It was now unleashed, after an earthquake bombardment by the American air force, and broke through the front and into Britanny, reaching Avranches by 31 July. It severely threatened the Germans, but Hitler now intervened to ensure that it would be fatal. The remnants of the ten German armored divisions in Normandy were concentrated and ordered to attack on 6 August through Mortain to Avranches, the idea being to pinch off the shaft of Patton's spearhead. But the Panzer divisions had long lost their cutting edge and were easily held at Mortain. Montgomery now changed his plan. He organized an attack due south by the British and Canadians from Caen but, decisively, ordered Patton to postpone his drive south into Britanny and instead to swing eastwards round the flank of the halted German Panzers at Mortain. By 14 August the two wings of the Allied armies were separated by only 15 miles on each side of Falaise and the bulk of the German army was inside what now came to be called the Falaise pocket. Kluge, who had replaced Rommel, bluntly told Hitler that his only hope of saving the fifty odd divisional remnants lay in immediate retreat, to which the Führer

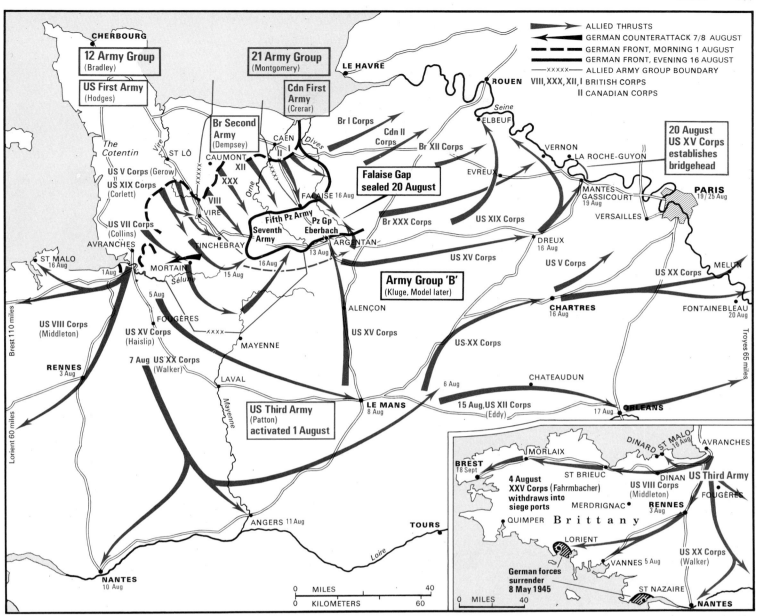

*Above:* The breakout from Normandy made the Allied victory in the West certain. France was cleared of Axis troops within two months.

*Right:* German snipers surrender to US troops in a French village

gave his consent. In the mouth of the pocket the Twelfth SS Hitler Youth Division sacrificed itself to hold open the route while the survivors made their escape to the Seine. Despite the destruction of the bridges, the Germans were able to activate ferries and by 19 August, when the Allies reached the line of the river, had evacuated them to the east bank. They then made their way at high speed out of France to the better defended Low Countries and Alsace-Lorraine. The Allies had won a victory as great as any achieved by the Russians.

### North Cape, Battle of, 1943

The battle of North Cape occurred on 26 December 1943 between the German battlecruiser *Scharnhorst* and the British Home Fleet led by the Commander in Chief, Admiral Sir Bruce Fraser in the battleship *Duke of York*. It took its name from the North Cape as it was fought between the northernmost tip of Norway and Bear Island in the Arctic.

A year before, Hitler had been so enraged by what he regarded as the *Kriegsmarine*'s incompetence in the Battle of the Barents Sea that he ordered the laying up of the surface fleet. In the Battle of the Barents Sea, a strong force composed of the *Lützow* and *Admiral Hipper* had failed to destroy a convoy defended by only eight destroyers. This led to the resignation of Admiral Raeder and his replacement by Admiral Dönitz, but it did not result in any important reduction in the strength of the Fleet, for Dönitz realized how valuable the heavy ships were in tying down British units badly needed elsewhere. Early in 1943 the new Commander in Chief even put forward a plan to Hitler to launch another attack.

In November 1943 the subject was raised again after two British convoys reached Murmansk unmolested, and Hitler agreed to a plan drawn up by Admirals Schniewind (Flag Officer, Group North) and Kummetz (Flag Officer, Northern Task Force). As the *Tirpitz* was still under repair there was only the *Scharnhorst* to support the Northern Task Force.

The battle which followed was brought on by British intelligence, which gave warning of the date and timing of the operation, and allowed Sir Bruce Fraser to dispose his forces to the best advantage. The first phase began at about 0840 hours on 26 December when the cruisers escorting convoy JW.55B picked up a radar contact. Twice the *Scharnhorst* tried to push past the cruisers but each time they fought her off without suffering serious damage gaining time for the *Duke of York* to close the gap from her distant covering position. The second phase began at 1617, when the German ship was taken completely unawares by salvoes from the *Duke of York*. Although action was broken off the British destroyers slowed the *Scharnhorst* down with torpedoes, allowing the *Duke of York* to finish her with gunfire at about 1945 hours.

The battle was the last major surface action fought in European waters and was unique in being the first fought entirely on radar plotting, the visibility was so poor that the British ships did not even see the *Scharnhorst* sink.

## Northern Burma Campaign, 1944–1945

The Allied overland offensive 'Capital' was a thrust to recapture Burma through Northern and Central Burma. The Allied advance was divided between General Slim's 14th Army and General 'Vinegar Joe' Stilwell's North Combat Area Command. In the first six months of 1944 the Japanese offensive to capture Kohima and Imphal had halted the advance of the 14th Army but Stilwell's advance, much further north, was unaffected.

The plan to capture Myitkyina was to use the Chindits as a Long Range Penetration Group to spearhead the thrust into Burma. The Chindits were to seize Indaw and the area around it on the Irrawaddy River, 150 miles north of Mandalay. Stilwell's Chinese troops were to march on Myitkyina. In February 1944 the 16th LRP Brigade set off overland from Assam and reached the Indaw area in mid-March. The 77th and the 111th LRP Brigades were transported by air to 'Broadway', a strip in the jungle 50 miles northeast of Indaw on 5 March. The plan was ill-conceived, the areas selected for landings were not suitable and Indaw was too remote to affect communications of Japanese operations in other areas. Then on 24 March Major General Wingate, the Commander of the Chin-

dits was killed in an air crash in the jungle. At first the Japanese, under General Hayashi, were taken by surprise but they were able to repulse the 16th LRP Brigade outside Indaw. Slim then decided that the Chindits should be used in the main offensive on Myitkyina, so they marched north and were transferred to his command on 16 May.

In March Stilwell's forces had secured Hukawng Valley with a Chinese tank unit and Merrill's Marauders. The Valley was half way to his objective but Stilwell was hampered because Chiang Kai-shek was not interested in fighting outside China's frontiers. However on 17 May Merrill's Marauders and Chinese troops captured Myitkyina airstrip and Stilwell assured Slim that he would capture Myitkyina in a quick thrust. The Japanese garrison resisted fiercely and Stilwell ordered that all men fit to press a trigger should return to the front. Stilwell's forces were at a standstill and Morrisforce (a detachment from the LRP Brigades) reached Waingmaw opposite Myitkyina on 29 May but was pushed back. The Japanese had increased their garrison to four times its original strength by 6 June so Stilwell made greater demands on the LRP Brigades. On 26 June, the 77th LRP Brigade captured Mogaung but the men were exhausted and despite Stilwell's complaints they were withdrawn from active service in July and August.

In mid-July the 36th Indian Division flew to Myitkyina with orders to concentrate south of Mogaung and soon undermined the Japanese positions in the area. This led to the isolation of Myitkyina and on 1 August the Japanese garrison commander committed suicide and two days later Stilwell's forces entered the city in force.

While Stilwell was advancing on Myitkyina, the Chinese 11th and 12th 'armies' in Yunnan took the offensive in late spring: this was after considerable pressure from the US. The Chinese wanted to open up the Burma road and make contact with Stilwell's forces. They spent the whole summer besieging two fortresses in the hills east of Lungling and when these were finally overcome in early September General Honda's Thirty-third Army launched a counteroffensive. This only allowed the Japanese to hold on to their positions and at the end of September Honda was ordered to withdraw south and protect the sector from Lashio to Mandalay. On 2 October Lord Mountbatten ordered that the North Burma roads be cleared so Stilwell's forces advanced from Myitkyina to Mongmit and the Chinese 11th and 12th armies advanced down the Burma road to reach the junction with the Ledo road.

In October Chiang Kai-shek put pressure on the Americans to recall Stilwell and he was replaced by General Wedemeyer. The British 14th Army was now approaching Mandalay and Meiktila. The Chinese New 1st Army (Stilwell's force) was held up at Bhamo and began to besiege it in November. After its garrison had withdrawn from Bhamo the Fiftysixth Division delayed the advance of the Chinese to Namhkam, which they only reached on 16 January 1945. On 20 January the Chinese 11th Army took Wanting and at last the Ledo-Burma road was open, restoring land communications with China. Honda had kept the two Chinese forces apart for eight months although he had been hopelessly outnumbered. All that was left for Allied forces was to clear the roads south.

(Refer back to map of Burma on page 43).

## Norway Campaign, 1940

Hitler decided to occupy Norway, despite its declared neutral status, in February, 1940. He had been outraged by the Royal Navy's capture of the *Altmark*, feared that the British might actually occupy Norway themselves, wanted its North Sea ports for his own Navy, and was anxious to protect the iron-ore traffic from Kiruna along the coast. Early on 9 April, German forces, under Falkenhorst began to land from the sea at Oslo, Kirstiansand, Bergen, Trondheim, and Narvik, and from the air at Sola (Oslo) and Stavanger airports. The landing at Oslo was hindered by the sinking of the carrier *Bhicker*, carrying most of the staff, which allowed the King and government to escape the capital, but other attacked ports fell quickly. Reinforcements followed and secured the southern and most densely populated region of the country quickly.

The Norwegian Army, a largely militia force, continued to mobilize, however, and was joined by contingents of British and French troops 13,000 strong, which landed at Namsos and Andalsnes after 16 April. The Armies' first operation was an attempt to recapture Trondheim by a pincer movement, but, despite initial success, it was defeated, so that by 3 May, Central Norway also was in German hands. The focus of fighting then shifted to Narvik, where the German Navy had already suffered heavy defeats at the hands of the British and continued to do so. The Allies managed to recapture the town but as a result of the German victory in France were withdrawn on 7 June. The Norwegians continued to resist until 9 June. Their effort, after an uncertain start and against great odds, had been remarkable.

## Norwegian Naval Campaign, 1940
see *Glorious* and *Hardy*

## Novikov, Colonel General Aleksandr A, 1900–1976

Novikov was Commander-in-Chief of the Soviet Air Force from 1942 to 1946. He played an important role in reorganizing the Red Air Force, after it had been knocked out in the first months of the war. Novikov was responsible for planning the air offensives on the Stalingrad Front, at the Battle of Kursk, and the Belorussian campaign.

## Nuremberg War Crimes Trial, November 1945 – October 1946

The International Military Tribunal was set up in May 1944 to try Nazi leaders on four charges of (1) the common plan (2) crimes against peace (3) war crimes and (4) crimes against humanity. The tribunal had US, British, French and Russian judges and heard much evidence of the Nazi terror and extermination camps. Among the accused were Bormann, Admiral Dönitz, Frank (Hans), Frick, Fritzsche, Funk, Goering, Hess, General Jodl, General Keitel, Kaltenbrunner, von Neurath, von Papen, Raeder, von Ribbentrop, Rosenberg, Sauckel, Schacht, von Schirach, Seyss-Inquart, Speer and Streicher. Only Fritzsche, Papen and Schacht were acquitted and the others received sentences ranging from 10 years imprisonment to death. In all, 177 people were indicted and sentences were given in October 1946.

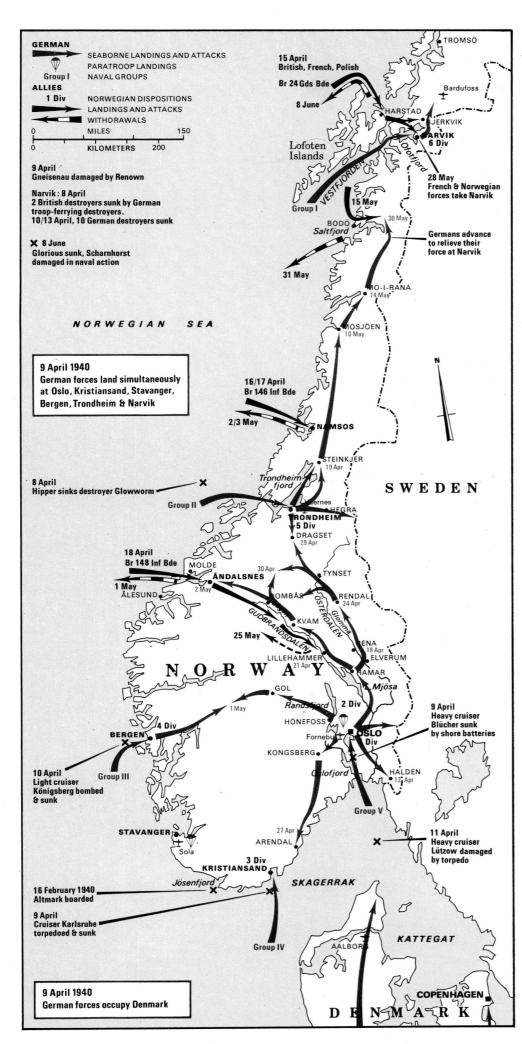

## Map annotations

**GERMAN**
- ➤ SEABORNE LANDINGS AND ATTACKS
- ⛨ PARATROOP LANDINGS
- Group I  NAVAL GROUPS

**ALLIES**
- 1 Div  NORWEGIAN DISPOSITIONS
- ➤ LANDINGS AND ATTACKS
- ◄ WITHDRAWALS

0 — MILES — 150
0 — KILOMETERS — 200

**9 April**
Gneisenau damaged by Renown

**Narvik : 8 April**
2 British destroyers sunk by German troop-ferrying destroyers.
10/13 April, 10 German destroyers sunk

**✕ 8 June**
Glorious sunk, Scharnhorst damaged in naval action

TROMSÖ
Bardufoss
15 April
British, French, Polish
Br 24 Gds Bde
8 June
HARSTAD
BJERKVIK
NARVIK 6 Div
Lofoten Islands
Otterfjord
28 May
French & Norwegian forces take Narvik
VESTFJORDEN
15 May
Group I
30 May
BODÖ
Saltfjord
Germans advance to relieve their force at Narvik
31 May
MO-I-RANA 14 May
MOSJÖEN 10 May

NORWEGIAN SEA

**9 April 1940**
German forces land simultaneously at Oslo, Kristiansand, Stavanger, Bergen, Trondheim & Narvik

16/17 April
Br 146 Inf Bde
2/3 May
NAMSOS
STEINKJER 19 Apr
SWEDEN

**8 April**
Hipper sinks destroyer Glowworm
Trondheim fjord
Group II
Vernes
HEGRA
TRONDHEIM 5 Div
DRAGSET 29 Apr

**18 April**
Br 148 Inf Bde
MOLDE
30 Apr
ÅNDALSNES
2 May
TYNSET
1 May
ÅLESUND
DOMBÅS
RENDAL 24 Apr
KVAM
GUDBRANDSDALEN
OSTERDALEN
Glomma
25 May
ENA 19 Apr
ELVERUM
LILLEHAMMER 21 Apr
HAMAR
NORWAY
GOL
Mjösa
Randsfjord
2 Div
1 May
HÖNEFOSS
Fornebu
OSLO Div
9 April
Heavy cruiser Blücher sunk by shore batteries
KONGSBERG
4 Div
BERGEN
Group III

**10 April**
Light cruiser Königsberg bombed & sunk
Oslofjord
HALDEN 12 Apr
Group V
27 Apr
ARENDAL

**11 April**
Heavy cruiser Lützow damaged by torpedo
STAVANGER
Sola
3 Div
KRISTIANSAND
Jösenfjord
SKAGERRAK

**16 February 1940**
Altmark boarded

**9 April**
Cruiser Karlsruhe torpedoed & sunk
Group IV
AALBORG
KATTEGAT
COPENHAGEN

**9 April 1940**
German forces occupy Denmark

DENMARK

## Obi
see Infra-red Target Detection Systems

---

## O'Connor, General Sir Richard, 1889–

Commander of 7th Division at the outbreak of war, O'Connor and his division were sent from Palestine to Egypt where he became commander of Western Desert Force. In September Egypt was invaded by Marshal Graziani's Italian troops from Libya. After a two-month pause, O'Connor launched a counteroffensive which drove them out and at Sidi Barrani encircled their retreating columns. He took over 100,000 prisoners, though having fewer than 30,000 troops of his own. His pursuit was then halted by the withdrawal of soldiers to send to Greece. Counterattacked by Rommel, his army was forced to retreat and, while reconnoitering forward, he was captured by a German patrol in April 1941. Released from captivity in Italy in 1943, he commanded 8th Corps in Northwest Europe.

---

## Odessa

Odessa stands for Organization for SS members. It was set up in 1947 as a 'charitable institution' but in fact helped SS men to escape from justice. The financing of the organization was probably arranged during the war when vast sums of money were transferred out of Germany.

---

## Odessa, Capture of, 1944
see Ukraine, Battle of the, December 1943–May 1944

---

## Oerlikon Gun

In 1939–40 the British Admiralty faced a desperate shortage of light automatic guns for the defense of ships against low-flying aircraft. The need had been foreseen prewar, and after long discussion the Swiss Oerlikon-Bührle Company's 20mm gun was chosen. It was light, simple to operate and, most important, it fired an explosive shell. The mounting was ideal for shipboard use being a simple pedestal with one man aiming and firing and a simple drum feed. Its cyclic rate of fire was 600rpm.

A total of 1500 guns was ordered from Switzerland just before the outbreak of war, but when the fall of France seemed imminent steps

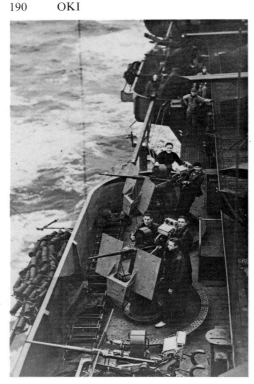

HMS *Trumpeter* fires her 20mm Oerlikon guns.

were taken to acquire the license, so that the guns could be made in England. Demand far exceeded production and the Admiralty even went to the length of making a special documentary film called *The Gun* for showing in armament factories to encourage faster production. The film was eventually shown in the USA in 1942 as part of the drive to get the US Navy to adopt it.

By 1945 the 20mm Oerlikon gun was no longer effective against the heavily armored aircraft in service and against kamikaze attacks. However, this was not to stop the weapon from remaining in service as a handy light surface weapon for another 30 years. During World War II it was used in a number of mountings, both manual and automatic.

## Okinawa, April-July 1945

The campaign to gain control of Okinawa was the last and largest amphibious operation mounted by the Central Pacific forces.

The island was defended by a garrison 100,000 strong of whom 77,000 were under Lieutenant General Ushijima. Since August 1944 Ushijima had supervised the building of an incredible maze of cave defenses. The US invasion fleet comprised 1300 vessels of all sizes and carried a total of 183,000 troops. Admiral Spruance was the Task Force Commander, Vice-Admiral Turner commanded the Amphibious force and Vice-Admiral Mitscher commanded the fast carrier force. The British Pacific Fleet of four carriers also took part in the operation in the Sakishima Gunto area. The new 10th Army was used in the operation, under the command of Lieutenant General Buckner.

As a preliminary to the operation, the 77th Division landed on the Kerama Retto group of islands on 26 March, so that it could be used as an advance base. Mitscher's force then made a series of raids to knock out the air threat but kamikaze pilots succeeded in knocking out the carriers USS *Franklin* and *Wasp* and also hit a battleship, cruiser, four destroyers and six other

ships. The kamikaze pilots had only a 14 percent rate of success. On 1 April US ships bombarded the island with 44,825 rounds of 5-inch and larger shells, 32,000 rockets and 22,500 mortar shells. On the same day troops landed on the west coast of the island where they met no opposition and by nightfall 60,000 men were ashore. On the next day the US drove to the east coast and captured two airfields. Buckner then sent three Marine divisions south and sent the 6th Marine Division north where they met some resistance in the Motubu Peninsula. They killed 2500 Japanese defenders and by 21 April the north had been cleared at the expense of 218 Americans killed and 902 wounded. On 6 April another kamikaze raid of 700 aircraft was launched and this resulted in thirteen US destroyers being sunk or damaged. The Japanese battleship *Yamato* had been sent on a mission to bombard the invasion fleet with its nine 18.1-inch guns and it only had enough fuel for the outward journey. Since it had no air cover, US aircraft located it off the southwest tip of the Kyushu Islands and sank it on 6 April.

Ushijima's main force was concentrated in the south of Okinawa but it was only on 4 April that the 24th Corps reached the defenses at Shuri. Despite reinforcements, the 24th Corps could not make a dent on these defenses and suffered a high casualty rate. The Japanese were safe in their caves which were not damaged by the constant artillery fire or naval bombardments. On 19 April Buckner ordered a more intensive bombardment but still there was no breakthrough. The Japanese did not like fighting on the defensive and on the night of 2 May Ushijima decided to launch a counter-offensive. Although the Japanese broke through at one point they were driven back with a loss of 5000 men. On 11 May Buckner ordered another offensive and Ushijima withdrew from the area. On 31 May Shuri was taken and the Americans reduced the defenses to rubble. On 21 June Ushijima issued his final order that the Japanese continue a guerrilla war – and then committed suicide. Fighting continued until the end of the month and for the first time in the war Japanese soldiers surrendered in large numbers, about 7400 in all.

Okinawa was the costliest operation in the Central Pacific. Some half a million men were involved in the fighting and it cost the Americans 49,000 in casualties of whom 12,500 died. More than 110,000 Japanese were killed on the island.

US landing craft on Okinawa.

## *Oklahoma*

The battleship *Oklahoma* (BB.37) was the sister of the *Nevada*. She was at Pearl Harbor on 7 December 1941 and was hit by five torpedoes. She capsized, leaving hundreds of men trapped inside the hull. In all 20 officers and 395 enlisted men lost their lives. Salvage began in March 1943 but when the *Oklahoma* was raised nine months later she was beyond repair. Stripped of guns and superstructure, she was sold for scrap in 1946 but sank while in tow from Pearl Harbor to San Francisco.

## Olbricht, General Friedrich, 1886–1944

Deputy to Fromm, the Commander of the Home Army, Olbricht was drawn into the military conspiracy against Hitler in February 1943. Olbricht's role was to move the Home Army troops to Berlin and he gave the orders to do so on 20 July 1944 under cover of an anti-foreign worker uprising exercise, Operation Valkyrie. When the plot failed, he was among the group whom Fromm had shot in the courtyard of the war ministry.

## Oldendorf, Rear Admiral Jesse B, 1887–

Oldendorf was the commander of Task Group 77.2 at the Battle of Leyte Gulf. His task was to prevent the Japanese forces from passing through the Surigao Strait. Early in the morning of 25 October Oldendorf's ships were able to devastate Vice-Admiral Nishimura's force with his torpedoes and radar-controlled gunfire. This was the first clear victory achieved in surface fighting against the Japanese.

During the invasion of Luzon, Oldendorf commanded the combat formations of the 7th Fleet and bore many kamikaze attacks.

## Omaha
see D-Day Landings 1944

## Onishi, Vice-Admiral Takijiro, 1891–1945

Onishi, with his friend the immensely talented Commander Minoru Genda, first came to prominence for carrying out a feasibility study of Yamamoto's concept of the attack on Pearl Harbor. These plans and studies date from as early as January 1941.

In October 1944 Onishi took command of the Fifth Base Air Force on Luzon with orders to support Admiral Kurita's attack on the US Leyte invasion force. As he had only 100 operational planes, he established a Kamikaze Special Attack Corps. Spontaneous kamikaze attacks had already occurred, but Onishi was the first to formally organize them as weapons.

Onishi, a fanatic, favored a suicidal last stand of the entire Japanese nation. He committed *harakiri* after the decision to surrender on 15 August 1945.

## Oppenheimer, J Robert, 1904–1967

Already a leading American nuclear physicist before the war, Oppenheimer was appointed director of the government laboratory at Los Alamos in 1942 and head of the team working to build the first atomic bomb. His scientific talent and personal powers of leadership brought the project to conclusion in time to use the weapon against Japan before having to risk an invasion of the home islands.

## *Orzel*

When Poland was overwhelmed by the German attack in September 1939 several of the modern warships in the Polish Navy escaped to England. However, the submarine *Orzel* was interned by the Estonian authorities and had to be disarmed. She escaped subsequently and evaded all the German efforts to find her as she made her way westwards through the Baltic. On 14 October she arrived at Rosyth in Scotland and joined the Polish naval forces operating with the Royal Navy. Her sister *Sep* was interned in Sweden.

## 'Oscar'
see Nakajima Ki-43

## Osmeña, President Sergio, 1878–1961

Osmeña was Vice-President of the Philippines until Quezon's death in August 1944 when he became President. Since Quezon was in poor health Osmeña sat on the Pacific War Council and on other boards planning the future of the Philippines throughout the war and went round the USA lecturing about the plight of the Philippines. Osmeña hated General MacArthur and had to be persuaded to accompany the invasion troops on Luzon in January 1945. He became head of the civil government once the Philippines were liberated.

## OSS
see Donovan, General William

## Ostwind

This was a German anti-aircraft tank consisting of the 37mm Flak 43 gun mounted in an armored rotating turret on top of a PzKw IV tank chassis. The turret was open-topped, but intended to give the gun crew better protection from ground fire that had previously been obtained by self-propelled anti-aircraft guns. Developed late in 1943, it is thought that relatively few were made.

## Owen Gun

This Australian submachine gun was designed by Lt Evelyn Owen and patented in 1941. As with the Austen gun, it was produced in answer to Australia's need for submachine guns, a need which could not be satisfied by production in Britain or the USA at that time. Although heavy and bulky in comparison with contemporary designs, the Owen was an extremely reliable weapon and highly spoken of by all who ever used it. Its mechanical features are rather unusual. In the first place the magazine is mounted on top of the gun which allows gravity to aid the feed and appears to prevent jamming. Secondly the construction is such that to dismantle the weapon it is necessary first to remove the barrel using a quick-release mechanism provided for this purpose. With a length of 32in with wooden stock, weighing 9lbs 5oz, the Owen fired the standard 9mm Parabellum cartridges at some 700 rounds a minute. Though less elegant than the Austen it was greatly preferred by the troops, and it was to remain in service until the 1960s.

## Overlord
see D-Day Landings

## Ozawa, Vice-Admiral Jisaburo, 1886–1966

Ozawa was Commander of the Japanese Mobile Fleet at the Battle of the Philippine Sea and at Leyte Gulf. He took over command in November 1942, when Admiral Nagumo was dismissed. During the Philippine Sea battle Ozawa's new flagship the carrier *Taiho* was sunk and he lost over 340 aircraft. He made the mistake of lingering near the battle and lost three more ships on the day after. He offered his resignation but Admiral Toyoda refused to accept it. At the Battle of Leyte Gulf Ozawa's Mobile Fleet acted as a decoy and he showed tremendous skill in drawing Admiral Halsey's Fleet away from the San Bernardino Strait.

## P–36 and Hawk 75, Curtiss

The first Hawk 75 was built by Curtiss as a private venture when it became clear that the company's famous family of Hawk biplanes was nearing the end of its useful life. In due course the US Army ordered 177 similar P–36As and 31 P–36Cs, each with a Pratt & Whitney R–1830 Twin Wasp engine and two or four 0.3in machine guns respectively. Four P–36As of the 46th Pursuit Squadron attacked a formation of Japanese bombers over Pearl Harbor on 7 December 1941, destroying two of them. Meanwhile, export versions, with fixed undercarriage, had seen action with both the Chinese and Siamese Air Forces. So had Hawk 75As of the French Air Force, which were generally similar to the P–36A. When France fell, 227 of the Hawks that had been ordered by that country were transferred to the RAF. They were held in reserve for a time; many were then sent to India, where one squadron remained operational on the Burma front until January 1944. RAF Hawks were named Mohawk and had Wright GR–1820 Cyclone engines. The Mohawk IV had a maximum speed of 302mph and armament of six 0.303in guns.

Curtiss P-36 fighter.

## P–38 Lightning, Lockheed

This US single-seat fighter and reconnaissance aircraft was operational in 1941–49. The RAF was not impressed with the Lightnings that it tested in 1941–42, and canceled its production orders. The Luftwaffe disliked the aircraft for a different reason. Having met it first in North Africa in late 1942, the Germans nicknamed the P–38 *Der Gabelschwanz Teufel* (the fork-tailed devil). In fact, it was more effective for ground attack than air combat, but the Japanese had reason for regretting that it possessed any interception capability. Their great Admiral Yamamoto was killed when Lightnings from

*Above:* P-38 Lightnings in formation.
*Right:* Lockheed Lightning P-38 H-5.

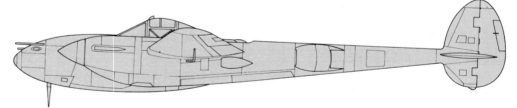

Guadalcanal, 550 miles away, shot down his transport after learning details of the Admiral's flight via an overheard radio message.

The prototype of the Lightning had been built to meet a US Army specification for a high-altitude interceptor, and flew for the first time on 27 January 1939. The first military airplane built by Lockheed, it was heavier than some contemporary bombers, with a weight of 14,800lb. It was also very fast, and the first small batch of P–38 production aircraft had a speed of 395mph. The last of them were delivered in the second half of 1941 as P–38Ds, considered the first aircraft of the type capable of operational use. The next model, the P–38E, dispensed with its predecessor's big 37mm gun, replacing it with a 20mm cannon and greater ammunition capacity. This was supplemented by four 'point fives', all armament being concentrated in the nose – a location made possible by the aircraft's unique twin-boom layout. All variants, up to P–38L, had Allison V–1710 engines of 1150 to 1475hp, fitted with turbo-superchargers. It was a refusal to export the 'blowers', with consequently reduced performance, that led to RAF rejection of the type. In Europe, P–38s were used primarily as long-range escorts for 8th Air Force medium bombers until superseded by Mustangs. They were then used mainly as fighter-bombers, although special variants were equipped as pathfinders, including a few with bomb-through-overcast radar in a bulbous nose. F–5 Lightnings, were the most used reconnaissance fighters of the war.

## P–39 Airacobra, Bell

This US single-seat fighter was operational from 1941 to 1944. No aircraft illustrates better than the Airacobra the perils of putting too many good, but untried, ideas into a single new airplane. Bell Aircraft designers were so captivated by the destructive power offered by American Armament Corporation's 37mm T–9 gun that they drew their new fighter around it. The only way the gun could be made to fire through the propeller hub, for optimum effectiveness, was to put the engine behind the pilot. A nose-wheel was introduced for the first time on a US Army single-seat fighter, filling the space under the propeller shaft where the engine normally went. Fuel tanks were made leakproof. The cannon was supplemented by two 0.5in machine guns in the nose, four 0.3in wing guns, and a 500lb bomb under the fuselage. The RAF, in urgent need of as many modern fighters as possible, ordered 675, most of which were released to the Russians and the USAAF in Britain. A single RAF squadron re-equipped with Spitfires after flying Airacobras for a few months as ground attack aircraft. The Americans lost six of the twelve P–39s sent on the first USAAF Airacobra mission in Europe in July

1942. Better success was achieved in the Pacific, and on ground attack duties in North Africa; but by early 1944, P–39 units were being re-equipped with later types. Only the Russians seem to have valued the Airacobra highly, perhaps because of its heavy armament; they had 4773 of the 9558 that were built. All had an Allison V–1710 engine of 1150–1200hp.

## P–40 Warhawk, Curtiss

This US single-seat fighter was operational from 1941 to 1945. A total of 13,738 P–40s were built between 1938 and 1944. The original version was little more than a re-engined P–36, with an Allison V–1710 supercharged in-line engine in place of the original radial. France ordered 140, which were taken over by the RAF as Tomahawk Is after the French collapse. Their modest performance, lack of self-sealing fuel tanks and armament of only two machine-guns caused them to be diverted mainly to Army Co-operation units. Curtiss took the hint, adding two guns on the Tomahawk IIA and two more on the IIB, as well as self-sealing tanks and increased armor. Thirteen RAF squadrons flew Tomahawk IIs. Others went to the USAAF as

*Above:* A P-40 on the Flying Tiger airfield.

Above: P-51H Mustang.

P–40Cs to Russia and to China, where they flew in the famous shark-tooth markings of the Flying Tigers, General Claire Chennault's American Volunteer Group, which destroyed 286 Japanese aircraft in seven months. The USAAF name for the P–40 was Warhawk; production variants up to P–40N had progressively more powerful V–1710 engines, from 1040 to 1360hp, and an armament of six wing-mounted 0.5in guns and a single 500lb bomb from the P–40E onward. Exceptions were the P–40F and L, with a 1300hp Packard-built Merlin engine, which gave a top speed of 373mph and improved high-altitude performance. Sturdy and adaptable rather than outstanding, the P–40s flew on almost all World War II battlefronts. More than 3000 Ds, Es, Ks, Ms and Ns were delivered to Commonwealth Air Forces, under the name Kittyhawk, serving mainly in the Western Desert, Italy and the Pacific area.

## P–47 Thunderbolt, Republic

This US single-seat escort fighter and fighter-bomber was operational from 1943–1955. A total of 15,683 Thunderbolts were built under USAAF contracts, of which the first were placed in September 1940. No other US fighter has ever been built in such numbers; and although 5222 were lost in action, the loss rate of

*Below:* P-51D Mustang.

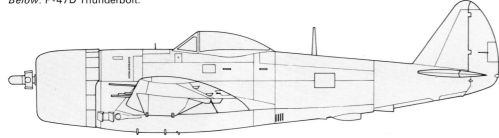

*Below:* P-47D Thunderbolt.

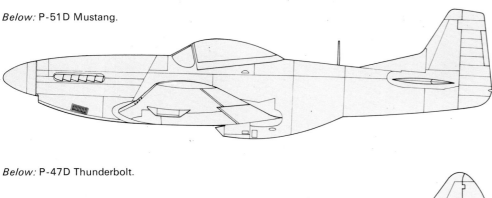

under 0.7 per hundred sorties was low by any standards, bearing in mind that Thunderbolts flew some 1.35 million combat hours. The last radial-engined fighter to serve in any numbers with the USAAF, the prototype XP–47B was designed around a 2000hp Pratt & Whitney R–2800 engine. The result was a very large fighter by the standards of the forties, and it became bigger and heavier as the war progressed. By 1945 the final-production P–47N had a 2800hp R–2800–77, an 18in longer span than earlier versions, a gross weight of 20,700lb, and armament of eight 0.5in machine guns plus two 1000lb bombs. It still managed a top speed of 467mph and, with 1266 gallons of internal and external fuel, could fly 2350 miles. Its purpose was to escort B-29s attacking Japan, so perpetuating the task undertaken by versions like the P–47C in Europe. The earlier P–47B, with a 13in shorter fuselage, had lacked maneuverability in combat: the P–47D proved most effective as a fighter-bomber, particularly after it had been adapted to carry ten underwing rockets. The 830 Thunderbolts supplied to the RAF, from September 1944, were used exclusively against the Japanese in Burma.

## P–51 Mustang, North American

This US single-seat fighter was operational from 1942. It is said that when Goering first saw Mustangs escorting USAAF day bombers all the way to Berlin he said that the war had truly been lost by Germany. Yet the prototype of this remarkable fighter, still first-line equipment in a few air forces in 1977, was designed and built in only 117 days. With the Battle of Britain newly won, an RAF Purchasing Commission in the USA had asked North American Aviation to produce an airplane embodying lessons learned in the Battle. The company's engineers wanted to embody innovations such as a laminar-flow wing and a rear-mounted belly radiator to reduce drag. They were told they could do so if the aircraft could be ready in 120 days. It was then April 1940. The prototype flew on 25 October, after a slight delay in getting its 1100hp Allison V–1710 engine. Production Mustang Is began to reach the UK in October 1941 and were a little disappointing. Overall performance was far superior to that of any other US fighter, but the power of the Allison fell off rapidly at height. The Allison-engined Mustang 1s, IAs and IIs were, therefore, used to supplant Tomahawks for armed tactical reconnaissance duties with Army Co-operation Command. They flew as far as Germany to attack ground targets, and carried out immensely valuable photo-reconnaissance work over Dieppe before the August 1942 Commando raid. First orders for the type were also placed by the USAAF after Pearl Harbor; but the Mustang was raised to an entirely new level of efficiency by the British suggestion that it should be re-engined with a Rolls-Royce Merlin, for which the US Packard company acquired license rights. Flight testing of the Merlin-powered prototypes in late 1942 showed that maximum speed had been increased by 50mph, to 441mph. Huge numbers were built for the USAAF and RAF, including 3738 P–51Bs and Cs, 7956 P–51Ds, 555 P–51Hs and 1337 P–51Ks. By VE-Day they had re-equipped all but one of the fighter escort groups of the USAAF 8th Air Force in Europe. P–51Ds escorted B-29s all the way to Tokyo and back from Iwo Jima. Some were modified to carry underwing rockets. Others were converted into two-seaters, and one of these was used by General Eisenhower as a personal high-speed transport round the Normandy beachheads after the D-Day landings. Fastest of all was the lightweight P–51H, with a 1380hp V–1650 Packard Merlin, which gave it a speed of 487mph. Armament of this version was six 0.5in guns and two 1000lb bombs or ten 5in rockets. In RAF service, Mustangs destroyed 232 V–1 flying bombs over the UK.

## P-61 Black Widow, Northrop

This US three-seat night fighter was operational from 1944–52. When news of the early successes achieved by RAF radar-equipped night fighters reached the USA, Northrop offered to build for the USAAF an aircraft to carry similar AI radar. Two prototypes were ordered on 11 January 1941, as XP–61s. A production order for 13 YP–61s followed within two months. By the time the first prototype flew on 26 May 1942, orders already totaled 575. The initial 200 production models were P–61As, named Black Widow because of their black overall paint-scheme and expected deadliness to an enemy. The first 'kill' by a P–61A was recorded in the South Pacific on 7 July 1944, and before long Black Widows had replaced P–40s in all USAAF night fighter squadrons. Production included 450 P–61Bs, of which 16 were converted to unarmed P–61G weather reconnaissance aircraft, and 41 P–61Cs, with 2800hp Pratt & Whitney R–2800–73 engines in place of the 2000hp R–2800–10s or 65s of the earlier versions. Maximum speed of the P–61B was 366mph. Armament comprised four forward-firing 0.5in guns, four 20mm guns in a remotely controlled upper turret, and four 1600lb bombs under the wings for night intruder missions.

## P-63 Kingcobra, Bell

The P–63 was basically a P–39 Airacobra with new laminar-flow wings, a more angular tail and a 1325hp Allison V–1710–93 engine. Most of the 1725 P–63As went to the Soviet Union, with a basic armament of one 37mm cannon firing through the propeller hub and two wing-mounted 'point fives'. Bombs or rockets could be carried under the wings. The Russians also received a high proportion of the 1227 P–63Cs, of which delivery started in December 1944, with uprated V–1710–117 engine and ventral fin. Another 300 went to the Free French air force. The Soviet Air Force used most of its 2421 Kingcobras for ground attack.

## P-80 Shooting Star, Lockheed

The first jet aircraft to become operational with the USAAF, this single-seat fighter flew for the first time on 8 January 1944. Two pre-production YP–80As were sent to Italy in the Spring of 1945, but the Shooting Star was too late to be used in action in World War II.

## Pacific Theater, Chronological List of Events

Pearl Harbor, 7 December 1941
Luzon, Fall of, 1941
Bataan, Defense of, 1942
Corregidor, Defense of, 1942
Hong Kong, Fall of, 1941
Malayan Campaign, 1941–42
Force Z, Sinking of, 1941
Singapore, Fall of, December 1941 – April 1942
Dutch East Indies, Fall of, 1942
Burma, Fall of, 1942
Lombok Strait, Battle of, 1942
Java Sea, Battle of, February 1942
Ceylon Raid, April 1942
Coral Sea, Battle of, May 1942
Midway, Battle of, 1942
Aleutians Islands Campaign, 1942–3

New Guinea. Port Moresby and Buna, March 1942 – January 1943
New Guinea. Milne Bay, August – September 1942
Guadalcanal, 1942
Savo Island, Battle of, 1942
Eastern Solomons, Battle of, 1942
Cape Esperance, Battle of, 11 October 1942
Santa Cruz Islands, Battle of, 1942
Guadalcanal, Naval Battle of, November 1942
Tassafaronga, Battle of, 1942
Arakan Offensive, Burma, December 1942 – April 1943
New Guinea. Huon Peninsula, 1943
New Georgia, 1943
Kula Gulf, Battle of, 1943
Kolombangara, Battle of, 1943
Vella Gulf, Battle of, 1943
Bougainville, 1943–44
Rabaul, 1943–44
Gilbert Islands, Battle for, 1943
Marshall Islands, 1944
Kohima and Imphal Offensives, 1944
New Guinea. Hollandia and Wewak, 1943–45
New Guinea. Biak and Wakde Islands, 1944
Philippine Sea, Battle of, 1944
Saipan, 1944
Tinian, 1944
Guam, 1944
Northern Burma Campaign, 1944–45
Palau Islands, 1944
Morotai, September 1944
Leyte Gulf, Battle of, 1944
Leyte, Battle for, 1944–45
Meiktila and Mandalay, The Battle for Burma, 1945
Rangoon, Capture of, 1945
Iwo Jima, February–May 1945
Okinawa, April–July 1945
Borneo Operations, 1945
Hiroshima and Nagasaki, Atomic Attack upon, 6 and 9 August 1945
Japan's Decision to Surrender

## Palau Islands, 1944

The Palau Islands had been used as an advance base for the Combined Fleet, but raids on the 30 and 31 March on the Palaus and the Western Carolines forced the Japanese to remove their HQ to Davao. The Palaus were to be invaded by Halsey's Central Pacific Force on the same day as Morotai. The Japanese had built strong defenses under the command of Lieutenant General Inone and had 6000 combat troops on the island of Peleliu. The US invasion was preceded by a heavy naval bombardment but it left the defenses intact. On 15 September, 1st Marine Division landed on the southwest cor-

Lt Clark Miller's torpedo bomber ran out of gasoline over Peleliu and became the first US plane to land on this captured airfield on 28 September 1944.

ner of Peleliu and it took them four days to take the airfield in the southern part of the island. The drive northwards was halted by heavy artillery on the Umurbrogol Mountain where the Japanese had dug themselves in. The battle became known as the Battle of Bloody Noose Ridge because resistance was worn down slowly and was finally overcome on 25 November.

Meanwhile on 17 September the 81st Infantry Division landed at Angaur and met little opposition because the Japanese commander would not commit his 1400 troops to what he thought was a diversionary landing. Within two days the island was overrun although resistance continued until 13 October.

The Marines' operation in Peleliu was very costly with 1792 US killed and 8011 wounded which represented a 40 percent casualty rate. The operation gave the Americans control of the Palau Islands.

## Panther Tank

After meeting the Soviet T–34 tank in late 1941 the German Army was considerably shaken to find that there was a tank better than its Panzer IV. After examining captured T–34s a specification was issued in November 1941 for a new design of tank with 60mm of frontal armor, a high velocity 75mm gun, and an all-up weight of 35 tons. Indeed, one school of thought advocated simply copying the T–34 as it stood, but this was turned down; it was, to say the least, unpatriotic, and, more to the point, there were mechanical features of the T–34 which made copying an impractical proposition for German manufacturers.

Designs were submitted by Daimler-Benz and MAN (Maschinenfabrik Augsberg-Nürnberg). The Daimler design featured a transversely mounted diesel engine, rear-drive, resilient steel wheels, spring suspension, and a number of other novelties which, while elegant engineering solutions, were not practical manufacturing propositions. The design was turned down in April 1942 before even the prototype was completed. The MAN design featured torsion-bar suspension, interleaved road wheels, rear engine and forward drive, and well-sloped armor. It was considered a better proposition than the Daimler design and orders were given for production in September 1942, but at the same time the specification was restated, increasing the frontal armor thickness to 80mm, a change which increased the weight from 35 to 44 tons. This was an unfortunate step, since by that time much of the detail design, of such things as wheels and suspension, had been completed and subcontractors were at work; increasing the weight by five tons threw additional strain on components designed for the original weight, and this, in due course, was to lead to problems of unreliability in action.

Panther was armed with a high velocity

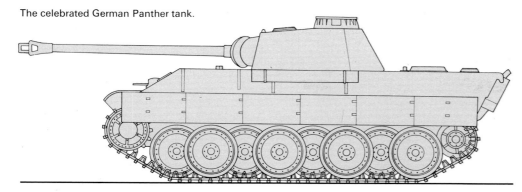

The celebrated German Panther tank.

75mm gun of 70 calibers length; this fired a 15lb piercing shell at 3068 ft/sec and could pierce 104mm of armor at 2000 meters range; firing tungsten-cored shot at 3937 ft/sec it could pierce 122mm at 2000 meters. Either of these projectiles was capable of dealing with a T–34 or KV at any practical fighting range. Moreover the high velocity meant a flat trajectory, which in turn meant less likelihood of missing the target due to a miscalculation of range, and this added up to a very high 'first-round hit probability factor' as the statisticians called it.

Production began in November 1942, using a 650hp engine; after 20 tanks had been built the engine was changed to a 700hp model in order to give better performance with the extra weight. From January 1943 the 'Ausführung D' (Model D) was the standard production model, incorporating some minor improvements such as a relocated commander's cupola and a new gearbox. Late in 1943 the 'Ausführung A' went into production; this lettering is an anomaly never explained, but the new model had such improvements as an armored cupola with periscopes, a ball mount for the hull machine gun and anti-bazooka side plates over the top run of the track. Finally, in July 1944, came the 'Ausf G' model which had a number of changes incorporated for the sake of manufacturing simplicity; the superstructure sides were altered and the slope of the armor increased, which, as a bonus, aided protection. In all, 4814 Panther tanks were produced before the war ended; it was undoubtedly Germany's best tank design, giving the almost ideal balance between armor, speed, weight and firepower.

An important derivative of the Panther was the Jagdpanther, a self-propelled anti-tank gun or 'tank destroyer' which used the chassis of the Panther to carry a superstructure having a limited-traverse 88mm gun at the front. Production began in 1944; 382 were made.

### Panzerfaust

This German recoilless anti-tank weapon was a light recoilless gun which fired an over-sized hollow-charge bomb.

In the summer of 1942 the appearance of the Russian T–34 tank in ever-increasing numbers led to a demand for a better anti-tank weapon for the individual soldier, and Dr Langweiler of the Hugo Schneider AG was given the task of developing a suitable weapon. His solution was the 'Faustpatrone', a simple 14in tube into which a fin-stabilized bomb was fitted, together with a small black-powder cartridge. This device could be held at arm's length and fired to discharge the bomb. It was, though, impractical as it stood since it could not be aimed. The device was therefore lengthened so that it could be tucked under the arm, allowing the rearward

blast of the cartridge to pass behind the firer, and the Panzerfaust was born.

The design eventually settled on a simple mild steel tube 31.5in long, in the front end of which the tail and flexible fins of the bomb could be fitted. This bomb had a 5.9in diameter hollow charge head and a tail tube about a foot long around which were four thin metal fins; these were wrapped around the tail tube so that the tail of the bomb could then be inserted into the launcher tube on top of a small black-powder charge. This was fired by a percussion cap and trigger unit on top of the launch tube. A simple rear sight was fitted to the tube, while a pin on the outside of the bomb warhead acted as a foresight.

The first models, known as the Panzerfaust Klein (with a small diameter bomb) and the Panzerfaust 30 (with the 5.9in bomb) were demonstrated to the army in March 1943, and in July 3000 of each type were ordered for active service trials in Russia. As a result of these tests, in October mass production was ordered at the rate of 100,000 Kleins and 200,000 Panzerfaust 30s every month, a rate not reached until April 1944.

The penetration performance of the Panzerfaust 30, with the 5.9in bomb, was more than adequate; it could go through 200mm of armor at a striking angle of 30°, more than enough to deal with any Russian tank, and thereafter development was concerned with improving the range. The range in meters was the number attached to the Panzerfaust title; thus the PZ 30 could reach 30 meters, the PZ 60 to 60 meters and so on. The PZ 60 was perfected in early 1944 and production of the two earlier models

A Panzerschreck in action.

was gradually switched to the PZ 60 during the summer of 1944. A PZ 100 was then developed, by careful re-design of the propelling charge, and this went into production late in 1944.

Until this time the Panzerfaust was the first throw-away weapon; it was issued complete and after the firer had launched the bomb he threw the empty tube away and obtained another Panzerfaust. This, though, was becoming a strain on German resources and the Panzerfaust 150 was intended to remedy this. The PZ 150 went into production in January 1945, and showed considerable improvement over the earlier models, the bomb being re-designed to give the same penetration with less explosive. In addition a fragmentation sleeve could be placed around the bomb to give splinters and make the weapon effective against personnel. It was then re-designed so as to be re-loadable in the field so that the user could re-load quickly and use the same launch tube up to ten times, but this development was not completed before the war ended.

Production of Panzerfaust ran into many hundreds of thousands, and it will be seen that this was not, as is often supposed, a last-ditch extempore weapon hurriedly produced as the war was ending. It was a well-thought-out and highly efficient device, capable of dealing with any tank then known.

### Panzers

In the 1920s, the German Army, seeking a formula for future warfare, embraced the theories currently being advanced by Liddell Hart, Fuller, Hobart and other British analysts and began the planning of an integrated armored force, the Panzers. To do this they inaugurated a program of tank development which, though it had its faults when viewed with hindsight, was nonetheless the most technically proficient and cost-effective tank program ever seen.

Work began in 1926 with contracts for experimental tanks being placed with several manufacturers; in order to comply with the letter of the Versailles Treaty these machines were officially termed 'tractors'. The 'Light Tractor' weighed ten tons, carried a 37mm gun and resembled the contemporary British Vickers tank; the 'Heavy Tractor' was a 20-tonner with two turrets, one forward with a 75mm gun, one at the rear carrying a machine gun. About ten

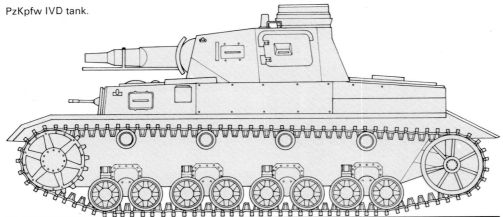

PzKpfw IVD tank.

prototypes, differing in various details due to the opinions of the different manufacturers, were built and tested secretly at the joint German-Soviet tank school at Kazan. Though production was contemplated, in the end they remained one-off machines, yielding valuable technical information which was used in the next series of designs, the *Neubaufahrzeug*.

The prototypes of this class were built in 1933–35; two types existed, the 'A' with 75mm and 37mm guns in the principal turret and machine guns in secondary turrets, and the 'B' with 105mm and 37mm main armament and secondary machine gun turret. Broadly speaking, both these designs were similar to the contemporary Vickers 'Independent' tank and they represented the then-popular vogue for multiple-turret vehicles, but they were soon seen to be far too complex and the idea was not pursued. The tanks were, however, retained as training vehicles and, in a brilliant propaganda stroke of 1940, were sent to Norway from whence newspaper photographs of the 'new German heavy tank' set Allied intelligence staffs on their ears.

In 1932, after much discussion and appraisal, specifications were issued for two types of tank to become the standard equipment of the new Wehrmacht, a light tank of about seven tons, armed with a 37mm gun, and a medium of 20 tons with a 75mm gun. But since development of these was to take some time, and since the Army wanted tanks on which to train, an even lighter design, influenced by the current designs of Carden-Loyd, was planned as a stop-gap. This was to be a five-tonner with a two-man crew and armed with two machine guns in the turret. Under the cover name of 'Agricultural Tractor' extensive contracts were let and the first *Panzer Kampf Wagen I Ausfuhrung A* (Armored Fighting Vehicle 1, Model A) entered service in the spring of 1934. These vehicles were scarcely combat-worthy but they could be turned out cheaply and quickly and served well to train the Panzers in maneuver and tactics.

The light tanks demanded in the original specification appeared in 1935 as the PzKpfw II; prototypes from various makers were tested and the design by MAN (Maschinenfabrik Augsberg-Nürnberg) selected for production. This tank weighed 7.2 tons and carried a 20mm cannon and a machine gun in the turret; with a crew of three men, it was powered by a 130hp gasoline engine and could reach 25mph on a good surface. There were numerous modifications to hull, suspension and turret before the design was perfected and mass production began in 1937, in the process of which the engine was uprated to 140hp and the weight increased to 9.5 tons.

The medium tank, which had been ordered at the same time as the PzKpfw II, entered service in 1937 as the PzKpfw IV, the jump in numbering being due to the fact that the tank to be known as PzKpfw III had been ordered (and christened) in 1936. The PzKpfw IV was to become the vital backbone of the Panzer force, more of this type being built than of any other. It was designed by Krupp, and weighed 17.3 tons; it was armed with a short 75mm gun in the turret, plus two machine guns, and had a crew of five men. The engine was a 250hp gasoline motor giving a speed of 18.5mph, while the armor protection ranged from 8 to 30mm in thickness.

Finally, in 1937 also, came the PzKpfw III, a Daimler-Benz design of light tank armed with a 37mm gun, powered by a 230hp motor and carrying a five-man crew. It weighed 15 tons, which was excessive for a 'light' tank at that time and in fact it differed from the PzKpfw IV very little except in armament, being almost the same size and appearance. This proved to be a blessing in later years when the size of the vehicle allowed heavier armament (5cm guns) to be mounted without major structural modifications.

These four tanks formed the combat strength of the Panzer arm at the outbreak of war; on 3 September 1939 there were 1445 PzKpfw I, 1226 PzKpfw II, 98 PzKpfw III and 211 PzKpfw IV plus about 200 specialized command and communication tanks – a total of 3195 combat vehicles. The Polish campaign, short and one-sided as it was, nevertheless allowed some conclusions to be drawn. The PzKpfw I was obviously useless as a combat tank, being too vulnerable and insufficiently armed. The PzKpfw II was of little value as an offensive vehicle, since its 20mm gun was by that time out-rated, but it still had its uses as a reconnaissance machine. The PzKpfw III was good but undergunned, and production of this model, armed with a heavier 5cm gun, was stepped up. But the PzKpfw IV was the outstanding tank, reliable, well-protected and with ample firepower, which makes it all the more incomprehensible that the Germans failed to appreciate its virtues and concentrate all their efforts into production of more of them at the expense of the II and III models.

The campaign of 1940 in France and the Low Countries convinced the Germans that they had the mixture right and that their armor was sufficient to cope with anything that was liable to confront them, as a result of which they opened the war against Russia with 3350 tanks and high hopes of success, in spite of their estimate that the Soviet tank strength was about 22,000. To some extent their optimism was

justified by events, since in the opening weeks of the campaign the Germans took or destroyed some 17,000 Soviet tanks for a loss of about 2700 of their own. But this initial euphoria was soon destroyed by the appearance of the Soviet KV and T–34 tanks, much superior in armor and performance to any German vehicle.

Due to their belief that the PzKpfw III and IV were so good as not to require replacement for some years, little development work had taken place in Germany since the outbreak of war. Now new specifications were hurriedly drawn up and issued to four manufacturers, demanding a medium tank of about 30 tons, armed with a 75mm gun to counter the Soviet T–34. Hitler, though, considered this to be insufficient, and he canceled the order with two companies and substituted a specification of his own, demanding a 45 tonner armed with the 88mm gun.

The original specification became the PzKpfw V 'Panther', probably the best German design of all. Designed by MAN, production began in November 1942. Design features included sloped armor to deflect shot, torsion-bar suspension, interleaved road wheels and a high-velocity 75mm gun which was capable of mastering any Soviet armor. With a crew of four it had armor 80mm thick, a 650hp gasoline engine, and could move its 43 tons at 28mph. For its time, it was an almost ideal mix of speed, maneuverability, protection and firepower.

The design which came from Hitler's specification became the PzKpfw VI 'Tiger', which probably became the most famous of all German tanks but was less technically successful. This was designed by Henschel, weighed 55 tons, carried an 88mm gun a crew of five and armor 25mm to 100mm thick. Driven by a 700hp motor it could travel at about 23mph. Production began in August 1942, but the early models had an unfortunate record of teething troubles – overheating, excessive fuel consumption, suspension problems – and before long a re-design was demanded. This resulted in the Tiger II or King Tiger, a 70-ton monster carrying an 88mm (later 128mm) gun and undoubtedly the most formidable fighting machine of World War II.

In addition to these standard designs the Panzer forces used a variety of captured tanks and, most important of all their 'outside' supplies, vast numbers of the Czech TNHP light tank, known in German service as the 'Panzer 38 (t)'. In the latter half of the war much attention was given to production of assault guns and self-propelled anti-tank weapons; this was due to both their tactical desirability and the fact that they were cheaper and quicker to produce than tanks largely because they lacked the complicated turret. Production of these vehicles reached large numbers and, to a great extent, interfered with the production of 'proper' tanks. The following figures give the best information available on the numbers of German tanks manufactured for the Wehrmacht.

| | |
|---|---|
| PzKpfw I | about 3000 |
| PzKpfw II | about 3580 |
| PzKpfw III | 5644 |
| PzKpfw IV | 9000 |
| PzKpfw V 'Panther' | 4814 |
| PzKpfw VI 'Tiger' | 1350 |
| 'King Tiger' | 484 |
| | 27,872 |

About 12,000 assault guns should be added to this number, though this figure is deceptive since many of them were conversions from super-annuated PzKpfw I, II and III tanks.

Production through the war years, compared with the other major nations:

| Year | Germany | USSR | Britain | USA |
|------|---------|--------|---------|--------|
| 1939 | 249 | | 969 | |
| 1940 | 1460 | 2794 | 1399 | 331 |
| 1941 | 3256 | 6590 | 4841 | 4052 |
| 1942 | 4278 | 24,668 | 8611 | 24,997 |
| 1943 | 5966 | 20,000 | 7476 | 29,497 |
| 1944 | 9161 | 29,000 | 5000 | 17,565 |

The numbers produced in 1945 were negligible and of little consequence to the course of the war.

## Panzerschreck
see Hollow Charge Weapons

## Papagos, General Alexander, 1883–1955

Commander in Chief at the time of Mussolini's invasion of Greece on 28 October 1940, Papagos repulsed it and chased the Italians back into Albania. He was unable to sustain, even with British assistance, the German invasion of April 1941, however, and, when defeat became inevitable, was removed from office by other officers, who offered terms to Germany. He was taken to Dachau as a hostage in 1943 and released by the Americans at the end of the war. He was again Commander in Chief during the successful post-war campaign against the left-wing guerrillas in northern Greece.

## Paris, the Liberation of, 1944

Eisenhower had decided during the battle of Normandy to bypass Paris to avoid the loss of life and destruction which a fight for the city would entail. Hitler for his part intended to turn the city into a 'fortress' and to burn it as the Allies approached. The French both inside the city and in the liberation army were determined to see that it was liberated quickly and cleanly. It was an uprising within the city on 19 August which decided the issue. Faced with the prospect of the city's destruction, Eisenhower dispatched the 2nd Free French Armored Division supported by American troops towards the city. The Germans meanwhile came to an agreement with the resistance leaders to cancel demolitions and although those outside showed fight the city fell to the Allies without great loss or damage on 25 August. General de Gaulle, who had set up his administration at Bayeux in June, immediately made a triumphal entry.

## Park, Air Marshal Keith, 1892–1975

Born in New Zealand, British Air Marshal Park, in 1939 was appointed Air Officer Commanding No 11 Group RAF Fighter Command. During the Dunkirk evacuation, his policy of maintaining a constant fighter shuttle from the Kent bases, aimed at preventing the Luftwaffe bombers from reaching the beaches, met with strong criticism from the surface forces who had expected 'umbrella' cover over the beaches themselves. However, considering the limited number of aircraft available to Park, his squadrons proved remarkably successful and the combat experience gained was invaluable.

Air Marshal Sir Keith Park.

Park was again criticized for his tactics during the Battle of Britain when certain fellow officers, notably Leigh-Mallory, disagreed with the essentially defensive nature of his squadrons' operations who were making no serious attempt at mounting an offensive. He was, nevertheless, fully supported by Dowding, Commander in Chief of Fighter Command.

In the autumn of 1941 he became Air Officer Commanding at Allied Headquarters in Egypt and in July 1942 was appointed AOC, Malta. The offensive tactics which he initiated, regular raids on German convoys to North Africa, seriously disrupted the passage of essential supplies to the Axis forces. His squadrons also provided air support for Operation Torch in November 1942. In January 1943 the Malta Command became part of the Mediterranean Air Command and by June of that year the greatly expanded Malta base was able to give substantial support to the Sicily landings, followed by those in Italy in September.

Park became Commander in Chief of Middle East Command in January 1944, later transferring to Southeast Asia Command in February 1945, where his squadrons gave vital air cover to the 14th Army in the capture of Rangoon and the Battle of Sittang Bend which occurred during the summer of 1945.

Park was a popular and sensitive Commander whose great initiative and drive inspired those whom he led.

## Patch, General Alexander McCarrell, 1889–1945

Patch achieved the distinction of winning the first American land victory of World War II on Guadalcanal in early 1943. In March 1944 he was designated commander of the US 7th Army which was earmarked for the invasion of Southern France in concert with the Overlord landings (Operation Anvil/Dragoon), and led it in the landings between Toulon and Cannes of 15 August 1944. Advancing up the Rhône Valley, he captured northern Alsace during the winter and the Saar in the following spring. In order to capture the mythical 'national redoubt', he made a headlong advance into South Germany in April 1945.

## Pathfinders
see Strategic Bombing Offensive in Germany

## Pattle, Squadron Leader M T St J,

A South African-born pilot, Pattle, with 41 confirmed victories, achieved the highest total of any fighter pilot serving with the RAF during World War II.

## Patton, General George, 1885–1945

An early enthusiast for the tank, a dashing extrovert and attractive character, Patton commanded the American forces which landed in Morocco in the Torch Operation in November 1942, and the 2nd Corps in Tunisia. He was commanding the 7th Army during the invasion of Sicily, and very successfully, when his anger with a 'battle-fatigued' soldier, over-publicized at home, led to his removal. Bradley, formerly his junior, became his superior for the invasion of Normandy, but as commander of the newly-formed 3rd Army, it was Patton who attracted the limelight in that campaign. Bursting out of the bridgehead on 25 July in Operation Cobra, he led – often indeed from the front – a swift and spectacular encirclement of the German Panzer divisions and then drove headlong into the interior of France. Shortage of gasoline, diverted to help Montgomery's advance into Holland during the Arnhem operation, brought him to a halt in Lorraine, where he fought a long and hard battle throughout the winter to break into Germany. He played a major part in the defeat of the Ardennes offensive and in the spring of 1945 directed the fastest and deepest drive into Germany, which arrived eventually in Czechoslovakia (from which he withdrew with reluctance and ill-humor). He was killed in a road accident shortly after the end of the war. Known as 'Old Blood and Guts' to his soldiers, he was the most flamboyant and effective American field commander of the European war.

General George Patton, Jr.

**'Paul'**
see Aichi E16A1 Zuiun

---

**Paul, Prince of Yugoslavia, 1893–**

Paul was the Prince Regent of King Peter II
from 1934–41. Paul felt that Yugoslavia had to
make an agreement with Hitler and in March
1941 convinced his government to agree to sign
on with the Berlin-Rome-Tokyo Axis. This provoked a fierce reaction throughout the country
and Paul was forced to resign.

---

**Paulus, Field Marshal Friedrich von, 1890–1957**

A promising general staff officer, Paulus transferred to the Panzer arm before the outbreak of
war and was appointed Chief of Staff to Reichenau in the Tenth and later Sixth Army. In
May 1940 he became Deputy Chief of the General Staff under Halder and then in January
1942 replaced Reichenau, who had been promoted to Army Group South, as Commander of
the Sixth Army. Its advance to Stalingrad culminated in its investment in the city in November and, when Manstein came to his relief in
December (Operation Winter Storm) he decided that his orders from Hitler prevented him
from breaking out to meet him. He was forced
to surrender on 30 January 1943, having been
promoted to Field Marshal the previous day.
Hitler vilified him for his decision, which was
unavoidable, and later the whole German army
joined Hitler in reprimanding him for his es-
pousal of the Russian-sponsored Free Germany
Movement, on behalf of which he broadcast
appeals to the Wehrmacht to give up the fight.
He settled in the Soviet zone of Germany after
the war.

---

**PAW (Panzer Abwehr Werfer)**
see High and Low Pressure Guns

---

**Pearl Harbor, 7 December 1941**

On Sunday 7 December 1941 Japanese aircraft
attacked the US Pacific Fleet at Pearl Harbor,
sinking four battleships and destroying 200 aircraft.
    Admiral Yamamoto's staff began planning
an operation to put the US Pacific Fleet out of
action, preparatory to any other operation in
June 1941. Yamamoto felt that Japan did not
have the resources to fight a long war against
the USA, so he wanted a surprise attack to
give Japan a decisive advantage. The US Navy
expected an attack on the Philippines or on
Malaya and had withdrawn the Pacific Fleet
to Pearl Harbor.
    On 26 November the Japanese fleet assem-
bled in the Kurile Islands under Admiral
Nagumo. It consisted of six carriers, two battleships, three cruisers, nine destroyers, three
submarines and eight accompanying tankers.
The carriers took 104 high-level bombers (equipped with torpedoes which could be launched
in only 30- to 45-foot deep waters and with
15- and 16-inch armor piercing shells with fins
which would explode on the decks of the ships),
135 dive-bombers, 40 torpedo bombers and 81
fighters. The fleet sailed due east from the Kurile
Islands until it was due north of Midway Island,
then it headed southeast to the Hawaiian Islands but was not detected by US shipping or

reconnaissance planes. The Japanese attack was
planned to coincide with a fourteen part message declaring war but the message was delivered
several hours after the attack because of the
slow translation of the text. Cordell Hull had
intercepted the message and had partially decoded it the day before. Admiral Harold Stark,
Chief of Naval Operations, had transmitted a
message of warning to Pearl Harbor authorities
to be on the alert, but it did not reach them in
time. The radar system spotted the Japanese
aircraft but mistook them for B-17s and no
alarm was raised. A further warning came when
a Japanese submarine was spotted outside the
harbor, but again this was disregarded. When
the Japanese aircraft struck, no anti-aircraft
guns were ready and the nine battleships were
without torpedo nets and made easy targets.
The Japanese had hoped to find at least two
aircraft carriers in the harbor but two were on
maneuvers in the Pacific, the *Lexington* was

*Top:* Battleship Row and Ford Island are hit on the
'Day of Infamy', 7 December 1941.
*Above:* Sailors on leave from Great Lakes NTC read
a Chicago newspaper announcing Pearl Harbor.

carrying aircraft to Midway Island and the *Enterprise* was on the same mission to Wake.
    The aircraft were launched in two waves. The
first left at 0600 local time and the bombing
began at 0755. In the first wave torpedoes hit the
*Arizona, Oklahoma, West Virginia* and *California* and sank them. The bombers also attacked
the five airfields known to Japanese intelligence
and found the aircraft close together on the
ground. The second wave was hampered by
smoke and did not do as much damage. By 1000
the attack was over. The Japanese aircraft had
sunk or damaged eighteen warships, destroyed
188 aircraft and killed or wounded 3581 sailors.
They left the harbor installations and oil tanks
intact.

Nagumo did not want to risk his carriers by launching a third wave, which would have ensured complete success. As it was, most of the ships were repaired and the Pacific Fleet received only a temporary setback. The attack achieved such unanimous support for Roosevelt's declaration of war on Japan that some people have even alleged that he himself staged it. This however was most definitely not the case. In their triumph, the Japanese lost only 55 men and less than 30 planes.

## Pedestal
see *Eagle* and Malta

## Peenemünde Arrow Shells

These were dart-like projectiles fired from special smooth-bore versions of standard artillery weapons, and were developed at the Aerodynamic Research Laboratories at Peenemünde, Germany, in 1942–45. They were originally developed as ultra-long-range shells for a 31cm smooth-bored version of the 28cm K5 railway gun. The shell was 75.2in long and 120mm caliber, with four fins at the rear end 31cm across and a 31cm sabot or discarding ring around the center of gravity. When fired this sabot fell away outside the gun muzzle, and the shell attained a velocity of 5000ft/sec and a maximum range of 93.8 miles. Two guns were made, one of which was used in action shelling the US 3rd Army at a range of about 78 miles.

The same type of projectile was then developed for the 105mm FLAK 39 anti-aircraft gun, the object here being to achieve a high velocity and thus a shorter time of flight to the target which would cut down the aiming errors. Experimental shells reached velocities of the order of 3500ft/sec but the work had to be abandoned since there was no production capacity available to make them in the large quantities demanded for combat use.

The Peenemünde arrow shell was 75.2 inches in length and 120mm caliber.

## 'Peggy'
see Mitsubishi Ki-67 Hirgu

## Peirse, Air Chief Marshal Sir Richard, 1892–1970

Peirse was the British Commander of Allied Air Forces in Southeast Asia. At the outbreak of the war Peirse was made an additional member of the Air Council and promoted acting Air Marshal. From April 1940 the post was made into Vice-Chief of Air Staff. From October 1940 until January 1942 Peirse was Commander in Chief of Bomber Command. His task was to improve the training of crews, who had little experience of night-flying, and to improve radar equipment. In January 1942 he became Allied Air Commander in the ABDA command but because of the rapid Japanese advance, the ABDA command was dissolved and Peirse became AOC-in-C in India. After the overwhelming defeat in Burma, Peirse had to re-

organize the air force and set up air bases in Bengal to prepare for the recapture of Burma. He set up his operational HQ in Calcutta and Delhi became a maintenance base. He also had to organize the airlifting of supplies from India over the 'Hump' to China. In December 1943 Peirse became Allied Air Commander in Chief of SEAC and he encountered some problems because Lord Mountbatten, the Supreme Commander of SEAC, had his HQ in Ceylon and communications were poor. His air force greatly contributed to the victory in Burma by airlifting supplies to the invading 14th Army. In November 1944 Peirse retired.

## Peltz, Lieutenant Colonel Dietrich,

A German Major General at the age of 29, Peltz directed bomber and dive-bomber units in the campaign against Poland and in the offensive against the UK between 1940 and 1941. He subsequently held a staff appointment concerned with the inspection of bombers and the organization of the bomber arm. His experience of ground-attack operations was put to good use against the Allies in the Mediterranean theater and from March 1943 he was responsible for a dive-bomber formation leaders course at Foggia in Italy.

In August 1943 he took command of Fliegerkorps IX, with control of all the Luftwaffe long-range bomber units based in northern France and the Low Countries. In addition, the whole of the long-range bomber force from Italy was sent to reinforce his command. He introduced pathfinder aircraft to improve accuracy. His task was to launch what was to prove the last major German strategic offensive of the war against Britain, following the devastating raid on Hamburg by the RAF in July 1943. Beginning on 21 January 1944, the resulting attacks on London, Hull and Bristol caused damage but failed to have any effect on British morale.

On 1 January 1945, in a last daring effort, he sent a force of approximately 800 fighters and fighter-bombers across the Rhine in support of the Ardennes offensive; but the lack of training and the inexperience of his pilots mitigated against success and the operation failed.

## *Pennsylvania*

The battleship *Pennsylvania* (BB.38) was built 1913–16 and served with the US Atlantic Fleet as the flagship of Admiral Henry T Mayo but did not cross the Atlantic in 1917 as the acute shortage of oil meant that only coal-burning battleships were needed for the Grand Fleet. On 7 December 1941 she was in dry dock at Pearl Harbor. Although not badly hit she was damaged and immobilized in the dock by the explosion of the two destroyers *Cassin* and *Downes* moored ahead of her.

The ship had to be recommissioned after repairs in August 1942 and returned to the Pacific. She was active in the Aleutian landings and took part in various bombardments but the climax of her career was on 24 October 1944 when she and other old battleships sank the Japanese battleship *Yamashiro* in the Battle of Surigao Strait (see Philippine Sea, Battle of). She was badly damaged aft by an aircraft torpedo while lying in Buckner Bay, Okinawa on 12 August 1945. Her repairs were cut short by the end of the war and her last voyage was to Bikini for the atomic tests in 1946. She won eight battle stars.

## Percival, Lieutenant General Arthur, 1887–1966

Percival was the British General in command of forces in Singapore at the time of the surrender to the Japanese in 1942.

Percival saw action in France under General Dill but was posted back to England before Dunkirk. In July 1941 he arrived in Malaya as GOC. The security of Singapore depended on British control of the sea. When the Japanese began their invasion of Malaya, Britain had two battleships, the *Repulse* and the *Prince of Wales*, but these did not have air support and were sunk on 10 December. The British forces in Northern Malaya could not stop the Japanese advance and on 27 January 1942 Percival ordered withdrawal to Singapore Island. Churchill ordered him to fight it out but by 15 February the water shortage on the island was so desperate that Percival surrendered along with 130,000 men.

Percival was interned in Manchuria but was present at the formal surrender of the Japanese on the USS *Missouri*.

## Persia, Occupation of, 1941

Both the British and the Russians suspected the ruler of Persia, Shah Reza Pahlevi, of sympathy for the Axis cause and, following the German invasion of Russia in June 1941, determined jointly to occupy the country. In August they did so, meeting no resistance, and in January the following year signed and issued a treaty guaranteeing their withdrawal from the country within six months of hostilities ceasing as evidence of their purely military motives. America acceded to the treaty in December 1943 at the Teheran Conference. The country provided one of the most important supply routes for western aid to the Soviet Union.

## *Perth*

This cruiser was built as HMS *Amphion* in 1934 but was transferred to the Royal Australian Navy in 1939 and renamed. After service in the Mediterranean, including action in the Battle for Crete, she was transferred to the Far East when war with Japan became imminent. The *Perth* was part of the American-British-Dutch-Australian (ABDA) force formed in December 1941, but met her end in the Battle of the Java Sea, being torpedoed by Admiral Nishimura's forces in the Sunda Strait on 1 March 1942.

## Pétain, Marshal Henri Philippe Omer, 1856–1951

After Foch the most honored French soldier of the Great War was Pétain for his defense of Verdun in 1916. Pétain was acting as Ambassador to Spain in 1940 when he was recalled by Reynaud to act as Vice-President of the Council (Deputy Prime Minister). He became convinced in early June that France must surrender and rejected Reynaud's proposal for a union with Britain, which he believed was also doomed to defeat. On that Reynaud resigned on 16 June and Pétain replaced him and at once offered the Germans an armistice which came into effect on 22 June. On 10 July the National Assembly under the leadership of Laval voted him emergency powers which he used to proclaim himself Head of a new *Etat Français*, replacing the Third Republic. He set up his capital at Vichy, in the zone left unoccupied by the Germans, and pursued a policy of collaboration with the Germans, which stopped short of entering the war on their side (as Laval wished). After the occupation of the unoccupied zone, consequent on the Allied invasion of French North Africa, his government became a puppet one and increasing age robbed him of his powers. He was taken to Germany in August 1944 but returned to France at his own wish in April 1945, where he was brought to trial and condemned to death. De Gaulle, who had served in Pétain's regiment at the outbreak of World War I, commuted the sentence to life imprisonment and he died on the remote Atlantic Ile d'Yeu at the age of 95. History will probably judge that his crime was not treachery but defeatism – a charge already made by some during World War I.

### 'Pete'

see Mitsubishi F1 M

### Peter II, King of Yugoslavia, 1923–1970

Peter II spent the war in exile and was deposed when peace was declared. In March 1941 he assumed full royal powers after his regent, Prince Paul, had been overthrown. Germany's prompt invasion forced Peter to flee and he eventually settled in London. Peter supported Mihajlović's Četniks in Yugoslavia but the Allies supported Tito's Partisan movement and this led to many disputes. He did not return to Belgrade when it had been liberated because he had agreed with Tito to set up a Regency council to represent him. Tito proclaimed a republic in November 1945 and Peter was deposed.

### Petlyakov Pe–2

This Soviet high-performance light bomber was operational from 1941. Vladimir Petlyakov was one of a number of top Soviet aircraft designers who were arrested in 1938 and were allocated the task of developing new combat aircraft in special prisons set up at aircraft factories. His particular responsibility was the VI–100, a fast high-altitude long-range two-seat fighter with pressurized crew accommodation. While the prototype was being built, its job was changed to high-altitude bombing. It flew for the first time on 7 May 1939, powered by two 1100hp M–105R supercharged engines, and had such slim, clean lines that it proved capable of 387mph at 33,000ft. It was less capable as a bomber, as accuracy proved impossible when bombs were dropped from its operating height of over 16,500ft. However, this did not matter as the Soviet High Command had ordered the VI–100's to be redesigned as the PB–100 dive-bomber following the successes achieved by Ju

Above: Pe-2s on a Soviet assembly line.
Below: Pe-8 Soviet heavy bomber.

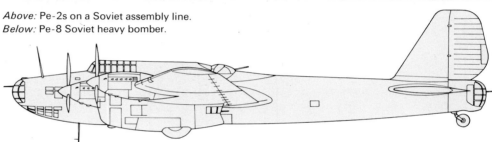

87s in the Spanish Civil War. The PB–100 prototype flew in early 1940 and was ordered into large-scale production in June. It was now a three-seater, with two crew-members under a blister canopy near the glazed nose, and a radio operator/rear gunner in a cramped position in the rear fuselage. The turbochargers that had been fitted to the engines of the VI–100 were no longer needed. Weapon load comprised six 220lb bombs in the fuselage bomb-bay, two more under each wing center-section, and two in the rear of the engine nacelles. Two 7.62mm machine guns were carried in the nose and one in the rear of the cabin; another could be fired under the tail by means of a periscope sight.

Production aircraft were designated Pe–2s. A total of 460 had been built by mid-1941, and were already popular with service pilots, who said they were easy to fly, stable in a dive and accurate in attack. Equally important when Germany invaded Russia, the Pe–2s were as fast as the German Bf 109E fighters that attempted to shoot them from the sky. When the Germans introduced the Bf 109F, Pe–2s had to fly at anything up to 23,000ft to elude it. Bombing results suffered until the observer's 7.62mm machine gun was exchanged for one of 12.7mm

in a turret, after which the dive-bombers could again hold their own in combat. At the end of 1942, the Luftwaffe replied with the Bf 109G–2. The Pe–2s were fitted with engines uprated to 1210 or 1260hp and the airframe was generally cleaned up, to raise their maximum speed by 25mph. Defensive armament was again increased and the Pe–2s retained their capability. Altogether 11,427 were built, remaining in production throughout the war. Variants included about 500 Pe–3 fighters, and Pe–2R reconnaissance aircraft.

### Petlyakov Pe–8

Only 79 of these Soviet four-engined heavy bombers were produced between 1938 and 1941, emphasizing the priority afforded to tactical bombing. Typical of aircraft produced under Tupolev supervision in the interwar years, the Pe–8 had a crew of 11 and wings thick enough for mechanic/air gunners to crawl inside to reach gun positions in the rear of each inboard engine nacelle. With four 1350hp AM–35 engines, the Pe–8 had a maximum speed of 274mph and could fly 2920 miles with 4400lb of bombs. Defensive armament comprised two 20mm, two 12.7mm and two 7.62mm guns in five turrets. Pe–8s equipped the 332nd Special Purpose Heavy Bomber Regiment, and most were flown initially by test pilots. The first night raid, on 19 July 1941, was directed against Königsberg. Eleven aircraft set out to attack Berlin on 11–12 August; one crashed through engine failure on take-off, four others suffered similar failures in varying degrees, and two were shot down by anti-aircraft guns.

Below: Side-view of a Pe-2.

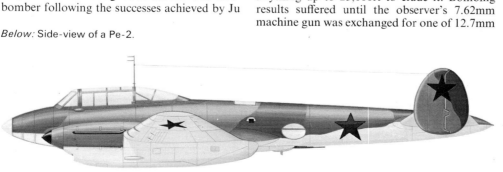

## Petrov, General Ivan Y, 1896–1950

Petrov was commander of the Caucasus Front, 1942–43. He commanded the 2nd Cavalry Division at Odessa and fought in its defense. He was then put in command of the land defenses at Sevastopol which fell in July 1942. From the North Caucasus Front he directed the operations which liberated Novorossiysk and the Taman peninsula. Then he drove his troops across to the Kerch peninsula and Crimea, but was removed from this command. In 1944 he was Commander of the 2nd Belorussian Front but was removed on Mekhlis's recommendation. From August 1944 to April 1945 he was in command of the 4th Ukrainian Front but was dismissed after the failure of the offensive on the Carpathians.

## Philippine Sea, Battle of the, 1944

The Battle of the Philippine Sea was the last occasion on which the Japanese Navy was able to challenge the US Pacific Fleet on equal terms. After the battle, the Japanese Navy had so few pilots and aircraft left that its aircraft carriers were virtually useless.

Admiral Toyoda's plan was to trap the US carrier force between Vice-Admiral Ozawa's carrier force planes and land-based aircraft from Guam in Operation A-Go. The Japanese force consisted of the Mobile Force which was divided into Force A with Ozawa's three carriers the *Taiho*, *Shokaku* and *Zuikaku* (which had 207 aircraft), Force B with another three carriers the *Junyo*, *Hiyo* and *Ryuho* (which had 135 aircraft) and a Van Force of Vice-Admiral Kurita's battleships.

Vice-Admiral Spruance's 5th Fleet assembled off the Marianas to protect the invasion force. He had Vice-Admiral Mitscher's Task Group 58, with fifteen carriers and 956 aircraft. The US fleet had overwhelming superiority in the air but the Japanese counted on their shore-based planes to tip the balance in their favor. On 11

*Below:* Japanese carrier *Zuikaku* and two destroyers under heavy aerial attack in the Philippine Sea.

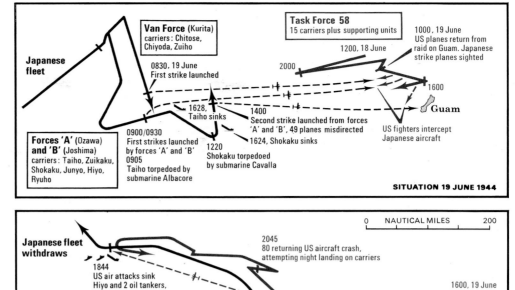

**SITUATION 19 JUNE 1944**

**SITUATION 20 JUNE 1944**

June the invasion began with the bombardment of airfields on Guam, and when Ozawa went into battle a week later he did not realize that the shore-based planes were out of action. On 19 June 1944 Ozawa sent out scout seaplanes which spotted part of Task Group 58, and at 0830 Ozawa sent in the first of four waves of aircraft. As the second wave was being launched the *Taiho* was hit by a torpedo from a US submarine, but the damage did not appear serious.

In the meantime Mitscher had sent out his planes to intercept the Japanese aircraft 50 miles ahead of the US Fleet. Only 20 Japanese planes in the second strike were able to break through and they could only inflict minor damage on the *Wasp* and *Bunker Hill*. The rest of the aircraft were shot down or missed their target and were brought down over Guam. At 1220 the *Shokaku* was recovering about 30 planes from these strikes when it was hit by a torpedo from the US submarine *Cavalla*. The *Shokaku* blazed for

three hours before sinking. Then at 1532 the *Taiho*, Ozawa's flagship, exploded and sank shortly afterwards. Ozawa thought that the planes which were missing had landed on Guam and had no idea of the failure of his attack. This battle is known as the 'Great Marianas Turkey Shoot' because of the very high Japanese losses in aircraft, about 300 in all.

The battle was not quite over. Ozawa did not withdraw until late afternoon on 20 June and at 1605 Mitscher decided to launch his aircraft against Ozawa's carriers. They sank the *Hiyo*, damaged the *Zuikaku* and holed the flight deck of the *Chiyoda*. Of the 216 American strike aircraft launched, 43 found their carriers in the night. However, many crashed in the sea and their crews were picked up, so only 16 pilots and 33 air crew were lost. Mitscher was disappointed that he had not been given a chance to attack the Japanese Fleet earlier, but the Battle of the Philippine Sea was a tremendous success for Spruance because Japanese air power was so completely wiped out. It was a dress rehearsal for the Battle of Leyte Gulf.

## Philippines
see Luzon and Leyte

## Piaggio P.108B

The only heavy bomber produced by Italy in World War II, the P.108B was powered by four 1500hp Piaggio P.XII engines and could carry up to 7716lb of bombs or three 18in torpedoes. Crew numbered seven, and eight 12.7mm machine guns were carried for defense, including a unique remotely controlled two-gun turret above each outer engine nacelle. P-108Bs made their first combat sortie against Gibraltar in 1942, flown by the 274th Long-Range Bomber Squadron. Subsequent operations took them over the Mediterranean, to North Africa and to Russia. Only 163 were built.

## PIAT
see Hollow Charge Weapons

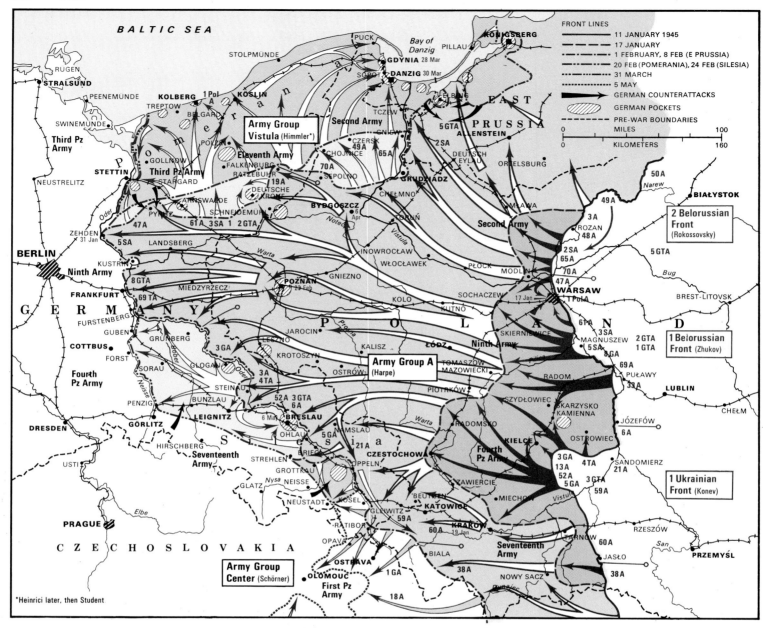

*Heinrici later, then Student

**Plate, Battle of the River**

see *Exeter*

---

**Pointblank**

see Strategic Bombing Offensive in Germany

---

**Pokryshkin, Alexander Ivanovich, 1913–**

This Russian airman was the second highest-scoring Soviet ace having destroyed 59 enemy aircraft.

---

*Pola*

Italian heavy cruiser of the *Zara* Class was sunk by gunfire and torpedoes at the Battle of Cape Matapan after having been disabled by an aerial torpedo earlier that day, 28 March 1941.

---

**Poland, Liberation of, 1944–45**

The Russians had swept the Germans out of Belorussia by mid-July 1944 and they pressed their advantage by attacking Poland. In the north Generals Chernyakhovsky and Zakharov

joined to take Bialystok on 18 July. South of the Pripet Marshes General Rokossovsky's 1st Belorussian Front crossed the Bug near Kovel on 22 July and swerved north to take Brest-Litovsk. On 24 July Rokossovsky marched into Lublin and sent his mobile troops to the Vistula and Warsaw. Here the Russians met stiff resistance and were checked at Siedlce. On 31 July Rokossovsky reached the outskirts of Warsaw but he needed to refuel, and stopped at Praga, a suburb of Warsaw. This encouraged the partisans to rise up against the Germans but it also allowed the Germans to bring up reinforce-

The Italian heavy cruiser *Pola*.

ments of three SS Panzer divisions from Italy. The front then stabilized along the Vistula. In the south General Konev launched his offensive on 16 July, on a 125 mile front and broke through the enemy lines near Luck to take Lvov on 27 July. He then built spearheads across the San at Jaroslaw and Przemysl on the next day. On 2 August the 1st Ukrainian Army made a bridgehead over the Vistula near Baranow.

General Model managed to halt the Russian offensive because it was running short of supplies and fuel and there followed a six-month

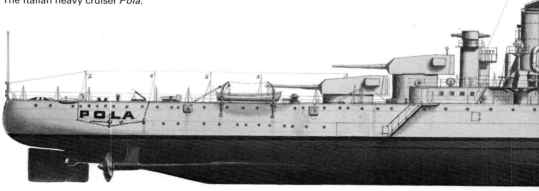

break in activities. On 12 January 1945 the Russians opened the final great offensive on a 750 mile front. Their forces were far superior to the Germans: they had a numerical superiority of five to one; their armored divisions now had Stalin tanks; Hitler had sent two Panzer Divisions to reinforce Hungary. Himmler had been appointed commander of Army Group Vistula. In the south Konev's armor crossed at Baranow and the left wing headed for Krakow while the center drove west for Oppeln. Konev's armor reached those cities on the 19 and 26 January and thus cut off the whole of Upper Silesia. Konev's right flank headed north to link up with Marshal Zhukov. Zhukov launched his attack across the Vistula on 14 January and bypassed Warsaw which fell on 17 January. Zhukov's armor bypassed all the fortresses which Himmler thought would have held up the advance. Hitler would not allow any withdrawal to consolidate positions but insisted on a rigid defense. Zhukov bypassed Torun which was later besieged by Rokossovsky and fell on 1 February. In late January Himmler relied on Poznan's defenses to check Zhukov, but the Russians bypassed the city and attacked the Warta positions which were poorly defended by the Volkssturm. On 30 January Zhukov crossed the Brandenburg frontier and was 100 miles from Berlin. In the north Rokossovsky broke through to the coast west of Danzig and trapped the German forces in East Prussia. Poland had been overrun by the Red Army in a month and the Red Army regrouped to prepare for the final assault on Berlin. Pockets of resistance at Torun, Poznan, Breslau and many other pockets of resistance held up further advance. Poznan resisted stubbornly until it fell on 23 February.

## Polikarpov I–15 and I–153

Successes achieved by I–15 biplanes during the Spanish Civil War, and against Japanese Navy Mitsubishi A5M monoplanes in China, prompted further development of the design

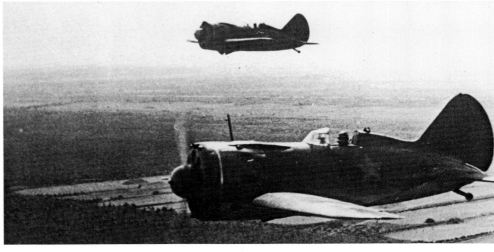

into the I–15*bis*, with uprated 750hp M–25V engine, four machine guns, and provision for two 165lb bombs; and the I–153 with M–62 or M–63 engine, provision for six rockets or two bombs, and a retractable undercarriage which helped to increase maximum speed to 267mph. Both types served in the campaigns against Finland, and were still operational in large numbers at the time of the German invasion, in June 1941. The I–15*bis* was used mainly in the dive-bomber role by that time. The I–153, which weighed only 4431lb fully loaded, was so maneuverable that it fared reasonably well against even the much faster Bf 109s of the Luftwaffe.

## Polikarpov I–16

This Soviet single-seat fighter was operational from 1935 to 1943. First flown on 31 December 1933, this tubby little fighter was the first single-seat low-wing monoplane fighter with retractable undercarriage to go into production anywhere in the world. In its original form, as the I–16 Type 1, it had an armament of two wing-mounted machine guns and was powered by a 450hp M–22 engine which gave it a speed of 224mph. Engine power and armament were gradually increased through a series of model changes, and the I–16 Type 10 which took part

Soviet I-16 fighters in formation in the Ukraine.

in the Spanish Civil War had a 750hp M–25V engine and four machine guns. It outperformed the Messerschmitt Bf 109Bs of the German Condor Legion in every respect except in a sustained 180 degree turn but began to be outclassed when the 109B was followed by the 109E. By the time the Germans attacked Russia in 1941, the standard versions in service were the I–16 Type 18 with an 850hp M–62 engine and the Type 24 with an M–63 of still higher rating and speed of 326mph. Armed with two machine guns and two wing-mounted 20mm cannon, these versions had been the most heavily armed fighters in the world in the late thirties. They bore the brunt of the initial German onslaught and were not retired from frontline duties until the Spring of 1943.

## Polish Campaign, 1939

The Polish campaign, lasting only 28 days, provided an excellent stage on which Hitler could show off the power and efficiency of his armored divisions. The campaign introduced a new concept of war: the Blitzkrieg. The German Army was deployed in 58 divisions of which fourteen were Panzers. They were opposed by the Polish Armed Forces under the Commander in Chief General Smigly-Rydz with 30 divisions, only one of which was motorized. Five powerful armies overran Poland from three directions on 1 September 1939: Third Army (General von Küchler) from East Prussia in the north; Fourth Army (General Kluge) from Pomerania; and Eighth (General Blaskowitz), Tenth (General Reichenau) and Fourteenth (General List) Armies from Silesia. Field Marshal Bock commanded the Army Group North and Field Marshal von Rundstedt the Army Group South.

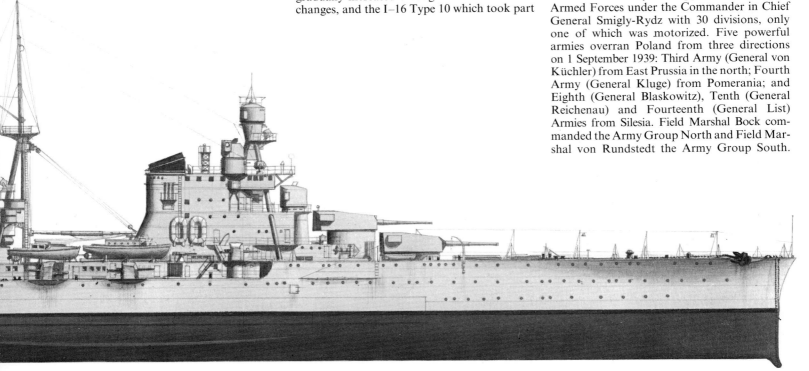

GERMAN ATTACKS 15/27 SEPTEMBER
POLISH BZURA POCKET
RUSSIAN ATTACKS 17/27 SEPTEMBER

For the first two days 1400 German planes attacked Polish airfields and destroyed some 900 planes before they had taken off. The Polish Army had only one tactic, to counterattack, and it was therefore placed in large groupings in the Danzig corridor and in front of Warsaw. By 8 September the Tenth Army reached Warsaw cutting off the Poles before they could cross the Vistula. Smigly-Rydz gave orders to retreat to southeast Poland on 10 September. Five days later the Third Army completed the northern arm of the pincer: the Fourth and Fourteenth Armies closed the pincer in the east on the 17. On that day the Russian Army invaded East Poland and took Vilnyus, reaching the Curzon Line within two days. On 18 September the Polish Government and High Command fled to Rumania. Warsaw however resisted until 27 September. On the German side 10,600 were killed, 30,000 were wounded and 3400 were missing. The Polish figures are not accurate, but at least 450,000 were taken prisoner and detained in camps. The German conquest of Poland gave Hitler complete hegemony over Central and Eastern Europe. The Germans now came face to face with the Soviets.

## Polish Home Army

The Polish Home Army was formed in 1939 under General Sikorski, but it was hampered by the growing impotence and discord of the Polish Government-in-Exile and the growth of the Communist PPR and People's Army. In January 1944 the PPR established a national committee in Warsaw which split the underground forces, and was later recognized by the USSR. The first contact between the Red Army and the

Home Army was in Yolhynia. The 27th Home Army division in the Kowel Sector agreed to coordinate operations with the Red Army but had to accept full operational subordination and reorganize its divisions into normal infantry divisions. This arrangement lasted for a time, but by April General Bor-Komorowski, Home Army Commander in Chief, was receiving information that the Red Army was co-operating with his forces only so long as they were fighting the Germans. They would then disarm the Home Army, arrest and sometimes kill the leaders and conscript the men into the Red Army. After each engagement Home Army divisions were offered the choice between incorporation into General Berling's Polish Army in Russia or disbandment.

On 6 April 1944 the Home Army independently carried out 'Operation Julia', disrupting railway lines, as a show of its efficiency and of its support for the Government-in-Exile. Then, on 1 August, it led the Warsaw uprising (in which the PPR and the People's Army co-operated) to pre-empt Russian occupation. Following Warsaw, the Home Army, now under Colonel Okulicki, engaged itself in anti-Soviet operations and its members were denounced as traitors. This phase culminated on 27 March 1945 in the arrest of sixteen underground leaders who were tricked into believing they were to negotiate with Zhukov. They were in fact flown to Lubianka jail. Their trial on 18–21 June showed how wide the gulf was between the Home Army and the Government-in-Exile, and they were convicted of anti-Soviet sabotage.

The Home Army was formally disbanded in July 1945, followed by a Provisional Government amnesty for Home Army and political prisoners.

## Popov, General Markian M, 1902–

Popov was Commander of the Bryansk Front in 1943 and the Baltic Front in 1944. Stalin did not really trust him. He was given the command of the armored divisions at Kharkov in May 1942, as part of Timoshenko's offensive but was pushed back. Popov worked out the Kutuzov Operation (Kursk) with Sokolovsky and after this success was appointed Commander of the 2nd Baltic Front. When his Front failed to take Riga, he was replaced by General Yeremenko.

## Portal, Air Marshal Sir Charles, 1893–1971

Portal was the British Air Marshal who was Chief of the Air Staff from 1940 to 1945 following a brief period as Commander in Chief RAF Bomber Command. His task was to direct the policy of the RAF and as the Air Member of the Chiefs of Staff Committee had an important role in the Allied conferences. For the greater part of the war he was a firm advocate of area strategic bombing, a view which was to bring him into direct conflict with the US strategic bomber Commanders who favored precision attacks. However, the respect in which he was held helped to make compromise possible at the Casablanca Conference in January 1943, when it was agreed that both forms should be allowed to go ahead in what came to be known as the *Combined Bomber Offensive*.

However, by the beginning of 1944 Portal became increasingly skeptical as to the effectiveness of area bombing. He, therefore, ordered RAF Bomber Command to make experimental night-time precision attacks and the resultant success of these led to the total commitment of the strategic units to Leigh-Mallory's Transportation Plan. Relations with Harris, Commander in Chief of Bomber Command, rapidly deteriorated with Harris doggedly maintaining a policy of area bombardment. The crisis point was reached in January 1945 with the Commander in Chief suggesting resignation. Portal, however, realized that the scandal such an act would occasion, together with the blow to Bomber Command's morale, would be wholly unacceptable and the matter was allowed to rest. A rather solitary figure, Portal was held in high esteem.

## Port Moresby
see New Guinea. Port Moresby and Buna

## Potato-Digger
see Marlin Machine Gun

## Potez 630

This French two/three-seat fighter was in service from 1938–44. In October 1934 several French companies began to design new aircraft to meet an *Armée de l'Air* requirement for a three-seat long-range fighter with two 20mm cannon suitable for bomber escort, fighter direction and the interception of enemy bombers. The aircraft built in quantity to meet this need was the Potez 631, first flown as the 630 in April 1936. Though bigger and heavier than most previous fighters, and far more costly, the twin-engined Potez was pleasant to fly and surprisingly maneuverable, and large orders were placed in 1937 for two main versions, the 630 with 580hp Hispano-Suiza 14AB radial engines and the 631 with 660hp Gnome-Rhône 14M engines of the same layout. Orders were also placed by Czechoslovakia, Finland, Greece, Romania, China and Japan, and production for the *Armée de l'Air* got into its stride as early as the spring of 1938. By May 1940 output of the nationalized SNCAN factories, which had taken over Potez, reached 121 aircraft, which was more than the rate at which the *Armée de l'Air* could form squadrons.

A trim and graceful machine, the 630 or 631 had a crew of two or three seated in tandem under a long 'greenhouse' canopy. In the nose were two 20mm Hispano HS–9 cannon (in early aircraft shortage of these resulted in four machine guns being substituted), while the rear cockpit had a single or pair of 7.5mm MAC 1934 machine guns for rear defense. In February 1940 the offensive firepower was greatly augmented by adding six MAC 1934 machine guns in blister fairings under the outer wings. In the hectic days of the spring of 1940, the 630 and 631 were the main long-range fighters, and virtually the only night fighter available (of course, it carried no radar). Seven squadrons were based in the fighting area in northern France but they only managed to shoot down 17 German aircraft; the much smaller number used by the Aéronavale (French Navy) shot down 12 more. From these fighters stemmed many other versions built in larger numbers, the most numerous of all being the 63.11 reconnaissance machine with a glazed nose and two-seat upper cockpit, which saw action on both sides until almost the end of the war.

## Potsdam Conference, 17 July–2 August 1945

At Potsdam, Churchill (replaced by Attlee midway), Truman and Stalin had to deal with a starving and demolished Germany and with the political fate of the liberated countries, especially those Eastern European ones already dominated by Russia.

The United States and Britain were not concerned with cash reparations from Germany so much as with rendering Germany self-supporting and harmless. They thus proposed that each power (including France) should receive reparations at its own discretion from its own zone of occupation. Russia would get additional credits from the other zones. There was little attempt at establishing a joint administration of Germany as a single unit.

Russia presented the conference with the de facto annexation of Eastern German lands by Poland. The Allies objected strenuously (especially because these lands were important suppliers of food for their sectors). But the main issue was the Yalta Declaration on Poland: Truman and Churchill would not recognize the Polish government as democratically based. A Polish delegation came to the conference, offering assurances of free elections, which were accepted despite Western Allies' police reports on events inside Poland. Stalin and the Poles agreed to broaden the Lublin Government to include other political parties. This issue was bound up with Soviet demands for recognition of their puppet governments in Rumania, Bulgaria and Hungary. The US and Britain demanded free elections with outside observers and press correspondents present in these three countries and Poland, but Stalin refused this as an insult to their integrity (and countering with arguments about the dubious legitimacy of the

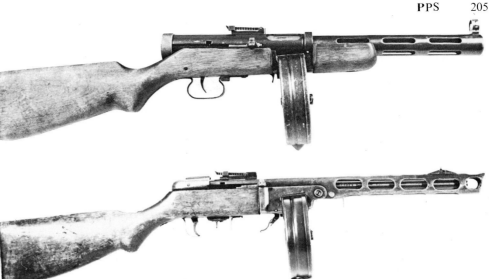

*Top:* PPD Model 1940 submachine gun. *Above:* The PPsH submachine gun. Both weapons were standard issue in the first stages of the Soviet defense of their country after the German invasion in June 1941.

present Italian government). The tension was increased by a military build-up in Yugoslavia, Bulgaria and Albania which were making territorial demands on Greece. Here the US and Britain finally took a stronger stand, defending Greece and claiming her to be within their sphere of influence.

Finally, on the subject of Japan, the USSR had been asked by that country to act as neutral intermediary between her and her enemies, but Stalin was getting ready to enter the war, demanding a share in the occupation of Japan and territorial concessions. He therefore did not pass on all the relevant information regarding Japanese peace-feelers. With the first atom bomb having been successfully tested just before the conference, the Potsdam Declaration was released, calling for the unconditional surrender of Japan and threatening the annihilation of that country without mentioning the new weapon.

The declaration proved a considerable stumbling block for the Japanese Cabinet, who wished to have the Emperor's position guaranteed before any Declaration of Surrender could be contemplated.

## Pound, Admiral Sir Dudley, 1877–1943

Promoted Admiral of the Fleet and First Sea Lord (Chief of the Naval Staff) in 1939 after having commanded in the Mediterranean, Pound also acted as chairman of the British Chiefs of Staff Committee until March 1942, when he was succeeded by Alanbrooke. Already in physical decline at the outbreak of the war, he over-strained himself by his methods of work, which kept him at the Admiralty night after night and drove him to interfere in the hour-to-hour handling of operations, sometimes with regrettable results, such as the attacks on Convoy PQ 17 in July 1942. He was by then suffering from the growth of an undetected brain tumor. He died in office, from which he should have been removed earlier, had his fine record and character not stayed the Prime Minister's hand.

## Poznan, Fall of
see Poland, Liberation of, 1944–45

## PP Submachine Guns

Soviet submachine guns were all identified by the letters PP for 'Pistolet Pulemet' or 'machine pistol', followed by a letter indicating the designer.

The first submachine gun to see use during the war years was the PPD 38/30, designed by Degtyarev. It appears to have been inspired by the German Bergmann MP28 and the Finn Suomi, a straightforward blowback weapon with wooden stock and perforated barrel jacket. It fed from a 25-round box magazine or from an unusual drum magazine which held 71 rounds and which had a box-like extension on its top surface so that it could be fitted into the magazine housing designed for the box magazine. Like all Soviet submachine guns which followed, it was chambered for the 7.62mm Soviet auto pistol cartridge and had the inner surface of the barrel chrome-plated.

The PPD 38/40 was used in the Winter War against Finland and when that was over Degtyarev made some changes in his design to produce the PPD 40 model. This did away with the unusual magazine arrangements and adopted a 71-round drum based on that of the Suomi and which could be slipped into place more easily than the type he had originally used. The rest of the gun was relatively unchanged from the 38/40 design, though some minor modifications had been made to simplify manufacture. But even incorporating these alterations, it was still a 'peacetime' weapon, well made by time-consuming processes.

When the German Army invaded in 1941 the Soviets lost vast amounts of material and weapons, and were faced with the problem of replacing these losses and also rapidly arming vast armies and putting them into the field with the minimum of delay in training. The submachine gun was tailor-made to solve these problems, if it could be designed for the cheapest and fastest possible production. The answer was the PPSh41, designed by Georgii Shpagin. It was cheap but effective, a simple blowback gun made of stamped and welded components and using the same 71-round magazine as the PPD40. The stamped barrel jacket was extended past the muzzle to form a rudimentary compensator to stop the muzzle climbing when fired automatically, and this was needed because most of these weapons made no allowance for the firing of single shots. About five million of these guns were turned out between 1941 and 1945 and whole Soviet units were often armed with no other weapon.

During the siege of Leningrad the shortage of weapons there began to cause alarm, and an engineer named Sudayev designed a sub-machine gun around the components and materials available within the besieged city. The result was the PPS–42, one of the simplest and cheapest guns ever made anywhere. It was entirely of stamped steel except for the barrel (which was half a rifle barrel and chromed), the bolt (a rectangular slab of steel) and a scrap of leather which acted as a shock absorber to stop the rearward travel of the bolt. Since there were no facilities for making the standard 71-round drum, the PPS used a curved box magazine holding 35 rounds, and it had no single-shot selector. It also had a folding buttstock similar to that used in the German MP38 and 40 designs. In spite of its crudity – most weapons had unground welds and machine marks on them – it was undoubtedly effective and, slightly improved on the PPS-43 model remained in service for the rest of the war.

## PPD Submachine Guns
see Degtyarev Machine Guns

## PQ17
see Admiralty, Convoys and *Tirpitz*

## *Prince of Wales*

This battleship was the second of the *King George V* Class to be commissioned but her *debut* was inauspicious. Arriving at Scapa Flow in May 1941, with Vickers' workmen still on board trying to cure teething troubles in her main armament and with a crew still unfamiliar with her vast hull and its intricacies, she had to sail to do battle with the *Bismarck*. On 24 May she followed her flagship, HMS *Hood* into action. Her main gunnery radar was out of action, and for a while she was forced to use a 15ft optical rangefinder, with the result that she shot poorly. As soon as the *Hood* blew up, the two German ships switched their fire to the *Prince of Wales*. She was hit seven times; three five-in shells, three eight-in, plus others. Fortunately only three exploded, and then with mild detonations, a poor comment on German shells and giving cause for doubt that it was a shell-penetration which sank the *Hood*. In fact the most damaging hit was a non-bursting 15in shell which went through the compass-platform, ricocheted off the binnacle and killed or wounded everyone except the Captain and a signalman.

The 14in guns were playing up too; the after-turret jammed when an error by the green crew allowed a 1400lb shell to fall out of the hoist and flooding put 'A' turret out of action. But the ship's fighting power was not seriously affected, for the jammed after-turret was put back into working order by its crew, who manhandled the errant shell back into the hoist. By switching over to the Type 281 air-warning radar set it was possible to give accurate ranges to the guns, and the sixth salvo was a 'straddle'. Before being ordered to break off action, the *Prince of Wales* scored two vital hits on the *Bismarck*, one which penetrated a fuel-bunker and another which caused flooding and put a boiler out of action. As a result the *Bismarck*'s oil fuel was contaminated and her speed was reduced by two knots, sufficient damage to cause the Atlantic sortie to be broken off.

After carrying the British Prime Minister to a transatlantic meeting with President Roosevelt the *Prince of Wales* was sent to the Far East with the old battlecruiser *Repulse* in an ill-judged attempt to deter the Japanese from attacking the British and Dutch possessions in the East Indies. On 10 December 1941 the two ships were attacked by the Japanese Twenty-second Air Flotilla, a force of about 30 bombers and 50 torpedo-bombers. High-level bombing attacks started after 1100 hours and then a single torpedo hit wrecked the *Prince of Wales*' steering.

This hit sealed the ship's fate, for the port outer propeller shaft was warped, and before the turbine could be stopped it churned up the engineroom bulkheads, allowing about 2500 tons of water to enter the machinery compartments. Then the shock effect of near-misses put the electrical generators out of action so that pumps began to fail and the AA guns could not be trained. Helpless by now, the battleship steamed slowly northwards and sank at 1320. If Pearl Harbor dealt a fatal blow to the supremacy of the battleship, this marked the end of any belief in the ability of capital ships to defend themselves against air attack. Henceforth battleships would rely on air cover, although their powerful AA batteries were still needed for the protection of task forces against aircraft which penetrated the screen.

## *Prinz Eugen*

This ship was the first of three improved *Hipper* Class heavy cruisers; her sisters *Lützow* and *Seydlitz* were stopped in 1940 and the hull of the *Lützow* was sold to the Soviet Union the same year. The *Seydlitz* began a conversion to a carrier in 1942 but this was incomplete when she was captured by the advancing Russian armies in 1945.

The *Prinz Eugen* had probably the most distinguished career of any major German warship in World War II. Launched on 22 August 1928, she entered service late in 1940. She escorted the battleship *Bismarck* in the sortie against Atlantic shipping in May 1941, and her eight-inch shells probably started the fire which led to the destruction of HMS *Hood*. During the long chase which followed, the *Prinz Eugen* ran short of fuel and so she broke away to Brest, leaving the battleship to fight it out alone. From Brest she and the battlecruisers *Scharnhorst* and *Gneisenau* carried out Operation Cerberus, the daylight dash through the English Channel on 12 February 1942. She later served on training duty in the Baltic and supported land opera-

*Prinz Eugen* in happier days in the North Atlantic.

tions against the Russians in the Eastern Baltic. On 15 October 1944 she rammed and severely damaged the cruiser *Leipzig* while evacuating troops, but her luck remained good, and in May 1945 she surrendered intact at Copenhagen, the only major *Kriegsmarine* unit left afloat and undamaged apart from the light cruiser *Nürnberg*.

On 17 June 1946 the *Prinz Eugen* was used as a target for nuclear tests and on 15 November 1947 the hulk was scuttled at Kwajalein.

## PT Boat
see Motor Torpedo Boats

## Puppchen

This German 88mm rocket launcher was mounted on wheels and resembled a cannon. It was unusual in that the rocket was loaded into the breech, which was then closed after it; since the gas generated by the rocket thrust was thus trapped in the gun barrel, it provided additional impulse to the rocket and improved the range and velocity above those figures produced by the same rocket fired from the more conventional form of open-ended launch tube. It was developed as a lightweight anti-tank weapon in late 1944, and fired a fin-stabilized hollow charge bomb capable of penetrating virtually any tank then known. Due to its late development, the number produced for service was relatively small.

## Pyle, Ernest, 1900–1945

Pyle was an American journalist who was the roving reporter for the Scripps-Howard newspaper chain. He first covered the Battle of Britain and his vivid description of London during the Blitz caught the imagination of his American readers. His accounts of the campaigns in North Africa, Sicily, Italy and France earned him the Pulitzer Prize in 1944. He wrote of the experience of the ordinary soldiers as well as of the generals. He accompanied US forces at Iwo Jima and Okinawa and was killed by Japanese fire on Ie Shima in April 1945.

## PZL P.7 and P.11

This Polish single-seat fighter was in service in 1932–35 (P.7) and 1934–39 (P.11). Zygmund Pulawski, chief designer of the Polish PZL company, created a series of gull-winged monoplane

fighters as good as any in the world. The P.7, powered by a license-built Jupiter engine, led in August 1931 to the P.11, powered by a 500hp Mercury. By 1933 the P.11a was in production for the Polish Air Force, followed a year later by the P.11c with redesigned fuselage and 645hp Mercury giving a top speed of 242mph. There was provision for four machine guns, though usually only two were fitted. By 1937 the fighter regiments had received 200 of these excellent warplanes, but when the Germans invaded in 1939 they were obsolescent. Nearly all were knocked out on the ground by bombing and strafing, but those that managed to get airborne claimed 128 victories. Large numbers were exported or made in other countries.

## PZL P.23

This Polish three-seat reconnaissance bomber was in service in 1936–39. The P.23A, named *Karaś* (Crucian Carp), was the chief tactical attack aircraft of the Polish Air Force in 1939, though it was by then obsolescent and about to be replaced by the P.46 Sum. Powered by a 580hp license-built Bristol Pegasus engine, the P.23A could reach 198mph and carry a bomb load up to 1543lb. It had three machine guns, one firing ahead, one in the rear cockpit and the third at the rear of the prominent ventral gondola for the bomb-aimer. In 1936 production switched to the P.23B, with 680hp Pegasus, and 210 of these were delivered. The more powerful P.43 was exported to Bulgaria. Most of the Polish machines were knocked out on the ground, but some managed to get into action and a few escaped to Rumania where the Rumanians took them over and in 1941 used them against the Soviet Union.

## PZL P.24

Last in the long line of Pulawski fighters, the P.24 was exported to Rumania and Greece. Both nations operated P.24s during World War II, the four Greek squadrons achieving notable successes against the German and Italian air forces.

## PZL P.37

This Polish three/four-seat heavy bomber was in service in 1938–39. Powered by two 925hp license-built Bristol Pegasus XX radial engines, the P.37 *Łoś* (Elk) was probably the best bomber in the world when it entered service in the fall of 1938. Capable of carrying up to 5688lb of bombs, it could reach 273mph, had long range and no blind spots (though it had only the usual armament of the day, with a total of three machine guns). Foolishly the Army tried to harm the program, cutting back production, but by mid-1939 about 30 had been delivered with single-fin tails (*Łoś* A) and 70 with twin fins (*Łoś* B). Many saw action, and 46 managed to escape to Rumania where they were impressed into the Rumanian Air Force and used against the Soviet Union in 1941. PZL received many export orders, but none of the aircraft for foreign customers could be delivered.

*Right:* The *Queen Elizabeth* with guns afire in the Mediterranean in 1941. Later in that year she was damaged by a human torpedo.

## Quebec Conference (First), August 1943

From 17 to 24 August 1943 Roosevelt, Churchill, Hopkins and the Combined Chiefs of Staff met at Quebec to discuss the outlined plan for the invasion of Normandy. This plan had been prepared by General Morgan and the COSSAC staff and was codenamed Overlord. The conference agreed on a target date for the plan of 1 May 1944, and worked out a command structure agreeing that the overall commander should be an American.

General Wingate attended the conference and the Combined Chiefs discussed strategy in the Far East. It decided that Operation Anakim (in Burma) was out of the question and that the only operation which could be mounted would be in China but they did agree that Wingate should try out his 'Long Range Penetration' groups in Burma.

## Quebec Conference (Second), September 1944

The Second Quebec Conference was a one-day consultation (10 September 1944) between Roosevelt and Churchill and the Combined Chiefs of Staff to discuss plans for the final defeat of Germany and Japan. It was at this conference that the notorious 'Morgenthau Plan' was discussed. The plan was to dismantle German industry and make Germany into a pastoral paradise. Roosevelt and Churchill did not commit themselves but Stimson and Hull argued strenuously against it and after a public outcry the plan was dropped.

### *Queen Elizabeth*

The *Queen Elizabeth* was the name-ship of a famous class of fast, heavily armed ships which included the *Warspite, Barham, Malaya* and *Valiant*. She was heavily reconstructed in 1937–40 and joined the Home Fleet. On 19 December 1941 she and the *Valiant* were badly damaged by Italian 'human torpedoes' in Alexandria harbor. In the technical sense, the two battleships were sunk, for they were lying on the bottom of the harbor, but as they lay upright in shallow water aerial reconnaissance did not reveal the extent of the disaster, and gave time for them to be refloated. She needed lengthy repairs which were made in the USA lasting until 1943.

## Quezon, President Manuel, 1878–1944

Quezon was President of the Philippines until he died in 1944. Quezon was a firm believer in co-operation with the US and he knew that it was only with US aid that the Philippines could fight the Japanese. When the Japanese landed on Luzon in December 1941, Quezon was already dying of TB but he tried to raise his country's morale. He accompanied MacArthur and his troops to the Bataan Peninsula and to Corregidor. In 1942 he went to the USA to plead his country's cause and to obtain more military aid for the Southwest Pacific Command and speed up the reconquest of the Philippines. In June he addressed the House of Representatives. He died in August 1944, three months before the landings on Leyte.

## Quisling, Vidkun, 1887–1945

The leader of the Norwegian Nazi party, the Nasjonal Samling, Quisling, a former army officer and government minister, proclaimed himself Head of Government on the German invasion of the country on 9 April 1940. He was disowned by most Norwegians and, his power proving nil, was removed from office until 1942. The Germans then reappointed him Minister President in February 1942 but he again failed to establish his authority though he clung to office until the end of the war. He then gave himself up to the police, stood trial and was executed for treason. Though vilified as the archetypal Nazi puppet, for which his name became a synonym, he was apparently convinced of his own patriotism.

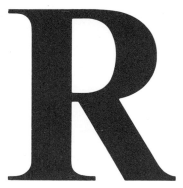

## Rabaul, 1943–44

Rabaul had fallen to the Japanese early in the war. It was subjected to heavy air attacks from Truk and from Admiral Nagumo's carrier force, and on 23 January 1942 troops landed at Rabaul on New Britain and at Kavieng on New Ireland. The small Australian garrison was soon overcome and both towns were developed as major bases for the Japanese Army. Rabaul had a garrison of 100,000 men protected by two air armies of 600 aircraft. The Japanese Eighth Fleet was stationed there and the Japanese built formidable defenses of mines, cement blocks and machine gun traps.

The American strategy was to isolate Rabaul and not attack it directly. To the north Admiral Nimitz took the Marshall Islands and knocked out Truk as a naval base. Rabaul was under heavy bombardment, but until the Americans had Bougainville as an air base in December 1943, bombers could only attack in the afternoon, when clouds obscured visibility. The first step in the reduction of Rabaul was the capture of Woodlark and the Trobriand Islands off Papua's southeast coast on 22–30 June 1943. These islands were then used as an air base for attacks on Rabaul. General MacArthur then planned to control the straits between New Guinea and New Britain by seizing Cape Gloucester on the southwest coast of New Britain. On 15 December 1943 Admiral Halsey's 3rd Fleet landed the 112th Combat Team near Arawe. The major amphibious landing by 1st Marines Division was at Cape Gloucester, 75 miles to the northwest on 26 December. After four days the Marines captured the Cape Gloucester airfield and built impressive defenses round it. The proximity of US airfields on New Britain and Bougainville meant that by mid-February Rabaul could no longer be used as an airbase and was short of air cover.

On 15 February the New Zealand 3rd Division took the Green Islands, 37 miles northeast of Buka in the Solomons. By 20 February its garrison had been knocked out and it could be used as a PT boat and light bomber base for attacks on Kavieng. Two weeks later the US 1st Cavalry Division landed on the east side of Los Negros in the Admiralty Islands. The Japanese were taken by surprise as they expected an invasion at Seeadler Harbor, and although they resisted strongly, they were overcome by 9 March. On 15 March the Americans proceeded to Manus and occupied the airstrip within two days. This meant that the Americans now controlled the Admiralties although the Japanese continued to fight until May. The Americans

had now cut off Rabaul's last supply route by sea and the base was left to wither on the vine. The fighting in the Admiralties cost the Japanese 3300 killed compared to US losses of 300 killed. To complete the encirclement, the 4th Marines regiment occupied the Emirau Islands in the Bismarcks on 20 March.

The Japanese still had 53,200 soldiers, 16,200 naval troops and 21,000 construction workers cut off in Rabaul. In November 1944 the Australian 5th Division arrived to relieve the Americans and they decided to establish themselves in a better position at the neck of the Gazelle Peninsula. They patrolled their lines uneventfully until the Japanese surrender.

---

## Radar

The basic principle of radar – the reflection of a radio wave from a target and the measurement of its travel so as to provide information on the range and direction of the target – appears to have been appreciated simultaneously in Britain, the USA and Germany, the germ in each case being early work in 'bouncing' signals from the upper atmosphere while performing basic radio research work. By the middle 1930s laboratory work was afoot in all three countries, under conditions of great secrecy, but the greatest progress was made in Britain under the stimulus of threatened bomber attack from Germany. By August 1938 a chain of radar stations were in operation covering the British coastline facing the North Sea and the Channel and this was augmented in the following year to cover almost the entire littoral. In Germany most of the work had been directed towards providing gunfire directing radar for the Navy, less effort going into the provision of early warning against air raids, while the USA had a handful of air warning sets undergoing trial.

All these sets were operating in metric wavelengths, and it soon became obvious that shorter wavelengths were needed in order to provide better and more accurate information from the radar signal. At the same time, high power was needed to obtain the maximum range, and these two requirements were not compatible, since no form of transmitting valve existed which could handle the requisite power at the frequencies demanded. The 'Klystron' valve, an American invention, held out some promise of raising the frequency, thus obtaining a wavelength of less than a meter, but it proved incapable of handling the power needed. In 1940 a group of scientists at Birmingham University, England developed the 'Magnetron', a cavity resonator which functioned as a transmitting valve at high frequencies and which could handle all the power needed. The magnetron was disclosed to the US in August by the Tizard Committee.

Not only did the magnetron allow powerful ground-based radar sets to be constructed, it also allowed sets of lower power but of more compact form to be built, enabling centimetric radar to be carried in aircraft. Aircraft radar was first developed in order to allow night fighters to detect targets; it was then expanded to provide bombers with a means of navigating, by reflections from the ground beneath which, in effect, built up a map of the area on a cathode ray tube in the aircraft. At the same time, ground-based radar could be used to track the aircraft very precisely and instruct the crew when to release its bombs. Radar was also a vital factor in airborne detection of U-Boats, which were in the habit of surfacing under cover

of darkness to charge their batteries and ventilate the boat. Using radar it was now possible to detect the U-Boat, close with it, then expose it in a powerful light to give visual command and permit bombs or depth charges to be dropped.

Ground-based radar was first employed solely as a warning device, detecting aircraft over the continent as they formed up to make bombing attacks on England; this gave the defensive forces sufficient warning to alert fighter aircraft and place them in the best position to effect an attack. As the accuracy of radar was improved it became possible to use the information on target range and direction to provide firing data for anti-aircraft guns, and a further technical improvement was the 'auto-follow' radar which, once 'locked on' to a target would continue to track it without human assistance, delivering a constant flow of data to the gun computers.

Radar was also used in a similar manner to direct coast defense guns, notably the large concentration of guns in the Dover area, and towards the end of the war trials were being carried out in the direction of ground artillery fire, though at that time there were considerable technical problems since the sets were not intended for terrestrial use. Another application was the adaptation of anti-aircraft radar to track trench mortar bombs in flight, from which data it was possible to construct the bomb's trajectory graphically and thus detect the position of the mortar, after which it could be fired on by counter-bombardment artillery.

In the sea war, radar was used both for air defense and for gunfire direction, though it was some time before the latter was perfected. In the action of the *Bismarck* versus *Hood* and *Prince of Wales*, all three ships had radar, but that of the German ship was superior due to the fact that the German development had concentrated on this form of radar for many years. The first really decisive use of naval radar seems to have been the engagement between the USS *Washington* and the Japanese *Kirishima* in November 1942, in which the *Washington*, in total darkness, scored nine 16in shell hits in eight minutes by radar direction at a range of 8400 yards, reducing the Japanese warship to a wreck.

It might be noted that the original term for radar was 'RDF' or 'Radio Direction Finding', an attempt to conceal the principle of operation; another term widely used was 'Radio Location', equally vague. The term 'radar' was coined in the USA and derived from 'RAdio Direction And Range', and it was adopted as a common Allied term late in 1944 when the system was first publicly revealed.

A German radar installation in the USSR, 1942.

## Radar (Naval)

Without radar the naval war would have been completely different. No single country could be said to have invented it, for scientists in Britain, France, Germany, Italy and the United States all stumbled on the principles in the mid-1930s while studying radio-waves. The Germans made good progress at first and had a gunnery fire-control set in the *Admiral Graf Spee* as early as 1936. The British followed with a surface search set in the same year and the US sent their first set to sea in 1937. But the early German promise led them to neglect the vital field of air-warning and surface search, whereas the USA and particularly Great Britain concentrated their efforts in this sector, with far-reaching benefits.

Known to the British as Radio-Direction Finding (RDF), a designation intended to mislead, radar was at sea in three of their ships in September 1939, but plans were already in hand to produce sets for anti-submarine aircraft and warships in quantity. The first action fought with radar was the Battle of the River Plate in December 1939 when the *Graf Spee* used her gunnery set and the *Bismarck* fired on destroyers at night using 'blind' fire. In 1941 the Type 291 surface search set was first used in an escort, and it soon proved to be a vital weapon against U-Boats by stopping the deadly night attacks on the surface. All British advances, particularly the resonant cavity magnetron which enabled the use of centimetric wavelengths, were made available to the United States, and there was even an ex-British radar set at Pearl Harbor in December 1941, although its readings were ignored.

By 1945 radar was applied in many ways not dreamed of four years before: to indicate targets, to navigate in poor visibility and to control friendly aircraft. What is known today as Electronic Countermeasures (ECM) was freely used to confuse enemy radar sets. In December 1943 the Battle of North Cape between the British Home Fleet and the German *Scharnhorst* marked the full realization of the potential of radar, for the entire action was fought by means of radar-plotting for the first time.

## Radom

Radom was the name of a Polish arsenal which gave its name to the 9mm VIS–35 pistol manufactured there from 1935 to 1944.

In the 1920s the Polish Army was provided with a heterogeneous collection of pistols of all types, and in the early 1930s the Polish Government announced a competitive trial to decide upon a standard pistol design. The design selected was by two Polish designers, Wilniewczyc and Skrzypinski, and went into production in 1935, giving rise to the official nomenclature of Pistol VIS, wz/35 (wz= *wzor* = model). In general it is of Browning pattern, using the same system of breech locking as the Colt M1911, but with a fixed cam beneath the breech instead of a swinging link. On the side of the slide was a catch which when depressed by the thumb, first blocked the firing pin and then lowered the hammer, allowing the pistol to be carried fully loaded and brought to readiness by simply thumbing back the hammer. A grip safety was also fitted, together with a catch on the rear of the frame which was used in stripping the pistol for cleaning.

Chambered for the 9mm Parabellum cartridge

Polish VIS-35 Radom pistol.

the Radom pistol was an extremely reliable and solid weapon, rather heavy (2lb 5oz) and thus with relatively low recoil force, making it a pleasant and accurate pistol to shoot. When Radom was occupied by the Germans in 1939 production continued, the pistols going to the German Army as their 'Pistole 35(p)'; these weapons are distinguished from the original Polish models since they carry German inspection stamps instead of the Polish eagle.

## Raeder, Admiral Erich, 1876–1960

A prewar commander of the German navy, he built the 'pocket' battleships and laid the foundations of Hitler's U-Boat fleet. But his real aim was to rebuild a High Seas Fleet, similar to the Kaiser's, in which he had served at the Dogger Bank and Jutland. Hitler was willing to build the necessary nucleus of big ships, but unwilling to add to them and, after 1942, unwilling to risk those built in oceanic operations. His and Raeder's views of naval strategy, therefore, increasingly diverged and the Grand Admiral was replaced by Dönitz in January 1943. Raeder was condemned to 10 years' imprisonment at Nuremberg.

## Raiders

In the naval context, a term used for any ship operating against Allied commerce. The major German warships were loosely called 'raiders', but it came to mean specifically the *hilfskreuzer* or auxiliary cruisers which were converted merchant ships, still in that disguise.

## Ram

This Canadian medium tank was developed after a decision in January 1941 to design and produce a medium tank in Canada. Co-operation between Britain, Canada and the USA over tank manufacture led to the adoption of the successful US M3 tank chassis as a basis and the design of a new superstructure to suit Canadian requirements. Design and construction were contracted to the Montreal Locomotive Works, a subsidiary of the American Locomotive Co.

The entire hull top and turret of the Ram were of cast armor, a remarkable design feat for 1941. The hull carried a main turret with two-pounder gun and also an auxiliary turret alongside the driver which carried a machine gun. A noticeable feature of the early Ram tanks was the provision of an escape door in the side of the tank, just above the tracks. Another unusual design feature was that the front of the turret was a bolted-on removable cast plate, so that

subsequent change of armament only required a new front plate and did not involve the production of a completely new turret. This feature was appreciated when the design was modified to use a six-pounder gun instead of the two-pounder, tanks so armed being known as Ram Mark 2.

The Ram tanks were issued to Canadian armored units in England and extensively used for training. During 1942–43 it was decided to terminate the Ram production in favor of production of the American M4A1 (Sherman) tank at Montreal; one reason for this was that it had proved impossible to up-gun the Ram by fitting a 75mm gun into the turret, in spite of the removable plate. Since the six-pounder was now virtually obsolescent, being superseded by 75mm and 76mm guns in all Allied tanks, production of the Ram came to an end in July 1943, and Canadian units had their tanks replaced by M4A1s prior to going into action on D-Day.

However, the Ram was yet to contribute to the war effort. The most important derivative was the 'Sexton' self-propelled gun, a 25-pounder gun mounted into a fixed armored superstructure on a Ram chassis. This became the standard self-propelled field artillery piece of the British Commonwealth, entering production in May 1943; when production came to an end in 1945, 2150 had been built and they were to serve for many years before being superseded in British service by the 'Abbott'; indeed, Sextons are still in service with the Portuguese, South African, Indian and Italian armies.

Other Ram variants included the 'Ram Kangaroo', a de-turreted Ram used for carrying infantry across bullet-swept ground, and the 'Skink' anti-aircraft tank which had four 20mm cannon mounted in a highly-modified Ram turret.

## Ramsay, Admiral Sir Bertram Home, 1883–1945

Ramsay organized the maritime side of the Dunkirk evacuation, when acting as Flag Officer in Dover. Subsequently he became responsible for Allied amphibious landings and planned the North African, Sicilian, D-Day and Walcheren landings. He was also naval Commander in Chief during the cross-channel invasion. He was killed in an air crash while flying to confer with Montgomery during the repulsion of the Ardennes offensive.

## 'Randy'
see Kawasaki Ki-102

## Rangoon, Capture of, 1945

Once the British had taken Meiktila and Mandalay at the end of March 1945 the race was now on to reach Rangoon before the monsoon broke. If General Slim's 14th Army could reach Rangoon its supply problem would be solved. Slim decided the best route would be the central railroad since this would also cut off the Japanese escape route to the Sittang area. He sent a small force from General Messervy's 4th Corps. General Stopford's 33rd Corps had orders to drive down the Irrawaddy and clear any Japanese resistance. If the 4th Corps did not reach Rangoon in time, then an amphibious plan to take Rangoon, 'Dracula,' would be launched by General Christison's 15th Corps.

General Slim (left), Vincent and Chambers at Government House after the recapture of Rangoon.

Messervy's force advanced south and by 14 April it reached Yamethin. On 13 April the 33rd Corps closed in on the Chauk-Yenangyaung oilfields and found the Japanese had abandoned Chauk. After a few days' fighting they took Yenangyaung. Messervy met little opposition and reached Toungoo on 24 April. The Japanese were now evacuating Southern Burma and as the area was full of rivers they had to leave much equipment and transport. Although the 4th Corps reached Pegu on 30 April, fifty miles north of Rangoon, their advance slowed down because the heat became unbearable and the rains came a week early on 2 May. Slim had already given the order to launch 'Dracula' on 27 April. The assault began with a parachute drop on Elephant Point. The amphibious troops landed to find the Japanese had left the area and they re-embarked and landed nearer Rangoon on 3 May. On the evening of 2 May engineers built a bridge over the Pegu River and Messervy's troops entered Rangoon on 6 May.

The 4th Corps had advanced 300 miles in 26 days and had lost 446 dead and 1706 wounded. The Japanese lost 6742 counted dead and 273 prisoners as well as much equipment.

### Razon

This American guided aerial bomb (the name derived from 'Range and AZimuth ONly') was an improvement on an earlier design AZON (AZimuth ONly). The bomb was a standard 1000lb General Purpose drop bomb with a gyro-stabilizing unit fitted to the tail so that the bomb was stable in flight and maintained a specific attitude after release. A radio receiver was connected to control surfaces on the bomb fins so that the bomb-aimer in the aircraft could watch the bomb as it fell and send radio signals to correct the flight. Since the bomb was stable in attitude – not spinning or rotating – it could be directed by command to either side or, by affecting the angle of fall, to a greater or lesser range – hence the name. It was used for precision bombing attacks in 1945, notably in cutting vital bridges in Burma.

### RDF
see Radar

### Red Army
see Soviet High Command and Barbarossa

### Reggiane Re 2001 Falco II

Development of the wartime Macchi and Reggiane single-seat fighters followed a similar pattern. The Italian Air Force did not place a production order for the original Re 2000 Falco, with a 1025hp Piaggio radial engine, although the little fighter had demonstrated that it could outmaneuver both the Macchi C.200 and the Messerschmitt Bf 109. Even when the radial engine gave way to a Daimler-Benz DB 601A in the Re 2001, raising the maximum speed to 337mph, only 252 were acquired, with 1175hp Alfa Romeo RA 1000 Monsone license-built DB 601s. The basic armament of two 12.7mm machine guns could be supplemented by two 20mm cannon in underwing fairings or a 1410lb bomb, according to model. The first Re 2001 operation was flown over Malta in May 1942. The cannon-armed Re 2001CN was used primarily as a night fighter in northern Italy.

### Reggiane Re 2002 Ariete

Intended for ground attack, this development of the Re 2000 retained a radial engine in a longer and stronger fuselage. The 1175hp Piaggio P.XIX gave it a top speed of 329mph, and it could carry 1430lb of bombs in addition to four machine guns. Between 40 and 50 Arietes were completed, serving with two Italian Air Force attack wings during the Allied landings in Sicily.

### Reggiane Re 2005 Sagittario

In much the same class as the Macchi C.205V, this superb fighter flew for the first time in September 1942. The 48 Sagittarios delivered to the Italian Air Force were used to defend Sicily and major Italian cities during the Allied advance northward, and ended up with the *Aviazione della RSI* as part of the final defense force for Berlin. The Re 2005 had a Fiat RA 1050 Tifone (license-built DB 605A). Armament comprised three 20mm cannon and two 12.7mm machine guns, plus up to 1390lb of bombs.

### Reichenau, Field Marshal Walter von, 1887–1942

A fervent Nazi by sentiment, if not party membership, from the early days, Reichenau was Hitler's choice to succeed Fritsch after his removal as Commander in Chief in 1938. From this he was dissuaded by Rundstedt, but he nevertheless continued to favor Reichenau, who commanded in turn the Tenth Army in Poland, the Sixth in Belgium, France and Russia and then, in December 1941, Army Group South succeeding Rundstedt. At the end of 1942 he died in an air crash while flying to hospital for treatment for a heart attack. A man of ruthless and overbearing temperament, feared as much as he was disliked by his colleagues, he had issued a 'Severity Order' to the Sixth Army which encouraged brutal treatment of Russians.

### Reising Submachine Gun

This weapon was designed by Eugene Reising and manufactured by the Harrington & Richardson Company for the US Marine Corps between 1941 and 1945. It was an unusual and unnecessarily complex design, firing from a closed bolt and using 12 or 20-round box magazines. While the design was technically sound, it was not well thought out from the combat point of view, and in service the gun was found to be extremely sensitive to dirt and dust, often jamming at inopportune moments.

The greater part of the production of the Reising submachine gun was taken by the United States Marine Corps and it was used extensively by them in the campaigns in the South Pacific. The British government also purchased a small number. However, it was not popular and was eventually relegated to be used as a training weapon and for use within the USA by factory guards and police forces.

### Renown

Originally a sister of the battlecruiser *Repulse*, the *Renown* underwent a complete modernization in 1936–39 which made her an ideal carrier escort or commerce protector. Her size did not permit armoring on a scale to suit her for the battle-line but she was nevertheless a valuable unit and was active throughout the war. With the carrier *Ark Royal* and the cruiser *Sheffield* she was the backbone of Force H from 1940 to 1942. She engaged the *Gneisenau* and *Scharnhorst* off Norway in April 1940 and drove the two ships off with damage, and she was in action against the Italians off Cape Spartivento later that year. She served with the Eastern Fleet in 1944 but returned to the Home Fleet in 1945 to release more modern ships for the Pacific.

### Repulse

The *Repulse* had been built in 1915–16 and, although partially re-armored after World War I to correct her more glaring deficiencies, and again in 1934–36, she was not a frontline unit in September 1939. She served with the Home Fleet until 1941, when the need arose for a fast ship to accompany the *Prince of Wales* to the Far East. This meant that an important refit planned in the US was canceled, thus robbing her of any chance of withstanding heavy air attack. Naval Staff wanted to send an aircraft carrier with the two ships – codenamed Force Z – but they were overruled by Churchill. When they arrived in Singapore they were immediately sent to intercept a Japanese invasion force.

Despite her age the *Repulse* was highly maneuverable, and she dodged the first waves of Japanese aircraft that attacked her off the coast of Malaya on 10 December 1941. But at 1223 hours a torpedo hit her steering, and shortly afterwards three more finished her off. She listed at an angle of about 65° to port, hung there for a moment and then rolled over and sank.

### Retchkalov, Grigorii Andreevich, 1918–

This Russian airman was the third highest-scoring Soviet ace with 58 victories.

### Reuben James

The *Reuben James* (DD.245) was a destroyer of World War I 'flush-decker' *Clemson* Class. On 31 October 1941 she was torpedoed and sunk by the German U-Boat *U.562* while escorting ships to Iceland. Although there was great indignation about the loss of life the incident was still insufficient to end American isolation.

## 'Rex'

see Kawanishi N1K1 Kyofu

## Rheinbote

This German long-range surface-to-surface free-flight rocket was developed in 1943 by the Rheinmetall-Borsig company, in order to meet an artillery requirement to carry 40kg of explosive to a range of 160 kilometers. As finally evolved Rheinbote was a four-stage rocket using diglycol propellant and launched from a simple rail projector on a trailer. Overall weight at launch was 3780lb and overall length 37.4ft. It attained a maximum range on test of 220 kilometers. Over 200 of these rockets were built and used operationally against Antwerp early in 1945.

## Rheintochter

This German ground-to-air guided missile was developed by the Rheinmetall-Borsig company from 1942 onwards. Firing tests began in August 1943 and by 5 January 1945 some 82 had been fired of which only four had failed. The propulsion involved a solid-fuel motor, with a solid-fuel boost unit used for initial launch. It was guided by radio command, the missile being optically tracked by means of flares attached to the fins. The warhead contained 330lb of high explosive and was detonated by a 'Kranich' acoustic proximity fuze. Rheintochter was originally designed for an altitude of 8000 meters, but when the design was completed the Luftwaffe turned it down, having decided that more altitude was necessary. The propulsion unit was therefore redesigned to use solid or liquid fuels, the boost motors slung alongside, and the missile was to be launched from a permanent emplacement in a pit. This was Rheintochter 3, and work began on it in May 1944. By January 1945 six had been built and fired, but the control system had not been perfected. Development was stopped on 6 February 1945, it being considered that it was unlikely to be completed in time to have any effect on the course of the war.

Rheintochter I ground-to-air missiles was based on solid-fuel.

## Rhine Crossings, 1945

Following the failure of the German Ardennes and Alsace offensives, the Allies gathered their forces for the advance to and crossing of the Rhine. The Canadians occupying the positions seized in Operation Market Garden, were already near the Rhine in Holland but still had ground to make. This they took in Operation Veritable, which began on 9 February. Simpson's 9th Army advanced to the Rhine in Operation Grenade, which began on 12 February. The British 2nd Army, positioned between, advanced to cover the gap. The 1st Army (Hodges) attacked with the 9th and reached Cologne on 5 March. Patton's 3rd Army, attacking through the difficult Eifel, did not reach the Rhine until 22 March but inflicted very heavy casualties on the Germans in the process and achieved its own surprise crossing of the Rhine at Oppenheim that night. The 7th Army meanwhile had cleared the Saar and the Palatinate and was up to the Rhine by 10 March. The most remarkable outcome of this preliminary campaign was the 1st Army's chance capture of the Ludendorff bridge at Remagen which gave Eisenhower a highway into the Rhineland. He used this, together with Patton's Oppenheim bridgehead, to provide the focus of his southern drive across the river and a deliberate British-Canadian-American assault around Wesel, co-ordinated with a major air-

American tank moves into a German town after the Allies crossed the Rhine.

borne descent, to start his northern drive. The offensives began on 25 and 23 March respectively and had as their preliminary objective the encirclement of the Ruhr. By 4 April they had joined hands, leaving Model, the 'Führer's Fireman', encircled with much of Army Group B, and were pressing onward. The British 1st Army reached the Elbe on 24 April, took Bremen after a week-long battle on 27 April and Lübeck on 2 May. Hamburg fell the following day, the last large objective in the British area. The Canadians meanwhile completed the liberation of northern Holland, an urgent task after the 'Hunger Winter' of 1944–45. The 1st and 9th Armies pressed straight ahead to the Elbe, which they reached on 13 April. The 9th Army seized a bridgehead by Magdeburg but were driven out of it by one of the few shows of strength made by the Germans at this stage of the campaign. Eisenhower did not react, since he had decided to await the arrival of the Russians on the Elbe, that being the eastern frontier of their agreed occupation zone. But he directed the 3rd and 7th Armies, with the 1st French on their outer flank, to hasten their advance into south Germany, where it was feared the Germans might try to hold a 'National Redoubt'. In fact Hitler's decision to remain to the end in Berlin canceled plans for a fight to the finish in the south. Patton's army drove into Czechoslovakia almost without opposition. The 3rd Army, not without a fight for Neckar and Nüremberg, entered Austria, while the French cleared Baden and Württemberg before entering Austria also. By 4 May the war in southern Germany was over. (See Germany, Surrender of, 1945.)

## Ribbentrop, Foreign Minister Joachim von, 1893–1946

A former champagne salesman whose 'von' was adopted, Ribbentrop owed his elevation to his early association with Hitler, who made him, after acceding to power, successively, Ambassador at large and then in 1936–38, Ambassador to Britain. His reports from that country did much to persuade Hitler that she would not honor her international guarantees. The consequences of that mistake were retrieved by his negotiation of the non-aggression pact with Russia (the Molotov-Ribbentrop Pact) of August 1939. He played no role of any importance during the war; his standing in the party and government progressively declined; and he was kept in office only at Hitler's behest. He was hanged as a war criminal at Nuremberg.

### *Richelieu*

The *Richelieu* and *Jean Bart* were authorized under the French Navy's 1935 Program, and they were followed by a slightly improved pair in 1938, to be called *Clemenceau* and *Gascogne*. The *Richelieu* was almost complete at the time of the fall of France in June 1940, and she steamed to Dakar in West Africa. Although she fired on British units which tried to attack Dakar with pro-de Gaulle forces she eventually joined the Allies in 1942. From there she went to the USA for repair and re-equipment for service in the East Indies in 1944–45. The opportunity was taken to give her more fuel capacity as she lacked endurance.

### Ridgway, Colonel Matthew Bunker, 1895–

Ridgway directed the airborne operations of the US 82nd Infantry Division in Sicily and Northwestern Europe. The first operation was in Sicily, in July 1943, when a glider regiment was used to parachute men onto the island. In fact weather conditions were so bad that many gliders were swept off course and many landed in the sea. Although the operation was tactically successful, casualties were high and it was obvious that the glider pilots needed more training. The 82nd Division was then sent to Britain to prepare for the Normandy invasion and it spearheaded the invasion of the Cotentin peninsula on 6 June 1944. Ridgway was then appointed Commander of the 18th Airborne Corps and took part in the airborne invasion of the Netherlands, the blocking of the Ardennes offensive and the offensive across the Siegfried Line. He was a man of great courage and respected by all who served with him.

### Rochling Shells

These special anti-concrete shells were developed by the Rochling Eisen und Stahlwerk, Dusseldorf, to be fired from the German Army's 21cm Mrs 18 howitzer. Rochling considered the normal anti-concrete shell – a shell of normal type, but with a blunt nose and base fuze – to be inefficient, and he proposed a shell which increased the impact blow by concentrating great weight into a small area. This was achieved by using a shell much longer than was conventional and stabilizing it with fins so that the mass of the shell was concentrated into a small diameter. The shell weighed 423lb and was 102in long; the conventional anti-concrete shell for the same weapon was 267lb in weight and 34.5in long. At the rear end of the Rochling shell were four flexible fins which, on loading, were wrapped around the tail of the shell and kept in place by a covering sabot. On leaving the muzzle, this sabot fell away and the fins sprang out into the air stream. The shell's maximum range was 12,330 yards.

During the development of the shell in 1940, tests were made against a captured Belgian fort; the shell penetrated 3.6 meters of concrete, a layer of broken stone, passed through the wall of an underground chamber, through the floor, and finally detonated several feet below the

floor. This seemed to justify Rochling's contentions and the shells went into production in 1942, and a stockpile was built up. However, Hitler was apprehensive that premature use of these shells might well disclose their secret to an enemy, whereupon the idea would be turned against Germany, and in a Führer Protocol of 5 January 1943 he ordered 'The Führer will decide personally on their operational employment in order not to give away to the enemy the construction . . .' As a result the Rochling shell was rarely used in combat.

### Rocket-assisted Shells

The German program of rocket development led to a great deal of accumulated knowledge on rockets; it was inevitable that soon there would be an attempt to ally the rocket with the conventional artillery shell in order either to increase the shell's range or to increase its velocity over a shorter range. After numerous development types had been tried, the best design was found to be a shell in which the forward section was occupied by a solid-fuel rocket motor and the rear section by the explosive content, while a blast pipe down the axis of the shell delivered the rocket efflux to the rear and provided thrust.

The first R-Granats (*Raketen-granat*) were issued for the 15cm heavy field howitzer 18 in the Russian campaign of late 1941, but these were more in the nature of experimental shells and the complicated instructions and warnings which went with them did nothing to inspire confidence in the gunners. A much improved model was later produced for the 28cm K5 railway gun; this weighed 546lb and carried 43lb of rocket propellant and 31lb of high explosive payload. It could reach a maximum range of 53 miles, but the accuracy was only such that the shell would land anywhere within a rectangle 3700yds long by 250yds wide. This inaccuracy, inherent with rocket assistance, is due to the fact that the rocket did not ignite until the shell was at the top of its trajectory; if the shell was

Rocket-assisted shells for a German rail gun. Left, the exterior; right, the time fuze and motor.

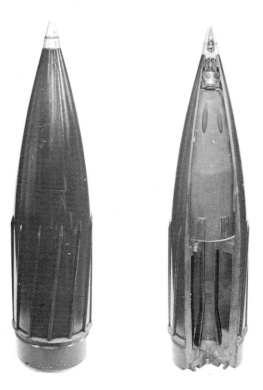

spinning perfectly symmetrically around its longer axis, then the shell would fly accurately; if, as was the general rule, the shell was yawing about its axis, then the sudden thrust of the rocket would alter the trajectory slightly, leading to inaccuracy.

An alternative to rocket assistance was the use of ram-jet assistance; this promised a more useful projectile since there would be less weight of propellant and a greater explosive payload. Several designs were drawn up and some experimental models made, but no practical results were achieved.

Rocket-assisted shells were also tried in Britain, a rocket unit being fitted to the base of coast defense 6in shells in an attempt to increase the range. However the same problem of inaccuracy arose. The project was dropped.

### Rockets

One of the major fields of development in all the combatant nations during the war was that of the free-flight (ie., without guidance) rocket, employed as an auxiliary artillery weapon.

The first to take interest were probably the Soviets who, in 1930, inaugurated a program of research at the Leningrad Gas Dynamics Laboratory under an engineer Petropavlovsky. After his death in 1935 the program continued under A Kostikov and resulted in an 82mm solid-fuel rocket carrying a 6.5lb high explosive warhead. This could be launched from an open-frame type launcher mounted on the bed of a 2.5 ton truck which carried 36 rockets. The launcher could be elevated and traversed like a gun, the rockets being launched over the truck cab which had to be protected by steel blast deflectors. These rockets had a maximum range of about 6000 yards. Known first as 'Kostikov's Gun' they were kept strictly secret until they were first used near Orsha in July 1941 against the Germans. They were later christened 'Stalin's Organ' by the German troops, due to the peculiar note emitted by the rocket as it flew, while the Soviet soldiers christened it 'Katyusha'. To preserve secrecy these weapons were always manned by NKVD troops, and very little hard information about them was ever released.

Shortly after the 82mm entered service it was followed by a heavier model of 132mm caliber, carrying a 40lb warhead and ranging to 9250 yards. This was also truck mounted, using a 16-rocket launcher unit and apparently some were also mounted on the chassis of obsolete tanks in order to give them better cross-country performance.

German rocket development also began in about 1930, under the control of the Army Weapons Department who set up the Kummersdorf West Experimental Station some 17 miles from Berlin. Here a solid-fuel rocket of 15cm caliber was developed together with a six-tube launcher mounted on a light trailer. This was issued to special units known (as a cover name) as Nebeltruppen (smoke troops), whose ostensible task was to provide smoke screens for the combat forces. The first units were activated in 1934 but, like the Soviet weapon, the weapons were not used in action until the Russian campaign and the first launcher was not captured by the Russians until January 1943. The rocket was an ingenious design which carried the propulsion motor in the nose and the explosive payload in the rear end, the exhaust for the rocket blast being in a ring of 26 venturis around

A dead German soldier almost loaded his 15cm Nebelwerfer in Tunisia.

the midsection of the weapon. The launcher was a simple arrangement of six tubes from which the rockets were fired electrically.

After the success of this weapon, a 21cm version was produced and there were also a number of 28cm and 31cm rockets which could be launched from individual launchers. By this time, though, the liquid-fuel rocket had captured the German imagination and most of the available manufacturing effort was being directed to the A–4 and FZG–76 missiles, as well as to a variety of missiles which never saw service.

British involvement with rockets began as a part of their anti-aircraft defense. In 1936 the demand for anti-aircraft guns was far beyond that which could be satisfied by the available finance or production facilities, and work began on a rocket which would carry a warhead equal in power to a 3in shell and deliver it to 10,000ft altitude in as short a time as a gun. The size of the rockets was determined by empirical factors; the smallest cordite charge which would produce an efficient rocket was 2in in diameter, while the largest charge which could be manufactured by existing machinery was 3in. As a result, 2in and 3in rockets became the standard types, the 3in as an AA rocket for the Army, the 2in as an AA device for the Royal Navy. Final trials were fired in Jamaica in early 1939 and by early 1940 several models had been standardized. The 3in went into abeyance since it was hoped that gun production would suffice, but it was later brought out and used most effectively as a barrage weapon, batteries of 64 twin-rocket launchers being installed around the coasts of Britain and manned largely by Home Guards. These rockets fired simple explosive shell warheads for the most part, though some were provided with the 'K' Rocket, an over-long device which carried two parachutes, 1000 feet of wire and a contact mine. Fired into the path of a raiding formation, up to 20,000 feet away, it would then deploy the parachute-supported cable and mine to sink slowly and then hopefully to become entangled with the raiders.

The 2in rocket was also used for a number of Parachute-And-Cable (PAC) devices used by the Royal and Merchant Navies for protection against dive bombers.

A 5in rocket was also developed as a possible carrier for poison gas, but this was abandoned and the warhead, filled with explosive, was used by the Royal Navy for shore bombardment from special rocket-carrying craft which could launch 1080 rockets in a matter of seconds. The same warhead, allied to a 3in motor, was then adopted by the Army for land bombardment, using a 16-tube launcher on a trailer.

The 3in rocket, carrying an armor-piercing head, was adopted by Naval Air as an anti-submarine measure, and this was later taken up by the RAF who used rockets in attacking tanks and other transport on the ground.

In the USA there was little or no work done until 1940 when research into spin-stabilized rockets began, resulting in an excellent 4.5in weapon. This carried the warhead in the nose with the motor in the rear and was vented through a ring of angled venturis which provided thrust as well as spinning to stabilize it in flight. A wide variety of launchers were available, mounted on trucks, tanks and trailers, and the rocket was also adapted to firing from fighter aircraft. A similar rocket using folding fins for stabilization was also developed in large numbers and used extensively in both Europe and the Pacific.

Probably the most famous of all American rockets was the 'Bazooka', a shoulder-fired 2.36in rocket with a hollow charge warhead used for anti-tank attack. This weapon can trace its descent from an experimental rocket launcher developed by the American scientist Robert Goddard in 1918. It was revived in 1941 and by 1942 had been perfected and was used in action in North Africa in November 1942.

## Rodney

The sister of HMS *Nelson*, the battleship *Rodney* was on her way to the United States for a long overdue refit in May 1941 when the news came of the *Bismarck*'s breakout. The *Rodney* left her convoy and sailed for the last-reported position, and so she was an opportune reinforcement for the *King George V* when she arrived. The two ships engaged the *Bismarck* on the morning of 27 May 1941. The *Rodney* maneuvered independently and went in close, as little as 3000 yards during the closing stages, in order to do as much damage to the German ship's hull as possible. She also fired her entire outfit of torpedoes and claimed a hit, the only known case of one battleship torpedoing another.

The *Rodney* never received a proper overhaul throughout World War II, with the result that she was in poor mechanical condition by 1945. Nevertheless she provided outstanding fire-support at Normandy in 1944.

## Rokossovsky, Marshal Konstantin K, 1896–1968

Rokossovsky led the Soviet Army that recaptured Poland. His first commands were in the Far East. During the Purges in 1938 he was imprisoned but later was reinstated. He came to the fore during the defense of Moscow in December 1941, where he commanded the Southern section of the Siberian army. He was then sent to the defense of Stalingrad and in December 1942 led the decisive breakthrough, overrunning the Rumanian and Italian flanks and surrounding Paulus's Sixth Army. At the Battle of Kursk he commanded the Central Front in the center of the Kursk salient. He commanded the 1st Belorussian Front against the German center and took Lublin and Brest-Litovsk in June 1944. However in July 1944 his advance faltered just outside Warsaw, and his troops did not advance for another six months. In August 1944 the Warsaw Uprising broke out and Rokossovsky's armies did nothing to help: Rokossovsky claimed that he had no supplies and that he faced a strong Panzer division. In January 1945 the Fronts were regrouped and he led the 2nd Belorussian Front which took Warsaw. He was then sent north and swept through northern Poland and arrived at the Gulf of Danzig on 26 January trapping the German armies in East Prussia. In May Rokossovsky reached the British forces at Lubeck. After the war he became Chief of the Armed Forces in Poland.

## Roma

see Fritz-X

## Rome, capture of, and Advance to the Gothic Line, 1944

The capture of Monte Cassino, held by the elite German First Parachute Division in May 1944, destroyed the integrity of Kesselring's Winter Line. Meanwhile the bulk of the 5th Army, now a Franco-American force, had been moved into the Anzio bridgehead and on 23 May, five days after the Poles had captured Cassino, it attacked out of the bridgehead. The German defenders of the Winter Line were now outnumbered, and the brilliant mountaineering of the French Moroccan troops east of Cassino, threatened them with envelopment as well. But instead of reaching out to join hands with the Moroccans, Mark Clark, commanding the 5th Army, decided at the last moment to switch the axis of his attack towards Rome thus allowing the Germans an escape route. Reacting with their usual efficiency, the Germans organized a rearguard operation in his path and held him for long

The bow of HMS *Rodney* in 1943.

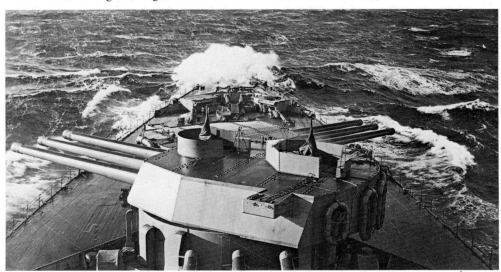

German troops in front of St Peter's in Rome shortly before its capture by the Allies in 1944.

enough to make good their escape. Rome fell to the 5th Army on 4 June but the German Tenth Army (Vietinghoff) had by then fallen back to a position north of the city where it could direct a series of attacks against half-prepared defensive positions spanning the peninsula. The Allies were therefore obliged to begin a fighting advance northward. Hitler was nevertheless forced to reinforce the front with eight divisions from outside Italy which he could not readily spare and, as the French and most of the Americans were soon withdrawn to mount the Anvil-Dragoon landing in the south of France, the Italian campaign now began to justify its rationale of diverting enemy formations from more important fronts. The outnumbered Anglo-Americans achieved the remarkable feat, in the circumstances, of keeping the Germans in motion for 64 days over a distance of 270 miles. They did not halt until they reached the outworks of the unfinished Gothic Line south of Florence on 4 August.

**Rommel, Field Marshal Erwin 1891–1944**

Holder of the highest Imperial decoration for bravery, the *Pour le Mérite*, Rommel was appointed in 1939 to command Hitler's escort and through that association got command of the Seventh Panzer Division for the attack on France in 1940. His crossing of the Meuse was a tactical triumph and, though he reacted with uncharacteristic panic when counterattacked at

Arras by the British on 21 May, he emerged from the campaign with an established reputation as a tank leader with real flair. Sent to North Africa in January 1941 to the assistance of the stricken Italians, he proceeded to win a reputation as a strategist and theater commander also. Though occasionally overbold, he retained the initiative in the fight with the British until the summer of 1942, when the balance of force shifted decisively in their favor, and even then he made Montgomery pay a high price for his victory at Alamein. He conducted a vigorous defense of Tunisia against the combined British and American armies but was evacuated before it fell. Next sent to France as commander of Army Group B under Rundstedt, he worked vigorously to improve the defenses of the Channel coast. He and Rundstedt disagreed over the location of the armor for the defensive battle but, despite losing the argument, he contained the Allied landings and blunted their early attempts at break-out. On 17 July, however, he was strafed in his staff car by a British fighter and severely wounded. Before he had fully recovered, he fell under suspicion of complicity in the Bomb Plot and was offered by Hitler the choice of disgrace or suicide. He chose the latter, was declared to have died of his wounds and buried with state pomp. Though never tested against the Russians, or at the highest level of command, the evidence suggests that Rommel was one of Germany's greatest soldiers. Even the Allies felt a rueful admiration for the 'Desert Fox'.

---

**Romulo, President Carlos P, 1901–**

Romulo was a pro-American Filipino, head of a publishing company. He became famous as the 'Voice of Freedom' broadcasting from Corregidor in 1942 and when he left the island in March he went on a lecture tour of the USA. He was made a Lieutenant Colonel and later a General of the Philippine Armed Forces and acted as General MacArthur's aide-de-camp. He was with MacArthur at the landing on Luzon in January 1945 and he set about incorporating the Filipino guerrillas into the Army. He became President of the Philippines after independence in 1946.

---

**Roosevelt, Anna Eleanor, 1884–1962**

Mrs Roosevelt was the wife of President Roosevelt and played an active part in keeping the morale of the American people as high as possible during the war. In September 1941 she became Director of the Office of Civilian Defense. She spent much of her time traveling and visited Britain, Australia and the South Pacific. She also visited Army camps in the USA. In recognition of her work she was (several times) US delegate to the UN General Assembly.

---

**Roosevelt, President Franklin Delano, 1882–1945**

Conscious of his people's deepseated hostility to involvement in World War II, Roosevelt nevertheless used their sympathy for the Allied and particularly the British cause to lend material support to them from soon after the outbreak. In March 1941 the Lend-Lease Act, which he had sponsored, made it possible for him to send Britain weapons and supplies on credit, a fac-

Roosevelt makes a broadcast wearing an armband in honor of his mother's death in 1941.

ility soon extended to Russia. In August he met Churchill, with whom he was in frequent communication, to agree on the Atlantic Charter for a postwar world, and, on Japan's attack on Pearl Harbor, began at once the dispatch of American forces to the theaters of war, in Europe as well as in the Pacific. Overriding the arguments of those, like Admiral King, who wished to make the major and greater effort against Japan, he stood by the agreement made with Churchill in August and confirmed in Washington in December, 1941 that put 'Germany First'. He also accepted the advice of the British, against that of Marshall and others, that it was too dangerous to attempt invasion of Europe in 1942 (and later in 1943 also) and cooperated in British plans to capture in turn French North Africa, Sicily and Italy. Perhaps his single most important influence upon the conduct of the war was to insist upon the 'Unconditional Surrender' of Germany and Japan, a principle which he had adopted at the Casablanca Conference of January 1943. He was also, however, the most important champion of Chinese interests in the Allied camp, and the propagator of a more conciliatory policy towards Stalin than Churchill wished. All in all, his greatness as a war leader lay in his concentration of all of America's mighty resources on the production and transmission of war material to the fighting fronts. Not only the American but the British, Chinese and Russian forces were supplied with weapons, munitions, vehicles and fuel in vast quantities, while their civilian populations benefited from generous shipments of food. Despite the material and numerical preponderance of Americans in the European and Pacific theaters of war, Roosevelt treated the British with the utmost tact and encouraged his subordinates to do likewise, thus fostering one of the most harmonious alliances of modern history. He lived to see his most cherished strategic project, the liberation of Europe, brought almost to fruition, under one of his favorite commanders, Eisenhower, and died before the latent strains of the alliance with Russia had marred the victory. A subtle if over-idealistic diplomatist and a charismatically popular leader, the appeal of his character transcended national boundaries.

## Rosenberg, Minister Alfred, 1893–1946

A Balt by origin, Rosenberg's writings on 'geopolitics', which argued the historic role of the German people and the superiority of an 'Aryan' race over all others, attracted, through their arresting mixture of fact and fable, the attention of Hitler, with whom he became associated at an early stage of the 'struggle for power'. In 1923–25 he was Deputy Leader of the party and later held the appointments of editor of the party newspaper, the *Völkischer Beobachter*, head of party education and director of overseas propaganda before the war. In 1941 he was made Minister for the Occupied Eastern Territories, but proved to lack executive talents. Real power in the east was wielded by others, notably Himmler and Sauckel. His influence was nevertheless judged criminal by the Nuremberg Tribunal and he was executed.

## Roslavl, Battle of, August 1941

After the Battle of Smolensk, Hitler and his generals began to hesitate over continuing their advance on Moscow. General Guderian's Panzer Division was rested and refitted and with Field Marshal Bock's assent was used to clear up the remaining Russian troops on the Central Front. Guderian was given a free hand. He started off with 14 divisions, of which four were armored, whereas the Russians at Roslavl only had the exhausted stragglers of 21 divisions, with very little ammunition. Guderian reached Roslavl and trapped the Russians in front of the town in an area of swamps. By August resistance had died down and 70,000 men and 200 guns were taken.

## Rostov, Capture of

see Caucasus, Battle of, July 1942–February 1943

## Rostov, Battle of, November 1941

After the Germans had secured the Ukraine, Field Marshal Rundstedt and his armies marched on to take Rostov. The weather was deteriorating and the rain and mud slowed down the German advance. On 21 November General Kleist's First Armored Army took Rostov by a frontal attack. Marshal Timoshenko then led the 37th Army and part of the 9th Army in a successful counterattack to oust the Germans from Rostov. Rundstedt had orders not to withdraw, so he resigned his command and the army retreated behind the River Mius.

## Royal Navy

In September 1939 the British Royal Navy was the largest in the world, despite two decades of retrenchment and limitation by international agreements. It had one priceless advantage over its enemies and rivals – its administration, personnel, ship design and methods had been victorious in a testing war only 20 years before, and weaknesses revealed in 1914–18 had been vigorously tackled. In one respect, however, the Royal Navy was tragically weak. In April 1918 it had lost control of its air power, and this had only been restored in 1936. Another problem was the number of old ships, for the international agreements limited the rate at

Plymouth, 1945: the USS *Augusta* passes the battlecruiser HMS *Renown*, which had been modernized after World War I and was one of the best-equipped capital ships of the Royal Navy.

which ships could be replaced. Fortunately a massive rearmament program had been started in 1937, and the first fruits of that expansion were ready by 1939–1940, just in time.

The basic strategic plan resembled the successful naval campaign of World War I, to contain German naval strength in the North Sea while mobilizing the British Empire and using industrial production to outstrip the Germans. This plan worked relatively well until the blitzkrieg of 1940 knocked out France. The French Navy had been entrusted with the task of containing the Italian Navy, but now the British had to divert ships to the Mediterranean for that task. At the same time, the German U-Boats now had bases on the Atlantic coast, putting them much closer to British shipping routes. This altered the strategic balance entirely, but in spite of all difficulties the British retained control of the Atlantic with an increasingly friendly United States providing war materials.

The attack on Pearl Harbor resulted in an immediate declaration of war on Japan by Britain, which was answered by a somewhat intemperate declaration of war by Germany on the USA. Immediately the US Navy pooled its resources in the Atlantic with the British and Canadians, but the requirements of the Pacific theater meant inevitably that the British and Canadians bore the main burden of fighting the Battle of the Atlantic, apart from the massive US shipbuilding program. The turning point of the naval war for the Royal Navy came in May 1941, for in that month the sinking of the *Bismarck* signaled the end of any serious surface threat to the Atlantic convoys, while in the Mediterranean the Italian failure to interfere with the evacuation of Crete confirmed the impotence of Italian seapower. Thereafter the Allies moved to the offensive, cautiously at first but with greater confidence each time. The U-Boat crisis of March–April 1943 was caused as much by a premature withdrawal of antisubmarine forces from the Atlantic to cover the invasion of North Africa, as any increase in the U-Boats' effectiveness, and as soon as reinforcements were provided the U-Boats suffered a severe defeat.

At the end of 1943 a long-standing threat to the Russian convoys was eliminated, when the *Scharnhorst* was sunk by the Home Fleet in the Battle of North Cape.

In the Far East the Royal Navy suffered catastrophically at the hands of the Japanese. The *Prince of Wales* and *Repulse* were sunk by Japanese aircraft three days after the elimination of the US Pacific Fleet at Pearl Harbor, and soon the supposedly impregnable bastion of Singapore fell to a numerically inferior Japanese army. Only Japanese vacillation prevented the loss of Ceylon as well, and British seapower did not re-establish itself in the East Indies until 1943–44. The steady rundown of the naval war in Europe released major warships for the Pacific fight in 1944, and finally the British Pacific Fleet was formed to join the Americans in the final assault on Japan.

*Strength of the Royal Navy in September 1939*
15 capital ships
7 aircraft carriers
15 heavy cruisers
46 light cruisers
181 destroyers
59 submarines
54 escorts

Despite its reputation for conservatism and love of tradition the Royal Navy showed that it had great capacity for innovation. Apart from its unique contribution to the development of radar, it also introduced a wide range of weapons and developed effective ships to use them. The armored carrier is only one example of successful ship-design.

## *Royal Oak*

This old battleship of the *Royal Sovereign* Class had fought at the Battle of Jutland in 1916, but had received no major modernization between the wars. On the night of 14 October 1939 she was the target for an attack by the German U-Boat *U.47* under the command of Kapitän-Leutnant Gunther Prien. The German U-Boat Commander had detected a gap in the blockships which protected the approaches to Scapa Flow, and Admiral Dönitz ordered *U.47* to attempt the hazardous operation to attack any heavy ships which could be found.

The first salvo of three torpedoes was unsuccessful; the single accurate torpedo either hit the anchor cable or (more likely) partially detonated without damaging the ship. Three-quarters of an hour later a second salvo of three torpedoes exploded under the *Royal Oak*, detonating her magazine and sending her to the bottom with the loss of 833 men.

Field Marshal von Rundstedt after his capture by American troops near Munich.

## Rundstedt, Field Marshal Karl Rudolf Gerd von, 1875–1953

One of the two most senior commanders of the German army in 1938, Rundstedt retired after the Blomberg-Fritsch crisis, but was recalled in 1939 to plan the Polish campaign, in which he commanded Army Group A. He held the same appointment for the campaign in the West in the following year. In this action his Army Group played the major role; he was responsible for persuading Hitler to make the crucial decision to halt the Panzer divisions outside the Dunkirk perimeter which eased the escape of the British Expeditionary Force. In 1941 he commanded Army Group South in the advance into the Ukraine, but was relieved by Hitler in the great purge of Generals in December 1941. Recalled again in 1942, he was made Commander-in-Chief in the west which until late 1943 was a quiet post. In November, however, he was urgently directed to strengthen the defenses of the Channel coast against an Anglo-American invasion. He disagreed with his subordinate, Rommel, as to how the battle should be fought and, when the invasion materialized, early formed the impression that resistance was hopeless. For his expressions of defeatism he was again retired but almost as soon again reappointed following the 'treachery' of Kluge. Between 5 September and 9 March 1945 the old Field Marshal was again *Oberbefehlshaber West* though he played little part in the operations in the theater – the 'Rundstedt Offensive' (the Ardennes offensive), for example, being entirely Hitler's work. His retirement in March was his last, but to the end Hitler treated him with respect. The reason, it has been suggested, is that even the dictator was impressed by his aristocratic 'old Prussian' demeanor. But others regard Rundstedt as an accomplished cynic, the Talleyrand of Hitler's *Generalität*.

## Russo-Finnish War, 1939

After Poland had been divided between Germany and the USSR, Stalin determined to extend the existing frontier with Finland so that Leningrad would be out of artillery range. On 14 October 1939 the Soviet government issued its territorial demands but the Finnish government refused to hand over part of the Karelian Isthmus and the Rybachi Peninsula in exchange for land in the center of Finland round Repola and Porajorpi. On the 28 October Stalin canceled the non-aggression pact with Finland and two days later the invasion began. The Finns checked the Russian advance on the Mannerheim Line and near Lake Ladoga. Further north two attacks against Salla and Suomussalmi were driven back.

The Russian plan had been to attack in the north to divert troops from the Mannerheim Line in the Karelian Isthmus. This had been achieved and when the armies had regrouped, the Russians renewed their attack with an artillery barrage in the South near Summa in February 1940. After two weeks General Meretskov broke through the Finnish defenses to threaten Viipuri. A second assault across the frozen Gulf of Finland to the rear of Viipuri led the Finnish government to sue for peace on the 6 March. On the 13 March a peace treaty was concluded and the terms were lenient because Stalin did not want to have a hostile neighbor, but the Finns had to concede the whole of the Karelian Isthmus.

The three-and-a-half month war had cost the Finns 24,923 dead and 61 airplanes; the Russians lost 200,000 men, 684 airplanes and 1600 tanks. The war showed how badly prepared the Red Army was. Their transport system had not allowed a sufficient reserve of munitions and equipment to be built up for the offensive. The Army had not been trained properly for the winter conditions and had faltered in the difficult terrain of Finland. Also, after the Purges, the Russian Generals, for example, Timoshenko were short of practical experience and had underestimated the power of the enemy. This was what led Hitler and the Western Powers to underestimate the fighting potential of the Red Army.

## Rybalko, General Pavel S, 1894–1948

Rybalko was Marshal of the Tank Corps and is generally credited with the liberation of Prague. He started off as a military instructor in 1941 and 1942. In the summer of 1942 he was Commander of the 5th Tank Army and then the 3rd Tank Army. He took part in the Liberation of the Don, Dniepr, Poland, Berlin and Prague.

## St Nazaire Raid, March 1942

In March 1942 the U-Boat offensive in the Atlantic was at its height and the Admiralty was afraid that the appearance of a powerful German surface raider in the Atlantic might destroy British morale. The *Tirpitz* was in Norwegian waters and if she was to operate in the Atlantic she would have to use the enormous dry-docks at St Nazaire. The Admiralty decided that if the dock was destroyed the *Tirpitz* would not try to break out to the Atlantic. Lord Mountbatten worked out the best plan for this operation: an old destroyer, laden with explosives, would ram the lock gates of the *Normandie* docks and then be scuttled, with three eight-hour fuzes on board to detonate the explosives.

The operation was codenamed Chariot and on 26 March a force was assembled at Falmouth. The HMS *Campbeltown* (ex-USS *Buchanan*) was used with a motor gunboat, 16 motor launches and one motor torpedo boat and 611 men were picked to carry out the raid. The German defenses at St Nazaire were powerful with 13 40mm guns and 28 20mm guns on the coast. By 0030 on 28 March the commando force had reached the Loire estuary undetected and at 0134 the *Campbeltown* rammed the lock gates, under heavy fire. By this time the Germans were fully alerted and only three craft succeeded in landing their men as planned, who blew up the dock installations. The fuzes on the *Campbeltown* were activated and the ship was scuttled but the evacuation of the commandos was confused and many were left behind. The Germans rounded up the men and as a party of officers were inspecting the *Campbeltown*, she blew up at about 1000. The raid was a great success and the lock gates were destroyed, but 144 men were killed and more than half the men were taken prisoner and spent the rest of the war in POW camps.

## Saipan, 1944

After the conquest of the Gilbert and Marshall Islands, Admiral Nimitz could knock out the Marianas, which would threaten Japanese communications. The three main islands of the group were Saipan, Tinian and Guam. Guam had been the HQ of Japan's Central Pacific Fleet, but in early 1944 there was only Admiral Ozawa's Striking Force stationed there. Admiral Koga had devised a plan to defeat the US Fleet in one battle – this was known as A-Go but Koga disappeared in a plane at the end of March 1944. His successor Admiral Toyoda also wanted a decisive battle with US naval forces and sent in as many ships as were available shortly after the Marines landed. In the Battle of the Philippine Sea the Japanese Navy was decisively defeated and lost some 450 aircraft.

While the battle for control of the sea was being fought out, the invasion of Saipan proceeded. Admiral Nagumo was the titular Commander in Chief of the 32,000-strong garrison on the island. In fact General Obata supervised the construction of the defenses on the island, but the defense of the island fell to Lieutenant General Saito, who was not known to have special gifts as a commander. The Japanese had not had enough building materials or supplies to construct a good defense, and were at a disadvantage because their orders were to fight on the beaches.

The American invasion force left Hawaii and Guadalcanal carrying 127,571 troops, of whom more than two-thirds were Marines. On 15 June 1944 Marine General Holland Smith's 5th Amphibious Corps landed south of Garapan in the extreme south of Saipan, covered by heavy naval shelling. By nightfall there were 20,000 troops ashore. Near Garapan the Japanese controlled the heights and the Marines advanced with difficulty. On the night of 16–17 June the 27th Infantry Division landed in the south and took Isley airfield, which meant that the Army P–47 Thunderbolts could be used. The Marines cut the island in half and on 22 June the Marines set about clearing the north while 27th Infantry cleared the south and then moved to the center to protect the overextended Marine lines. In the north the Marines faced savage fighting, but by the night of 26 June, after Mount Tapotchau had been captured, the Japanese in that area only had 1200 troops left and three tanks. General Holland Smith felt the army was not advancing quickly enough and he dismissed its commander, Ralph Smith. The Marines and the Army did not co-operate well. The Marines approached the northern end of the island and on 6 July Nagumo and Saito committed suicide to encourage their troops to fight to the last. Two days later there were suicidal counterattacks by Japanese troops on the beaches. The civilian population also committed suicide en masse by jumping off the cliffs at Marpi Point, or else blowing themselves up with grenades, like the soldiers. Of the garrison of 32,000 only 1000 Japanese soldiers survived, and 22,000 civilians also died. The US casualties were high: 10,347 Marines and 3674 soldiers of whom 3426 died. The Marines went on to Tinian and Guam. The failure of the Japanese to hold on to the Marianas led to the resignation of General Tojo's government on 18 July.

## 'Sally'
see Mitsubishi Ki-21

## Salo Republic, 1943–45

The Salo Republic was the Italian puppet government (also known as the Italian Social Republic) created by Mussolini when, prodded by Hitler, he was forced to return to Italy after his abduction by Otto Skorzeny. His government was a shadowy affair, nominally in control of non-Allied occupied Italy, but actually controlled by the Wehrmacht. It collapsed with the fall of Germany and the assassination of Mussolini in April-May 1945.

## Samar Sea, Battle of
see Leyte Gulf, Battle of, 1944

## San Francisco Conference, 25 April–26 June 1945

This conference was called to finalize the arrangements of the Dumbarton Oaks Conference for the United Nations. Few changes were made from the previous conference (except on the subject of colonial trusteeship). The major confrontation was once again over Poland: the United States and Britain did not recognize the Soviet-sponsored Warsaw Government as representative and Russia did not recognize the Polish Government in Exile. The conference ended with the signing of the United Nations Charter.

## Santa Cruz Islands, Battle of, 1942

When the land battle on Guadalcanal opened in October 1942, the US naval forces could only play a defensive role. The only carriers in the area were the *Hornet* and the hastily-repaired *Enterprise*. The surface force, Task Force 64, under Rear Admiral Lee consisting of the battleship *South Dakota*, cruisers *Portland* and *San Juan* was sent to block the 'Tokyo Express.'

Admiral Yamamoto sent the Combined Fleet of five carriers, two battleships, and more than 30 destroyers under Admirals Kondo and Nagumo to hold the sea approaches to Guadalcanal and occupy Henderson airfield when General Maruyama's forces had recaptured it. The Marines held on to Henderson Field and the Japanese fleet turned away. The *Enterprise* carrier group with *South Dakota* under Rear Admiral Kinkaid joined with the *Hornet*, and when they spotted two Japanese carriers Kinkaid launched a strike which did not find its target. On 25–26 October Kinkaid again received a report on the Japanese and at 0730 the first strike of dive bombers, torpedo planes and Wildcats left the *Hornet*. Admiral Nagumo had anticipated this and sent a strike force at 0710 but he could not launch a second. The US planes attacked and the *Zuiho* was put out of action. The Japanese dive bombers attacked the *Hornet* and within ten minutes she was ablaze.

Japanese 'Val' makes a crash dive on the USS *Hornet* in the Battle of the Santa Cruz Islands.

At 0930 the *Shokaku* was seriously damaged and out of action for nine months. A second wave of dive bombers attacked the *Enterprise* but only hit with two bombs and her speed was not affected. Japanese pilots were not experienced and scored fewer hits.

The *Enterprise* recovered the majority of her planes and withdrew from the battle leaving the *Hornet*. The *Zuikaku* and *Junyo* were undamaged, but they had lost so many aircraft that they did not launch a final assault on the *Hornet* until 1515. A torpedo crippled her and she was finally sunk by Japanese destroyers. This was a costly victory for the Japanese who could ill-afford to lose so many pilots.

## *Saratoga*

The USS *Saratoga* was laid down as battlecruiser CC.3 after World War I, a sister of the *Lexington*, but she too was converted to an aircraft carrier (CV.3) and completed in 1927. She missed the debacle at Pearl Harbor but was torpedoed off Hawaii on 11 January 1942 and so missed both the Coral Sea and Midway battles. She was torpedoed again by the submarine *I.26* off Guadalcanal on 31 August 1942 but was repaired in time to take part in the Battle of the Eastern Solomons. She supported the landings on Bougainville, the Gilbert Islands, Kwajalein, Eniwetok and Iwo Jima, earning the affectionate nickname of 'Sara'.

In 1944 she took part in the Pacific raids and operated for a while with the British Eastern Fleet in the spring to mount a strong offensive against the Japanese in the East Indies. She provided Avengers, Dauntlesses and Hellcats for a strike against Sabang on 19 April and another against the oil-refinery at Surabaya in Java on 17 May. She was badly damaged off Iwo Jima on 21 February 1945 by a kamikaze and returned to the US for repairs. She ended her days as a target at Bikini.

## Sarin

This German poison gas was discovered in 1938 and is properly known as isopropyl methyl phosphoro-fluoridate. It was one of the original 'Nerve Gases', but was found to be exceptionally difficult to manufacture; only a pilot plant existed at the war's end, no operational production having been achieved.

## Sauckel, Ernst, 1894–1946

Sauckel became important in 1942 when he was appointed Plenipotentiary General for the Allocation of Labor. Between that date and the end of 1944, he was responsible for the deportation of some five million people from their homes to Germany, of whom he frankly admitted 'not even 200,000 came voluntarily'. He ordered that the deportees be exploited 'to the highest possible extent at the lowest conceivable degree of expenditure'. He was found guilty of crimes against humanity at Nuremberg and hanged.

## Saul, Air Vice-Marshal Richard E,

Commander of No 13 Group RAF Fighter Command during the Battle of Britain, Saul was responsible for the defense of the northern area of the United Kingdom.

## Savoia-Marchetti S.M.79

This Italian four/five-seat bomber and torpedo dropper, was in service 1936–1944. The prototype of this three-engined aircraft flew in late 1934. It was one of the first aircraft in Europe to have such modern features as retractable landing gear, flaps, and variable-pitch propellers, though it had an old-fashioned structure of aluminium, steel tube, wood and fabric. After capturing many speed records the S.M.79 went into production as a bomber for the Regia Aeronautica, first seeing action in the Spanish Civil War in 1937. Named Sparviero (Hawk), it did extremely well in Spain, and soon built up a great reputation, so that its crews fiercely resented any later aircraft. Built in large numbers for an Italian aircraft (about 1200), the S.M.79 was flown with great courage and skill by its crews on all kinds of missions against cities, battleships and troops. Throughout most of World War II it flew more missions than all other Italian bombers combined, and many experts also think it was the best of all land-based torpedo bombers of its day. Most were powered by three 1000hp Piaggio P.XI radial engines, reaching a speed of up to 267mph. The bomb load was normally 2200lb, or two externally slung small torpedoes; various defensive armaments were carried, usually with a 12.7mm gun firing ahead from the hunchbacked roof over the cockpit and three other machine guns aimed by hand. Rumania used a very different S.M.79–JR with two (not three) 1220hp Jumo 211 engines. These had glazed noses and served on the Eastern Front in 1941–44.

## Savoia-Marchetti S.M.84

The S.M. 84 was a development of the S.M.79 with a more refined airframe, three 1000hp Piaggio P.XIbis engines, and up to 4410lb of bombs or two torpedoes.

## Savo Island, Battle of, 1942

This was the first naval battle to take place off Guadalcanal. When the Japanese received news of the Guadalcanal landings, Vice-Admiral Mikawa was sent on 8 August 1942 with five heavy cruisers, two light cruisers and a destroyer to attack the transports. An Allied cruiser force under Rear Admiral Crutchley was stationed off Savo Island to protect the transports which should have had several warnings about the night attack – Mikawa's force was spotted by an aircraft, but the pilot thought they were Allied ships. Furthermore, two Allied destroyers on patrol did not spot the Japanese heavy ships on their radar.

Allied ship-to-ship communications (TBS) were not working well. At 0138, 9 August, Mikawa's ships opened fire and hit the Canberra and Chicago. The Canberra was put out of action, but Chicago pulled out of the battle in pursuit of a Japanese destroyer. The Japanese then illuminated the Astoria, Vincennes, and Quincy which were slow to respond. The Astoria was hit several times. The Quincy sank with 370 men lost and Vincennes sank with 332 men lost and 258 men wounded. The Japanese force circled round Savo Island but did not attack the transports because Mikawa was afraid of being attacked by aircraft. He did not know that Admiral Fletcher's carrier force had been withdrawn. The Japanese had sunk four cruisers: the Canberra, Astoria, Vincennes and Quincy, with only 111 casualties and slight damage to their ships.

## Schacht, Hjalmar, 1877–1970

Schacht was President of the Reichsbank, 1933–39, Minister of Economics, 1935–37, and Hitler's 'economic wizard'. He joined Hitler's entourage in 1930 (though never joining the Nazi party) and advised him on economic policy. As President on the Reichsbank, Schacht saw to the financing of German rearmament through monetary manipulations. He was dismissed from his bank presidency after a disagreement with Hitler but he retained a position in the Cabinet as Minister without Portfolio until 1943. He was not trusted by the Nazis and expounded the view that the German economy could not support a war of any length. He lived privately until 1944, when he was arrested on (unfounded) suspicion of complicity in the bomb plot and confined in Flossenburg. He was tried at Nuremberg and acquitted and has since amassed a second fortune and has acted as adviser to many underdeveloped countries.

The 31,800-ton Scharnhorst battlecruiser, sporting nine 11-inch guns.

## Scharnhorst

In 1933 the German Navy announced its intention to build a battlecruiser of 26,000 tons to match the French Dunkerque, in place of a fourth 'pocket battleship'. The ship actually displaced 31,800 tons in standard condition, which enabled her to have armor on a battleship-scale. However the 11in (28cm) guns and turrets for the fourth, fifth and sixth 'pocket battleships' (six mountings in all) had been ordered, and so it was decided to appropriate these for the new battlecruiser and her sister to be built later. The armament was weak for a ship of such size, and the 11in was quite outclassed by the 15in and 16in guns of the major navies' battleships. Aware of this, the designers allowed for eventual upgunning by replacing the triple 11in mounting with the new twin 15in (38cm) at a later date. The ship was to be called Scharnhorst, while her sister Gneisenau was ordered in secret under the 1934 Program; the revival of the names of Graf Spee's cruisers was a calculated gesture of defiance cast in the direction of the Treaty of Versailles.

With her sister, the Scharnhorst operated successfully against British shipping in the Atlantic in 1939–40, sinking the Armed Merchant Cruiser Rawalpindi on 23 November 1939 southeast of Iceland. On 8 June 1940 they sank the carrier HMS Glorious at the end of the Norwegian campaign but one of the escorting destroyers hit the Scharnhorst with a torpedo just before the destroyer sank. In 1941 the two ships sank 22 ships, totaling 115,622 tons, but by February they had taken refuge in Brest where they were subjected to heavy bombing. On 12 February 1942 she and the Gneisenau in company with the Prinz Eugen made a bold dash through the Channel in daylight in the face of attacks by aircraft, coast defense guns and surface ships without damage apart from striking a mine at the end of the day.

Although Operation Cerberus may have been a slap in the face to the British who were taken by surprise, the retreat of the two capital ships from their base at Brest removed a dangerous threat to the Atlantic convoys. The Scharnhorst was now something of a liability, and when she was repaired she was sent north to Norway to

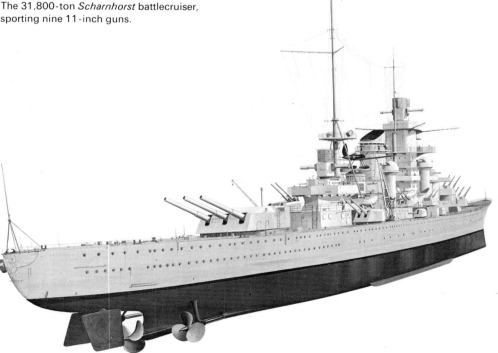

join the *Tirpitz* in balefully watching the convoys to Russia. On 6 September 1943 she bombarded Spitzbergen with the *Tirpitz* and in December put to sea on a final, ill-planned sortie against the British convoys JW.55B and RA.55A. Admiral Dönitz told Hitler on 19 December 1943 that the *Scharnhorst* would attack a convoy soon if the circumstances were favorable.

The circumstances were far from favorable, for the convoys they chose to attack on 26 December were covered by the flagship of the Home Fleet, the battleship *Duke of York* and a strong force of cruisers and destroyers. We now know that the British had decoded the orders to the *Scharnhorst* and so she ran into a hot reception. The cruisers with the convoy damaged her radar and fire-control, but she was still a formidable adversary. While her attention was distracted in a gun-duel with the *Sheffield* and *Norfolk*, the *Duke of York* approached unobserved to within 12,000 yards before opening fire. The *Scharnhorst*'s aim was not good, and she scored only two minor hits on the *Duke of York*, whereas she herself was hit repeatedly. She was attacked by four destroyers, which hit her with four torpedoes, slowing her down for the *Duke of York*. Finally the *Scharnhorst* was torpedoed by the cruiser *Jamaica*, and sank with the loss of her entire crew except for 36 men. A handsome ship, the *Scharnhorst* was the pride of the German Navy.

### Schirach, Baldur von, 1907–1974

Schirach was head of the Hitler Youth and later Gauleiter of Vienna. On Hitler's accession to power, Schirach had been appointed Reich Youth Leader and succeeded in bringing all youth movements, including the boy scouts and religious movements, under his control. He served as an infantryman in France in 1940, and then was appointed Gauleiter and governor of Vienna, which was regarded as a trouble spot by the Nazis. At Nuremberg he was accused of deporting Viennese Jews and of executing arbitrary justice and was sentenced to 20 years.

### Schlüsselburg, 1941-44
see Leningrad, Battle and Siege of

### Schmeisser
see Erma and Maschinen Pistole

### Schmetterling

This German anti-aircraft missile was developed in 1941 by Professor Wagner and was refused by the Luftwaffe on the grounds that it was a defensive weapon. Wagner received no official backing until 1943. Then the Henschel company was given a development contract with production to begin in February 1945. Due to bomb damage interrupting the work, the development was incomplete when the war ended; of 59 experimental launchings, 34 had failed for various reasons.

Schmetterling was a bomb-shaped missile with fins, with two take-off booster rockets attached to the outside. The boost rockets were solid-fuel types, while the internal sustainer motor was a liquid-fuel rocket fueled by a hydrocarbon/nitric acid mixture. After launch the missile settled down to a speed of 537mph and was radio controlled and visually tracked

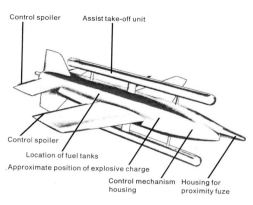

The Schmetterling anti-aircraft missile was designed in 1941.

by a ground controller. It had an effective range of about 10 miles with a ceiling of 35,000 feet. The warhead carried 55lb of high explosive and was fitted with a 'Fox' proximity fuze.

### *Schnellboote*
see German Navy and Motor Torpedo Boat

### *Schnellfeuerpistole*
see Mauser Arms

### Schörner, Field Marshal Ferdinand, 1892–1973

An able soldier though an even more talented sycophant, Schörner's ostentatious Nazism won him very rapid promotion during the war. His speciality was the meticulous execution of unrealistic orders. He remained in command of Army Group North, isolated in the Courland pocket, for six months, July 1944 to January 1945, and then took command of Army Group Center in Czechoslovakia, whence, far from communicating the gravity of its predicament to Hitler, Schörner fed him with promises of victory. For his soft words he achieved the height of his ambition: the by-then-empty title of Commander-in-Chief of the German Army, which he held for the ten days between Hitler's suicide and the surrender.

Supermarine Spitfires flying in formation over HMS *Indomitable*.

### Scoones, General Sir Geoffrey, 1893–1975

Scoones led British resistance in fierce fighting in defense of Imphal in Assam. In 1939 Scoones served on the General Staff at Allied HQ in India and later became Director of Military Operations and Intelligence. On 29 July 1942 Scoones was made commander of the 4th Corps (stationed at Imphal). The British could not undertake any offensive action until communications had been improved and until the command had been reorganized. SEAC was set up and Scoones was under General Stilwell's command. His task was to advance into central Burma across the Chindwin. Early in 1944 it became obvious that the Japanese were planning an offensive and Scoones was ordered to hold the Imphal Plain. Scoones withdrew all his divisions back to Imphal by April 1944 – although at times it looked as if it could not be done. Although his troops at Imphal were cut off they had five weeks' supplies and defended their positions vigorously. The Japanese ran out of supplies and by 23 June Scoones's troops could begin the advance into central Burma. On 7 December 1944 Scoones was appointed GOC, Central Command India and on 14 December he was knighted along with Generals Slim, Christison and Stopford.

### Seafire, Supermarine

Seafires began as carrier-based versions of RAF Spitfires of various marks. The initial Seafire Mk IB was a conversion of the Spitfire VB, with two 20mm and four 0.303in guns and, sometimes, clipped wings. Like the Seafire IIC, built from the start as a naval fighter, it had a deck arrester hook but not folding wings. The IICs had a 'universal' armament wing, capable of carrying four 20mm guns, and operated in fighter, low-altitude fighter and photo-reconnaissance forms. Next came the Seafire III, with double-folding wings which enabled it to use carrier deck-lifts, a 1585hp Merlin 55M engine and provision for take-off rockets. Again there were LF and FR variants, and the Mk III could carry 500lb of bombs. After about 1770 of these Merlin-engined Seafires had been delivered, production switched to Griffon-powered versions, but these were too late to play any part in World War II.

## Sealion, Operation

On 16 July 1940, Hitler issued his Führer Directive No 16 for the Conduct of the War. Its key sentence read, 'As England, in spite of the hopelessness of her military position, has so far shown herself unwilling to come to any compromise, I have therefore decided to begin to prepare for and, if necessary, to carry out an invasion of England'. The operation was codenamed *Seelöwe* (Sealion) and planned in two versions. The first called for the landing of 13 divisions in the first wave on a front of 225 miles from Lyme Regis to Dover, with 26 divisions to follow up. The Navy and the Luftwaffe rightly pointed out, however, that they were unable to protect a crossing on such a wide front and a second plan was produced in August. It reduced the front of attack to that between Worthing and Dover and the force to 9 divisions in the first wave and 7 in the follow-up, which were to hold the lodgment area for up to 16 days while the third wave was assembled and transported. All depended, however, on the ability of the Navy to transport the Army in the face of the Royal Navy, which depended in turn on the Luftwaffe's ability to secure air superiority over the Channel. As it could not do until it had won the Battle of Britain, which had begun on 10 July, Sealion had to await the outcome. Hitler, meanwhile, displayed a remarkable lack of interest in the project, taking his first and only holiday of the war during its preparation. When it became clear, at the end of September, that the Battle of Britain had been lost, he lost interest in the project altogether, ordering on 12 October that preparations be continued merely as means of bringing diplomatic and military pressure to bear. The invasion fleet, which had been assembled from all the north European ports and rivers but had suffered heavily from RAF attacks, was dispersed at the end of September and never reassembled.

## Selassie, Haile, Emperor of Abyssinia, Lion of Judah, King of Kings, 1891–1976

On the successful Italian invasion of his country in 1936, Haile Selassie was driven into exile but, following the ill-judged Italian attack on British Somaliland in 1940, was brought back to his throne in the wake of the British counter-offensive, which liberated his kingdom in a short and brilliant campaign. An effective and impressive autocrat, he was overthrown by a coup in 1974 and died in custody.

## Semovente

This was an Italian term for a self-propelled gun, though in general it was applied to a 75mm assault gun mounted on the chassis of the M/13 tank. This was copied from the German idea and consisted of a fixed armored superstructure on the tank hull which carried the gun mounted frontally and with limited traverse. Other versions were developed mounting 90mm and 149mm guns, but they were relatively few in number and made little contribution to the war.

## Serov, General Ivan A, 1905–

Serov was responsible for the deportations from Estonia, Lithuania, and Latvia. Serov's NKVD was responsible for shooting Russian soldiers

suspected of deserting. In 1945 he was Deputy Chief of Smersh and made General of Security Troops. He also became Deputy Supreme Commander of Soviet forces in Germany.

## Sevastopol, Battle of, May–June 1942

In May 1942 the Germans held all of the Crimea except the Eastern part, the Kerch peninsula and Sevastopol. On 8 May the Germans launched an offensive using dive-bombers and were able to overcome Russian resistance. The Red Army lost 100,000 prisoners and 200 tanks. The only remaining resistance was at Sevastopol. General Vlasov had launched an attack on the Germans outside the fortress, but he was unable to enlarge his flanks. He got no support from his headquarters and after five days he was encircled and allowed himself to be taken by the Germans. On 7 June General Manstein's Eleventh Army launched a final assault and after a month of heavy fighting Sevastopol surrendered on 4 July.

## Sevastapol, Capture of
see Crimea, Battle of the, 1941–44

## Sexton
see Ram

## Seyss-Inquart, Arthur, 1892–1946

Seyss-Inquart was Hitler's secret Austrian representative and became Chancellor of Austria in 1939. He built up the Nazi movement in Austria so that Hitler's troops could take over the country without difficulty. In May 1940 he was made Commissioner of the Netherlands, a post he held until the end of the war. He had control of the whole administration of the country and set about using the Dutch economy solely for the German war effort. He carried out a vigorous campaign against the Jews and deported some 117,000 of them; he also tried to wipe out the resistance movement with some success. He was arrested by the Canadians in May 1945 and was executed for war crimes.

## SG-43
see Goryunov Machine Gun

## Shaped Charge Munitions
see Hollow Charge Weapons

## Shaposhnikov, Marshal Boris M, 1882–1945

Shaposhnikov was an important military theorist. In 1940, he put forward to Stalin a plan to hold the Russian armies behind the old borders, on the Stalin Line instead of leaving them thinly deployed on an extensive frontier. He was overruled and dismissed from his post of Chief of General Staff. In July he was reappointed but he recommended withdrawal and so bore the brunt of Stalin's anger. In November 1941 he fell ill and was replaced by General Vasilevsky. He was able to help in the planning of the defense of Moscow and was against the offensive at Kharkov in 1942, feeling it to be premature. From June 1943 until his death he was Commandant of the Voroshilov Military Academy.

## *Sheffield*

HMS *Sheffield* was one of the most famous British warships of World War II, with a remarkably active and lucky career. She was a six-inch gunned cruiser of the *Southampton* Class, built to match the Japanese *Mogamis* but destined never to engage a Japanese warship of any kind. She operated with the Home Fleet in 1939–40 and fought in the Norwegian Campaign. Then in August 1940 she joined Force H, and for the next two years her name was always linked with the *Renown* and *Ark Royal*. During the search for the *Bismarck* in May 1941 she was attacked in error by Swordfish torpedo-bombers, but this mischance proved a blessing in disguise. The *Sheffield* was able to radio to the *Ark Royal* that the rough weather was detonating the magnetic fuzes of the torpedoes prematurely, and so the second strike against the *Bismarck* had the setting changed to 'contact'.

On 31 December 1942 the *Sheffield* and *Jamaica* were acting as the distant escort for a convoy to Russia when the convoy was attacked by the *Lützow* and *Admiral Hipper*. After the destroyers of the close escort had fought a gallant delaying action the *Sheffield* and *Jamaica* came up and put the two heavy cruisers to flight, sinking the destroyer *Friedrich Eckholdt* in the process. On 26 December 1943 the *Sheffield* was part of the cruiser force which held off the *Scharnhorst*.

## Sherman

'Sherman' is the British name for the US tank M4 and its numerous variants. Production of the Sherman during the war totaled 48,347 tanks, the greatest production of any single model ever achieved before or since, and to this figure may be added over 8000 chassis used for other weapons and almost 6000 tanks reworked and sent back into service.

The M4 story began in March 1941 when the US Ordnance Department, having completed work on the M3 series, immediately began to plan its replacement. By April five tentative designs had been produced, and one, the Medium Tank T6, was selected by the Armored Force because of its simplicity. It was to have a chassis and mechanical layout based on earlier designs, a turtle-shaped cast hull and a cast turret mounting a 75mm gun. Twin machine guns were to be mounted in the hull front firing on fixed lines, another machine gun alongside the driver in a ball mount, a co-axial machine gun in the turret and side exit doors completed the design, and a wooden mock-up was approved in May 1941.

By this time the British Tank Mission in the USA had amassed experience from combat reports and made some suggestions which resulted in the fitting of the radio in the turret, instead of in the hull which had been US practice up to that time, and in the fitting of smoke dischargers in the turret. In October 1941, after a prototype had passed trials, the design was standardized as the Medium Tank M4 and plans laid for production to begin early in 1942. The side doors were eliminated, since this would give a stronger hull, but the casting of the massive hull led to production problems and an alternative design using a welded hull was approved as a suitable design for plants without facilities for heavy casting. Eleven plants were designated for construction of the M4, including the Detroit Tank Arsenal operated by Chrysler

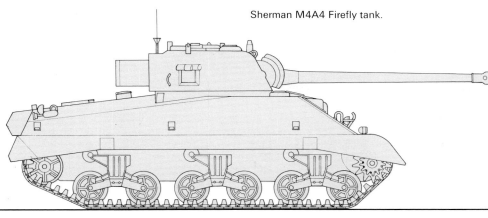

Sherman M4A4 Firefly tank.

M36 self-propelled 90mm gun on an M6 Sherman chassis.

Motors and the similar, purpose-built, tank plant at Grand Blanc, Michigan operated by Fisher Bodies.

The principal bottleneck threatened to be the supply of engines; the designated engine was the Wright Continental radial air-cooled engine which had been derived from an aviation design, but these could not be produced in the vast quantity required and alternative engines were therefore tested and approved. This led to a variety of different models, according to the engine fitted and the type of hull construction:

Section of a Sherman M4A4 tank.

**M4** The alternative design with welded hull but with the original Continental radial engine.
**M4A1** The original design with cast hull and Continental engine.
**M4A2** Welded hull and with a General Motors diesel engine. The majority of these appears to have been sent to Soviet Russia in 1942. Others were used by the US Marines and by the British Army and a few by the US Army.
**M4A3** Welded hull, Ford 500hp V–8 tank engine. This had been specially developed as a tank engine to replace the Continental and became the standard tank unit. The M4A3 was almost entirely used in US Army service.

**M4A4** Welded hull, fitted with a Chrysler multi-bank engine built up from five 6-cylinder engines arranged around a common crankshaft. The majority of these were supplied to the British Army.
**M4A5** US Army designation for the Canadian 'Ram' tank (qv).
**M4A6** Welded hull, fitted with a Caterpillar diesel engine, which necessitated lengthening the hull.

The original armament for the M4 was a 75mm gun capable of firing AP shot or high explosive shells. As the war progressed this gun became out-dated, and in February 1944 approval was given to the fitting of a slightly larger turret with a 76mm high-velocity gun, a weapon with far better performance than the short-barreled 75mm weapon. In British service about 600 M4s of various types were modified by removing the 75mm or 76mm guns and replacing them with the British 17-pounder, as great an improvement over the 76mm as that had been over the 75. These were known as 'Sherman Fireflies' and were used in northwest Europe.

In order to provide a close support tank, a number of M4 and M4A3 tanks were fitted with 105mm howitzers in the turret. This was a modification of the standard US field artillery piece, firing the same ammunition, and providing the tanks with powerful fire ability.

The outstanding features of the M4 series were its simplicity, ease of maintenance and mechanical reliability. Towards the end of the war it was outclassed by the last German and Soviet developments, but this was balanced by its vast production and quick replacement, its speed and maneuverability and, to some extent, by its improved armament. Shermans can still be found in service with various armies in the middle 1970s, a testimony to the excellence of their design and construction.

Because of this basic soundness the chassis was selected as the basis for a number of specialist armored vehicles. Notable among these were the M7B1 105mm self-propelled gun, the M10 Tank Destroyer mounting a 3in gun in an open-topped turret, the M36 tank destroyer similar to the M10 but with a 90mm gun, the M40 self-propelled 155mm gun, and the M43 self-propelled 8in howitzer.

---

**Sherman, Rear Admiral Fred, 1888–1957**

Sherman was the captain of the *Lexington* during the Battle of Coral Sea and had to abandon ship after she blew up. He then commanded the *Saratoga-Princeton* carrier group which Admiral Nimitz lent to General MacArthur and he participated in numerous raids on Rabaul at the end of 1943. He rejoined the 5th Fleet and took part in the Battle of the Philippine Sea and Leyte Gulf. During the Battle of Leyte Gulf the *Princeton* was hit by a dive-bomber and sank.

---

**Shigemitsu, Mamoru, 1881–1957**

Shigemitsu had a long career in Japanese foreign affairs which began as Minister to China in 1930. In 1932 in Shanghai he lost a leg due to a bomb thrown by a Korean patriot. He was ambassador to Russia from 1936 to 1938 and to London from 1938 to 1941, where he tried to appear anti-militarist and to convince Westminster that the Tripartite Pact need not lead to war between Japan and the Allies.

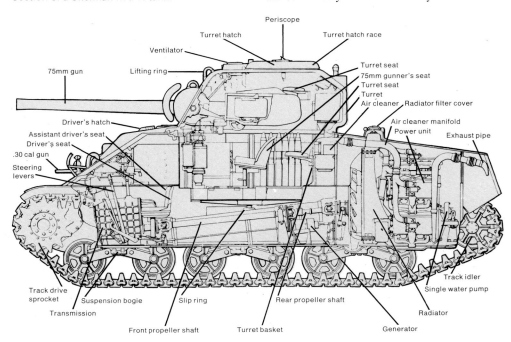

Periscope
Turret hatch    Turret hatch race
Ventilator
75mm gun    Lifting ring    Turret seat
                            75mm gunner's seat
                            Turret seat
                            Turret
                            Air cleaner    Radiator filter cover
Driver's hatch                          Air cleaner manifold
Assistant driver's seat                 Power unit
Driver's seat                                   Exhaust pipe
.30 cal gun
Steering
levers
Track drive                                     Track idler
sprocket    Suspension bogie    Slip ring    Rear propeller shaft    Single water pump
    Transmission                                      Radiator
        Front propeller shaft    Turret basket    Generator

Two days after Pearl Harbor, Shigemitsu was appointed Ambassador to the Nanking puppet government. With his experience of Chinese affairs, he was always an opponent of the occupation of China as a colony, feeling this to be inconsistent with Japan's role as anti-imperialist liberator of the East. He favored abolishing the unequal treaties with Nanking and offering unrestricted economic aid. Prime Minister Tojo supported the Shigemitsu plan after 1941 and had won over the army by early 1943. Shigemitsu therefore became Foreign Minister (April 1943–45), in which capacity he advocated political freedom for all East Asia and an end to military occupation, a 'good neighbor' policy. Shigemitsu was a member of the surrender cabinet and led the Japanese delegation which signed the surrender on the *USS Missouri*. After several years imprisonment for war crimes, he returned to politics as Deputy Prime Minister and Foreign Minister 1954–56.

## *Shinano*

This, the third battleship of the *Yamato* Class was suspended at the outbreak of war in December 1941, but after Midway the recasting of the building program to replace the lost carriers led to a new design being prepared. She was not to be a conventional fleet carrier but a huge repair and maintenance ship for other carriers. She would carry a small number of fighters for defense but be capable of arming, fueling and repairing a much larger number.

The ship was launched in October 1944 in an advanced state, but it was decided that she should be moved from Yokosuka to the Inland Sea out of reach of air attacks. Despite being only partially complete and lacking trained men who were familiar with the working of the ship, she was sent on her maiden voyage to Matsuyama near Kure. She left Yokosuka at 1800 hours on 28 November 1944 escorted by three destroyers. Next morning she showed up as an echo on the radar screen of the US submarine *Archerfish*, and after a long chase the submarine got into a firing position at 0317. At least four out of the full salvo of six torpedoes hit the giant target, but instead of an orderly process of damage control, chaos ensued aboard the *Shinano*. Watertight doors were left open, welded joints began to open under pressure, and some vital pumps were found to be missing. The captain seemed to have been content to regard his ship as unsinkable, until she finally rolled over at 1017.

## Sho-Go
see Leyte Gulf, Battle of, 1944

## *Shoho*

Under the 2nd Reinforcement Program of 1934 the Japanese Navy planned a subterfuge to enable them to increase their tonnage of aircraft carriers beyond that allowed under the international treaties. Two submarine tenders, the *Takasaki* and *Tsurugizaki* were planned, but were specially strengthened and laid out internally so that they could be rapidly converted to carriers. The *Tsurugizaki* was completed in 1939 but the *Takasaki* lay incomplete from 1936 to 1940.

When work started on conversion in 1940 it was decided to re-engine the ships with geared steam turbines as the original high-speed diesels had proved a failure due to poor design. The incomplete *Takasaki* was converted in 1940 and was renamed *Zuiho*: her sister underwent conversion between January 1941 and January 1942 and became the *Shoho*. She carried 27 operational aircraft and three spares. The *Shoho*'s career was short, as she was earmarked for the Port Moresby landings which brought on the Battle of the Coral Sea. She was sunk by aircraft from the *Lexington* and *Yorktown* on 7 May 1942. Two 1000lb bombs hit her on the flight deck, then 11 more bombs and a possible seven torpedoes struck. She sank in 10 minutes.

## Sibuyan Sea, Battle of
see Leyte Gulf, Battle of, 1944

## Sicily, Invasion of, 1943

Operation Husky, the invasion of Sicily, had been decided on at the Casablanca Conference in January 1943. Detailed planning began in April and the forces were ready in July. They were commanded by General Eisenhower and consisted of two armies, the US 7th commanded by Patton and the British 8th commanded by Montgomery, together forming the 15th Army Group under General Alexander. The size of the invading force was 140,000, carried in 3000 ships and landing craft. They were to be opposed by the Italian Sixth Army, commanded by General Guzzoni, which numbered 275,000 men in units of mixed quality, and also contained the German Fifteenth Panzer Grenadier and Hermann Goering Panzer Divisions. The Allied air forces had available about 3700 aircraft to the enemy's 1400.

The Allied plan was to land in the extreme south of the island, the British east of Cape Passero and the Americans west of it, seize the ports of Syracuse and Licata respectively, secure the airfields around Catania and then advance to Messina, opposite the toe of Italy, which would be captured by Montgomery with Patton guarding his left flank. Heavy weather on the night of 9–10 July caught the armada at sea and nearly forced a postponement of the landings but it also caused the defenders to relax their vigilance and so helped the invaders ashore with light loss. However, numbers of aircraft and gliders which were carrying airborne troops

Just after dawn 10 July 1943 British troops land on Sicily and unload.

to landing zones near Syracuse and Licata dropped their parachutists or slipped their tows out to sea, with consequent loss of life. Despite this setback, the Axis counterattack on 11 July, mounted by the German Panzer divisions, was driven off and between 12 and 15 July the Allies united their bridgeheads and secured their initial objectives. Guzzoni now ordered his troops out of western Sicily and concentrated them for the defense of the Catania plain under Mount Etna. The move successfully blocked Montgomery's efforts to pass east of Etna towards Messina between 15 and 19 July. German reinforcements including the Twenty-Ninth Panzer Grenadier and First Parachute Divisions were now reaching the island and Alexander accordingly made a change of plan. Montgomery was to cease his frontal attack towards Catania and instead seek to pass between it and Etna, while Patton, on whose front the resistance was weaker, was to drive along the coast to Messina. This strategy, assisted by a series of amphibious 'end runs' by the Americans along the north coast, progressively unhinged the enemy defense and, after bitter fighting, brought the Allies to Messina on 17 August. Skillful rearguard action and clever use of ferries under cover of darkness had allowed the enemy to get most of their surviving soldiers away, about 100,000 in all; they had lost 164,000.

## Siegfried Line

The Siegfried Line was the more common name for Germany's line of fortifications on its western frontier, the West Wall. It was hurriedly constructed in 1936 as an answer to the Maginot Line and was finished in May 1940, north of Aachen. After the successful campaign in France, 1940 the Line was dismantled and neglected but in 1944 it was restored to hold up the Allies' advance into Germany.

## Sikorski, General Wladyslaw, 1881–1943

Sikorski was the Prime Minister of the Polish government-in-exile from 1939 until his death in 1943. Sikorski was in Paris when Germany invaded Poland and he became Premier of the Polish provisional government and Commander-in-Chief of its armed forces. By spring 1940 the Poles had an army of 100,000 men but when France fell the Poles left for Britain. Sikorski had to negotiate with friendly

countries to obtain recognition for his government and aid for the underground movement in Poland. In July 1941 he opened up negotiations with the USSR to secure recognition of the pre-1939 boundaries and to obtain an amnesty for Polish prisoners in the USSR. These negotiations allowed General Anders to recruit a Polish Army in the USSR and inquire into the fate of the Polish officers who had been deported. In 1942 Sikorski reached an agreement with Roosevelt which allowed him to recruit US citizens of Polish extraction into his army.

In 1943 Anders was able to report that he could not trace many Polish citizens in the USSR and in April Sikorski raised the matter of the murdered Poles at Katyn with Churchill. Churchill was anxious to have smooth relations with Stalin and disregarded Sikorski's evidence. Relations between the USSR and the Polish government-in-exile were very strained. Sikorski died in a plane crash off Gibraltar on 4 July 1943.

## Simonov Automatic Rifle

During the early 1930s the US Army adopted the Garand Automatic rifle, a step which spurred several other armies into closer study of this type of weapon. Among them was the Soviet Army who had been experimenting off and on for several years, and who in 1936, adopted the Simonov design known as the AVS–36. This was a gas-operated rifle using a piston mounted above the barrel to unlock and retract the bolt. It fired the standard 7.62mm Soviet rifle cartridge from a 15-shot detachable magazine, and the mechanism was arranged to permit automatic fire in the light machine gun role. Although adopted in some numbers, it soon exhibited defects. The muzzle blast and recoil were excessive so a muzzle brake was fitted to reduce them. The action was open to dust and dirt which led to the mechanism clogging. And the bolt locking system appears not to have been as reliable as hoped. As a result the rifles were phased out starting in 1938 when a replacement, the Tokarev SVT–38, appeared. Nevertheless, a number remained in service (since the replacement was slow in taking place) during the war.

## Singapore

Singapore had been chosen as the main fleet base for a powerful Far Eastern Fleet as long ago as 1919, but little was done until very late to even complete the defenses. Expenditure on the 'Bastion of the Far East' became a subject for political wrangling, and work was stopped and restarted more than once in the 1930s, but all concerned seem to have forgotten Admiral Jellicoe's original warning that a base was only a haven for a strong fleet. In the event the failure to provide a strong fleet allowed the Japanese free access to the Malay Peninsula, and so exposed the landward flank of the fortress to attack.

Mention must be made of the persistent myth that the Singapore guns could only fire seaward. This is quite untrue, despite Churchill's statements, for the 15in gun batteries not only covered the mainland approaches to Singapore Island but fired on the advancing Japanese. What was wrong, however, was the assumption that the guns would only have to fire against ships; they had only been issued with armor-piercing shells, which were nearly useless against troops

advancing through jungle. It is also interesting to note that the Admiralty's requests for medium and light guns to cover the Causeway and to prevent small assault boats from crossing the Johore Strait were vigorously opposed by the RAF, which wanted money diverted from fixed defenses to air defenses, as the decisive battle for Malaya would be fought in the north. Events proved the RAF right; the battle for Malaya was fought in the north but the RAF lost it, leaving the fortress of Singapore to bear the brunt of a conventional land assault.

## Singapore, Fall of, 1942

After the fall of Malaya General Arthur Percival had at his command 70,000 combatant and 15,000 noncombatant troops, but all his battalions were under-strength. General Yamashita had three divisions in hand and he decided to attack the northwest corner of the island of Singapore.

On 8 February after an air and artillery bombardment, assault troops of the Japanese Fifth and Eighteenth Divisions landed in darkness and attacked along an eight-mile stretch, the section held by three battalions of the 22nd Australian Brigade. Some 13,000 Japanese assault troops landed safely. The Australians then withdrew from the causeway, which allowed the Japanese to make a deeper penetration along the main road. A third Japanese division was then landed, increasing their strength on the island to 30,000. The British abandoned the Jurong Line and fell back to protect the city. However they lost most of their supplies. A prolonged siege was impossible because water supplies were extremely low. Therefore, on 15 February Percival surrendered with some 130,000 men to Yamashita. The British had not had adequate air cover to protect their naval base, which was in any case designed to withstand a naval, not land-based, attack. The whole campaign had cost the Japanese less than 10,000 men. This was the most ignominious capitulation in the history of British arms.

## Sirte, Battle of
see *Littorio*

## 'Skink'
see Ram

## Skorzeny, Colonel Otto, 1908–1976

A German commando teader and best known for his daring rescue of Mussolini from the peak of the Gran Sasso in the Abruzzi in September 1943, Skorzeny also kidnapped the son of the Hungarian dictator, Horthy, in 1944, thus nullifying the father's plans to make a separate peace with the Russians. In December 1944 as part of the Ardennes offensive, he led a force of English-speaking Germans into American lines where they spread confusion and destruction. He was the most successful German irregular soldier of the war.

## Skua, Blackburn

This British, carrier-based dive bomber was in service from 1938 to 1941. Powered by an 830hp Bristol Perseus, this two-seater shot down a Do

18 flying boat off Norway just after the start of World War II, and later bombed and sank the light cruiser *Königsberg*. Apart from this the 165 built saw little action. The 136 Rocs, a fighter version with four-gun turret, saw even less.

## SLC
see Human Torpedoes

## Slessor, Air Marshal Sir John, 1897–1979

At the outbreak of war Slessor was Director of Plans Branch at the Air Ministry, and in 1940 went on a special mission to the USA with Army and Navy officers to meet their American counterparts. The most important result of these discussions was an agreement that should the USA and Japan become involved, the Allies would concentrate initially on defeating Germany and that Japan should be contained until that time.

Following a period as Air Officer Commanding No 5 Bomber Group RAF Bomber Command, he was appointed to the new post of Assistant Chief of the Air Staff (Policy) in 1942, attending the main Allied conferences. A year later he became head of RAF Coastal Command; in this capacity, working in close cooperation with the Royal Navy and the US forces, he played a major part in the defeat of the German U-Boats in the Battle of the Atlantic. From January 1944, he was Commander in Chief of the RAF units in the Mediterranean and Deputy Commander in Chief Allied Air Forces in that theater.

He became Chief of the Air Staff in the postwar period.

## Slim, General Sir William, 1891–1970

Slim became famous for restoring the morale of British forces after the fighting retreat from Burma, and for reconquering Burma in 1944–45.

Early in the war Slim was in command of the 5th Indian Division in the Sudan on the Eritrean frontier and was wounded in the first offensive against the Italians at Gallabat. He recovered to take command of the 10th Indian Division in

General Sir William Slim.

Iraq in 1941. His division was sent to Iran where it routed the enemy and made contact with Russian troops at Teheran.

In 1942 Slim was sent to Burma to command the 1st Corps (Burcorps) but he found a desperate situation and could only cover the long retreat from Rangoon to India before the monsoon broke. He was then appointed to command the 18th Corps in India and he set about building up the men's morale. Late in 1943 a new army, the 14th, was formed to fight in Burma although this was low in the Allies' list of priorities. One of the important factors in the campaign now was the use of guerrilla units behind Japanese lines (Merrill's Marauders and Wingate's Chindits) and also the supply of troops by airplane.

In February 1944 the British offensive began. Although the Japanese had scored a tactical victory, the British managed to hold on to Arakan. The 14th Army went on to drive the Japanese out of Imphal and Kohima in two months of heavy fighting. During the monsoon in 1944 the Japanese withdrew to the Chindwin. In spite of this, the Japanese Army did not collapse and Slim still had to fight his way through Burma before reaching Rangoon. Although Slim did not have air cover, he used air supply to provision his troops. He advanced across the Irrawaddy and took Mandalay in the third week of March 1945. Rangoon fell shortly afterwards in May and Slim arrived to find the town deserted. There were still some Japanese trapped west of the Sittang who had to be dealt with. Slim was made Commander in Chief of Allied Land Forces in Southeast Asia and was planning the reconquest of Malaya when the Japanese surrendered. In August 1945 Slim was made a General.

### Slot
see Cape Esperance, Battle of

### Smigly-Rydz, Marshal Edward, 1886–1943

Smigly-Rydz was Commander in Chief of the Polish Armed Forces in 1939. He deployed his forces throughout Poland and when it was clear that they could not resist German might, he ordered them to fall back on the southeast. However the USSR then invaded eastern Poland.

He fled to Rumania where he was imprisoned and dismissed from his post. In 1941 he escaped and went back to Poland where he joined the underground and was probably killed by the Germans.

### Smith, General Walter Bedell, 1895–1961

A staff officer who had risen from the ranks, he became, at the outbreak of the war, secretary of the US Joint Chiefs of Staff and American secretary of the Anglo-American Combined Chiefs of Staff. In September 1942 he went to England to become Chief of Staff to Eisenhower, with whom he remained to the war's end. Eisenhower enormously valued his services and talents, which were those of the perfect soldier-diplomat. He laid the basis for the negotiation of the Italian armistice of 1943 and arranged the surrender of the German forces in the west in May 1945. Smith proved a tactful, persistent and highly capable administrator of war plans.

### Smith, Major General Holland, 1882–1967

'Howlin' Mad' Smith was the Marine commander of the 5th Amphibious Corps which captured the Aleutian Islands, the Gilbert Islands, the Marianas and Iwo Jima. He was a tough general who forced his men on relentlessly and did not seem affected by the high casualty rates. After the great losses at the Gilbert Islands he argued that taking Tarawa was unnecessary and that the Islands should have been avoided. At Iwo Jima he was faced with the problem that Marines and Army would not cooperate.

### SMK
see KV Tanks

### SMLE
see Lee Enfield Rifle

### Smolensk, Capture of, 1944
see Dniepr, Battle of the, August-December 1943

### Smolensk, Battle of, July 1941

The German advance through the USSR in 1941 was not as smooth as appears at first sight. In June and July bad roads and mud slowed down the trucks carrying vital supplies of fuel and ammunition. Also the Russians had blown up crucial bridges which held back some of the heavier armored vehicles, and there were minefields, especially along the Stalin Line. In early July the German army had plans to make a pincer movement behind General Timoshenko's army at Smolensk, by crossing the Dniepr. This meant breaking through the Stalin Line, which proved easy as the Russians had not constructed any defenses along this line. On 12 July the Germans breached the Stalin Line from Rogachev to Vitebsk. Generals Guderian and Hoth's Panzer Divisions outstripped their infantry, which could not advance because of the mud. The German army entered Smolensk on 16 July, but Guderian and Hoth had crossed the Dniepr and were far enough ahead to threaten the Bryansk army at Roslavl. Russian counterattacks by well-trained cavalry scored some local victories. The Panzers were

Scorched Earth: Vitebsk aflame, taken by the Germans in the battle for Smolensk.

low on ammunition and had no infantry to support them so some Russian divisions escaped encirclement. By 5 August resistance in the pocket round Smolensk was broken and 309,000 men, 3000 guns and 3205 tanks were taken. This operation was not as successful as it could have been, because of the strained relations between Field Marshal Kluge, in command of the Fourth Army, and Guderian, who was commanding the Panzers for Kluge.

### Smuts, Prime Minister Jan Christiaan, 1870–1950

A member of the British War Cabinet during World War I, Smuts was Prime Minister of his own country during World War II. He was responsible for bringing South Africa into the war at the outset. He supported Churchill, and remained one of his closest confidants – as he had been in the earlier war – to the end. He attended the opening of the United Nations in San Francisco and the 1946 peace conference, the only man present who had also taken part in the peace conference of 1919.

### Sokolovsky, Marshal Vasiliy D, 1897–1968

Sokolovsky was commander of Soviet forces in Germany after the war. In 1941–43 he was Chief of Staff of the Western Front, where he worked with General Konev. He helped in the preparation of Operation Kutuzov (Kursk), and operations at Smolensk, Lvov, the Vistula-Oder and Berlin. From 1944 to 1945 he was Chief of Staff on the 1st Ukrainian Front and was held responsible for the failure to advance from north of the Pripet Marshes in February 1944. He was then made Marshal Zhukov's Deputy Front Commander on the 1st Belorussian Front.

### Soman

This German poison gas was discovered in 1944 and was the third of the original 'Nerve Gas' group. Correctly known as pinacolyl methyl phosphoro-fluoridate, it was never taken beyond the laboratory stage.

### Somervell, General Brehon, 1892–1955

Somervell was the US Commanding General of the Army Service Forces from August 1942 until he retired at the end of the war. He was

involved in the mobilization and war production of the US war effort. He attended all the major planning meetings and was responsible for supplies and equipment and the co-ordination of resources.

## Somerville, Admiral Sir James Fownes, 1882–1949

As Commander of Force H, the fleet of capital ships based at Gibraltar, it was Somerville's unhappy task in July 1940 to deliver the ultimatum to the commander of the French fleet in Mers-el-Kebir and Oran that it must be sailed at once to waters out of reach of the Axis. On the expiry of the ultimatum period, he was obliged to sink the fleet at its moorings by gunfire, with heavy loss of life. In 1941 he led Force H in pursuit of the *Bismarck* and helped hunt it to destruction. In 1942 he went to Ceylon as Commander of the Eastern fleet. From 1944 he was Head of the British naval mission in Washington. He was the most successful British surface fleet commander of the war.

## Somua S–35

This French cavalry tank was developed in 1935 and at the outbreak of war was considered to be one of the best tanks then in service in any nation. It was the first service tank ever to use a completely cast hull and turret; the turret was traversed by electric power; the steering and transmission involved a very advanced double differential system; the engine was a 190hp V–8; and the armor was 55mm thick. All features were well in advance of the general run-of-tank designs of the time. It was armed with a 47mm gun and coaxial 7.5mm machine gun in the turret which had to be operated by the solitary occupant of the turret, the tank's commander. This was a fundamental flaw in all French tanks and it greatly nullified the otherwise excellent features of the S–35. About 500 were built prior to 1940 and their combat record appears to have been good. Numbers of them were taken over by the German and Italian armies and used both as tanks and as chassis for mounting various self-propelled guns.

## Sonar
see Asdic

## 'Sonia'
see Mitsubishi Ki-51

## Sorge, Richard, 1895–1944

By birth and upbringing a German, Sorge had been converted to communism in his youth and entered the Soviet Secret Service in the 1920s. Concealing his role, he was accepted by the German Ambassador in Tokyo, where he worked as a journalist, as a confidant and through him was able to transmit news both of German–Japanese dealings and of the intentions of both Axis powers to Moscow. His most important message warned of the attack on Pearl Harbor and assured the Russians that their Siberian border was unthreatened and allowed them to transfer their Far Eastern army westward in the winter of 1941 and thus win the Battle of Moscow in December. Sorge had been arrested in October, however, and after a lengthy interrogation, was hanged in 1944. He was posthumously named a Hero of the Soviet Union. He may well have been the most successful spy in history. He was certainly one of the coolest.

## Soviet High Command

The Red Army had been considerably weakened by the Purges of 1937–38. Two Marshals survived: Budenny and Voroshilov, neither of whom were to show outstanding military leadership during the war. The 1934 Military Soviet had comprised 80 members and in September 1938 only five of them were still alive. All eleven Deputy Commissars for Defense had disappeared. Every Commander of the military districts had been executed. As a result, there were not many experienced leaders and there was no dominant personality, aside from Stalin, to decide on overall strategy to face the Germans. On 22 June 1941 there was no High Command for the commissariats of Defense and Navy. General Timoshenko proposed that a High Command be initiated and on the day after the German Invasion a High Command, called the Stavka, was set up with Timoshenko as Chairman, a nominal post. On 30 June Stalin decided to change the system and created a Committee of Defense of the State: GKO, which was to be responsible for all aspects of the war. Its members were Stalin, (the President), Molotov, Malenkov, Voroshilov and Beria. The GKO issued orders which were put into effect by the People's Commissariats. The Stavka remained as a unit to direct military operations and on 10 July was reorganized with Stalin as Chairman, and Molotov, Timoshenko, Budenny, Voroshilov, Shaposhnikov and Zhukov as members. On 8 August Stalin then named himself Supreme Commander of the Armed Forces of the USSR, replacing Timoshenko. After all these changes Stalin could oversee all military matters. He left the planning of operations to his generals but the final decision lay in his hands. One of the problems early on in the war was bad communications, which meant that orders from the Stavka did not get through – generals waited for orders and lost time. The Germans could break their communications code and knew what moves were being planned.

## Spaatz, General Carl, 1891–1974

Spaatz was an American General who was in command of the USAAF in Europe and the Pacific. In 1940, before the US entered the war, General Carl 'Tooey' Spaatz was an official observer in London, there witnessing the Battle of Britain. Following Pearl Harbor he was appointed Chief of the Air Force Combat Command; then, in March 1942, Commanding General of the 8th Air Force.

Anticipating a major assault on northwest Europe in 1943, Spaatz's units transferred to the UK in July 1942 and were in action within six weeks against targets in France, including participation in the Dieppe Raid. From January 1943, the 8th Air Force pursued its daytime precision bombing missions as part of the *Combined Bomber Offensive* against Germany. Spaatz, meanwhile had been temporarily detached from his command to become Deputy for Air Operations in the North African theater, with responsibility for co-ordinating the operations of the Eastern Air Command and the 12th Air Force. His role was extended in February 1943, with the formation of the Mediterranean Air Command when he became Commander of the Northwest African Air Forces for the drive through Tunisia into Sicily and up through Italy.

With the formation of the United States Strategic Air Forces in Europe (USSAFE), Spaatz was given the task of co-ordinating the strategic bombing activities of the 8th AF in the UK and the 15th AF in Italy, and of bringing them within the aegis of the *Overlord* command. This last point was, however, to bring about a conflict of ideas and personality. In common with his British counterpart, Sir Arthur Harris, Commander-in-Chief of RAF Bomber Command, he believed that the strategic forces could best benefit Operation Overlord by pursuing their strategic objectives. This view was contrary to that of Leigh-Mallory, Commander of the Allied Expeditionary Air Force, and of the Deputy Supreme Commander, Sir Arthur Tedder. Moreover, like Harris, Spaatz refused to co-operate in any way with Leigh-Mallory. However, the policy of the two strategic commanders differed essentially with regard to the targets to be attacked. Spaatz believed firmly in precision bombing, whereas Harris advocated the area offensive. Spaatz, in fact, devised a plan which adapted his force's strategic role to suit Overlord requirements. Issued on 5 March 1944, his 'Oil Plan' recommended attacks against Germany's vital oil installations which would not only damage her resources but would also force the Luftwaffe into the air to defend them. Although this plan was rejected as an immediate measure in favor of Leigh-Mallory's Transportation Plan, it was officially sanctioned in September 1944, with oil targets assuming priority over those connected with communications.

Spaatz was transferred to the headquarters of the Army Air Force in March 1945 being sent subsequently to command the US Strategic Air Forces in the Pacific in July of the same year, with the 8th and 20th AFs based in the Marianas and on Okinawa. He also directed the heavy bombers operating against the Japanese mainland destroying 60 percent of the ground area of the 60 largest cities. The last devastating action of the war was carried out under his command with the dropping of atomic bombs on Hiroshima and Nagasaki; attacks which proved beyond doubt the war-winning capabilities of the strategic bombers.

## Speer, Minister Albert, 1905–

Universally admitted to be the most able of Hitler's servants, Speer first joined his entourage as his personal architect, in which capacity he designed the Nuremberg stadium but, after the death of Todt in an air accident, was appointed to fill his place as Armaments Minister. It was a brilliant appointment. Speer had both the technical and adminstrative skill and the personal self-confidence to impose correct solutions of the war supply problem on German industry as well as on Hitler himself. Despite the growing impact of Allied bombing from 1942 onwards he actually increased output on a rising curve until September 1944. Thereafter he became convinced that Germany must try to lose the war, as she was bound to do, with the least possible long-term damage to her economy and, when he became aware of Hitler's nihilistic

*Above:* Albert Speer emerges from a captured Soviet T-34 tank.

intentions, did what he could to thwart them – towards the end with decreasing care for secrecy. Hitler probably became aware of Speer's disloyalty but allowed his long-standing affection for his only 'artistic' subordinate to get the better of his (by then almost instinctive) vindictiveness. Speer's conversion came, however, too late for the Allies who insisted on noticing that he had used slave-labor on some of his schemes and arraigned him at Nuremberg. He was sentenced to twenty years' imprisonment. During his term he wrote what will undoubtedly remain the single most arresting account of life and politics within Hitler's entourage. The story of the life of the man himself, well-born, brilliant, charming and handsome, is itself the stuff of Faustian drama.

### Sperrle, Field Marshal Hugo, 1885–1953

This German Field Marshal commanded the Luftwaffe units in the west, known corporately as Luftflotte III, from January 1939. During the Spanish Civil War he had been the first Commander of the German Condor Legion, later relinquishing the post to General Volkmann.

With promotion to Lieutenant General in 1937 he became General of Aviators, subsequently taking command of Luftflotte III. In 1940, he was promoted to Generalfeldmarschall. The units of Luftflotte III provided support for the army in its victorious 'blitzkrieg' across western Europe. During the Battle of Britain he directed jointly with Kesselring, Commander of Luftflotte II, the Luftwaffe assault on the UK, his bombers perpetrating the night-time attacks. At this time Luftflotte III

was based in northern France with Sperrle's headquarters in Paris, although it was alleged that the greater part of the operational planning fell to his Chief of Staff, Günther Korten.

In 1944 the weight of the Allied air offensive in preparation for, and during, the D-Day operations fell on Luftflotte III, with the result that on D-Day itself Sperrle's units were able to offer no effective opposition to the invading forces.

A man who had worked his way up from humble origins to become one of the Luftwaffe's highest-ranking officers, he is said to have possessed greater talents as a bully than as a strategist or a military planner.

---

### Spitfire, Supermarine

This British single-seat fighter was operational from 1938 to 1954. One of the most renowned and elegant aircraft in flying history, the Spitfire was designed by R J Mitchell in the light of experience gained with his racing seaplanes which won the Schneider Trophy for Britain in 1927/31. The prototype, which flew first on 5 March 1936, looked so small and fast that a senior German officer dismissed it contemptuously as 'a toy'. Initial production was slow, not helped by the complex structure. Only sufficient aircraft for nine squadrons had been delivered by the outbreak of war. By the start of the Battle of Britain, 19 squadrons had received some 1400 aircraft. When production ended in 1947, the grand total of all Spitfires produced for the RAF was 20,351. Over a full decade, the power of the aircraft's succession of Rolls-Royce Merlin and Griffon engines had doubled. Weight had increased by 40 percent, speed by 35 percent to 454mph, and rate of climb by 80 percent. Remembered for their semi-elliptical 'pointed' wings, Spitfires sometimes had the wingtips clipped squarely for low flying, or extended to an even sharper point for high flying. Beginning with an armament of eight 0.303in Browning machine guns, they progressed, via four 0.303s and two 20mm cannon, to four 20mm guns plus 1000lb of bombs or rockets. The final postwar Mk 24 Spitfire represented an almost total redesign by comparison with the Mk I; yet it was unmistakably related. As an interceptor, the 355mph, Merlin-engined Mk I shared victory in the Battle of Britain with the Hurricane. Subsequently, it superseded the 'Hurri' in almost every theater of war, from Malta to Burma, although it never appealed greatly to the Russians. When the Mk V was outclassed by the German Fw 190, the imbalance was remedied by the Mk IX with the two-speed, two-stage supercharged Merlin 61 of 1660hp. With armament removed, Spitfires could fly fast enough to elude most enemy fighters at high or low altitude, and performed valuable reconnaissance duties throughout the war. In particular, they did much to confirm the German use of radar in the early months, and later enabled Bomber Command to assess the results of its attacks and potential targets.

The Supermarine Spitfire.

### Spruance, Vice-Admiral Raymond A, 1886–1969

Spruance was one of the most successful admirals in the Pacific War. As Nimitz's Chief of Staff at Midway he took over the direction of the battle when Fletcher's *Yorktown* was put out of action and inflicted a severe defeat on the Japanese Navy. After this he played a major part in the planning and directing of operations in the Central Pacific.

At the outbreak of the war Spruance was in command of a cruiser division at Midway Island. In June 1942 he was sent as commander of Task Force 16 to stop the Japanese invasion of Midway. As a result of brilliant timing Spruance's bombers put ten Japanese ships out of action – they lost four aircraft carriers. Admiral Nimitz, Commander-in-Chief of the Pacific Fleet, made him his Chief of Staff and Spruance helped to plan many campaigns. In August 1943 he assumed command of the 5th Fleet. In November 1943 Spruance commanded the bombardment of Tarawa in the Gilbert Islands and although the US suffered terrible losses, was successful. Two months later Spruance led the successful leapfrogging campaign to take Kwajalein, in the Marshalls. On 17 February 1944 he led the attack on Truk in the Carolines while Admiral Kelly Turner attacked Eniwetok.

He developed the use of the fleet train which kept carrier forces in operation for several months. He sent Mitscher to attack in the Marianas and took tactical command of the three-pronged attack on the Palau Islands, and on Yap Island and the Ulithi atoll in the Carolines. All these operations were accomplished successfully with few losses. Spruance directed operations at the Battle of the Philippine Sea and was criticized for not ordering his planes to follow up the attack on Admiral Ozawa's carriers. He then directed the assault on Iwo Jima and was planning attacks on the coast of Japan when the surrender was announced.

---

### Stalingrad, Battle of, 1942–43

General Paulus had instructions from Hitler to take Stalingrad, but it was unclear whether this was a covering operation for General Kleist's offensive in the Caucasus or an important operation in its own right. Hitler changed his mind: first, diverting the Fourth Panzer Army away from Paulus's advance and then ordering it to turn around and attack Stalingrad from the south. These maneuvers delayed Paulus's army by a few weeks.

Paulus's first attack was launched on 19 August 1942 and within a few days he had broken through the northern suburbs and reached the Volga. The Fourth Panzer Army could not link up with the main attack but by 12 September the Russians had been forced within a perimeter of 30 miles. By 13 October the Fourth Panzer Army reached the Volga in the

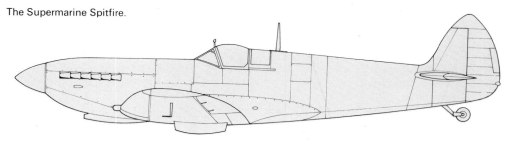

south but the Soviet Guards Division arrived and blocked further progress. Stalin was most disappointed at his troops' failure to hold the Germans or to launch a successful counter-attack with General Moskalenko's army. From September onwards Generals Zhukov, Vasil-ievsky and Stalin planned a massive counter attack from north of the Don. The Sixth Army had been ordered to bombard Stalingrad but if anything, the Russians under Chuikov found it easier to defend the rubble. On 19 November the Russian counterattack was launched from the north by the newly-formed Southwest Front under General Vatutin, whose attack con-centrated on Serafimovich, Dumitrescu's Rum-anian army base. Delayed by fog, Yeremenko's Stalingrad Front attacked the day after from the south while General Rokossovsky's Don Front was involved in a holding operation. Stalin and Zhukov directed these operations from Mos-cow and had direct communications with frontline commanders. On 23 November Yeremenko's and Vatutin's armies joined up, trapping 20 German and two Rumanian divis-ions. General Weichs's army had withdrawn in time. Hitler had refused to allow Paulus to with-draw after Goering had extravagantly prom-ised to supply the army with 500 tons of fuel and food per day. The Soviet generals under-estimated the number of troops trapped and did not at first use sufficient force to break through the defenses. In December Rokossovsky re-newed the attack of the Don Front and drove the Germans back another 20 miles towards the Volga. Weichs urged Paulus to break out but the latter refused to disobey Hitler. Manstein was then selected to launch an operation to relieve the Sixth Army with an attack on Yeremenko's line in the south. By 23 December Manstein's Group Hoth and Operational Group Hollidt were within 25 miles of Paulus. At this point they were checked by the newly arrived 2GA and 7th Tank Corps. On 25 De-cember the Russians started an artillery and Katyusha rocket barrage to the northeast of the Kessel, killing 1300 Germans. Stalin handed over Yeremenko's divisions outside Stalingrad to Rokossovsky and gave him sole charge of operations. Rokossovsky continued the artil-

Soviet gun crew fires at the enemy during the defense of Stalingrad in December 1942.

lery barrage and broke through the German lines. Once the Pitomnik airstrip had fallen (on 16 January) there was little hope and Paulus surrendered to General Shumilov. More than 94,000 Germans surrendered with him but at least 147,000 had died within the city and a further 100,000 died outside. Two Rumanian, one Italian and one Hungarian army were de-stroyed.

This battle was a turning point in the war on the Eastern Front. Paulus's Sixth Army was the first German army to surrender. After this the Germans had to retreat. The struggle at Stalin-grad did hold the Red Army up and gave Kleist's army a chance to escape from the Caucasus. Stalingrad showed what the Red Army could achieve when operations were properly planned.

---

### Stalin, Joseph, 1879–1953

Stalin was dictator of the USSR and Commander-in-Chief of its Armed Forces. Im-mediately before the German invasion of the USSR Stalin had pursued a policy which gave the Red Army time to reorganize. Earlier Stalin had greatly weakened his Army by purging its ranks. He had control of army appointments but he had neglected equipment: Russian tanks and aircraft were greatly inferior to the Ger-mans (until the appearance of the T-34 in De-cember 1941). In order to buy time Stalin made a pact with Hitler in 1939, which completely reversed his policy of encouraging communist parties in Eastern Europe. The Hitler-Stalin Pact agreed on the partition of Poland and in Sep-tember 1939 the Red Army marched into eastern Poland. Stalin's attack on Finland in November 1939 also provoked much criticism from the Western powers.

In June 1941 Hitler's army swept over the USSR's frontiers. Stalin had insisted on station-ing his divisions along the USSR's western bor-der, where they had no defense lines and the local divisions were taken unawares. The first six months of war probably cost Stalin more than 3.5 million in casualties and prisoners. The war could have been lost in those months had it not been for the fact that there was enough industrial machinery and plants beyond the Urals to build the tanks and aircraft needed to

The attack on Stalingrad gave the German Sixth Army most of the city, but the Russians held and counter-attacked. It was the turning point of the war.

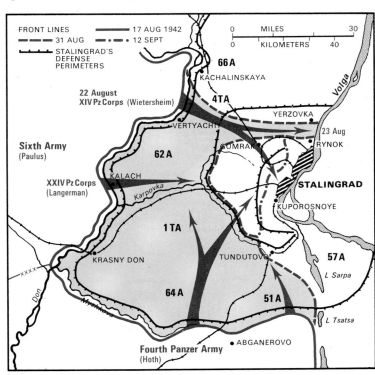

defeat the Germans. It was only in December that the German offensive stopped short of Moscow and Stalin's scorched-earth policy began to pay off. Stalin remained in Moscow throughout the first winter and directed General Zhukov's counterattack. Zhukov and Shtemenko later said 'Stalin did not decide . . . important military questions personally, for he well understood the necessity for collective work in these complicated questions'; he allowed his generals plenty of tactical and sometimes strategic freedom. However, generals were often unwilling to report their mistakes and Stalin sometimes had a completely false impression of the situation. However the success of Zhukov's counterattack made Stalin overconfident and he overreached himself in May 1942, when the Red Army tried to re-enter the Ukraine and was beaten back. The operation to relieve Stalingrad at the end of 1942 was directed by Stalin with the close collaboration of Zhukov and General Vasilievsky. In 1944 the Red Army swept over the Ukraine, Belorussia and the Baltic States and cleared the Germans out of the USSR in a brilliant operation for which Stalin takes much of the credit.

After the German invasion, the USSR became Allies of Great Britain and later of the USA. Stalin showed great skill in his handling of President Roosevelt and Churchill. Stalin pressed demands for a second front as soon as possible from 1941 onwards, he implied that had it not been for France and Britain's failure to hold Western Europe Hitler would not have been successful in the USSR. His constant demands for a second front made relations among the Allies somewhat tense. Churchill and Roosevelt felt there was always the possibility that the USSR would make a separate peace with Germany. At the Teheran Conference (November–December 1943) Stalin promised his support for Operation Overlord and the war against Japan. As the Red Army swept over Eastern Europe it became clear that Stalin intended to interfere in local politics. In Poland he encouraged the Lublin committee (a Communist group) to declare itself the provisional government and recognized it before attending the Yalta Conference which was to discuss the issue. At Yalta he agreed that the Lublin government would have to expand its base of support and hold free elections but this was not carried out. At the Potsdam Conference the question was again raised and Churchill and Roosevelt also wanted free elections in Hungary, Rumania and Yugoslavia but Stalin refused. At the end of the war the USSR had established puppet regimes in Eastern Europe and the Western Powers had to accept them.

Stalin was a great war leader and managed to get large concessions out of his Allies. Roosevelt felt that he knew how to deal with Stalin, but Stalin outmaneuvered him at the diplomatic conferences. Under Stalin's leadership, the USSR emerged as the most powerful military nation, alongside the USA.

## Stalin Line

In the 1930s Marshal Tukhachevski had developed the idea of building a system of fortifications on the lines of the Maginot Line in France. This was in accord with US strategy of the time, which led him to think in terms of defensive warfare as opposed to a more advanced school of thought in Britain, which believed in highly mobile tank offensives. Tukha-

chevski paid frequent visits to France and the French gave him much advice and aid in the building of the Line. It was a combination of concrete field works, natural obstacles, tank traps, minefields, etc. It used trees, lakes and marshes as cleverly as possible but it was by no means a continuous line. Around main cities Pskov, Minsk, Korosten and Odessa fortifications were extensive but in between there were many gaps. After the occupation of Poland, Bessarabia and the Baltic States, the Stalin Line was no longer the main line of defense. Soviet troops were moved up to the frontiers of these countries and dispersed.

## Stangl, Franz

Commandant of the Treblinka concentration camp near Warsaw, Stangl was responsible for the extermination of 700,000 people. The figure represented the total number of people sent to the camp, of whom only 40 survived when the camp was demolished. The Nazi authorities thought it wise to destroy the evidence of Treblinka by demolishing the camp, and at the same time they thought first to remove possible witnesses, SS guards included, by sending them to fight the partisans in Yugoslavia. Stangl survived this and returned to his family in Austria in 1945. He was arrested by the Americans who were unaware of his connection with Treblinka and was sent to be tried by the Austrian courts. He escaped from a working party in Austria and disappeared to South America.

## Stargrad Attack
see East Germany, Liberation of, 1945

## Stark, Admiral Harold, 1880–1972

In 1939 President Roosevelt made Stark US Chief of Naval Operations and Stark took part in secret discussions with Britain about the war. He extended US naval patrols to protect US shipping from German submarines. At the end of 1941 he put the Navy on a war footing but he failed to give Admiral Kimmel at Pearl Harbor sufficient warning. Stark was one of the principal advocates of the Hitler-first strategy and in March 1942 Stark was sent to London as Commander of US naval forces in European waters. This was mainly an administrative post and throughout the war Stark continued to be involved in planning at the various Allied conferences.

## Stauffenberg, Colonel Count Claus von, 1907–1944

Son of a South German family of Catholic aristocrats, Stauffenberg – known as the 'Bamberger Reiter' in his prewar cavalry regiment for his resemblance to the handsome sculpture of that name – was badly wounded in the Western Desert and transferred in 1942 to a staff appointment with the Home Army in Berlin. He was soon drawn into the circle of military conspirators against Hitler but also quickly formed the opinion that they lacked resolution. Thus it was that he took it upon himself, as someone with access to Hitler's conferences but so disabled as to escape body search, to smuggle a bomb into the Führer's conference room, a feat he achieved on 20 July 1944. Unfortunately,

though he made good his escape from the Rastenburg headquarters, the Berlin conspirators failed to act with resolution during his return flight to the city and, by the time he had arrived, had lost irretrievable time. By evening the coup had foundered and Stauffenberg, with others, was shot in the courtyard of the War Ministry by Fromm, who hoped thereby to remove the evidence of his own complicity. Stauffenberg's courage and purity of character have made his name one of the best known and respected in modern German history.

## Sten Gun

This British submachine gun became known as the epitome of cheap and ugly weapons. It was developed by two men called Sheppard and Turpin at the Royal Small Arms Factory, Enfield, and thus took its name from a combination of the initials of the men and the location.

In 1940 Britain needed submachine guns desperately and the only source of supply was the USA from whence Thompson guns were bought in small quantities and at a high price. Numerous designs had been assessed and it was eventually decided to manufacture a copy of the German Bergmann MP28 as the 'Lanchester', but while this weapon was being evaluated two designers appeared with their idea of a submachine gun. It was tried, approved, and put into production forthwith, and before the war ended over four million had been made. It was never a popular weapon with the troops. In the first place, to a generation brought up on weapons built by the traditional gunmaking methods, it looked terrible – slab-sided, welded together, roughly finished. In the second place, it soon gathered a reputation for being unsafe due to its habit of firing when dropped or otherwise severely mishandled – though this defect was soon cured. Thirdly, it had a habit of jamming at inopportune moments due to the poor design of magazine copied from the German MP38. But for all that, it was a war-winning weapon, and was used to equip partisans and resistance workers all over Europe, some of whom used them as a pattern to produce their own models.

There were several models of the Sten gun, but all used the same basic mechanism, a massive bolt inside a tubular casing with the barrel fixed to the front and the magazine feeding from the left side where it could be supported on the firer's forearm. The Mark 1 had a wooden filling in the metal butt, a wooden fore-end and a folding hand grip. These luxuries were soon discarded with the advent of the Mark 2, the most common model. This used a simple metal strut and welded plate for a butt; the barrel was retained by a perforated screw-on sleeve which also acted as the hand grip; and the whole weapon could be easily and rapidly dismantled into its component parts for concealment or carriage, a distinct advantage for partisans and underground fighters. A Mark 2S was also made, fitted with a large Maxim-pattern silencer; this was extensively used by Commandos and similar raiding parties. The Mark 3 reverted to the Mark 1 pattern having a fixed barrel surrounded by a sheet-metal jacket. The Mark 4 was a short pattern intended for use by airborne troops but was not adopted. Finally, the Mark 5 was the 'luxury' model which was put into production after the early desperate needs had been satisfied; it had a wooden stock based on that of the Lee-Enfield rifle and also had the end of the barrel designed to accept the standard bayonet. A wooden pistol grip was fitted and the general finish was much better. But for all the cosmetic treatment it was still the same old Sten and had the same old vices. There was also a Mark 6, which was the silenced version of the Mark 5. The Sten remained in service with the British Army until the 1960s and several hundred thousand are still scattered about the world.

## Stettinius, Edward, 1900–1949

Stettinius was a US industrialist and he succeeded Hull as Secretary of State. President Roosevelt brought him into his government in January 1941 as director of the Office of Production Management. From October 1941 until September 1943 Stettinius acted as special assistant to Roosevelt and his task was to look after war production, see that raw materials were not wasted and generally manage a war economy. In 1943 he became Under-Secretary of State and played a major part in solving Anglo-American differences in London (April 1944) and in organizing the Dumbarton Oaks Conference. In November 1944 Roosevelt made him Secretary of State and his chief adviser at Yalta. He attended the San Francisco Conference where he was chairman of the US delegation, but in July 1945 he resigned to become the first US delegate to the UN. Stettinius was an influential man who worked hard to insure that the UN would be a success after the war.

## Stilwell, General Joseph, 1883–1946

Stilwell, and American General, spent most of the World War II as Chiang Kai-shek's Chief of Staff in China. He was a vitriolic and argumentative man often at odds with Generals Wavell, Slim and Wingate, men with whom he was supposed to co-operate in Burma. He also had bitter arguments with Brigadier General Chennault, commander of the 14th USAAF in China. These arguments earned him the nickname 'Vinegar' Joe.

Before the war Stilwell acted as military attache at the US Embassy at Peking from 1932–1939. He went back to the USA but returned to China when war broke out and on 10 March 1942 Stilwell was made Chiang Kai-shek's Chief of Staff. He was sent to Burma with the Chinese 5th and 6th armies (equivalent to two western divisions) but he could do little to prevent the Japanese from gaining control of the Burma Road. He rescued the encircled Chinese garrison at Toungoo and then retreated to India, traveling on foot.

'Vinegar Joe' Stilwell.

Bombs are loaded on a Stirling.

With the establishment of the new Southeast Asia Command in August 1943, Stilwell was appointed Deputy Supreme Allied Commander under Vice-Admiral Mountbatten. He built up his forces for an offensive in Northern Burma and on 21 December he assumed direct control of operations to capture Myitkyina. The city did not fall until August 1944 and Stilwell blamed the British 'Long Range Penetration Groups' for not obeying his orders promptly enough. When Slim said the men were exhausted and should be withdrawn, he would not agree until the men had undergone a medical examination. During 1944 the Japanese put into operation Ichi-Go and overran US air bases in Eastern China, so the Joint Chiefs of Staff wanted Stilwell to be Commander of all Chinese forces. Chiang Kai-shek blamed Stilwell for the Japanese success and pressed the Americans to recall him. In October 1944 Stilwell returned to the USA. His last active command occurred when he replaced General Buckner in the last stages of the conquest of Okinawa in June 1945.

Although Chiang Kai-shek had Stilwell dismissed, he recognized Stilwell's contribution to the Burma Road campaign by renaming part of the Burma Road the Stilwell Road.

## Stimson, Henry L, 1867–1950

In July 1940 President Roosevelt called Stimson back into the government at the age of 72 as Secretary of War. Stimson was one of the two Republicans in Roosevelt's war cabinet, having served President Hoover as Secretary of State, 1929–33. His task was to oversee mobilization, training and military operations. His first important step was to introduce the first compulsory service laws in peacetime. He also established the autonomy of the US Air Corps. He was the first advocate of Lend-Lease and did his utmost to increase aid to Great Britain. He wanted an invasion of France as soon as possible but accepted Churchill's argument for a postponement at talks in July 1943. Stimson took part in all the major Allied conferences.

Another of his important responsibilities was the organization of scientific research and he kept the President informed of progress on the Manhattan Project. In 1945 he recommended the use of the atomic bomb.

## Stirling, Colonel David, 1915–

A Scots Guards officer, Stirling joined the commandos in 1940 and in 1941 in the Western Desert, raised his own force for raiding behind the Axis lines which became known as the Special Air Service. Operating with the Long Range Desert Group, it inflicted much material destruction and some loss of life on the enemy, particularly at desert airfields. After his capture in 1943 the SAS continued to use the methods of warfare the 'Phantom Major' had pioneered.

## Stirling, Short

This British heavy bomber was operational from February 1941 to September 1944. Designed from the start as a four-engined bomber, to Specification B.12/36, the Stirling reflects the farsightedness of RAF policymakers in the mid-thirties. However, while recognizing the importance of massive attack being able to carry up to seven tons of bombs, they imposed strange limitations. Insisting that the aircraft should be small enough to go into standard RAF hangars, they compelled the designers to restrict wing span to 99ft 1in. This enforced the use of a low aspect ratio, and the aircraft had a service ceiling of only 17,000ft, which proved a great handicap operationally. The bomb-bay was divided into sections, giving insufficient room for bombs of more than 4000lb weight. And the tall, complex undercarriage not only gave a steep ground angle but proved unreliable in service. Despite its shortcomings, the Stirling often operated in daylight, without fighter escort. Its range was sufficient to reach Berlin, Pilsen in Czechoslovakia and even northern Italy by night. It was used mainly against less heavily defended targets from mid-1943, and for the next year spent many nights minelaying and using ECM devices to jam enemy radars in support of the main force of Lancasters and Halifaxes. More than 1750 Mk 1 and Mk III Stirling bombers were built, with 1595/1650hp Bristol Hercules engines. They were followed by 450 Mk IVs, which gave good service in 1944–45 as glider tugs and transports, and by the Mk V, built from the outset as a transport.

## Stopford, General Sir Montagu, 1892–1971

Stopford's 33rd Indian Corps raised the siege of Kohima in Assam and opened the road to Imphal. The Corps then advanced through Central Burma to take Mandalay. In November 1943 Stopford went to India to take command of the 33rd Corps. When the Japanese launched their offensive to capture Kohima and Imphal, Stopford's troops crossed India with speed to reach the battlefront. Stopford was given command of the Dimapur-Kohima area on 2 April 1944. The British garrison at Kohima was 1500 strong and four to one but it held out until the 33rd Corps broke the roadblock into the town and relieved the garrison. Stopford's troops then marched along the road to Imphal and met up with Scoones's 4th Corps. His 33rd Corps then cut its way across the Burmese mountains to Shwebo and attacked Mandalay from the north in March 1945, shortly after the fall of Meiktila. His troops then followed the Irrawaddy River to take the Yenangyaung oilfields.

## *Strasbourg*

This French battlecruiser was a sister of the *Dunkerque* and was authorized in 1934, as soon as it was known that the Italians were to go ahead with the *Littorio* Class. She escaped from Mers-el-Kebir without damage by skillful handling and with the aid of covering fire from the Santon fortress. She reached Toulon on 4 July 1940 where she remained until 27 November 1942. On that day German assault troops tried to storm the dockyard and seize the French Fleet, but true to his promise to his Allies, Admiral Darlan's fleet immediately scuttled itself.

An Italian salvage team under Ing Generale Giannelli managed to raise the *Strasbourg* by July 1943, but it was little more than a useless hulk that was recovered. After a period of nominal Italian ownership the hulk was ceded back to the French in 1944, but was sunk once more in an Allied bombing raid on Toulon on 18 August 1944.

## Strategic Bombing Offensive against Germany, 1941–45

During the interwar years the RAF had maintained its independence from the Army and the Navy by using the argument that the strategic bombing of specific targets was a powerful offensive weapon. Although there had been much talk of building up Bomber Command, when World War II broke out there were only 33 operational bomber squadrons and half of them were obsolescent. British bombers were used on daylight raids but by fall 1940 it was decided to send them out on night-time raids because losses during the day were very high. In January 1941 Bomber Command decided to attack Germany's synthetic oil supplies, but as reports came back it was found that only 20 percent of these bombers reached within a five-mile radius of their target. Bomber Command began to advocate area-bombing (for example, raids on semi-precise targets, such as railways) in order to wear down German morale. Lord Cherwell supported this argument and calculated that it would take fifteen months to make one-third of the German population homeless. This was challenged by many, including Sir Henry Tizard, who wanted Bomber Command to step up attacks on U-Boats and

bases. Air Marshal Harris decided that the only way to cut losses was to increase the concentration of bombers and '1000 bomber' raids were made on Cologne, Essen and Bremen in May and June 1942. These were very successful, in that there was only a 3–5 percent loss rate and civilian morale was badly damaged by the extensive damage to the cities. There were also frequent raids on the Krupp works at Essen.

In 1942 the bombers got new navigational aids – Gee (March), Oboe (December) and $H_2S$ in January 1943. The Pathfinders force was also set up in August 1942 to mark out targets for the bombers. Although bombers were finding it easier to pick out their targets they were under increasing pressure from the Luftwaffe, whose fighters were now equipped to fight at night. The Americans also began to organize raids on Germany but their pilots were trained for daylight precision bombing and there was little co-ordination of bombing strategies. At the Casablanca (January 1943) and Washington (May 1943) Conferences it was decided that strategic bombing should be used to prepare the way for the land invasion and that a combined bombing offensive, Pointblank, should be aimed at knocking out the Luftwaffe and German industry.

From March to July 1943 Bomber Command undertook 43 major raids in the Battle of the Ruhr. There was very little precise bombing but the most spectacular raid was the breaching of the Möhne and Eder dams by the 'Dambuster' 617 Squadron in May 1943. From July to November 1943 there were 17,000 bombing sorties in the Battle of Hamburg in which over 42,000 people are thought to have been killed. The Americans threw their full weight into the bombing offensive after their day-time losses were reduced when the P–51 Mustang became operational and drove the German fighters from the skies. At the end of 1943 there were raids on Mannheim, Frankfurt, Hannover and Kassel. There were also 123 raids on Berlin which was out of the range of Oboe and there were very heavy bomber losses. Although 200,000 tons of bombs were dropped in 1943, these raids did not produce the desired results. German morale stiffened under the bombing raids and German industry was successfully re-

organized so that productivity only dropped by 9 percent and armaments' production rose.

In 1944 the bombing offensive was diverted from the area bombing of Germany to helping Overlord, by disrupting the German transport network in France. These raids gave Bomber Command a chance to reconsider its strategy against Germany and led it to decide in favor of attacking Germany's war economy. By April 1944 the Luftwaffe no longer had control of the air, thanks to the Mustang fighter and the bombing of oil plants. Both the British and the 8th USAAF stepped up their raids on oil plants as far afield as Rumania, where the Ploesti oilfields were hit in April 1944. The British distribution of bombing offensives in 1944 was 53 percent on towns, 14 percent on oil plants and 15 percent on the transport network. In the early months of 1945 the bombing campaign was stepped up so that Berlin was under daily attack. In February Dresden was attacked and 1600 acres of the town were devastated and more than 40,000 civilians were killed (some say the total was as high as 100,000). By March 1945 Speer no longer thought in terms of rebuilding damaged industrial plants or replacing the transport network; the German war economy could no longer function.

The bombing offensive did not bring about the immediate collapse of either the German army or the civilian morale, despite the fact that about 593,000 people had died.

## Strategic Bombing Offensive against Japan, 1944–45

The USAAF began to bomb Japan using B-29s from bases in China and India but these raids did not do much damage and stopped early in 1945. In October 1944 bases in the Marianas were ready and the B-29s were sent on daytime, precision bombing raids on the industrial towns in Japan. The early results were disappointing and General Lemay decided to switch to night-time low altitude attacks, dropping incendiary

The ruins of Tokyo after the fire raids of 1944–45. On one night more than 190,000 bombs were dropped on Tokyo itself.

bombs. Until the end of the war 65 major Japanese cities were bombed and a total of 153,887 tons of bombs were dropped. The most spectacular raid was on the night of 9–10 March when 279 B-29s swept over Tokyo during a gale, and dropped 190,000 incendiary bombs. Forty percent of the capital was burned out, seventeen square miles were destroyed and 72,000 people were killed.

The effect of the bombing campaign was the breakdown of an already failing war economy. There were extreme food shortages and the daily ration was fixed at 1500 calories; the railway system broke down and there were frequent power cuts. Civilian morale was badly shaken and the large-scale evacuation of towns began, so that some 8,500,000 people fled to the countryside. Japanese civilian casualties during the six months of bombing were twice as high as the total number of casualties suffered by their armed forces in three and a half years of intensive fighting.

## Streicher, Julius, 1885–1946

Streicher was the self-styled 'Jew-baiter Number One'. He was the editor and proprietor of *Der Stürmer*, the principal anti-semitic paper in Germany. He promoted the Nuremberg decrees against the Jews in 1935. Until 1940 he was Gauleiter of Franconia but he was forced to retire when a Nazi commission found him guilty of misappropriating confiscated Jewish property. Hitler allowed him to live out the war on his farm and he was tried at Nuremberg, found guilty and hanged.

## Stuart Tank

This was the British name for the US light tanks of the M2, M3 and M5 series. They were the first US tanks to see combat being used by the British 8th Army at Sidi Rezegh in November 1941 and by US forces in the Philippines in 1941/42. More notably, they were the only prewar design of light tank to see the war through; every other design was found to be useless in combat.

The design of the M2 tank dated back to 1933 when, under the orders of General MacArthur, the US Cavalry took over the development of armored vehicles. MacArthur demanded a tank which would function in the traditional cavalry role, that of fast raiding into and behind enemy lines, together with rapid support for infantry, and for these purposes he demanded a light, fast tank in which speed and firepower was more important than armor protection. From this request came the T2 tank, with a .50 machine gun in its turret and a .30 machine gun in the hull, driven by a converted airplane engine of 250hp and weighing about 6.5 tons. Since the National Defense Act of 1920 laid down that only infantry could have 'tanks', the cavalry vehicles were called 'Combat Cars' though they looked remarkably like tanks.

This design, which had been developed at the Rock Island Arsenal, was gradually improved throughout the 1930s, small numbers being built as financing was available, until in the spring of 1939 the M2A4 was designed. This had a 37mm gun in its rotating turret and the armor thickness had been increased to 25mm; two machine guns were mounted in sponsons at the sides of the hull and a third in the turret alongside the 37mm gun; and a new syncromesh gearbox installed. This might well have followed the same course as its predecessors and perhaps only a dozen might have been built, but for the fact that in September Germany invaded Poland and the USA suddenly found some money with which to equip its army. The M2A4 tank went into production in April 1940; a total of 375 were eventually built.

After the lightning campaign in France in 1940 the US Ordnance Department set about redesigning the M2A4 in the light of reports from the battle area. The armor was increased to 37mm thickness which, bringing the weight up to over 13 tons, necessitated a lengthened suspension and track. Other modifications were made so that it eventually became a completely new vehicle – on 5 July 1940 this was standardized as the Light Tank M3, the first model passing from the production line in March 1941.

With the approach of war and the hastening of the US armament program, many automobile manufacturers were brought into the tank production field bringing with them considerable expertise in mass-production and utilization of components which was new to the armored vehicle world. One such company, Cadillac Division of General Motors, suggested mounting two Cadillac engines and a Hydromatic transmission in the M3 tank to compensate for the shortage of Continental engines. In October 1941 the company converted a tank and drove it 500 miles to a proving ground to demonstrate it. The trip alone was sufficient to prove the soundness of the idea, and the M3, fitted with the Cadillac engines and transmission, extra thickness of armor and some other changes, was standardized in November 1941 as the Light Tank M5.

It can be seen from the foregoing that all three tanks were closely related, which is why they were called 'Stuart' in British service without any distinction being made. All had a crew of four, a driver, assistant driver/hull gunner, turret gunner and commander; all mounted a 37mm gun as their principal armament; all had a narrow, boxy hull and a top speed of about 35mph.

Although designated 'light tanks' they were, in fact, rather heavier than most of that class and closely approximated in speed, armament and protection the British 'cruiser' class, which is why the British adopted them in the Western Desert. They could be quickly and cheaply built,

General Student, inspecting paratroopers.

easily maintained, and were extremely reliable and nimble vehicles, features which endeared them to their crews. While they were outclassed as primary combat tanks by the middle of the war, they were still of great value as training vehicles and they remained in frontline service until the end of the war, in armored reconnaissance regiments in Europe and as fighting tanks in the Pacific, where their light weight was of value in amphibious operations.

## Student, General Kurt, 1890–1978

A World War I pilot, Student joined the Luftwaffe at its formation and was commissioned to raise a force of parachute troops. Using both parachutes and gliders his force achieved some remarkable successes in Belgium and Holland during the 1940 campaign but its landings in Crete the following year, though leading to the capture of the island, were judged too costly by Hitler for him to permit a repetition. The *Fallschirmjäger*, which eventually grew to ten divisions, became, therefore, a ground force of an elite character, much respected by its enemies. Student, by happenstance, was commanding in Holland at the time of the Arnhem operation in September 1944 and it was his particular understanding of airborne operations, assisted by a lucky capture of crucial documents, which did much to thwart the enterprise. For his success he was promoted to command Army Group G in the area, which he did to the end of the war.

## Stuka
see Junkers Ju 87

## Stumpff, General Hans-Jürgen,

This German Air Force officer commanded Luftflotte V based in Oslo from the Spring of 1940 until January 1944. Following a disastrous operation against the north of Britain on 15 August 1940 during the Battle of Britain, Luftflotte V was never again committed to attack that area.

## Sturmgeschütz (Assault Guns)

While fully alive to the mobile warfare theories of the Panzers, the German Army was sufficiently realistic to know that this was not the total answer to all problems, and in view of their experiences in World War I they demanded some mobile form of artillery which could accompany the infantry and destroy strong points and other obstacles by direct fire, notably during the period in a battle when the conventional supporting artillery was otherwise engaged or could not be brought into action due to moving up. From this request the Assault Gun came into being, light or medium artillery pieces mounted on tracked chassis from current production tanks. The nomenclature adopted was a blend of the parent tank and the gun which was mounted; thus, the first to appear (in 1940) was the Sturmgeschütz III mit 7.5cm Kanone, implying a modified PzKpfw III chassis with a 75mm gun. As with subsequent designs (which were all more or less modifications or improvements on this original) the tank hull was built up into a fixed superstructure and the gun was mounted in the front plate. This vehicle, and its two successors, mounted a short-barreled 75mm gun which was adequate for dealing with 'soft' obstacles, but experience soon showed that it would be an advantage to have a gun capable of dealing with tanks. In early 1942 the StuG III 7.5cm L/43 appeared, mounting the long-barreled gun normally found on tanks; indeed, it was little more than a tank with a fixed gun instead of a turret. This had almost as good a performance as a tank, given its limitations of field of fire, and was a good deal cheaper to make, and for this reason the manufacture of assault guns increased until more were being made than tanks.

While the 7.5cm high velocity gun could cope with most problems, there was still a need for a heavier weight of shell, and a number of Sturmgeschütz were built mounting 105mm howitzers. The first of these was no more than the standard 10.5cm le FH18 field howitzer minus its wheels bolted down into an open-topped superstructure on a PzKpfw III chassis, but few of these were built before a 'proper' design, with roofed-in superstructure, was produced. The heaviest gun to be mounted was the 150mm Infantry Howitzer Model 33 placed on PzKpfw IV chassis, known as the 'Grizzly Bear' (Brummbar) of which over 300 were built.

The heaviest assault weapon was the 'Sturm Tiger' a highly modified Tiger tank chassis carrying a 38cm short-barreled rocket projector which could be breech-loaded from inside the armored superstructure. Twelve rockets could be carried inside the vehicle, and it was intended for close-range bombardment of strong fortifications. Only ten were made in 1944; it weighed 68 tons and could fire the 760lb rocket to a range of 6000 yards.

---

## Sturmgewehr

Literally meaning 'Assault Rifle', this German development in the small arms field had considerable influence on postwar designs. During the early 1930s a number of German officers began to question the conventional design of infantry rifle. In general, such rifles dated from the turn of the century and had been designed in response to demands which no longer appeared valid. They were built to fire a powerful cartridge capable of sending a bullet up to two miles–with reasonable accuracy up to at least one mile. Analysis of actions in World War I indicated that the infantry soldier rarely fired his rifle at ranges greater than about 400 yards, and that it was exceptional for a soldier to be able to recognize or even aim at a target at greater ranges in the confusion of battle. In such a case there was a good argument for reducing the size and power of the cartridge, abandoning the useless mile-plus capability and providing just sufficient power and accuracy to deal with targets up to about 750 yards away. With such a reduced cartridge it would be possible to reduce the size of the weapon and, since they would weigh less, the soldier could carry more ammunition. (There seems to have been no chance of the soldier being allowed to carry the same amount of cartridges and thus reduce his load.)

A short cartridge with a 7mm bullet was developed successfully, but with war approaching it was felt that a complete change of caliber would prejudice the chance of having the idea accepted, and the cartridge was redesigned based on the standard 7.92mm service caliber, the bullet being slightly shorter than normal. In 1940 development of a suitable weapon, known as the Maschinen Karabiner 42 (MKb42) was begun by the firms of Walther and Haenel, both of which produced weapons suitable enough to be tried in combat on the Russian front in 1942–3. With a few modifications the MKb42 as made by Haenel was selected for production and first deliveries were made in June 1943.

The prototype rifles had been well-received on the Russian Front and the Army was clamoring for them, but the development now ran into a snag; Hitler disapproved of the weapon since, basing his opinion on his World War I service, he considered it to have insufficient range. In vain did the proposers try and argue that this was practically their thesis; but the answer was still no, clinched by the argument that there were tens of millions of the normal 7.92mm cartridges in stock. The proposers now faced a dilemma since they had already tooled up and were actually producing the weapon, though not in the quantities they would have liked. So they resorted to subterfuge; the weapon continued in production but was re-christened the Machine Pistol 43, and the production figures were shown in the monthly returns under the 'Machine Pistol' (ie., submachine gun) heading, which concealed the weapon's existence and, into the bargain, pleased Hitler by artificially boosting the submachine gun production figures.

Eventually the cat leapt out of the bag at a conference of infantry commanders from the Russian front; when Hitler asked what they needed, they all asked for more of the 'new rifles'. After a monumental uproar, Hitler was finally convinced of the weapon's utility, solemnly re-named it the 'Assault Rifle' and gave it his blessing; but this was late in 1943 and although the production was expanded, there were never sufficient weapons to meet demand.

The StuG 43 (as it was now known) was a gas-operated rifle which could also be fired in the automatic mode as a light machine gun at 500rpm. It was 37in long and weighed 11lb, a creditable bulk for such a useful weapon. Much of it was made from stamped metal and plastics, foreshadowing the postwar tendency towards designs aimed firstly at production facility and secondly at durability. Approximately 80,000 rifles were made, and after the war they were retained in service by the East German Border Police for some years.

---

## Submarine

The characteristics of submarines differed little from one navy to another. The more modern ones had diesel electric drive on the surface, diesel generators providing current for electric motors on the surface, and batteries as the power-source when submerged. Endurance on the surface varied according to the amount of fuel and the size of the submarine, but in all types, submerged endurance was only a matter of a few hours at modest speed. After that the submarine had to surface to recharge her batteries.

In all navies but the Japanese the big cruiser-submarines with medium-caliber guns and the aircraft-carrying freaks of the 1920s had been discredited, and most navies favored boats ranging from 500 to 1000 tons. The British had developed the concept of the heavy bow-salvo as a means of attacking well-defended targets from a safe range and their latest 'T' Class boats could fire 10 torpedoes forward. The standard Type VII U-Boat, by comparison, fired only four tubes forward and the US Navy's *Gato* Class fired six.

The size depended on the theater of operations. The US Navy favored a 1500-ton boat with good habitability and range for the Pacific, but without the floatplane and heavy gun-armament of Japanese submarines. The Germans, on the other hand, chose a 750-ton design

Sturmgeschütz III with its 75mm gun.

as the basis for mass-production, a choice which proved rather cramped for Atlantic operations.

The stress of anti-submarine measures by the Allies led to radical and far-reaching improvements in the design of U-Boats. In 1940 the Germans had found an air-mast in Dutch submarines, intended to improve ventilation. Ignored at first, it was adopted in 1943 as the *schnorchel* in a desperate attempt to find a way for U-Boats to charge their batteries under water. At the same time designers came up with two improved designs, one the so-called 'electro-submarine' with streamlined hull and enlarged batteries for fast-running, and the second the hydrogen-peroxide propelled Walter submarine. As with so many other experimental equipment, the German High Command was more impressed by the unproven high technology of the Walter boat, which suffered from very low endurance, and did not give sufficient emphasis to the practical and efficient 'electro-submarine' or Type XXI. The result was that no Walter boat was operational by May 1945 and only three Type XXI boats.

*Top:* A Dekabrist Class Soviet submarine.
*Above:* USS *Tinosa* returns to Pearl Harbor in 1944 after a successful patrol.

nations which led to war, particularly in the breakdown of negotiations between Japan and America: It was Sugiyama who imposed deadlines as to when negotiations must end and war begin onto Konoye and Togo. He and Nagano (Navy Chief of Staff) pushed for war throughout September-November 1941. Directing operations from Tokyo throughout the war, he was promoted to Field Marshal and resigned as Chief of Staff in February 1944 when Tojo absorbed this position in his consolidation of political and military power. Sugiyama became War Minister again under Koiso, until that cabinet resigned. He shot himself to death after the Allied occupation.

A Short Singapore flying boat.

## Sugiyama, General Hajime, 1880–1945

Sugiyama was Army Chief of Staff throughout the war until 1944, and an important advocate of war, supporting a strike south. He attended the Disarmament Conference in Geneva (1926–28); became a member of the Supreme War Council in 1935; was appointed War Minister 1937–38 during which time he oversaw the 1937 China campaign; and then became Army Chief of Staff. In the latter capacity, he played a central role in the political machi-

## Sunderland, Short

This British long-range maritime reconnaissance-attack flying-boat was operational from 1938 to 1959. Evolved from Imperial Airways' famous 'C' Class Empire flying-boat, to meet official Specification R.2/33, the prototype Sunderland flew for the first time on 16 October 1937. A total of 739 were built over the next eight and a half years, earning great distinction as the last of a series of superb flying-boats operated by the RAF. Powered by four radial piston-engines, each of 1065 to 1200hp according to Mk, the Sunderland was a large, graceful aircraft, with a crew of 13. On patrol missions it could remain airborne for 13.5 hours, cruising at 134mph. The first to make wartime headlines were two Sunderlands which landed on rough seas to pick up 34 survivors from a torpedoed ship. Belying their unaggressive appearance, aircraft of this type not only destroyed enemy submarines located visually or by radar but could also defend themselves so well, with anything up to fourteen guns, that they were nicknamed 'Flying Porcupine' by the Luftwaffe. One Sunderland, attacked by six Ju 88s, shot down one, forced another to land and drove off the rest. On another occasion, a Sunderland shot down three of eight attacking Ju 88s.

## Superfortress
see B-29 Superfortress, Boeing

## *Surcouf*

The French submarine *Surcouf* was the world's largest in 1939. She had been designed for extended commerce-raiding and carried not only a floatplane in a hangar but twin eight-inch guns. She escaped from Brest on 18 June 1940 and reached Plymouth on her electric motors only, as her diesels were dismantled for overhaul. She was one of the ships which was seized shortly afterwards, but she was recommissioned under the Free French flag on 27 August. She was sent to Halifax in February 1941 to act as an escort for convoys, but later

that year she was refitted for service in the Pacific. On 19 February 1942 she was on her way to the Panama Canal when she was rammed at night by the US freighter *Thomson Lykes*. There is no historical basis for a rumor that she was sunk by the Allies after being discovered playing a double game, refueling U-Boats in the Caribbean.

## Surigao Strait, Battle of
see Leyte Gulf, Battle of, 1944

## Sutherland, Lieutenant General Richard, 1893–1966

Sutherland was General MacArthur's Chief of Staff during the war. His arrogance antagonized many senior officers, including General Kenney. In March 1943 he presented the outlines of MacArthur's Elkton plan. He also attended all the discussions to co-ordinate war effort with the other Pacific Commands. In MacArthur's absence he took all major decisions.

## Suzuki, Admiral Kantaro, 1867–1948

A naval college graduate who had served in Korea in the 1890s and in the Russo-Japanese War and had already retired by 1927, Suzuki was an old man when war broke out. Having avoided both the army and navy cliques in his long career, he was very valuable as a compromise figure in public affairs. Thus in 1929 he became Grand Chamberlain (a position very close to the Emperor) and member of the Supreme War Council. He miraculously survived an assassination attempt in the 1936 coup in which he was a prime target as an anti-militarist. In August 1944 he was elected President of the Privy Council, being reactivated as a political figure to be used to head a peace-seeking cabinet: thus in April 1945 he became Prime Minister, engaged in a delicate game of juggling factions in order to bring the war to a close while maintaining order between the armed forces and the Emperor on the throne. He resigned on 14 August 1945 when Japan surrendered to the United States.

## Swordfish, Fairey

This British carrier-based bomber and torpedo carrier was in service between 1936–45. Though outwardly obsolete before the war began, the Swordfish was so robust and reliable, and flown with such courage and skill, that it established a wonderful wartime record against the German, Italian and Japanese fleets, and even served in the close-support role firing rockets and drop-

ping bombs. Flown by a crew of from one to four, but usually two or three, the Swordfish could reach about 139mph on a 690hp Pegasus, and carried a torpedo or up to about 2000lb of bombs or mines, depth charges or rockets. Late models had radar between the landing gear. In 1940 they sank many warships at Taranto; in 1941 they sank more at Cape Matapan and crippled the *Bismarck*; in 1942 they almost suicidally made the only possible close attacks on the German fleet making its 'Channel dash'; and by 1943 it had helped RN submarines virtually eliminate Axis sea power from the Mediterranean. Altogether 2391 were built, and they outlasted the Albacore, intended as their replacement.

## *Sydney*

Three cruisers of the *Amphion* Class were ordered for the Royal Navy under the 1931–32 Programs, to an improved *Leander* design. The *Phaeton* was transferred on completion to the Australian Navy and became HMAS *Sydney*, while the *Apollo* became the *Hobart* in 1938 and the *Amphion* became the *Perth* a year later.

The *Sydney* distinguished herself by sinking the Italian six-inch gunned cruiser *Bartolomeo Colleoni* off Crete in July 1940, but she also suffered the ignominy of being the only regular warship to be sunk by an armed merchant cruiser. She was disabled by gunfire and torpedoed by the German auxiliary cruiser *Kormoran* in the southwestern Pacific on 19 November 1941. She was last seen on fire and drifting away from the sinking *Kormoran*, and no crew members were found apart from one dead seaman some months later.

## Syria, British Occupation of, 1941

Syria and the Lebanon, both French mandated territories, remained under the control of the Vichy government following the capitulation of 1940. Their strategic situation made them highly desirable both to the British and the Germans and when, in the spring of 1941, it became clear to the British that the Germans were actively suborning the neutrality of French officers there, they decided to forestall a coup. On 8 June British and Free French troops entered the country from Palestine and Iraq, which the British had also just occupied. At first they met no resistance, until they were obliged to fight on the line Chameh-Merjayoun-Mount Hermon. Resistance, though emotionally painful, since it entailed Frenchmen fighting Frenchmen, was not strong and on 21 June the Free French entered Damascus. The British installed friendly regimes in both Syria and Lebanon.

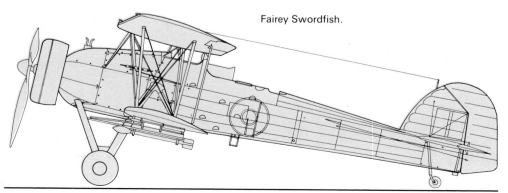
Fairey Swordfish.

## T–34 Tank

The T–34 tank was the standard Soviet medium battle tank throughout the war years and, in the opinion of most experts, was probably the best tank design of the war.

After some ten years of experimenting and designing, in 1939 the Soviets laid down a specification for their '1940–41 Tank Program' for a medium tank which was to be fitted with a powerful diesel engine, provided with sloped armor to deflect shot, welded armor instead of riveted, and with a high-velocity 76mm gun as the main armament. And, of course, the whole design had to be done with an eye to simple mass production and simple maintenance in the field. In August 1939 the 'Medium Tank Design Group' set to work to synthesize all their past experience and produce the ideal medium tank. Their work was completed by December, and two prototypes were immediately built by the Kharkov Tank Factory. After a long traveling trial to test the suspension and engine, followed by firing trials, these two prototypes were sent to join the war in Finland, to be tried in combat. By the time they arrived in March 1940, the war was over, but it was so obvious that the design was sound that production began at the Kirov Tank Factory in Leningrad in May, the first production model coming from the line in June.

In the next twelve months about 1200 tanks were produced, though there were some initial teething troubles to be overcome; the production of the new diesel engine could not keep pace with the production of hulls, and some tanks were fitted with older gasoline engines; transmission failure was a common fault, so that it was not unusual to see a T–34 going into action with a spare transmission lashed to the engine covers.

The existence of the T–34 was a closely guarded secret (though, unaccountably, some visiting American pressmen were allowed to see some T–34s at the Stalin Tank School in May 1941) and its appearance in battle after the German invasion in June 1941 was a severe shock to the Panzers; Germans complained that their shells simply bounced off the T–34. The first one to be met by the Seventeenth Panzer Division tore through the German front and left a nine-mile swath of destruction in its wake before it was stopped by a field artillery howitzer at short range.

Since the total strength of serviceable T–34s at the start of the Russian campaign was about 1100, the first priority was production; the initial German advance had overrun or at least threatened most of the tank plants, and they

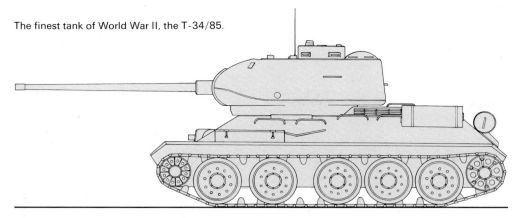

The finest tank of World War II, the T-34/85.

were hurriedly moved east and reorganized. A combination of evacuated works was brought together at Nizhni-Tagil to form the 'Ural-mashzavod' which became one of the principal producers of T–34 tanks. By the end of the war, an estimated 40,000 had been produced.

After their initial shock, the Germans concentrated on producing more powerful anti-tank guns and tanks, and the Soviets in their turn began to make improvements to the T–34. The first move was to improve its firepower by fitting a longer-barreled 76mm gun improving the armor-piercing performance. Then the turret was redesigned to do away with the rear overhang, which the Germans had found to be a weak spot in the design; a skillfully thrown Tellermine could be lodged beneath this overhang, so that on detonation it would wreck the turret. Moreover it acted as a shot trap. Other improvements included increased fuel capacity and improved welding techniques in the assembly.

Next came a larger turret mounting an 85mm gun derived from an anti-aircraft gun. This turret had, in fact, been developed for the KV series of heavy tanks and allowed three men to occupy it, which made life easier for the tank commander who could now concentrate on commanding instead of having to divide his time between command and gunnery. Armor thickness was increased to 110mm on the front and 90mm on the turret, and a new five-speed gearbox was installed.

In addition to the battle tanks, the T–34 hull and chassis were used as a basis for a variety of specialist vehicles, such as flame-throwing tanks, mine-rollers and recovery tanks, and for the SU–85 and SU–100 self-propelled guns. It continued in production after the war and was supplied to many satellite countries. It is still widely used, a testimony to the soundness of the original design.

## 'Tabby'
see Infra-red Target Detection Systems

## Tabun

This was the first of the German 'Nerve Gases'. Properly known as Ethyl-dimethyl-amido-phosphoro-cyanidate, it was discovered by Dr Gebhardt Schraeder in 1936 in the course of experiments into organic phosphorus compounds for weed-killers. It was found to be ten times more poisonous than Phosgene, previously considered the most lethal of war gases. Instead of attacking the respiratory system as did most war gases until that time, Tabun attacked the central nervous system so that the body's functions were no longer under the

brain's control. Exposure to the gas meant death within a few minutes.

After considerable difficulty, manufacture of Tabun began at a special factory at Dyhernfurth on the River Oder, the planned production being 1000 tons per month from mid-1942. Difficulties arose, however, and it is believed that the total production was in the region of 15,000 tons before the factory was captured by the advancing Soviet Army. Since that time nothing further has been heard of the plant and it is believed to have been dismantled and taken back to Russia in 1945. All the gas in the plant was filled into various munitions and moved out before the Russians arrived, however, and upwards of half a million artillery shells and over 100,000 aircraft bombs filled with the gas were discovered in German ammunition dumps as the war came to an end.

## Taisho 14
see Nambu Pistols

## Taper Bore
see Coned Bore Gun

## Taranto

Taranto was the main fleet base of the Italian Fleet, in the Gulf of Taranto next to the 'heel' of Italy. Although the *Regia Navale* had shown no great energy since June 1940 the Italian intentions towards Greece changed the strategic situation. As soon as Mussolini's ultimatum was presented to the Greek Government the British decided to move reinforcements from North Africa to Greece, and this put the supply line between Greece and Alexandria within reach of the Taranto Fleet.

Admiral Cunningham, Commander-in-Chief of the British Mediterranean Fleet, planned a quick strike for 21 October 1940 to celebrate the anniversary of Trafalgar Day but the operation was postponed until 11 November. It was nothing less than a torpedo-bomber strike from aircraft carriers, the first in history. It worked brilliantly, for only 21 aircraft and a total of 11 torpedoes disabled the Italian Fleet. The new battleship *Littorio* was sunk, with the *Conte di Cavour* and *Duilio*, in return for only one aircraft shot down.

The shallowness of the harbor meant that the ships could be salvaged without too much difficulty, but at a crucial moment three out of four Italian capital ships were out of action. What was more important was that Italian confidence was shaken at a time when some boldness could easily have brought substantial rewards. The initiative was never regained.

## Tarawa
see Gilbert Islands

## Tassafaronga, Battle of, 1942

Admiral Tanaka tried to make another supply run to Guadalcanal on 30 November 1942 in the Second Destroyer flotilla. Tanaka planned to float drums of supplies onto the shore but his force was spotted by Rear Admiral Wright in the cruiser *Minneapolis* with four other cruisers and seven destroyers. Tanaka's flotilla prepared to launch its drums not realizing that Wright's force was nearby. Wright hesitated before giving his destroyers the order to fire and then opened up with guns from the *Minneapolis* and *New Orleans*. Tanaka's ships hastily regrouped but the *Takanami* was hit and sank. As the US ships hesitated they were perfect targets because their guns lit up the ships. The Japanese launched their 'Long-Lance' torpedoes and hit the *Minneapolis, New Orleans* and *Pensacola*. The Japanese destroyers fired another round of torpedoes and hit the cruiser *Northampton*, which sank. The Japanese flotilla escaped with little damage.

## TBS
see Savo Island, Battle of, 1942

## Tedder, Air Marshal Sir Arthur (1st Baron) 1890–1967

At the beginning of the war Tedder was Director General of Research and Development at the Air Ministry. In 1941, following a period as Deputy Commander of Middle East Command, he was appointed its Air Commander in Chief. Faced with depleted air strength, he set up a mobile repair organization which restored damaged aircraft, thereby filling the supply gap until reinforcements could arrive by sea. With Allied fortunes constantly fluctuating in that theater, he considered inter-Service co-operation to be essential and was especially successful in the relationship he established with the Army Commanders.

German success in Greece and Crete demonstrated conclusively that air supremacy was a vital factor in any surface campaign. Tedder accordingly set about establishing this condition, giving it priority over the direct support

Air Marshal Sir Arthur Tedder.

of land and sea operations. This policy contributed significantly to the success of the El Alamein offensive in October 1942.

Following the Casablanca Conference in January 1943, Tedder became Commander-in-Chief of the newly-formed Mediterranean Air Command, responsible for all Allied air operations. Co-operating closely with General Eisenhower, Supreme Commander for Torch and the successive campaigns, he effected a complete integration of land/sea/air operations. The Allied invasions of Tunisia, Sicily and Italy were preceded by concentrated assaults on Axis air-strength and by long-range strategic bombing of communications, thereby affording a tactical advantage by isolating the battle area. The technique of close support, known as 'Tedder's carpet', involving the intensive bombing of enemy forces immediately in front of the Allied armies, was to play a significant part in the Salerno landings.

Tedder's well-tried relationship with General Eisenhower was extended when he was appointed the latter's Deputy for Operation Overlord in 1944. Once again he fostered the vital integration of the US and British Services, drawing on his immense experience and personal tact to weld together the diverse resources at his disposal and to gain the co-operation of Commanders who often held strong personal differences. The successful implementation of the Transportation Plan, which effectively isolated the invasion zone for D-Day, owed much to Tedder's ability to manipulate his Commanders into accepting a common policy.

When control of the Strategic Air Forces reverted to the combined Chiefs of Staff, Tedder took over the direction of the Tactical Air Forces, following Leigh-Mallory's transfer to the Middle East. On 9 May 1945 he signed the instrument of surrender on behalf of General Eisenhower.

## Teheran Conference, 28 November – 1 December 1943

From early 1943, relations between Russia and her Western Allies were tense and mistrustful, Churchill and Stalin carrying on a vitriolic correspondence until June.The conference therefore took a year to organize. Stalin felt his Allies were playing a delaying game and letting the full weight fall on Russia by fighting in the non-essential Italian front and refusing to open the promised second front in Europe (northern France), until a later date. Stalin also felt the United States and Britain were making decisions without him, yet he could not leave Russia.

The Teheran Conference was preceded by the Moscow Conference of Foreign Ministers, 19–30 October, which settled problems of convoys between England and Russia, and which finally convinced Stalin of the utility of the Italian campaign and of the genuineness of Allied intentions to launch the promised cross-channel invasion.

At Teheran a tentative date and general outlines were arranged for Operation Overlord in Normandy and the supplementary Operation Anvil in the South of France. There was still disagreement over the importance of the Italian campaign. Churchill felt that the more Allied forces there were in Italy, the fewer Germans there would be in Normandy. The United States considered the Italian terrain too difficult for a quick, decisive campaign and therefore wanted

maximum manpower concentrated in France. It was decided to limit the campaign to capturing Rome, advancing to the Pisa–Rimini line with no subsequent advance to the Balkans. Teheran also saw a Four Power declaration pledging continued Allied collaboration after the war and calling for the establishment of an international peace-keeping organization. They also issued a declaration of intention to conduct legal trials of Nazi war criminals. A further proposed declaration pledging a resolution of self-government to liberated countries (cf. Yalta Conference) foundered on the Polish question. Though the three Powers agreed that Poland should lie between the Oder and the Curzon Line (thus annexing part of Germany and leaving the problem of Lvov, Vilnyus and Königsberg unsettled), they would not finalize such matters until after the war. The Polish Government-in-Exile would not agree to it, and the Soviets would not recognize the Polish Government unless they did.

## Tellermine

This German anti-tank mine became one of the most ubiquitous weapons of the war. The name (teller means plate) derives from its flat, plate-like shape. The original model was the T-Mine 35, introduced in 1935, 13in in diameter, just under 4in high, and containing 11.4lb of TNT. The explosive was in a light steel container well sealed against damp, and the mine was covered by a spring-loaded upper plate carrying a fuze unit. The mine was buried in the ground and lightly covered with dirt, after which any pressure on the top plate of approximately 350lb or more would operate the fuze and detonate the explosive charge. It was sufficiently powerful to disable any combat tank of the time.

In 1942 a new model, the T-Mine 42, appeared. This was somewhat simpler in design, had a smaller-diameter cover plate, was loaded with 10lb of Amatol, and weighed 17lb as against the 30lb of the T-Mine 35. This meant that they were easier and quicker to make, and also easier and quicker to transport and lay, without any loss of effectiveness. The only tactical change was that they now required a heavier pressure (about 550lb) to set them off, but this was an advantage in that they were less likely to be fired by 'soft' vehicles, reserving their effect for the tanks.

In 1943 a further simplification was made to produce the T-Mine Pilz 43 (Pilz means mushroom), a name presumably derived from the new shape of the cover plate. In essentials it was much the same as the T-Mine 42.

In addition to being fired by the pressure of a passing tank all Tellermines had sockets in the sides and bottom into which booby-trap igniters could be fitted to detonate the mine if any attempt was made to lift it.

## Tempest, Hawker

This British single-seat fighter was operational from Spring 1944 until 1949. Sydney Camm realized quickly that many of the Typhoon's troubles stemmed from the fact that it was fast enough to be affected by the compressibility shock-waves that threatened to make flying near the speed of sound extremely hazardous. Even in a high-speed dive at Typhoon speeds, air flowing over the thick high-lift wings was speeded up so much that accidents resulted. The

answer was to fit thinner wings, and the Tempest was known initially as the 'thin-wing Typhoon'. First to fly, on 2 September 1942, was the prototype Tempest V, with a Sabre engine. It entered service with Wing Commander R P Beamont's three-squadron Tempest Wing, in Kent, just in time to deal with the V–1 flying-bomb assault on southern England. With a cruising speed much higher than other RAF fighters, the Tempests had no difficulty in catching their robot targets, claiming 638 of the 1771 brought down by the RAF between 13 June and 5 September 1944. The Tempest achieved fame also as train-busters and ground-attack fighters. When the first Me 262 jet fighters were flown into action by the Luftwaffe, at least 20 were destroyed by Tempest pilots in air combat. Production of the Tempest V ended in August 1945, after a total of 800 had been completed. Other versions were built after the war, some flying as target tugs until 1953. All versions were armed with four 20mm guns, plus underwing bombs or rockets.

## Tennessee

The Tennessee (BB.43) was the sister of the battleship California, and was launched on 20 November 1919. Commissioned on 3 June 1920, a year later she joined the Pacific Fleet. She was moored at Berth F–6 inboard of the West Virginia in 'Battleship Row' on the morning of 7 December 1941. She went to General Quarters when Japanese aircraft were sighted at 0755 hours but could do little but fire at them as she was blocked by the West Virginia. Burning oil and debris from the explosion of the Arizona started fires aft, and two bombs hit her turrets.

A hurried refit at Puget Sound Navy Yard was completed in March 1942, and the Tennessee returned to Pearl Harbor to guard Hawaii during the period leading up to the Battle of the Coral Sea and Midway. With the crisis over she was sent back to Puget Sound for a total reconstruction which took until May 1943. She bombarded Kiska in the Aleutians in August and Tarawa in November. In the Battle of Surigao Strait on 25 October 1944 she fired 69 rounds of 14in ammunition in only 12 minutes, as the six battleships annihilated Admiral Nishimura's force.

During the Okinawa landings the Tennessee was the target for repeated kamikaze attacks. On 12 April she was attacked by six aircraft, one of which hit on the starboard side and killed 25 men and wounded 104. Repairs were completed at Ulithi by 3 May and the old battleship returned to the gun-line at Okinawa.

## Terauchi, Field Marshal Hisaichi, 1879–1945

Terauchi was given command of the Southern Army (comprising four armies, including those of Homma and Yamashita) on 6 November 1941, with orders to seize all US, Dutch and British possessions in the southern area as soon as possible, commencing on 8 December. Stationed in Saigon, he accomplished the invasion of Indochina, Siam and Malaya so quickly that he could invade Java a full month ahead of schedule.

Terauchi, a tough-minded man, was responsible for the construction of a 250-mile Burma Road, during which one-third of the 50,000 man work-force of Allied POWs died in brutal conditions. He censured both Homma (of Bataan Death March fame) and Imamura (in the Dutch East Indies) for their liberal and lenient policies toward the natives. He was one of the three men (along with Koiso and Hata) suggested to replace Tojo, having been promoted to Field Marshal the year before.

In 1944–45 he had the impossible task of defending the vast area from New Guinea to Burma with his Southern Army. He also commanded at Leyte, where he refused to give up the lost battle despite the desperate need of his troops at Luzon and despite the loss of an entire convoy of 10,000 men due to Allied bombing.

On 12 September Terauchi suffered a stroke and was unable to sign the surrender at Singapore.

## Ter Poorten, General Hein, 1887–1948

In October 1941 General ter Poorten was made Commander-in-Chief of land forces in the Dutch East Indies. He was an artillery specialist and an experienced pilot and although he had 125,000 well-trained soldiers in his army he knew that he did not have sufficient artillery, planes or transport to fight a campaign. He had oil wells mined in preparation for Japanese attacks.

In January 1942 Japanese troops landed at Sarawak, the Celebes and at Tarakan in Borneo. Although the Dutch forces were backed up by the Allied forces they could not match the Japanese in fire power and the US bombers withdrew for lack of fighter support. In April 1942 Ter Poorten surrendered near Bandung.

## Thompson Submachine Gun

The 'Tommygun' beloved of Hollywood was designed by a team headed by General John T Thompson and made up of the design staff of the Auto-Ordnance Company. Thompson's idea, in his own words, was to make a 'trench broom' which could be used in World War I but the war ended before his design was perfected. It owed nothing to any other design, using the much-disputed 'Blish' system of delayed blowback operation in which a wedge held the breech closed while chamber pressure was high but slipped free after the bullet left the barrel and allowed the bolt to recoil and perform the necessary loading cycle. It was also a most luxuriously made weapon, carefully machined and finished to a high specification, which, in turn, meant it was expensive. In the 1920s and 1930s a handful was sold by normal weapon production standards; 15,000 were made by Colt, under license, and many of these were still in stock in 1939. In November of that year the British and French ordered quantities of the guns, the US Army followed suit (the US Marines had used a few in 1928) and by August 1941, 318,900 guns had been ordered. By this time Thompson had died and the company had passed into other hands. A factory was acquired and fitted out, and, in addition, the Savage Arms Corporation was licensed to make the guns. Between the two, these plants eventually produced 90,000 guns a month, the total wartime production being 1,383,043 weapons.

The original Thompson pattern, with the Blish delayed blowback system, was known in service as the M1928A1. This used a 50-round drum magazine as standard, though box magazines of various sizes were also made. British troops in 1940 found that the .45 cartridges in the drum tended to slap back and forth and make a noise, advertising the presence of night patrols, so they abandoned the drum and began using the box, a measure which was almost universally adopted.

As supplied in 1939 the M1928A1 cost $209. The Savage company, seeking to speed up production, experimented with removing the Blish locking wedge and found that the gun worked equally well as a simple blowback; another modification removed the separate firing pin and adopted a pin fixed in the bolt, simplifying assembly; the muzzle compensator which countered the upward climb of the gun when fired automatically was dropped, and the characteristic fore-end pistol grip was replaced by a plain wooden fore-end stock. With these changes the weapon became the M1 submachine gun in 1942 and production was speeded up; more to the point, the cost came down to $45, complete with a kit of spares in 1944.

The Thompson was heavy and large compared with most other submachine guns of the war years, but it had one outstanding virtue in the soldiers' eyes – it was utterly and unquestionably the most reliable machine of its type ever made. When cheaper machine guns came along, many men refused to part with their Thompson as long as they could obtain the ammunition for it. It became so firmly identified with Commandos, Rangers and other special service troops that it was incorporated into the badge of the British Combined Operations Command, the only submachine gun ever to earn heraldic distinction.

## 'Thor'
see Karl

## Thousand Bomber Raid
see Strategic Bombing Offensive against Germany

## Thunderbolt
see P-47 Thunderbolt, Republic

## Thursday
see Kohima and Imphal Offensives, 1944

## Tigercat, Grumman F7F

This twin-engined fighter was built for the US Navy during the late war years as both the F7F–1 single-seat tactical support fighter and F7F–2 two-seat night fighter. Both versions reached Marine squadrons too late for operational use.

## Tiger Tank

The most famous German battle tank, though not the best, the Tiger generated an aura of invincibility giving it a psychological advantage of great value. After its appearance in battle, few Allied troops were ever attacked by mere tanks – they invariably reported that they were being attacked by a Tiger. This reputation was justified by events such as the action in which SS-Obersturmführer Wittmann commanding a Tiger on the Villers Bocage road in Normandy on 13 June 1944, destroyed 25 half-tracks and tanks, effectively blocking the road and halting the advance of a complete armored division. Furthermore he had already destroyed 119 Soviet tanks in his service on the Russian front.

The Tiger was developed by the Henschel company, and it was the culmination of a long series of experimental vehicles dating from 1937. Weighing 56 tons, it carried armor up to 100mm thick and was armed with the 8.8cm KwK 36 gun, the tank version of the celebrated '88' anti-aircraft and anti-tank gun. This weapon could pierce 105mm of armor at 1000 meters, more than adequate to deal with any Allied tank.

The hull was box-like, scorning the advantage of the sloped plate and relying entirely on thickness. The turret was thick and massive, with vertical sides, and so heavy that it needed low-geared hand operation to turn it, the gunlayer having to make 720 revolutions of a handwheel to rotate the turret through 360 degrees. A foot-operated hydraulic traversing gear was also fitted but it too was slow, and this led to a tactical disadvantage since it was possible to sneak up on a Tiger from the side or rear and loose off a quick shot or two before the gunner could bring the ponderous turret and gun to bear on his assailant.

Power was provided by a 21-liter (1281 cu in) V–12 Maybach gasoline engine, later changed to a 24-liter (1464 cu in) model delivering 700 horsepower. This was driven through an eight-speed preselector gearbox to a transverse transmission unit in the nose, driving the front sprockets of the 28·5in wide track. Suspension was maintained by overlapping road wheels sprung by torsion bars, which gave an extremely comfortable and stable ride. Arrangements for submersion were included in the design, and the first Tigers could submerge to a depth of 13 feet and remain there up to 2·5 hours, a facility which proved extremely useful when crossing some of the larger Russian rivers. This facility, though, was expensive and difficult to provide and was abandoned after the first 495 tanks had been made.

The Tiger's reputation in attack was not good; in its first combats in Russia it was invariably

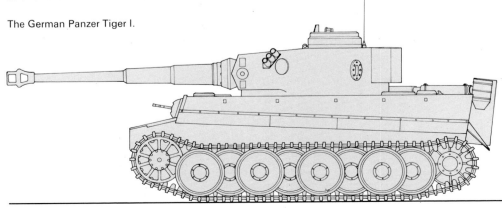

The German Panzer Tiger I.

sent into action on difficult ground, on forest tracks through marshland, in conditions where well-handled anti-tank guns could usually get the better of it. Similarly, in North Africa in 1942 the first Tiger attack was stopped by two British six-pounder guns who held their fire until the Tigers were less than 500 yards away and thus defeated both tanks. But in Normandy, in 1944, the reputation in defense was practically invincible; a Tiger which picked its spot and waited for the Allies to blunder onto it could execute enormous destruction.

The Tiger remained in production for two years, from August 1942 until August 1944, when it was superseded by the 'King Tiger'. A total of 1350 tanks were made in that time, indicative of the fact that the Tiger, good as it was, was conceived primarily as a fighting machine and not as a mass-production machine.

The *Tirpitz* in the Norwegian fjord where she was sunk by British Lancasters.

## Timoshenko, Marshal Semion K, 1895–1970

Timoshenko was of peasant origins and made his career in the Cavalry. He took part in the Soviet occupation of Poland 1939–40 and commanded the Karelian troops in the Russo-Finnish War. On 7 May 1941 he was made Marshal and took over from Voroshilov, the task of reorganizing the Red Army. He put into operation many schemes to improve training and discipline. As Commander of the Western Front at the outbreak of the war, he could do little to halt the German advance. He allowed his armies to be trapped at Smolensk. He was made Commander of the Southwestern Front in September 1941. In May 1942 he planned an offensive against the Germans at Kharkov. He timed the offensive, unwittingly, to take place a week before the Germans planned theirs. His army was routed and he was transferred to the Northwestern Front, where he did not play such a major role. He took part in planning operations and was the Stavka representative in the Baltic and the Balkans, but Stalin no longer respected his judgment.

## Tinian, 1944

On 24 July Marine divisions from Saipan were transported to a small beach on Tinian and took the Japanese commander, Admiral Kakuda, and his garrison of 9000 by surprise. By the evening the Marines had established a beach-head and 1200 Japanese died when they tried to drive the Marines back. The 2nd Marine Division cleared the northern part of the island while the 4th Marines attacked the southern part and within a week the island was in American hands. The US lost 327 killed and 1771 wounded, but the Japanese lost their entire garrison.

## *Tirpitz*

The *Tirpitz* was nearly identical to her sister *Bismarck*, apart from having extra AA guns and eight torpedo-tubes. Although never in a surface action she was a constant threat to the Allied convoys to North Russia, and so was the object of numerous attacks. On 16 January 1942 she sailed from Wilhelmshaven for Norway, and there she remained for the rest of her career. On 4 July 1942 a mere shift of berth was sufficient for the First Sea Lord, Sir Dudley Pound, to order the convoy PQ17 to scatter. On 6 September 1943 with the *Scharnhorst* and ten

destroyers she bombarded shore installations on Spitzbergen, and on 20 September she was attacked in Altenfjord by British midget submarines (X-craft). The shock effect put her main armament and machinery out of action for seven months.

On 9 March 1942 she made one of her rare trips to sea, and was 'jumped' by Albacore torpedo-bombers from HMS *Victorious*. On this occasion the *Tirpitz* was lucky to escape unscathed, but the consequence was that Hitler forbade the ship ever to put to sea if it was known that an enemy carrier was at sea. On 3 April 1944 she was hit by a bomb during a strike from the carriers *Victorious, Furious, Emperor, Fencer, Pursuer* and *Searcher*. In all, 16 air strikes were made, seven by the RAF and nine by the Fleet Air Arm. The reason for the poor return was not any special immunity enjoyed by the *Tirpitz* but rather the unique problems posed by the terrain. By hiding the *Tirpitz* deep in a Norwegian fjord the Germans made it almost impossible to mount a conventional air attack; either the aircraft did not see the target until too late or they risked flying into the sides of the fjord.

Another problem was the great distance between the British Isles and Northern Norway, which made it necessary for land-based bombers to fly from Russia. On 15 September 1944 a force of Lancaster bombers damaged the *Tirpitz* with 12,000lb 'Tallboy' bombs, and although she was not sunk the damage could not be repaired so far north. In any case Hitler wanted her to become a floating battery to defend Norway from the invasion which he was sure would come. The battleship was moved to Tromsö, and there she was within reach of bombers based in Britain. On 12 November 1944 another force of Lancasters surprised her without any defending fighters in the air. In perfect visibility the bombers hit her with three 'Tallboys' and she capsized.

## Tiso, President Joseph, 1887–1946

Monsignor Joseph Tiso was the President of Slovakia from 1938–44. Tiso became leader of the Slovak People's Party in August 1938 and he immediately pressed the Czechoslovak government in Prague to give Slovakia autonomy. The Czechs tried to arrest him but under pressure from Hitler were forced to give up control of Slovakia. Tiso negotiated a pact with Hitler in

March 1939 and was recognized by the USSR, Britain and France. Tiso set up concentration camps but he had to be threatened by the Germans before he agreed to intern all the Jews in camps. Before the Red Army reached Slovakia partisans proclaimed an uprising in August 1944. Tiso was removed from power and the Germans took over the administration of the country. Tiso was tried after the war and was hanged on 3 December 1946.

## Tito, Josip Broz, 1892–

Tito was leader of the Yugoslav Partisans who fought German occupation troops throughout the war. After the German invasion of Yugoslavia, Tito began to organize a partisan network and in August 1941 he left Belgrade to take charge of Partisan operations in Serbia. His forces successfully cleared most of Serbia by mid-September but he was then involved in negotiations with General Mihajlović's Cetniks. These negotiations broke down and the Partisans were involved in clashes with the Cetniks so that by December the Germans once again controlled Serbia and Tito withdrew to eastern Bosnia. The Partisans gradually fought back with a little assistance from the British and by May 1943 they had four lightly equipped divisions. During this period the Cetniks were cooperating with the Axis forces and Tito's troops were nearly cut off on several occasions in Montenegro (January and May 1943). In the summer of 1943 Tito got full support from the British and officers and equipment were sent for his force which was now 250,000 strong. In May 1944 Tito was almost killed when German paratroops attacked his HQ at Drvar and he left for Vis, an island off Dalmatia. In August 1944 Tito went to Moscow and met Stalin. He met Churchill in Italy who promised more aid and Tito received more Anglo-American aid than any other person in Europe. Tito returned and soon his Partisans had the Germans in retreat. In October the partisans and the Red Army entered Belgrade but it was only in May 1945 that the partisans met the British 8th Army at Trieste. Tito made an agreement with Peter II's government in November 1944 which would pave the way for Peter's return but in March 1945 Tito set up a provisional government with himself as Prime Minister and a republic was declared in November 1945.

## Tobruk
see Crusader Operation, 1941

## Togo, Shigenori, 1882–1950

A very blunt and straightforward diplomat, Togo was Foreign Minister under Tojo until war began. He was strongly opposed to the excessive demands of the militarists and therefore sincerely strove to come to an agreement with the Americans. However he was severely hampered by the military, who placed deadlines on his negotiations after which, they claimed, war must begin. They also refused to even consider any withdrawal from Indochina; Togo said this was America's minimum requirement. Togo was also hampered by American misconceptions and misinformation: for example, Cordell Hull received inaccurate translations of Togo's proposals and diplomatic instructions which greatly exaggerated their belligerence.

Togo was also strongly against initiating war with a surprise attack, wanting instead to give due warning. He argued with Nagumo but made no headway. Togo soon resigned in protest against Tojo's 'dictatorial policies'.

In April 1945 Suzuki appointed Togo Foreign Minister to seek peace. He stood staunchly against those militarists who preferred national suicide. He opposed negotiating through Russia, which was in reality something less than neutral. He demanded that the Potsdam Declaration be publicized in Japan to show the Allies that the Japanese were considering it seriously. Togo resigned in August 1945.

---

## 'Tojo'
see Nakajima Ki-44 Shoki

---

## Tojo, General Hideki, 1884–1948

By 1937 Tojo had become Chief of Staff of the Kwantung Army in Manchuria. During the next year he received an Imperial dispensation which allowed him to hold his military command and serve in the Cabinet. He became Vice-Minister of War in Konoye's administration and Minister of War in 1940. On 17 October 1941 when a new military government came to power, Tojo became Prime Minister with the support of Sugiyama as Chief of Army General Staff and Nagano as Chief of Naval Staff.

As Minister of War Tojo had helped negotiate the Tripartite Pact with Hitler and Mussolini. Tojo now embarked on a policy which led to war. He forced the Vichy French regime to allow Japanese troops to occupy French Indo-China. After receiving the Premiership, Tojo was preparing for war and sent a Strike Force to attack Pearl Harbor. War was declared on 8 December 1941.

Tojo remained Prime Minister until the fall of the Marianas, when he took responsibility for defeat and was forced to resign. After the Battle of Midway Imperial General HQ had refused to recognize that US power was increasing. After the fall of the Marianas, liberals and Navy men joined to force Tojo out and he was succeeded by Koiso, another general who was not as fanatical as Tojo. After Japan's surrender Tojo tried to commit suicide. He recovered to face trial as a war criminal and was hanged on 23 December 1948.

Tojo was a hard-working and hard-headed man who was nicknamed 'the Razor'. He was greatly feared by the civilian members of the prewar administration because of his popularity in the Army. He took the blame for having lost the war.

---

## Tokarev Pistol

This standard Soviet 7.62mm automatic pistol was designed by Feodor V Tokarev, a gunsmith who became technical manager of various arsenals and who had designed a number of successful military weapons. Development of the pistol took place in the late 1920s and it was ahproved for service in 1930, being called the TT–30 (Tula-Tokarev 1930, Tula being the arsenal selected to make it.) Basically it was a Browning pattern using the swinging link system for locking the breech, similar to that of the US Army's Colt M1911 pistol, but with some modifications to improve reliability and simplify maintenance and manufacture. The principal innovations were three; the hammer and lockwork were placed in a separate module which made initial assembly and subsequent repair much easier; the magazine was formed without feed lips so that the feeding into the chamber was controlled by 'lips' machined into the pistol frame; there was no grip or applied safety catch, the only safety measure was a half-cock notch on the hammer.

In 1933 the design was slightly changed. In the original pattern the barrel had two locking lugs machined on its upper surface to lock into recesses in the slide. This was now changed to two circumferential bands passing completely round the barrel; the functioning of the breech lock remained the same but the lock lugs could now be cut on the lathe which finished off the barrel instead of having to be done in a separate machining operation. This design became known as the TT–33.

As well as serving as the standard Soviet pistol the Tokarev was widely adopted by satellite countries after the war and copies were produced in Poland, China and Yugoslavia.

Tokarev M.1933 pistol.

---

## Tokyo Bombing
see Strategic Bombing Offensive against Japan

---

## Tokyo Express
see Guadalcanal, 1942

---

## Tokyo Rose (Mrs Iva Ikuko Toguri d'Aquino) 1916–

'Tokyo Rose' made daily broadcasts to Allied soldiers in the East, in which she tried to demoralize the soldiers. Tokyo Rose had been brought up in the USA and had a zoology degree from UCLA. When the war broke out she had been visiting a sick aunt and to avoid working in the factories she worked with the Japanese Broadcasting Corporation. She was trained by a POW, a US Army captain and started to make broadcasts in which she told

---

how the Japanese were winning the war and how the people in the USA were enjoying themselves. In 1948 she was taken to court and sentenced to ten years imprisonment and fined $10,000. The captain was never tried. Mrs d'Aquino is living now in Chicago and still claims that she was not Tokyo Rose. In January 1977 President Gerald Ford pardoned her.

---

## Tolbukhin, Marshal Fyodor I, 1894–1949

Tolbukhin led the Soviet armies that liberated the Crimea, the Ukraine, Rumania, Yugoslavia, Hungary, Austria and Bulgaria. He graduated from the Frunze Military Academy in 1934. From 1942 to 1943 Tolbukhin commanded the 57th Army in the defense of Stalingrad. In 1943 he was given command of the South Front and captured the towns at the mouth of the Donets. In April 1944 he led the offensive to recapture the Crimea and broke through the German defenses. He became a Marshal in 1944 after the successful defeat of a German army of 200,000 at Jassy-Kishinev. In 1945 and 1946 Tolbukhin was the Supreme Commander of troops in Bulgaria and Rumania.

---

## 'Tony'
see Kawasaki Ki-61

---

## Torch, Operation, Allied landings in North Africa, 1942

Despite long discussions at the First Washington Conference and in the summer of 1942, the British and Americans failed to co-ordinate their views about the timing of a full-scale invasion of the continent of Europe. Determined for reasons of public morale, and to avert the transfer of troops to the Pacific so that American troops should see action somewhere in the west in 1942, Roosevelt eventually agreed to a British plan to invade French North Africa. It was still under the control of Vichy, whose local troops were not expected to fight the Allies, and its occupation would defeat Rommel's efforts to wrest control of the North African coast from the British. Three task forces, under the command of General Eisenhower, were created to make the landings, which were dispatched by sea from the United Kingdom: Eastern, largely British, to seize Algiers; Central, American, to take Oran; and Western, also American, commanded by Patton, to occupy French Morocco. The landings were synchronized to begin on 8 November. The British got ashore with little difficulty, thanks to the forbearance of French sympathizers, but the French forces at Oran and in Morocco did not surrender until 10 and 11 November respectively.

A confused political situation ensued. Admiral Darlan, commander of the Vichy armed forces, was in Algeria, and agreed to a ceasefire. He insisted, however, that he must receive the assent of Pétain, whose foreign minister, Laval, was striving to deter Hitler from using the Allied landings as a pretext to enter unoccupied France. When Hitler insisted on Pétain agreeing to German forces entering Tunisia, which the Torch forces had not yet occupied, Laval prevaricated, Hitler ordered the occupation of the Vichy zone, and Darlan broke with Pétain. Some French commanders in Tunisia therefore decided not to obey Darlan's orders to side with the Allies and allowed German forces to enter

An Italian column in retreat through the Tunisian desert.

the country unopposed. British and American troops hastened towards it, as Montgomery was doing from the other end of the North African coast in pursuit of Rommel, and the bulk of the French garrison concentrated inland, but the Germans were able to land the advance guard of an expeditionary force under General Nehring. Meanwhile the French fleet had scuttled itself at Toulon and the Italians had occupied Corsica. These developments determined that the possession of North Africa was to be contested bitterly.

## Torpedo

The standard weapon of the submarine and the destroyer was the torpedo, a self-propelled fish which detonated against an enemy ship's side below the waterline. As it had proved in 1914–1918 the torpedo was the most destructive naval weapon and accounted for many more ships sunk than either bombs or gun-fire.

The basic torpedo had changed very little in 40 years, but during the war many improvements were made. The German Navy adopted electric propulsion and a magnetic influence exploder to detonate the torpedo underneath the target's keel. Similar devices were developed by the British and Americans, but they proved to be of dubious reliability. The Germans and Americans were plagued by faulty torpedoes in the early part of the war, but eliminated the problems later. A most important advance for the Allies was an anti-submarine homing torpedo, known as 'Fido' or the Mark 24 mine, while the German Zaunkönig or the GNAT (German Naval Acoustic Torpedo) was used against convoy escorts.

The torpedo was also used by aircraft and again torpedo bombing proved far more effective than dive-bombing.

## Tovey, Admiral Lord John Cronyn, 1885–1971

Flag officer of the Home Fleet at Scapa Flow, 1940–43, Tovey's greatest success was the hunting and destruction of the *Bismarck* in May 1941. He also covered the Russian convoys in 1942–43 from stations off Iceland and attempted without success, to bring to battle and sink the *Tirpitz*. He criticized the Admiralty for laying emphasis on his duty to cover the convoys because he felt to sink the *Tirpitz* was more important. In 1945 he was responsible for safety of convoys to Amsterdam.

## Toyoda, Admiral Soemu

Toyoda was Commander at the Yokosuka Naval Base until he was appointed Admiral Koga's successor as Commander in Chief of the combined Navy. He was well known for being meticulous and sarcastic. He believed in the concept of the 'Decisive Battle' which would destroy the US Fleet. He planned operation A-Go which involved luring the American fleet from the Marianas to a point near the Palaus because his ships were short of fuel and could not go out in chase. His plan resulted in the disaster at the Battle of the Philippine Sea. Even after this he planned the destruction of the US Fleet at Leyte Gulf. Exaggerated reports from pilots on bombing raids against American ships raised Toyoda's hopes but in the end he did not have sufficient air power to fight the Americans. He then sent the *Yamato* on its suicide mission to Okinawa and this left him with no main line ships fit for battle. Together with Umezu and Anami, he was opposed to Japan's unconditional surrender but he continued as Navy Chief of Staff until after the war.

## Treblinka
see Holocaust

## Tresckow, Major General Henning von, 1901–1944

Tresckow was one of the leading conspirators against Hitler. He served successively as Chief of Staff to the Army Group commanders of the Eastern Front, von Kluge, von Bock, and von Manstein. In March 1943 he obtained and planted bombs in Hitler's aircraft but they failed to detonate. Tresckow originated the Valkyrie Plan for the July Plot, 1944, and when this failed he committed suicide by walking into the Russian field of fire.

## Truk
see Marshall Islands, 1944

## Truman, President Harry S, 1884–1972

Elected Vice-President at Roosevelt's fourth election in 1944, Truman found himself within five months of his inauguration the most powerful man in the world. He was the first to admit his lack of necessary experience but was overmodest about his political talents, which were considerable. Though unable to prevent Stalin's institution of a new imperialism in eastern Europe before the end of the war, and in

defiance of Allied agreements on the subject, he early formed the opinion that Russian territorial ambitions must be contained and acted to do so. He also took the awesome decision to use the atomic bomb against Japan. Truman's greatness as a President dates, however, from the postwar years rather than his months as wartime Commander in Chief.

## Tunisia, Campaign in, 1942–43

Initial contact between the Germans and the Allies in Tunisia following the successful Torch landings, occurred between 17–23 November. The British 1st Army concentrated its strength on the coast intending to drive to Tunis some 30 miles away, while the French 19th Corps and the American 2nd Corps advanced to take positions to its south. The southern flank remained open in the direction of Mareth, towards which Rommel was making his way from Libya, pursued by Montgomery's British 8th Army. On 25 November the 1st Army struck at Tunisia and reached to within ten miles but was counterattacked by Nehring whose troops enjoyed air superiority and drove the British Army back to its start line. By the time the Allies were ready to try again in early December, the German Fifth Army, under von Arnim (consisting of the Three Hundred and Forty-Fourth Infantry, Tenth Panzer and the elite Hermann Goering Panzer Divisions) had arrived and was deployed to make a battle of it. The Germans repulsed a drive on Tunis by the 1st Army in late December and, seizing the initiative, attacked and damaged the French 19th Corps in the mountains to the south throughout January and the first half of February.

Worse was to come. Rommel had now arrived at Mareth, a highly defensible position, via Tobruk (left 13 November), Benghazi (20 November) and Tripoli (23 January), and he persuaded Arnim to mount a counteroffensive against the Americans as soon as possible. The plan was that the US 2nd Corps should be attacked frontally at Sidi Bou Zid in front of the Kasserine Pass, and then in the flank by his own Afrika Korps from Gafsa. The attack was launched on 14 February and inflicted a major defeat on the Americans all the more humiliating for being unplanned. The inexperienced Americans broke in several places, and in others were surrounded and obliged to surrender. It was only confusion and lack of decision on how best to exploit their success on the part of the Germans which averted a disaster. Had Rommel been allowed his head, he might well have brought it about, and it was fortunate for the Allies that he was not made theater commander until the day after the Kasserine battle ended.

Rommel's command now consisted of the German Fifth Army and the Italian First, which contained some German units. The former launched its own attack against the British on the coast outside Tunis on 26 February and gained some ground, but suffered losses which the Germans could no longer afford. Rommel's preferred plan was to maintain pressure further from Tunis, which he did by attacking the British south of the Mareth Line at Medenine on 6 March. The battle, his last with Montgomery in Africa, was a serious failure which cost him a third of his tanks. Three days later he left Africa a sick man returning command to Kesselring, the air force general who was to prove himself here and later in Italy a formidable land commander.

The British now took the offensive. Assisted by a diversionary offensive by Patton commanding US 2nd Corps, towards Gafsa, Montgomery attacked the Mareth Line on the night of 20–21 March. The frontal assault by 30th Corps was held and repelled by the Fifteenth Panzer Division but the New Zealand Division, driving round the flank, unhinged the whole line and obliged the Germans to leave it between 26 and 31 March. Patton and Montgomery maintained the pressure and on 6 April the Italian General Messe, commanding his First Army, withdrew to Enfidaville, fifty miles south of Tunis.

The Axis now controlled only a pocket around Tunis itself. A month of bitter fighting followed as the Allies strove to win a quick victory to release their armies for the assault on Sicily, the objective which Churchill and Roosevelt had selected at the Casablanca Conference in January. It began on 19 April, with a British attack, was followed on 23 April with a spectacular American advance towards Tunis by Bradley's US 2nd Corps and culminated in a decisive push towards Tunis by the British 1st Army on 6 May. The next day that city and Bizerta fell. The Axis troops had orders to fight until the last shot but many fired in the air. On 13 May the last Axis troops still in the field, the Italian First Army, surrendered. In all 275,000 Axis prisoners passed into Allied hands. Many of them had entered Africa only six months before. Their loss had brought Hitler almost no advantage whatever.

## Tupolev, General Andrey N, 1888–1972

General Tupolev was a gifted designer of airplanes. He designed the TB-3 (ANT-6), a four-engined heavy bomber with a bomb load of not less than two tons which could strike deep into the enemy's territory. He also designed the SB-2 (ANT-40), an all-metal light bomber with a speed not exceeding 250 mph. This emphasis on bombers meant that by 1936 about 60 percent of the aircraft of the VVS (Red Air Force) were bombers. In 1938 he was arrested but while in jail designed the TU-2, a dive-bomber which was mass-produced during the war. He then went on to design passenger planes and torpedo launches.

## Tupolev SB–2

This Soviet high-performance bomber was operational from 1936. When SB–2s appeared in Spain during the Civil War, their top speed of 264mph comfortably exceeded that of any other production bombers in the world. Above 16,000ft they could outfly the Luftwaffe's Bf 109B fighters. The rate of climb was superior at all altitudes to that of the American Boeing P–26A interceptor, and better than that of the Italian Fiat C.R.32 above 21,000ft. An improved version, the SB–2bis, with M–103 engines, appeared in 1938. Maximum speed was now 280mph and range 1430 miles with 1100lb of bombs. Armed with four machine guns, in nose, dorsal and ventral positions, it was built in very large numbers, taking part in border fighting against the Japanese in Mongolia in 1938–39 and in the winter campaign against Finland in 1939–40. It was unfortunate for units equipped with SB–2s that these once-unrivaled aircraft were still operational as night bombers at the time of the German attack on Russia.

## Turner, Admiral R Kelly, 1885–1961

Turner was with the War Plans Division of the Department of the Navy and participated in negotiations with the Japanese before the war.

In July 1942 Turner was put in command of the South Pacific Amphibious Force, TF 62, although he had no first-hand experience of island fighting. He organized the transport of the Marines to Guadalcanal and was caught off-guard in the Battle of Savo Island. After this operation he caught malaria but returned to prepare the invasion of New Georgia.

He was then transferred in 1944 to the Central Pacific Area under Spruance. In the Marianas campaign Turner landed the 2nd and 4th Marine Divisions. In August Turner established an air base on Saipan for the B-29s in order to attack the Philippines. In February 1945 he led the expeditionary force which took Iwo Jima.

## Twining, General Nathan F, 1897–

From 1942 to 1943 Twining was Chief of Staff to the Commander in the South Pacific. He was then appointed to command the US 13th AF, one of the most formidable air formations of the war. His outstanding successes in directing air operations included the conflict at Guadalcanal. In 1944 he transferred to Italy as Commander of the US 15th AF which was engaged in the strategic offensive against Germany and Eastern Europe. He subsequently returned to the Pacific to lead a force of B–29s in an attack on Japan.

Twining's tough and determined nature was coupled with a vast knowledge of the technicalities of strategic bombing and with an ability to exploit situations to the full.

## Typhoon, Hawker

This British single-seat fighter was operational from 1942 to late 1945. Built around a mighty 2180hp 24-cylinder Napier Sabre engine, the Typhoon marked Hawker's final transition to metal monocoque construction. The prototype flew on 24 February 1940, and it was expected that production aircraft would be in service by the summer of that year as RAF Fighter Command's first 400mph interceptors. With Fw 190s already in production for the Luftwaffe, there was desperate need for an aircraft that would match their performance. Early engine problems, and accidents resulting from structural failure at the tail, almost led to cancellation of the whole Typhoon program. Just in time, it was realized that the fighter had truly outstanding performance at low altitude. So, from the Spring of 1942, 'Tiffies' began dealing with the Fw 190s that had been eluding Spitfires during tip-and-run attacks on southern England. Next they switched to the attack, becoming the first fighters to carry two 1000lb bombs under their wings. Airfields and communications were prime continental targets, with up to 150 railway locomotives destroyed each month by mid-1943. However, it is for ground attack with rockets that Typhoons are best remembered. Before D-Day they destroyed vital German radar stations; afterwards, adopting their famous 'cab rank' technique, they maintained standing patrols over the battle area, from which they could be called in by radio for a line-astern attack on any targets that were notified by ground controllers. Altogether, 3330 Typhoons were built.

### U.47

This Type VIIB U-Boat was commanded by K/Lt Gunther Prien. Apart from his other successes, which made him an 'ace', Prien is remembered for his daring attack on Scapa Flow in October 1939, when he torpedoed the British Battleship *Royal Oak*. He was finally sunk on 7 March 1941 in the North Atlantic by the corvettes *Arbutus* and *Camellia*.

### U.48

The highest scoring U-Boat of World War II, *U.48* sank 51 ships (310,407 tons gross) between September 1939 and June 1941.

### U.110

This U-Boat was forced to the surface on 9 May 1941 by the corvette *Aubrietia* and the destroyers *Bulldog* and *Broadway*. Boarding parties recovered vital information about the 'Enigma' coding machine and U-Boat ciphers before *U.110* sank in tow. The value of this find was so great that nothing was revealed about it for another 20 years.

### U.505

The big Type IXC U-Boat *U.505* was captured and boarded by a US task force comprising the escort carrier *Guadalcanal* and DEs *Chatelain*, *Jenks* and *Pillsbury*, northwest of Dakar. She was towed to the USA and after lengthy trials was presented to the Chicago Museum of Science and Industry.

### U.570
see Graph

### U.652
see *Greer*

## U-Boat

Derived from *Unterseeboot* or 'underwater boat', U-Boat was the German naval term for a submarine in both World Wars. German U-Boat design was officially banned under the Versailles Treaty, but as early as 1922 the talented team of Krupp's Germania Yard at Kiel had

U-Boat under attack from US naval aircraft.

been reunited in Holland, with the task of carrying out research. All the future U-Boats were designed by this team, and the contracts which were obtained by the front-organization, *Ingenieurs scheepsbouwkantoor*, for Finland, Spain and Turkey, were used as prototypes for future U-Boats. The Navy was primed by Hitler's promises of future expansion to place secret orders for U-Boat material before the public renunciation of the Versailles Treaty. As a result a startled world was confronted by an apparently miraculous expansion of the U-Boat Arm. By September 1939 65 U-Boats had been started, and a further 1097 were completed by May 1945.

Between 3 September 1939 and 8 May 1945 785 U-Boats were sunk. The personnel of the U-Boat Arm had comprised some 39,000 men of whom 32,000 were dead. But they had exacted a fearful price. The Allies and neutral countries lost 2828 ships totaling 14,687,231 tons to the submarines of Germany, Italy and Japan, and by far the greatest proportion of those losses were inflicted by the German U-Boats. A further 175 Allied warships were sunk by submarines.

Despite the appaling losses suffered, the morale of the U-Boat Arm did not waver. In May 1943 they suffered so heavy a defeat that they had to be withdrawn from the Battle of the Atlantic but as soon as new tactics and weapons were ready, the battle was on again. A similar comeback was planned for 1945, and was only averted by the Allied armies overrunning the shipyards and centers of production. This astonishing resilience can be attributed to the drive and leadership of Admiral Karl Dönitz, first head of the U-Boat Arm, then head of the Navy and finally *Führer*.

### Udet, General Ernst, 1896–1941

German Air Force General and World War I ace, Udet as Director General of Equipment of the Luftwaffe, controlled much of the power formerly invested in Milch. Udet was responsible for the Luftwaffe's concentration on single-engined fighters such as the Bf 109, and on dive-bombers and light and medium bombers in the early part of the war.

In November 1941, following a serious quarrel with Goering, an old, established friend, he committed suicide, though his death was officially reported as the result of an aircraft accident.

### U-Go

see Kohima and Imphal Offensives, 1944

### Ukraine, Battle of the, July-August 1941

At the outbreak of the war, General Kirponos was in command of the Russian forces in the south facing General Rundstedt's army. Kirponos's army was the only Soviet army to provide any resistance to the Germans and checked them between the Pripet Marshes and the Carpathian Hills. Kirponos wasted his mechanized corps which were no match for General Kleist's Panzers. The reserve mechanized corps with a few T-34s were called up but they were exhausted from their march and inexperienced, so they did not fight in formation as the Germans did. Despite heavy casualties the Russians managed to inflict heavy losses on the Germans.

German troops warmly greeted in Ukraine, 1941.

On 10 July Marshal Budenny was made Commander in Chief of all the troops in the Southwest Front. He had one and a half million soldiers in two concentrations at Uman and Kiev. On 15 and 16 July Kleist took Berdichev and Kazatin and drove a wedge between the two armies. At this stage it would have been advisable to withdraw to the Dniepr and avoid encirclement, but Budenny continued to send troops, equipment and even General Tyulenev out to Uman. On 18 July Kleist took Belaya Tserkov and intercepted Soviet communications about mounting a counterattack. On 20 July the Russians launched their attack, which was quickly repulsed by the Germans, who went on to take Novo Ukraina on 25 July. On 30 July General Manteuffel's tanks took Kirovograd. The troops at Uman counterattacked and thought they had successfully diverted General Schobert and his troops; in fact Schobert had completed their encirclement. By 8 August the Russians were surrounded and by 22 August all resistance in that pocket had been crushed. The next task for the Germans was to take the troops at Kiev. Guderian's march south took the Russians by surprise. On 12 September Kleist broke through the 38th Soviet Army and Model's Panzer Division made contact with Guderian, some 150 miles east of Kiev. On 16 September the encirclement was complete and Stalin would not allow any withdrawal. After five days of resistance some 665,000 men surrendered, according to the Germans. Although this was a major German victory, the fact that troops had been diverted from the offensive on Moscow meant that the Germans reached Moscow in the midst of winter instead of two months earlier.

### Ukraine, Battle of the, December 1943–May 1944

After the capture of Kiev the Germans and Russians awaited reinforcements. On 24 December 1943 General Vatutin's 1st Ukrainian Front launched the main Russian winter offensive and recaptured Zhitomir and Korosten. On 3 January 1944 the Russian mobile forces captured the junction of Novigrad Volynsk, 50 miles beyond Korosten, and on the next day

crossed into Poland despite the blizzards and bad road conditions. Vatutin's left wing reached General Konev's 2nd Ukrainian Front right wing and encircled 10 German divisions at Korsun-Shevchenkosy. Konev thought he had trapped the mass of the German army and had tanks positioned in strategic points. General Manstein sent his tanks to relieve the trapped forces but they failed to break through and it was left to the divisions in the pocket to break out, although they had little artillery support against the Russian T-34s. The operation probably cost Manstein the lives of 20,000 men, many wounded and used all his reserves.

On 5 February Vatutin captured Rovno and was heading south to cut Manstein's command in two. In the south, General Kleist's position was not much better. General Tolbukhin (4th Ukrainian Front) took Nikopol on the east bend of the Dniepr on 8 February and then he moved south to take the Crimea. On 22 February General Malinovsky (3rd Ukrainian Front) pushed to Krivoi Rog. In early March Vatutin was fatally wounded by partisans and Marshal Zhukov took command of the 1st Ukrainian Front, and launched the Russian spring offensive from Shepetovka despite the mud, because of his improved transport: he now had US trucks. On 7 March his troops reached Tarnapol and outflanked the lines on the Bug. Konev struck from Uman and reached the Bug on 12 March. He crossed the river and with General Rotmistrov's tanks widely deployed, he was able to take the German bridgehead over the Dniestr at Mogilev. Zhukov backed this up by moving south from Tarnapol and joined up with Konev at Jassy on the Prut at the end of March. This maneuver finally separated the Fourth Panzer Army from the First.

In the south Malinovsky had kept pace with this by driving across the mouth of the Dniepr and Bug and taking Kherson on 13 March and Nikolayev on 28 March. These disasters, coupled with the threat to the Crimea, caused Hitler to dismiss Manstein, who was replaced by Field Marshal Model.

Model's answer to this threat to the Balkans was to occupy Hungary. Then Model launched a counteroffensive along the Dniestr and regained the railway junction at Delatyn. This front was stable from April till July to the east of Lvov.

Since he was blocked along the Rumanian frontier, Konev headed south and combined with Malinovsky to threaten Odessa. Kleist had to fall back on the town but on 5 April Malinovsky shut the routes out of Odessa. Nonetheless the Germans managed to escape and the town fell on 10 April. Hitler then dismissed Kleist and Schörner became the Commander of Army Group South Ukraine. At this point the Russian offensive in the south also ground to a halt, whilst waiting for supplies and resting. However in early May Konev made a heavy attack west of Jassy with Stalin tanks but did not advance very far as Schorner had strong panzer reserves under General Manteuffel. In the ensuing battle the Russians were repulsed and there was no more activity on this front for four months.

This long battle for possession of the Ukraine was finally resolved in the north by the battle of Brody-Lvov in July, and in the south by the battle of Jassy-Kishinev in August.

**Uman Pocket**
see Ukraine, Battle of the, July-August 1941

**Umezu, General Yoshijiro, 1882–1949**

Umezu was made Army Chief of Staff to succeed General Tojo. He was a staunch opponent of unconditional surrender but was eventually convinced to accept the Potsdam Declaration. He was one of the few top Japanese politicians to attend the surrender ceremony at Tokyo Bay in September 1945.

**United Nations Conference**
see San Francisco Conference

**United Nations Declaration**

The United Nations Declaration was signed on 1 January 1942 by the USA, the UK, the USSR, China, Australia, Belgium, Canada, Costa Rica, Cuba, Czechoslovakia, the Dominican Republic, El Salvador, Greece, Guatemala, Haiti, Honduras, India, Luxembourg, the Netherlands, New Zealand, Nicaragua, Norway, Panama, Poland, South Africa and Yugoslavia. Subsequent signers were Bolivia, Brazil, Chile, Colombia, Ecuador, Egypt, Ethiopia, France, Iceland, Iran, Iraq, Liberia, Mexico, Paraguay, Peru, the Philippines, Saudi Arabia, Turkey, Uruguay and Venezuela.

The Declaration endorsed the Atlantic Charter, pledged that each country would not come to a separate agreement with the Axis powers, and ensured that each would co-operate militarily and economically in the war.

**US Army**

The US Army, like the British, was very small at the beginning of the war and professionally and technically even more backward. It had few reserves, and the volunteer National Guard, equivalent to the British Territorial Army, was badly undertrained and equipped. The country, however, had vast reserves of fit and technically adept men, whose familiarity with machinery made them ideal material for training in the new machine warfare, and a vast and vigorous industry from which to equip them. At the outset, the War Department took the decisions to raise 90 divisions, four million men in all, in a carefully proportioned blend of infantry, armor and airborne, and to win the war with that force. The American Navy, in the United States Marine Corps, had an alternative army of many divisions, eventually numbering 500,000, with which the assault stages of the Pacific war were very largely fought.

American equipment initially was in very short supply and deficient. The prewar tanks, in particular, were quite inadequate. Within a year of going to war, however, the Americans had begun mass production of one of the most successful models of the conflict, the Sherman. They also produced a successful tank-destroyer, the M–10, with a 3in gun. Their artillery was excellent, with fine 105mm and 155mm howitzers and a 155mm gun of notable accuracy and range. Small arms were of the most modern kinds, with a semi-automatic rifle, the Garand, as standard, and a whole range of automatic weapons from the .45 Thompson to the .5 Browning for the infantry. Munitions never lacked. The Americans adopted from the outset the policy of using firepower to save lives and were prepared to use land and air bombard-

ment of the enemy on a scale which no country could ever match.

The American president is constitutionally Commander in Chief of the Armed Forces, but Roosevelt did not intervene in the conduct of operations, though he laid down the broad lines of policy. Grand strategy was decided by the inter-service Joint Chiefs of Staff working with the British Chiefs of Staff as the Combined Chiefs of Staff. Foremost among them was General Marshall, Army Chief of Staff, a soldier of enormous professional competence and complete dominance over his army colleagues and subordinates. He established nevertheless a relationship of complete trust with his principal theater commander, Eisenhower, and allowed him relative freedom of conduct of operations. Eisenhower delegated the same freedom both to his own and his British army commanders. The system of command was therefore much looser than that prevailing in the German or Russian Armies.

A notable feature of the American command system was that the Air Force remained part of the Army until the end of the war. Marshall cleverly arranged for a common service command to underpin both the land and the air forces.

**Ushijima, Lieutenant General Mitsuru, 1887–1945**

After having served on Iwo Jima, Ushijima, the quiet and competent former commandant of the Military Academy, arrived on Okinawa Island towards the end of 1944. Starting with a base force of 21,000 troops, he organized all available men of all ages until, by March, he had a force of over 100,000. He built defense lines in depth, fortresses, caves, correctly predicting the American invasion plans.

He conducted a primarily defensive campaign against the 183,000 Allies who landed on Okinawa, except for two counteroffensives (13 April and 3 May) which his subordinates convinced him to launch against his better judgment; they both failed with enormous losses. In constant heavy rain, Ushijima and his troops retreated southward throughout May, where the fighting was continued from caves. Toward the end, almost 1000 Japanese were killed every day. Ushijima committed suicide on 22 June as the Americans approached his cave. Most of his 110,000 troops were dead by this time, though the fighting continued until 2 July. In addition, 75,000 civilians died; the Americans suffered about 50,000 casualties.

**US Navy**

The United States Navy was bound by the same treaties as the British, and although smaller in numbers in the lesser categories, the US had parity in capital ships up to 1939. Time had softened the virulent anti-British sentiments of the early 1920s, and by the late 1930s no-one in Washington seriously considered the idea of Great Britain as a future opponent. Increasingly attention was focused on Japan as the principal adversary, and inevitably this led to an emphasis on naval aviation and submarines to counter the Japanese opposite numbers. In other respects, however, the US Navy had lagged behind, notably in anti-submarine warfare, and like the other Western democracies, the years of financial stringency had prevented vital research from being pursued.

USS *South Dakota* and USS *Alabama* pass the guns of the British Home Fleet. The *South Dakota* took part in the Naval Battle of Guadalcanal.

In 1940 Congress passed the 'Two-Ocean Navy' Bill, allowing the building of 1,325,000 tons of new warships, a timely measure which allowed the gradual rebuilding of industrial resources. President Roosevelt made it clear that his sympathies lay with Great Britain and France rather than the Axis, and throughout 1940 and 1941 aid was given to the British in all forms, culminating in the Lend-Lease Act, which allowed the USA to 'lend' war material to Great Britain at the price of leasing bases around the world. As British warships were repaired in US naval shipyards these yards were soon proficient at coping with battle-damage, and the free exchange of technical information worked to the advantage of the United States in much the same way. Nevertheless, the transition of the US economy from peacetime to full war-production was a staggering achievement, and in 1942 warships and merchant ships began to pour from the shipyards to replace ships lost to the U-Boats' depredations.

The destruction of the Pacific Fleet at Pearl Harbor forced the US Navy to place more reliance on carrier strike tactics than had been foreseen, and soon an entire fleet of fast carriers was under construction. But these were not ready in time for two crucial battles, Coral Sea in May 1942 and Midway a month later. The first was a tactical defeat even if a strategic victory but the second was one of the decisive sea battles of history, a finely judged affair which achieved its effect without reckless hazarding of ships and men.

After Midway the US Navy went over to the offensive and the first counterstroke was to invade Guadalcanal in the Solomon Islands. This revealed an alarming weakness in the American night-fighting organization. The Japanese had a most devastating torpedo, the 'Long Lance' and knew how to use it in the misty conditions found in the South Pacific. Only the possession of radar enabled the American and Allied ships to hold their own, but after a series of disasters and near-disasters the Allies' persistence and weight of firepower overcame Japanese resistance.

As the fast carrier task forces were built up the US Navy hit at the Japanese garrisons across the Pacific in a series of raids and amphibious assaults. The 'island-hopping' technique was developed so that strong garrisons

were isolated. All the while the Japanese Fleet lurked behind its defensive perimeter, hoping to lure the US Fleet into a final decisive battle. The Battle of the Philippine Sea in June 1944 was a big carrier battle, and in the ensuing 'Marianas Turkey Shoot' the skilled Navy pilots shot down nearly 300 aircraft losing only a tenth of that number themselves. Then came the series of battles in the area known as Leyte. This was the Japanese Navy's last throw, but it resulted in the destruction of nearly all the major units left, and was the greatest conflict in the history of naval warfare, in terms of numbers and tonnage of ships involved.

The final stage of the drive on the Japanese homeland was marked by a new and sinister development, the kamikaze or suicide air attack, but the US Navy survived even this. The dropping of the atom bombs on Hiroshima and Nagasaki made an invasion of the Japanese islands unnecessary, but the destruction of Japan's air and naval forces had also made the end inevitable. Surrender might have been delayed for a few more months, but the strangulation of Japan's food and raw material imports had robbed her of the means to continue the war.

In the war against Japan the US Navy achieved two remarkable things. First, it showed that carrier-borne aircraft could take on and defeat a land-based air force, which had been thought impossible before the war. Second, its submarines fought the only *successful* undersea campaign; even if the tonnage sunk was much lower than that sunk by the U-Boats in the Atlantic, the US submarine campaign was a complete success. In other ways, too, the USN showed great originality. Its minelaying campaign, with that of the Air Force, played a big part in the destruction of Japanese seapower, and its naval aviators' expertise reached an almost fabulous degree of perfection.

*Strength of the US Navy – December 1941*
16 battleships
7 aircraft carriers
18 heavy cruisers
19 light cruisers
6 anti-aircraft cruisers
171 destroyers
114 submarines

**Utah**
see D-Day landings, 1944

**V-1**
see FZG-76

**V-2**
see A-4 Rocket

**V-3**
see High Pressure Pumps

**'Val'**
see Aichi D3A

**Valentine Tank**

This British battle tank took its name from the fact that the initial design was submitted by Vickers Limited to the War Office just before St Valentine's Day 1938. The first models came off the line in May 1940. Thereafter over 8000 were built before production stopped in 1944. As well as being made in Great Britain by Vickers (6855 tanks) they were made in Canada by the Canadian Pacific Railway Co (1420 tanks) and about 2500 of these were sent to Russia to be used on the Eastern Front.

The basic Valentine was a 17-tonner with armor of up to 65mm thick. The turret mounted a two-pounder (40mm) gun which, like all its kind, could fire only armor-piercing shot and not high explosive shells. A 7.92mm BESA machine gun was also mounted in the turret which was notoriously cramped; different models of Valentine used two- or three-man turrets, but none was particularly comfortable and none was provided with any form of cupola, which meant that the commander had to fight his tank with his head and shoulders outside the turret; a highly vulnerable position. Towards the end of the production run a number of tanks were up-gunned to take the six-pounder and later types had a 75mm gun; one defect of the up-gunning was that when the six-pounder was fitted it took up so much space that the machine gun had to be omitted. Mechanically, the Valentine was outstanding among British tanks of its time, being extremely reliable and easily serviced. As a result, the chassis was extensively used for a variety of specialist vehicles, among them the 'Bishop' self-propelled 25-pounder field gun, the 'Archer' SP 17-pounder anti-tank gun, flame-throwers, mine-clearing tanks, observation tanks for artillery, armored searchlight tanks, and the first types of Duplex Drive swimming tanks.

*Valiant*
see *Queen Elizabeth*

## Vandegrift, Lieutenant General Alexander A, 1887–1972

Vandegrift was commander of land forces in the Solomons campaign. On 8 August 1942 he landed unopposed on Guadalcanal. He had no knowledge of Guadalcanal. On 13 September he beat off fierce fighting by the Japanese in what is known as the Battle of Bloody Ridge. The US lost control of the sea and were very short of supplies. Finally the 7th Marines were sent as reinforcements and Vandegrift could defend Henderson Field properly.

By 3 November he was on the offensive and surrounded 400 Japanese troops at Point Cruz. He left Guadalcanal on 9 December and Major General Patch replaced him. He returned to the USA and in July was made Lieutenant General, commanding officer of 1st Marine Amphibious. On 1 November 1943 he led landings at Bougainville. He then reported back to Washington and was made Commandant of the Marine Corps.

## Vandenberg, Arthur, 1884–1951

Vandenberg was a Republican Senator from Michigan. He was an isolationist but at the end of the war he was converted to internationalism. He was a delegate to the San Francisco Conference and he ensured that the Senate ratified the United Nations Charter.

## Vasilievsky, Marshal Aleksandr M, 1895–1977

Vasilievsky was the representative of HQ responsible for co-ordinating military activities of Fronts or major strategic flanks. He graduated from the Frunze Military Academy in the early 1930s. He held important posts in the Commissariat of Defense. From 1941 to 1942 he was Deputy Chief of Operations Control and then became Chief of General Staff of the USSR Armed Forces. He was responsible for co-ordinating the different Fronts at Stalingrad and also masterminded the actual offensive. In 1944 he co-ordinated the 2nd and 3rd Fronts in Belorussia and East Prussia. He was in constant touch with Stalin through his representative in Moscow, Antonov. When Stalin was at Yalta, Vasilievsky took his place in Moscow. He took part in all major planning conferences. In 1945 he was sent to the Far Eastern Front where he was appointed Commander in Chief.

## Vatutin, General Nikolay F, 1901–1944

Vatutin led the Russian armies which liberated Stalingrad, the Ukraine and Kiev. He graduated from the Frunze Academy in 1929 and went on to train at the Academy of General Staff. He was one of Stalin's military advisers on the Stavka and was head of General Staff Operations in 1941. He was Vasilievsky's deputy and a friend of Zhukov, but Stalin disliked him. Nonetheless he asked to be given his first important command on the Voronezh Front in 1942. In November 1942 he led his newly-formed Southwest Front in the operation to cut off the Sixth Army at Stalingrad. At Kursk he halted Manstein's advance and counterattacked to take Kharkov. He then led his forces into the Ukraine and captured Kiev. In early March 1944 he was fatally wounded while leading an operation to take Rovno.

## Vella Gulf, Battle of, 1943

On 6 August 1943 Rear Admiral Wilkinson received news that the 'Tokyo Express' was about to make another run to Kolombangara. He decided to send a small force of six destroyers under Commodore Moosbrugger, which arrived at Vella Gulf at 2200. The Japanese force consisted of four destroyers of which three were carrying troops and supplies. The Japanese were not ready for the attack and three destroyers were immobilized after a short time. Rear Admiral Shigura escaped and managed to fire eight torpedoes, but none hit the US ships. The three Japanese destroyers *Arashi*, *Hagikasi* and *Kawakaze* sank. This success for the US Navy led to the cancellation of the Tokyo Express.

## Ventura, PV–1 and PV–2 Harpoon, Lockheed

Clearly related to the Model 14 Hudson, the Ventura was a similar military adaptation of the larger commercial Model 18 Lodestar. The RAF ordered 675 in the Summer of 1940 with deliveries to begin in March 1941. In fact, the first Ventura did not fly until 31 July 1941, and the type was unable to make its first operational flight with RAF Bomber Command until 3 November 1942. Venturas were quickly found to be unsuited to daylight raids over Europe and were withdrawn from Bomber Command in 1943. From the fall of that year, they were transferred to Coastal Command as Ventura G.R.Is, and were supplemented later by G.R.Vs. The US Navy operated similar aircraft as PV–1s. These were followed in 1944 by the improved PV–2 Harpoon, with increased span, larger tail surfaces, an armament of five or eight forward-firing 0.5in guns, a two-gun turret and two ventral guns, up to four 1000lb bombs or depth charges located internally and two more externally.

## Veritable
see Rhine Crossings, 1945

## Vian, Admiral Sir Philip, 1894–1968

Leader of the daring raid to free the prisoners of the *Graf Spee*'s commerce raiding, the operation known as the *Altmark* incident of 1940, Vian went on to take part in a whole series of more or less unorthodox Royal Naval operations: the evacuation of Namsos in May 1940 when the *Afridi* was sunk under him; the hunt for the *Bismarck* in which he commanded a flotilla of destroyers; the raid on Spitzbergen in July 1941; and the two Mediterranean battles of Sirte. He commanded a squadron of aircraft carriers in the Italian landings and the Eastern Task Force in the Cross-Channel invasion. At the end of the war he took the Eastern Fleet's squadron of aircraft carriers into the central Pacific for the campaign against Japan, in which their armored decks helped them to play a vital part in the battle with the kamikaze pilots defending Okinawa. His record was the most colorful and varied of any British Admiral of the war.

## Vichy France
see Pétain, Marshal

## Vickers Gun

This was the standard medium machine gun of the British and Commonwealth Armies from 1912 to 1965. The basic design was even older originating from the Maxim Gun, first used by the British Army in 1888. The Vickers company made slight modifications in 1912, reversing the motion of the lock, lightening the weapon and using less expensive and lighter metal in the manufacture.

It was a recoil-operated machine gun, water cooled and belt fed and using a toggle lock to secure the breech at the instant of firing. It weighed 40lb without its tripod and fired the standard .303 British cartridge at about 450rpm. Like all the Maxim breed it was reliable beyond question; records exist of phenomenal feats of endurance in both world wars. The most famous instance occurred on the Somme in 1916 when ten Vickers guns delivered twelve hours of continuous fire to deny a stretch of ground to the Germans, using up a million rounds of ammunition, a hundred spare barrels and keeping two men doing nothing but filling ammunition belts.

Not just an infantry gun, the Vickers was turned out in several variant models for use in aircraft and tanks, both in .303 and .50 calibers. The guns were essentially the same, the differences being matters of method of cooling (aircraft guns were air cooled), feeding (some aircraft guns fed the belt from the right, some from the left), or mounting. Innumerable Vickers guns are still in use in various countries to this day, and probably will be for many years to come.

*Victorious*
see *Illustrious*

## Vildebeest, Vickers

This two-seat torpedo-bomber biplane entered service with the RAF in 1933. Its replacement was overdue when World War II began, and the 156mph Vildebeest was, in fact, Coastal Command's only operational torpedo-bomber. The last two squadrons suffered heavy losses when the Japanese invaded Singapore in 1941.

## Vishinsky, Andrei, 1883–1955

Vishinsky was Vice-Commissar of Foreign Affairs in the USSR. He was Molotov's deputy and specialized in manipulating governments in countries under Soviet occupation. In June 1940 he nominated a provisional government in Latvia to supervise elections. He was Molotov's spokesman on Polish policy and he announced that the USSR would not allow US aircraft to use airbases in its territory to help the Warsaw Uprising. In February 1945 he was sent to Rumania where he bullied King Michael into dissolving the government and setting up a Communist administration. After the war he became Foreign Minister 1949–53.

## Vistula-Oder, Battle of
see Poland, Liberation of, 1944–45

## Vittorio Veneto

The second battleship of the *Littorio* Class battleships was completed on 28 April 1940, a week before her sister. She escaped damage at Taranto and led an active career. She was in the indecisive skirmish known as the Battle of Cape Spartivento. She was the unwitting cause of the Battle of Cape Matapan in March 1941, for at 1521 hours on 28 March she was torpedoed by a British Albacore torpedo-bomber from HMS *Formidable*. She limped homewards, and the Commander in Chief ordered other ships to screen her. One of these, the heavy cruiser *Pola* took another torpedo-hit, and it was while trying to save her that the *Fiume* and *Zara* fell in with Admiral Cunningham's battleships that night.

The *Vittorio Veneto* was back in action by the end of the year, but in December she was torpedoed once more, this time by the British submarine *Urge*. Her luck improved after that, for she escaped without damage when the *Littorio* was damaged by British air attack in June 1942, and although she suffered slight damage while lying in La Spezia, she was not hit by German glider-bombs when her sister *Roma* blew up in September 1943. She was moved from Malta to Egypt with the *Littorio* and lay there until 1946.

## Vlasov, Lieutenant General Andrey A, 1900–1945

Vlasov led the anti-Stalin movement of Russians in Germany during the war. He had been adviser to Chiang Kai-shek from 1938 to 1939. He proved his courage in his defense of Kiev in August 1941, when encircled by the Germans. Stalin gave him permission to withdraw and he was given command of a force defending Moscow. He was then captured by the Germans at Sevastopol in May 1942 when he refused to fly out. At first he made propaganda broadcasts, he voiced the distrust of Stalin felt by the army. In November 1944 Himmler let him form an Anti-Stalinist Committee for the Liberation of the Peoples of Russia. He recruited soldiers from the POW camps and among those who had been brought back from Russian territories as forced labor. He was to set up three divisions of Russian soldiers and on 14 November he published a manifesto in Prague, which attacked Stalin's annexation of foreign territory and his policy on nationalities. At the end of the war one division was involved in fighting the Red Army at Frankfurt-on-the-Oder. Another division marched into Prague before the US and defeated the SS garrison. The troops surrendered to the US but were handed over to the Soviet Army and many committed suicide. General Vlasov was arrested by the Soviet authorities on Czech soil in May 1945 and in August he was shot for treason and espionage.

## Volkssturm Gewehr

Late in 1944 the Germans inaugurated a *Primitiv-Waffen-Programm*, an attempt to develop and turn out a large number of cheap but effective weapons with which to arm the 'Volkssturm' or 'People's Guard' and various other last-ditch and guerrilla organizations which, in the event, failed to materialize.

For a submachine gun the answer was simply to copy the British Sten gun, with slight modifications to suit German methods of manu-

Volkssturm Gewehr.

facture and use – eg., the magazine fitted in the bottom of the gun instead of into the side. But to provide a cheap rifle it was necessary to start from scratch. The design was done by an engineer Barnetzke of the Gustloffwerke, Suhl, who based his design on a system of delayed blowback on which he had been working for some time. The barrel was surrounded by an annular sleeve, to which the bolt was attached. The weapon fired the 7.92mm short cartridge which had been adopted for the MP43 assault rifle, and, indeed, the assault rifle's 30-round magazine was used to simplify production.

On firing, a proportion of the propelling gas was allowed to pass through four vents some 2.5in ahead of the chamber and this gas entered the space between the barrel and the annular sleeve. In the normal course of events, the recoil of the cartridge would tend to blow the bolt open, but this movement was now resisted by the gas pressure pushing on the forward end of the sleeve, thus delaying the opening of the bolt until such time as the gas pressure dropped. When the bolt finally began to open, the annular sleeve was allowed to vent the trapped gas to the open air after which the bolt carried out the usual loading cycle.

The only defect of this design was that the exterior of the barrel and the interior of the sleeve had to be carefully machined to give an almost gas-tight fit, and, inevitably, gas fouling tended to jam the action. But apart from this it was a brilliant design not only in its mechanical layout but also in that it was easily put together by non-specialist factories from non-essential materials. By the time production began, however, the war was coming to an end and relatively few of these weapons were made.

A similar design, also by Barnetzke, was the 'Volks Pistole' a 9mm pistol intended for mass-production. This used the same system of gas-induced delay, venting gas from the chamber into the interior of the slide; it was hammer fired and used the magazine of the Walther P–38, for production convenience. Only prototypes of this pistol were made before the war ended.

## Voronezh, Battle of, June 1942

Following the successful capture of Kharkov, General Hoth led his Fourth Panzer Army and the Second Hungarian Army on an offensive to reach the Don and take Voronezh, thus covering the Don-Donets corridor for General Paulus's advance to Stalingrad. They met some resistance from General Golikov's tanks but reached their objective on 5 July. The Fourth Panzer Army was then sent south to take part in the Caucasus campaign and it had to cross the path of Paulus's Sixth Army, wasting valuable time. Golikov was dismissed but was restored to his command of the Voronezh Front in December 1942.

## Voronov, General Nikolay N, 1899–

Voronov was a Marshal of artillery who directed major operations. He played an important part in the re-equipping of artillery and in the development of its tactical application. In the Russo–Finnish War he used the artillery to breach the Mannerheim Line. He directed artillery on the Leningrad Front in 1941 and Stalingrad offensive. At Kursk he helped plan the deployment of artillery and anti-aircraft guns.

## Voroshilov, Marshal Kliment E, 1881–1969

Marshal Voroshilov was associated with Stalin and Budenny during the Civil War, when they set up the 1st Cavalry Army. In 1934 he was Commissar for Defense and saw to the mechanization of the Red Army. In May 1940 he was replaced by Timoshenko and was appointed Deputy Chairman of the Defense Committee. In July 1941 he was Commander of the armies of the Northwest Front, near Leningrad. He failed to check the German advance because of his lack of military knowledge, although his task was not facilitated by the fact his troops were badly trained and inexperienced. He showed personal courage in the defense of the city but Stalin removed him and he had a staff appointment for the rest of the war. As a member of the State Defense Committee he attended many of the Allied conferences. In August 1942 during Churchill's visit to Moscow, Voroshilov acted as military spokesman in talks with Generals Brooke and Wavell. They discussed the possibility of establishing an Anglo-American air force in Transcaucasia but this was eventually rejected by the Russians in May 1943. In November 1943 Voroshilov attended the Teheran conference. At the end of the war he signed the armistice on behalf of the Allies with Hungary and then became head of the Soviet Control Commission in Hungary.

## Vyazma-Bryansk, Battle of, October 1941

Following the Battle of the Ukraine, the German High Command was ready to resume the offensive against Moscow. General Höpner's Panzer Gruppe had been sent from Leningrad and General Hoth and General Guderian's Panzer Armies were ready to challenge the last of the USSR's great armies: the 32nd and 3rd. The Panzers had no trouble breaking through. Guderian took Orel in the first week of October and Höpner forced Konev's Western Front into the path of the infantry of Generals Kluge and Strauss. In the north of this sector Hoth broke through to the south and took Vyazma. This meant that there were two pockets and 650,000 men were trapped. After some fierce fighting the Soviet 3rd Army at Vyazma surrendered on the 14 October and the 32nd at Bryansk surrendered on the 20 October.

# W

## Waffen SS

The Waffen SS were fully militarized combat formations of the SS and had 40 divisions in the field at the end of World War II. The Waffen SS were notorious for their cruelty towards the civilian population, for example, their behavior during the Warsaw ghetto uprising and during the Warsaw uprising, 1944. The Waffen SS began recruiting for their training schools in 1935 and they were supposed to be an elite armored division and also a unit of the Nazi party. Although many of the officers were regular ex-Army, some were convicted criminals such as Oskar Dirlewanger, the notorious Butcher of Warsaw, and others had a reputation for tremendous cruelty such as General Bach-Zelewski, Theodore Eicke and Franz Jeckeln. In 1943 there were four SS divisions and after one, the Adolf Hitler division, had stopped the Russian advance at Kharkov, it was decided to go through with a plan of rapid expansion by conscripting foreigners. New divisions were sent to stem the Red Army's advance in Hungary under SS General Dietrich and fought a retreating battle through Hungary to Austria.

Finnish members of the Waffen SS on maneuvers near Leningrad.

## Wainwright, Major General Jonathan H, 1883–1953

When General MacArthur left Bataan, Wainwright took over command of land troops and held out in Corregidor until 6 May 1942.

Wainwright had arrived in the Philippines in September 1940 and in December 1940 he had orders to defend the northern part of Luzon. As the Japanese landed in Lingayen Gulf, Wainwright made a quick retreat to prevent his forces from being cut off and fell back to Bataan. After MacArthur left, Roosevelt made him Lieutenant General on 19 March 1942.

Although the Japanese air power was generally superior, Wainwright held out in Bataan until 8 April then withdrew to Corregidor. After Corregidor Wainwright was forced to order all troops in the Philippines to stop fighting.

Wainwright was on the Bataan Death March and survived it to be a POW in Manchuria until the end of the war. Haggard and gaunt, he was at MacArthur's side on board the USS *Missouri* to accept the Japanese surrender.

## Walcheren, Assault on
see Antwerp, September-November 1944

## Wallace, Vice-President Henry, 1888–1965

Wallace was President Roosevelt's Vice-President and a close adviser. He attended the Washington Conferences and sat on various Boards including the Economic Defense Board and the Top Policy Group which discussed the scientific effort. In 1944 Roosevelt chose Harry Truman as his running mate because Wallace had antagonized some influential Democrats because of his allegedly pacifist views vis-à-vis the Soviet Union and postwar policy.

## Wallbuster Shell
see Burney Guns

## Wallis, Sir Barnes, 1887–1979

As an airship engineer he designed the successful R.100, and then as an airplane designer he invented the 'geodetic' fuselage used for the Wellington. During the war Barnes turned his thoughts to the design of bombs, both large and specialized. His most celebrated invention was the 'bouncing' bomb, a spherical device with which the Möhne and Eder dams were destroyed in May 1943. He later designed the 'Tall Boy' and 'Grand Slam' bombs, monster weapons used at the end of the war to destroy viaducts and bridges.

## Walther

Carl Walther GmbH of Zella-Mehlis, Thuringia was a major German manufacturer of pistols and sporting arms. The company's principal wartime reputation rested upon the P–38 pistol which became the standard Wehrmacht pistol in 1938, replacing the long-established Luger. The reason for replacement was that the Luger, good as it was, was ill-suited to mass production and too expensive, and in the middle 1930s the German Army called for designs for a replacement. In 1936 the Walther factory produced their *Armee Pistole* or Model AP as a possible

military weapon; this was evaluated by the Army who turned it down on the grounds that it employed a concealed hammer, a device which the Army considered unwise since it was not possible to see whether the gun was cocked. The design was modified to include a visible external hammer, and in this form was accepted.

The P–38 was a remarkable pistol in that it was the first military pistol to adopt the 'double-action' type of action. In most automatic pistols of the time it was necessary to pull back the slide and release it, chambering a cartridge. This left the hammer cocked; the next step was to apply the safety catch, or, carefully, lower the hammer onto the loaded chamber. Either way was conducive to accidents, and it was usual to carry the pistol with the chamber empty, relying on sufficient warning to allow time to draw it, operate the slide, and thus bring it to the active condition. The Walther design changed all this; the slide was operated to charge the chamber, after which the safety catch was applied; this dropped the hammer but also locked the firing pin so that there was no danger of the pistol firing. It could now be carried in perfect safety. When needed, the only action was to draw it, release the safety catch and pull the trigger. This lifted the hammer to the full-cock position and then released it to fire the cartridge, an action similar to that of a revolver. Thereafter the action was just the same as any other automatic.

The breech was locked by a wedge beneath the barrel, which locked the slide until a short recoil had taken place. Another innovative feature was a signal pin in the rear of the slide which protruded, giving both visible and tactile indication of a cartridge in the chamber.

Upwards of a million P–38 pistols were made, several other companies being involved in production in order to meet the demand. It was adopted by the Swedish Army in 1939 though the outbreak of war soon put an end to their supply. In postwar years production was resumed by the new Walther factory at Ulm, and it is currently the standard pistol of the Bundeswehr under the title 'P–1'.

The Walther company were, of course, involved in other armament production during the war, notably the Gewehr 41 automatic rifle (which was not a success), the MKb 42, prototype of the MP43 assault rifle, the Gewehr 43 automatic rifle and various machine guns.

## Warhawk
see P-40 Warhawk, Curtiss

## Warsaw Uprising, 1 August–3 October 1944

By late July 1944, the German Army in Poland appeared to be routed as Rokossovsky reached the Vistula and the suburbs of Warsaw. The Polish Government in Exile and General Bor-Komorowski of the Home Army decided to raise Warsaw against the Germans and pre-empt the Russians and the Communist PCNL. They knew of the USSR's disinclination to aid them, and since they had not consulted the Red Army, they did not know that the Russian offensive in Poland was coming to an end. The Germans had not been routed and had retired to strong defenses behind the Vistula, and had reinforced Warsaw on 29 July with the Goering Panzer Division.

Nonetheless 42,500 Home Army troops, plus civilians and the Communist People's Army, with great unity, discipline and enthusiasm won two-thirds of the city in twenty hours on 1 August. The Germans counterattacked on 4 August, under SS Commander Bach-Zelewski, a specialist in partisan uprisings. By 10 August the Poles were isolated into three small areas and the German dive-bombers and heavy artillery had command of the skies. The Allies had to air-drop supplies to partisans outside Warsaw, who smuggled them into the city through the sewer system which served the Poles' for communications. However the Germans discovered the Poles' extensive use of the sewers during the siege of Stare Miasto in early September. Bor therefore evacuated the area. All this time Prime Minister Mikolajczyk was attempting to negotiate Russian aid for Warsaw, but the Polish Government would not agree with Stalin's terms which included agreement with the PCNL. Stalin would not allow the Western Allies to use the Russian bases for air-drops and even disarmed Home Army troops making their way to Warsaw, claiming he would not aid those antagonistic to the Soviet Union.

On 10 September the Russians attacked Praga, occupying it on 15 September. This was followed by nightly air-drops by the Russians (from 14 September) and Americans (from 18 September) which boosted Polish morale. On 20 September communications were finally established between Warsaw and the Red Army. Two battalions of the Kosciuszko Division (PPR) were sent. Nonetheless, the Poles lost Czerniakow on 23 September and Mokotow on 27 September and declared themselves unable to continue unless the Red Army attacked Warsaw by 1 October. On 3 October Bor signed an armistice with the Germans: the Home Army, but not the People's Army, were given combatant status (and, therefore, normal POW treatment) and the principle of collective responsibility was not to be applied to civilians.

On the Polish side, 15,000 were killed; on the German side, 10,000 killed, 7000 missing and 9000 wounded.

## Warspite

The *Warspite* was a legend in her lifetime, a veteran of two World Wars and the most distinguished British fighting ship of the 20th Century. As a unit of the *Queen Elizabeth* Class she had covered herself with glory at the Battle of Jutland in 1916, when she fought seven German battleships after her steering had jammed. She was the first British battleship to undergo full modernization, in 1933–36, and so despite her age found herself in the frontline in 1939. She played a supporting role at the Second Battle of Narvik in April 1940, using her 15in guns with deadly effect in the confines of Narvikfjord and using her floatplane to reconnoiter for the destroyers.

The entry of Italy into the war in June 1940 forced the Admiralty to reinforce the Mediterranean Fleet, and the *Warspite* began her famous association with Admiral A B Cunningham as his flagship. She damaged the *Giulio Cesare* badly with a single 15in shell who she hit at 24,600 yards (14 miles) and led the line at the Battle of Cape Matapan. She was badly damaged by dive-bombers during the Battle for Crete and had to be extensively repaired in the USA but returned for the invasion of Italy in 1943. While lying off Salerno she was nearly sunk by two glider-bombs, but after a nightmare journey in the care of seven tugs, including a passage *sideways* through the Straits of

HMS *Warspite*, veteran of Jutland, fires her guns off Catania on the Sicilian coast.

Messina,she made port. She was allocated to the Normandy Invasion bombardment force, and despite further damage from a magnetic mine while passing through the English Channel, she performed excellently. Her last assignment was the bombardment of Walcheren, after which she was decommissioned. If ever a ship can be said to have had a personality it was the *Warspite*, and although perverse it made her a much loved ship. There were few regrets when she cheated ordained fate by running aground on the way to be scrapped.

## Warwick, Vickers

The Warwick was a scaled-up development of the Wellington, which it was intended to replace. The prototype flew on 13 August 1939 powered by two Rolls-Royce Vultures. Abandonment of this engine led to the decision to fit the Bristol Centaurus. This was in short supply, so the Warwick Mk I eventually went into production with 1850hp Pratt & Whitney Double Wasps. By that time, it was clearly outdated as a bomber so the Warwick saw wartime service as an air/sea rescue aircraft carrying an airborne lifeboat, and as a transport aircraft.

## Washington Conference (First), December 1941 – January 1942

This conference took place immediately after the USA had declared war on Japan and was the first attempt by the Allies to co-ordinate operations.

General Marshall and Admiral Stark put forward a plan which accepted that the Philippines, Guam and Wake Island would fall to Japan and that the main strategy should be directed at wearing Germany down. The Americans were anxious to prepare operations and plan an offensive in Europe as soon as possible in 1943. The British did not think this would be possible and preferred to discuss intermediate projects. Churchill proposed a North West Africa Project, a landing in Algeria and an attack on Morocco but the US did not agree on its importance. The British and US were also at odds over the question of the ABDA command in the Far East. The British felt that if a British general was appointed overall commander, he would be

forced to take the responsibility for an inevitable defeat at the hands of the Japanese. Eventually they agreed that General Wavell should be made overall commander.

The conference made two important decisions: it decided that military and economic resources should be pooled under the direction of the Allied Chiefs of Staff and that it should pursue a 'Germany First' policy.

## Washington Conference (Third), May 1943

This conference was called at Churchill's insistence and gave Britain and the USA a chance to discuss their strategical differences. The Americans felt that the invasion of Italy was unnecessary and should come second to the invasion of Normandy. The question was left undecided and settled at a later date. Generals Stilwell and Chennault attended the conference to discuss the Far East and they clashed bitterly. Chennault wanted greater emphasis on *air* support for the Chinese Army whereas Stilwell wanted to build up the Army. It was finally decided that more aircraft would be sent to China.

## Wasserfall

This was a German radio-controlled supersonic guided missile for anti-aircraft use. It was developed in reply to a demand for a missile which would destroy aircraft flying at 65,000ft altitude at 550mph and at ranges up to 30 miles from the launch point, a highly advanced specification for the early 1940s. The intention was to deploy batteries of these missiles to defend the centers of population, an estimated 200 batteries being necessary to cover Germany.

Work began at the Peenemünde test station in 1942; the design borrowed a great deal from the contemporary A–4 missile. The first firing tests took place across the Baltic in February 1944, in which the rocket reached an altitude of 23,000ft. By July 1944 seven more had been made and fired. Development was stopped in February 1945; although some sources have suggested that some of the trial missiles were actually fired against Allied aircraft, there is no evidence to support this.

The Wasserfall weighed 7800lb at takeoff, was 26ft long and carried a 674lb warhead of high explosive fitted with a proximity fuze. Had it been completed sooner, it would have been a formidable addition to Germany's air defenses.

**Watchtower**
see Guadalcanal, 1942

## Watson-Watt, Sir Robert, 1892–1973

A government scientist, Watson-Watt became interested in the possibility of using radio waves to locate the position of unseen aircraft in 1935. Tests having proved the theoretical possibility, Watt developed a method of 'radio direction finding' by measuring the time taken for the echo of a radio beam to return to its transmitter. By 1939 RDF, or radar as it came to be called, had been developed to the point where a chain of transmitting towers covered the approaches to the south coast from Sheerness to the Isle of Wight. It made it possible to win the Battle of Britain. He spent the rest of the war refining his invention and extending its use to many functions; night air interception, maritime range-finding, ground acquisition from the air and the distinction of friendly from enemy aircraft. Tedder called Watt 'one of the three saviors of Britain'.

**Wavell, General Sir Archibald, 1883–1950**

Wavell was one of the most respected British commanders of World War II. His main contribution to the war effort was in fighting in Egypt 1940–41 when with limited resources he was able to push the Italians back.

Wavell became Commander-in-Chief in the Middle East in July 1939 and his main duty was to build up defenses in the Middle East and North Africa. His command extended over the Eastern Mediterranean. On 13 September 1940 the Italian Tenth Army advanced into Egypt and were 60 miles inside the border by 18 September. On 9 December Wavell's Desert Force began to drive them back, although they were outnumbered by the Italians. The 6th Australian Division captured Benghazi on 6 February and the Allies controlled Cyrenaica. This was the Allies' only victory in the Middle East until Alamein.

In February 1941 Wavell launched a series of offensives to drive the Italians out of East Africa and after heavy fighting the Italians surrendered Addis Ababa on 6 April. In February Wavell had had to send a large part of his troops to

Greece and had kept one infantry division and one armored division to protect Cyrenaica. This was a risk because his forces were not well-equipped and when General Rommel's Afrika Korps arrived in North Africa they could out-maneuver the British. On 11 April the Axis forces had reached the Egyptian border.

In November 1941 Churchill had become impatient at Wavell's reluctance to take the offensive and he transferred him to the position of Commander-in-Chief in India. When Japan entered the war, Wavell was appointed Allied Supreme Commander but he had insufficient air cover to prevent the Japanese from overrunning Malaya and the Dutch East Indies and in February 1942 Wavell resigned his command. He returned to India where he marshaled his resources to prepare an offensive on Burma. In December 1942 his troops advanced in the Arakan but they made no breakthrough, especially since Wavell insisted on frontal assaults. In January 1943 Wavell was made Field Marshal and in June he became Viceroy of India. Churchill did not appreciate Wavell's gifts as military commander and thus gave him a political appointment, which meant he played no further part in military planning.

## Wedemeyer, Major General Albert, 1897–

Wedemeyer replaced General Stilwell as Chiang Kai-shek's Chief of Staff. From 1941–43 Wedemeyer worked in the War Department General Staff and was regarded as an expert in war plans. In August 1943 he was appointed US Deputy Chief of Staff under Admiral Mountbatten and in October 1944 he was sent to China to try out a new American policy: to work for co-operation between Chiang and the Communists. President Roosevelt no longer insisted that an American General should be Commander in Chief of Land Forces in China and Wedemeyer's main task was to ensure that US aid was being correctly used. The Kuomintang Army was so corrupt that officers did not give their men proper rations and there were black market dealings in war supplies.

## Wellesley, Vickers

Like the later and more famous Wellington, this two-seat general-purpose bomber had wings and fuselage of geodetic construction, combining strength with lightness. To avoid having to

Vickers Wellesley over East Anglia.

cut too many holes in the 'basketwork' structure, up to 2000lb of bombs could be carried in unique underwing containers. Power plant was a 925hp Bristol Pegasus radial engine giving the Wellesley a speed of 228mph. Armament comprised one forward firing machine gun and another in the rear cockpit. Only four Wellesleys remained operational with Bomber Command at the outbreak of war; 100 others had been despatched to the Middle East, where they operated successfully against the Italians. On the first day of the East African campaign, they bombed Massawa in Eritrea, following up with a raid on Addis Ababa on 18 August. They remained in use for shipping reconnaissance until 1941.

## Wellington, Vickers

This British long-range night bomber was operational from 1938 to 1945. Known universally as the 'Wimpey' – after the cartoon character J Wellington Wimpey – the Wellington bore the burden of Bomber Command's heavy night offensive until the task could be taken over progressively by the four-engined aircraft ordered under the 1936 program. The prototype flew on 15 June 1936. Two months later the Air Ministry ordered 180 production Wellington Is, with 1000hp Bristol Pegasus radial engines; and before the end of 1938, No 99 Squadron was already equipping with the type at Mildenhall. By the outbreak of war there were six squadrons; production contracts covered many more, including Mk IIs with two 1145hp Merlin X engines and Mk IIIs with 1375hp Hercules IIIs. Initial attempts to use unescorted Wellingtons in daylight, protected by the crossfire of colleagues in formation, proved disastrous. Many aircraft were lost and the only consolation was the discovery of how much damage the unique basketwork geodetic airframe structure could absorb and still hold together. A switch was made to night bombing, to little effect in that era before the development of radio and radar navigation/bombing aids.

During the Winter of 1941–42, the number of operational Wellington squadrons in Bomber Command rose to 21, and there were still 599 'Wimpeys' in the force which carried out the first 1000-bomber raid on Cologne in the following May. Altogether 11,461 were delivered, including a large number of maritime reconnaissance and anti-submarine variants for service with Coastal Command and in the Mediterranean theater. Some were equipped as torpedo-bombers; others began to exert a major

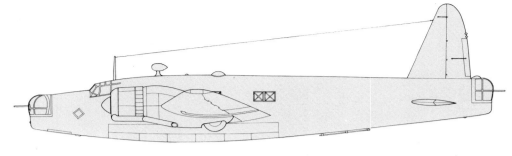

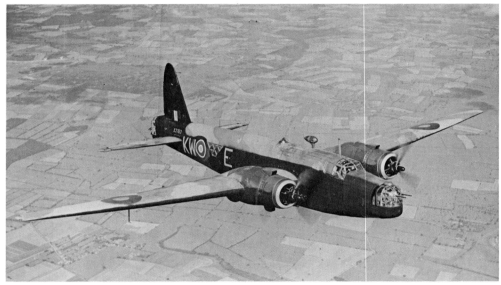

*Top:* Vickers Wellington 1C.
*Above:* Wellington bomber on its way to bomb Germany.

influence on the tide of war in North Africa when fitted with radar to locate, and searchlights to illuminate, their shipping targets by night as well as day. Early in the war, Wellington D.W.Is had been flown with 48ft diameter metal hoops attached to their wings and fuselage to explode the magnetic mines that represented Hitler's first 'secret weapon'. A few were tested with strange cigar-shape fuselages and pressure cabins in the soon-abandoned hope that this would put them beyond the reach of German fighters. Many ended their career as postwar crew trainers.

---

*Weserübung Nord*
see Norway Campaign, 1940

---

*Weserübung Sud*
see Denmark, Occupation of

---

*West Virginia*

The battleship *West Virginia* (BB.48) was the third unit of the *Maryland* Class and was launched in 1921. She was torpedoed and set on fire at Pearl Harbor in December 1941, and was completely rebuilt on the lines of the *California* and the *Tennessee*, unlike her two sisters. She was one of Admiral Oldendorf's bombardment force which had to stop the Japanese at the Battle of Surigao Strait in October 1944. Like the other modernized battleships she returned to the Pacific relatively late, but was inactive at Lingayen Gulf, Iwo Jima and Okinawa. She was slightly damaged by a kamikaze in April 1945 and again by a bomb in June.

**West Wall, Defense of, 1944–45**

Rundstedt, who had been restored as Commander-in-Chief West on 5 September after being removed two months before for suggesting that the war was lost, found Germany's western defenses in a perilous state. He had 63 divisions under command, but none was at better than half strength and they were scattered along a four hundred mile front from the mouth of the Scheldt to the Swiss frontier. The West Wall, which followed the line of Germany's 1939 frontier as far as the Dutch boundary, had been left unfinished and was in a poor state of repair. He had few tanks and the Allies enjoyed air superiority. His only advantages were the difficult terrain, the approaching bad weather, the Allied supply difficulties compounded by their failure to take Antwerp's river approaches in early September and the spiritual fillip conferred by the failure of the Market Garden Operation to cross the last of the great Dutch water obstacles. He was nevertheless condemned to fight a completely defensive battle against great material superiority. The campaign effectively resolved itself into three actions. The British in the north were occupied throughout October and November with the clearing of the Scheldt estuary, culminating in the amphibious assault on Walcheren. They had no strength to fight in Holland. The Ardennes was regarded as unpromising for an offensive effort. Attacks were therefore left to the US 9th and 1st Armies, which attacked and captured Aachen in October and drove into the Hürtgen forest and towards the Roer river in November. In Lorraine, Patton attacked throughout October and November, capturing Metz on 22 November and breaching the West Wall. By 15 December it had bridgeheads across the river Saar and was poised to advance to the Rhine when the German Ardennes offensive upset the Allied timetable. South of Patton, Devers' 7th US Army and de Lattre's 1st French Army, which had made the advance from the Mediterranean, fought side by side in Alsace. Breaking across the line of the Meuse on 13 November they took Strasbourg on 23 November, and outflanked Colmar to reach the Rhine. The onset of the Ardennes offensive and the German counteroffensive in Alsace (Operation *Nordwind*) then brought their advance to a halt.

---

**Western Desert, Rommel's First Offensive, 1941**

The arrival in Tripolitania, Libya of the German Africa Korps commanded by General Erwin Rommel in March 1941 reversed the tide of events which had been running in favor of the

British troops in the Desert fire their 5.5in long-range gun.

British. Already weakened by the dispatch of many units to fight in Greece, they were now faced by a force of formidable fighting strength. Moreover, although his orders were to stand on the defensive, Rommel had decided that in the circumstances, attack was the best form of defense. He began by probing at the British forward positions at El Agheila on 24 March and, finding them lightly defended, pushed on along the coast to Benghazi which he took on 3 April and Tobruk, reached on 11 April. Wavell, the British theater commander, decided to hold that port, still protected by its Italian entrenchments, as a fortress, garrisoned by the Australian 9th Division. Rommel twice tried to breach the defenses, 13–17 April and 30 April – 4 May, but then was forced to bypass it. Advancing to the Egyptian frontier, which had been hastily reinforced, he beat off an improvised British counterattack at Halfaya, 15–17 May, and captured the place on 27 May. He had now advanced 450 miles in two months and overextended his lines of supply. His first offensive was brought to an end.

**Western Front, Chronological List of Events**

Norway, Campaign, 1940
Holland, Invasion of, 1940
Belgium, Invasion of, 1940
Eben Emael, Capture of Fort, 1940
Ardennes, Passage of, 1940
Arras, Battle of, 21 May 1940
France, Battle of, 1940
Dunkirk, Retreat to and Evacuation from, 1940
Sealion, Operation, 1940
Britain, Battle of, 1940
St Nazaire Raid, March 1942
Dieppe Raid, 1942
Sicily, Invasion of, 1943
Italy, Capitulation of, 1943
Italy, Invasion of, 1943
Italy, Winter Line Campaign, 1943–44
Cassino, Battle of Monte, 1944
Anzio, 21 January 1944
Rome, Capture of, and Advance to the Gothic Line, 1944
D-Day Landings, 1944
Normandy, Breakout from, 1944
Paris, Liberation of, 1944
Anvil, 15 August 1944
West Wall, Defense of, 1944–45
Antwerp, September-November 1944
Arnhem (Operation Market Garden), September, 1944
Bulge, Battle of, 1944
Alsace, German Offensive in, 1944
Rhine Crossings, 1945
Gothic Line and Surrender in Italy, 1944–45
Germany, Surrender of, 1945

**Weygand, General Maxime, 1867–1965**

A man of mysterious origins whose father has been variously identified (both King Leopold II of Belgium and the Emperor Maximilian of Mexico have been mentioned), Weygand was born in Brussels but was allowed to join the French army, in which he served during World War I as Chief of Staff to Foch. He had retired before 1939 but was recalled to service (he chose those words as the title of his memoirs) in the Lebanon at the outbreak of war and then summoned urgently home by Reynaud at the height of the battle of France to relieve Gamelin. He arrived on 20 May to find the front already too

decayed to be mended, but nevertheless bravely announced his intention to defend a 'Weygand Line' along the Somme. Using what troops he had left after the destruction of the field armies in the north he held the tide for a few days in early June but was then obliged to advise the seeking of an armistice. After its signing he was made Vichy Minister of War and then Delegate-General in North Africa, where his policy was so anti-German that Hitler insisted on his dismissal. Arrested by the Gestapo in 1942, he was imprisoned after the Liberation but exonerated and released in 1948. An old, but brave and patriotic man, he had been asked to do the impossible in 1940.

**Weygand Plan**
see France, Battle of, 1940

**Whirlwind, Westland**

This British single-seat fighter was operational from December 1940 to 1943. The prototype Whirlwind flew on 11 October 1938 and was considered such a revolutionary design that its existence was kept secret until well into the war years. It was the first single-seat twin-engined fighter ordered for the RAF and, when designed, had an unprecedented heavy armament of four 20mm cannon closely grouped in its nose to give a great concentration of firepower. Unfortunately, it was also unique in having two 885hp Rolls-Royce Peregrine engines, which proved troublesome. Added to its high (for the time) landing speed, which restricted the number of airfields from which it could operate, this led to production being restricted to 112 aircraft and withdrawal from service after only three years. Whirlwinds were judged to be of little use as interceptors, as performance fell off rapidly at height. The maximum speed lower down was 360mph, and range sufficiently good to make them useful as escort fighters for fast day bombers; but their best service was given as fighter-bombers during low-level raids across the Channel, with Hurricanes, in 1942–43.

Grumman F4F Wildcat.

A 2000lb bomb is loaded into a Whitley prior to going on a raid over Germany.

**Whitley, Armstrong-Whitworth**

This British five-seat heavy bomber and maritime patrol aircraft was in service from 1937 to 1945. Built to a 1934 specification, the Whitley did at least have stressed-skin construction, but it was designed to have a very thick wing set at such an angle that the aircraft normally flew in an odd nose-down posture. Its chief attributes were great strength and the heavy bomb load of 7000lb carried in the fuselage and inner wings. Nearly all also had the first power-operated rear turret in the world to carry four machine guns; another gun was in the nose turret. In 1939–40 hundreds of Whitleys, almost all of them Mk Vs powered by the 1145hp Merlin, droned across Germany on long and freezing missions dropping leaflets and, from May 1940, bombs. This was a period when, in the words of a Bomber Command captain 'They used to tell us to bomb Krupps works, but we were lost as soon as we left the airfield'. The last of 1737 Whitleys was delivered in June 1943, by which time all had been transferred to Coastal Command, as the ASV-radar-equipped Mk VII, or to such non-operational duties as paratrooping and glider towing. The 119 paratroopers who made the brilliant 1942 Bruneval raid were dropped from Whitleys. A few of these tough and well-liked machines served until the end of 1944 carrying electronic countermeasures.

**Wildcat/Martlet, Grumman F4F**

This US single-seat carrier-based fighter was operational from 1941 to 1945. This tubby little monoplane, with wheels retracting into the front fuselage as on earlier Grumman biplanes, was the only carrier-based fighter available to the US Navy during the first half of the war in the Pacific. In some respects, its performance was inferior to that of the Japanese Zero. Yet, over the whole wartime period, it achieved 6.9 'kills' for every USN Wildcat lost in air combat, thanks to its sturdy construction, armament of six 0.5in guns, and the better training of its

pilots. Many of these victories were scored against bombers and transports, perhaps easier but often more vital prey than the Zeros. The F4Fs supplied to Britain, and used mainly from carriers fighting German long-range bombers and U-Boats in the Atlantic, were known as Martlets until 1944, when the US name was standardized. Final version for both navies was the FM–2, built by Eastern Aircraft and known in Britain as the Wildcat VI. By changing to a Wright R–1820 engine, which was lighter in weight than the original 1200hp R–1830 though giving an extra 150hp, the FM–2 offered the improved take-off performance needed to operate from the shorter decks of escort carriers. Maximum speed was 332mph.

## Willkie, Wendell, 1892–1944

Willkie was a Democrat who opposed the New Deal and joined the Republican Party in 1938. In 1940 he was surprisingly chosen as Republican candidate for the Presidency and he substantially reduced Roosevelt's winning margin. After war had been declared he was very critical of the Darlan agreement on the grounds that it was dictated by expediency. Willkie was a convinced internationalist and expounded his idealistic vision of the world after the war in his best seller *One World*. In 1942 he went on a good-will visit round the world (with Roosevelt's approval) and visited more than thirty countries. In China and the Near East he visited the front lines. In 1944 he withdrew from the primaries after a humiliating defeat in Wisconsin and died a few months later.

## Wilson, Field Marshal Sir Henry Maitland, 1881–1964

Wilson, little known in Britain during the war, commanded in the Mediterranean theater. General Officer Commanding in Egypt at the outbreak he oversaw both the Cyrenaican and early Libyan campaigns, commanded the Greek operation and then occupied Iraq and Syria. In 1942 he commanded in Persia-Iraq and in February 1943 succeeded Alexander as British Commander in Chief Middle East. In January 1944 he succeeded Eisenhower as Allied Supreme Commander Mediterranean and in November, on the death of Dill, went to Washington to head the British military mission. A military diplomat and strategic adviser rather than a commander, the longevity of his appointment is evidence of his talent. He was universally known as 'Jumbo' because of his large and ungainly frame.

## Winant, John, 1889–1947

Winant was US Ambassador to Great Britain from 1941 until after the end of the war. He replaced Joseph Kennedy and immediately worked to improve Anglo-American relations. He helped Harry Hopkins in working out Lend-Lease arrangements. In 1943 he helped plan the Moscow Foreign Ministers' Conference which resulted in the setting up of a European Advisory Commission. Winant was the US representative to the Commission which discussed the future of Germany. He also attended the Casablanca and Teheran Conferences and was the US representative to the first meeting of the UN.

## Wingate, Major General Orde, 1903–1944

Wingate was a very controversial figure. His guerrilla force the 'Chindits' fired the imagination of the British in 1943. Wingate had had experience of guerrilla warfare in Israel in 1936 when he had founded the 'Special Night Squads'. In fall 1940 he was summoned from England to organize a guerrilla campaign in Ethiopia. After a successful campaign Wingate was sent back to England to a minor staff post and while suffering from malaria and depression he tried to kill himself. While recovering from this Wingate was summoned by General Wavell to the China-Burma-India theater. Wavell had been impressed by Wingate's methods in Ethiopia and wanted him to try out 'Long Range Penetration Groups' in the Burmese jungle.

Wingate decided to train a unit, the size of a brigade, to fight behind Japanese lines; their main task would be to disrupt communications. The unit would be supplied by air. Wingate called the unit the Chindits after a mythical beast the Chinthe, after which the Chindwin River was named.

The first Chindits operation set out in February 1943 and crossed the Chindwin River to attack Japanese outposts, railway lines and blow up bridges. By mid-March they crossed the Irrawaddy River but the Japanese hit back, and when the unit withdrew to India a third of its force and much equipment had been lost. Wingate became the hero of the British public and the operation was hailed as a great success. In fact it did not achieve as much as was claimed by the press in 1943. It did convince the Japanese that their line along the Chindwin was not strong enough and led to the offensive against Kohima and Imphal. The British Army learned the value of supplying soldiers cut off from the Bengal bases by air.

Wingate wanted to try his 'Long Range Penetration' tactics with a larger force six brigades strong but before he could see this put into operation he was killed in an air crash in the jungle on 24 March 1944. The 2nd Chindits operation was badly planned and not a success.

Wingate's contribution to the war effort is difficult to assess. He provoked extreme reactions in people: professional soldiers were suspicious of his plans but politicians, especially Churchill encouraged him to develop his ideas. After his death the British Army in Burma did not train any more special units.

## Winter Line
see Italy, Winter Line Campaign, 1943–44

## Witzleben, Field Marshal Erwin von, 1881–1944

Witzleben was among the 12 generals promoted to Field Marshal in the victory celebrations of 18 July 1940. He had commanded the First Army in France and penetrated the Maginot Line. He was retired in 1942, after a period of static command in the West, and at once resumed plotting to bring about the downfall of Hitler as he had tried, without real resolution, to do before the war. The 'Bomb Plotters' of 1944 planned to make him Commander in Chief should their coup succeed. When it did not he was arrested and hanged. Ironically it was a false report that he had been seen in uniform on the morning of 20 July which first put the men loyal to Hitler in Berlin on their guard.

## X-series Missiles

These were German wire-guided missiles. The first to be developed was the X–4, an air-to-air missile, work on which began in June 1943. It was a finned missile with a wingspan of 6ft 6in, driven by a bi-fuel liquid rocket at 550mph. Bobbins of wire were carried in the wing tips, which unwound as it flew, and guidance signals were sent down the wire to function spoiler tabs on the wing surfaces which caused it to alter direction. The warhead carried 44lb of explosive and a 'Kranich' acoustic proximity fuze. Prototypes were flown successfully in September 1944 but the wire link from aircraft to missile was considered too restricting, and work then began on two alternative versions, one using the 'Pudel' acoustic homing system in which the missile would find its own way to the noise of the target's engines, and one using a radio link system of guidance. Neither of these had passed the development stage when the war ended.

As an off-shoot of the X–4 program, it was decided to develop a wire-guided ground-to-ground missile for anti-tank use; this became known as the X–7. It was gyro-stabilized and wire-guided in the same manner as the X–4 but carried a hollow charge warhead fitted with an impact fuze. It was propelled by a two-stage solid propellant rocket motor, weighed 22lb, had a range of 1000 meters and could penetrate over 200mm of armor.

The X-series were developed by the Ruhrstahl AG company of Düsseldorf, but none was ever brought to sufficient perfection to begin production before the war ended. Nevertheless, the company deserve recognition for being the originators of the wire-guided anti-tank missile which is today in the armories of every nation, and, except for relatively small refinements, is made to the same specifications as the X–7.

X-4 guided missile.

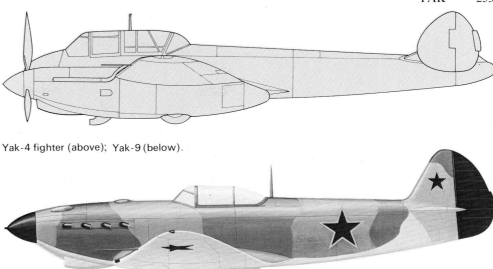

Yak-4 fighter (above); Yak-9 (below).

### Yakovlev, Aleksandr S, 1906–

Yakovlev was an aeronautical engineer who specialized in the design of piston-type aircraft and jets. He designed a single-seat fighter YAK-1, which was a high-speed fighter and mass-produced until the war. This was modified and developed into YAK-3, YAK-7 and YAK-9 which were produced from 1943 to 1947. Yakovlev then developed supersonic planes.

### Yakovlev Yak–1

Impressed by the Spitfire and Bf 109, which he had seen during visits to Europe, Alexander Yakovlev decided to match something of their small size, light weight, high power and heavy armament with the maneuverability and simplicity characteristic of Soviet fighters. He designed his I–26 (Yak–1) prototype around an M–105P engine of 1050hp, although the prototype had to be fitted with a standard M–105 at the time of its first flight, on 1 January 1940. It proved to have a speed of 373mph and was ordered into immediate production; 8721 were built, including Yak–1Ms. Except for early production aircraft, Yak–1s were powered by a 1240hp M–105PF engine and armed with a 20mm cannon, firing through the propeller hub, and two 7.62mm machine guns or one of 12.7mm.

*Below:* Yakovlev Yak-1 Soviet fighter.
*Bottom:* Yak-3 Soviet fighter.

### Yakovlev Yak–3

This Soviet single-seat fighter was operational from 1943. In spite of its designation, the Yak–3 was a later aircraft than the Yak–9. It owed its existence to the fact that pilots of the latter aircraft sometimes found themselves at a disadvantage when fighting the latest German Bf 109Gs. They could climb more rapidly to 16,000ft and had better maneuverability than the Messerschmitts; but the Bf 109G was more than 25mph faster than the Yak above 20,000ft and Yak–9 crews tried to avoid combat above 13,000ft. To counter the 109G, the Russians first produced the Yak–1M, differing from the standard Yak–1 in having reduced span, a cut-down rear fuselage and all-round-view canopy, a smaller radiator and armament of only two 12.7mm machine guns. From the Yak–1M was evolved the Yak–3, with a VK–105PF–2 engine uprated to 1290hp, the oil cooler removed from under the nose to the port wingroot, and other design refinements. Even after the 20mm gun had been put back, the Yak–3 flew 31mph faster than a Yak–9 and 25mph faster than a Bf 109G; but the German aircraft remained superior above 20,000ft. At low levels the story was very different, and many a Focke-Wulf 190 stalled and crashed when trying to match the tight turning circle of the Yak. An all-metal version, known as the Yak–3U, was put into production towards the end of 1944, but was not used operationally in World War II.

### Yakovlev Yak–4

The Yak-4 was a twin-engined light bomber contemporary of the Yak–1, with which it had much in common. With two 960hp M–103 engines, crew of two, 880 to 1325lb of bombs and armament of two machine guns or 20mm cannon, it had a maximum speed of 336mph and range of 500 miles with 880lb of bombs. Only a few were used operationally.

### Yakovlev Yak–7

At the same time as he was developing the Yak–1, Yakovlev designed a two-seat conversion trainer, designated Yak–7V, of very similar configuration. From this were evolved two single-seat night fighters, the Yak–7A and 7B, with 1240hp M–105PF engine and armament of one 20mm cannon and one 12.7mm machine gun.

### Yakovlev Yak–9

This Soviet single-seat fighter was operational from 1942. The prototype of the Yak–9 was tested initially in July 1942 as the Yak–7DI, a long-range fighter evolved from the Yak–7 trainer. Its designers achieved the space and weight saving for additional fuel by changing the spars from wood to steel in an otherwise standard Yak–7B plywood-covered wing. The production version was given a cut-down rear fuselage and all-round-view canopy, like those of the Yak–1M, and an armament of one 20mm cannon and two 12.7mm machine guns. The power plant was a 1240hp VK–105PF in-line engine. Like other new Soviet combat aircraft, it entered service during the key Battle for Stalingrad in the winter of 1942–43. It proved an efficient interceptor below 10,000ft and was used also in a ground attack role. Many special versions were produced, starting with the Yak–9T and 9K which had a 37mm or 45mm gun respectively to attack German tanks; even the famous Tiger and Panther tanks proved vulnerable to such formidable weapons. The Yak–9B (bomber) had an internal weapon bay for four vertically-stowed 220lb bombs. The Yak–9R was a photo-reconnaissance variant. The Yak–9D had additional fuel tanks for a range of 870 miles, the outcome of a personal challenge from Stalin that Yakovlev should produce an escort fighter with the range of a

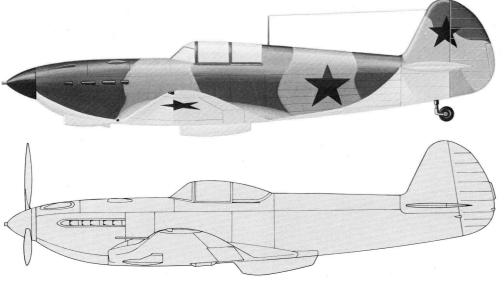

Spitfire. With still more internal fuel and a drop-tank, the Yak–9DD of 1944 was able to fly nonstop the 1120 miles from the Ukraine to Bari in Italy, to provide support for Tito's Yugoslav partisans; it also escorted USAAF B–17s and B–24s used on shuttle-bombing raids against Germany and the Balkans.

Despite its designation, the Yak–9U, of which a prototype flew in January 1944, was really a new type, with an all-metal airframe, a longer fuselage, and a 1700hp VK–107A engine which raised the maximum speed to 434mph at 18,000ft. It became available in time to take part in the final air battles of the war, as did the Yak–9P interceptor, which remained in service with the Soviet Union and its allies well into the jet age. When production ended, no fewer than 36,732 Yakovlev piston-engined fighters had been built, including 8721 Yak–1s, 6399 Yak–7s, 16,769 Yak–9s and 4484 Yak–3s. Their pilots included the Free French Normandie-Niemen Regiment, which fought on the Russian front, and the Soviet women's fighter regiment which claimed 38 enemy aircraft in 4419 sorties.

## Yalta Conference, 4–11 February 1945

(Preceded by a short Anglo-American conference on Malta.) With victory in Europe close at hand, there was much to be settled. Roosevelt wanted Russia to fight in the Pacific, which she agreed to, in return for territorial concessions. Both England and America were concerned over how Stalin intended to use his military power in Eastern Europe. On the subject of Germany, the Allies agreed to the principle but not the details of dismemberment. Stalin wanted full reparations to be paid by Germany, 50% ($10,000 million) to be paid to Russia, plus the removal of all German heavy industry to Allied nations. Britain especially felt this figure was outrageous and would entail America and Britain paying for Germany's imports in order to keep her alive while others received the reparations: the debate was postponed.

France was refused representation at Yalta, due to the United States, who did not agree with England's desire to build France into a Great Power again. However both Allies supported giving France a zone of occupation in Germany. The US declared at Yalta her intention of removing all her troops from Europe after only two more years. Furthermore, the three rejected Italy's appeal for Allied status and more financial aid because France and other liberated nations had priority, and because free elections must be held in Italy first.

The conference agreed to give full representation in the United Nations to only two Soviet Republics and agreed to grant veto power to Great Powers except when acting as interested parties to a dispute. They called for and set a date for a conference to write a United Nations Charter in San Francisco.

The most pressing problem was still Poland. Russia had already established its puppet 'Lublin Government' at Warsaw, which was liquidating its opposition: the Polish Government in Exile could do nothing, nor could the United States or England until they recognized the Lublin Government. This was impossible until a free election was held. The most they could do was obtain Russia's signature to the Yalta Declaration on Liberated Europe, in which the Allies pledged to help nations 'solve by democratic means their pressing political and economic problems' by (1) forming broadly representative interim governments, pledged to free elections, and (2) facilitating such elections.

## Yamamoto, Admiral Isoroku, 1884–1943

Yamamoto was Japan's most brilliant naval tactician. He was the architect of the successful raid on Pearl Harbor and an exponent of combined air and sea power.

Yamamoto was opposed to the idea of war against the USA. He felt that Japan could achieve an initial victory in the first year but was bound to lose in the face of the USA's greater wealth and resources. Yamamoto was Minister of the Navy from May 1938, Commander-in-Chief of the First Fleet from 1939 and later of the Second Fleet. He concentrated on improving the efficiency of the Navy.

After the success of the Pearl Harbor attack which his staff had planned a year in advance, Yamamoto decided on a plan to fight a decisive battle with the US fleet in the Pacific. Yamamoto prepared an operation to destroy the US fleet off Midway Island, which involved eight separate task forces but because the US had broken the Japanese Fleet code they were able to inflict a heavy defeat on the Japanese. Yamamoto then became involved in the attempt to hold Guadalcanal and his Navy scored many successes against the badly-trained US Fleet.

In April 1943 the US intercepted a radio signal giving details of Yamamoto's special inspection tour of the Solomon Islands. Fighters from Henderson Field shot down his plane, which crashed in the jungle. Yamamoto was regarded as a special hero by the Japanese and his death was a great blow to morale.

## *Yamashiro*

This Japanese battleship, flagship of Admiral Nishimura, took many torpedo-hits and heavy shells in the Battle of Surigao Strait on the night of 24–25 October 1944. She finally capsized and sank at 0419 on the morning of 25 October, the last battleship to fight other battleships.

## Yamashita, Lieutenant General Tomoyuki, 1885–1946

Yamashita, the 'Tiger of Malaya,' scored Japan's most decisive land victory of the war in Malaya. Yamashita was Inspector General of the Imperial Army Air Forces when he was sent on a military mission to Germany in 1940. His report stated that Japan should not declare war on the USA or Britain until the Army and Air Force was modernized.

However in December 1941 war was declared and Yamashita commanded the Twenty-fifth Army which landed on the Thai Peninsula. British resistance was disorganized and the Japanese had overwhelming air superiority. In February 1942 Yamashita reached Singapore and succeeded in bluffing General Percival into believing the Japanese forces were much stronger than in fact they were. Percival surrendered unconditionally on 15 February 1942.

After the fall of Singapore, Prime Minister Tojo transferred Yamashita to command First Army Group in Manchuria and train soldiers. This meant Yamashita was out of the public eye, but after Tojo's fall Yamashita was appointed Commander of the Fourteenth Area Army and his task was to defend the Philippines. When the Americans invaded Leyte, Field Marshal Terauchi and Imperial GHQ ordered Yamashita to make a stand there, believing the false claims of their pilots that US air power had been destroyed. Yamashita could not oppose the American forces on the beaches of Luzon when they invaded in January 1945, but managed a counterattack after a week. Yamashita lost many men and supplies in a hopeless battle. His main group made a last stand in the north. Yamashita gave orders not to fight for Manila but Vice-Admiral Iwabuchi disobeyed him. Yamashita continued fighting in the Philippines until he heard of the Japanese surrender on 2 September 1945. In February 1946 Yamashita was executed for war crimes.

## *Yamato*

In 1934 the Japanese Naval Staff drew up plans for a super-battleship which would do two things: be invincible in battle against any existing ships, and be so large that any American reply to her would be too big to pass through the Panama Canal. The Japanese reasoned that if they could build a fleet of such ships in secret, to appear after the lapse of the disarmament treaties, it would take the US so long to widen the Panama Canal that the Japanese would be able to win a fleet action or persuade the Americans to accept parity.

The result was that the largest and most heavily armed and armored battleships in the world were built: 64,000 tons, nine 18in guns and armor rising to 25in in thickness. Originally seven were authorized; however, three were never started, Number 4 was canceled in 1941, and Number 3 became an aircraft carrier. The *Yamato* commissioned on 16 December 1941 and the *Musashi* followed in August 1942. The two ships had been built in total secrecy; although both US and British intelligence had some idea about the 18in guns they did not have any idea of just how big the two ships would be.

The *Yamato* was in the Battle of Midway, the Philippine Sea and Leyte Gulf, and survived a number of bomb-hits. Her end came in April 1945 when a scheme was drawn up to give her sufficient fuel for a one-way trip to Okinawa. The idea was that she would smash her way past the Allied surface fleet, run herself on the beach and use her 18in guns to destroy the invasion fleet. But long before she got anywhere near Okinawa she was attacked by wave after wave of carrier planes, and sank after scores of torpedo- and bomb-hits.

## Yeremenko, Marshal Andrey I, 1892–1970

Yeremenko directed operations at Stalingrad, Smolensk and later in Czechoslovakia. In August 1941 he was appointed Commander of the Bryansk Front but was seriously wounded and out of action for a year. In August 1942 he was again wounded but became Commander of the Southeast Front. At Stalingrad he led the encirclement operation but Stalin then gave General Rokossovky the order to clear up the Sixth Army. Yeremenko was to check Field Marshal Manstein's forces. In 1943 he was sent to command the Independent (Black Sea) Maritime Front and cleared the Germans out of the Crimea. In 1944 he led the 2nd Baltic Front which took Dvinsk and threatened Riga. He was then sent to the Carpathian Front.

## Yokosuka D4Y Suisei

Although 2319 D4Ys of all models were built, the Suisei ('Judy') never achieved great success in its intended role as a dive-bomber. Early versions, with a 1200hp Aichi Atsuta Vee engine, were plagued by structural deficiencies and maintenance problems and were used for reconnaissance. The Suisei ended its career as a suicide aircraft, packed with 1765lb of high explosive and fitted with take-off rockets to help it become airborne.

## Yokosuka MXY–7

This Japanese-piloted missile was in service from 1944 to 1945. One of the strangest and most frightening aerial weapons of World War II, the MXY–7 was specially designed as a piloted bomb to be carried under a bomber – invariably a G4M2e – until within about 50 miles from the target and then released. The pilot steered to the target in a fast glide and then, when quite close, he pushed over into a violent dive, while igniting the three-chambered rocket engine to plummet into the target at well over 500mph. The whole forward fuselage was a huge warhead, containing 2645lb of explosive. About 755 were delivered together with various lower-powered turbojet and trainer versions, and somewhat different models for catapulting from land bases or the decks of submarines.

## Yokosuka P1Y1 Ginga

Known to the Allies as 'Frances', this elegant naval bomber entered service in the spring of 1944, but was prevented from reaching its full potential by engine problems and shortage of skilled assembly workers and pilots at that stage of the war. When they worked properly, the two 1820hp Homare engines gave the Ginga a speed of 347mph at 20,000ft. It could carry two 550lb bombs internally, with smaller bombs under the wings; a single 1870lb or 1765lb torpedo under the fuselage; or two 1100lb bombs under the center-section. Armament comprised a 20mm cannon in the nose and a 12.7mm dorsal machine gun, although a few aircraft had two 20mm or 12.7mm guns in a dorsal turret. Operating mainly from Japan, Gingas sank at least one US carrier. Some were employed in a suicide role at Okinawa. Production totaled 1002.

## York

The heavy cruiser HMS York was an experimental prototype, the first British attempt to break away from the expensive and oversized 10,000-ton cruisers built after the Washington Treaty. Although in many ways a more successful ship than the earlier 'County' Class, the York did not achieve enough savings on manpower and running costs to make her a worthwhile alternative. A modified version was built, HMS Exeter.

HMS York served with the Home Fleet in 1939–40 but went to the Mediterranean. While lying in Suda Bay, Crete, she was hit by an Italian explosive motor boat (26 March 1941) and had to be beached to avoid sinking. Salvage work began, and she was within 24 hours of completion despite constant air attack, when the German paratroop attack started. She was therefore blown up and abandoned on 22 May.

## Yorktown

The aircraft carrier Yorktown (CV.5) and her sister Enterprise were the first of a new departure in US carriers. All the lessons of the previous 20 years were assimilated and worked into the new design, with the result that the new class was smaller than the Lexington Class, and yet carried as many aircraft. One school of thought in the US Navy wanted smaller carriers like the Ranger (CV.4) to spread the risk, but another school maintained that as aircraft were the carrier's main weapon, the more the better. This argument won the day with the Yorktown, and in 1932 Congress was asked to approve the construction of two 20,000-ton carriers under Fiscal Year 1934, to be paid for by the Public Works Administration as a way of boosting employment in the depressed shipbuilding industry.

The main features of the Yorktown Class were incorporated into future carriers, and the Essex design was little more than an enlarged version. The hangar was designed for maximum capacity, and was open to the ship's side. A weak point was that the hangar ventilation was linked to the ship's main system, but the stowage of avgas was effective in reducing the risk of fire. Armor was fitted on the hangar deck, but the flight deck was made of six-inch wide hardwood planks laid athwartships. Three high-speed elevators brought aircraft up from the full-length hangar.

In the Battle of the Coral Sea the Yorktown was the flagship of Rear-Admiral Fletcher, and she had embarked 71 aircraft of CVG–5, comprising VF–42, VS–5, VB–5 and VT–5. On 8 May 1942 she was attacked by nine B5N 'Kates', but the single bomb which hit inboard of the island did not affect the ship's efficiency as the fires were soon put out. The carrier returned to Pearl Harbor after the battle and was in dry dock on 27 May for repairs when the news came through that the Combined Fleet was heading for Midway.

The Japanese knew that Yorktown had been hit, and understandably concluded that she was incapable of putting to sea in time. But the Pearl Harbor Navy Yard workmen achieved the impossible by repairing her in three days. Her air group's losses had been made good with experienced aircrew from the Lexington. The Americans now had three carriers, whereas all Japanese planning presupposed that they were

USS Yorktown under attack

facing only two, the fatal flaw which resulted in other wrong decisions being made during the Battle of Midway.

The Yorktown's VT–5 was badly mauled in an attack on the Japanese carriers on 4 June without scoring any hits, but 17 dive-bombers returned safely. Although the Enterprise air group knocked out three of the Japanese carriers, the one still undamaged, the Hiryu, immediately flew off a strike against the Yorktown, which was the nearest American carrier. Although only eight 'Val' bombers penetrated the curtain of AA fire and the defending fighters, they hit her with three 250 kg bombs. One hit the deck and set parked aircraft ablaze; the second hit the stack and blew out five of the six boiler-fires; the third penetrated three decks and ignited the avgas. The avgas fire was dealt with by flooding the magazines and damping the fuel tanks with $CO_2$ gas, but one boiler could not keep the Yorktown moving. However, by 1320 hours the ship was under way at 20 knots on three boilers, still burning but able to start fueling her fighters once more.

At 1420 another strike was detected; this time it was Hiryu's torpedo-bombers. Only eight of the defending fighters had been fueled, and these were flown off, but they were not enough to stop a superbly executed attack. Four 'Kates' bracketed the Yorktown with torpedoes on either bow at only 500 yards, and two hit her on the port side amidships. The ship soon listed 26° to port as she took on hundreds of tons of water. But still the Yorktown refused to sink.

At dawn on 5 June efforts began to save the Yorktown, and a minesweeper and two destroyers came alongside to tow her and fight the fires. All day and all night they toiled to save the carrier, and by noon on 6 June Captain Buckmaster could report that there was hope of getting her to port. But the position had been reported by Japanese reconnaissance planes to the submarine I.168, and at 1330 she put two torpedoes into the starboard side of the carrier and one into the destroyer Hamman lying alongside. The Yorktown died gamely next morning at 0501, after sustaining more damage than most battleships were ever called upon to endure.

## Yukikaze

This Japanese destroyer of the Kagero Class seemed to lead a charmed life. She went through the entire war without being hit, although all her sisters were sunk. She was involved in nearly all the important actions in the Pacific.

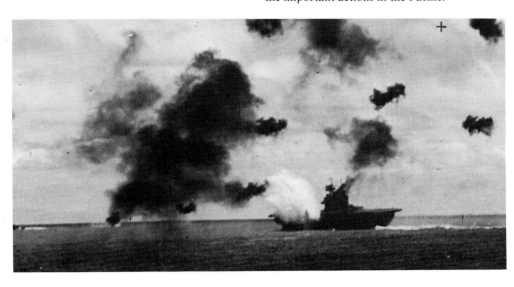

# Z

## Zeitzler, General Kurt, 1895–1963

After service as Chief of Staff of the First Panzer Army in Russia in 1941, Zeitzler was chosen to replace Halder as Chief of the Army Staff (OKH) in September 1942. His main achievement, during Hitler's loss of confidence in his strategic judgment following the fall of Stalingrad, was to persuade him to authorize the Kursk attack in the summer of 1943. Conceived as a means of restoring German freedom of action on the Eastern Front, it in fact wiped out the *Ostheer*'s strategic reserve of armor, thus obliging him thereafter to conform to Russian strategic dictates. Zeitzler, who was a more amenable character than Halder had been, was nevertheless kept on at OKH until July 1944, when the combined effect of the Destruction of Army Group Center, the Bomb Plot and his own ill-health led to his dismissal.

## 'Zero'

see Mitsubishi A6M

## Zhukov, Marshal Georgii K, 1896–1974

Zhukov was Commander-in-Chief of the Red Army for most of the war and was its most respected general. He was closely associated with General Timoshenko and had fought in the Far East, where he had observed Japanese military methods. In August 1939 he commanded the Soviet counteroffensive at Khalkhin-Gol, Mongolia and successfully defeated the Japanese. He was appointed Chief of Staff of the Red Army in the final stages of the Russo-Finnish War. In October 1941 Zhukov was sent to assist Marshal Voroshilov in Leningrad and after the latter's failure, replaced him. His main task though, was to build a Reserve Front to protect Moscow. After the Germans had been exhausted by the blizzards and the bad road conditions, Zhukov was able to launch a counteroffensive with fresh troops from Siberia on 6 December 1941. Zhukov maintained the offensive and occupied territory up to 40 miles from Moscow. In the fall of 1942 Zhukov planned the counteroffensive at Stalingrad with Vasilievsky. He was a cautious general, unwilling to risk his troops in maneuvers they were not trained or prepared for. He limited his objectives to taking Stalingrad and at first did not realize that the whole of the Sixth Army was trapped there. Zhukov advised Stalin to let General Rokossovsky take Stalingrad, while General Yeremenko dealt with Field Marshal Manstein's forces. Anxious not to overextend his armies, he failed to cut off General Kleist's army in the Caucasus.

Zhukov was present at the preparations for the Battle of Kursk in July 1943 and directed the Soviet sweep across the Ukraine. He became more daring but always overestimated the Germans. In March 1944 he was made Commander of the 1st Ukrainian Front and his armies advanced at a rate of 30 miles a day, because there was little resistance. His army crossed the Dniestr and took Kolomya and Cernauti. On April 1 the advance was halted at the Yablonica or Tartar Pass, the entrance to Hungary, because supplies were not getting through. Once the railways had been restored and the Red Army had been regrouped, Zhukov led the 1st Belorussian Front which took Warsaw in a pincer movement (17 January 1945). His army then took Lodz and advanced through Prussia at a rate of 100 miles a week. By a skillful maneuver Zhukov's forces unexpectedly advanced up the corridor between the Vistula and the Warta. On 31 January Zhukov took Landsberg, but his supplies failed again and German resistance stiffened as the army approached Berlin. On 16 April the Soviet army broke out of a bridgehead across the Oder and by 25 April Berlin was encircled. On 8 May Zhukov signed the German surrender in Berlin.

## *Zuiho*

This Japanese carrier was a sister of the *Shoho*, and had been converted from the incomplete submarine tender *Takasaki* in 1940. She survived until 1944, and was sunk by aircraft from the *Essex, Lexington, Franklin, Enterprise* and *San Jacinto* in the Battle of Cape Engaño. She had formed part of Admiral Ozawa's decoy force which had lured Admiral Halsey's forces away from Leyte Gulf to allow Admiral Kurita to destroy the invasion fleet.